JN040737

英語日記
パーフェクト
表現辞典

改訂版

石原真弓 著
（英語学習スタイリスト）

Gakken

はじめに

私が英語で日記を書き始めたのは、留学した初日、1991年9月16日のこと。渡米前夜にプレゼントされた5年連用日記帳をアメリカへ持って行ったことがきっかけです。英語に自信があったわけではありませんが、「人に見せるわけではないし、せっかく留学したのだから英語で書こう」と、気軽な気持ちで始めました。以来、1日も欠かさず書き続け、愛用している5年連用日記帳は現在7冊目です。

当時の日記を読み返すと、単純な文法ミスや単語の誤りなどが散見され、思わずクスッとしてしまいます。一方で、年を追うごとに正しい英語で書けるようになり、こなれた表現や気持ちを的確に表した英文が交じっていく変化も見てとれます。

英語で日記を書く習慣は、実生活にも効果をもたらしてくれました。会話の際、頭の中で英文を作ってから話していた私ですが、日記で書き慣れている事柄はパッと口をついて出てくるようになったり、友人とのおしゃべりから自分のミスに気づきやすくなったり。また、かっこいいネイティブ表現を耳にしたときは書き留めておき、日記に取り入れてみるなど、インプット、アウトプットの双方向で英語のアンテナが敏感になったように思います。1日1～2文でも、完璧な英語でなくても、毎日続けることで徐々に力がついていったことを確信できます。

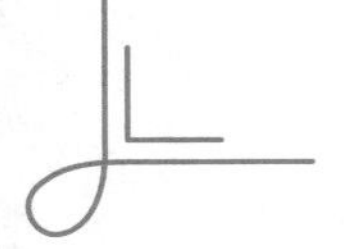

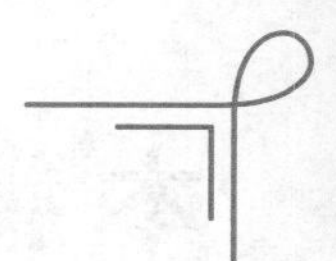

このような実体験から、20年以上にわたって拙著やセミナーで英語日記を広めてきました。実際に日記を書き始めた方からお手紙をいただくこともあり、うれしく思います。それと同時に、「書きたいことがうまく英語にできない」「ニュアンス表現でつまずく」「いつも似た英文で進歩がない」といった独習のもどかしさも聞かれました。

そこから「日常的な日記表現を網羅した辞典のような本があれば、そのような悩みが多少なりとも解決されるのではないか」と考え、『英語日記パーフェクト表現辞典』を出版したのが2013年のことです。「表現を写すだけでも勉強になる」「単語を入れ替えたり、文を組み合わせたりするだけで日記が完成する!」「書いているうちに英文のコツがつかめてきた」といった感想が届き、本書に意義があったことを心うれしく感じています。また、長く読み継がれていることは私にとって大きな励みであり、感謝の気持ちでいっぱいです。

あれから10年が経ち、世の中が移り変わりました。新しい習慣やサービスが生まれ、流行や社会的感覚も多様化しました。それに伴い、全体的に表現を見直し、時代に合わせて更新したのが本書です。書きたいことが見つかる1冊として、英語日記はもちろん、SNSで発信したり、会話を楽しんだりする際に本書が身近な存在となり、より充実した「英語のひととき」の助けとなれば幸いです。

石原真弓

本書の特長

本書では、英語日記を書く上で役立つ文法や構文、フレーズなどを１冊にまとめました。この本を手元に置いて、いつでも必要なときにめくってみてください。きっと、英語日記を楽しく続けられるはずです。

1章 英語日記フレーズ集

日常のさまざまなことについて英語で書くときに使える表現を収録。そのまま書き写すだけでも、立派な英語日記になります。会話やメールなどでも使える表現ばかりなので、いつでも手元に置いて参照してください。

こんなときに

▶さっと英語日記を書きたい！
▶自然な英語表現を身につけたい！
▶会話力も上げたい！

01
天気・季節

天気

天気を表す単語

晴れた	sunny		
快晴の	bright［ブゥライㇳ］		
曇りの	cloudy	虹	rainbow
雨の	rainy	風が強い	windy
小雨	light rain	風が心地いい	breezy
大雨、豪雨	heavy rain	気持ちのいい風	nice breeze
にわか雨	(light) shower	暖かい	warm
雪の	snowy	暑い	hot
大雪	heavy snow	肌寒い	chilly
粉雪	powder snow	涼しい	cool
霧の	foggy［フォギー］	寒い	cold
あられ、ひょう	hail［ヘイゥ］	乾燥した、カラッとした	dry
雷、雷鳴	thunder	じめじめしている	humid［ヒューミッㇳ］
雷、稲光	lightning	蒸し暑い	muggy［マギー］
台風	typhoon	うだるように暑い	boiling hot
竜巻	tornado	凍えるように寒い	freezing cold

晴れ

今日はいい天気だった。	The weather was nice today.
今日は快晴だった。	It was very bright out today.
雲一つない青空だった。	There wasn't a single cloud in the clear, blue sky.
穏やかな日だった。	It was a calm day. ＊calm［カーム］＝穏やかな

28

1章：英語日記フレーズ集

さわやかな天気だった。	The weather was refreshing.
3日ぶりに晴れた。	It was the first clear day in three days. ＊first ... in ～ days＝～日ぶりの…
台風一過の秋晴れだった。	After the typhoon passed, it was a nice autumn day.
明日は晴れるといいな。	I hope the weather is nice tomorrow.
僕は晴れ男（晴れ女）だ。	It's always sunny when I go out. ＊直訳は「私が出かけるときはいつも晴れる」

曇り

今日は曇りだった。	It was cloudy today.
一日中曇っていた。	It was cloudy all day.
どんよりした一日だった。	It was an overcast day. ＊overcast［オウヴァキャスㇳ］＝どんよりした
曇りの日が続くなぁ。	It has been cloudy for several days now.
空に雲が立ち込めていた。	The sky was full of clouds. ＊full of ～＝～でいっぱいで
午後から雲が出てきた。	It got cloudy in the afternoon.

雨

今日は雨だった。	It was rainy today.
今日もまた雨だった。	It was rainy again today.
4日も雨が続いてる。	It has been raining for four days.
夕方になって雨が降り始めた。	It started raining early in the evening.
朝、にわか雨が降った。	There was a light shower in the morning.
午後はどしゃ降りだった。	It poured in the afternoon. ＊pour［ポーァ］＝（雨が）激しく降る

29

英語日記フレーズは項目ごとに分類されているので、目当ての例文が探しやすくなっています。意味や発音がわかりづらい表現には注釈を付けています。英語日記を書くときに便利な単語リストも、ぜひ参照してください。

2章 英語日記に役立つ文法

英文を書く上で知っておきたい基本的な文法を丁寧に解説しています。英文法をもう一度おさらいしたいときや、日記に書いた英文の文法が正しいか確認したくなったときなどに、開いてみましょう。

こんなときに

▶文法をおさらいしたい！
▶英語日記を書いていて、文法が正しいか迷う……。

3章 英語日記でよく使う構文

日常的な英語表現でよく使う 74 の構文を収録。豊富な例文と解説を通じて、各構文の使い方がしっかり理解できます。さまざまな構文を身につけることで、日記に書く英文のバリエーションがより豊かになります。

こんなときに

▶英語日記でよく使う構文をおさらいしたい！
▶日記に書く英文のバリエーションを広げたい！

さあ、あなたも今日から
英語日記を書いてみましょう！

英語日記パーフェクト表現辞典 [改訂版]

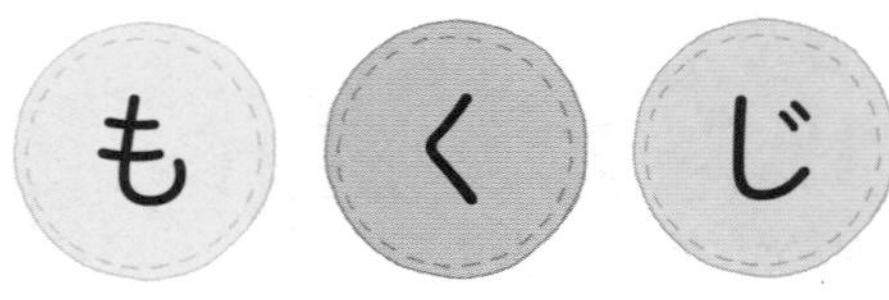

03　行事・イベント …… 72

04　人間関係 …… 94

05　気持ち・感想 …… 120

09 電話・郵便 …… 192

10 家事 …… 210

11 仕事 …… 222

12　学校生活 …… 260

13　大学・専門学校 …… 290

19　趣味・習いごと …… 408

20　スポーツ …… 428

26　出産・育児 …… 552

27　ペット …… 580

2章 英語日記に役立つ文法 …… 645

3章 英語日記でよく使う構文 …… 695

英語日記を書く前に

❶ 英文を書くときの簡単ルール

文頭は大文字に

英文を書くときは、文の冒頭を大文字にします。また、I（私は・私が）は、文の途中でも必ず大文字で書きます。単語と単語の間は、読みやすいように、アルファベット１文字分くらいのスペースをあけましょう。

例 学校に行った。
I went to school.

文頭は大文字に　単語と単語の間にはスペースを

コンマやピリオドの付け方

文の意味の切れ目にはコンマ（,）を、文の終わりにはピリオド（.）を書きます。コンマは、英文が短い場合など特に必要がなければ書かなくて構いません。疑問を表す文にはクエスチョンマーク（?）、気持ちを強く表したいときなどにはエクスクラメーションマーク（!）を、文の終わりに書きます。

例 具合が悪かったので、家にいた。
I was sick, so I stayed at home.

意味の切れ目にはコンマ　文の終わりにはピリオド

つづりがわからなくても気にしない！

英語日記を書いていると、単語のつづりに自信が持てないことがあるかもしれません。そんなとき、辞書で調べるのはもちろんよいことですが、あまり気にせず、あやふやなまま書いてしまっても大丈夫です。気軽に取り組むほうが長続きしますよ。

ローマ字で書いてもOK

英語で何と表現すればいいのか迷うときは、ローマ字で書いても構いません。特に、日本ならではの行事や習慣、食べ物などは、英語で表すのが難しいもの。無理に英語にする必要はありません。

例 昼食にきつねうどんを食べた。
I had kitsune udon for lunch.

② 日付と時間の書き方

英語で年月日を書くとき、アメリカ式では「月、日、コンマ（,）、年」の順に書くのが一般的です。日付と曜日だけを書く場合は、「曜日、コンマ（,）、月、日」の順番が一般的。下の表にあるように、「月」と「曜日」は短縮形で書くこともよくあります。

英語で時間を表すときは、24時間制（13時など）よりも12時間制（午後1時など）が一般的です。午前か午後かを表すなら、10 a.m.（午前10時）や2 p.m.（午後2時）のように、「時刻＋a.m./p.m.（午前／午後）」の形で書きましょう。a.m.やp.m.は、am/A.M./AMのように書いても構いません。ただし、日記は自分だけが見るものですから、24時間制のほうが慣れているという人は、無理に12時間制で書かなくても大丈夫です。

例 2023年8月12日→ **August 12, 2023**（または **Aug. 12, 2023**）
10月16日 月曜日→ **Monday, October 16**（または **Mon., Oct. 16** など）
14時30分→ **2:30 p.m.**

「月」の書き方

1月	**January（Jan.）**
2月	**February（Feb.）**
3月	**March（Mar.）**
4月	**April（Apr.）**
5月	**May**
6月	**June**
7月	**July**
8月	**August（Aug.）**
9月	**September（Sep./Sept.）**
10月	**October（Oct.）**
11月	**November（Nov.）**
12月	**December（Dec.）**

「曜日」の書き方

月曜日	**Monday（Mon.）**
火曜日	**Tuesday（Tue./Tues.）**
水曜日	**Wednesday（Wed.）**
木曜日	**Thursday（Thu./Thur.）**
金曜日	**Friday（Fri.）**
土曜日	**Saturday（Sat.）**
日曜日	**Sunday（Sun.）**

※（　）内は短縮形の例です。短縮形は、最後にピリオド（.）を付けて書くのが一般的です。また、「月」の5～7月には、短縮形はあまり用いられません。

❸ こんなふうに書いてみよう

英語日記には、特別なルールはありません。日本語の日記と同じで、その日あったことやこれからの予定、自分が考えていることなど、好きなことを好きなように書いてOK。まずは、1～3文程度の短い日記から書き始めてみましょう。大切なのは、楽しみながら英語日記を続けることです。

下は、私が書いた日記のサンプルです。英語が苦手と感じている人も、これなら続けられそうだと思いませんか？

❶Sunday, Sep.23
❷sunny

❸
I bought a bag.
It was 70 percent off!
I was ❹soooo happy. ❺ :)

❻

訳 バッグを買った。7割引！ スゴクうれしい。

❶その日の日付や曜日を書きましょう。

❷文字やイラストで、天気を記しておくのもおすすめです。

❸1章「英語日記フレーズ集」も参考にしながら、日記を書いてみましょう。

❹soをsooooと表すなどして、意味を強調してもいいですね。

❺❻顔文字やイラストを描くのもGOOD。

日記帳はどんなものを使ってもOK！

英語日記を書くための日記帳やノートは、どんなものを使っても構いません。自分が書きやすいと感じるものを選んでみましょう。ちなみに私は、5年分の日記が書ける「5年連用日記帳」を、もう30年以上も愛用しています。1ページに同じ日付の日記が5年分並ぶ形式なので、過去の同じ日に何をしていたかが一目でわかって、とても面白いですよ。

▲私が愛用している「5年連用日記帳」。もう7冊目に入りました。

4 何を書くか迷ったときは

「日記に書くことがない」――そう感じている人の多くは、「日記には特別なことを書かなくてはいけない」と、自らハードルを高くしてしまっているように思います。でも、その日の天気や食事の内容など、ちょっとしたことを書くだけでも立派な日記になります。あまり気張らず、気楽に取り組んでみましょう。

簡単に続けられる日記のテーマ例として、以下に「ごはん日記」「健康日記」「育児日記」を紹介します。このほか、その日あったうれしい出来事をつづる「幸せ日記」、お気に入りのレシピを英語でメモする「レシピ日記」など、アイデア次第でいろいろな日記が書けます。ぜひ、楽しく続けられるテーマを見つけてくださいね。

ごはん日記　毎日の食事を書き留める日記。栄養バランスのチェックにも GOOD！

I had some toast and coffee for breakfast.
I went to a Chinese restaurant for lunch.
I had curry with rice and some salad for supper.

訳 朝食はトーストとコーヒー。ランチは中華料理店に行った。夕飯はカレーライスとサラダを食べた。

健康日記　体重や体脂肪率などの健康に関する情報や、その日の運動などを記録。

Weight : 55kg (↑ 0.5kg)
Waist : 72cm
Pedometer : 6238 steps

I had some cookies late at night.
Oh NOOOOO!!!

訳
体重：55kg（↑ 0.5kg）
ウエスト：72cm
歩数計：6238 歩

夜中にクッキーを食べちゃった。
ああ、ヤバーイ !!!

育児日記　授乳や子どもの送り迎えなど、育児にまつわる出来事を書く日記。

I took Maiko to the preschool at 8:30 a.m.
I picked her up around 3 p.m.
She went to bed around 8:30 p.m.

訳 朝８時半に、マイコを幼稚園に連れていった。午後３時ごろ、彼女を迎えに行った。マイコは夜８時半ごろ、布団に入った。

本書における表記

・本書では、原則としてアメリカ英語を使用しています。また、日本語のニュアンスを自然な英語で表すために、意訳している表現もあります。

・本書に掲載しているフレーズは、自分の状況に合わせて、名詞の単数・複数、冠詞（a/an、the）、時制（現在・過去・未来など）、人称代名詞（I、you、we、they、he/she）、固有名詞などを、適宜変更してお使いください。

例 **She is kind.** → **He is kind.**
（彼女は優しい）　（彼は優しい）

I borrowed some books. → **I borrowed a book.**
（何冊か本を借りた）　（本を1冊借りた）

・数字や単位については、日記での書きやすさを考慮して、本来スペルで書くものであっても［アラビア数字＋単位記号］で表している場合があります。

例 **three kilos → 3kg**
ten centimeters → 10cm
20 degrees Celsius → 20℃

・それぞれの言語の特徴やニュアンスを考慮して、日本語の文と英文で異なる時制（現在・過去・未来など）を採用している表現もあります。

例 息子の首がすわった。　**He can now hold his head up.**

・「息子は」「娘は」は、my son や my daughter などのほかに、he や she と人称代名詞で表している場合もあります。

・so を soooo と書いて感情を強調したり、♪♡などの記号を用いて日記らしさを出したりしている表現もあります。

・カタカナの発音表記は参考用です。ご了承ください。

・「インスタ」および「インスタグラム」「Instagram」は登録商標です。

・X（ツイッター）は、2023年8月現在、通称として広く用いられている「Twitter」ならびに「ツイッター」の表記を主に採用しています。

1章

英語日記フレーズ集

普段の生活について英語で書くときに使える表現を、たっぷり収録。
そのまま書き写すだけでも、立派な英語日記になります。

01 天気・季節

天気

天気を表す単語

晴れた	sunny		
快晴の	bright［ブゥライト］		
曇りの	cloudy	虹	rainbow
雨の	rainy	風が強い	windy
小雨	light rain	風が心地いい	breezy
大雨、豪雨	heavy rain	気持ちのいい風	nice breeze
にわか雨	(light) shower	暖かい	warm
雪の	snowy	暑い	hot
大雪	heavy snow	肌寒い	chilly
粉雪	powder snow	涼しい	cool
霧の	foggy［フォギィ］	寒い	cold
あられ、ひょう	hail［ヘイゥ］	乾燥した、カラッとした	dry
雷、雷鳴	thunder	じめじめしている	humid［ヒューミッド］
雷、稲光	lightning	蒸し暑い	muggy［マギィ］
台風	typhoon	うだるように暑い	boiling hot
竜巻	tornado	凍えるように寒い	freezing cold

晴れ

今日はいい天気だった。
The weather was nice today.

今日は快晴だった。
It was very bright out today.
＊out＝外は

雲一つない青空だった。
There wasn't a single cloud in the clear, blue sky.

穏やかな日だった。
It was a calm day.
＊calm［カーム］＝穏やかな

さわやかな天気だった。	**The weather was refreshing.**
3日ぶりに晴れた。	**It was the first clear day in three days.** ＊first ... in ～ days＝～日ぶりの…
台風一過の秋晴れだった。	**After the typhoon passed, it was a nice autumn day.**
明日は晴れるといいな。	**I hope the weather is nice tomorrow.**
私は晴れ男（晴れ女）だ。	**It's always sunny when I go out.** ＊直訳は「私が出かけるときはいつも晴れる」

曇り

今日は曇りだった。	**It was cloudy today.**
一日中、曇っていた。	**It was cloudy all day.**
どんよりした一日だった。	**It was an overcast day.** ＊overcast[オウヴァキャスト]＝どんよりした
曇りの日が続くなぁ。	**It has been cloudy for several days now.**
空に雲が立ち込めていた。	**The sky was full of clouds.** ＊full of ～＝～でいっぱいで
午後から雲が出てきた。	**It got cloudy in the afternoon.**

雨

今日は雨だった。	**It was rainy today.**
今日もまた雨だった。	**It was rainy again today.**
4日も雨が続いてる。	**It has been raining for four days.**
夕方になって雨が降り始めた。	**It started raining early in the evening.**
朝、にわか雨が降った。	**There was a light shower in the morning.**
午後はどしゃ降りだった。	**It poured in the afternoon.** ＊pour[ポーァ]＝(雨が)激しく降る

だんだん雨脚が強まっていった。 **The rain got heavier and heavier.**

＊「弱まっていった」なら、got lighter and lighter

外は霧雨が降っている。 **It's drizzling outside.**

＊drizzle＝霧雨が降る

今朝、小雨が降った。 **It sprinkled this morning.**

＊sprinkle＝小雨が降る、雨がぱらつく

今にも雨が降りそうだ。 **It looks like it's going to rain any time now.**

雨が小降りになってきた。 **The rain is letting up.**

＊let up＝（雨などが）弱まる

午後に雨が止んだ。 **It stopped raining in the afternoon.**

早く雨が止まないかなぁ。 **I hope it stops raining soon.**

ここのところ雨ばかりで、憂うつだ。 **It has been raining a lot lately, and I'm feeling down.**

雨だったので、出かけるのをやめた。 **It rained, so I decided not to go out.**

私、雨女（雨男）なのかなぁ？ **Am I a rain bringer?**

＊rain bringer＝雨を連れてくる人

傘を持っていない日に限って、雨が降る。 **It only rains on days when I don't have my umbrella.**

足元がびしょぬれになった。 **My feet were soaking wet.**

＊soaking wet＝びしょぬれで

全身ずぶぬれになった。 **My whole body was wet.**

雪・みぞれ

雪が降った。 **It snowed.**

雪が降り始めた。 **It's starting to snow.**

みぞれが降った。 **It sleeted.** ＊sleet＝みぞれが降る

粉雪だった。 **It was powder snow.**

ぼたん雪だった。 **The snowflakes were really big.**

＊snowflake＝雪片、雪の1片

初雪が降った。 **We had the first snow of the season.**

今年の初雪は、例年より 10 日遅かった。 **The first snow of the year was ten days later than usual.**

雪が降りそうな寒さだ。	**It's cold enough to snow.**
ドカ雪が降った。	**It snowed very heavily.**
8年ぶりの大雪らしい。	**I hear it's the first heavy snowfall in eight years.** ＊first ... in ～ years：～年ぶりの…
起きたら雪が積もっていた。	**When I woke up, there was snow on the ground.**
雪が30センチも積もった。	**We had as much as 30cm of snow.**
雪はすっかり溶けてしまった。残念！	**All the snow melted. Too bad!** ＊「安心した！」なら、Too bad!をPhew!［フュー］に
雪はすぐに溶けてしまった。	**The snow melted right away.**
家の前の雪かきをした。	**I cleared away the snow in front of my house.**
2回も滑って転んでしまった。	**I slipped and fell twice.** ＊slip＝滑る　fall＝転ぶ。過去形はfell
雪で多くの車が立ち往生した。	**A lot of cars got stuck in the snow.** ＊get stuck＝立ち往生する、抜け出せなくなる

風

風が心地よかった。	**The breeze felt nice.**
そよ風が気持ちいい日だった。	**It was a nice breezy day.**
風が冷たかった。	**The wind was cold.** ＊「暖かかった」なら、coldをwarmに
風のない穏やかな一日だった。	**It was a calm, windless day.**
風が激しい日だった。	**It was a gusty day.** ＊gusty［ガスティ］＝風の強い
ものすごい風で、吹き飛ばされそうになった。	**I was almost blown away by the strong wind.** ＊blown＝blow（～を吹き飛ばす）の過去分詞
向かい風が強くて、自転車が前に進まなかった。	**The strong headwind pushed against my bike.** ＊headwind＝向かい風
強風で、傘が折れてしまった。	**The strong wind broke my umbrella.**

強風で、傘が使い物にならなかった。	My umbrella was useless in the strong wind. ＊useless［ユースレㇲ］＝使い物にならない

豪雨・台風

帰宅途中、夕立に遭った。	I got caught in a shower on my way home. ＊get caught in 〜＝〜に巻き込まれる　shower＝にわか雨
激しい雷雨だった。	It was a violent thunderstorm. ＊violent＝激しい、猛烈な
ゲリラ豪雨に見舞われた。	I got caught in a sudden downpour. ＊downpour＝どしゃ降り
台風が近づいているらしい。	I hear there's a typhoon coming.
台風の影響で、すごい雨だった。	It rained heavily because of the typhoon.
台風の進路がそれて、ひと安心。	I'm glad the typhoon has changed the course.
今年は台風が多いな。	We're having a lot of typhoons this year.
スコールのようだった。	It was like a squall.　＊squall［スクウォーオ］
バケツをひっくり返したようだった。	It was like a bucket of water had been turned over. ＊turn over 〜＝〜をひっくり返す

雷・ひょう

雷がゴロゴロ鳴った。	I could hear the thunder rumbling. ＊rumble＝（雷などが）ゴロゴロ鳴る
雷が鳴って、怖かった。	The thunder scared me. ＊scare＝〜をおびえさせる
家の近所に雷が落ちた。	The lightning hit in my neighborhood.
少しの間、停電した。	The power was out for a little while. ＊power＝電力
すごい音だった。	The sound was really loud.
遠くに稲光が見えた。	I could see the lightning in the distance.

ピカピカ、ドーン！ **Flash and boom!**
＊**boom**＝（雷などの）とどろく音

午後、ひょうが降った。 **It hailed in the afternoon.**
＊**hail**＝ひょうが降る

暑い

暑かった。 **It was hot.**

めちゃくちゃ暑かった。 **It was boiling hot.**

蒸し暑い一日だった。 **It was really hot and humid.**
＊**humid**＝蒸し蒸しする

ダラダラと汗が出た。 **I sweated a lot.**

暑くて死にそう。 **It's so hot that I feel like I'm going to die.**

この暑さには参るなぁ。 **This summer heat makes me sick.**

このところ毎日、焼けつくような暑さだ。 **It has been burning hot every day lately.**
＊**burning**＝焼けつくように

ゆうべは蒸し暑くて眠れなかった。 **It was too muggy to sleep last night.**
＊**muggy**［マギィ］＝蒸し暑い

暑くて、一歩も外に出たくなかった。 **It was so hot that I didn't want to take a step outside.**

1週間連続で真夏日だ。 **It has been over 30℃ for a week.**

今日は猛暑日になった。 **It reached over 35℃ today.**

ゆうべも熱帯夜だった。 **It was a hot and humid night again yesterday.**

気温は38℃まで上がった。 **The temperature went up to 38℃ .**

エアコンなしなんてムリ。 **I would die without an air conditioner.**

扇風機をつけた。 **I turned on my electric fan.**
＊**turn on ～**＝～（電気など）をつける

寒い

寒かった。 **It was cold.**

凍える寒さだった。 It was freezing cold.

寒くて死にそう。 I'm freezing to death.

＊to death＝死ぬほど、とても

この寒さはいつまで続くんだろう？ I wonder how long it's going to be this cold.

少し肌寒かった。 It was a little chilly.

日が落ちた途端に寒くなった。 As soon as the sun went down, it got cold.

朝晩はだいぶ冷え込む。 It's pretty cold in the morning and at night.

気温が氷点下まで下がった。 The temperature went down to below zero.

手がかじかんだ。 My hands were numb.

＊numb［ナム］＝かじかんだ、感覚を失った

手足が冷たかった。 My hands and feet were cold.

こたつから離れられないよ。 It's hard to get out of the kotatsu.

使い捨てカイロは必需品だ。 Hand warmers are a must-have.

＊「使い捨てカイロ」はhot packsとも言う

湯たんぽで足があったかい。 My hot water bottle keeps my feet warm.

家の中でも着込んでいる。 I wear extra clothes even in the house.

暖かい

暖かい一日だった。 It was a warm day.

暖かくなってきた。 It's starting to get warm.

今日はポカポカ陽気だった。 It was nice and warm today.

小春日和だった。 We had an Indian summer today.

＊Indian summer＝小春日和

3月にしては暖かかった。 It was warm for March.

涼しい

涼しかった。 **It was cool.**

だんだん涼しくなってきた。 **It's getting cooler.**

だいぶ涼しくなってきた。 **It has cooled down considerably.**
＊considerably＝かなり、ずいぶん

夕方になって涼しくなった。 **It cooled down early in the evening.**

7月にしては涼しかった。 **It was cool for July.**

じめじめ・乾燥

今日はじめじめしていた。 **It was humid today.**

湿気で髪がまとまらなかった。 **My hair was a mess due to the humidity.**
＊humidity＝湿気

肌がベタついて不快だった。 **My skin was sticky and uncomfortable.**

洗濯物が乾かなくて困る。 **I can't get my laundry to dry.**

空気が乾燥していた。 **The air was dry.**

空気が乾燥して、のどが痛い。 **I've got a sore throat because of the dry air.**
＊sore［ソァ］＝痛い　throat［スロウト］＝のど

肌がかさかさだ。 **My skin is dry.**

天気予報

天気予報が当たった。 **The weather forecast was right.**

天気予報が外れた。 **The weather forecast was wrong.**

明日の予報は、晴れのち曇り。 **It'll be clear, then cloudy tomorrow.**

降水確率は60パーセント。 **There's a 60% chance of rain.**
＊chance＝可能性

傘を持っていったほうがよさそうだ。 **I'd better take an umbrella with me.**

今日の最高気温は33℃だった。 **Today's high was 33℃.**

今日の最低気温は−1℃だった。	**Today's low was -1°C.**
明日は寒くなるらしい。	**They say it's going to be cold tomorrow.** ＊「さらに寒くなる」なら、coldをcolderに
明日は暖かくなるらしい。	**They say it's going to be warm tomorrow.** ＊「さらに暖かくなる」なら、warmをwarmerに
明日から暑さが厳しくなるらしい。	**They say it's going to be hotter from tomorrow.**
明日は雨になりそうだ。	**It looks like it's going to rain tomorrow.**
週末、晴れるかなぁ。	**I wonder if it'll be sunny on the weekend.**
今週末、雨が降らないといいな。	**I hope it doesn't rain this weekend.**
来週は雪の予報なので、冬用タイヤに換えた。	**They say it's going to snow next week, so I changed my tires to winter tires.**
車にチェーンを付けた。	**I put snow chains on my tires.**

気象

今年は異常気象だ。	**The weather is really strange this year.**
この暑さは異常だ。	**This heat is unusual.**
1月にこの暖かさはちょっと不気味。	**It's a bit strange to have such warm weather in January.**
やっぱり、地球温暖化が進んでいるのかな。	**Maybe it's because global warming is getting worse.**
毎年これじゃ、もはや異常気象とは言えないな。	**If it's like this every year, then we can't really say it's unusual weather anymore.**
はっきりとした四季がなくなりつつある。	**Our four distinct seasons are becoming indistinct.** ＊distinct＝はっきりした　indistinct＝はっきりしない

明日は大寒波が来るらしい。	**They say a major cold wave is coming tomorrow.** ＊cold wave＝寒波
10年ぶりの寒波らしい。	**This is the first cold wave in ten years, I hear.**

季節

春

春が来た！	**Spring has come!**
桜が五分咲きだった。	**The cherry trees were at half-bloom.** ＊bloom＝開花
来週あたりに満開になりそう。	**I think they'll probably be in full bloom next week.** ＊in full bloom＝満開で
桜が満開だった！	**The cherry trees were in full bloom!**
お花見日和だった。	**It was a perfect day to see the cherry blossoms.**
庭でチョウを見かけた。	**I saw a butterfly in my yard.**
公園にいろいろな花が咲いていた。	**There were various flowers blooming in the park.**
春の新緑って好き。	**I like the fresh green leaves in spring.**
花粉症さえなければ、春は最高の季節なのに。	**Spring would be the perfect season if I didn't have hay fever.** ＊hay fever＝花粉症
春一番が吹いた。	**We had our first spring gale of the year.** ＊gale＝強風
今日は黄砂がすごかった。	**There was a lot of yellow sand today.**

夏

もう梅雨に入ったのかな？	**I wonder if the rainy season has already started.**

今年の梅雨はやけに長いな。	The rainy season this year is really long.
早く梅雨が明けないかなぁ。	I hope the rainy season is over soon. ＊over＝過ぎて
夏はもう、すぐそこだ。	Summer is just around the corner.
すごく暑いけど、やっぱり夏が好き。	It's really hot, but I still like summer.
熱中症に気を付けないと。	I need to be careful not to get heat stroke. ＊heat stroke＝熱中症
今年は珍しく冷夏だ。	This summer is unusually cool.

秋

もう秋だ。	It's already fall.
秋の風が心地いい。	The autumn breeze feels nice.
まだまだ残暑が厳しい。	The lingering summer heat is still severe. ＊lingering＝長引く severe［スィヴィァ］＝厳しい
各地で紅葉が見頃だ。	We can see the autumn colored leaves everywhere.
虫の声が聞こえる。	I can hear the insects.
食欲の秋。ついつい食べ過ぎちゃう。	My autumn appetite is here. I can't help overeating. ＊appetite［アパタイト］＝食欲 can't help ～ing＝つい～してしまう、～せずにはいられない
秋は何でもおいしいな。	Everything tastes great in the fall.
読書の秋。	Autumn is the season for reading.
スポーツの秋。	Autumn is the season for sports.
芸術の秋。	Autumn is the season to enjoy the arts.
今日は運動会日和だった。	It was a perfect day for a sports festival. ＊「運動会」は、field dayとも言う

冬

軒先につららができていた。	**There were icicles hanging off the eaves.** ＊icicle［アイスィコゥ］＝つらら　eaves［イーヴズ］＝軒
霜柱を踏んだら、サクサクと音がした。	**When I stepped on the frost, I could hear it crackling.** ＊frost＝霜　crackle＝バリバリ音を立てる
手が霜焼けになった。	**I got chilblains on my hands.** ＊chilblains＝霜焼け。重度の場合はfrostbite
雪だるまを作った。	**I made a snowman.**
かまくらを作った。	**I made a snow house.**
童心に返って雪合戦をした。	**I was in a snowball fight and felt like a kid again.**
今年は暖冬だ。	**This winter is unusually warm.**

空・天体

日が長い・短い

日が短くなってきた。	**The days are getting shorter.**
だいぶ日が長くなった。	**The days are much longer now.**
今日は夏至、1年で一番日が長い日だ。	**Today is summer solstice, the longest day of the year.**
今日は冬至、1年で一番日が短い日だ。	**Today is winter solstice, the shortest day of the year.**
家を出たとき、まだ外は真っ暗だった。	**It was dark when I left my house.**
朝5時には、もう空が明るい。	**It's already light outside at 5 a.m.**
夜7時になっても、まだ明るかった。	**It was still light outside at 7 p.m.**

雲

うろこ雲が広がってきれいだった。	**The sky was beautiful with cirrocumulus clouds.** ＊cirrocumulus［スィロウキュームラス］ clouds＝うろこ雲

大きな入道雲が見えた。 **I saw big thunderheads.**
＊thunderhead＝入道雲、積乱雲

一直線に雲が伸びていた。 **The clouds were stretched out in a line.**
＊stretched out＝伸びて

飛行機雲が見えた。 **I saw a contrail.**
＊contrail＝飛行機雲

雲がすごい速さで流れていた。 **The clouds were moving so fast.**

太陽

太陽がまぶしかった。 **The sun was really bright.**

朝日がきれいだった。 **The rising sun was beautiful.**
＊「夕日」なら、rising sunをsunsetに

夕日がすごく大きく見えた。 **The sunset looked enormous.**
＊enormous[イノーマス]＝大きい、巨大な

今日は日食だった。 **There was a solar eclipse today.**
＊solar eclipse[ソウラー イクリプス]＝日食

明日は26年ぶりの皆既日食だ。 **Tomorrow will be the first total solar eclipse in 26 years.**
＊first ... in ～ years＝～年ぶりの…

悪天候で皆既日食が見られなかった。 **We couldn't see the total solar eclipse because of the bad weather.**

いつか金環日食を見てみたいなぁ。 **I want to see the annular eclipse someday.**
＊annular[アニュラー]＝環状の

月

月がきれいだった。 **The moon was beautiful.**

お団子を供えてお月見をした。 **We offered dango and did moon viewing.**

おぼろ月が見えた。 **The moon looked hazy.**
＊hazy＝かすみがかった

三日月だった。 **It was a crescent moon.**
＊crescent[クレスント] moon＝三日月。「半月」はhalf moon、「満月」はfull moon、「新月」はnew moon

今日は月食だった。 **There was a lunar eclipse today.**
＊lunar eclipse[ルーナー イクリプス]＝月食

皆既月食を見た。 **We saw a total lunar eclipse.**
＊「部分月食」は、partial lunar eclipse

星

星座を表す単語

おひつじ座	Aries［エアリーズ］	いて座	Sagittarius［サジテァリアス］
おうし座	Taurus［トーラス］	やぎ座	Capricorn
ふたご座	Gemini［ジェマナィ］	みずがめ座	Aquarius
かに座	Cancer	うお座	Pisces［パイスィーズ］
しし座	Leo	オリオン座	Orion［ァラィアン］
おとめ座	Virgo［ヴァーゴゥ］	カシオペア座	Cassiopeia［キャスィアピーア］
てんびん座	Libra	おおぐま座	Ursa［アーサ］Major
さそり座	Scorpio	こぐま座	Ursa Minor

星がきれいだった。　**The stars were beautiful.**

流れ星を見た。　**I saw a shooting star.**
＊「流れ星」は、falling starとも言う

あっという間に消えちゃった。　**It was gone in no time.**

急いで願い事をした。　**I hurried to make a wish.**

願い事を言い終える前に消えてしまった。　**It disappeared before I could make a wish.**

天の川が見えた。　**I was able to see the Milky Way.**

オリオン座がくっきりと見えた。　**I saw Orion really clearly.**

しし座流星群を見た。　**I saw the Leonids meteor shower.**
＊Leonids meteor［ミーティアー］ shower＝しし座流星群

冬の夜空はきれいだな。　**The winter night sky is beautiful.**

虹

雨が上がって、虹が見えた。　**When the rain stopped, I saw a rainbow.**

久しぶりに虹を見た。　**It's been a long time since I last saw a rainbow.**

二重の虹が見えた。ラッキー！　**I was lucky to see a double rainbow! Lucky me!**

天気・季節について
英語日記を書いてみよう

日々の天気について、英語で書いてみましょう。

ポカポカ陽気

It was nice and warm today. I couldn't help nodding off while watching TV.

訳

今日はポカポカ陽気だった。テレビを見ながら、ついウトウトしてしまった。

ポイント

「今日はポカポカ陽気」は nice and warm today（心地よく暖かい日）で、「つい～してしまう」は can't help ～ing（～せずにはいられない）で表すとよいでしょう。「ウトウトする」は nod off と表します。「～しながら」は、while ～ing を使いましょう。

また雨！

It has been raining for five days now. My laundry won't dry and I feel blue. I hope it's sunny tomorrow.

訳

5日連続の雨。洗濯物はなかなか乾かないし、気持ちも憂うつ。明日は晴れてほしいな。

ポイント

It has been ～ing は現在完了進行形で、「ずっと～の状態が続いている」という継続の意味を表します。My laundry won't dry の won't は will not の短縮形で、「どうしても～しない、～しようとしない」という意味。I hope it's ... は、I hope it'll be ... でも OK です。

暑〜い！

Today's high was 37.6℃. It was unbelievably hot. This month's electricity bill will probably go through the roof. (Sigh)

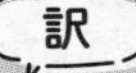

今日の最高気温は37.6°C。信じられないくらい暑かった。今月の電気代、すごいことになりそう。（はぁ〜）

「今日の最高気温」はtoday's high。「今日の最低気温」ならtoday's lowとします。「信じられないくらい暑い」はunbelievably hotと表しましたが、really hot（本当に暑い）でもOKです。go through the roofは「（価格などが）非常に高くなる」という意味。

強風で…

It was really windy today. The headwind pushed against my bike and messed up my hair before I got to school. It was terrible!

訳

今日は風がとても強かった。向かい風で自転車は前に進まないし、学校に着く前に髪はボサボサになるし。もう最悪！

「向かい風」はheadwindで、「追い風」ならtailwindです。「向かい風で自転車が前に進まない」は意訳して、The headwind pushed against my bike（向かい風が私の自転車を押した）と表現しました。mess up 〜は「〜をめちゃくちゃにする」の意味。

02
体調

体調について

体調がいい

今日は体調がよかった。	**I felt great today.**
最近、体調がいい。	**I've been in good shape lately.** ＊in good shape＝調子がいい。「体調が悪い」なら、in bad shapeに
だんだん体調がよくなってきた。	**My health is getting better.**
体が軽い気がする。	**My body feels light.**
祖父は今日、体調がよさそうだった。	**Grandpa looked well today.**
隣のカジシマさんは90歳でピンピンしている。	**My next-door neighbor, Kajishima-san, is 90 and is alive and kicking.** ＊alive and kicking＝元気はつらつで、ピンピンして
コタロウは元気いっぱいだった。	**Kotaro was full of energy.**

体調が悪い

今日は体調があまりよくなかった。	**I didn't feel very well today.**
最近、どうも体調が悪い。	**I've been under the weather lately.** ＊under the weather＝体調が優れない、元気がない
一日中、具合が悪くて寝ていた。	**I was sick in bed all day.**
寒気がする。	**I have the chills.** ＊chill＝寒気
マリコは具合が悪そうだった。	**Mariko looked sick.**
今日は仮病を使っちゃった。	**I faked being sick today.** ＊fake＝〜のふりをする
昔より体が弱くなったなぁ。	**I'm not as strong as I used to be.**

病名を表す単語

風邪	cold
インフルエンザ	flu［フルー］
新型コロナウイルス	COVID / COVID-19
頭痛	headache
腹痛	stomachache
歯痛	toothache
生理痛	cramps
はしか	measles［ミーズォズ］
水ぼうそう	chicken pox
おたふく風邪	mumps［マンプス］
ぜんそく	asthma［アズマ］
気管支炎	bronchitis［ブランカイタス］
花粉症	hay［ヘィ］ fever
中耳炎	otitis［オウタイティス］ media
外耳炎	external otitis
脳卒中	stroke
がん	cancer
心臓発作	heart attack
胃かいよう	stomach ulcers［アゥサーズ］
肺炎	pneumonia［ニューモウニァ］
糖尿病	diabetes［ダイアビーティス］
高血圧（症）	hypertension
低血圧（症）	hypotension
貧血	anemia［アニーミア］
結膜炎	conjunctivitis
白内障	cataract［キャタラクト］
緑内障	glaucoma［グラゥコゥマ］
うつ病	depression
更年期障害	menopausal disorder
帯状疱疹	shingles［シンゴゥズ］

体の部位を表す単語

頭	head
髪	hair
額	forehead
顔	face
まゆ毛	eyebrow
まつ毛	eyelash
まぶた	eyelid
目	eye
鼻	nose
耳	ear
ほお	cheek
口	mouth
唇	lip
舌	tongue［タン］
口ひげ	mustache［マスタッシュ］
あごひげ	beard［ビアード］
あご	chin
首	neck
胸部	chest
胸、乳房	breast
肩	shoulder
腕	arm
ひじ	elbow
手	hand
親指	thumb［サム］
人差し指	index finger
中指	middle finger
薬指	ring finger
小指	little finger / pinkie
足の指	toe
つめ	nail
背中	back
腰	lower back / hip
おなか	belly
へそ	bellybutton / navel
おしり（全体）	buttocks / butt
脚（足首より上）	leg
ひざ	knee［ニー］
関節	joint
足先	foot

風邪

風邪気味だ。
I have a slight cold.

風邪をひいちゃった。
I have a cold.

風邪をひいたみたい。
I think I have a cold.

ひどい風邪だ。
I have a bad cold.

会社でうつされたのかもしれない。
I might have caught it at work.
*caught[コート]はcatch(～[病気]にかかる)の過去分詞

風邪が長引いている。
I have a persistent cold.
*persistent＝継続する、なかなか治らない

風邪が治った。
I got over my cold.
*get over ～＝～(病気)から回復する

最近、風邪がはやっている。
There's a cold going around these days.
*go around＝(病気などが)広がる

風邪をひかないようにしなきゃ。
I need to be careful not to catch a cold.

外出時はマスクをしよう。
I'm going to wear a mask when going out.

手洗いとうがいを忘れないようにしよう。
I need to remember to wash my hands and gargle.
*gargle＝うがいをする

今年の風邪はのどにくるらしい。
I hear this year's cold affects the throat.
*affect＝～に変調をきたす

今年の風邪は長引くらしい。
I hear this year's cold is persistent.

インフルエンザ・感染症

最近、インフルエンザがはやっている。
A lot of people have been coming down with the flu lately.
*come down with ～＝～(病気)にかかる
flu＝インフルエンザ

今年はA型インフルエンザがはやっているらしい。
I heard the type-A flu is going around this year.

インフルエンザの予防接種を受けた。
I got a flu shot.
*shot＝注射

来月、ワクチンの接種予約を入れた。	**I made a reservation to get the vaccine next month.** ＊vaccine［ヴァクスィーン］＝ワクチン
インフルエンザにかかったかも。	**I might be coming down with the flu.**
インフルエンザにかかった。	**I have the flu.**
ノロウイルスに感染した。	**I caught the norovirus.**
新型コロナウイルスに感染した。	**I caught COVID.**
症状が軽くてよかった。	**I'm glad I only have mild symptoms.** ＊symptom＝症状
自宅療養になった。	**I had to isolate myself at home.** ＊isolate＝～を隔離する
リョウの学校でクラスターが発生してしまった。	**There was a cluster at Ryo's school.**
高齢の母が感染しないよう、自分もしっかり予防しよう。	**I'll make sure to take precautions so my elderly mother won't get infected.** ＊precaution＝用心、備え　elderly＝年配の
店の入り口にある手指消毒液で手を消毒した。	**I disinfected my hands with the hand sanitizer at the shop entrance.** ＊disinfect＝～を消毒する
マスクを着けた顔しか知らない人がいる。	**There are people whose faces I only know with a mask on.**

頭痛

朝からずっと頭が痛い。	**I've had a headache since this morning.**
一日中、頭が痛かった。	**I've had a headache all day.**
頭が重かった。	**My head felt heavy.**
頭がズキズキ痛んだ。	**My head was throbbing.** ＊throb［スロッブ］＝ズキズキする
頭がガンガンする。	**I have a pounding headache.** ＊pounding＝(頭が)ガンガンするような
ひどい頭痛だ。	**I have a bad headache.**
今もまだ頭が痛い。	**My head is still aching.** ＊ache［エイク］＝痛む

このところ、片頭痛が続いている。 I've been having migraines.
＊migraine［マイグレイン］＝片頭痛

頭痛薬を飲んだ。 I took medicine for my headache.

薬を飲んでしばらくしたら、頭痛が治まった。 Some time after I took the medicine, the headache was gone.

発熱

なんだか熱っぽい。 I feel a little feverish. ＊feverish＝熱っぽい

高熱が出た。 I had a high fever. ＊「微熱」は、slight fever

38℃の熱が出た。 I had a fever of 38℃.
＊「38℃近い熱」なら、a fever of almost 38℃

おでこに保冷剤を当てた。 I put an ice pack on my forehead.

熱にうなされた。 The fever made me delirious.
＊delirious＝(熱などで)うわごとを言う

熱が全然下がらない。 My fever won't go down.

解熱剤を飲んだ。 I took a fever reducer.

熱が下がってきた。 My fever is going down.

腹痛

急におなかが痛くなった。 I suddenly got a stomachache.

夕食後、おなかが痛くなった。 I got a stomachache after dinner.

食べ過ぎておなかが痛くなった。 I got a stomachache from eating too much.

脇腹が痛い。 I feel a pain in my side. ＊side＝脇腹

おなかに差し込むような痛みを感じた。 I felt a sharp pain in my stomach.

胃がシクシク痛んだ。 I had a dull pain in my stomach.
＊dull＝鈍い

食中毒で具合が悪くなった。 I got sick from food poisoning.
＊food poisoning＝食中毒

胃薬を飲んだ。 I took medicine for my stomachache.

下痢

おなかを下している。	**I have the runs.** ＊the runs＝下痢
一日中、おなかがゴロゴロいっていた。	**My stomach has been rumbling all day.** ＊rumble＝（おなかなどが）ゴロゴロ音を立てる
便がゆるかった。	**My stool was watery.** ＊stool［ストゥーゥ］＝便通、大便
何度もトイレに駆け込んだ。	**I dashed to the restroom a hundred times.** ＊a hundred times＝何度も
下痢止めを飲んだ。	**I took medicine for my diarrhea.** ＊diarrhea［ダイアリーア］＝下痢

便秘

便秘だ。	**I'm constipated.** ＊constipated［カンスティペイティッド］＝便秘で
最近、便秘ぎみだ。	**I get constipated a lot these days.**
もう3日も出ていない。	**I've been constipated for three days now.**
おなかが張っている感じがする。	**My stomach feels tight.**
トイレで20分頑張ったけど、ダメだった。	**I sat on the toilet for 20 minutes, but nothing happened.**
便秘薬を飲んだ。	**I took medicine for my constipation.**

吐き気

吐き気がした。	**I felt like throwing up.** ＊throw up＝吐く、戻す
戻しそうだった。	**I was about to throw up.** ＊be about to ～＝まさに～するところだ
もう少しで戻すところだった。	**I almost threw up.** ＊threw［スルー］＝throwの過去形
吐き気を我慢した。	**I tried not to throw up.**
吐いてしまった。	**I threw up.**
食べた物を全部戻してしまった。	**I threw up everything I ate.**

船酔いしてしまった。	**I got seasick.**
車酔いしてしまった。	**I got carsick.**
バスに乗る前、娘に酔い止めを飲ませた。	**I gave her anti-nausea medicine before we got on the bus.** ＊anti-nausea［アンタイ ノーズィア］＝酔い止めの

胸焼け・胃もたれ

胃がムカムカした。	**I had an upset stomach.** ＊upset＝（胃の）調子がおかしい
胃がもたれた。	**My stomach felt heavy.**
胸焼けした。	**I had heartburn.** ＊heartburn＝胸焼け
脂っこい物を食べ過ぎたようだ。	**I think I ate too much greasy food.** ＊greasy＝脂っこい
消化不良を起こしたみたいだ。	**I think I have indigestion.** ＊indigestion［インダイジェスチョン］＝消化不良

二日酔い

ひどい二日酔いだった。	**I had a terrible hangover.** ＊hangover＝二日酔い
二日酔いで頭が痛かった。	**I had a headache because of my hangover.**
飲み過ぎて気持ちが悪くなった。	**I felt horrible from drinking.**

生理・生理痛

生理になった。	**I'm on my period.** ＊period＝生理
今日は２日目だったので、つらかった。	**I was on the second day of my period, so it was rough.** ＊rough［ラフ］＝つらい、苦しい
生理で一日中、眠かった。	**I was sleepy all day because of my period.**
生理痛がひどい。	**I have really bad cramps.** ＊cramps＝生理痛
生理痛の薬を飲んだ。	**I took medicine for my cramps.**
生理が終わった。	**My period is over.**

生理不順なのが心配。	**I'm worried that my period is irregular.**
予定より生理が早かった。	**My period came early.** ＊「遅かった」なら、earlyをlateに
生理が１週間遅れている。	**My period is a week late.**
生理前のイライラがひどい。	**I have bad PMS.** ＊PMS＝premenstrual syndrome（月経前症候群）
気分が落ち込んでいる。	**I'm feeling down.**

食欲がある・ない

食欲がない。	**I don't have an appetite.** ＊appetite［アパタイト］＝食欲
最近、あまり食欲がない。	**I don't have much of an appetite these days.**
何も食べる気がしなかった。	**I didn't feel like eating anything.**
食欲が出てきた。	**I worked up an appetite.** ＊work up an appetite＝食欲をかき立てられる
最近、食欲が旺盛だ。	**I have a big appetite these days.**
私って、ホント大食い。	**I really am a big eater.**
彼女は小食だ。	**She eats like a bird.**

貧血・立ちくらみ

最近、貧血気味だ。	**I've been feeling anemic recently.** ＊anemic［アニーミック］＝貧血の
貧血で倒れてしまった。	**I fainted from anemia.** ＊faint＝気を失う　anemia＝貧血
頭がぼーっとした。	**My head felt fuzzy.**
めまいがした。	**I felt dizzy.**
めまいがひどい。	**I have severe dizziness.**
立ちくらみがした。	**I got dizzy when I stood up.**
もっと鉄分を取らないと。	**I need to get more iron.** ＊iron［アイアン］＝鉄分

疲労

なんだか体がだるいなぁ。	**I feel kind of sluggish.** ＊sluggish［スラギッシュ］＝活気のない、のろのろした
一日中、体がだるかった。	**I felt sluggish all day.**
体が重かった。	**My body felt heavy.**
疲れがたまってるみたいだ。	**I think my fatigue is building up.** ＊fatigue［ファティーグ］＝疲労
疲れ過ぎて、起き上がれなかった。	**I was too tired to get up.**

寝不足

最近、寝不足だ。	**I haven't been getting enough sleep lately.**
寝不足で頭がふらふらした。	**The lack of sleep made me light-headed.** ＊light-headed＝頭がふらふらする
寝不足で集中できなかった。	**I couldn't concentrate because I didn't get enough sleep.** ＊concentrate＝集中する
このところ、寝付きが悪い。	**I've been having a hard time falling asleep.**
夜中に何度も目が覚めてしまう。	**I keep waking up in the middle of the night.**
昨日は３時間しか眠れなかった。	**I only slept for three hours last night.**
睡眠リズムが崩れている。	**My sleep rhythm is all messed up.** ＊be messed up＝めちゃくちゃである
朝、スッキリ起きられない。	**I don't wake up feeling refreshed.**
朝起きるのがつらい。	**It's tough to get out of bed in the morning.**

花粉症・アレルギー

花粉症の季節がやってきた。	**The hay fever season has already begun.** ＊hay［ヘィ］fever＝花粉症
もしかして、花粉症になったかも。	**I might have hay fever.**

ついに今年、花粉症になってしまったようだ。
Hay fever finally caught up with me this year.
＊catch up with ～＝～を悩ませ始める。caughtはcatchの過去分詞

花粉症はつらい。
Hay fever is unbearable.
＊unbearable［アンベアラボゥ］＝耐えられない

今日は花粉が多くてつらかった。
All of the pollen was killing me today.
＊pollen［パールン］＝花粉

今日は花粉が少なくて楽だった。
It was easier today because there wasn't much pollen.

今年は花粉がかなり多いらしい。
The pollen count is expected to be quite high this year.
＊pollen count＝花粉飛散数。「少ない」なら、highをlowに

今年は去年より花粉が多いらしい。
The pollen count is expected to be higher this year than last year.

今年の花粉は例年並みだ。
The pollen count is going to be the usual amount.

目がかゆかった。
My eyes were itchy.
＊itchy［イッチィ］＝かゆい

目がかゆくて、涙が出た。
My eyes were itchy and teary.
＊teary［ティアリィ］＝涙の

鼻も耳もかゆい。
Both my nose and ears are itchy.

くしゃみが止まらなかった。
I kept sneezing.

鼻水が止まらなかった。
My nose wouldn't stop running.
＊run＝（鼻水が）出る

一日中、鼻が詰まっていた。
My nose was blocked all day.

花粉のせいで、肌が荒れている。
My skin is rough because of pollen.
＊rough＝荒い、ざらざらの

外に出るときはマスクが必需品だ。
I can't go out without wearing a mask.

スギ花粉のアレルギーだ。
I'm allergic to Japanese cedar pollen.
＊allergic［アラージッㇰ］ to ～＝～に対するアレルギーの
cedar［スィーダー］＝スギ

ハウスダストのアレルギーだ。
I'm allergic to house dust.

猫アレルギーだ。
I have a cat allergy.
＊allergy［エラジィ］＝アレルギー

アレルギーでそばが食べられない。	**I can't eat soba because I'm allergic.** ＊be allergic[アラージック]＝アレルギーである
夕食の後、じんましんが出た。	**I broke out in hives after dinner.** ＊break out in ～＝～(発疹など)が突然出る hives＝じんましん

目の不調

左目が痛い。	**My left eye hurts.**
朝起きたら、まぶたがはれていた。	**When I woke up this morning, my eyelids were swollen.** ＊swollen[スウォウルン]＝はれた
朝から目が充血している。	**My eye has been bloodshot since this morning.** ＊bloodshot＝充血した
目がゴロゴロする。	**I have something in my eye.**
ものもらいになってしまった。	**I have a sty on my eye.** ＊sty[スタィ]＝ものもらい
1日、眼帯をして過ごした。	**I wore an eye patch all day.**
ドライアイだ。	**My eyes are dry.**
視力が落ちてきた。	**My eyesight is getting worse.** ＊eyesight＝視力
最近、目がかすむ。	**My eyesight has been getting cloudy.**
遠くのものが見えづらい。	**I'm near-sighted.** ＊near-sighted＝近視の
近くのものが見えづらい。	**I'm far-sighted.** ＊far-sighted＝遠視の
小さい文字が見えにくくなった。	**I'm having a hard time reading small letters these days.**
老眼になってきたかも。	**Maybe I'm getting far-sighted with age.**
老眼鏡を作った。	**I got reading glasses.**
わぁ、老眼鏡をかけたらよく見える！	**Wow, I can read really well with my reading glasses on.**
乱視気味だ。	**I have slight astigmatism.** ＊astigmatism[アスティグマティズム]＝乱視

使い捨てのコンタクトレンズを使い始めた。 **I started using disposable contact lenses.** ＊contact lensesは、contactsとしてもOK

コンタクトって快適。 **Contact lenses are comfortable.**

コンタクトを片方、なくしちゃった。 **I lost a contact lens.**

コンタクトを入れると目が痛くなる。 **My eyes hurt when I wear contact lenses.**

家では眼鏡をかけよう。 **I'll wear my glasses in the house.**

レーシックの手術、受けてみようかな。 **I'm thinking about getting LASIK surgery done.** ＊surgery［サージュリィ］＝手術

耳の不調

耳が聞こえづらい。 **I'm finding it hard to hear.**

補聴器を買ったほうがいいかな？ **Should I get a hearing aid?** ＊hearing aid＝補聴器

耳がかゆい。 **My ears are itchy.** ＊itchy［イッチィ］＝かゆい

中耳炎になった。 **I got an inner-ear infection.** ＊infection＝伝染、感染。「中耳炎」はotitis mediaとも言う

外耳炎になった。 **I got external otitis.** ＊external otitis［オウタイティス］＝外耳炎

耳鳴りがする。 **My ears are ringing.**

鼻の不調

鼻が詰まっている。 **I have a stuffy nose.** ＊stuffy＝詰まった

鼻水が出る。 **I have a runny nose.**

鼻水が止まらない。 **My nose won't stop running.**

鼻がむずむずする。 **My nose is itchy.**

慢性的な鼻炎だ。 **I have chronic nasal inflammation.** ＊chronic＝慢性的な　nasal［ネイゾォ］inflammation＝鼻炎

鼻血が出た。 **I got a nosebleed.**

歯・口の不調

歯が痛い。	**I have a toothache.** ＊toothache［トゥーセイク］＝歯痛
親知らずが痛い。	**My wisdom tooth hurts.** ＊「親知らず」が複数なら、toothをteethに
親知らずを抜いてもらった。	**I had a wisdom tooth pulled out.**
歯がズキズキ痛む。	**I have a throbbing toothache.** ＊throb［スロブ］＝ズキズキする
マズい、虫歯になったかも。	**Oh, no. I think I have a cavity.** ＊cavity＝虫歯
虫歯になっちゃった。	**I have a cavity.**
治療しなきゃ。	**I must get it fixed.**
歯が１本、ぐらぐらしている。	**One of my teeth is loose.** ＊「奥歯」なら、teethをmolars（奥歯）に
歯のクリーニングをしてもらおう。	**I should get my teeth cleaned.**
歯石を取ってもらわなきゃ。	**I need to have the tartar removed from my teeth.** ＊tartar＝歯石
口臭が気になる。	**I'm worried about bad breath.**
歯みがきをしていたら、歯茎から血が出た。	**My gums bled when I brushed my teeth.** ＊gum＝歯茎　bled＝bleed（出血する）の過去形
歯周病かも。	**I think I have gum disease.**
口内炎ができた。	**I have a canker sore.** ＊canker sore＝口内炎
口内炎が痛い。	**My canker sore hurts.**
歯槽のう漏になった。	**I got pyorrhea.** ＊pyorrhea［パイアリーァ］＝歯槽のう漏
歯に詰め物をしてもらった。	**I got a filling.**
歯の詰め物が取れちゃった。	**My filling fell out.**
歯並びが悪いのが気になる。	**I don't like my crooked teeth.** ＊crooked［クルーキッド］＝曲がった、ゆがんだ
歯の矯正をしようかな。	**Maybe I should get braces.** ＊braces＝歯列矯正器具

のどの不調・せき

のどが痛い。 **I have a sore throat.** ＊sore［ソァ］＝痛い

つばを飲み込むとのどが痛い。 **My throat hurts when I swallow.**

せきがひどい。 **I have a bad cough.** ＊cough［カーフ］＝せき

夜中じゅう、ずっとせきをしていた。 **I was coughing all night.**
＊cough＝せきをする

のどがいがらっぽい。 **My throat is scratchy.**
＊scratchy＝（のどが）いがらっぽい

たんがからむ。 **My throat is full of phlegm.**
＊phlegm［フレム］＝たん

首・肩の不調

首が回らない。 **My neck is really stiff.** ＊stiff＝こわばった

首を寝違えた。 **I got a crick in my neck while sleeping.** ＊crick＝筋違え

首を左に動かすと痛む。 **It hurts when I move my head to the left.**

むち打ちになってしまった。 **I have whiplash.**
＊whiplash［ウィップラッシュ］＝むち打ち

肩こりがひどい。 **My shoulders are stiff.**
＊首に近いところなら、My neck is stiff.

肩が痛くて、右腕が上がらない。 **I can't raise my right arm because of the pain in my shoulder.**

これって四十肩かな？ **Have I gotten a frozen shoulder?**
＊frozen shoulder＝四十肩、五十肩

スマホを見過ぎているから、多分「スマホ首」だな。 **It's probably a text neck since I'm using my phone too long.**
＊text neck＝スマホなどの携帯デバイスを長時間使用したことで現れる、首の痛みなどの症状

肌荒れ・虫刺され

最近、肌が荒れている。 **My skin is rough these days.**

ニキビができた。 **I got pimples.** ＊pimple＝ニキビ

日焼けでヒリヒリする。 My skin stings from the sunburn.
＊sting＝ひりひりする

化粧水が肌に合わないみたい。 I think my face lotion doesn't suit my skin.
＊suit＝～に合う

手指消毒液で手が荒れちゃった。 My hands are rough from hand sanitizer.
＊sanitizer＝消毒剤

肌が乾燥している。 My skin is dry.

背中に湿疹ができた。 I got a rash on my back.
＊rash＝湿疹、吹き出物

息子にあせもができた。 My son got a heat rash.
＊heat rash＝あせも

ダニに刺されたみたい。 I think I got bitten by mites.
＊bite＝～をかむ・刺す。過去分詞はbitten
mite＝ダニ

私、いつも蚊に刺される！（はぁ～） I always get bitten by mosquitos! (Sigh)

私には虫よけスプレーは効き目ゼロ。 Mosquito repellent doesn't work for me at all.
＊repellent［リペレント］＝虫よけ

蚊に刺されたところがかゆくてたまらない。 These mosquito bites are so itchy.
＊bite＝刺された跡

足の不調

足がしびれた。 My feet went numb.
＊numb［ナム］＝しびれた

足がむくんだ。 My legs are swollen.
＊legは、ひざ（またはもも）から足首まで。足首から下はfoot（複数形はfeet）で表す

右足がつった。 I got a cramp in my right leg.
＊cramp＝（筋肉の）けいれん、引きつり

最近、足がつりやすい。 These days, I get leg cramps easily.

靴ずれした。 I got a blister on my foot.
＊blister＝（皮膚の）まめ、水ぶくれ

あの靴は私の足に合わない。 Those shoes don't fit me right.

外反母趾で、靴選びが大変。 I have bunions, so it's hard to choose shoes.
＊bunion［バニオン］＝外反母趾

足の巻き爪が痛い。 My ingrown toenail hurts.
＊ingrown＝内向きに伸びた　toenail＝足のつめ

足にうおのめができた。 I got a corn on my foot.
＊corn＝うおのめ、たこ

水虫だったら嫌だなぁ。 I hope it's not athelete's foot.
＊athlete's foot＝水虫

体の痛み

痛い！ Ouch! ＊Ow![アゥ]とも言う

体中が痛かった。 My body ached all over.
＊ache[エイク]＝痛む

右ひざがすごく痛い。 My right knee hurts really bad.
＊hurt＝痛む。過去形もhurt

右腕が痛かった。 My right arm hurt.

痛みを我慢できなかった。 I couldn't stand the pain.
＊can't stand ～＝～を我慢できない

もう痛くなくなった。 It doesn't hurt anymore.

腰痛

腰が痛い。 My lower back hurts.
＊「腰」は単にbackとも言う

最近、腰痛がひどい。 I've been having bad lower-back pain recently.

姿勢が悪いからだな。 It's because I have bad posture.
＊posture＝姿勢

ぎっくり腰になってしまった。 I strained my back.
＊strain＝～(筋など)を違える

椎間板ヘルニアかもしれない。 Maybe I have a hernia.
＊hernia[ハーニァ]

腰が痛くて、前かがみの姿勢を取れない。 I can't bend over because of my back pain. ＊bend over＝上半身を曲げる、かがむ

筋肉痛

筋肉痛になった。 My muscles are sore. ＊sore[ソァ]＝痛い

全身、筋肉痛だ。 I have sore muscles all over.

久々の山歩きで、足が筋肉痛だ。 My leg muscles are sore from my first trekking in a while.
＊trekking＝山歩き、トレッキング

筋肉痛が2日遅れで来た。 The muscle pain appeared two days later.

筋肉痛で、歩くのがつらかった。 It was hard to walk because my muscles were very sore.

筋肉痛がだいぶよくなった。 My sore muscles are much better.

骨折・打撲・ねんざ

歩いていて転んじゃった。 I fell when I was walking.

階段から落ちた。 I fell down the stairs.

左足を骨折した。 I broke my left leg.

全治1カ月だって。トホホ。 It'll take a month to heal completely. Boo-hoo.
*boo-hoo[ブーフー]=トホホ、えーん(泣)

左足をギプスで固定した。 My left leg is in a cast. *cast=ギプス

しばらくは松葉づえで歩かなきゃならない。 I have to walk with crutches for a while. *crutch=松葉づえ

骨にひびが入っていた。 The bone was cracked.
*「足の骨に」なら、My leg bone was cracked.

骨折していなくてよかった。 I'm lucky my bone wasn't broken.

足首をねんざした。 I sprained my ankle.
*sprain=〜をねんざする

右脚が肉離れになった。 I pulled a muscle in my right leg.

右肩を打撲した。 I bruised my right shoulder.
*bruise[ブルーズ]=〜を打撲する

左手首をひねってしまった。 I twisted my left wrist.

左の人さし指を突き指した。 I sprained my left index finger.

左腕が赤くはれ上がった。 My left arm was red and swollen.
*swollen[スウォウルン]=はれた

青いあざができた。 There was a bruise.
*bruise[ブルーズ]=あざ

知らない間に、腿にあざができていた。 I got a bruise on my thigh without noticing it. *bruise=あざ thigh[サィ]=腿

額にたんこぶができた。 **I have a bump on my forehead.**
＊bump＝たんこぶ

切り傷・すり傷

包丁で人さし指を切っちゃった。 **I cut my index finger with a knife.**

転んでひざをすりむいてしまった。 **I fell and grazed my knee.**
＊graze＝〜をすりむく

指にとげが刺さった。 **I pricked my finger on a thorn.**
＊prick＝〜を刺す thorn[ソーン]＝とげ

血が出た。 **It was bleeding.** ＊bleed＝出血する

なかなか血が止まらなかった。 **It wouldn't stop bleeding.**

マオは額を３針縫った。 **Mao got three stitches on her forehead.**

痕にならないといいな。 **I hope it won't leave a scar.**
＊leave＝〜を残す scar＝痕、傷痕

やけど

左手をやけどした。 **I burned my left hand.**
＊burn＝〜をやけどさせる

すぐに冷水で冷やした。 **I cooled it down with cold water.**

水ぶくれができちゃった。 **I got a blister.** ＊blister＝水ぶくれ

やけどしたところがまだ痛む。 **It still hurts where it got burned.**

やけどが痕になっちゃった。 **The burn left a scar.**

やけどがだいぶよくなった。 **The burn is much better now.**

病院・医院

病院にまつわる単語

※「～科」はdepartment of ～で表します。～には、以下の単語が入ります（「麻酔科＝anesthesiology」まで）。

内科	internal medicine
外科	surgery
小児科	pediatrics
産婦人科	obstetrics and gynecology / OB/GYN
眼科	ophthalmology
耳鼻咽喉科	ENT (ear, nose, throat の略)
整形外科	orthopedic surgery
皮膚科	dermatology
心療内科	psychosomatic internal medicine
呼吸器内科	respiratory medicine
循環器内科	cardiology
精神科	psychiatry［サイカイアトリィ］
脳外科	cerebral surgery
神経外科	neurosurgery
泌尿器科	urology［ユラロジィ］
放射線科	radiology
麻酔科	anesthesiology［アネスィズィオロジィ］
総合病院	hospital
医院	clinic
内科医	physician
外科医	surgeon
眼科医	eye doctor
産科医	obstetrician
皮膚科医	skin doctor
歯科医	dentist
漢方医	herb doctor
薬剤師	pharmacist
手術室	OR (operating room の略)
救急処置室	ER (emergency room の略)
頭痛外来	headache clinic
発熱外来	fever clinic
薬局	pharmacy

病院に行く

病院に行かなきゃ。
I need to see a doctor.
＊see a doctor＝医者に診てもらう、病院に行く

何科に行けばいいんだろう？
Which department should I visit?

評判のいい整形外科はどこだろう？
I wonder which orthopedic surgery has a good reputation.
＊reputation＝評判

近所で評判のいい耳鼻科を調べた。
I searched for a good ENT clinic in my neighborhood.

病院に行こうと思ったのに、今日は休診だった。
I planned to go to the hospital, but it was closed today.

明日、皮膚科に行こうっと。	**I'll see a skin doctor tomorrow.** ＊英語では「～科医に診てもらう」と表すことが多い
火曜の10時に、病院を予約した。	**I made a hospital appointment at 10:00 on Tuesday.**
明日は2時に歯医者だ。	**I have a dentist appointment at 2:00 tomorrow.**
今朝一番で、タカハシ医院に行った。	**I went to Takahashi Clinic first thing this morning.** ＊first thing in the morning＝朝一番で
今日の午前中、足のリハビリに行った。	**This morning, I went to rehab for my leg.** ＊ rehabは、rehabilitation（リハビリテーション）の略
病院は混んでいた。	**The hospital was crowded.**
3時間も待たされた。	**I had to wait for three hours.**
待ち時間は漫画を読んでいた。	**I read a comic while I waited.**
外に出て時間を潰した。	**I killed time waiting outside.**
アプリで待ち時間がわかるので、便利。	**It's convenient that I can check the wait time on the app.**

救急車

救急車を呼んだ。	**I called an ambulance.** ＊ambulance［アンビュランス］＝救急車
救急車はすぐに来てくれた。	**The ambulance came right away.**
救急車で病院に運ばれたのは初めて。	**It was my first time to be taken to the hospital by ambulance.**
救急隊員の人たちが頼もしかった。	**The paramedics were reliable.** ＊paramedic＝救急隊員
救急指定病院に駆け込んだ。	**I rushed to an emergency hospital.**

診察

タカハシ先生が診察してくれた。	**Dr. Takahashi examined me.** ＊examine［イグザミン］＝～を診察する
診察は5分ほどで終わった。	**The examination was about five minutes long.** ＊examination＝診察

とても話しやすい、いい先生だった。	**The doctor was very nice and friendly.**
丁寧な診察だった。	**It was a thorough examination.** ＊thorough［ソーロゥ］＝徹底的な
スズキ先生の診察は信頼できる。	**I can trust Dr. Suzuki's examinations.**
無愛想な先生だった。	**The doctor was blunt.** ＊blunt［ブラントｔ］＝ぶっきらぼうな
いい医者を見つけるのは難しい。	**It's tough to find a good doctor.**
ただの風邪だった。	**It was just a cold.**
インフルエンザだった。	**It was the flu.**
ストレス性の胃炎と診断された。	**I was diagnosed with stress-related gastritis.** ＊be diagnosed［ダイアグノウストｔ］ with ～＝～と診断される　gastritis＝胃炎
念のため、別のお医者さんにも診てもらおう。	**I'll get a second opinion from another doctor just in case.** ＊just in case＝念のため

健康診断

来週は会社の健康診断だ。	**My company checkup is next week.** ＊checkup＝健康診断。physicalとも言う。「市の健康診断」なら、companyをcityに
健康診断までに、少しでも体重を減らしたい。	**I want to lose a little weight before the checkup.**
明日は健康診断だから、今夜はお酒を飲めない。	**I have my checkup tomorrow, so I can't drink alcohol tonight.**
健康診断を受けた。	**I had a checkup.**
年に１度は健康診断を受けないとね。	**It's good to have a checkup once a year.**
人間ドックを受けた。	**I had a full checkup.**
前日の夜から食事禁止だった。	**I wasn't allowed to eat anything from the night before.**

これから健康診断が終わるまで、何も食べられない。	**I can't eat anything until after my checkup.**
健康診断の結果が心配だ。	**I'm worried about my checkup results.**
がん検診を受けた。	**I was screened for cancer.** ＊screen＝～を検査する　cancer＝がん
婦人科検診を受けた。	**I had a gynecological exam.** ＊gynecological［ガイナカロジコゥ］＝婦人科の
血液検査をした。	**I had a blood test.**
視力検査をした。	**I had an eye exam.**
視力は右が 1.2、左が 1.0 だった。	**My eyesight is 1.2 in the right eye and 1.0 in the left eye.**
裸眼は、両目とも 0.7 だった。	**My naked eyesight is 0.7 for both eyes.**
息子は視力検査でC判定だった。	**My son got a C on his eye exam.**
聴力検査をした。	**I had an ear exam.**
尿検査をした。	**I had a urine test.**　＊urine［ユーリン］＝尿
検便をした。	**I had a stool test.**　＊stool［ストゥーゥ］＝便
メタボ気味だと言われた。	**I was told that I'm close to having metabolic syndrome.**
将来、生活習慣病の恐れがあるらしい。	**I might have a lifestyle-related disease in the future.**
医者から食生活についての指導を受けた。	**The doctor advised me on what to eat.**
血圧を測った。	**They checked my blood pressure.**
血圧が少し高かった。	**My blood pressure was a little high.** ＊「低かった」なら、highをlowに
血圧は正常だった。	**My blood pressure was fine.**
血圧は上が 125、下が 86 だ。	**My blood pressure is 125 over 86.**

鼻から胃カメラを入れた。	**They inserted a gastric camera through my nose.** ＊gastric＝胃の
内視鏡検査はつらかった。	**The endoscopy was painful.** ＊endoscopy＝内視鏡検査
バリウム検査を受けた。	**I had a barium swallow test.**
胸部のレントゲンを撮った。	**I had a chest X-ray.** ＊X-ray＝レントゲン撮影
マンモグラフィー検査を受けた。	**I had a mammogram.**
再検査になっちゃった。	**I have to get checked again.**
大きな病院で精密検査をすることになった。	**I need to get a detailed exam at a big hospital.**

入院

明日から入院することになった。	**I'm checking into the hospital tomorrow.**
入院は1週間の予定だ。	**I'll be in the hospital for a week.**
病院に行って、そのまま入院した。	**I went to the hospital and ended up being admitted.** ＊be admitted＝入院する
検査入院した。	**I was admitted for several exams.**
4人部屋だった。	**It was a room for four people.**
個室に移った。	**I moved to a private room.**
差額が高いけど、仕方ない。	**It's a lot more expensive, but it can't be helped.**
病院食はあまりおいしくない。	**Hospital food doesn't taste very good.**
ここの病院は、ご飯がおいしくてうれしい!	**I'm glad the food at this hospital tastes so good!**
入院中は退屈だ。	**Being in the hospital is boring.**
この病院はWi-Fiが使えるから助かる。	**It's helpful that this hospital has Wi-Fi.**

友達がお見舞いに来てくれた。	**My friend came to visit me.**
入院している母のお見舞いに行った。	**I went to see my mom in the hospital.**
タナカさんのお見舞い、何を持っていこうかな。	**I wonder what I should take for Tanaka-san.**

手術

白内障の手術をした。	**I had cataract surgery.**
盲腸の手術をした。	**I had an appendectomy.** ＊appendectomy［アペンデクトミィ］＝虫垂切除術
明日は手術だ。緊張する。	**I'm having an operation tomorrow. I'm nervous.** ＊operation＝手術
簡単な手術らしい。	**They say it's an easy operation.** ＊「難しい」なら、easyをdifficultに
母の手術がうまくいきますように。	**I hope my mother's operation goes well.** ＊go well＝うまくいく
手術が終わるまで落ち着かなかった。	**I couldn't relax during the operation.**
手術は無事、成功した。	**The operation was successful.**
手術は２時間ほどかかった。	**The operation took about two hours.**
６時間の大手術だった。	**It was a major operation that took six hours.**

退院

あさって、退院できることになった。	**I'll be able to leave the hospital the day after tomorrow.**
早く退院したいなぁ。	**I want to leave the hospital soon.**
どのくらいで退院できるのかなぁ。	**I wonder when I can leave the hospital.**
今日の午後、退院した。	**I left the hospital this afternoon.**
セイラが退院した。よかった！	**Good news! Seira was discharged from hospital!** ＊be discharged＝退院する

整体・しんきゅう院

整体に行った。	I went to see a seitai chiropractor. ＊chiropractor＝カイロプラクティック療法士
整骨院に行った。	I went to an osteopathic clinic. ＊osteopathic＝整骨療法の
カイロプラクティックに行った。	I went to see a chiropractor.
しんきゅう院に行った。	I went to an acupuncture and moxibustion clinic. ＊acupuncture［アキュパンクチュァ］＝はり moxibustion［マクサバスション］＝きゅう
おきゅうをしてもらった。	They did a cauterization on me. ＊cauterization［コーテライゼィション］＝きゅうを据えること
腰のマッサージをしてもらった。	I got a lower back massage.
肩の痛みが和らいだ。	It eased the pain in my neck. ＊ease＝～を和らげる。英語で「肩が痛い」は「首が痛い」と表現することが多い
全身のコリがほぐれた。	The stiffness in my whole body was eased.
スッキリした。	I felt refreshed.
あまり効果を感じなかった。	I didn't really feel any difference.
ほかの所に行こうかな。	Maybe I should go somewhere else.
定期的に通うほうがいいと言われた。	He advised me to go there regularly.

薬・手当て

薬

ドラッグストアで頭痛薬を買った。	I bought headache medicine at the drugstore.
1週間分の薬を出してもらった。	I got medicine for one week.
薬局に処方せんを持っていった。	I took my prescription to the pharmacy. ＊prescription=処方せん
お薬手帳を持っていくのを忘れた。	I forgot to bring my medicine book.

アプリのお薬手帳を使い始めた。 **I started using an app-based medicine book.**

漢方薬をもらった。 **I got herbal medicine.**

抗生物質が処方された。 **The doctor prescribed an antibiotic.**
＊prescribe＝～を処方する　antibiotic＝抗生物質

薬を飲んで、しばらく様子を見てみよう。 **I'll take the medicine and see what happens.**
＊see＝～を見てみる・確かめる

この薬、すごくよく効く！ **This medicine really works!**

食後に薬を飲んだ。 **I took the medicine after my meal.**

昼食後の薬を飲み忘れちゃった。 **I forgot to take my medicine after lunch.**

市販の頭痛薬を飲んだ。 **I took over-the-counter headache medicine.**
＊over-the-counter＝（薬が）市販の、店頭販売の

痛み止めを飲んだ。 **I took pain medicine.**

目薬を差した。 **I used eye drops.**

点鼻薬を差した。 **I used nose drops.**

座薬を入れた。 **I used a suppository.**
＊suppository［サパザトリー］＝座薬

けがの手当て

傷口にばんそうこうを貼った。 **I put a Band-Aid on the cut.**
＊Band-Aid（バンドエイド）は商標

傷口に軟こうを塗った。 **I put ointment on the wound.**
＊ointment＝軟こう　wound［ウーンド］＝傷

傷口を消毒した。 **I disinfected the wound.**
＊disinfect＝～を消毒する

タオルで傷口を押さえて止血した。 **I pressed a towel to the wound to stop the bleeding.**

右腕に包帯を巻いた。 **I put a bandage on my right arm.**
＊bandage＝包帯

腰に湿布を張った。 **I put a compress on my back.**
＊compress＝湿布。「温湿布」なら、hot compress

体調について 英語日記を書いてみよう

その日の体調について、英語で書いてみましょう。

体調がよさそう

I went to see my father-in-law in the nursing-care facility. He looked well today and recognized me. I was happy.

義父に会いに介護施設へ行った。今日は体調がよさそうで、私のこともわかってくれた。うれしかった。

「義父」は father-in-law で、「義母」なら mother-in-law です。「介護施設」は nursing-care facility としましたが、assisted living でも OK です。「～の顔を見てわかる、～が誰だかわかる」というときの「わかる」は、recognize を使います。

花粉症で目がかゆい

My eyes were really itchy because of my hay fever. I don't like this time of the year. I wish I could go out to enjoy the beautiful cherry blossoms.

花粉症で目がすごくかゆかった。この時期はイヤ。外に出て花見を楽しめたらいいのになぁ。

「花粉症」は hay fever と言います。「この時期」は this time of the year としましたが、this season と表すこともできます。I wish I could ～ は「(実際はそうできないけれど) ～できたらいいのになぁ」という意味。cherry blossoms は「桜の花」です。

ぎっくり腰になった

I strained my back when I tried to pick up something off the floor. It's really painful and I can't move. Even just lying down in bed is unbearable.

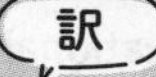

床に落ちた物を拾おうとして、ぎっくり腰になった。めちゃくちゃ痛くて動けない。ベッドに横になっているだけでもツライ。

「ぎっくり腰になった」は strained my back。strain は「～（筋など）を違える」の意。「拾おうとして」は「～しようとしたときに」と考えて、when I tried to ～とします。lying は lie（横たわる）の -ing 形。「ツライ」は unbearable（耐えられない）と表現しました。

気管支炎と診断

I went to see a doctor because I couldn't stop coughing. I was diagnosed with bronchitis. The doctor prescribed antibiotics for it.

せきが止まらなかったので病院へ行った。気管支炎と診断された。抗生物質を処方された。

「せきが止まらなかった」は couldn't stop coughing（せきを止められなかった）と表します。「～だと診断された」は was diagnosed with〈as〉～。「抗生物質を処方された」は、I got antibiotics.（抗生物質をもらった）でも OK。prescribe は「～を処方する」の意味です。

03
行事・イベント

祝日・行事を表す単語

元日	New Year's Day
成人の日	Coming-of-Age Day
建国記念の日	National Foundation Day
天皇誕生日	The Emperor's Birthday
春分の日	Vernal Equinox Day
昭和の日	Showa Day
憲法記念日	Constitution Day
みどりの日	Greenery Day
こどもの日	Children's Day
海の日	Marine Day
山の日	Mountain Day
敬老の日	Respect-for-the-Aged Day
秋分の日	Autumnal Equinox Day
スポーツの日	Health and Sports Day
文化の日	Culture Day
勤労感謝の日	Labor Thanksgiving Day
振替休日	substitute holiday
正月休み	New Year's (holiday)
新年会	New Year's party
節分	Setsubun
バレンタインデー	Valentine's Day
ひな祭り	Doll Festival
ホワイトデー	White Day
花見	cherry blossom viewing
端午の節句	Boy's Festival
母の日	Mother's Day
父の日	Father's Day
七夕	Star Festival
花火大会	fireworks show
お盆休み	Obon holiday
ハロウィーン	Halloween
七五三	Shichi-Go-San
クリスマス・イブ	Christmas Eve
クリスマス	Christmas
忘年会	year-end party
大みそか	New Year's Eve

お正月

新年を迎えて

あけましておめでとう！ **Happy New Year!**

新しい年の始まりだ。 **A new year has started.**

いい一年になりますように。 **I hope this will be a good year.**

家族が健康でいられますように。	**I hope my family stays healthy.**

お正月の過ごし方

今年も寝正月だ。	**I'm spending the New Year's holiday relaxing at home this year again.**
お正月は、実家に帰省しただけ。	**All I did was go to my parents' home for New Year's.**
子どもたちが帰ってきたので、忙しかった。	**I was busy because my children came back home.**
おじいちゃんの家に、新年のあいさつに行った。	**I went to my grandpa's for a New Year's visit.**
両親に会いに帰省したかったな。	**I wanted to go home to see my parents.**
両親に電話をかけた。	**I called my parents.**
みんなでおせち料理を食べて、テレビを見た。	**We ate osechi and watched TV.**
家族で箱根駅伝を見た。	**My family watched the Tokyo-Hakone Intercollegiate Long Distance Relay Race.** ＊intercollegiate＝大学間の、大学対抗の
高校の同窓会に出席した。	**I joined my high school reunion.**
海外で過ごすお正月は、何だか特別だ。	**It's really great to spend New Year's overseas.**
たまには海外でお正月を過ごしてみたい。	**I'd like to spend New Year's overseas sometimes.**
お正月休みは、たっぷり休むことができた。	**I had a good rest during my New Year's holiday.**
お正月休みも今日で終わりか。（はぁ〜）	**Today is the last day of the New Year's holiday. (Sigh)** ＊sigh［サィ］＝ため息
お正月気分がなかなか抜けない。	**I can't get out of the New Year's mood.**

年賀状・新年のあいさつ

年賀状が 30 枚来ていた。	I got 30 New Year's cards. ＊「年賀状」は、New Year's greeting cardとも言う
思ったよりたくさん年賀状が来た。	I received more New Year's cards than I expected.
最近は年賀状をもらう枚数も少なくなったな。	Recently I don't receive that many New Year's cards.
ツツミさんから年賀状がきていた。	I got a New Year's card from Tsutsumi-san.
私はツツミさんに出してない。マズい！	I didn't send one to Tsutsumi-san. Oops!
すぐに返事を出した。	I wrote him a reply right away.
今年は喪中なので、年賀状が出せなかった。	This year I'm in mourning, so I couldn't send any New Year's cards. ＊mourning＝服喪、喪中
面倒くさくて、年賀状を出さなかった。	I couldn't be bothered to send New Year's cards. ＊can't be bothered to ～＝面倒なのでわざわざ～したくない
もらった人にだけ出すことにしよう。	I'll only send New Year's cards to those who sent them to me.
ユウコの年賀状がすてきだった。	The New Year's card from Yuko was beautiful.
年賀はがきで「切手シート」が３枚当たった。	I won three sheets of stamps from the New Year's postcard lottery. ＊lottery＝くじ
年賀はがきは全部はずれた。(あ～あ)	I didn't win anything in the New Year's postcard lottery. (Sigh)
年が明けた瞬間、彼から LINE が来た。	I got a LINE message from him just as the new year began.
みんなに新年のあいさつを LINE した。	I sent New Year's greetings to everyone via LINE. ＊via ～＝～によって

初詣

明治神宮に初詣に行った。
I went to Meiji Shrine for my first shrine visit of the year.
＊「近所の神社」なら、Meiji Shrineをa shrine nearbyに

おさい銭として100円入れた。
I put 100 yen in the offering box.
＊offering box＝さい銭箱

いい一年になるよう祈った。
I prayed for a good year.

家族の健康を祈った。
I prayed for my family's health.

レオが大学に合格するよう祈った。
I prayed that Reo will pass the college entrance exam.

おじいちゃんの病気が早くよくなるよう祈った。
I prayed for my grandpa's quick recovery.
＊recovery＝回復

おみくじは大吉だった。
The omikuji said, "Great Luck."
＊omikujiは、fortune paperとしてもOK

おみくじは凶だった。最悪！
The omikuji said, "Unlucky." That's the pits!
＊the pits＝ひどい状況、最低

おみくじを境内の木に結んできた。
I tied the omikuji to a tree branch at the shrine.
＊tie＝～を結ぶ　branch＝枝

厄年・おはらい

今年は厄年だ。
This is an unlucky year for me.

今年は前厄だ。
This is the year before my unlucky year.
＊「後厄」なら、beforeをafterに

おはらいをしてもらったほうがいいかな。
Maybe I should get a purification ceremony at the shrine.
＊purification[ピュリフィケイション]＝浄化、清め

おはらいに行った。
I had a rite of purification performed at the shrine.
＊rite＝儀式

今年は厄年だけど、気にしない。
This is an unlucky year for me, but I don't mind.
＊mind＝～を気にする・心配する

初日の出

高尾山へ初日の出を見に行った。
I went to Mt. Takao to see the first sunrise of the year.

初日の出がきれいだった。 The first sunrise of the year was beautiful.

曇っていて、初日の出は見えなかった。 It was cloudy, so I couldn't see the first sunrise of the year.

今年は初日の出が見えなくて残念。 It's too bad that I didn't get to see the first sunrise of the year.

初夢

初夢はいい夢だった。 My first dream of the year was great.

初夢に富士山が出てきた！ I dreamed of Mt. Fuji in my first dream of the year!

大金持ちになった夢を見た。 I dreamed that I became super rich.

初夢は大した夢じゃなかった。 My first dream of the year was pretty ordinary. ＊ordinary＝普通の、平凡な

何の夢も見なかった。 I didn't dream anything.

お正月の食事

おせちを食べた。 I ate osechi. ＊osechiは、Japanese New Year's dishesでもOK

デパートで注文した高級おせちを食べた。 I ate fancy osechi from a department store. ＊fancy＝高級な、極上の

洋風おせちもおいしいな。 Western-style osechi is good too.

もうおせちは食べ飽きた。 I'm tired of eating osechi every day.

雑煮を食べた。 I ate zoni. ＊zoniは、rice cakes in soupとしてもOK

白みそ仕立ての雑煮だった。 The zoni was in white miso soup. ＊「すまし仕立て」なら、clear soup

お餅を食べ過ぎた。 I ate too many mochi.

甘酒がおいしかった。 The amazake tasted good.

おとそでほろ酔い気分になった。 The New Year's sake made me tipsy. ＊tipsy＝ほろ酔いの

お年玉

お年玉を６人分用意しなきゃ。	**I need to prepare otoshidama for six children.**
お年玉で懐がさみしいなぁ。	**I gave a lot in otoshidama, so I'm low on money.** ＊low on ～＝～が乏しい
今年から、お年玉をあげる番だな。	**This year, it's my turn to start giving otoshidama.**
お母さんにもお年玉をあげた。	**I gave otoshidama to my mom too.**

初売り・福袋

明日はデパートの初売りだ！	**Department stores are having their New Year's opening sales tomorrow!**
福袋を買いに行かなきゃ！	**I should go get a lucky bag!**
福袋を買うために、朝８時から並んだ。	**I stood in line at 8:00 in the morning to get a lucky bag.**
今年はネットで福袋をゲット。	**I got a lucky bag online this year.**
オンラインで予約した福袋が届いた。	**The lucky bag I reserved online arrived.**
お目当ての福袋が買えてうれしい！	**I'm so happy that I got the lucky bag I wanted!**
福袋には、すてきな服がたくさん入っていた。	**There were lots of nice clothes in my lucky bag.**
福袋に入っていた物は、あまり気に入らなかった。	**I didn't really like the stuff in my lucky bag.** ＊stuff［スタッフ］＝物
福袋はハズレだった。	**No luck with my lucky bag.**
福袋は売り切れていた。残念！	**All the lucky bags were already sold out. Too bad!**

いろいろな行事

成人式

今日は成人の日だった。	**It was Coming-of-Age Day today.**
振り袖姿の人をたくさん見かけた。	**I saw a lot of girls in their long-sleeved kimonos.**
朝早くから美容院に行った。	**I went to the hair salon early in the morning.** ＊hair salonは、beauty salonやhairdresser'sでもOK
メイクと着付けをしてもらった。	**I had my makeup and hair done and got dressed in a kimono.**
花模様の赤い着物を着た。	**I wore a red kimono with a flowery design.** ＊flowery＝花の
初めて振り袖を着て、うれしかった。	**I was happy to wear a furisode for the first time in my life.**
スーツでビシッとキメた。	**I got dressed up in a suit.**
ワンピースを着た。	**I wore a dress.**
成人式に出席した。	**I attended the Coming-of-Age ceremony.**
昔の同級生と顔を合わせて、懐かしかった。	**It was really good to see my old classmates.**
娘の晴れ着姿がかわいかった。	**My daughter looked adorable in her kimono.** ＊adorable［アドーラボォ］＝かわいい、愛らしい

節分

今日は節分だった。	**Today was Setsubun.**
家で豆まきをした。	**We did bean-throwing at home.**
鬼は外、福は内！	**Out with the demon! In with good fortune!** ＊demon＝悪魔、鬼　fortune＝運

子どもたちと一緒に鬼のお面を作った。	**The kids and I made demon masks.**
夫は、お面をかぶって鬼の役をした。	**My husband put on a mask and played the role of the demon.**
子どもたちが鬼に豆を投げつけた。	**The kids threw beans at the demon.**
サユリは鬼を怖がって、泣いてしまった。	**Sayuri was so scared of the demon that she cried.**
歳の数だけ豆を食べた。	**I ate as many beans as my age.**
今年の恵方は東北東。	**This year's lucky direction is east-northeast.** ＊direction＝方角
北北西の方角を向いて、恵方巻きを食べた。	**I ate my ehomaki sushi roll facing north-northwest.**
スーパーの恵方巻きはすごく高かった。	**The ehomaki at the supermarket were so expensive.**
家で恵方巻きを作った。	**I made ehomaki at home.**

バレンタインデー

今日はバレンタインデー。	**Today is Valentine's Day.**
今年はチョコを手作りしようかな。	**Maybe I'll try making homemade chocolate this year.**
デパートにチョコを買いに行った。	**I went to a department store to buy chocolate.**
人気のチョコは売り切れていた。あ～あ！	**The popular chocolate was sold out. Oh no!**
パッケージがすてきなチョコを買った。	**I bought beautifully packaged chocolate.**
自分へのご褒美に高級チョコを買った。	**I treated myself to high-class chocolate.**
お目当てのチョコが買えて満足。	**I'm happy I could buy the chocolate I wanted.**

近所のスーパーで、6人分のチョコを買った。 **I bought chocolate for six people at the nearby supermarket.**

上司と、同僚3人にチョコをあげた。 **I gave chocolate to my boss and three co-workers.**
＊co-worker＝同僚

夫とヒデユキにチョコをあげた。 **I gave chocolate to my husband and Hideyuki.**

カナエとチョコを交換した。 **Kanae and I gave each other chocolate.**

フユコと一緒にブラウニーを焼いた。 **I baked brownies with Fuyuko.**

ミオは同級生のマサキくんにチョコをあげていた。 **Mio gave chocolate to her classmate Masaki-kun.**

今年はチョコを何個もらえるかな？ **I wonder how much chocolate I'll get this year.**

今年はチョコをもらえなかった。 **No chocolate for me this year.**

1つしかもらえなかった。 **I only got one box of chocolate.**
＊ここでの「1つ」は「1箱」の意味

ユイカからチョコをもらった。 **Yuika gave me chocolate.**

会社で8個、チョコをもらった。 **I got eight pieces of chocolate at work.**
＊piece＝～個、～粒

ユウトは何箱かチョコをもらったみたい。 **It seems Yuto received several boxes of chocolate.**

本命チョコはなしか…。 **No true-love chocolate for me ...**

社内の義理チョコなんて、やめればいいのに。 **I wish they would end the custom of giri-choco in the office.**
＊custom＝習慣

ひな祭り

おひなさまを飾った。 **We displayed our hina-dolls.**

ひなあられを食べた。 **We ate hina-crackers.**

ひな祭りのパーティーを開いた。 **I threw a doll festival party.**
＊threw［スルー］＝throw（～を催す）の過去形

みんなでちらしずしを食べた。	**We ate chirashi-zushi.**
おひなさま、早く片付けなくちゃ。	**I need to hurry up and put away the dolls.**

ホワイトデー

バレンタインのお返し、面倒くさいなぁ。	**Giving candy in return for Valentine's chocolate is a real pain.** ＊in return＝お返しに　pain＝苦痛
社員向けにクッキーを買った。	**I bought some cookies for the staff at the office.**
リナが欲しがっていたピアスをあげよう。	**I'm going to buy Rina the pair of earrings she wanted.**
妻に小さな花束を贈った。	**I bought my wife a small bouquet.** ＊bouquet［ボウケィ］＝花束、ブーケ
ユウキがホワイトデーにマカロンを1箱くれた。	**Yuki gave me a box of macaroons for White Day.**

花見

近所の公園に花見に行った。	**I went to the nearby park to see the cherry blossoms.**
今日は会社の花見だった。	**Our office had a cherry-blossom-viewing party today.**
朝から場所取りをした。	**I went in the morning to reserve a spot.**
桜は七分咲きだった。	**The cherry blossoms were 70% out.**
満開の桜がきれいだった。	**The cherry trees in full bloom were gorgeous.**
桜は少し葉が出てきていた。	**Some of the cherry trees had leaves sprouting.** ＊sprout［スプラウト］＝芽を出す
公園は花見客でいっぱいだった。	**The park was full of cherry blossom viewers.**
桜の下で飲むお酒は最高だ。	**Drinking under the cherry blossoms is so much fun.**

こどもの日

ベランダにこいのぼりを飾った。
We put up carp streamers on the balcony. ＊carp＝こい　streamer＝吹き流し

部屋によろいかぶとを飾った。
We put a set of samurai armor on display in our room. ＊armor＝よろい、かっちゅう

両親が五月人形を贈ってくれた。
My parents gave us a doll for the Boy's Festival.

ちまきとかしわ餅を食べた。
We ate chimaki and kashiwamochi.

新聞紙でかぶとを折った。
We folded a newspaper into a samurai helmet.

しょうぶ湯に入った。
I took a bath with sweet flag blades. ＊sweet flag blade＝しょうぶの葉

母の日・父の日

母の日にカーネーションをあげた。
I gave my mom some carnations for Mother's Day.

母にワインをあげた。
I gave my mother a bottle of wine.

ネットで母に花を贈った。
I sent flowers to my mom online.

タダシから花束が届いた。
Tadashi sent me a bunch of flowers. ＊a bunch of ～＝～の束

手作りのカードをもらった。
I got a handmade card.

毎年、息子が母の日を忘れずにいてくれてうれしい。
I'm happy that he always remembers Mother's Day.

父の日にネクタイをあげた。
I gave my dad a tie for Father's Day. ＊tie[タイ]＝ネクタイ

父の日に似顔絵をもらった。
I got a portrait of myself for Father's Day. ＊portrait＝肖像、似顔絵

感激して、泣きそうになった。
I was so touched that I almost cried. ＊touched＝感動して

ヤバい！　父の日を完全に忘れてた。 **Uh-oh! I totally forgot about Father's Day.**

七夕

明日は七夕だ。 **Tomorrow is the Star Festival.**

短冊に願い事を書いた。 **I wrote my wishes on strips of colored paper.** ＊strip of paper＝細長い紙切れ

縁側にササの葉を飾った。 **I put up a bamboo branch on the veranda.** ＊veranda＝縁側

折り紙で輪つなぎを作った。 **I made a paper chain with origami paper.**

商店街にササが飾ってあった。 **The shopping area was decorated with bamboo branches.**

夫の願い事は「宝くじが当たりますように」だって。 **My husband's wish was to win the lottery.**

お盆・帰省

お盆は何日に帰省しようかな。 **What day should I go back home for Obon?**

新幹線が満席だった。 **The shinkansen seats were completely full.**
＊shinkansenは、bullet［ブレット］trainでもOK

やっぱり実家は落ち着く。 **There's nowhere more relaxing than my parents' home.**

義実家は落ち着かない。 **I don't feel comfortable at my in-laws' home.** ＊in-law＝姻族

夏休み

明日から夏休みだ。 **My summer vacation starts tomorrow.**

子どもたちと盆踊りに行った。 **My kids and I went bon-dancing.**

縁日で金魚すくいをした。 **I scooped goldfish at the festival.**
＊scoop＝～をすくい取る

ゲーム屋台がたくさんあった。	**There were so many carnival games.** ＊carnival game＝（お祭りなどの）ゲーム屋台
どのゲームも行列ができていた。	**There were lines for all the games.**
屋台で焼きそばを買って食べた。	**I bought yakisoba from a food stall and ate it.**
久々に浴衣を着た。	**I wore a yukata for the first time in ages.** ＊for the first time in ages＝久しぶりに
フミに浴衣を着せてあげた。	**I dressed Fumi in a yukata.** ＊dress＝～に服を着せる
花火大会に行った。きれいだった！	**I went to the fireworks show. It was amazing!**
ハルトと昆虫採集に行った。	**Haruto and I went insect catching.** ＊insect＝虫
セミ取りに行った。	**We went to catch cicadas.** ＊cicada［スィケイダ］＝セミ

敬老の日

敬老の日に、おばあちゃんにスカーフをあげた。	**I gave my grandma a scarf for Respect-for-the-Aged Day.** ＊grandmaは、grandmother（おばあちゃん）の略語
おじいちゃんに電話した。	**I called my grandpa.** ＊grandpaは、grandfather（おじいちゃん）の略語
おじいちゃん、おばあちゃんとビデオ通話でおしゃべりした。	**I enjoyed chatting with my grandparents via video call.** ＊via ～＝～によって
おじいちゃんの肩をもんであげた。	**I gave my grandpa a neck massage.** ＊neck massageは、neck rubとしてもOK
おじいちゃんとおばあちゃんが、元気で長生きしますように。	**I hope my grandparents live a long and happy life.**

ハロウィーン

子どもたちとかぼちゃのランタンを彫った。	**My kids and I carved a jack-o'-lantern out of a pumpkin.** ＊carve＝～を彫る　lantern＝ランタン、ちょうちん
ハロウィーンの仮装パーティーに参加した。	**I participated in the Halloween costume party.** ＊participate in ～＝～に参加する

保育園でハロウィーンのパーティーがあった。	**The nursery school had a Halloween party.** ＊nursery (school)＝保育園
街のハロウィーン・イベントに参加した。	**I joined the town Halloween event.**
ルイはフランケンシュタインの仮装をした。	**Rui dressed up as Frankenstein.**
ヒナコは魔女の仮装をした。	**Hinako dressed up as a witch.**
「トリック・オア・トリート！」と言いながら近所の家を回った。	**We went around the neighborhood saying, "Trick or treat!"** ＊Trick or treat.＝「お菓子をくれなきゃいたずらするぞ」
お菓子をたくさんもらった。	**We got lots of candy.**

七五三

マリエの７歳の七五三だった。	**It was Marie's 7-year-old Shichi-Go-San.**
記念写真は夏に前撮りしてある。	**We had the photos taken early during summer.**
晴れ着がよく似合っていた。	**She looked gorgeous in her kimono.**
娘は着物がきゅうくつだと文句を言っていた。	**My daughter complained that the kimono was tight.**
神社にお参りに行った。	**We went to the shrine.**
娘は千歳あめをもらってうれしそうだった。	**She looked happy to get some chitose-ame.**
家族で記念撮影をした。	**We had family photos taken.**
ヘアメイクも着付けも込みのプランだった。	**It was a plan that included hair, makeup and dressing.**
息子は緊張して、あまり笑顔が出なかった。	**My son was nervous and didn't really smile.**

クリスマス

メリークリスマス！	**Merry Christmas!** **Happy Holidays!**

イブは彼女と過ごしたいな。	**I want to spend Christmas Eve with my girlfriend.** ＊「彼氏と」なら、with my boyfriend
今年も独りのクリスマス。	**I'll be all by myself again this Christmas.**
あ～あ。明日はクリスマスなのに、何の予定もないや。	**Ah ... Tomorrow is Christmas, and I have no plans.**
クリスマスケーキを予約した。	**I ordered a cake for Christmas.**
クリスマスケーキ、今年は手作りしよう。	**I'm going to bake a cake for Christmas this year.**
ブッシュ・ド・ノエルが上手にできた。	**My yulelog cake turned out really well.** ＊yulelog［ユーォログ］cake＝ブッシュ・ド・ノエル
ローストチキンを予約した。	**I ordered a roasted chicken.**
ノリコの家でクリスマスパーティーを開いた。	**We had a Christmas party at Noriko's.**
子どもたちとクリスマスツリーの飾り付けをした。	**My kids and I decorated our Christmas tree.**
テツシへのクリスマスプレゼント、何がいいかなぁ。	**I wonder what I should get Tetsushi for Christmas.** ＊「子どもたちへ」なら、Tetsushiをmy kidsに
リョウは自転車が欲しいって。	**Ryo told me he wants a bike.**
子どもたちは、サンタさんからのプレゼントを楽しみにしている。	**The children are looking forward to getting presents from Santa Claus.**
子どもたちの枕元にプレゼントを置いてきた。	**I left presents for the children by their pillows.** ＊pillow＝枕
明日の朝、子どもたちがどんな反応をするのか楽しみ。	**I'm looking forward to seeing their reactions tomorrow morning.**
プレゼントに財布をもらった。	**I got a wallet as a present.**
ウエスト一家にクリスマスカードを送った。	**I sent a Christmas card to the West's.**
ケントからクリスマスカードが届いた。	**I got a Christmas card from Kent.**

年末

今年も残すところあと3日か。
There are only three days left in the year.
＊left＝残って

今日も忘年会、明日も忘年会。
I have another year-end-party today. And another one tomorrow.

今日は納会だった。
We had the year-end corporate luncheon today.
＊luncheon＝昼食会

今日で仕事納めだった。
Today was the last working day of the year.

大掃除、面倒くさいな。
Year-end cleaning is a pain.

大掃除で家中ピカピカになった。
I finished my year-end cleaning, so now my house is spick-and-span.
＊spick-and-span＝こざっぱりした、こぎれいな

年末ジャンボ、当たるといいな。
I hope I win something in the year-end lottery.

おせちの準備を始めなくちゃ。
I need to get ready to make osechi.

今年はおせちを手作りすることにした。
This year, I've decided to cook osechi myself.

デパートのおせちを予約した。
I ordered osechi at a department store.

今年は初めて洋風おせちを頼んだ。
I ordered Western-style osechi for the first time this year.

有名シェフ監修のおせちを注文した。
I ordered osechi supervised by a famous chef.

年賀状を書かなきゃ。
I need to write New Year's cards.
＊「年賀状」は、New Year's greeting cardとも言う

やっと年賀状を書き終えた。
I've finally finished writing my New Year's cards.

今年は早めに年賀状を出せた。
I was able to mail my New Year's cards early this year.
＊mail＝～を投かんする

ようやく年賀状を出せた。	**I've finally sent out my New Year's greeting cards.**
	＊send out ～＝～を発送する。sentはsendの過去形
年賀状を 50 枚出した。	**I sent 50 New Year's greeting cards.**
年越しそばを食べた。	**We ate soba for New Year's Eve.**
テレビで「紅白歌合戦」を見た。	**We watched Kohaku on TV.**
除夜の鐘が聞こえてきた。	**Now I can hear the temple bells ringing on New Year's Eve.**
カウントダウンコンサートで年を越した。	**I spent the New Year at a countdown concert.**
今年も一年、無事に過ごせてよかった。	**I'm glad we made it through another year in health and safety.**
	＊make it through ～＝～をうまくやり遂げる

誕生日

誕生日おめでとう！	**Happy birthday!**
今日は私の 38 歳の誕生日。	**Today is my 38th birthday.**
もう祝ってもらうような年じゃないけど。	**At my age, I don't really expect anyone to celebrate my birthday.**
いくつになっても、誕生日はうれしいな。	**Birthdays are special no matter how old you are.**
	＊このyouは、「一般的な人々」を指す
誕生日に革のブックカバーをもらった。	**I got a leather book cover for my birthday.**
友達や家族が誕生日をお祝いしてくれて、うれしかった。	**I was happy my friends and family celebrated my birthday.**
レストランで誕生日のディナーを食べた。	**We had my birthday dinner at a restaurant.**
店員さんがハッピーバースデーの歌を歌ってくれた。	**The staff at the restaurant sang happy birthday to me.**
ちょっと恥ずかしかったけど、うれしかった。	**I was a little embarrassed but happy.**

誕生日なのに、ヒロは電話もくれなかった。	**Hiro didn't even call to wish me a happy birthday.**
ハナの7歳の誕生日だった。	**It was Hana's seventh birthday.**
息子ももう20歳かぁ。	**My son is already 20.**
ユリの誕生日パーティーに、友達がたくさん来てくれた。	**A lot of friends came to Yuri's birthday party.**
ユウヤの誕生日ケーキを焼いた。	**I baked a birthday cake for Yuya.**
彼に誕生日プレゼントをあげた。	**I gave him a birthday present.**

記念日

今日は15回目の結婚記念日だ。	**Today is our 15th wedding anniversary.** ＊anniversary＝記念日
明日は結婚記念日だ。	**Tomorrow is our wedding anniversary.**
明日は花を買って帰ろう。	**I should get some flowers on the way home tomorrow.**
結婚記念日のディナーに、レストランを予約しようかな。	**Maybe I should make a reservation for our anniversary dinner.**
今日で、マユと付き合い始めて1周年。	**Today is my first anniversary with Mayu.**

結婚式 （→ p. 541「結婚」を参照）

お葬式・法事

今日はおじいちゃんのお葬式だった。	**Today was Grandpa's funeral.**
どうか安らかに。	**May his soul rest in peace.** ＊rest＝（遠回しに）永眠する
母は天寿を全うした。	**My mother died of natural causes.** ＊die of ～＝～で死ぬ　cause＝原因
ゆっくりお別れできてよかった。	**I'm glad we could take our time to say goodbye.**
安らかな顔をしていた。	**His face looked peaceful.**

みんなでお棺に花を手向けた。 Everyone placed flowers in the casket.

たくさんの弔問客が来た。 Lots of condolence callers came.
＊condolence caller＝弔問客

お焼香の仕方で戸惑った。 I was confused by how to offer the incense. ＊incense＝お香

お経が長かった。 The sutra was too long.
＊sutra＝（仏教の）経典

喪服がキツくなっていた。 My mourning dress was tight.
＊スーツの喪服なら、dressをsuitに

最近は家族葬が増えたなぁ。 We have more and more family funerals these days.

今日は祖父の命日だった。 Today was the anniversary of my grandfather's death.

今日は祖母の三回忌だった。 Today was the second anniversary of my grandma's death.
＊「三回忌」は、英語では「2回目の記念日」と表す

祖母のお墓参りに行ってきた。 I visited my grandmother's grave.
＊grave＝墓

飲み会・パーティー

飲み会

飲み会だった。 I had a drinking session today.

いつものメンツで飲み会をした。 I had a drinking session with my usual buddies. ＊buddy＝仲間、相棒

朝まで飲んだ。 We drank till dawn. ＊dawn＝明け方

三次会まで付き合った。 I went along with them to the third drinking session.

終電前に切り上げた。 We finished before the last train.

飲み会の幹事をした。 I was the organizer of the drinking session.

今回は飲み会への参加を控えた。 **I refrained from attending the drinking session this time.**
＊refrain from ～ing＝～するのを控える

カラオケ（→ p. 416「カラオケ」を参照）

パーティー・お祝い

国際交流パーティーに参加した。 **I took part in an international exchange party.**
＊take part in ～＝～に参加する。tookはtakeの過去形

立食パーティーだった。 **It was a buffet-style party.**
＊buffet-style＝立食形式の

フォーマルなパーティーだった。 **It was a formal party.**

父の還暦のお祝いをした。 **We celebrated our father's 60th birthday.**

祖母の米寿のお祝いをした。 **We celebrated our grandma's 88th birthday.**

ホームパーティー

家に友人たちを招いて、パーティーを開いた。 **I invited some friends and had a house party.**

1人1品ずつ持ち寄った。 **Everyone brought one dish.**

ハヤセさんがおいしいワインを持ってきてくれた。 **Hayase-san brought a nice bottle of wine.**

サトウさんの引っ越し祝いにお呼ばれした。 **I was invited to Sato-san's housewarming party.**
＊housewarming（party）＝新居披露パーティー

ユウジの家で鍋パーティーをした。 **We had a hot-pot party at Yuji's place.**
＊hot-pot＝鍋

行事・イベントについて英語日記を書いてみよう

さまざまな行事やイベントについて、英語で書いてみましょう。

娘の運動会

Misaki has her sports festival tomorrow. Hope she finishes first in the race. I'm looking forward to it!

明日はミサキの運動会。かけっこで１位を取れるといいな。楽しみ！

「～だといいな」は、未来のことでも I hope ～（現在形の文）で表すのが一般的ですが、I hope (that) she'll finish first のように、will（短縮形は～'ll）を使っても構いません。また、日記などでは主語を省略して、Hope she ... のように表すことも多いですよ。

もうすぐひな祭り

The Doll Festival is just around the corner. The kids helped me set up the hina dolls. We're all set!

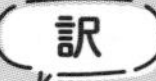

もうすぐひな祭り。子どもたちと一緒にひな人形を飾った。準備はバッチリ！

「もうすぐ～だ」と間近に迫っているイベントは、～ is (just) around the corner と表します。２文目は、「子どもたちがひな人形を飾るのを手伝ってくれた」と考えて、help ～（人）...（動詞の原形）で表しました。be all set は「準備完了」という意味です。

もちつき大会

We went to the annual rice-cake pounding and eating event. The rice cakes that had just been pounded were so good! ☺

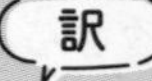

家族で毎年恒例の餅つき大会へ行った。つきたてのお餅は最高においしかった！ ☺

「家族で」は、we（私たちは）を主語にすればOK。日記では、これで誰のことかわかりますよね。「毎年恒例の」は annual。「餅つき大会」は、rice-cake pounding and eating event（餅をついて食べるイベント）と表しました。pounding は making でもOKです。

高校の同窓会

We had our high school reunion at The Okura Tokyo. I didn't recognize Nami-chan at first. She looked really beautiful. We had a great time talking about the old days.

オークラ東京で高校の同窓会があった。最初、ナミちゃんが誰だかわからなかった。すごくきれいになっていた。昔の話に花が咲いて楽しかった。

「高校の同窓会」は、high school reunion と表します。recognize は「（外見や特徴などから）～だと識別できる・見分けがつく」という意味です。a great time と talking about the old days（昔の話をして）で、「昔の話に花が咲いて」のニュアンスを出すことができます。

04

人間関係

出会い

タナカさんという人と知り合った。	**I got to know a person named Tanaka.**
B 社のヨシダさんと知り合った。	**I got to know Yoshida-san from B Company.**
今日のパーティーでは、大勢の人と知り合った。	**I met a lot of people at the party today.**
一度に大勢の人と出会ったので、名前を覚えられなかった。	**I met a lot of people at one time, so I couldn't remember all their names.**
ソダさんが友達を紹介してくれた。	**Soda-san introduced her friend to me.**
新しい友達ができた。	**I made a new friend.**
彼女と知り合えてうれしかった。	**It was nice to get to know her.**
彼と話ができてよかった。	**I'm glad I was able to talk with him.**
彼女には、以前から会いたいと思っていた。	**I've always wanted to meet her.**
ようやく彼女に会えてうれしかった。	**I was happy to finally meet her.**
彼女には初めて会ったような気がしなかった。	**It didn't feel like my first time to meet her.**
私たちは昔からの友人のように、意気投合した。	**We got along great as if we were old friends.** ＊get along＝気が合う

彼に見覚えがあった。	**He looked familiar.**
また彼女に会いたい。	**I want to see her again.**
近いうちにまた彼女に会いたい。	**I want to see her again sometime soon.**
思いがけない出会いだった。	**It was a chance meeting.** ＊chance＝思いがけない、偶然の
すてきな出会いだった。	**It was a wonderful meeting.**
最近、新しい出会いがないなぁ。	**I'm not meeting new people these days.**
初対面の人と話すのって、苦手。	**I'm not good at talking to people when I first meet them.**
最近、人と会うのが面倒くさい。	**I feel too lazy to meet people these days.**

相手の外見

容姿

彼女は美人だ。	**She's beautiful.**
彼女はものすごい美人だ。	**She's a real knockout.** ＊knockout＝すごい美人
彼女はかわいらしい人だ。	**She's a cute person.**
彼はルックスがいい。	**He's good-looking.**
彼はかっこいい。	**He's cool.**
彼はハンサムだ。	**He's handsome.**
彼はたくましくていい男だ。	**He's a hunk.** ＊hunk［ハンク］＝たくましくセクシーな男性
彼女は笑顔がすてきだ。	**She has a great smile.**
彼女はとても魅力的だ。	**She's charming.**
彼女は顔が小さい。	**She has a small face.**

彼女は目が大きい。 She has big eyes.

彼女は目鼻立ちがはっきりしている。 She has clear-cut features.

彼女はきめの細かい肌をしている。 She has fine, smooth skin.

彼女は肌がきれいだ。 She has beautiful skin.

彼は肌が荒れている。 He has rough skin.

彼女は色白だ。 She has fair skin.

彼女は日焼けしている。 She's tanned.

彼は血色が悪い。 He has a poor complexion.

＊complexion［コンプレクション］＝顔色

彼女は（具合が悪くて）顔色が悪い。 She looks pale.

彼は（運動をしていて）健康的だ。 He's fit.

＊fit＝健康的な

彼女は髪がきれいだ。 She has beautiful hair.

彼は歯並びがきれいだ。 He has good teeth.

彼女は歯並びが悪い。 She has crooked teeth.

＊crooked［クルーキッド］＝曲がった、ゆがんだ

彼女はロングヘアだ。 She has long hair.

彼女はセミロングヘアだ。 She has medium-length hair.

彼女はショートヘアだ。 She has short hair.

彼は角刈りだ。 He has a crew cut.

＊crew cut＝角刈り

彼はぼさぼさ頭だ。 He has messy hair.

彼は頭のてっぺんが薄い。 He's thinning on top.

＊thin［スィン］＝薄くなる

彼は生え際が後退しかけている。 He has a receding hairline.

＊recede［リスィード］＝後退する

彼女は化粧が濃かった。 She wore heavy makeup.

＊「薄かった」なら、heavyをlightに

彼女はすっぴんでもかわいかった。 She was pretty without makeup.

体型

彼は中肉中背だ。 **He has a medium build.**
＊build＝体格、体型

彼女は背が高い。 **She's tall.**

彼は背が低い。 **He's short.**

彼女は大柄だ。 **She's large.**

彼女はふくよかだ。 **She's full-figured.**

彼女はすらっとしている。 **She's slender.**

彼はとてもやせている。 **He's really thin.**

彼は筋肉質だ。 **He has a muscular build.**
＊muscular＝筋骨たくましい

彼は引き締まった体をしている。 **He has a lean body.**
＊lean［リーン］＝脂肪の少ない

彼女はスタイルがいい。 **She has a nice figure.**
＊女性について用いる

彼は体格がいい。 **He has a nice build.**
＊男性について用いる

見た目の印象

彼は華がある人だ。 **He has a star aura.**
＊aura［オーラ］＝雰囲気、オーラ

彼女は華やかな人だ。 **She's glamorous.**

彼はパッとしない人だ。 **He looks plain.**

彼女は目つきの鋭い人だ。 **She's sharp-eyed.**

彼女は真面目そうな人だ。 **She looks like a serious person.**

彼は優しそうな人だ。 **He looks kind.**

彼女は厳しそうな人だ。 **She looks strict.**

彼は利口そうな人だ。 **He looks smart.**

彼はファッションセンスがいい。 **He has good taste in fashion.**

彼女は身なりがきちんとしていた。	**She was well-dressed.**
彼は見苦しい格好だった。	**He didn't look presentable.** ＊presentable＝見苦しくない
彼女は寝癖がついていた。	**She had bed hair.**
彼は姿勢がよかった。	**He had good posture.** ＊posture＝姿勢
彼は姿勢が悪かった。	**He had poor posture.**
彼は猫背だ。	**He's slouching.** ＊slouch＝前かがみになる
彼女は金持ちそうだ。	**She looks rich.**
彼は若く見える。	**He looks younger.**
彼女は子どもがいるようには見えなかった。	**She didn't look like she had a child.**
彼は実際の年齢より上に見える。	**He looks older than he actually is.**
彼女は大人っぽく見える。	**She looks mature.** ＊mature［マチュア］＝成熟した、大人の

相手の性格

付き合いやすい性格

彼女は楽しい人だ。	**She's fun.** ＊「とても楽しい人」なら、a lot of fun
彼は一緒にいて楽しい人だ。	**He's fun to be with.**
彼女は社交的な人だ。	**She's outgoing.**
彼は魅力的な人だ。	**He's attractive.**
彼女は人を引きつける性格だ。	**She has a magnetic personality.**
彼は人付き合いがうまい。	**He's a good mixer.**
彼女は明るい〈陽気な〉人だ。	**She's cheerful.**
彼女は活発な人だ。	**She's active.**

彼は気さくな人だ。	**He's friendly.**
彼はおしゃべりだ。	**He's talkative.** ＊talkative＝話し好きな
彼女はユーモアがある。	**She has a good sense of humor.** ＊humor［ヒューモァ］
彼は感じがいい。	**He's pleasant.**
彼女は愛きょうがある。	**She's lovable.**
彼女は子どものように無邪気だ。	**She's pure-hearted, like an innocent child.**
彼は笑顔を絶やさない人だ。	**He's always smiling.**
彼女は性格がいい。	**She's good-natured.**
彼は話し上手だ。	**He's a good talker.**
彼女は聞き上手だ。	**She's a good listener.**
彼は話しやすい。	**He's easy to talk to.**
彼女は腰が低い。	**She's humble.** ＊humble＝謙虚な、つつましい
彼は優しい。	**He's kind.** ＊kindは、niceとしてもOK
彼女は思いやりがある。	**She's thoughtful.**
彼女は寛大だ。	**She's generous.**
彼はおおらかだ。	**He's big-hearted.**
彼女は温厚だ。	**She's mild-tempered.**
彼女は（金銭的に）気前がいい。	**She's generous with her money.**
彼はさっぱりとした性格だ。	**He's refreshingly frank.** ＊refreshingly＝すがすがしく
彼女はハキハキと話す。	**She talks clearly and briskly.** ＊briskly＝きびきびと
彼は自然体だ。	**He's spontaneous.** ＊spontaneous［スポンテイニアァ］＝自然な
彼女は裏表がない。	**She's sincere.** ＊sincere＝裏表のない、正直な

彼は率直だ。	**He's straightforward.** **He's frank.**
彼女は純粋だ。	**She's a pure-hearted person.**
彼は誠実だ。	**He's honest.**
彼女は真面目だ。	**She's nice and earnest.** ＊earnest だけだと、「冗談も言わないような真面目な人」というネガティブなイメージになることもある
彼は律儀だ。	**He's dutiful.** ＊dutiful［デューティフォ］＝義理を守る
彼女は冷静だ。	**She's calm and controlled.** ＊calm［カーム］＝落ち着いた
彼は聡明だ。	**He's bright.**
彼女は頭の回転が速い。	**She's a quick thinker.**
彼は思慮分別がある。	**He's a sensible person.**
彼女は物わかりがいい。	**She's understanding.**
彼は斬新な考えを持っている。	**He's full of new ideas.** ＊full of ～＝～がいっぱいで
彼女はプラス思考だ。	**She's a positive person.**
彼は融通が利く。	**He's flexible.** ＊flexible＝柔軟な
彼女は野心的だ。	**She's ambitious.**
彼は勇敢だ。	**He's brave.**
彼女は意志が強い。	**She's strong-willed.**
彼は責任感が強い。	**He has a strong sense of responsibility.**
彼女は有言実行の人だ。	**She's as good as her word.**
彼は自信を持った人だ。	**He's self-confident.**
彼女は信頼できる。	**She's reliable.**
彼はしっかりしている。	**He's a together person.** ＊together＝落ち着きのある、しっかりした

彼女は良識がある。	**She has a good head on her shoulders.** ＊have a good head on one's shoulders＝常識がある
彼は礼儀正しい。	**He's well-mannered.**
彼女は丁寧な人だ。	**She's polite.**
彼女はおしとやかだ。	**She's graceful.**
彼女は協力的だ。	**She's cooperative.**
彼は時間に正確だ。	**He's punctual.**
彼女は（仕事や勉強に）熱心だ。	**She's hardworking.**

付き合いにくい性格

彼は強引な人だ。	**He's pushy.** ＊pushy［プッシー］
彼女は失礼な人だ。	**She's rude.**
彼は礼儀をわきまえない。	**He has no manners.**
彼女は口が悪い。	**She has a dirty mouth.**
彼は言葉遣いが悪い。	**He uses foul language.** ＊foul［ファオゥ］＝汚い
彼女は偉そうだ。	**She's bossy.**
彼は横柄だ。	**He's arrogant.** ＊arrogant［アラガント］
彼女は人使いが荒い。	**She's a slave driver.**
彼は図々しい。	**He has a lot of nerve.** ＊nerve［ナーヴ］＝厚かましさ、図太さ
彼女は自信過剰だ。	**She's too self-confident.**
彼はうぬぼれが強い。	**He's conceited.** ＊conceited［カンスィーティッド］
彼女は自意識過剰だ。	**She's overly self-conscious.** ＊self-conscious［カンシャス］
彼は目立ちたがり屋だ。	**He's an attention-seeker.**
彼女は承認欲求が強い。	**She wants approval from others.**

彼は自慢話ばかりする。	**He's always bragging about himself.**
彼はお高くとまっている。	**He's snobbish.**
彼女は性格が悪い。	**She has a bad personality.**
彼は暗い性格だ。	**He's a gloomy person.**
彼女は冷たい。	**She's cold.**
彼は思いやりがない。	**He's heartless.**
彼女はマイナス思考だ。	**She's a negative person.**
彼はムスッとしている。	**He's unfriendly.**
彼女は気難しい。	**She's hard to please.** ＊please＝～を楽しませる
彼は話しかけづらい。	**He's hard to talk to.**
彼女は人付き合いが下手だ。	**She's a bad mixer.**
彼は協調性に欠けている。	**He isn't a team player.**
彼女はぶっきらぼうだ。	**She's blunt.** ＊blunt［ブラント］＝ぶっきらぼうな
彼は短気だ。	**He has a short-temper.**
彼女は気分屋だ。	**She's moody.**
彼は変な人だ。	**He's weird.** ＊weird［ウィアード］＝変な、奇妙な
彼女は裏表がある。	**She's two-faced.**
彼はうそつきだ。	**He doesn't tell the truth.** ＊liar（うそつき）を用いてHe's a liar.とすると、かなり強い響きになる
彼女は疑い深い。	**She's a skeptic.** ＊skeptic［スケプティック］＝疑い深い人
彼は意地悪だ。	**He's mean.**
彼女は陰険だ。	**She's sneaky.**
彼はずるがしこい。	**He's a cunning person.**

彼女は欲深い。	**She's greedy.**
彼は攻撃的だ。	**He's an aggressive person.**
彼女は批判好きだ。	**She's judgemental.**
彼は辛らつだ。	**He has a sharp tongue.** ＊tongue［タング］＝話しぶり
彼女は自分勝手だ。	**She's selfish.**
彼は融通が利かない。	**He's stubborn.** ＊stubborn［スタバン］＝強情な
彼女は頑固だ。	**She's bullheaded.**
彼は神経質だ。	**He's too sensitive.**
彼女はとても内気だ。	**She's really shy.**
彼は優柔不断だ。	**He's indecisive.** ＊indecisive［インディサイスィヴ］＝優柔不断な
彼女は鈍感だ。	**She's thick-skinned.** ＊thick-skinned＝（非難などに）鈍感な、無神経な
彼は保守的だ。	**He's a stick-in-the-mud.** ＊stick-in-the-mud＝保守的な人
彼女は無責任だ。	**She's irresponsible.**
彼女は言うこととやることが違う。	**She's the type of person who says one thing and does another.**
彼はおせっかいだ。	**He's a busybody.** ＊busybody［ビズィバディ］＝おせっかいな
彼女は口やかましい。	**She's a nag.**
彼女は人のことにいちいち口出しする。	**She's a backseat driver.** ＊backseat driver＝余計な口出しをする人
彼は一言多い。	**He says one word too many.**
彼女はへりくつばかり言う。	**She's such a quibbler.** ＊quibbler［クイブラー］＝つべこべ言う人
彼はしつこい。	**He's persistent.**
彼女はケチだ。	**She's stingy.**
彼は知ったかぶりをする。	**He's a know-it-all.**

彼女は偏見を持っている。	**She's prejudiced.**
	＊prejudiced［プレジャディスト］
彼は不注意だ。	**He's careless.**
彼女は真面目過ぎる。	**She's too serious.**
彼は度量が狭い。	**He's narrow-minded.**
彼女は細かなことにうるさい。	**She's picky.**
彼は重箱の隅をつつくタイプだ。	**He's a nitpicker.**
彼女はずけずけものを言う。	**She's too outspoken.**
彼は時間にルーズだ。	**He's not punctual.**
	＊punctual＝時間を厳守する
彼女は口が軽い。	**She's a big mouth.**
彼女は詮索好きだ。	**She's nosy.**
彼はごますりタイプだ。	**He's an apple polisher.**
	＊apple polisher＝ご機嫌取り
彼女はあきらめが悪い。	**She doesn't know when to give up.**

いろいろな性格

彼女は外向的だ。	**She's extroverted.**
彼は内向的だ。	**He's introverted.**
彼女は大胆だ。	**She's bold.**
彼はおとなしい性格だ。	**He has a quiet personality.**
彼女は繊細だ。	**She's delicate.**
彼は静かだ。	**He's quiet.**
彼女はサバサバした性格だ。	**She has an easy-going personality.**
彼はのんびりした性格だ。	**He has a relaxed personality.**
彼女はナルシストだ。	**She's a narcissist.**
彼はロマンチストだ。	**He's a romanticist.**

彼女は現実的だ。	**She's a realist.**
彼は楽観的だ。	**He's an optimist.**
彼女は悲観的だ。	**She's a pessimist.**
彼は粘り強い。	**He's tenacious.** ＊tenacious＝粘り強い
彼女は飽きっぽい。	**She's easily bored.**
彼は負けて文句を言うタイプだ。	**He's a bad loser.**
彼女は負けっぷりが潔い。	**She's a good sport.** ＊sport＝（試合などで）潔い人
彼は自分のことを棚に上げるタイプだ。	**He's a pot-calling-the-kettle-black type.** ＊pot-calling-the-kettle-blackの直訳は、「鍋がやかんを黒いと言うような」

相手のプロフィール

相手の名前・年齢

彼女はオオサキマリコさんという。	**Her name is Mariko Osaki.**
彼はヤマグチさんという。	**His name is Mr. Yamaguchi.**
彼女は 42 歳だ。	**She's 42 years old.** ＊years oldは省略可
彼は 50 代くらいだ。	**He's probably in his 50s.**
彼女は 20 代だ。	**She's in her 20s.**
彼は 30 代前半だ。	**He's in his early 30s.**
彼女は 40 代半ばだ。	**She's in her mid-40s.**
彼は 50 代後半だ。	**He's in his late 50s.**
彼女は私と同年代だ。	**She and I are of the same generation.**
彼は私ぐらいの年齢だ。	**He's about my age.**

彼女は私より少し若いだろう。	**She's probably a little younger than me.** ＊「少し年上」なら、youngerをolderに
彼、いくつくらいだろう。	**I wonder how old he is.**
彼女は年齢不詳だ。	**You can't tell her age from the way she looks.** ＊このyouは、「一般的な人々」を指す
私たちは同い年だとわかった。	**I learned we were the same age.** ＊learn＝～と聞いて知る
彼、私より年上には見えなかった。	**He didn't look older than me.**
彼女が私より年下だなんて、信じられなかった。	**I couldn't believe she was younger than me.**

相手の家族構成

家族を表す単語

両親	parents
父	father / dad
母	mother / mom
祖父母	grandparents
祖父	grandfather / grandpa
祖母	grandmother / grandma
子ども	child / kid
息子	son
娘	daughter [ドーター]
孫	grandchild / grandchildren
孫（男）	grandson
孫（女）	granddaughter
兄・弟	brother
姉・妹	sister
（男女の区別なく）きょうだい	sibling
義理の父	father-in-law
義理の母	mother-in-law
義理の兄・弟	brother-in-law
義理の姉・妹	sister-in-law
おじ	uncle
おば	aunt
いとこ	cousin [カズン]
おい	nephew [ネフュー]
めい	niece [ニース]
親戚	relative
夫	husband
妻	wife
婚約者（男）	fiancé
婚約者（女）	fiancée
元夫	ex-husband
元妻	ex-wife
継父	stepfather
継母	stepmother
継息子	stepson
継娘	stepdaughter
はとこ	second cousin
曽祖父	great-grandpa
曽祖母	great-grandma
ひ孫	great-grandchild

彼は1人暮らしだ。	**He lives by himself.**
彼は、妻と義理の両親と暮らしている。	**He lives with his wife and his parents-in-law.**
彼らは4人家族だ。	**They're a family of four.**
彼女のところは大家族だ。	**She has a large family.**
彼は一人っ子だ。	**He's an only child.**
彼女には姉が2人と弟が1人いる。	**She has two sisters and a brother.**
彼女は3人姉妹の末っ子だ。	**She's the youngest of three sisters.** ＊「一番上」なら**the oldest**、「真ん中」なら**the middle**
彼には4人のきょうだいがいる。	**He has four siblings.** ＊**sibling**＝（男女の区別なく）きょうだい
彼には双子の妹がいる。	**He has a twin sister.**
彼女の息子さんは中学2年生だ。	**Her son is in the eighth grade.**
彼女の息子さんは来年、高校受験だそうだ。	**I heard her son is going to take high school exams next year.**
彼の娘さんが大学を卒業したそうだ。	**I heard his daughter graduated from college.**
彼女の息子さんが就職したそうだ。	**I heard her son started working.**
彼の息子さんが結婚したそうだ。	**I heard his son got married.**
彼女は旦那さんより7歳年上だ。	**She's seven years older than her husband.**
彼は結婚していて子どもが2人いる。	**He's married with two children.**
彼女は既婚で子どもはいない。	**She's married with no children.**
彼は犬を飼っている。	**He has a dog.**

国・地域名を表す単語

アイルランド	Ireland
アメリカ	America / the U.S.
イギリス	Britain / the U.K
イタリア	Italy
インド	India
インドネシア	Indonesia
ウクライナ	Ukraine
エジプト	Egypt
エチオピア	Ethiopia
オーストラリア	Australia
オーストリア	Austria
オランダ	Holland / the Netherlands
カナダ	Canada
韓国	South Korea
カンボジア	Cambodia
ケニア	Kenya
シンガポール	Singapore
スーダン	Sudan
スイス	Switzerland
スウェーデン	Sweden
スペイン	Spain
タイ	Thailand
台湾	Taiwan
中国	China
デンマーク	Denmark
ドイツ	Germany
トルコ	Turkey
ニュージーランド	New Zealand
ネパール	Nepal
ノルウェー	Norway
ハンガリー	Hungary
フィリピン	the Philippines
フィンランド	Finland
ブータン	Bhutan
ブラジル	Brazil
フランス	France
ベトナム	Vietnam
ベルギー	Belgium
ポーランド	Poland
ポルトガル	Portugal
香港	Hong Kong
マダガスカル	Madagascar
マレーシア	Malaysia
南アフリカ	South Africa
メキシコ	Mexico
モロッコ	Morocco
ロシア	Russia

都市名を表す単語

アテネ	Athens［アースィンズ］	ニューヨーク	New York
アムステルダム	Amsterdam	パリ	Paris
ウィーン	Vienna［ヴィエナ］	バンクーバー	Vancouver
エルサレム	Jerusalem［ジェルーサレム］	バンコク	Bangkok
オタワ	Ottawa	フィレンツェ	Florence
キャンベラ	Canberra	ブリュッセル	Brussels
広州	Guangzhou	北京	Beijing
コペンハーゲン	Copenhagen	ベルサイユ	Versailles［ヴェアサィ］
サンフランシスコ	San Francisco	ベルリン	Berlin［バーリン］
シアトル	Seattle	マドリード	Madrid
シカゴ	Chicago	ミュンヘン	Munich［ミューニク］
シドニー	Sydney	ミラノ	Milan
上海	Shanghai	メルボルン	Melbourne
ジュネーブ	Geneva［ジェニーヴァ］	モスクワ	Moscow［マースカウ］
ソウル	Seoul	リオデジャネイロ	Rio de Janeiro
チューリッヒ	Zurich［ズーリック］	ローマ	Rome［ロウム］
デリー	Delhi	ロサンゼルス	Los Angeles
ドバイ	Dubai	ロンドン	London
ナポリ	Naples［ネイポォズ］	ワシントン	Washington D.C.

彼は奈良の出身だ。　**He's from Nara.**

彼女は大阪生まれの横浜育ちだ。　**She was born in Osaka and raised in Yokohama.**

彼は東京に住んで８年になるそうだ。　**He has lived in Tokyo for eight years now.**

彼女は５年前まで、福岡に住んでいたそうだ。　**She lived in Fukuoka up until five years ago.**

彼とは同郷だとわかった。　**I found out that he and I come from the same town.**

＊find out ～＝～とわかる。foundはfindの過去形

彼はカナダのカルガリー出身だ。　**He's from Calgary, Canada.**

彼女はアメリカからの交換留学生だ。　**She's an exchange student from America.**

彼女は先月、来日したばかりだ。	She just came to Japan last month.

相手の職業

職業を表す単語

正社員	full-time worker
契約社員	contract employee
派遣社員	temporary worker / temp
アルバイト	part-timer
自営業者	self-employed
フリーランス	freelancer
社長	president
会社役員	company executive
会社員	office worker
公務員	public employee
受付係	receptionist
秘書	secretary
エンジニア	engineer
プログラマー	programmer
会計士	accountant
税理士	tax accountant
弁護士	lawyer
行政書士	administrative scrivener
建築家	architect
医師	doctor
看護師	nurse
薬剤師	pharmacist
教師	teacher
教授	professor
保育士	nursery school teacher
介護士	care worker
社会福祉士	social worker
デザイナー	designer
編集者	editor
報道記者	reporter
通訳者	interpreter
翻訳者	translator
俳優	actor
歌手	singer
ユーチューバー	YouTuber
インフルエンサー	influencer
政治家	politician
漁師	fisher
農業従事者	farmer
警察官	police officer
消防隊員	firefighter
建設作業員	construction worker
美容師	hairdresser
理容師	barber
販売員	sales clerk
（飲食店の）接客係	server
レジ係	cashier
主婦、主夫	homemaker

彼女は保育士だ。	She's a nursery school teacher.
彼は主夫だ。	He's a homemaker. ＊homemaker＝主婦、主夫
彼は会社員だ。	He's an office worker. ＊「会社員」は、company workerとも言う
彼は IT 企業に勤めている。	He works for an IT company.
彼女は貿易関係の仕事をしている。	She works in trade.

彼女は食品業界が長い。
She has been in the food industry for years.
＊for years＝何年も

彼は、以前はアパレル関係の仕事をしていた。
He used to be in the apparel industry.

彼は医療機器の営業をしている。
He sells medical equipment.
＊equipment＝機器

彼は経理を担当している。
He's in charge of accounting.
＊in charge of ～＝～を担当して　accounting＝会計

彼女はパートで事務をしている。
She does office work part time.
＊part time＝パートタイムで

彼はジムのインストラクターだ。
He's an instructor at a gym.

彼はプログラミングのエキスパートだ。
He's a programming expert.

彼女は社長だ。
She's the president of a company.

彼は会社を経営している。
He runs a business.
＊run＝～を経営する

彼女は飲食店を経営している。
She runs a restaurant.

彼はベテラン教師だ。
He's an experienced teacher.

彼女は小学３年生を受け持っている。
She's a third-grade teacher.

彼は高校で数学を教えている。
He teaches math in high school.

彼は定年退職している。
He's retired from work.

彼女は最近、転職したばかりだ。
She has recently changed jobs.

彼は派遣社員だ。
He's a temp.
＊tempは、temporary worker（派遣社員）の略

彼女はアルバイトで働いている。
She works part time.

彼は法政大学の２年生だ。
He's a sophomore at Hosei University.
＊sophomore［サフォモー］＝（大学の）2年生

彼女は法学専攻だ。
She majors in law.
＊major in ～＝～を専攻する

人付き合い

友人・知人に会う

午後、ミユカと会った。	I met Miyuka this afternoon.
2時に東京駅で待ち合わせた。	We met at Tokyo Station at 2:00.
シンジとお茶した。	Shinji and I had some coffee. ＊some coffeeは、some teaとしてもOK
ジムでハヤシさんを見かけた。	I saw Hayashi-san at the gym.
スーパーで偶然、カイヌマさんに出くわした。	I ran into Kainuma-san at the grocery store. ＊grocery［グロウサリー］store＝生鮮食料品店
帰宅途中、アサノさんに会った。	I saw Asano-san on the way home.
電車の中でクボさんに会った。	I met Kubo-san on the train.
オオモリさんが家に寄った。	Omori-san dropped by my place.
カクタさんの家にお邪魔した。	I visited Kakuta-san at her house.
あんな所で彼女に会うとは驚いた。	I didn't expect to see her there.

久しぶりの再会

久しぶりにアオイと会った。	I met Aoi for the first time in ages.
キムラさんと3カ月ぶりに会った。	I saw Kimura-san for the first time in three months.
カタギリさんと会うのは、去年の9月以来だった。	I met Katagiri-san for the first time since last September.
親戚が久しぶりに集まった。	My relatives got together for the first time in a while.
おいっ子のユウが大きくなっていた。	My nephew Yu has gotten bigger.
ヒカリは、もうお母さんの背を超していた。	Hikari is already taller than her mother.

4組のクラス会があった。	There was a reunion for Class 4.
高校の同級生に会った。	I met some friends from high school.
久しぶりに会う人ばかりだった。	I saw a lot of my classmates for the first time in a long while.
最初、彼が誰だかわからなかった。	I didn't recognize him at first.
彼女は元気そうだった。	She looked great.
シズナの赤ちゃんに会えて、うれしかった。	I was so happy to meet Shizuna's baby.
みんな全然変わっていなかった。	They haven't changed a bit.
みんなに「変わらないね」と言われた。	They told me that I looked the same.
みんなに「だいぶ変わったね」と言われた。	They told me that I looked very different.
「きれいになったね」と彼に言われた。	He told me I had become beautiful.
彼女はすごくきれいになっていた。	She has become really beautiful.
彼女はやせたように見えた。	She looked like she had lost weight.
彼はだいぶ太っていた。	He gained a lot of weight.
彼、髪が薄くなっていた。	He was losing his hair.
彼女は白髪が増えていた。	She had more gray hair.
お互い老けたなぁ。	We both looked older.
旧交を温めた。	We caught up with each other. ＊catch up with ～＝～(久しぶりの人)と話す
中学校時代の思い出話に花が咲いた。	We had a great time talking about our junior high school days.
また会う約束をした。	We promised to get together again.
これからも連絡を取り合うことにした。	We decided to keep in touch. ＊keep in touch＝連絡を取る

近所付き合い

隣のアキヤマさんに、リンゴをお裾分けした。	**I gave some apples to my next-door neighbor, Akiyama-san.**
お返しにジャガイモをいただいた。	**I got some potatoes in return.**
ワタナベさんに、カナダ旅行のお土産を渡した。	**I gave Watanabe-san a gift from Canada.**
シバタさんと立ち話をした。	**I stood chatting with Shibata-san.**
町内会の集まりがあった。	**We had a gathering of our neighborhood association.**
マンションの自治会の会議に出た。	**I attended the condo association meeting.** ＊condoは、condominium（分譲マンション）の略
回覧板が回ってきた。	**The neighborhood bulletin was passed around to me.** ＊bulletin［ブレティン］＝広報、会報
回覧板をタナベさんに回した。	**I passed the neighborhood bulletin to Tanabe-san.**
コウダさんは来月、大阪に引っ越すそうだ。	**Kouda-san is moving to Osaka next month.** ＊move＝引っ越す
寂しくなるな。	**I'll miss her.** ＊miss＝～がいなくて寂しく思う
隣の人が引っ越しのあいさつに来た。	**My new neighbor came to say hi.** ＊say hi＝あいさつをする
いい人そうでよかった。	**I'm glad she looked nice.**
出がけに隣の人と顔を合わせたので、あいさつした。	**When I was leaving, I saw a neighbor and greeted her.** ＊neighbor＝隣人、近所の人
隣には、どんな人が住んでいるんだろう？	**I wonder what kind of people live next-door.**
うちのマンションは、近所付き合いがほとんどない。	**People living in my condo don't really associate with each other.**

人との別れ

人と別れる

5時に彼女と別れた。
I said bye to her at 5:00.
＊say bye to ～＝～と別れる。saidはsayの過去形

駅でハナと別れた。
I said bye to Hana at the station.

息子を空港で見送った。
I saw my son off at the airport.
＊see ～ off＝～を見送る。sawはseeの過去形

彼女を駅まで送った。
I saw her off at the station.

笑顔で彼を見送った。
I saw him off with a smile.

別れ際、つい泣いてしまった。
I couldn't help crying when I saw her off.
＊can't help ～ing＝～せずにはいられない

「バイバイ！」と手を振った。
I waved good-bye to him.
＊wave＝手を振る

人との死別

祖父が亡くなった。
My grandfather passed away.
＊pass away＝亡くなる

父は72歳で亡くなった。
My dad passed away at the age of 72.

祖母は97歳で大往生した。
My grandmother passed away peacefully at 97.

彼はぽっくり逝った。
He dropped dead.
＊drop dead＝ぽっくり死ぬ

安らかな死だった。
It was a peaceful death.

彼は早過ぎる死を迎えた。
He died too early.

彼女は死にひんしている。
She's dying.

いとこが肝臓がんで亡くなった。
My cousin passed away from liver cancer.

隣人が自死した。
A neighbor of mine committed suicide.

おいが交通事故で亡くなった。	**My nephew was killed in a car accident.**
彼のことを思って祈っている。	**My thoughts and prayers are with him.** ＊thought[ソート]＝思い　prayer＝祈り
ヤマダさんのお母さまのご逝去の報に触れ、悲しみに暮れている。	**I'm very sorry to hear about Yamada-san's mother's death.**
彼の死は、言葉では表せないほど悲しい。	**His death has saddened me beyond words.** ＊sadden＝〜を悲しませる
彼女が他界して12年になる。	**It's been 12 years since she passed away.**
私はピンピンコロリがいいな。	**I want to die suddenly and painlessly while I'm active and healthy.**

Memo

人間関係に関することを、メモしておきましょう。

人間関係について 英語日記を書いてみよう

人間関係にまつわるあれこれを、英語で書いてみましょう。

友達とケンカ

Yohei and I had an argument. I apologized by LINE, but I haven't gotten a reply yet. Maybe I should've said sorry to him in person.

ヨウヘイとケンカをしてしまった。LINEで謝ったけど、まだ返事が来ない。直接謝るべきだったかなぁ。

「言い争い（のケンカ）」は argument か quarrel［クワレゥ］、「殴り合いのケンカ、激しい口論」は fight と表します。Maybe I should've ～（動詞の過去分詞）は「～すべきだったかな」、in person は「（メールや電話などではなく）直接」という意味です。

上階の人の足音

The man upstairs makes noise when he walks. I wish I could ask him to walk quietly but I can't as I sometimes run into him in the parking lot.

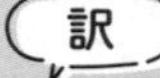

上階の男性の足音がうるさい。静かに歩くように言いたいけど、たまに駐車場でばったり会うから言えないな。

「上階の」は upstairs、「下階の」なら downstairs。I wish I could ～は「～できたらいいけれど（実際はできない）」という意味。この文の as ～は「～なので」という意味を表します。run into ～は「～にばったり会う」、parking lot は「駐車場」のことです。

気を遣うのって疲れる

I don't want to go along with my husband to his parents' home during the Obon holiday. I get so tired trying to be nice to my in-laws.

訳

お盆休みに夫の実家へ帰省するの、嫌だなぁ。義母や義姉に気を遣うのって、すごく疲れる。

ポイント

「夫の実家へ帰省する」は、go along with my husband to his parents' home（夫と一緒に彼の両親の家に行く）と表しました。「義母」は mother-in-law、「義姉」は sister-in-law のように言いますが、ここでは in-laws（姻戚）とまとめています。

ありがたいママ友

Marina's teacher called me to come pick her up because she had a fever. But I was in a meeting and I couldn't. Ms. Kondo kindly picked her up for me.

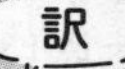

訳

マリナの先生から、マリナが熱を出したから迎えに来るように電話があった。でも、私は会議中で行けなかった。ご親切に、コンドウさんが代わりに迎えに行ってくれた。

ポイント

pick up は「～を迎えに行く」という意味です。「ご親切に～してくれた」は kindly ～（動詞の過去形）で表します。この kindly は動詞の直前に置きます。覚えておきましょう。「～の代わりに」は for ～を用います。

05

気持ち・感想

いろいろな気持ち

好き

この色、好きだな。 **I like this color.**

このバンド、大好き！ **I love this band!**

京都は、お気に入りの都市。 **Kyoto is my favorite city.**

私、チョコレートに目がないんだよね。 **I love chocolate more than anything.**

＊more than anything＝ほかの何よりも

嫌い

この俳優、好きじゃない。 **I don't like this actor.**

コーヒーは、あまり好きじゃない。 **I don't really like coffee.**

＊don't really 〜＝あまり〜でない

飛行機に乗るのって、本当に苦手。 **I really don't like flying.**

＊fly＝飛行機に乗る

ゴキブリ、大嫌い！ **I hate cockroaches!**

＊cockroach（ゴキブリ）は、くだけてroachと略すことも

うれしい・幸せ

やった！ **Yes!**
I did it!

すごくうれしい！ **I'm so happy!**

本当に幸せ。 **I'm really happy.**

最高にうれしい。 **I couldn't be happier.**

＊「これ以上うれしいことはない」というニュアンス

言葉では表せないくらいうれしい。	**I have no words to express how happy I am.**
わ～すごい、信じられない！	**Wow, this is too good to be true!** ＊too good to be trueは、「話がうま過ぎる」という疑い深いニュアンスで使われることも多い
うれしい知らせが届いた！	**I got some good news!**
彼女、本当にうれしそうだったなぁ。	**She looked really happy.**
彼のことは私にとってもうれしい。	**I'm happy for him.**
私って世界一の幸せ者だ。	**I'm the happiest person on earth.**
僕って、なんて幸せなんだろう。	**I'm such a lucky guy.** ＊このluckyは「恵まれていて幸せ」の意味。女性なら、guyをwomanに
夢みたい！	**It feels like a dream!**
ラッキー！	**Lucky me!** **I'm so lucky!**
運がいい。	**I'm in luck.**
今日はツイてたなぁ。	**I lucked out today.**

楽しい・面白い

楽しかった。	**It was fun.** **I had fun.**
めちゃくちゃ楽しかった。	**I had a ball.** **I had a great time.** ＊ball＝素晴らしいひととき
すっごく楽しい。	**It's a lot of fun.**
楽しい一日だった。	**It was a great day.** ＊great dayは、fun dayとしてもOK
期待していなかったけど、意外と笑えた。	**We didn't expect it, but it WAS funny.** ＊WASと大文字で書くことで、意味を強調できる
超うける！	**That's hilarious!** ＊hilarious［ヒラリアス］＝爆笑ものの
超笑えた！	**It cracked me up!** ＊crack ～ up＝～を大笑いさせる

爆笑した！	**I laughed out loud!** ＊loud＝大声で
おなかがよじれるほど笑った。	**I laughed until my sides ached.** ＊side＝脇腹　ache［エイク］＝痛む
笑い過ぎて涙が出た。	**I laughed to tears.**
思い出すたびに笑ってしまう。	**I chuckle whenever I remember it.** ＊chuckle＝くすくす笑う　remember＝〜を思い出す

悲しい

悲しい。	**I'm feeling sad.**
とても悲しい。	**I'm really sad.** **I'm heartbroken.**
泣きそう。	**I'm close to tears.** ＊close［クロウス］to 〜＝今にも〜しそうで
泣きたい気持ちだった。	**I felt like crying.**
泣きたい気持ちを必死に抑えた。	**I tried really hard to hold back my tears.** ＊hold back 〜＝〜を抑える
涙があふれてきた。	**Tears welled up in my eyes.** ＊well up＝わき出る、あふれる
涙が止まらない。	**I can't stop crying.**
なんて残酷な！	**How cruel!** ＊cruel＝残酷な、むごい
胸が張り裂けそうだった。	**I felt heartbroken.**
彼女が悲しんでいるのを見て、胸が張り裂けそうだった。	**It broke my heart to see her sad.**

寂しい・むなしい

寂しいな。	**I'm feeling lonely.**
彼に会えなくて寂しい。	**I miss him.**
心にぽっかりと穴が空いたようだ。	**It's like there's a hole in my heart.**
突然、寂しさがこみ上げてきた。	**All of a sudden, I was hit by a wave of loneliness.**

息子に寂しい思いをさせて申し訳ない。	**I'm very sorry I'm making my son feel lonely.**
むなしい。	**I feel empty.** ＊empty＝むなしい、空虚な
毎日同じことの繰り返しで、むなしくなる。	**I feel empty doing the same thing every day.**
今日は誰とも口をきかなかった。	**I didn't talk to anyone today.**
世界で自分だけひとりぼっちの気分だ。	**I feel like I'm all alone in the world.**
こんなとき、マユがいてくれたらなぁ。	**At times like this I wish Mayu were here.**
人生なんて、こんなもんだ。	**That's the way it is.** **That's life.**

憂うつ・うんざり

憂うつだなぁ。	**I'm feeling low.** **I feel depressed.** ＊lowは、blueでもOK。depressedは、downでもOK
最近、やる気が出ないなぁ。	**I don't have any motivation these days.** ＊motivation＝やる気
何もやる気がしない。	**I don't feel like doing anything.**
何もかも嫌になった。	**I'm sick and tired of everything.**
もう嫌になっちゃう。	**It's driving me crazy.** ＊drive ～ crazy＝～の気を変にさせる
絶望的だ。	**It's hopeless.**
もううんざりだ。	**I'm sick of it.**
何もかも台無しだ。	**I really messed up everything.** ＊mess up ～＝～を台無しにする
お先真っ暗。	**The road ahead is pitch-dark.** ＊pitch-dark＝真っ暗闇の
なんでいつもこんな目に遭うのかな。	**How come this always happens to me?**
人生に疲れた。	**I'm tired of life.**

期待・楽しみ

楽しみ！	**I can't wait!**
明日が楽しみ。	**I can't wait for tomorrow.** **I can hardly wait for tomorrow.**
次の試合が楽しみ。	**I'm looking forward to the next game.**
ワクワクしてきた。	**I'm getting excited.**
ワクワク、ドキドキ。	**I'm excited and nervous.**
早く土曜日にならないかな。	**I wish it were Saturday already.**
興奮して、なかなか眠れなかった。	**I was too excited to sleep.**
この映画には、すごく期待してる。	**I really have high expectations for this movie.**
期待を裏切りませんように。	**I hope it doesn't disappoint me.** ＊「人」に対する期待なら、itをhe/she/theyなどに

がっかり・残念

あ〜あ、がっかり。	**What a letdown!** ＊letdown（期待外れ）は、disappointmentとしてもOK
彼には本当にがっかりした。	**I was really disappointed in him.**
あと少しでうまくいきそうだったんだけどな。	**It looked like it was just about to turn out okay.** ＊turn out 〜＝〜という結果になる
期待外れだった。	**It was a letdown.**
イマイチだった。	**It wasn't good enough.**
期待したほどよくはなかった。	**It wasn't as good as I expected.**
期待したのが間違いだった。	**I shouldn't have expected so much.**
残念だなぁ！	**That's too bad!** **That's a shame!** ＊shame＝残念なこと

つまらない

つまんないなぁ。	**It's boring.** **I'm bored.**
つまらない本だった。	**It was a boring book.**
退屈だった。	**It was a drag.** ＊drag＝退屈なこと・人
とても退屈だったので、途中でテレビを消した。	**I turned off the TV because it was really boring.**
めちゃくちゃ退屈。	**I'm bored to death.**
日々の生活に退屈してる。	**I'm bored of my everyday life.**
全然面白くなかった。	**It was no fun at all.**
何か面白いことないかなぁ。	**I wonder if there's anything exciting going on.**
時間の無駄だった。	**It was a waste of time.**

感動した

感動した。	**I was moved.** ＊movedは、touchedとしてもOK
深く感動した。	**I was really moved.**
感動で涙が出た。	**I was moved to tears.**
彼の優しさに感動した。	**I was moved by his kindness.**
心を揺さぶられた。	**I was touched.**
刺激を受けた。	**I was inspired.**
もらい泣きしちゃった。	**I cried in sympathy.**
彼のスピーチに深く感銘を受けた。	**I was really impressed with his speech.**
最後のシーンにグッときた。	**I was deeply touched by the last scene.**

怒り

腹立たしい。	**This is annoying.** ＊annoying［アノィイング］＝気に障る、迷惑な
超むかつく！	**I'm so pissed off!** ＊下品な表現
まだ怒りが収まらない。	**I'm still mad.**
思い出したらまた腹が立ってきた。	**Just remembering it made me angry again.**
つまらないことでカッとなった。	**I got mad over nothing.**
堪忍袋の緒が切れた。	**I couldn't take it any longer.** **I've lost my patience.** ＊take it＝我慢する　patience＝我慢、忍耐
怒りで体中が震えた。	**My whole body shook with anger.**
ストレス発散したい！	**I need to let off some steam!** ＊let off steam＝うっぷん晴らしをする
誰かに全部話してしまいたい。	**I want to tell everything to someone.**
夫に八つ当たりしちゃった。	**I took it out on my hubby.** ＊take it out on 〜＝〜に八つ当たりする。tookは takeの過去形　hubby＝husband（夫）
いい加減にしてよ！	**Give me a break!** ＊いらいらするような発言などに対して、「いい加減にしてよ！」「ちょっと待ってよ！」といったニュアンス
ほっといてほしい。	**Just leave me alone.**
余計なお世話だよ。	**It's none of his business.** ＊相手が女性なら、hisをherに
彼女の態度にカチンときた。	**Her attitude got on my nerves.** ＊attitude［アティテュード］＝態度
彼とはもう絶交だ。	**I'm done with him.** ＊be done with 〜＝〜と関係を絶つ
彼女のこと、一生許さない！	**I will never forgive her!**
どうしても許せない！	**It's absolutely unforgivable!**
彼のことはもう信用しない。	**I won't trust him anymore.**
彼女とは二度と口をきかない！	**I will never talk to her again!**

彼の顔を見るのも嫌。	I can't stand the sight of him. ＊stand＝～を我慢する
彼女に言い返せばよかった。	I should've said something back to her.

驚き

あ～、びっくりした。	Oh, I was surprised.
本当に驚いた。	I was really surprised.
うそみたい。	I just can't believe it.
マジで？	No kidding!
すごい偶然！	What a coincidence! ＊coincidence［コウインスィデンス］＝偶然
なんて一日だ！	What a day! ＊よい意味でも悪い意味でも使う
信じられない！	Unbelievable!
いまだに信じられない。	I still can't believe it.
こんなことになるなんて、信じられない。	I can't believe this is really happening.
自分の目を疑った。	I couldn't believe my eyes. ＊「耳を疑った」ならeyesをearsに
（彼女の話を聞いて）心臓が止まるかと思った。	She almost gave me a heart attack. ＊ニュースを見聞きした場合などは、SheをItにする
事実は小説よりも奇なり。	Truth is stranger than fiction.

自信がある・ない

自信満々だ。	I'm really confident.
準備万端だ。	I'm all set. Everything is ready. ＊set＝準備万端で
こんなの朝飯前だよ。	This is a piece of cake. This is as easy as pie. ＊1文目は、単にPiece of cake.としてもOK
うまくやれる自信がある。	I'm confident that I'll do well.

5 気持ち・感想

まあまあ自信がある。	**I'm pretty confident.**
自分に自信が持てない。	**I'm not confident in myself.**
何だか自信がなくなっちゃった。	**I'm no longer confident for some reason.**
もっと自分に自信を持ちたい。	**I want to be more confident in myself.**
自分を信じなきゃ。	**I should believe in myself.**
ちょっとずつ自信が付いてきた。	**I'm becoming more confident.**
過信しないように気を付けよう。	**I'll try not to be overconfident.** ＊overconfident＝自信過剰な、うぬぼれた
私って自信過剰かな？	**Am I overconfident?**

不安・緊張

心配だなぁ。	**I'm worried.**
すごく不安。	**I'm feeling really uneasy.** ＊uneasy＝不安な、心配な
不安で夜も眠れない。	**I'm too anxious to sleep at night.**
緊張してる。	**I'm nervous.**
緊張してきた。	**I'm getting tense.** ＊tense＝緊張した
超ドキドキ！	**I have butterflies in my stomach.** ＊have butterflies in one's stomach＝（緊張などで）ドキドキする
明日の演奏会を前に、神経が高ぶっている。	**I'm keyed-up about the music performance tomorrow.** ＊keyed-up＝（大きな出来事を前に）興奮・緊張して
胃が痛くなってきた。	**I'm getting knots in my stomach.** ＊knot＝（不安などによる胃やのどの）締めつけられる感じ
私には無理かも。	**I don't think I can do it.**
何だか嫌な予感がする。	**I have a bad feeling about this.**
ホントにうまくいくのかなぁ。	**I wonder if it'll go well.** ＊go well（うまくいく）は、work outとしてもOK
うまくいくといいな。	**I hope it goes well.**

すごく緊張した。 I was really nervous.

声が震えてしまった。 My voice got shaky.

手が震えていた。 My hands were shaking.

心臓がバクバクしていた。 My heart was beating fast.

頭が真っ白になった。 My mind went blank.
＊go blank＝（頭の中が）真っ白になる

顔が真っ赤になっていたと思う。 I think my face was red.
I think I was flushed.
＊flushed＝赤面した

彼は不安そうな顔をしていた。 He looked nervous.

安心

安心した。 I'm relieved.

ほっとひと安心！ What a relief!

何とかなってよかった。 I'm glad I managed it.
＊manage＝～を何とかやり遂げる

何とか間に合った。 I barely made it.
＊barely＝何とか～する　make it＝間に合う

これで安心して眠れる。 Now I can sleep with an easy mind.

しっかり準備したから、安心だ。 I feel at ease because I'm fully prepared.

子どもの顔を見ると安心する。 I feel relieved whenever I see my kid's face.

家に帰るとほっとする。 I feel relieved when I get back home.

満足

すごく満足している。 I'm fully satisfied.

言うことなしだ。 I'm perfectly satisfied.

大満足のセミナーだった。 I was completely satisfied with the seminar.

みんなが喜んでくれて、大満足。	**I'm happy that everyone enjoyed it.**
充実した一日だった。	**I had a fruitful day.** **I had a fulfilling day.** ＊fruitful＝実りの多い　fulfilling＝充実感のある
頑張ったかいがあった。	**My hard work paid off.** ＊pay off＝成果が出る。paidはpayの過去形
やれることはすべてやった。	**I did all I could do.**
自己評価はＡ！	**My self-assessment is an A!**

不満

すごく不満だ。	**I'm not satisfied at all.**
いまひとつ満足していない。	**I'm not really satisfied with this.**
心の中がモヤモヤする。	**I have pent-up feelings.** ＊pent-up＝（感情などが）抑え付けられた
あんなので満足できるわけない！	**How could I be satisfied with that?**
そのレストランには満足できなかった。	**I wasn't satisfied with that restaurant.**
この不満をどこにぶつければいいの？	**Where should I go to complain?**
最近、私、愚痴ってばかりだな。	**I'm always griping these days.** ＊gripe[グライプ]＝（ダラダラと）不平を言う
なるべく不満は口にしないようにしなきゃ。	**I should keep my complaints to myself.** ＊complaint＝不平、不満
不平を言うの、や～めた！	**Okay, that's it. No more complaining!** ＊that's it＝そこまでだ　complain＝不平を言う

怖い・不快

すごく怖い。	**I'm so scared.** **It's so scary.**
ちょっと怖いな。	**I'm a little scared.**
死ぬかと思った。	**I thought I was going to die.**
もう耐えられない。	**I can't take it anymore.** ＊take it＝我慢する

もうあんな思いはしたくない。	**I don't want to go through that again.**
身の毛もよだつ体験だった。	**It was a hair-raising experience.**
怖くて叫び声も出なかった。	**I was too scared to scream.**
足が震えた。	**My legs were trembling.** ＊tremble＝震える
血の気が引いた。	**I turned white.**
鳥肌が立った。	**I had goosebumps.** ＊goosebumps＝鳥肌
閉所恐怖症だ。	**I'm afraid of enclosed spaces.** ＊enclosed＝囲まれた
高所恐怖症だ。	**I'm afraid of heights.** ＊heights＝高い所
暗闇が苦手だ。	**I'm afraid of the dark.** ＊「高い所が苦手」なら、darkをheightsに
ぞっとした。	**It was creepy.**
すごく気持ち悪かった。	**It was so gross.** ＊gross［グロウス］＝気持ち悪い
虫が大っ嫌い！	**I hate bugs!**
何回乗っても飛行機は怖い。	**I'll never get used to flying.** ＊get used to ～＝～に慣れる

後悔

なんでこうなっちゃったんだろう。	**How did it end up like this?** ＊end up＝結局～になる
なんでいつもこうなるんだろう。	**Why do I always end up like this?**
こんなはずじゃなかったのに。	**This wasn't how it was supposed to be.** ＊be supposed to ～＝～するものとされている
あんなことするんじゃなかった。	**I shouldn't have done that.**
取り返しのつかないことをした。	**I did something I can't undo.** ＊undo＝～(したこと)を元に戻す
軽率だった。	**It was careless of me.**
やり過ぎちゃったかな。	**Maybe I went a bit too far.** ＊go too far＝度を超す。wentはgoの過去形

余計なこと言っちゃったかな。	**I might have said one word too many.**
みんなに迷惑かけちゃった。	**I caused my friends a lot of trouble.** ＊「みんな」が同僚なら、friendsをco-workersに
もっと早くからやっておくんだった。	**I should've done it sooner.**
もっと準備しておけばよかった。	**I should've been more prepared.**
ホント後悔してる。	**I really regret it.** ＊regret＝～を後悔する
後悔はしていない。	**I have no regrets.** ＊regret＝後悔
後悔しても仕方がない。	**It's too late for regrets.**
済んだことは仕方ない。	**What's done is done.**
後悔先に立たず、だな。	**It's too late to be sorry.**
あの頃に戻れたらいいのに。	**I wish I could turn back the clock to those days.**
人生やり直したい。	**I wish I could redo my life.** ＊redo＝～をやり直す

恥ずかしい

（決まりが悪くて）恥ずかしかった。	**I was embarrassed.**
（自分の行為が道徳的に）恥ずかしい。	**I'm ashamed.**
（内気で）恥ずかしい。	**I'm shy.**
（人前で恥をかかされて）恥ずかしかった。	**I was humiliated.** ＊humiliated［ヒューミリエイティッド］
みんなに笑われちゃった。	**Everyone laughed at me.**
もう最悪！	**It really sucks!** ＊suck［サック］＝（物事が）ひどい、最低だ
思い出したくもない。	**I don't want to remember it.**
早く忘れたい。	**I just want to forget about it.**

嫌な記憶を消してしまいたい。	**I want to blot out the bad memories.** ＊blot out ～＝～を消し去る
穴があったら入りたい。	**I wish I could sink into the floor.** ＊sink into ～＝～に沈み込む
顔が真っ赤になっちゃった。	**I went bright red in the face.** ＊go red＝赤くなる。wentはgoの過去形
顔から火が出そうだった。	**My face burned with shame.** ＊burn＝ほてる　shame＝恥ずかしさ
思い出すだけで赤面しちゃう。	**Just remembering it makes me blush.**
聞くは一時の恥、聞かぬは一生の恥。	**Better to ask the way than go astray.** ＊astray＝道に迷って
恥を忍んで彼女に助けを求めた。	**I swallowed my pride and asked her for help.**

感謝する

カオル、ありがとう。	**Thanks, Kaoru.**
ユウト、本当にありがとう。	**Thanks so much, Yuto.**
ありがたいことだ。	**I'm grateful.** ＊gratefulは、thankfulとしてもOK
彼女には感謝している。	**I'm grateful to her.**
彼女にはいくら感謝しても足りない。	**I can't thank her enough.** ＊直訳すると「十分に感謝することができない」
彼への感謝の気持ちは、言葉では表せない。	**There are no words to express how grateful I am to him.**
明日、彼に感謝の気持ちを伝えよう。	**I'll show him my gratitude tomorrow.** ＊gratitude＝感謝
手伝ってくれたみんなに感謝。	**I'm grateful for everyone's help.**
健康に恵まれてありがたい。	**I'm thankful for my good health.**
今年も無事に過ごせたことに感謝したい。	**I'm thankful nothing bad happened throughout the year.**

謝罪する

申し訳ない。	**I'm sorry.**
本当に申し訳なく思う。	**I'm really sorry.**
彼には申し訳ないことをした。	**I feel terrible for what I did to him.**
みんなに謝りたい。	**I want to apologize to everyone.** ＊apologize［アパロジャイズ］＝謝罪する
彼女にちゃんと謝らないと。	**I need to give her a proper apology.** ＊proper＝適した、ふさわしい　apology＝謝罪
明日、彼女に謝ろう。	**I'll tell her I'm sorry tomorrow.**
彼に謝罪の手紙を書こう。	**I'll write him a letter of apology.**
ひたすら謝った。	**I kept apologizing.**
彼女におわびの品を持っていった。	**I went to see her with an I'm-sorry gift.** ＊「おわびの品」は、apology giftとも言う
彼に許してもらえるといいな。	**I hope he forgives me.**
謝ってほしい！	**I want an apology!**
これは謝って済むことじゃない。	**This isn't something that can be apologized away.**
謝るくらいなら、最初からしないでほしい。	**If you're going to apologize, then don't do it in the first place.**
彼女が謝ってくれた。	**She apologized to me.**
彼が謝ってくれて、腹の虫が治まった。	**He apologized, and I calmed down.** ＊calm down＝落ち着く
彼は謝ってくれたけど、やっぱり許せない。	**He apologized, but I just can't forgive him.**

褒める

私、よく頑張った！	**I did a good job!**
やればできる！	**If I try, I can do it!**
自分を褒めてあげたい。	**I want to praise myself.** ＊praise［プレイズ］＝～を褒める

自分にご褒美をあげよう。	**I should give myself a treat.** ＊treat＝楽しみ、喜び
ミサコに拍手を送りたい。	**I want to give a big hand to Misako.** ＊「自分に」なら、Misakoをmyselfに
モリタさんは本当に偉い。	**Mr. Morita is truly a great person.**
たまには夫を褒めてあげなきゃ。	**I should compliment my husband once in a while.** ＊compliment＝〜を褒める　once in a while＝時々
英語を褒められてうれしかった。	**I was glad he complimented me on my English.** ＊compliment 〜 on ...＝…について〜を褒める
お世辞でもうれしかった。	**I was flattered.** ＊flattered＝(褒められたりして)うれしい、気をよくする
褒め言葉と受け取った。	**I took it as a compliment.** ＊compliment＝褒め言葉

祝う

おめでとう！	**Congratulations!** ＊くだけて、Congrats!とも言う
ヨシキ、おめでとう！	**Congratulations, Yoshiki!**
誕生日おめでとう！	**Happy birthday!**
卒業おめでとう！	**Congratulations on your graduation!**
就職おめでとう！	**Congratulations on finding a job!**
昇進おめでとう！	**Congratulations on your promotion!**
結婚おめでとう！	**Congratulations on your marriage!**
出産おめでとう！	**Congratulations on your new baby!** ＊new babyは、性別に合わせてbaby boy(男の子)やbaby girl(女の子)としてもよい
本当におめでたい。	**I'm really happy for them.**
2人の門出を心から祝いたい。	**I really wish them happiness in their new life.**
私たちの結婚記念日に乾杯！	**Here's a toast to our wedding anniversary!** ＊toast＝祝杯、乾杯

励ます

大丈夫、大丈夫。	**It's all right.**
今まで通りやれば大丈夫。	**It'll be okay if I keep doing what I'm doing.**
落ち着け、自分。	**Calm down, Mayumi.** ＊Mayumiのように、自分の名前を入れる
私なら絶対やれる。	**I'm sure I can do it.**
自分を信じて頑張ろう。	**I'll believe in myself and give it my best shot.**
絶対うまくいくはず！	**I'm sure it'll go well!**
ダメでもともと。	**I have nothing to lose.** ＊lose＝～を失う
マサヤ、頑張れ！	**Hang in there, Masaya!** ＊hang in there＝踏ん張る
彼らには頑張ってほしい。	**I want them to do their best.**
彼女を陰ながら応援している。	**I'm supporting her behind the scenes.** ＊behind the scenes＝陰で
努力はいつか報われるはず。	**My efforts will pay off eventually.** ＊effort＝努力　pay off＝報われる
彼の言葉に励まされた。	**His words cheered me up.** ＊cheer ～ up＝～を励ます

慰める

気にしない、気にしない。	**Don't worry about it.**
あまり気にしないようにしようっと。	**I'll try not to let it bother me.**
誰にだってあることだ。	**It happens to anyone.**
誰だってミスをする。	**Everybody makes mistakes.**
完璧な人なんていない。	**Nobody's perfect.**
私だけが悪いわけじゃない。	**I'm not the only one at fault.** ＊fault[フォールト]＝責任、落ち度
ただついていなかっただけ。	**It just wasn't my day.**

今度から気を付ければいいさ。 **Just be careful next time.**

次はきっとうまくいくよ。 **Better luck next time.**

疑う

本当かな？ **Is it really true?**

半信半疑だ。 **I'm doubtful.**
＊doubtful［ダウトフォゥ］＝確信がない

そんな話は信じない。 **I don't buy that story.**
＊buy＝～を受け入れる・信じる

そんなにうまい話があるかな。 **It's too good to be true.**

そう簡単には信じられない。 **I can't believe it just like that.**
＊just like that＝簡単に

疑いの気持ちが消えない。 **I still have my doubts.**
＊doubt［ダウｔ］＝疑い、疑念

だまされないぞ。 **I'm NOT going to be fooled.**
＊fool＝～をだます

それは疑いようがない。 **No doubt about it.**

うそじゃないかと疑っている。 **I wonder if it's a lie.**

彼女はうそを言っている気がする。 **I have a feeling she's lying.**

うらやむ・ねたむ

サナはいいなぁ！ **Sana is so lucky!**

彼がうらやましい。 **I'm jealous of him.**

彼女みたいになりたい。 **I want to be like her.**

ユミに彼氏ができて、うらやましい。 **Yumi got a boyfriend. I'm jealous.**

彼の会社はボーナスが出た。いいな！ **His company gives bonuses. Lucky him!**

彼をねたんでしまう。 **I can't help being jealous of him.**
＊can't help ～ing＝～せずにいられない

ずるいよ。 **It's not fair.**
＊fair＝公平な

彼女は人をうらやんでばかりいる。 **She's always so envious of others.**
＊envious［エンヴィアｽ］＝ねたみ深い

自分を人と比べるのはやめよう。	I should stop comparing myself to others.

賛成する

私は賛成だな。	I agree.
彼の意見に賛成。	I agree with him.
それには賛成。	I'm for it.
おおむね賛成だな。	I basically agree.
全面的に賛成だな。	I completely agree.
まったく異論はない。	I have no objections whatsoever. ＊objection＝反対　no 〜 whatsoever＝少しの〜もない
反対する理由はないよ。	I don't have any reason to disagree.
いい考えだと思う。	I think it's a good idea.

反対する

私は反対だな。	I have to disagree.
それには反対。	I'm against it.
妻の意見に反対だ。	I don't agree with my wife.
賛成できない。	I can't agree.
そのやり方には賛成できない。	I can't agree with that approach. ＊approach＝方法、やり方
もう一度考え直したほうがいい。	I think it needs to be reconsidered. ＊reconsider＝〜を考え直す・再検討する
認めるわけにはいかない。	I can't allow this. ＊allow＝〜を許す・認める
反対の意志を伝えた。	I came out against it.

どちらでもない

私はどちらでもいい。	I'm okay either way. ＊either way＝どちらの方法でも
私は中立の立場だ。	I'm neutral.

どちらとも言えないな。 **I can't really say.**
＊I can't say.は、「私にはわからない」というニュアンス

どちらでも変わらない気がする。 **I don't think they're any different.**

どちらに転んでも、うまくいくさ。 **It'll be all right either way.**

考えがまとまらない。 **I can't make up my mind.**
＊make up one's mind＝決心する

どうすべきか決めかねている。 **I haven't decided what to do.**

私って優柔不断だな。 **I'm such an indecisive person.**

もう少し考えてみたい。 **I need a little more time to think.**

みんなの意見に従おう。 **Let's go with the general opinion.**
＊general＝一般的な、全員の

あきらめる

まっ、仕方ないか。 **Well, it can't be helped.**

もうあきらめよう。 **OK, it's time to give this up.**

あきらめたほうがいいよね。 **I think I should just stop.**

あきらめも肝心だ。 **Sometimes giving up is the best choice.**

すっぱりあきらめることにした。 **I decided to give it up.**

無理なものは無理なんだ。 **Some things can't be changed.**

別のやり方を探すほうがよさそうだ。 **I'd better find another way.**

気持ちを切り替えよう。 **I'll put this behind me.**
＊put ～ behind＝～を忘れる

前に進まなきゃ！ **I should move on!**

どうしてもあきらめられない。 **I just can't forget about it.**

我慢する

あと少し我慢しよう。 **I'll be patient just a little longer.**
＊patient＝我慢強い

彼にはあと少し我慢してもらおう。	**I'll ask him to be patient just a little longer.**
もっと我慢強くならなきゃ。	**I have to be more patient.**
そろそろ我慢の限界だ。	**I'm running out of patience.** ＊run out of ～＝～を使い果たす　patience＝我慢
もう我慢できない。	**I can't take it anymore.** ＊take it＝我慢する
それ以上我慢できなかった。	**I couldn't bear it anymore.** ＊bear＝～に耐える
彼にはもう我慢できない。	**I can't put up with him anymore.** ＊put up with ～＝～を我慢する
私にだって我慢の限界がある！	**There's a limit to my patience!**
どうして私ばかり我慢しなきゃならないの？	**Why do I always have to take this?**
まだまだ我慢が足りないのかな？	**Maybe I have to learn to be more patient.**
彼女は本当に我慢強い。	**She's really patient.**

気持ちを表すショートフレーズ

すごい！	**Great!** **Awesome!**　＊awesome［オーサム］
わぁ、すごい！	**Wow!**
最高！	**Terrific!**
かっこいい！	**Cool!**
その調子！	**Way to go!**
いいぞ！	**Right on!**
よっしゃー！	**YES!!!**
よくやった！	**Good for her!** ＊使う相手に合わせて、herをhim/them/usなどに
まったくもう！	**Come on!** **Shoot!**

くそっ！／ちぇっ！ Darn it!
Damn it!
＊itはどちらも省略可。Damn it![デァーミット]は、下品な表現

あり得ない！ No way!
That's impossible!

マジで？ Seriously?

最悪！ This sucks!
This is terrible!
＊suck[サック]=(物事が)ひどい、最低だ

まいったなぁ！ Oh no!

ウゲッ！ Yuck!
Gross! ＊yuck[ヤック] gross[グロウス]

超気持ち悪い！ Disgusting! ＊disgusting[ディスガスティング]

あっちへ行け！ Go away!

わぁ～ん。／（泣） Boo-hoo.
＊boo-hoo[ブーフー]は、大声で泣く様子

やれやれ。 Oh my.
Oh dear.

ま、仕方ないか。 Oh well.

あっ、しまった。 Uh-oh. ＊uh-oh[アッオー]

おっと。 Oops. ＊oops[ウーップス]

いてっ！ Ouch!
Ow! ＊ouch[アウチ] ow[アウ]

ふぅ～。／ホッ。 Phew.
Whew. ＊phew[フュー] whew[フュー]

はぁ…。 Sigh ... ＊sigh[サイ]=ため息

あ～あ。 Ah ... ＊ah[アー]

やっぱりね。 I knew it.
No wonder.
＊No wonder.は、「不思議ではない」というニュアンス

5 気持ち・感想

気持ち・感想について
英語日記を書いてみよう

さまざまな気持ちや感想を、英語で書いてみましょう。

合格してうれしい！

I passed Grade 2 of the STEP test at last! I did it! I'm so happy I passed it before graduating from high school.

ようやく英検２級に合格した！　やったぁ！　高校卒業前に合格できて、すごくうれしい。

STEP は Society for Testing English Proficiency の略で、「日本英語検定協会」のこと。単に Eiken としても OK です。I did it!（やったぁ！）は、I made it! や Yes! と表すこともできます。「すごくうれしい」は really〈extremely〉happy などと表現してもいいですね。

あの2人が別れたなんて

I was shocked to hear Nanako and Atsushi broke up. They were so lovey-dovey with each other. I wonder what happened to them. I just can't believe it.

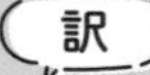

ナナコとアツシが別れたと聞いて、かなり驚いた。あんなにラブラブだったのに、何があったんだろう。ホント信じられない。

shocked は「かなり驚いて、衝撃を受けて」という意味。「（恋人や夫婦が）別れる、離婚する」は、break up を使います。「AとBが別れた」は、A and B broke up、または A broke up with B と表します。lovey-dovey は「ラブラブの、アツアツの」という意味。

うっかりしてた

When I got home and unlocked the front door, I carelessly left the key in the lock. A passer-by kindly rang the doorbell and let me know. Whew.

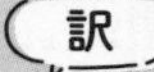

帰宅して玄関のカギを開けたのはいいけど、うっかりカギをドアに差し込んだままにしてしまった。親切にも、通りすがりの人がベルを鳴らして教えてくれた。やれやれ。

「うっかり」は carelessly（不注意にも）と表します。「カギをドアに差し込んだままにしてしまった」は left the key in the lock。この left は leave（～を置き忘れる）の過去形です。Whew（Phew ともつづる）は、「やれやれ、ほっ」と安心した気持ちを表します。

どうして私だけ？

Mari and I whispered during class, and the teacher told me off. Why only me? It's not fair! Just remembering it made me angry again.

マリと授業中ひそひそおしゃべりしていたら、私が先生に叱られた。どうして私だけ叱られるわけ？　ずるいよ！　思い出したら、また腹が立ってきた。

tell off で「～を叱りつける」という意味。I was told off by the teacher と受け身で表しても OK です。fair は「公平な」。not fair で「公平でない＝ずるい」となります。made me angry は「私を怒らせた」で、make ～ ... で「～を…にさせる」という意味です。

06

感覚

味覚

おいしい

おいしかった。	**It was good.** ＊goodは、tastyとしてもOK
とてもおいしかった。	**It was really good.** **It was delicious.**
ほっぺたが落ちそうだった。	**It was absolutely scrumptious.** ＊scrumptiousは、deliciousと同じ意味のカジュアルな語
風味が豊かだった。	**It had a rich flavor.** ＊rich＝豊かな、芳醇（ほうじゅん）な
後味がよかった。	**It left a pleasant aftertaste.**
口の中に神戸牛の味わいが広がった。	**The taste of Kobe beef spread through my mouth.** ＊spread＝広がる。過去形もspread
今まで食べた中で一番おいしかった。	**It was the most delicious thing I had ever had.**
間違いなく、あそこのラーメンが一番おいしい！	**Without a doubt, they have the best ramen!** ＊without doubt［ダウㇳ］とも言う
そこの料理は、言葉で表せないくらいおいしい。	**Their food is delicious beyond words.** ＊beyond words＝言葉で表現できない
やっぱりカレーは２日目がおいしい。	**Curry tastes even better on the second day.**
風呂上がりの冷たいビールは最高！	**A cold beer after a bath is great!**
お母さんの手料理に勝るものはない。	**There's nothing like my mom's home cooking.**

おなかがすいてるときは、何を食べてもおいしい。　**Everything tastes good when you're hungry.** ＊このyouは、「一般的な人々」を指す
Hunger is the best sauce. ＊直訳は「空腹は一番のソース」

おいし過ぎて、やめられない。　**It tastes so good that I just can't stop eating.**

まずい

おいしくなかった。　**It wasn't good.** ＊goodは、tastyとしてもOK

あまりおいしくなかった。　**It wasn't very good.**

まずかった。　**It was terrible.**
It tasted awful. ＊awful［オーフォ］

とてもまずかった。　**It was really awful.**
It was horrible.

口に合わなかった。　**I didn't like the taste.**

我慢して全部食べた。　**I put up with it and ate it all up.** ＊put up with ～＝～に耐える

傷んだような味がした。　**It tasted a little rotten.** ＊rotten［ラットゥン］＝腐った

食べられたものじゃなかった。　**It just wasn't edible.** ＊edible［エディボォ］＝食べられる

おいしそうには見えなかった。　**It didn't look appetizing.** ＊appetizing＝食欲をそそる、おいしそうな

オエッて感じだった。　**It was yucky.** ＊yucky［ヤッキー］＝気持ち悪い、すごくまずい

普通の味

味はまあまあだった。　**It was okay.**

おいしくもなく、まずくもなかった。　**It wasn't good or bad.**

普通の味だった。　**It was nothing out of the ordinary.** ＊out of ～＝～の範囲を超えて　ordinary＝普通の、平凡な

普通の味が一番だ。　**Normal taste is best.**

甘い

甘かった。　**It was sweet.**

甘過ぎた。	**It was too sweet.**
甘辛かった。	**It was sweet and salty.**
甘酸っぱかった。	**It was sweet and sour.**
ほどよい甘さだった。	**It was moderately sweet.**
甘くておいしかった。	**It was sweet and tasty.**
自然な甘さだった。	**It had a natural sweetness.**

しょっぱい

しょっぱかった。	**It was salty.**
しょっぱ過ぎた。	**It was too salty.**
ほどよい塩加減だった。	**It was nicely salty.**
もう少し塩味が利いているほうが好きだな。	**I prefer a little more salt in it.**

辛い

辛かった。	**It was spicy.** ＊spicyは、hotとしてもOK
ピリ辛だった。	**It was a little spicy.**
辛過ぎた。	**It was too spicy.**
カレーは「中辛」が好きだ。	**I like moderately hot curry.**
「大辛」のカレーを注文した。	**I ordered super hot curry.**
あまりの辛さに汗が出た。	**It was so spicy that I sweated.**
辛くて舌がひりひりした。	**It was so spicy that my tongue was burning.** ＊tongue[タング]＝舌

そのほかの味

酸っぱかった。	**It was sour.**
苦かった。	**It was bitter.**

渋かった。	It was bitter.
脂っこかった。	It was oily.
こってりしていた。	It was thick. It tasted rich. ＊thick＝濃厚な
あっさりしていた。	It was light. It had a light taste.
本格的な味だった。	It had an authentic flavor. ＊authentic［オーセンティック］＝本物の
独特の風味だった。	It had a unique flavor.
珍しい味だった。	It tasted different.
変な味だった。	It had a funny taste.
まろやかな味だった。	It had a mild taste.
素朴な味でおいしかった。	It tasted nice and simple.
舌がピリピリした。	My tongue was tingling. ＊tingle＝ひりひりする
薄味だった（おいしかった）。	It was mild.
薄味だった（おいしくなかった）。	It was tasteless. It was bland. ＊blandは、病院食などの味が薄い食べ物について言う
味が濃かった。	It had a strong taste.
薄いコーヒーだった。	It was mild coffee. ＊mildは、weakとしてもOK
濃いコーヒーだった。	It was strong coffee.
コクのあるコーヒーだった。	It was rich coffee.
酸味の利いたコーヒーだった。	The coffee was acidic. ＊acidic＝酸味のある
コクのあるワインだった。	It was a full-bodied wine.
フルーティーなワインだった。	It was a fruity wine. ＊fruity＝（ワインなどが）果物の風味がある
渋味のあるワインだった。	The wine was astringent. ＊astringent＝酸味の強い

6 感覚

すっきりした味わいのビールだった。 It was a refreshing beer.

辛口のビールだった。 It was a dry beer.

芳醇(ほうじゅん)な味わいだった。 It was a mellow flavor.
＊mellow＝芳醇な、熟成した

濃厚なチーズケーキだった。 The cheesecake was rich.

ヨーグルトのような味だった。 It tasted like yogurt.

想像した通りの味だった。 It tasted exactly as I had expected.

味付け

彼の料理は、いつも薄味だ。 His food is always mild.
＊「味が濃い」なら、mildをtoo strongに

味付けが濃過ぎると娘に言われた。 My daughter said I flavor my food too strongly.
＊flavor＝〜に味を付ける

彼女の味付けは、私の好みにピッタリ。 She flavors her food exactly the way I like it.

年のせいか、最近は薄味が好きになってきた。 Maybe because I'm getting older, I prefer a lighter taste now.

何かひと味足りない気がした。 It tasted like there was something missing.

全然味がしなかった。 It was flavorless.

何のだしを使っていたんだろう？ I wonder what kind of stock they used.
＊stock＝だし

煮物は、よく味がしみていた。 The nimono had a rich flavor.

隠し味の砂糖が利いていた。 I noticed the subtle taste of sugar.
＊subtle［サトォ］＝かすかな

家庭的な味だった。 It tasted like home cooking.

歯ごたえ・食感

サクサクしておいしかった。 It was nice and crisp.

しっとりしておいしかった。 It was nice and moist.

フワフワだった。 **It was fluffy.**
＊fluffy［フラッフィー］＝フワフワの

パサパサしていた。 **It was dry.**

もちもちしていておいしかった。 **It was nice and soft.**

とろみがあっておいしかった。 **It was thick and tasty.**

スープが水っぽかった。 **The soup was watery.**

うどんは、コシがあっておいしかった。 **The udon was nice, with a chewy texture.**
＊chewy［チューウィ］＝コシのある texture＝歯ごたえ

外はサクサクで中はジューシーだった。 **It was crisp outside and juicy inside.**

とろけるように柔らかい牛肉だった。 **The beef was meltingly tender.**
＊meltingly＝とろけるように

ゴムみたいな歯ごたえの肉だった。 **The meat was chewy like rubber.**

タコはコリコリしていた。 **The octopus was chewy and crunchy.**

ほくほくしておいしい焼き芋だった。 **It was a nice, steaming baked sweet potato.**

サラダはシャキシャキだった。 **The salad was crisp.**
＊crisp＝（野菜などが）新鮮な、パリッとした

嗅覚

いい香り

いいにおいがした。 **It smelled nice.**

おいしそうなにおいがした。 **It smelled appetizing.**
＊appetizing＝食欲をそそる、おいしそうな

香ばしい香りがした。 **It had a savory smell.**
＊savory［セイヴァリィ］＝香りのよい

入れたてのコーヒーの香りがした。 **There was an aroma of fresh coffee.**

台所から、ケーキの焼けるにおいがした。 **I could smell a cake baking in the kitchen.**

紅茶はかすかにリンゴの香りがした。	**The tea had an apple scent.** ＊scent［セント］＝ほのかな快い香り
あの香水のにおい、好きだな。	**I like the smell of that perfume.**
彼の香水が甘く香った。	**I caught a whiff of sweet cologne from him.** ＊whiff［ウィッ］＝一瞬のにおい　「香水」は男性の場合はcologne、女性の場合はperfumeを用いることが多い
キヨハラさんは、いい香りがした。	**Kiyohara-san smelled nice.**
香水は何をつけてるんだろう？	**I wonder what perfume she wears.**
今日は何のアロマをたこうかな？	**What aroma should I burn today?**
ティートゥリーにしようっと。	**I'll use tea tree.**
かんきつ系の香りがした。	**It smelled of citrus.** ＊citrus［スィトラス］＝かんきつ類
ラベンダーの香りは落ち着く。	**The smell of lavender makes me relax.**
グレープフルーツの爽やかな香りがした。	**There was a refreshing fragrance of grapefruit.**
新しいシャンプーは、いい香り。	**My new shampoo smells nice.**
甘い香りのするせっけんだった。	**The soap smelled sweet.**

いやなにおい

臭かった。	**It was smelly.** **It stank.** ＊stink＝悪臭を出す。過去形はstankまたはstunk
ひどいにおいがした。	**There was an awful smell.** ＊awful［オーフォ］＝ひどい
変なにおいがした。	**There was a weird smell.** ＊weird［ウィアード］＝変な、奇妙な
鼻にツンときた。	**There was a pungent smell.** ＊pungent＝（においや味が鼻や舌を）強く刺激する
ガス臭かった。	**It smelled like gas.**
カビ臭いにおいがした。	**There was a moldy smell.** ＊moldy＝カビ臭い
焦げ臭かった。	**I smelled something burning.**

たばこ臭かった。 It smelled like cigarettes.

服がたばこ臭くなった。 My clothes smelled of cigarette smoke.

焼肉のにおいが取れないな。 I can't get rid of the yakiniku smell.
＊get rid of ～＝～を取り除く

なんだか生臭かった。 Something smelled fishy.
＊fishy＝生臭い

脇のにおいが気になる。 I'm worried that my armpits are smelly.
＊armpit＝脇の下

シャツが汗臭かった。 The shirt smelled of sweat.

彼、ニンニク臭かった！ He had garlic breath!

お父さんの足が臭かった。 My dad's feet smelled bad.

娘に臭いって言われちゃった。 My daughter said I smell.

もしかして加齢臭？ Could it be old person smell?

隣のおじさんの口臭がキツかった。 The man next to me had really bad breath.

隣の人の香水がキツかった。 The person next to me had really strong perfume.

柔軟剤の香りが強過ぎる。 The scent of the softener is too strong.

思わず鼻をつまんでしまった。 I couldn't help holding my nose.
＊hold＝～をつかむ

鼻が曲がりそうだった。 It smelled awful.
＊awful＝不快な

ソファに消臭剤をスプレーした。 I sprayed deodorizer on the sofa.
＊deodorizer＝消臭剤

聴覚

静かだった。 It was quiet.

うるさかった。 It was noisy.

よく聞こえなかった。	**I couldn't hear very well.**
ドン、という音がした。	**I heard a boom.** ＊boom＝ドーン、ゴロゴロなどの大きな音
嫌な音だった。	**It was an unpleasant sound.** ＊unpleasantは、annoying［アノィイング］としてもOK
サイレンが聞こえた。	**I heard sirens.**
耳をつんざくような雷鳴がした。	**There was deafening thunder.** ＊deafening［デフェニング］＝耳をつんざくような
どこかから赤ちゃんの泣き声が聞こえた。	**I heard the sound of a baby crying somewhere.**
騒がしいレストランは好きじゃない。	**I don't like noisy restaurants.**
物音一つしなかった。	**There wasn't a single sound.**
会場はシーンとしていた。	**There was silence in the hall.** ＊hallは「会場（建物）」のこと
会場はザワザワしていた。	**I could hear murmuring in the hall.** ＊murmur［マァマァ］＝ざわめく
風の音が聞こえた。	**I could hear the wind blowing.**
外から虫の声がした。	**I could hear the insects outside.**
耳に心地よい音楽だった。	**The music was really pleasant.**
彼女の歌声を聞くと落ち着く。	**Her singing helps me relax.**
流れる川の音が心地よかった。	**The sound of the river was relaxing.**
彼女、地獄耳だな。	**She has sharp ears.** ＊have sharp ears＝地獄耳である
耳が遠くなったなぁ。	**I don't hear as well as I used to.**
耳鳴りがした。	**My ears were ringing.**
お父さんに補聴器を買ってあげようかな。	**Maybe I should buy my dad a hearing aid.** ＊hearing aid＝補聴器
扉がカチッと開いた。	**The door clicked open.** ＊click＝カチッと音がする
ドアがガチャンと閉まった。	**The door clanged shut.** ＊clang＝ガチャンと音を立てる
彼はピシャッとドアを閉めた。	**He slammed the door.** ＊slam＝～をピシャリと閉める

ドアを開けるとキーキーいう。	**The door makes a squeaking sound when I open it.**
誰かがボールペンをカチカチさせていた。	**Somebody clicked a ballpoint pen continuously.** ＊click＝〜をカチッといわせる
時計のチクタクいう音で集中できなかった。	**I couldn't concentrate because of the tick-tock of the clock.** ＊concentrate＝注意を集中する
周りがうるさくて勉強に集中できなかった。	**I couldn't concentrate on my studies because the surroundings were so noisy.**
ヘッドホンから音漏れしている男性がいた。	**There was a guy with loud music coming from his headphones.**
ダイスケは指をポキポキ鳴らす癖がある。	**Daisuke has a habit of cracking his knuckles.** ＊crack＝〜を鳴らす　knuckle＝指の関節
子どもたちがザブーンとプールに飛び込んだ。	**The kids made big splashes as they dived into the pool.**
ドスドス歩く足音が聞こえた。	**I could hear pounding footsteps.** ＊pounding＝ドンドン打つような

視覚

はっきり見えた。	**I could see it clearly.**
あまりよく見えなかった。	**I couldn't see it clearly.**
何も見えなかった。	**I couldn't see anything.**
よく目をこらして見た。	**I strained my eyes to see it.**
富士山がきれいに見えた。	**I was able to see Mt. Fuji clearly.**
彼のことをちらっと見た。	**I took a glance at him.** ＊glance＝ちらりと見ること
涙で彼の顔がにじんで見えた。	**His face looked blurry through my tears.** ＊blurry［ブラーリー］＝にじんだ
目を閉じた。	**I closed my eyes.**

目をそらした。	**I looked away from it.**
見ないようにした。	**I tried not to see it.**
じろじろ見られて不快だった。	**I was uncomfortable being stared at.** ＊stare at ～＝～をじっと見る
背中に視線を感じて振り向いたら、リサがいた！	**I felt someone's eyes on my back and turned around, and there was Lisa!** ＊turn around＝振り返る
外はまぶしかった。	**It was bright outside.**
スマホの使い過ぎで目が疲れた。	**My eyes are tired from using my smartphone too much.**
目がしばしばする。	**I'm bleary-eyed.** ＊bleary＝（目が）かすんだ

触覚

コーヒーは熱かった。	**The coffee was hot.**
スープは温かかった。	**The soup was warm.**
お風呂のお湯がぬるかった。	**The bath water was lukewarm.** ＊lukewarm［ルークウォーム］＝ぬるい
ちょうどいい湯加減だった。	**The water was at the right temperature.**
海の水は冷たかった。	**The sea water was cold.**
痛かった。	**It hurt.**
赤ちゃんの肌みたいに柔らかかった。	**It was as soft as a baby's skin.**
手がガサガサになっちゃった。	**My hands got really dry and rough.**
布団がフカフカになった。	**The futon got fluffy.**
ウサギの毛はフワフワだった。	**The rabbit's fur was fluffy.**
その耳当てはあったかくてモフモフしていた。	**The earmuffs were warm and fluffy.**

その布はざらざらした感触だった。	**The material felt rough.**
シルクのような手触りだった。	**It felt like silk.**
新しく買ったマフラー、チクチクする。	**My new scarf is prickly.** ＊prickly＝チクチクする
セーターを洗濯したら、ごわごわになってしまった。	**The sweater got stiff when I washed it.** ＊stiff＝硬い
陶器はつるつるの手触りだった。	**The china was glossy and smooth.** ＊china＝磁器、陶器　glossy＝光沢のある
風呂場の床がぬるぬるした。	**The bathroom floor was slippery.**
テーブルがベタベタしていた。	**The table was sticky.**

感覚について 英語日記を書いてみよう

さまざまな感覚について、英語で書いてみましょう。

 新鮮なノドグロ

Tecchan and I went to Hokuriku to enjoy fresh fish. All the fish were sooooo good, but we loved the rich and tender nodoguro best.

てっちゃんと新鮮な魚を味わいに北陸へ行った。どれもすご～くおいしかったけど、中でも特に脂ののったノドグロは最高だった。

「すご～くおいしい」は sooooo good で表しました。「脂ののった」は rich ですが、これだけだと「くどい、しつこい」という意味にもなるので、and tender（そして柔らかい）を加えました。これで「脂がのって美味な」というニュアンスが出ます。

 アロマセラピーでリラックス

I started to use an aroma lamp and some essential oils about a week ago. Since then, I've been able to relax and sleep better. I'll use lavender tonight.

1週間ほど前から、アロマライトと精油を使い始めた。それ以来、とてもリラックスできるし、よく眠れる。今夜はラベンダーにしようっと。

aroma lamp は「（コンセントタイプの）アロマライト」。キャンドルをたくタイプなら、aroma oil burner。sleep well は「よく眠れる」、sleep better は「今までよりさらによく眠れる」というニュアンスです。

サイレンが鳴り響く

Several police cars and ambulances hurried away with their sirens screaming. I wonder if there has been a big accident.

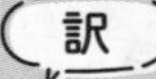

何台ものパトカーと救急車が、サイレンを響かせながら、ものすごい勢いで過ぎていった。大事故でも起きたのかな。

1文目は、意味の固まりで分けるとわかりやすいです。several police cars and ambulances（何台ものパトカーと救急車が）、hurried away（急いで過ぎていった）、with their sirens screaming（サイレンを鳴り響かせて）となります。自問自答の「～かな」はI wonder ～で。

眼鏡の度が合っていないかも

I can't see very well these days. Maybe my glasses aren't right for me. I guess I should see an eye doctor one of these days.

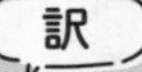

最近、ものがよく見えない。眼鏡の度が合っていないのかも？ 近いうちに、眼科に行ったほうがよさそうだ。

「最近」はthese days。過去形や完了形の文なら、recentlyで表します。「眼鏡の度が合っていない」は、my glasses aren't right for meでOK。I guess I should ～（動詞の原形）は「～したほうがよさそうだ」、one of these daysは「近いうちに」。

07
一日の生活

朝

起床

7時半に起きた。	**I woke up at 7:30.** **I got up at 7:30.** ＊woke upは「目が覚めた」、got upは「布団から出て起き上がった」ことを表す
今朝は早起きした。	**I woke up early this morning.**
いつもより早く起きた。	**I got up earlier than usual.**
早起きすると気分がいい。	**It feels good to wake up early.**
「早起きは三文の得」だ。	**The early bird catches the worm.** ＊catchesは、getsにしてもOK
爽やかな朝だった。	**It was a refreshing morning.**
今朝は目覚めが悪かった。	**I got up on the wrong side of the bed this morning.** ＊got upは、woke upでもOK。wrongをrightにすると「目覚めがよかった」の意になる
よく眠れた。	**I had a good night's sleep.** **I slept well.**
今日も頑張るぞ！	**I'm going to work as hard as always!** ＊work hard＝しっかり働く、しっかり勉強する
今日は何だかいいことありそう。	**I have a feeling something nice will happen today.**
母に起こされた。	**My mom woke me up.** ＊wake ～ up＝～の目を覚まさせる、～を起こす
珍しく自然に目が覚めた。	**Unusually for me, I woke up by myself.**

朝日がまぶしくて目が覚めた。 The bright morning sun woke me up.

工事の音で目が覚めた。 The construction noise woke me up.

鳥の声で目覚めて、最高の朝だった。 It was a wonderful morning because I woke up to the sound of birds.
＊wake up to ～＝～で目を覚ます

寒くて布団から出られなかった。 It was so cold that I had trouble getting out of bed.

寝過ぎなのかも？ Maybe I sleep too much?

コーヒーで目を覚ました。 I had coffee to wake me up.

シャワーを浴びて目を覚ました。 I took a shower to wake me up.

朝寝坊

今朝は寝坊しちゃった。 I overslept this morning.
＊oversleep＝寝坊する。過去形はoverslept

30分寝坊しちゃった。 I overslept half an hour.

今朝はいつもより遅くまで寝ていた。 I slept in this morning.
＊sleep in＝遅くまで寝ている

本当は6時に起きる予定だった。 I was supposed to wake up at 6:00.

起きたら7時だったので、焦った。 I woke up at 7:00, so I was in a rush.

慌てて目覚まし時計を確認した。 I hurriedly checked my alarm.
＊alarmは、alarm clockとしてもOK

アラームが鳴らなかったみたい。 It seems my alarm didn't go off.
＊go off＝（目覚まし時計や警報器などが）鳴る

アラームを止めちゃってたみたい。 It looks like I stopped my alarm.

スヌーズを何度も繰り返した。 I pressed snooze over and over.

眠くて仕方なかった。 I was really sleepy.

午前中はずっと眠かった。 I was sleepy all morning.

あとちょっとだけ寝たかった。 I wanted to sleep a little more.

「あと５分だけ」と二度寝した。	**I told myself, "Just five more minutes," and went back to sleep.**
起きたら２時間たっていた。	**I woke up two hours later.**

朝食

軽く朝食を取った。	**I had a light breakfast.**
朝食をガッツリ食べた。	**I had a big breakfast.**
朝食をかき込んだ。	**I bolted down my breakfast.** ＊bolt down ～＝～をかまずに飲み込む・大急ぎで食べる
急いで朝食を取った。	**I ate breakfast in a hurry.** ＊in a hurry＝急いで
ゆっくり朝食を取った。	**I took my time eating breakfast.** ＊take one's time ～ing＝ゆっくり～する
遅い朝食を食べた。	**I had a late breakfast.** **I had brunch.**
朝食を抜いた。	**I skipped breakfast.** ＊skip＝～を抜かす
朝食はご飯とみそ汁、目玉焼き。	**I had rice, miso soup and eggs sunny side up for breakfast.** ＊eggs sunny side upは「片面焼きの目玉焼き」
朝は玄米を食べる。	**I eat brown rice in the morning.**
トーストにジャムを塗って食べた。	**I ate some toast with jam.** ＊jam＝ジャム
最近の朝食は、栄養価の高いオートミール。	**My breakfast these days is highly nutritious oatmeal.**
朝食は前の晩の残り物。	**I had last night's leftovers for breakfast.** ＊leftover＝残り物
朝ご飯にはコーヒーだけ飲んだ。	**I only had coffee for breakfast.**
朝食抜きは体によくないとわかってるけど…。	**I know it's not healthy to skip breakfast, but ...**
朝は食欲がないんだよな。	**I'm not hungry in the morning.**
朝食を取りながらニュースをチェックした。	**I checked the news while I had breakfast.**

身だしなみ

顔を洗った。	**I washed my face.**
歯を磨いた。	**I brushed my teeth.**
朝、シャワーを浴びた。	**I took a shower in the morning.**
朝風呂に入った。	**I took a bath in the morning.**
着替えた。	**I changed my clothes.**
ネクタイを締めた。	**I wore a tie.**
髪型がイマイチ決まらなかった。	**I couldn't set my hair right.**
寝癖がひどかった。	**I had bad bed hair.** ＊bed hair＝寝癖
髪をとかした。	**I combed my hair.** ＊comb[コーム]=(髪を)くしでとかす
コテを使って髪を巻いた。	**I used a curling iron to curl my hair.**
化粧をした。	**I put on makeup.**
５分で化粧を済ませた。	**I finished putting on makeup within five minutes.**
化粧をする時間がなかった。	**I didn't have time to put on makeup.**
化粧のりが悪かった。	**I couldn't get my makeup right.**
マスカラを塗るのを忘れた。	**I forgot to put on mascara.**
ひげをそった。	**I shaved my face.** ＊my faceは、省略してもOK

出かける準備・持ち物

遅刻しそうだった。	**I was almost late.** ＊almost＝もう少しで
朝はいつも慌ただしい。	**I'm always in a hurry in the morning.**

5分早く家を出るようにしよう。	**I should leave home five minutes early.**
テレビのニュース番組を見た。	**I watched the news on TV.**
スマホでニュースをチェックした。	**I checked the news on my phone.**
お父さんがトイレを占領していて困った。	**I had to wait because my father was in the bathroom.**
念のため、傘を持って出た。	**I had my umbrella with me just in case.** ＊just in case＝念のため
お弁当を持って出た。	**I took my lunch with me.**
ハンカチを忘れた。	**I forgot my handkerchief.**
書類を忘れて、途中で家に取りに帰った。	**I forgot my documents, so I went back home to get them.**

通勤・通学

いつもより1本早い電車に乗った。	**I took one train earlier than the one I usually ride.**
7時ごろだと、電車がすいてるなぁ。	**The train isn't so crowded at around 7:00.**
電車に乗り遅れた。	**I missed the train.** ＊miss＝～に乗り遅れる
ギリギリセーフだった。	**I barely made it.** ＊barely＝何とか～する　make it＝間に合う
電車に乗り遅れそうだったけど、ギリギリ間に合った。	**I almost missed my train, but I made it just in time.** ＊just in time＝ギリギリで間に合って
混んでいたので、乗るまでに2本の電車を見送った。	**The trains were so full that I had to wait for two to pass before I could get on.** ＊pass＝通過する
電車の中でTOEICの勉強をした。	**I studied for the TOEIC exam on the train.**
電車の中で英語のニュースを聞いた。	**I listened to the news in English on the train.**

電車の中で英語のニュース記事を読んだ。	**I read news stories in English on the train.**
スマホで音楽を聞いた。	**I listened to music on my phone.**
スマホで英単語の音声を聞いた。	**I listened to English vocabulary audio on my phone.**
足を踏まれた。	**Someone stepped on my foot.**
電車の中に傘を忘れちゃった。	**I left my umbrella on the train.**
電車で寝過ごしちゃった。	**I fell asleep on the train and missed my stop.**
あそこの踏切は、いつも長い。	**That railroad crossing always takes a long time.**
「開かずの踏切」だ。	**The railroad crossing gate wouldn't open.**
通勤に 40 分かかった。	**It took 40 minutes to get to work.**
学校まで 15 分歩いた。	**I walked 15 minutes to school.**
遅刻しそうだったので、学校まで走っていった。	**I thought I was going to be late, so I ran to school.**
朝から走って疲れちゃった。	**I had to run this morning, so I was tired.**
また遅刻しちゃった。	**I was late again.**
バスはちょうど行ったところだった。	**The bus had just left.**
今日はバスがすいていたので、座れた。	**The bus wasn't so crowded, so I got a seat.**
バスが全然来なくて、焦った。	**I got really worried when the bus didn't come for a long time.**
バスの中で、オダさんに会った。	**I saw Oda-san on the bus.**
今朝は道が混んでいた。	**The road was crowded this morning.**

いつもと違う道で行った。	**I took a different route.**
抜け道を使った。	**I took a shortcut.** ＊shortcut＝近道
自転車通勤に変えようかな。	**Maybe I should go by bike instead.**
会社まで自転車で行った。	**I rode my bike to work.**
自転車通勤を始めてから、体調がよくなった。	**I've been in better shape since I started riding my bike to work.**
強風の中、自転車をこぐのはキツかった。	**It was really hard pedaling my bike in the strong wind.** ＊pedal＝～(自転車など)をこぐ
雨だったので、自転車でなくバスで行った。	**It was raining, so I took the bus instead of riding my bike.**
雨だったので、レインコートを着て自転車に乗った。	**It was raining, so I wore a raincoat while riding my bike.**

昼

家での昼食

お昼は、昨日の残り物で済ませた。	**For lunch, I had leftovers from yesterday.**
焼きそばを作って食べた。	**I had fried noodles that I made.**
冷蔵庫にある材料で、ささっと作った。	**I made something simple with things in my fridge.**
テレビで紹介していたスパゲティを作った。	**I made some spaghetti that I saw on a TV show.**
レトルトのカレーを食べた。	**I had instant curry.**
イトウベーカリーのパンを食べた。	**I had some bread from Ito Bakery.**
冷蔵庫に何もなかったので、弁当を買いに行った。	**There wasn't anything in my fridge, so I went and bought a bento lunch.**
お弁当を買ってきて、家で食べた。	**I bought a bento lunch and ate it at home.**

ピザの出前を取った。	**I had a pizza delivered.**
Uber Eatsでタイ料理を頼んだ。	**I ordered Thai food from Uber Eats.**

家事 （→ p. 210「家事」参照）

日常生活の買い物 （→ p. 314「食料品・日用品を買う」参照）

夜

帰宅

7時ごろ家に帰った。	**I got home at around 7:00.**
今日は早く帰れた。	**I was able to get home early today.**
家で帰りを待っていてくれる人がいるのって、いいなぁ。	**It's nice to have someone at home waiting for me.**
コウイチは5時ごろ帰ってきた。	**Kouichi got home at around 5:00.**
マサミの帰りがいつもより早かった。	**Masami got home earlier than usual.**
塾の日は息子の帰りが遅いので、心配になる。	**My son gets home late on cram school days, so I worry about him.**
最寄り駅まで娘を迎えに行った。	**I went to pick up my daughter at the nearest station.**
ジュンはずいぶん帰りが遅かった。	**Jun got home pretty late.**
10時半なんて、遅過ぎる。	**10:30 is too late.**
どこに行ってたんだろう？	**I wonder where he was.**
カラオケに行っていたらしい。	**He said he had been to karaoke.**
定時に退社した。	**I left the office on time.**
今日はまっすぐ帰った。	**I came straight home today.**
残業で帰りが遅くなった。	**I had to work overtime and got home late.**

7 一日の生活

もっと早く帰れると思ったのに。	**I thought I would be able to get home earlier.**
電車が止まっていて、帰りが遅くなった。	**The trains had stopped, so I got home late.**
午前様になってしまった。	**I came home after midnight.**
タクシーで帰宅した。	**I took a taxi home.**
夫の帰りが遅かったので、ちょっと心配した。	**My husband came home late, so I was a little worried.**
飲みに行っていたらしい。	**He said he had been to a drinking session.**
電話くらいしてくれればいいのに。	**I wish he had called.**
LINE くらいできると思う。	**He could have at least sent me a LINE message.**

料理する （→ p. 375「料理する」を参照）

夕飯

帰ってから夕飯を作った。	**I fixed dinner after I got home.** ＊fix＝～(食事など)を作る・準備する
スーパーでお総菜を買った。	**I bought some prepared food at the supermarket.**
夕飯は外で食べて帰った。	**I went home after eating dinner.**
帰ったら、カレーのにおいがした。	**When I got home, I smelled curry.** ＊smell＝～のにおいを感じる
夕飯はすき焼きだった。	**We had sukiyaki for dinner.**
1人で夕飯を食べた。	**I ate dinner alone.**
息子が帰るまで夕食を待った。	**I waited for my son to come home before we had dinner.**
家族そろって夕食を取った。	**All my family had dinner together.**
久しぶりにみんなで夕飯を食べた。	**We ate dinner together for the first time in a while.**

夕飯はみんなでファミレスに行った。	**We went to a family restaurant for dinner.**

お酒（→ p. 379「お酒」を参照）

お風呂

夫がお風呂を入れてくれた。	**My husband ran a bath for me.**
9時ごろ、お風呂に入った。	**I took a bath at around 9:00.**
私が一番に入った。	**I took a bath first.** ＊「最後に」なら、firstをlastに
リナと一緒にお風呂に入った。	**I took a bath with Rina.**
今日はさっとシャワーだけ浴びた。	**I took a quick shower today.**
1時間、半身浴をした。	**I took a half body bath for an hour.**
お風呂にスマホを持ち込んだ。	**I brought my phone to the bath with me.**
湯に漬かりながらマンガを読むのは至福のひとときだ。	**Reading manga in the bathtub is bliss.** ＊bliss＝至福
お風呂の中でうたた寝しちゃった。	**I nodded off in the bathtub.** ＊nod off＝ウトウトする
肩コリに効く入浴剤を入れてみた。	**I added some bath powder to help soothe my stiff neck.** ＊soothe［スーズ］＝～（痛みなど）を和らげる stiff＝こわばった
今日の入浴剤は、ヒノキの香りにした。	**Today, I chose the Japanese cypress-scented bath powder.** ＊～-scented＝～の香りのする
ちょうどいい湯加減だった。	**The bath was at the right temperature.**
お湯がちょっと熱過ぎた。	**The water was a little too hot.**
ああ、いい湯加減だった。	**Ah, the hot water felt great.**
ああ、すっきりした。	**Ah, I feel refreshed.**
長湯してのぼせちゃった。	**I stayed in the water too long and got dizzy.**

ドライヤーで髪を乾かした。	**I blow-dried my hair.**
風呂上がりにビールを飲んだ。	**I grabbed a beer after my bath.** ＊grab＝～(飲み物)をのどに流し込む
風呂上がりの冷えたビールは最高！	**There's nothing better than a cold beer right after a bath!**

だんらん

みんなで大河ドラマを見た。	**We watched the Taiga drama.**
お父さんはいつも、チャンネルをころころ変える。	**My father always flips through the channels.** ＊flip through ～＝～(チャンネルなど)を素早く変える
お気に入りのドラマの続きを見た。	**I watched the next episode of my favorite drama.**
YouTube をダラダラ見た。	**I chilled out watching YouTube.** ＊chill out＝くつろぐ、落ち着く
子どもたちは YouTube 動画を見るのが大好きだ。	**My kids love watching YouTube videos.**
子どもたちとおしゃべりした。	**My children and I had a chat.**
子どもたちとトランプをして遊んだ。	**I played cards with my kids.** ＊play cards＝トランプで遊ぶ
子どもたちの宿題を見てあげた。	**I helped the kids with their homework.**
1 時間ほどテレビゲームをした。	**I played video games for about an hour.**
ケンタがテレビゲームばかりしているので、叱った。	**Kenta was just playing video games, so I told him off.** ＊tell ～ off＝～を叱りつける。tellの過去形はtold
妻の肩をもんであげた。	**I gave my wife a neck massage.** ＊ここでのneckは「(首に近い部分の)肩」を指す
タカコが肩をもんでくれた。	**Takako massaged my neck.**
お父さんにマッサージしてあげた。	**I gave my father a massage.**
お母さんの白髪を抜いてあげた。	**I pulled out my mother's gray hairs for her.** ＊pull out ～＝～を抜く

寝る前に

全身にボディローションを塗った。	**I rubbed lotion on my whole body.** ＊rub＝〜を塗る・すり込む
明日の持ち物を準備した。	**I got my things ready for tomorrow.**
寝る前にちょっと晩酌。	**I had a nightcap.** ＊nightcap＝寝る前に飲む酒
布団を敷いた。	**I laid out my futon.** ＊lay out 〜＝〜を広げる。layの過去形はlaid
目覚ましを6時にセットした。	**I set my alarm clock for 6:00.**
今夜は何のアロマにしようかな。	**What scent should I use tonight?** ＊scent［セント］＝香り
快眠には、やっぱりラベンダーがいい。	**I think lavender is the best for a good night's sleep.**
娘を寝かしつけた。	**I put my daughter to bed.** ＊put 〜 to bed＝〜を寝かしつける
子どもたちにおやすみのキスをした。	**I kissed my kids good night.**

就寝・睡眠

もう11時だ。	**It's already 11:00.**
そろそろ寝よう。	**I should hit the sack soon.** ＊hit the sack＝寝る。go to bedと同じ意味
もう寝なきゃ。	**I need to go to sleep.**
眠くなってきた。	**I'm getting sleepy.**
あくびが止まらない。	**I can't stop yawning.** ＊yawn［ヤーン］＝あくびをする
もう2時なのに、全然眠くない。	**It's already 2:00, but I'm not sleepy at all.**
明日は休みだから、まあいいか。	**Well, it's OK. I have tomorrow off.**
明日は早く起きなきゃ。	**I have to wake up early tomorrow.**
硬めのマットレスに変えようかな。	**Maybe I should change to firm mattress.**
フカフカの布団は最高だ。	**There's nothing better than a fluffy futon.**

7 一日の生活

低反発枕、気持ちいい～！	**My posturepedic pillow is comfy!** ＊posturepedic［パスチャーピディック］＝低反発の
オーダーメイドで枕をあつらえた。	**I got myself a custom-made pillow.**
暑くて寝られなかった。	**I couldn't sleep because it was too hot.**
夜中に数回、目が覚めた。	**I woke up a couple of times in the middle of the night.**
夫が夜、うなされていた。	**My husband was groaning in his sleep last night.** ＊groan［グロウン］＝うなる、うめく
夫のいびきがひどかった。	**My husband's snoring was awful.** ＊snore［スノァ］＝いびきをかく
私、寝言を言っていたらしい。	**I was told that I was talking in my sleep.**
歯ぎしりをしていたと妻に言われた。	**My wife told me that I was grinding my teeth.** ＊grind［グラインド］＝～をきしらせる
ケンは寝相が悪い。	**Ken tosses and turns.** ＊toss＝激しく動く
夜中に蹴られて起きた。	**His kick woke me up in the middle of the night.**
寝汗をかいた。	**I sweated in my sleep.**
変な夢を見た。	**I had a strange dream.**
いつの間にか寝ていた。	**I fell asleep without knowing it.**
ゆうべはぐっすり寝た。	**I slept well last night.**
ゆうべはなかなか寝付けなかった。	**I had a hard time falling asleep last night.**
最近、寝付きが悪い。	**I have trouble falling asleep these days.**
7時間寝た。	**I slept for seven hours.**
4時間しか眠れなかった。	**I only slept for four hours.**
最低6時間は寝たい。	**I want to sleep at least six hours.**

一日を振り返って

今日も疲れた。	**I got tired again today.**
いい日だった。	**Today was a good day.** **I had a good day.**
忙しい日だった。	**Today was a busy day.** **I had a busy day.**
今日はバタバタだった。	**Today was hectic.** **I had a hectic day.** ＊hectic［ヘクティック］＝てんてこ舞いの
大変な日だった。	**Today was a rough day.** **I had a rough day.** ＊rough［ラフ］＝つらい、大変な
充実した日だった。	**I had a fulfilling day.** **I had a productive day.**
何もかもうまくいく日だった。	**I had a good hair day.** ＊「髪型が決まった日」という意味もある
今日のことは忘れないだろう。	**I'll never forget about today.**
思い通りにならない日だった。	**I had a bad hair day.** ＊「髪型が決まらなかった日」という意味もある
何をやってもうまくいかない日だった。	**Today was one of those days.** ＊one of those days＝何をやってもうまくいかない日
今日はあっという間だった。	**Today was over so fast.**
結局、一日だらだらしてしまった。	**I ended up doing nothing all day.**
今日も一日、無事に過ごせてよかった。	**I'm glad I made it through the day okay.** ＊make it through ～＝～をうまくやり遂げる
明日もいい日でありますように。	**I hope tomorrow is another good day.**

一日の生活について 英語日記を書いてみよう

日々の生活のあれこれについて、英語で書いてみましょう。

ゆっくり寝られた

I slept in this morning since it was my day off. I caught up on my sleep and felt so refreshed.

訳

仕事が休みだったので、今朝はいつもよりゆっくり寝られた。これで寝不足解消。気分もすっきりした。

ポイント

sleep in は「(休みの日などに)いつもより遅くまで寝ている」という意味で、I slept in till 10:00.(10 時まで寝ていた)のようにも使います。catch up on ～(～[仕事や睡眠など]の遅れ・不足を取り戻す)を用いると、「睡眠不足解消」のニュアンスが出ます。

朝寝坊

I overslept. I left home in a hurry and dashed to the station. I barely made it for my train. I was all sweaty and out of breath. I felt embarrassed.

訳

寝坊した。急いで家を出て駅まで猛ダッシュ。何とかいつもの電車に乗れたけど、汗だくで息切れ。恥ずかしかった。

ポイント

make it は「間に合う」の意。「恥ずかしい」は embarrassed(失態で決まりが悪く恥ずかしい)、ashamed(道徳的に間違ったことをして恥ずかしい)、humiliated(人前で恥をかかされて恥ずかしい)、shy(性格が内気で恥ずかしい)と使い分けます。

お弁当作りは大変だけど…

I get up at 5:00 every morning and make four lunch boxes. It's tough, but every time they bring back their boxes empty, I feel happy.

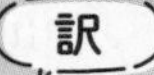

毎朝5時に起きて、4人分のお弁当作り。大変だけど、空っぽになった弁当箱を見るとうれしい。

get up（起きる）や make（作る）などの日課は、現在形で表します。「今日に限ってしたこと」なら過去形に。every time ～は「～するたびに」。they bring back their boxes empty は、直訳すると「彼らが弁当箱を空の状態で持って帰ってくる」です。

子どもたちの宿題を見た

I was able to come home early, so I helped the kids with their homework. Kaoru's writing is getting better and Tomoki is good with numbers.

早く帰れたので、子どもたちの宿題を見てあげた。カオルは字がうまくなっているし、トモキは算数がよくできるようだ。

「宿題を見る」は、ただ見ているだけではなく、教えたり指摘したりして「手伝う」ので help を使います。「～の…を手伝う」は help ～（人） with …（物事）で表します。「算数」は numbers。ほかに、math や arithmetic、figures（計算）とも言います。

08
交通・外出

電車

電車にまつわる単語

駅	(train) station
改札	ticket gate
ホーム	platform
車掌	conductor
駅員	station employee
運賃	fare
IC カード	IC card
切符	ticket
片道切符	one-way ticket
往復切符	round-trip ticket
1日乗車券	one-day pass
定期券	commuter pass
通学定期券	student commuter pass
電車	train
普通列車	local train
急行	express train
特急列車	limited express
新幹線	bullet train
車両	car
5号車	car No. 5
自由席	non-reserved seat
指定席	reserved seat
グリーン車	Green Car
女性専用車両	women-only car
優先席	priority seat
始発	the first train
終電	the last train
通勤ラッシュ	commuter rush
始発駅	starting station
終着駅	terminal station
人身事故	fatal accident
遅延証明書	delay certificate
痴漢	sexual molester
時刻表	timetable
路線図	railroad map
踏切	railroad crossing

運賃・切符

Suica を買った。 **I bought a Suica card.**

ICOCA に 3000 円分、チャージした。 **I charged 3,000 yen to my ICOCA.**

梅田まで 270 円だった。 **It cost 270 yen to get to Umeda.**

Suica を忘れたので、券売機で切符を買った。 **I forgot my Suica, so I bought a ticket at the machine.**

1日乗車券を買った。 **I bought a one-day pass.**

静岡まで片道切符を買った。 **I bought a one-way ticket to Shizuoka.** ＊「往復切符」なら、round-trip ticket

切符をなくしてしまった。 **I lost my ticket.**

電車に乗る

電車で仙台駅まで行った。 **I went to Sendai by train.** **I took a train to Sendai.**

電車で15分かかった。 **It took 15 minutes by train.**

各駅停車に乗った。 **I took a local train.**

急行に乗った。 **I took an express train.**

阪急宝塚線に乗った。 **I took the Hankyu Takarazuka Line.**

池袋行きの電車に乗った。 **I took a train bound for Ikebukuro.**
＊bound for ～＝～行きの

駆け込み乗車をしてしまった。 **I made a dash for the train.**
＊make a dash＝ダッシュする、突撃する

危ないから、もうしないようにしよう。 **It's dangerous, so I won't do it again.**

1両目に乗った。 **I got in the first car.**

ホームで20分ほど待った。 **I waited on the platform for about 20 minutes.**

なかなか電車が来なかった。 **The train wouldn't come.**

乗り過ごしてしまった。 **I missed my stop.** ＊stop＝停車駅

寝ていて終点まで行ってしまった。 **I fell asleep and rode to the end of the line.**
＊ride＝（乗り物などに）乗って行く。過去形はrode
line＝路線

違う電車に乗ってしまった。 **I got on the wrong train.**

8 交通・外出

反対方向の電車に乗ってしまった。 I got on the train going in the opposite direction.

舞浜で降りた。 I got off at Maihama.

降りる駅を間違えた。 I got off at the wrong station.

車内にて

冷房が効き過ぎだった。 The air conditioning was too strong.

暖房が効き過ぎだった。 The heater was too high.

混んでいた。 It was crowded.

すし詰め状態だった。 We were packed in like sardines.
＊sardine＝イワシ

電車の中は、ムシムシしていた。 It was really humid on the train.
＊humid＝ムシムシした

すいていた。 It wasn't crowded.

ガラガラにすいていた。 It was almost empty.

座れなかった。 I couldn't get a seat.

ずっと立っていた。 I stood the whole way.

座れてラッキーだった。 I was lucky to get a seat.

ほかの人たちが席を詰めてくれた。 They scooted over and made room for me.
＊scoot over＝座席を詰める　room＝場所、空間

おばあさんに席を譲った。 I gave up my seat to an old lady.

若い男性が席を譲ってくれた。 A young man gave up his seat to me.

窓から見る景色を楽しんだ。 I enjoyed looking at the scenery from the window.

小さな男の子が、外の景色に夢中になっていた。 A little boy was absorbed in the view outside.

飯田線は景色がいい。 The Iida Line has a nice view.

熟睡してしまった。	**I fell fast asleep.** ＊fast asleep＝ぐっすり眠って
車内はとても静かだった。	**It was very quiet in the train.**
隣の男性が大きな音で音楽を聞いていた。	**The man next to me had his music on too loud.**
電車の中で化粧するのって、やめてほしい。	**I don't like it when people put on makeup on the train.**
痴漢に遭った。最悪！	**Someone groped me. It was horrible!** ＊grope＝～に痴漢行為をする
気分の悪そうな人がいた。	**There was someone who looked sick.**
駅員を呼んだ。	**I called a station employee.**

特急・新幹線

13時40分発の自由席を２枚買った。	**I bought two non-reserved tickets for the 13:40 train.**
京都までの指定席を２枚買った。	**I bought two reserved seat tickets to Kyoto.**
指定席はすべて満席だった。	**All the reserved seats were booked.** ＊book＝～を予約する
グリーン車にした。	**I bought a Green Car ticket.**
自由席は混んでいた。	**The non-reserved cars were crowded.**
自由席はすいていた。	**The non-reserved cars weren't crowded.**
空席がすぐに見つかってよかった。	**I was lucky to find a seat quickly.**
誰かが私の席に間違えて座っていた。	**Someone sat in my seat by mistake.**
駅で駅弁を買った。	**I bought a bento box at the station.** ＊「駅弁」は、boxed mealとしてもOK
乗ってすぐ、駅弁を食べた。	**I started eating my bento box as soon as I got on the train.**

電車の中で食べる弁当って、なんであんなにおいしいんだろう。
Why do bento boxes taste so good on the train?

車内販売でアイスクリームとコーヒーを買った。
I bought ice cream and coffee from the on-board vendor.
＊vendor=売る人

新幹線の中で仕事をした。
I got some work done while I was on the Shinkansen.
＊Shinkansenは、bullet[ブレット] trainとしてもOK

コンセントが使える座席だった。
I had a seat with a power outlet.

乗り換え

新宿駅で、各駅停車に乗り換えた。
I transferred to a local train at Shinjuku.

京浜東北線から丸ノ内線への乗り換えは遠過ぎる。
The transfer from the Keihin-Tohoku Line to the Marunouchi Line is too far.

駅構内は迷路のようだった。
The station was like a maze.

乗り換えがわかりづらかった。
Changing trains was complicated.

乗り換えが面倒だった。
Changing trains was a bother.

連絡（乗り継ぎ）が悪かった。
It was a bad train connection.

そこへ行くのに電車を３回乗り換えた。
I changed trains three times to get there.

事故・遅延

谷町線は事故で遅れていた。
The Tanimachi Line was late because of an accident.

大雪で電車が遅れた。
The train was delayed by heavy snow.
＊delay＝～を遅らせる

大雨のため、静岡付近で新幹線が止まった。
The bullet train had to stop near Shizuoka due to the heavy rain.

四ツ谷駅で人身事故があったらしい。
I heard there was a fatal accident at Yotsuya Station.
＊fatal accidentは直訳すると「死亡事故」。「人身事故」は、serious accidentとも言う

三宮駅で線路内に人が立ち入ったらしい。	**Someone apparently got on the tracks at Sannomiya Station.** ＊apparently＝どうやら〜らしい
車内で急病人が出たらしい。	**They said someone on the train suddenly got sick.**
目の前で男性が倒れた。	**A guy collapsed in front of me.** ＊collapse＝突然倒れる
急いで駅員さんを呼んだ。	**I hurried off to call a station employee.**
周りの乗客と一緒に介抱した。	**The other passengers and I looked after him.**
彼が無事でよかった。	**I'm glad he was okay.**
なかなか運転再開しなかった。	**It was a long while before the train service resumed.** ＊resume＝再開する
急いでいたので、困った。	**It was frustrating because I was in a hurry.** ＊frustrating＝イライラさせるような
電車って、急いでるときに限って遅れる。	**Trains are only late when you're in a hurry.** ＊このyouは、「一般的な人々」を指す
会社に電話して、電車が遅れていると伝えた。	**I called the office and let them know the train was late.**
ああいう時は慌てても仕方がない。	**There's no point in panicking at a time like that.**
振替輸送で名鉄線に乗った。	**I was transferred to the Meitetsu Line.**
30 分後、ようやく電車が動き出した。	**The train finally started moving again 30 minutes later.**
遅延証明書をもらった。	**I got a train delay certificate.** ＊trainは省略してもOK

車（→ p. 424「車・バイク」も参照）

バス

バスで病院まで行った。	**I took a bus to the hospital. I went to the hospital by bus.**
なかなかバスが来なかった。	**The bus took forever to come.**
雨のせいか、バスが遅れていた。	**Maybe because of the rain, the bus was late.**
渋滞で、バスがなかなか進まなかった。	**There was a traffic jam, so the bus was very slow.** ＊traffic jam＝交通渋滞
バスって、時間通りに来たためしがない。	**I've never seen a bus arrive on time.** ＊on time＝時間通りに
6つ目の停留所で降りた。	**I got off at the sixth bus stop.**
一番後ろの席に座った。	**I sat in the very back.**
バスはたいてい座れるからうれしい。	**It's nice because I almost always get a seat on the bus.**
バスだと、街の風景が見られるのがいい。	**It's nice that you can look outside and see the view from the bus.** ＊このyouは、「一般的な人々」を指す
運賃は420円だった。	**It cost 420 yen.** ＊costは過去形もcost
新宿から松江まで高速バスに乗った。	**I took the highway bus from Shinjuku to Matsue.**
夜行バスに乗った。	**I took an overnight bus.**
深夜バスで帰宅した。	**I came home on the late-night bus.**
深夜バスは料金が倍だ。	**The bus fare doubles late at night.**

タクシー

タクシーで吉祥寺駅まで行った。	**I went to Kichijoji Station by taxi. I took a taxi to Kichijoji Station.**

遅刻しそうだったので、タクシーを使った。	**I took a taxi because I was running late.** ＊be running late＝遅れている
駅のタクシー乗り場でタクシーに乗った。	**I got a taxi from the station's taxi stand.**
タクシー乗り場に長い行列ができていた。	**There was a long line at the taxi stand.**
電話でタクシーを呼んだ。	**I called a taxi.**
アプリでタクシーを呼んだ。	**I got a taxi via app.** ＊via ～＝～によって
道でタクシーをつかまえた。	**I hailed a taxi on the street.** ＊hail＝～（タクシー）を呼び止める
タクシーはすぐにつかまった。	**It wasn't long before I got a taxi.**
なかなかタクシーがつかまらなかった。	**I had to wait a long time to get a taxi.**
トランクに荷物を入れた。	**I put my baggage in the trunk.** ＊baggage［バギッジ］＝荷物
後部座席に乗った。	**I sat in the back seat.**
助手席に乗った。	**I sat in the front passenger seat.**
運転手と世間話をした。	**I made small talk with the taxi driver.**
運賃は1200円だった。	**It cost 1,200 yen.**
5000円もかかっちゃった。	**It cost as much as 5,000 yen.**
深夜料金だったので、高くついた。	**The fare was high because of the late-night rate.**
領収書をもらった。	**I got a receipt.** ＊receipt［リスィート］＝領収書、レシート

自家用車

車でディズニーランドに行った。	**We drove to Disneyland.** **We went to Disneyland by car.**

1号線を走って、30分ほどで着いた。	**I went on Route 1 and got there in about 30 minutes.**
道に迷ってしまった。	**I got lost on the way.**
カーナビのおかげで迷わずに済んだ。	**Thanks to my car GPS, I didn't get lost.** ＊GPSは、global positioning systemの略
スマホのナビを使った。	**I used the GPS on my smartphone.** ＊smartphoneは単にphoneでもOK
スマホのナビのほうが正確かも。	**The smartphone GPS seems more accurate.**
電柱に車をこすっちゃった。	**I scraped my car on a telephone pole.** ＊scraped＝〜にすり傷をつける
私って、運転が下手だなぁ。	**I'm a terrible driver.**
道の駅に立ち寄った。	**We stopped at a roadside station.**
仕事の後、ナオコを車で迎えに行った。	**I picked up Naoko after work.** ＊pick up 〜＝〜を車で迎えに行く
イシカワさんが駅まで迎えに来てくれた。	**Ishikawa-san picked me up at the station.**
セイカを家まで車で送っていった。	**I drove Seika home.**
ヒデユキを駅で降ろした。	**I dropped Hideyuki off at the station.** ＊drop 〜 off＝(車で)〜を降ろす

カーシェアリング

カーシェアリングのサービスを契約した。	**I signed up for a car-sharing service.**
いつも車に乗るわけじゃないから、自家用車は必要ない。	**I don't always use a car, so I don't need to have my own.**
近所にステーションがあるから便利だ。	**There's a car-sharing station in my neighborhood, so it's convenient.**
いろいろなステーションで乗れるから便利だ。	**There are lots of places you can use it from, so it's convenient.**

週末にカーシェアの車を予約した。	**I reserved a share car for the weekend.**
予約しようとしたら、もう借りられてた。あ〜あ。	**I planned to reserve a car, but they were all taken. Oh no!**
少し遠いステーションの車を予約した。	**I reserved a car from a station farther away.**
ピカピカの車で気分がよかった。	**The nice shiny car put me in a good mood.**
前の人があまりきれいに使っていなかったみたい。	**The person before me left the car in a mess.** ＊leftはleaveの過去形　mess＝散らかった状態
やっぱり自家用車のほうがいいかも。	**Maybe it's better to have my own car after all.**
返却時間に間に合わなさそうで焦った。	**I thought I wouldn't make the return time so I hurried.** ＊make＝〜に間に合う
予約時間を延長した。	**I extended the rental time.**
延長料金が高かった。	**The extension fee was too expensive.**

道路状況

道が混んでいた。	**There was a traffic jam.** **The traffic was heavy.** ＊traffic jam＝交通渋滞
渋滞に巻き込まれた。	**I ran into a traffic jam.** ＊run into 〜＝〜にぶち当たる。runの過去形はran
事故で渋滞していた。	**An accident caused a traffic jam.** ＊cause＝〜を引き起こす
下水道工事で渋滞していた。	**There was a traffic jam because of sewer construction.** ＊sewer［スーアー］＝下水道
迂回（うかい）しなければならなかった。	**I had to take a detour.** ＊detour［ディートァ］＝迂回路
渋滞で、全然進まなかった。	**Traffic came to a standstill.** ＊standstill＝停止、休止
帰省ラッシュに巻き込まれた。	**I got stuck in a heavy homecoming exodus.** ＊get stuck＝立ち往生する exodus［エクソダス］＝集団移動

高速は大渋滞だった。	**The traffic on the expressway was heavy.**
高速は意外とすいていた。	**The traffic on the expressway was lighter than I expected.**
何度も信号につかまった。	**I kept getting stuck at red lights.**
一方通行だった。	**It was a one-way street.**
新しい道路ができていたなんて知らなかった。	**I didn't know there was a new road.**

高速道路

高速に乗るか、一般道で行くか。どっちが速いかな？	**Which is faster, the expressway or the local roads?** ＊「高速道路」は、super-highwayやthruwayとも言う
高速で行って正解だった。	**Taking the expressway was the right choice.**
一般道で行けばよかったな。	**I should've taken the local roads.**
帰りは高速に乗った。	**I took the expressway back home.**
海老名で高速に乗った。	**I got on the expressway at Ebina.**
浜松で高速を降りた。	**I got off the expressway at Hamamatsu.**
大雪で高速道路が通行止めだった。	**The expressway was closed due to the heavy snow.**
2時ごろ、パーキングエリアで休憩した。	**I took a break at a parking area at around 2:00.** ＊take a break＝休憩を取る
サービスエリアでラーメンを食べた。	**I ate ramen at a rest area.** ＊「サービスエリア」は、rest stopとも言う
刈谷ハイウェイオアシスのトイレが超豪華で驚いた。	**I was surprised that the restroom at Kariya Highway Oasis was so gorgeous.**

ガソリンスタンド

ガス欠になりそうだった。	**I was about to run out of gas.** ＊run out of ～＝～がなくなる　gas[ギャス]＝ガソリン

ガソリンスタンドがなかなか見つからなかった。	**I had a hard time finding a gas station.**
ガソリンスタンドで給油した。	**I filled up at a gas station.** ＊fill up＝(車を)満タンにする
セルフのガソリンスタンドだった。	**It was a self-serviced gas station.**
ガソリンがどんどん値上がりしてる。(はぁ～)	**Gas is getting more and more expensive. (Sigh)** ＊sigh［サイ］＝ため息
ハイオク満タンで入れてもらった。	**I asked for a full tank of premium.** ＊premium＝ハイオクガソリン
レギュラー満タンで 5000 円だった。	**A full tank of regular gas cost 5,000 yen.**
充電スポットで電気自動車に充電した。	**I charged my electric car at a charging spot.**
電気自動車の充電を待つ車が 3 台いた。	**There were three people waiting to charge their electric cars.**
この車は燃費がいいのでうれしい。	**I'm glad that my car is fuel efficient.** ＊fuel［フューエォ］efficient＝燃費のいい
洗車してもらった。	**I got my car washed.**

駐車・駐車場

モールの駐車場に車を停めた。	**I parked in a parking lot of a shopping mall.**
駐車場が全然見つからなかった。	**I couldn't find a parking lot.**
駐車場はすぐに見つかった。	**It was easy to find a parking lot.**
駐車場はどこもいっぱいだった。	**All the parking lots were full.**
事前にアプリで駐車場を予約した。	**I had reserved a parking lot via app beforehand.**
路上駐車をした。	**I parked on the road.** ＊park＝駐車する
すぐに戻ったのに、駐禁を切られてしまった。	**I got a parking ticket even though I went back to my car right away.** ＊parking ticket＝駐車違反切符

レッカーされていた。最悪！	**My car got towed. It sucked!** ＊tow＝～をけん引する　suck＝(物事が)ひどい、最低だ
駐車するときに右側をこすっちゃった。	**I scraped the right side of my car while parking.** ＊scrape＝～をこすり付ける
駐車って苦手。	**I'm not good at parking.**
一発できれいに駐車できた。	**I parked perfectly on my first try.**
駐車場が広くて、どこに停めたかわからなくなった。	**The parking lot was so big that I forgot where I parked.**
駐車料金が無料でうれしかった。	**I was glad that the parking was free.**

車のトラブル

車が故障した。	**My car broke down.**
タイヤがパンクしちゃった。	**I had a flat tire.** ＊flat tire＝パンクしたタイヤ
エンストした。	**The engine stalled.** ＊stall＝(エンジンが)止まる
エンジンがかからなかった。	**The engine didn't start.**
バッテリーが上がっちゃった。	**The battery was dead.**
ヘッドライトの消し忘れが原因だ。	**It was because I forgot to turn off the headlights.**
オーバーヒートしてしまった。	**The engine overheated.**
エンジンルームから煙が出た。	**There was smoke coming from the engine compartment.**
オイルが漏れていた。	**Oil was leaking.** ＊leak＝漏れる
キーを車内に入れたままロックしちゃった。	**I locked my key inside the car.**
車上荒らしに遭った。	**I had a car break-in.** ＊break-in＝侵入窃盗
すぐに警察を呼んだ。	**I called the police right away.**

車のメンテナンス・買い換え

洗車した。	**I washed my car.**
タイヤが減ってきた。	**The tires are getting worn out.** ＊worn out＝すり切れた
そろそろ交換の時期だ。	**I need to get them replaced soon.**
スタッドレスタイヤに交換した。	**I replaced the tires with studless tires.**
オイル交換をした。	**I got an engine oil change.**
もうすぐ車検の時期だ。	**It's almost time for a car inspection.** ＊inspection＝検査
車検に出した。	**I took my car in for an inspection.** ＊take ～ in for ...＝～（車など）を…（整備）のために持ち込む
車検のタイミングで車を買い換えようかな。	**I might buy a new car around the time when the inspection is due.** ＊due＝～することになっている
古い車を下取りに出して新車を買った。	**I traded in my old car and bought a new one.**

飛行機 （→ p. 464「飛行機」を参照）

自転車・スクーター

自転車で図書館に行った。	**I biked to the library.** **I went to the library by bicycle.** ＊bike＝自転車で行く
サイクリングに出かけた。	**I went for a bike ride.**
絶好のサイクリング日和だった。	**It was perfect weather for cycling.**
買ったばかりの自転車に乗った。	**I rode my brand-new bicycle.** ＊bicycleは、bikeとしてもOK
雨だったので、慎重に運転した。	**It was raining, so I rode carefully.**
電動自転車はラク～♪	**I find it so easy to ride an electric bike♪**
タイヤに空気を入れた。	**I put air in the tires.**

前輪がパンクしていた。	**The front wheel was flat.** ＊flat＝パンクしてぺちゃんこになった
自転車を整備してもらった。	**I had my bicycle serviced.**
自転車をレンタルした。	**I rented a bicycle.**
自転車用のヘルメットを買った。	**I bought a helmet for cycling.**
スクーターで買い物に行った。	**I went shopping on my scooter.**

歩く

駅まで 20 分歩いた。	**I walked 20 minutes to the station.**
歩いて 30 分かかった。	**It took 30 minutes on foot.**
早足で歩いた。	**I walked briskly.** ＊briskly＝活発に、足早に
のんびりと歩いた。	**I walked leisurely.** ＊leisurely＝のんびりと
公園まで歩いていった。	**I walked to the park.**
川沿いを歩いた。	**I walked along the river.**
家の近所を散歩した。	**I took a walk around the neighborhood.**
リンカと一緒に保育園まで歩いた。	**Rinka and I walked to her nursery.** ＊nursery (school)＝保育園
歩き過ぎて足が疲れた。	**My legs are tired from walking too much.**

道に迷う・道案内

道に迷う

道に迷ってしまった。	**I got lost.**
僕って、本当に方向音痴。	**I really have no sense of direction.**
地図を読むのが苦手だ。	**I'm bad at reading maps.**
ビルの場所がわからなかった。	**I couldn't find the building.**

改札がいくつもあって、迷ってしまった。 **There was more than one ticket gate, so I got lost.**

違う改札から出てしまった。 **I went out through the wrong ticket gate.**

待ち合わせ場所がわからなかった。 **I couldn't find the meeting place.**

地図アプリを頼りに道を探した。 **I used my map app to find the way.**

近くの人に道を尋ねた。 **I asked a passer by for directions.**
＊passer by［パッサーバィ］＝通行人

交番で道を尋ねた。 **I asked for directions at a police box.**

親切に道を教えてくれた。 **They kindly gave me directions.**
＊give 〜 directions＝〜に道を教える

道案内する

外国人観光客に道を聞かれた。 **A foreign tourist asked me for directions.**

外国人観光客に秋葉原への行き方を聞かれた。 **A foreign tourist asked me how to get to Akihabara.**

ホテルまでの道を教えてあげた。 **I gave him directions to his hotel. I showed him the way to his hotel.**
＊2文目は、実際に案内したり図を描いたりしたときに使う

ホテルまで案内してあげた。 **I guided him to his hotel.**

私も道がわからなかった。 **I didn't know the way, either.**

交番で尋ねて教えてあげた。 **I asked at a police box, and then I told him.**

英語で道案内するのは緊張した。 **I was nervous about giving directions in English.**

うまく案内できた。 **I was able to give directions well.**

何とか案内できた。 **I managed to give directions.**
＊manage to 〜＝何とか〜する

彼にすごく感謝された。 **He really appreciated my help.**
＊appreciate＝〜を感謝する

役に立ててよかった。 **I was happy to be of help.**
＊be of help＝役に立つ

交通・外出について 英語日記を書いてみよう

外出したことや交通手段について、英語で書いてみましょう。

散歩がてらギャラリーへ

The weather was very nice, so my husband and I walked to the art gallery to see Mr. Kondo's watercolor paintings. We also enjoyed the cherry blossoms on the way.

天気がとてもよかったので、コンドウさんの水彩画を見に夫とギャラリーまで歩いていった。途中、桜もキレイだった。

「～まで歩いていく」は go to ～ on foot よりも、walk to ～が自然な言い方。「水彩画」は watercolor painting、「油絵」は oil painting。「鉛筆やペンなどで描いた絵」なら drawing です。この enjoy は「花や景色を楽しむ」というニュアンス。on the way は「(～へ行く)途中」。

交通渋滞にはまる

We had a good time shopping at the outlet mall, but on the way back, we got stuck in a traffic jam. It took over two hours to get home. We were worn out.

アウトレットモールでの買い物は楽しかったけど、帰りに渋滞にはまって、家に着くのに２時間以上もかかった。もうクタクタ。

on the way back は「帰り道で」という意味。「渋滞にはまる」は、get stuck in traffic、be caught in a traffic jam といった表現もあります。「(～の)時間がかかった」は、It took ～(かかった時間)で表します。「クタクタ」は、exhausted や really tired でも OK。

タクシーで京都旅行

We chartered a taxi for half a day. The driver guided us around Kyoto. He explained the historical background and it was easy to understand.

半日タクシーをチャーターして、運転手さんに京都を案内してもらった。歴史的な背景を説明してくれて、わかりやすかった。

charter は「[時間単位、一日単位などで]～(乗り物)を貸し切る」という意味。「案内してもらった」は、The driver guided us (運転手が私たちを案内した)と表せば OK。「わかりやすい」は easy to understand、「わかりにくい」なら hard to understand です。

乗り換えがわからない

Kana and I went to Disneyland by train. At Tokyo Station, we couldn't find the Keiyo Line. There were people everywhere. It was a hassle, but Disneyland was great fun!

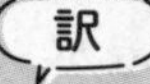

カナちゃんと電車でディズニーランドへ行った。東京駅では、京葉線がどこにあるのかわからなかった。どこも人だらけ。大変だったけど、ディズニーランドはとても楽しかった！

「京葉線がどこにあるのかわからなかった」は、we didn't know where the Keiyo Line was (京葉線がどこにあるのか知らなかった)でも OK。hassle は「大変なこと」。fun を強調するときは、great fun や a lot of fun とします。

09 電話・郵便

電話

電話をかける

夜、サトウくんに電話した。	I called Sato-kun in the evening.
彼の自宅に電話した。	I called him on his home phone.
明日、トクダさんに必ず電話しよう。	I'll make sure to call Mr. Tokuda tomorrow.
たまには母に電話しようかな。	Maybe I should call my mom sometimes.
父に折り返し電話した。	I called my dad back.
電車を降りてから彼にかけ直した。	I called him back once I got off the train.
誰も出なかった。	Nobody answered.
留守電につながった。	I reached the voice mail.
留守電にメッセージを残した。	I left a voice mail.
レストランに予約の電話をした。	I called the restaurant to make a reservation.
レストランに電話して、営業時間を尋ねた。	I called the restaurant to ask what time they're open.
美容院に電話して、日曜日の予約を入れた。	I called my hairdresser and made an appointment for Sunday.
電話でピザを注文した。	I ordered a pizza by phone.

注文した商品について電話で問い合わせた。	I called them to ask about the stuff I ordered. ＊stuff＝物

電話を受ける

ユリちゃんから電話があった。	I got a call from Yuri.
アキに男の子から電話がかかってきた。	Aki got a phone call from some boy. ＊some＝ある～
お父さんから２回、着信があった。	I had two missed calls from my dad. ＊missed call＝不在着信
知らない番号から着信があった。	I got a missed call from a number I didn't know.
最初、彼女が誰だかわからなかった。	I couldn't recognize her voice at first.
非通知の電話がかかってきた。	I got a call from a blocked number. ＊blocked＝未公表の
電話に出なかった。	I didn't answer the phone.
忙しくて電話に出られなかった。	I was too busy to answer the phone.
彼は留守電を残していなかった。	He didn't leave a message.
用件は何だったのかな。	I wonder what it was about.
息子ったら、たまには電話してくれたらいいのに。	I wish my son would call me every once in a while. ＊every once in a while＝たまに、時々
久しぶりの電話だった。	It was the first call in a while.
息子からの電話を振り込め詐欺かと思った。	When my son called, I thought it was a phone scam. ＊phone scam＝電話による詐欺
最近、間違い電話が多いな。	I often receive wrong number calls these days. ＊wrong number call＝間違い電話
最近は固定電話をほとんど使わないなぁ。	I don't really use my landline these days. ＊landline＝固定電話

電話で話す

孫からの電話は、いつでもうれしい。
It's always nice to get a call from my grandson.
＊孫が女の子なら、grandsonをgranddaughterに

ジュンコの声を聞くとほっとする。
I feel relaxed when I hear Junko's voice.

彼女の声を聞くだけでうれしい。
Just hearing her voice makes me happy.

キヨミと1時間、電話でおしゃべりした。
Kiyomi and I talked on the phone for an hour.

最近、ハルミが長電話ばかりしている。
Harumi is always making long phone calls these days.

誰と話してるんだろう？
Who is she talking to?

どうやら彼氏と電話しているみたいだ。
It seems she's on the phone with her boyfriend.

電話を切る

9時ごろ、電話を切った。
I hung up at around 9:00.
＊hang up＝電話を切る。hangの過去形はhung

お母さんがうるさいので、電話を切った。
I hung up because my mom was nagging me.
＊nag＝〜にうるさく小言を言う

電話を切るのが名残惜しかった。
It was hard to hang up.

一方的に電話を切られた。すごく失礼！
He hung up on me. How rude!
＊相手が女性の場合は、HeをSheに

電話がつながらない

ヤマグチさんに電話したけど、つながらなかった。
I tried calling Mr. Yamaguchi, but I couldn't reach him.

電話をかけたけど、話し中だった。
I called, but the line was busy.
＊line＝回線　busy＝話し中で

最近、リョウくんがあんまり電話に出ない。
Ryo-kun hardly ever answers his phone these days.
＊hardly ever 〜＝めったに〜しない

忙しいのかな？
I wonder if he's busy.

着信拒否されてるわけじゃないよね？
It's not because he's blocked my number, is it?
＊block＝～を拒否する

予約の電話が一向につながらなかった。
I couldn't connect to the reservation center for hours.
＊for hours＝何時間も

セールス電話

午後、セールスの電話が３件もかかってきてうんざり。
I got three sales calls this afternoon. I'm sick of them.

最近、勧誘の電話がよくかかってくる。
I'm getting a lot of cold calls these days.
＊cold call＝勧誘電話

出張買取に来るというリサイクル店からの電話だった。
It was a call from a second-hand shop that would come here to buy my things.

不動産営業の電話だった。
It was a call from a real estate agent.

どこから電話番号が漏れているんだろう？
I wonder how they got my number.

無言電話・いたずら電話

無言電話があった。
I got a silent call.
＊silent call＝無言電話

いたずら電話があった。
I got a prank call.
＊prank call＝いたずら電話

気味が悪いな。
It was creepy.

電話に出たら、すぐ切れてしまった。
Somebody called and then hung up when I answered.
＊hang up＝電話を切る。hangの過去形はhung

振り込め詐欺

息子を名乗る電話がかかってきた。
Someone called me and claimed to be my son.
＊claim to be ～＝～と主張する

私に息子はいないのに！
I don't have a son!

母のところに、娘を名乗る電話がかかってきたらしい。 It seems someone pretending to be her daughter called my mom.
＊pretend to be ～＝～のふりをする

母から確認の電話がかかってきた。 My mom called me to check.

母が振り込め詐欺にだまされないか心配だ。 I'm worried that my mom might fall for a bank transfer scam.
＊bank transfer＝銀行振替　scam=詐欺

父はもう少しでだまされそうになったらしい。 My dad said he was almost scammed.
＊scam= ～を詐欺にかける

高齢者をだまそうとするなんて、許せない！ Scamming elderly people is unforgivable!

実家の電話にナンバー・ディスプレイを付けた。 I got caller ID for my home phone.
＊caller ID＝発信者番号通知

電話をいつも留守電にしておくよう母に伝えた。 I told my mom to always set her phone to voicemail.

電話のトラブル

彼の声が遠かった。 I couldn't hear him well.

彼の声がプツプツ途切れた。 His voice broke up on the phone.

電話を盗聴されている気がする。 I think my phone is being tapped.
＊tap＝～(他人の電話)を盗聴する

電話代

電話代が高過ぎる。 My phone bill is too high.

えっ！　今月の電話代、１万円も!? My gosh! My phone bill for this month is 10,000 yen!
＊My gosh!＝えっ！、しまった！

格安スマホに変えようかな。 Maybe I should switch to a budget smartphone.
＊budget＝安い

プランの見直しをしてもらおう。 I'll ask them to revise my payment plan.
＊revise＝～を見直す

今月の電話代、そんなに高くなかった。ホッ。 My phone bill wasn't so high this month. Phew!
＊Phewは、Whewともつづる

電話代は6000円以内に収めたい。	**I want to keep my phone bill within 6,000 yen.**
長電話はやめよう。	**I'll stop making long calls.**
無料ビデオ通話のおかげで、電話代は基本料金のみ。	**I only pay the basic monthly fee for my phone thanks to the free video chat.**

国際電話

カナダのメアリーに電話をかけた。	**I called Mary in Canada.**
オーストラリアのマイケルから電話があった。	**I got a phone call from Michael in Australia.**
朝8時に電話して、向こうは夕方5時だった。	**I called at 8:00 in the morning, and it was 5:00 in the evening on the other end.**
時差の関係で、エイミーになかなか電話できない。	**It's hard to call Amy because of the time difference.** ＊time difference＝時差
アプリを使って国際電話がかけられるんだ！	**I didn't know you could make international calls using an app!**
スーザンから、誕生祝いの国際電話があった。	**Susan called me from abroad on my birthday.**

ビデオ通話

ドイツのイマイさんとビデオ通話をした。	**I had a video call with Imai-san in Germany.**
友達とオンライン飲み会をした。	**I had an online drinking party with my friends.**
明日は8時に孫とビデオ通話だ。	**I'm having a video chat with my grandson at 8:00 tomorrow.**
相手の顔を見ながら話せるって、すごい。	**It's amazing that we can see each other's faces when we're talking.**
相手を身近に感じられる。	**It feels like the person is really close.**

いつでも孫の顔が見られる。 I can see my grandchildren's faces any time I want.

故郷の父も、ビデオ通話を使えるようになった。 Even my dad back home can do video calls now.

両親はしょっちゅう、孫の顔が見たいと言って電話してくる。 My parents are calling all the time to see their grandkids.

ビデオ通話なら、料金は無料だ。 Video calls are free.

便利な時代になったなぁ。 This is the age of convenience.

ファクス

ファクスで申し込み書を送った。 I faxed in the application.
＊fax in ～＝～をファクスで送る

店の地図がファクスで送られてきた。 They faxed the store map to me.

ファクスの用紙が切れちゃった。 I ran out of fax paper.
＊run out of ～＝～を切らす。runの過去形はran

ファクスって意外と便利。 Fax is more convenient than you think.

最近はファクスを使わなくなった。 We don't use fax much recently.

携帯電話・スマートフォン

契約・解約

スマホの契約をした。 I got a smartphone.
I signed a contract for a smartphone.
＊sign a contract＝契約する

新しいiPhoneの注文をした。 I ordered a new iPhone.

ネットで注文できた。 I could order it online.

新しいiPhoneを受け取った。 I got my new iPhone.

お母さんにスマホを契約してあげた。 I got my mom a smartphone.

携帯のキャリアを変えようかな。 I'm thinking of changing to another cellphone carrier.

au からソフトバンクに乗り換えた。	**I moved from au to SoftBank.**
スマホをもう1台、契約しようかな。	**I think I should get an extra phone.** ＊「スマートフォン」は、phoneだけでもOK
スマホを解約した。	**I canceled my phone.**
2台のうち、1台を解約した。	**I canceled one of my two phones.**
キャンペーン中で、解約手数料を払わずにすんだ。	**There was a campaign, so I didn't have to pay the cancellation fee.**

新機種・機種変更

スマホの機種変更をしようかな。	**I'm thinking of getting a new phone.**
スマホの機種変更をした。	**I got a new phone.**
オンラインで機種変更を申し込んだ。	**I applied for a new phone online.**
前のスマホのほうが使いやすかったかも。	**My old phone was easier to use, I guess.**
最新のスマホ、かっこいいんだよな。	**The latest smartphone model is so cool.**
赤いのが欲しいなぁ。	**I want a red one.**
品切れで、1カ月待ちだ。	**The phone is out of stock, so I have to wait for a month.** ＊out of stock＝品切れで
新しい機種がどんどん出て、ついていけないよ。	**New phones keep coming out and I can't keep up with them.** ＊keep up with ～＝～（流行など）に遅れずについていく

各種手続き

料金プランの変更をした。	**I got a different payment plan.**
より安いプランに変更してもらった。	**Now I'm on a cheaper payment plan.**
家族割引の手続きをした。	**I got the family discount.**
キャンペーン中で、手数料が無料だった。	**There was a campaign, so there was no handling fee.** ＊handling fee＝手数料

キャンペーン中で、5000円もお得だった。	**There was a campaign, so I saved 5,000 yen.**
スマホの修理を依頼した。	**I asked them to fix my phone.** ＊fix＝～を修理する
代替機をもらった。	**I got a temporary replacement.** ＊temporary＝一時的な　replacement＝代替品
手続きカウンターは混んでいた。	**The service counter was crowded.**
順番が来るまで、結構待った。	**I waited for a long time for my turn.** ＊turn＝順番
店員さんの説明が丁寧だった。	**The shop assistant explained it thoroughly.** ＊thoroughly＝徹底的に、じっくり

機能・性能

スマホって、ホント便利。	**Smartphones are really convenient.**
スマホは必需品だ。	**Smartphones are a must.**
新しいスマホは、写真撮影の性能がすごく上がったらしい。	**I hear that the camera on the new smartphone has improved a lot.**
スマホでもこんなにきれいな写真が撮れるんだ。	**It's amazing that you can take such good photos on a smartphone.**
どこでも好きな音楽が聞けて便利だな。	**It's convenient to be able to listen to my favorite music wherever I want.**
スマホに決済アプリが入っている。	**I have a payment app on my phone.**
今は財布を持たずに出かけられる。	**Now I can go out without my wallet.**
待ち時間にスマホでドラマの続きを見た。	**I watched the next drama episode on my smartphone while I waited.**
帰宅途中の電車でTikTokを見た。	**I watched TikTok videos on the train going home.**

テキストメッセージ

レイコにメッセージを送った。	**I texted Reiko.** ＊ text＝～にテキストメッセージを送る
ヒデからメッセージが届いた。	**I got a text from Hide.** ＊text＝(スマホなどの)メッセージ

お母さんから、メッセージで買い物リストが送られてきた。	**My mom texted me the shopping list.**
マキちゃんに写真を送った。	**I sent Maki-chan some photos.**
スマホでノリくんにお店のリンクを送った。	**I sent Nori-kun the store link by phone.**
レンの動画を撮って母に送った。	**I took a video of Ren and sent it to my mom.**
迷惑メールがたくさん来る。	**I'm getting a lot of spam.**
迷惑メール、うざい。	**The spam is really annoying.** ＊annoying＝気に障る、迷惑な
メアドを変えたほうがいいかな？	**Maybe I should change my e-mail address.**

LINE

トウゴに LINE を送った。	**I sent Togo a LINE message.**
ユカリから LINE が来た。	**Yukari LINE'd me.** ＊このLINEは「～にLINEする」という動詞の意味
コウタに LINE したのに、既読にならないなぁ。	**I sent Kota a LINE message, but it's not marked as read.**
彼はスマホ見てないの？	**Doesn't he check his phone?**
彼にずっと未読スルーされてる。	**He doesn't even read my messages.**
彼女に既読スルーされてるのかな？	**Is she ignoring my messages even though she's read them?**
学生時代の仲間とグループ LINE を作った。	**I made a LINE group for my school friends.**
グループ LINE のメッセージが多過ぎて疲れる。	**I'm tired of too many group messages.**
グループ LINE で話が盛り上がった。	**We had fun chatting in the LINE group.**
みんなあまりグループ LINE に投稿しない。	**No one really posts anything in the LINE group.**

9 電話・郵便

グループ LINE、なんだか険悪な雰囲気。	**There's a tense feeling in the LINE group.** ＊tense＝緊迫した
娘と LINE 通話をした。	**I called my daughter on LINE.**
みんなで LINE ビデオ通話をした。	**We had a video call on LINE.**
新しい LINE スタンプを買っちゃった。	**I bought new LINE stamps.**
２人でお互いにスタンプを送りまくった。	**We sent each other stamps back and forth.** ＊back and forth＝行ったり来たり
ハルナのスタンプがかわいかった。	**Haruna's stamps were so cute.**

アプリ

人気のゲームアプリをダウンロードしてみた。	**I downloaded a popular game app.** ＊appは、applicationの略
最近、いろいろなアプリを試してる。	**I've been trying different apps recently.**
無料アプリでも結構楽しめる。	**Even the free apps are pretty fun.**
英単語アプリを使い始めた。	**I started using an English vocab app.** ＊vocab=語彙。vocabularyと同じ
今はアプリで勉強できる。	**These days, we can study with apps.**
会員証はアプリに切り替えてる。	**I've been switching my membership cards to an app.**
いろいろな店の会員証を全部持ち歩かなくて済む。	**I don't have to carry all kinds of membership cards anymore.**

スマホのトラブル

スマホをなくしてしまった。	**I've lost my phone.**
どこで落としたのか、見当が付かない。	**I have no idea where I might have dropped it.** ＊have no idea＝まったくわからない
タクシーの中に置いてきたのかも。	**I might have left it in the taxi.**

スマホがないと困るなぁ。	**Not having a phone is such an inconvenience.**
交番に届けてくれた人がいた。よかった！	**Someone took it to the police. Thank goodness!**
スマホをトイレに落としちゃった！	**I dropped my phone in the toilet!**
スマホが故障した。	**My phone broke.**
画面にひびが入った。	**My screen is cracked.** ＊crack＝ひびが入る
画面がきれいに映らなくなった。	**The display isn't working well.**
電源が入らない。どうしよう？	**It won't turn on. What should I do?** ＊turn on＝電源が入る
データが全部消えちゃったかも。	**I might have lost all the data.**
みんなの連絡先がわからなくなっちゃう！	**I won't be able to contact anyone!** ＊contact＝～に連絡を取る
バックアップを取っておいてよかった。	**Good thing I had a backup.**
会議中に電話が鳴って少し焦った。	**I panicked a little when my phone rang during the meeting.**
マナーモードにするのを忘れた。	**I forgot to set it to silent mode.**

電波が悪い

彼、電波の悪い場所にいたみたい。	**He seemed to be in a place with bad reception.** ＊reception＝（電波の）受信状態
電波が悪くて、途中で切れてしまった。	**The call ended because of poor reception.**
電波が悪くて、電話をかけられなかった。	**I couldn't call because of the terrible reception.**
職場は電波が悪いので、不便だ。	**The reception at work is terrible. It's such a pain.** ＊pain＝悩みの種
早く電波状況を改善してほしい。	**I want them to improve the reception quickly.**

電池・充電

電池のもちが悪い。	The battery doesn't last long. ＊last long＝長持ちする
充電が切れてしまった。	The battery died. ＊die＝(電池が)切れる
慌ててショップに駆け込んで、充電した。	I hurried to a shop to charge the battery.
駅でレンタル充電器を使った。	I used a rental charger at the station.
コンビニでスマホの充電器を買った。	I got a phone charger at a convenience store.

郵便・宅配便

郵便・宅配便にまつわる表現

切手	stamp
記念切手	commemorative stamp
はがき	postcard
年賀状	New Year's greeting card / New Year's card
暑中見舞い	summer greeting
寒中見舞い	winter greeting
クリスマスカード	Christmas card
手紙	letter
封筒	envelope
便せん	letter paper
あて先	addressee
差出人	sender
郵便ポスト	mailbox
書留郵便で	by registered mail
速達で	by express mail
航空便で	by airmail
船便（地上便）で	by surface mail
親展の	confidential
小包	package
冷蔵便	refrigerated delivery
冷凍便	frozen delivery
宅配ボックス	delivery box
置き配	package drop
不在票	delivery notice
～を元払いで送る	send ～ through prepaid shipping
～を着払いで送る	send ～ by COD

郵便を出す

近所のポストに手紙を投函した。	I put the letters in a nearby mailbox.
また手紙を出し忘れてしまった。	I forgot to mail the letter again.

慌てて出しに行った。 I rushed to mail it.
＊rush to 〜＝慌てて〜する

父に書留で5万円送った。 I sent my father 50,000 yen by registered mail. ＊registered mail＝書留郵便

請求書を速達で送った。 I sent the invoice by express mail.
＊invoice＝請求書 express mail＝速達

アリーに手紙を書いた。 I wrote a letter to Allie.
＊a letterは、省略してもOK

フィレンツェから家族に絵はがきを送った。 I sent a postcard to my family from Florence. ＊Florence＝フィレンツェ

郵便局で、84円切手を20枚買った。 I bought twenty 84-yen stamps at the post office.

記念切手を買った。 I bought some commemorative stamps. ＊commemorative stamp＝記念切手

郵便を受け取る

郵便物がいくつか来ていた。 I got some mail. ＊mail＝郵便物

ワタナベさんから手紙が届いた。 I got a letter from Mr. Watanabe.

電話代の請求書が届いた。 I got my phone bill. ＊phone bill＝電話代

息子から書留が届いた。 I got registered mail from my son.
＊registered mail＝書留郵便

年賀状が53枚届いた。 I got 53 New Year's greeting cards.
＊「年賀状」は、New Year's cardsとしてもOK

ペギーからクリスマスカードが届いた。 I got a Christmas card from Peggy.

イザワさんからすてきな暑中見舞いが届いた。 I got a beautiful summer greeting card from Izawa-san.

エンドウさんからお礼状が届いた。 I got a thank-you letter from Mr. Endo.

旅行のパンフレットが速達で届いた。 A travel brochure was sent to me by express mail.
＊brochure［ブロウシュア］＝パンフレット

郵便受けに、チラシがたくさん入っていた。 There were a lot of flyers in my mailbox. ＊flyer＝チラシ。flierともつづる

珍しく、郵便物が一つもなかった。 I didn't receive any mail, which was unusual.

そろそろ届いてもいいころなのに、おかしいな。 It should have been delivered by now. I wonder what happened.

郵便が届くまでに、以前よりだいぶ時間がかかるようになった。 It takes a lot longer for mail to be delivered these days.

ああ、今日は土曜日だから配達がないのか。 Ah, there's no delivery today because it's Saturday.

宅配便を出す

小包を２個出した。 I sent two packages.

２つで 1900 円だった。 It cost 1,900 yen for two.

郵便局で小包を出した。 I sent a package at the post office.

めいに小包を送った。 I sent a package to my niece.

コンビニに小包を出しに行った。 I went to the convenience store to send a package.

宅配便の営業所に荷物を持ち込んだ。 I took my package to the courier's office.
＊courier［クーリエ］＝宅配便業者

書類を宅配便で送った。 I sent some documents through a package delivery service.

明日には到着するはずだ。 It should arrive tomorrow.

配達日時を、木曜日の 14 ～ 16 時に指定した。 I set the delivery for Thursday between 14:00 and 16:00.

カニを冷凍便で送った。 I sent crab by frozen delivery.
＊frozen delivery＝冷凍便

ケーキを冷蔵便で送った。 I sent cake by refrigerated delivery.
＊refrigerated delivery＝冷蔵便

荷物を着払いで送った。 I sent a package by COD.
＊COD＝cash on delivery（着払い）の略

自宅まで集荷に来てもらった。 I asked them to pick up the package at my house.

宅配便を受け取る

午後、小包を受け取った。	**I received a package in the afternoon.**
注文していた服が届いた。	**The clothes I ordered were delivered.** ＊deliver＝～を配達する・届ける
海外から本が届いた。	**The book arrived from overseas.**
ヒトミがリンゴを送ってくれた。	**Hitomi sent me apples.**
荷物を置き配で受け取った。	**I had my package left by the door.**
スッピンで髪もボサボサだったので、玄関前に置き配してもらった。	**I had my package left by the door because I didn't have my makeup on and my hair was messy.** ＊messy＝乱雑な
宅配ボックスは便利だなぁ。	**A delivery box is useful.** ＊集合住宅や駅などの宅配ボックスならdelivery lockerに
荷物をコンビニで受け取った。	**I got my package at the convenience store.**
配達日時を指定したのに、届かなかった。	**I specified a delivery date and time, but the package never arrived.** ＊specify＝～を指定する
宅配便の不在票が入っていた。	**I found a missed-delivery notice.** ＊missed-delivery notice＝不在配達通知
再配達してもらわなきゃ。	**I need to ask for a redelivery.** ＊redelivery＝再配達
午前中に再配達してもらった。	**I had it redelivered this morning.** ＊redeliver＝～を再配達する
再配達を頼んでたのに、忘れてた！	**I requested redelivery, but I forgot about it!**
配達員さん、ごめんなさい。	**Sorry, delivery person.**
こんな大雨の日に配達してもらって、申し訳ない。	**I feel sorry they had to deliver it on such a rainy day.**

電話・郵便について 英語日記を書いてみよう

電話や郵便、宅配便などについて、英語で書いてみましょう。

ユウコと長電話

Yuko called me for the first time in about five years. We just talked and talked about our school days. It was fun remembering the good old days.

5年ぶりくらいに、ユウコから電話があった。学生時代のことをひたすら話し続けた。思い出話に花が咲いた。

「〜ぶりに」は、for the first time in 〜（期間）を使って「〜の期間で初めて」と表現します。just talked and talked は「ひたすら話した」。we talked away とも言えます。最後の英文の直訳は、「古き良き時代を思い出して楽しかった」です。

スマホをいじってばかり

Miku is always on her phone and isn't studying hard. If her grades drop, I'll need to limit her screen time.

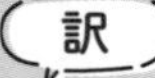

ミクはスマホをいじってばかりであまり勉強していない。成績が下がったら、スマホの使用時間を制限しなきゃいけないな。

「〜してばかり」は always（いつも）で表せます。「スマホをいじる」は be on one's phone。phone だけでも smartphone のことだとわかります。成績が「下がる」は drop、「上がる」は improve。screen time は「（スマホなどの）使用時間」です。

クリスマスカード

I got a Christmas card from Deanna. She sounded really excited about becoming a grandmother in April. I'll send her a New Year's greeting card in return.

ディアナからクリスマスカードが届いた。4月におばあちゃんになることに、すごくワクワクしているようだった。私も年賀状の返事を出そうっと。

「〜が届いた」は、I received 〜（〜を受け取った）と表現できます。「〜のようだった」と書きたい場合は、手紙を読んで感じたなら sounded を、写真などを見て感じたなら looked を用います。「おばあちゃんになること」は being a grandma とも表せます。

食材配達を利用してみたい

Aiko told me that she has food delivered every week. It comes with recipes, so you don't need to think hard about what to cook. I want to try it, too.

アイコが毎週食材を配達してもらっていると言っていた。レシピが付いてくるから、献立に悩む必要もないらしい。私も利用してみたいな。

「〜を…してもらう」は have 〜（人や物事）…（動詞の過去分詞）で表します。ここでは、she has food delivered としています。come with 〜は「〜が付いてくる」、think hard は「真剣に考える」、what to cook は「何を料理するか（＝献立）」という意味です。

10
家事

食事の用意・後片付け

食材の買い出し (→ p. 314「食料品・日用品を買う」を参照)

料理 (→ p. 375「料理する」を参照)

食器を洗う

夕飯の後、食器を洗った。
I did the dishes after dinner.
＊do the dishes＝食器を洗う。wash the dishesでもOK

トモが食器を洗ってくれた。
Tomo did the dishes for me.

私が食器を洗って、トモがふいた。
I washed the dishes and Tomo dried them.

トモが洗い物を手伝ってくれた。
Tomo helped by giving me a hand with the dishes.
＊give ～ a hand＝～(人)を手伝う

たまには娘が食器洗いを手伝ってくれたらいいのに。
I wish she could help with washing the dishes sometimes.

台所が汚れた食器の山になっていた。
The dirty dishes in the kitchen were piling up.
＊pile up＝山積みになる

洗うのに1時間以上もかかった。
It took more than an hour to wash them.

ふきんを漂白剤につけておいた。
I soaked the dishcloth in bleach.
＊soak ～ in ...＝～を…につける

油汚れがなかなか落ちなかった。
The grease didn't come off easily.
＊grease＝油脂

カップに茶渋が付いていた。
The teacup was stained.
＊stained＝シミの付いた

洗剤で手が荒れた。
My hands got chapped from the detergent.
＊get chapped＝(肌などが)荒れる

また茶わんを割っちゃった。	**I broke another rice bowl.**
お気に入りのお皿を割っちゃった。ショック！	**I broke my favorite plate. What a shock!**
台所がきれいだと気持ちがいい。	**It feels nice when the kitchen is clean.** ＊cleanは、spick-and-span（こざっぱりとした）でもOK

食洗機

食洗機が欲しい。	**I want a dishwasher.**
食洗機を買おうかな？	**Maybe I should buy a dishwasher.**
食洗機用の洗剤を買ってこなくちゃ。	**I need to get dishwasher detergent.**
食器を食洗機に入れた。	**I put the dishes in the dishwasher.**
食洗機を買ってから、皿洗いが本当にラク。	**Washing dishes got really easy after I bought the dishwasher.**
食洗機に食器が入りきらなかった。	**The dishes wouldn't fit in the dishwasher.**
食洗機を設置したけど、ほとんど使っていない。	**I put in a dishwasher, but I haven't used it much.** ＊put in ～＝～を取り付ける
手で洗ったほうが早いや。	**It's faster to do the dishes by hand.**
夫はいまだに食洗機の使い方がわかっていない。	**My husband still doesn't know how to use the dishwasher.**
また「食洗機不可」の食器が入れられていた！	**There were "not-dishwasher-safe" dishes in there again!**

洗濯・衣類の手入れ

洗濯する

午前中に洗濯した。	**I did the laundry in the morning.** ＊do the laundry＝洗濯をする
2回、洗濯した。	**I did two loads of laundry.** ＊load＝1回分の量　laundry＝洗濯物

洗濯物がだいぶたまっている。	**The laundry has really piled up.** ＊pile up＝山積みになる
色物と白物を分けて洗った。	**I washed the colors and the whites separately.**
手洗いコースで洗った。	**I used the hand-wash setting.**
久しぶりにシーツを洗った。	**I washed my sheets for the first time in a while.**
下着を手洗いした。	**I hand-washed my underwear.** ＊hand-wash＝～を手洗いする
セーターが縮んじゃった。	**The sweater shrunk.** ＊shrink＝縮む。過去形はshrunk
Ｔシャツが色落ちしちゃった。	**The T-shirt faded.** ＊fade＝(色などが)薄れる
ジーンズの色が白いシャツに移っちゃった！	**The color from the jeans stained the white shirt!** ＊stain＝～にシミを付ける
白いシャツが水色になっちゃった！	**My white shirt turned light blue!** ＊turn ～＝～に変わる
ナオキはまた、服を泥だらけにして帰ってきた。	**Naoki came home with his clothes all muddy again.** ＊muddy＝泥だらけの
夫がポケットにティッシュを入れっぱなしにしていた。	**My husband left tissues in his pocket.**
洗濯物が全部ティッシュまみれになった。	**Now all the laundry is covered in bits of tissue.** ＊bits of ～＝～の破片
洗濯する人の気持ちになってほしい。	**He should think about the person that has to wash his clothes.**
洗濯は１日おきでよし！	**Doing the laundry every other day is just fine!**

洗濯物を干す・取り込む

洗濯物を干した。	**I hung up the laundry.** ＊hang up ～＝～を干す。hangの過去形はhung
洗濯物を室内に干した。	**I hung up the laundry inside.**
セーターを陰干しした。	**I hung up my sweater in the shade.** ＊shade＝日陰
洗濯物を取り込んだ。	**I brought in the laundry.** ＊bring in ～＝～を中に入れる。bringの過去形はbrought

洗濯物を畳んだ。 I folded the laundry. ＊fold＝～を畳む

洗濯物が雨にぬれてしまった。 The laundry got wet in the rain.

最近、雨ばかりで洗濯物がなかなか乾かない。 It's been raining all the time, so the laundry won't dry.

ジーンズはまだ半乾きだった。 The jeans were still half dry.

生乾きのにおいがした。 They smelled damp. ＊damp＝湿った

Tシャツが庭に落ちていた。 The T-shirt had fallen onto the lawn. ＊lawn＝芝生

洗い直さなきゃ。 I need to wash them again.

乾燥機

洗った服を乾燥機にかけた。 I dried the laundry in the clothes dryer.

乾燥機を3時間かけた。 The clothes dryer took three hours.

洗濯乾燥機は便利だな。 Washer-dryers are convenient.

洗濯から乾燥まで全部お任せ。 I can have it do everything from washing to drying.

夜、寝ている間に洗濯と乾燥が済んじゃう。 The washing and drying finish overnight while I'm asleep.

ニットを乾燥機にかけたら縮んじゃった。 I put knitwear in the dryer and it shrank. ＊shrink＝縮む。過去形はshrunk

お気に入りだったのに…。 It was my favorite ...

少し大きめだったから、まあいいか。 It was a little big for me, so I guess it's fine.

乾燥機にかけるとふんわり仕上がる。 Clothes come out of the dryer nice and fluffy.

洗濯物を干す時間が節約できる。 I can save on the time I spend hanging up laundry.

洗濯洗剤

洗剤を変えてみた。	I used a different detergent. ＊detergent［ディタージェント］＝洗剤
新しい柔軟剤、とてもいい香り。	I really like the smell of the new softener. ＊softener［ソフナー］＝柔軟剤
最近の洗剤はコンパクトだなぁ。	Detergent these days is really compact.
もう柔軟剤がない。	I ran out of softener. ＊run out of ～＝～を使い果たす。runの過去形はran
蛍光漂白剤だと知らずに使っちゃった。	I used fluorescent bleach without realizing. ＊fluorescent［フローレスント］＝蛍光性の
このせっけん、汚れがよく落ちる！	This soap cleans dirt so well!
デリケート洗剤でスカートを洗った。	I washed my skirt with delicate detergent.

アイロンがけ

ハンカチにアイロンをかけた。	I ironed my handkerchief. ＊handkerchiefは、くだけてhankyとも言う
スチームで服のシワを伸ばした。	I steamed my clothes to get rid of the wrinkles.
スーツのズボンをプレッサーにかけた。	I used a press iron on my suit trousers.
私、アイロンがけが下手だなぁ。	I'm not good at ironing.
アイロンでやけどしちゃった。	I burned myself with the iron.
アイロンがけって面倒くさいな。	Ironing is a bother. ＊bother＝厄介なこと
シャツのアイロンがけって、結構大変。	It's really difficult to iron shirts.
アイロンがけのいらないシャツは、ラクでいいな。	Non-iron shirts are easy to take care of. ＊take care of ～＝～の手入れをする
給食着にアイロンをかけるのが苦痛。	Ironing the school lunch outfit is a pain.

クリーニング

スーツをクリーニングに出した。	**I took my suit to the cleaners.** ＊cleaners＝クリーニング店
この店は、次のシーズンまで保管もしてくれる。	**This store can keep clothes until the next season.**
シミがきれいに落ちてよかった。	**I'm glad the stain came out.** ＊stain＝シミ
クリーニング店にワンピースを取りに行った。	**I picked up the dress from the cleaners.**
私のスーツが見当たらなかった。	**They couldn't find my suit.**
ほかの店舗に送られてしまったらしい。	**It turned out it had been sent to another store.**
ドライクリーニングって、意外とお金がかかる。	**Dry cleaning can be quite expensive.**
クリーニング代もバカにならない。	**The dry cleaning fee is not insignificant.** ＊insignificant＝わずかの
第3木曜日はドライ品が30パーセントオフ！	**Dry cleaning is 30% off on the third Thursday of the month!**
デリケートな素材って、毎回クリーニングに出すのが面倒。	**It's a hassle to take delicates to the cleaners every time.** ＊hassle＝面倒なこと　delicates＝デリケートな衣類
洗濯機で洗える服が一番。	**Machine washable clothes are the best.**
セーターはホームクリーニングで十分。	**Sweaters can be washed at home.**

服の手入れ

服のシミ抜きをした。	**I removed the stains from the clothes.**
服の毛玉を取った。	**I removed the fluff balls from the clothes.** ＊fluff ball＝毛玉
セーターの穴を補修した。	**I stitched up the hole in my sweater.** ＊stitch up ～＝～を繕う・縫う

10 家事

ジーンズの裾上げをしてもらった。 I had the hem taken up on my jeans. ＊hem＝縁、裾

ジーンズの裾上げをした。 I hemmed up my jeans. ＊hem up ～＝～を裾上げする

取れてしまったボタンを付けた。 I sewed on a button that came off. ＊sew［ソゥ］on ～＝～を縫い付ける

夏服に衣替えをした。 I changed my wardrobe for the summer. ＊「冬服」なら、summerをwinterに

防虫剤を入れて、冬服をしまった。 I added insect repellent and put away my winter clothes.

祖母の着物をきんちゃく袋にリメイクした。 I made my grandmother's kimono into a drawstring pouch. ＊drawstring pouch＝きんちゃく袋

片付け・掃除

片付け

部屋が散らかってる。 The room is messy. ＊messy＝散らかった

片付けなきゃ。 I'd better tidy up. ＊tidy up＝片付ける、整頓する

いらないものを全部捨てた。 I threw away everything that I didn't need. ＊throw away ～＝～を捨てる。throwの過去形はthrew

コタツを押し入れにしまった。 I put the kotatsu in the closet.

本棚の整理をした。 I arranged the books on the shelf. ＊arrange＝～をきちんと並べる

いらない本を古本屋さんに売った。 I sold the books I don't want to a secondhand bookstore. ＊secondhand＝中古の

掃除

自分の部屋を掃除した。 I cleaned up my room.

トイレを掃除した。 I cleaned the toilet.

家中を掃除した。 I cleaned the entire house.

大掃除をした。 I cleaned up everything.

掃除機をかけた。	**I vacuumed.** ＊vacuum［ヴァキューム］＝掃除機をかける
ロボット掃除機をかけた。	**I used the robot vacuum.**
床を水ぶきした。	**I wiped the floor with a wet cloth.** ＊「からぶき」なら、wet clothをdry clothに
テーブルをふいた。	**I wiped the table.** ＊wipe＝～をふく
窓ガラスをふいた。	**I wiped the windows.**
網戸を洗った。	**I cleaned the screen door.**
玄関を掃いた。	**I swept the entrance.** ＊sweep＝～を掃く。過去形はswept
家具にハタキをかけた。	**I dusted the furniture.** ＊dust＝～のほこりを払う
フローリングワイパーでペットの抜け毛を掃除した。	**I cleaned pet hair off the floor with the wiper.**
床にワックスをかけた。	**I waxed the floor.**
床にコロコロをかけた。	**I used a roller on the floor.**
台所の換気扇を掃除した。	**I cleaned the kitchen fan.**
エアコンのフィルターを掃除した。	**I cleaned the air conditioner filter.**
ピカピカになって気持ちいい！	**It feels great when everything is clean.** ＊cleanは、spick-and-span（こざっぱりした）でもOK

10 家事

そのほかの家事

シャンプーを詰め替えた。	**I refilled the shampoo bottle.**
廊下の電球が切れていた。	**The hall light burned out.** ＊burn out＝燃え尽きる
風呂場の電球を交換した。	**I replaced the bathroom light bulbs.** ＊light bulb＝電球
布団を干した。	**I aired out my futon.** ＊air out ～＝～を外気にさらす
布団を乾燥機にかけた。	**I aired my futon with the dryer.**
名もなき家事にうんざり。	**I'm sick of the endless, thankless housework.** ＊endless＝終わりのない　thankless＝感謝されない

雪かき

雪かきをした。	**I shoveled the snow.** *shovel＝～をシャベルでかく
家の前の道路の雪かきをした。	**I cleared the snow from the front walk.** *clear＝～を片付ける・きれいにする
イトウさんが雪かきを手伝ってくれた。	**Ito-san helped me clear the snow.**
屋根の雪下ろしをした。	**I cleared the snow from the roof.**
今年の冬は雪が多くて、雪かきが大変。	**There has been a lot of snow this year, so clearing it is hard work.**
除雪車が通った後の雪のかたまりを片付けた。	**I cleaned up the snow left by the snowplow.** *snowplow＝除雪車

ごみ・不用品

ごみにまつわる単語

ごみ	garbage［ガービッジ］
可燃ごみ	burnable garbage
不燃ごみ	non-burnable garbage
生ごみ	kitchen garbage
資源ごみ	recyclable garbage
粗大ごみ	oversized waste
缶	can
びん	glass bottle
ペットボトル	plastic bottle
プラスチック	plastic
ガラス	glass
ダンボール	cardboard
古紙	wastepaper
牛乳パック	milk carton
古着	used clothes
電池	battery
ごみ箱	garbage can
ごみ袋	garbage bag
ごみ集積所	garbage collection point
ごみ収集車	garbage truck

ごみ出し

明日の朝、必ずごみを出さなきゃ。	**I have to remember to take out the garbage tomorrow morning.**
今日は不燃ごみの日だった。	**It was collection day for non-burnable garbage today.**

可燃ごみを出した。	**I took out the burnable garbage.**
ダンボールを資源ごみに出した。	**I took out the cardboard as recyclable garbage.** ＊cardboard＝ダンボール
今朝、ごみを出し忘れちゃった。	**I forgot to take out the garbage this morning.**
ごみの分別は面倒くさい。	**It's a hassle to separate the garbage.** ＊hassle＝面倒なこと
市指定のごみ袋を切らしちゃった。	**I ran out of city-approved garbage bags.**
ごみ出しのルールを守らない人がいる。	**Someone doesn't follow the rules for taking out their garbage.** ＊follow＝～に従う
すごいごみの量になった。	**It's an awfully large amount of garbage.** ＊awfully＝とても、ものすごく
うちって、どうしてこんなにごみが出るんだろう？	**I wonder why we have so much garbage.**
カラスに生ごみを荒らされた！	**The crows messed up the kitchen garbage!** ＊mess up ～＝～を散らかす
粗大ごみの収集をネットで申し込んだ。	**I arranged a pickup for the oversized waste online.**
収集は18日だ。	**The collection date is the 18th.**

リサイクル

まだ使える家具は、リサイクル店に持っていこう。	**I'll take the reusable furniture to a secondhand shop.** ＊reusable＝再利用可能な　furniture＝家具
いらない食器は売ろう。	**I'll sell the tableware I don't need.**
不要品をアプリで売った。	**I sold my unwanted items via an app.** ＊via ～＝～によって
全部で2万円になった。やった！	**I got 20,000 yen for everything. Yay!**
キムラさんが机をもらってくれることになった。	**Kimura-san is going to take my desk.**

家事について 英語日記を書いてみよう

日々の家事について、英語で書いてみましょう。

食洗機、大助かり！

I bought a dishwasher. Now I can save some time. It was a bit expensive, but I think it's worth it.

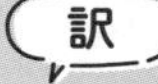

食洗機を買った。これで少し時間ができる。ちょっと高かったけど、その価値はあると思う。

「これで少し時間ができる」の「これで」は now、「少し時間ができる」は「少し時間を節約できる」と考えて、I can save some time と表します。「ちょっと高かった」の「ちょっと」は、a little でも OK。「その価値がある」は、it's worth it と表現します。

重曹の威力

Yuki told me she uses baking soda for cleaning, so I cleaned the kitchen sink with it. It made it spotless and sparkly. It also got rid of the bad smell. It was great!

ユキが重曹を掃除に使っていると聞いて、私も重曹で台所の流し台を掃除してみた。ピカピカになるし、においも取れた。最高！

「ユキが～と聞いて」は「ユキが～と教えてくれた」と考えて、Yuki told me (that) ～とすると、「ユキ」が情報源であることがはっきりします。「ピカピカ」は spotless（シミ・汚れのない）と sparkly（ピカピカの）を一緒に用いて、強調してみました。

換気扇の掃除が面倒

The kitchen fan got really greasy, but it's a pain in the neck to take it off and wash it.

台所の換気扇の油汚れがひどい。でも、取り外して洗うのは面倒くさいなぁ。

「台所の換気扇」は kitchen fan。「換気扇の油汚れがひどい」は、get greasy（油で汚れた状態になる）と really（とても）を組み合わせて、The kitchen fan got really greasy とすれば簡単です。「面倒くさい」は a pain in the neck で。in the neck は省略 OK です。

セーターが縮んじゃった…

I dried a sweater in the dryer by mistake and it shrunk. I just bought it this winter ... I'm too careless.

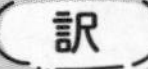

間違えて、セーターを乾燥機に入れたら縮んでしまった。この冬買ったばかりなのに…。私って、本当に不注意だな。

「～を乾燥機に入れる」は put ～ in the dryer ですが、これだと入れる行為のみを指します。入れて乾かしたので縮んだという状況から、ここでは put（～を入れる）ではなく dry（～を乾かす）を用いました。「縮む」は shrink。過去形は shrunk または shrank です。

11 仕事

仕事全般

部署名を表す単語

※部署名の英語表記は、会社により異なります。
dept.はdepartment(部)の略です。

秘書室	secretarial office	渉外部	client relations dept.
経営企画室	corporate planning office	営業部	sales dept.
人事部	personnel dept.	企画部	planning dept.
総務部	general affairs dept.	マーケティング部	marketing dept.
法務部	legal affairs dept.	編集部	editorial dept.
経理部	accounting dept.	海外事業部	overseas dept.
広報部	public relations dept.	生産管理部	production control dept.

職業 (→ p. 110「職業を表す単語」を参照)

仕事への意気込み

もっと仕事を頑張るぞ!	**I'm going to work harder!**
早く仕事を覚えたい。	**I want to get used to my job soon.** ＊get used to ～＝～に慣れる
集中して仕事に取り組もう。	**I should focus and buckle down to my job.** ＊buckle down to ～＝～に身を入れる
お客さんに信頼されたい。	**I want to gain the trust of the customers.**
いい商品を開発したい。	**I want to develop good products.** ＊develop＝～を開発する

売り上げナンバーワンを目指すぞ！ I will aim for top sales!
＊aim［エイム］for ～＝～を目指す

仕事の調子

最近は仕事が順調だ。 Work has been going well lately.

最近、絶好調だ。 I'm in top condition these days.

最近、不調だ。 I'm in a slump these days.

だんだん仕事をうまくこなせるようになってきた。 I've been getting better and better at my job.

仕事がたまっている。 I have a pile of work to take care of.
＊a pile of ～＝山積みの～

今日は仕事がはかどった。 I got a lot of work done today.

今日は効率よく仕事できた。 I worked efficiently today.
＊efficiently＝効率的に

生産的な1週間だった。 I had a productive week.

私って手際が悪いんだろうな。 I think I'm inefficient.
＊inefficient＝非効率的な、要領の悪い

仕事の悩み・トラブル

仕事量が多過ぎる。 I have too much work.

仕事で大きなミスをしてしまった。 I made a huge mistake at work.

過労で倒れそう。 I'm going to break down from overwork.
＊break down＝壊れる、倒れる

うつになりそうだ。 I feel like I'm getting depressed.
＊get depressed＝うつになる

この仕事に向いていないと思う。 I don't think I'm cut out for this job.
＊be cut out for ～＝～に向いている

今の会社は自分に合わない。 This company doesn't suit me.
＊suit＝～に合う

職場の人間関係がぎくしゃくしている。 Interpersonal relationships at our office are really awkward.
＊awkward＝ぎくしゃくした、気まずい

同僚とケンカをしてしまった。 I had an argument with a co-worker.
＊argument＝口論

サトウさんは会社を休みがちだ。 **Sato-san is often absent from work.**

部下が指示に従ってくれない。 **My workers won't listen to me.**

＊one's worker＝〜の部下

フカイさんのパワハラに悩まされている。 **Ms. Fukai's harassment makes me feel frustrated.**

サナダさんって、セクハラ発言が多い。 **Mr. Sanada says a lot of things that are inappropriate.**

＊inappropriate（不適切な）は、「道徳的、倫理的に間違った」という含みがあり、セクハラを暗示する

上司と部下との板挟みだ。 **I'm torn between my boss and junior worker.**

＊be torn between 〜 and ...＝〜と…の板挟みになる

やる気が出ない

はぁ、明日は月曜日か〜。 **Aw, tomorrow is blue Monday.**

＊blue Monday＝（休み明けの）憂うつな月曜日

会社に行きたくないな。 **I don't want to go to work.**

最近、どうもやる気が出ない。 **I haven't had any motivation lately.**

＊motivation＝やる気

5月病かな？ **Maybe I'm having the so-called "May blues."**

＊so-called＝いわゆる　blues＝憂うつ

今の仕事に情熱を持てない。 **I just can't get excited about my current job.**

＊current＝現在の

忙しい

今日はかなり忙しかった。 **I was extremely busy today.**

今日はやけにバタバタしていた。 **It was awfully hectic today.**

＊awfully＝ひどく　hectic＝てんてこ舞いの

今週は忙しくなりそうだ。 **I think this week is going to be busy.**

繁忙期で忙しい。 **It's a busy period and we're going crazy.**

＊period＝期間　go crazy＝狂乱状態に陥る

決算期なのですごく忙しい。 **It's an accounting period, so it's really busy.**

＊accounting period＝決算期

貧乏暇なしって感じ。 The poor have no time for leisure, I guess.
＊leisure［リージャー］＝余暇、暇

仕事に追われている。 I'm swamped with work.
＊be swamped with ～＝～に忙殺される

新プロジェクトで忙しい。 I'm busy with the new project.

最終報告書の作成で忙しい。 I'm busy writing the final report.

忙しさもひと段落だ。 Things have finally settled down.

人手不足

人手が足りない！ We don't have enough manpower!

人手を増やしてほしい。 We need more manpower.

うちの部は、慢性的な人手不足。 Our department is chronically understaffed.
＊chronically＝慢性的に　understaffed＝人員不足の

猫の手も借りたいくらいだ。 We need all the help we can get.

辞める人が多過ぎる。 There are too many people quitting.
＊quit［クイット］＝辞める

誰か新しい人が入るのかな。 I wonder if we'll get any new employees.

人事部が欠員を補充してくれない。 The personnel department hasn't replaced them yet.

アルバイトを入れてほしい。 I wish they would consider hiring some part-timers.
＊consider ～ing＝～することを検討する

日々の仕事

通勤（→ p. 162「通勤・通学」を参照）

出社

8時半に出社した。 I got to work at 8:30.

いつもより早く、8時に出社した。 I got to work at 8:00, earlier than usual.

まだ誰も来ていなかった。 No one had come yet.

誰もいないオフィスは、仕事がはかどる。 I can get a lot of things done when there's no one else in the office.

ヨコタさんがもう出社していた。 Ms. Yokota was already at work.

寝坊して、11 時に出社した。 I overslept and got to work at 11:00.

＊oversleep＝寝坊する。過去形はoverslept

朝礼に遅刻してしまった。 I was late for the morning meeting.

A 社に立ち寄ってから出社した。 I stopped by A Company before I went to work.

病院に寄ってから出社した。 I stopped by the hospital on my way to work.

リモートワーク

今日は在宅勤務の日だった。 I worked from home today.

出社は週に 2 日だけ。 I only go to the office two days a week.

着替えも化粧もいらないからラク〜。 I don't need to get dressed or put on makeup, it's great!

すっかり服を買わなくなってしまった。 I hardly ever buy clothes anymore.

＊hardly ever do＝ほとんど〜しない

オンとオフの切り替えが難しい。 It's hard to switch on and off.

今日は誰とも話さなかった。 I didn't talk to anyone today.

オフィスでの雑談が恋しいな。 I miss the office chatter.

＊chatter＝無駄話、おしゃべり

上司に小言を言われなくて済むのはうれしい。 I'm happy I don't need to listen to my boss's complaints.

チャットで監視されてる気分。 I feel like they are watching me through the chat.

会社のムダな飲み会がなくなって、快適！ It's great that the pointless work drinking parties have disappeared!

たまには会社のみんなと食事にでも行きたい。	**I'd like to have a meal with people from work now and then.** ＊now and then＝時々、たまに
1日1回は外に出ないとダメだね。	**It's no good if you don't go outside at least once a day.**

仕事の電話

今日は電話が多かった。	**I got a lot of calls today.**
電話対応ばかりで、仕事がはかどらなかった。	**I spent all day answering phones and didn't get much work done.**
会社の電話を受けるのが苦手だ。	**I'm not good at taking calls at work.**
内線と外線を間違えちゃった。	**I mixed up the internal and external lines.** ＊mix up ～＝～を取り違える
保留したつもりで切ってしまった。	**I tried to put them on hold, but I ended the call.** ＊put ～ on hold＝～を電話口で待たせる
タカノさんと、電話で1時間も話した。	**I talked with Ms. Takano on the phone for an hour.**
商品に関する問い合わせの電話を受けた。	**I got a call about one of our products.**
クレームの電話を受けた。	**I got a complaint call.** ＊complaint＝クレーム
クレーム電話の対応に追われた。	**I spent all my time answering complaint calls.**
社用携帯が故障した。	**My company phone broke.**
うちの会社はまだファクスが現役だ。	**We still use fax at my company.**

報告書・資料

午後は報告書を2本、書き上げた。	**I wrote two reports this afternoon.**
パワポで会議用の資料を作った。	**I made the materials for the meeting using PowerPoint.** ＊material＝資料
カトウさんに報告書を提出した。	**I submitted a report to Mr. Kato.** ＊submit＝～を提出する

報告書まで手が回らなかった。	**I couldn't get around to the report.** ＊get around to ～＝～に取りかかる余裕ができる
明日には報告書をまとめなきゃ。	**I have to finalize my report tomorrow.** ＊finalize＝～をまとめる
レポートを書くのもひと苦労だ。	**Writing the report is a struggle.** ＊struggle＝苦労
資料の準備は間に合った。	**I got the materials ready just in time.**
オオクラさんがまとめた資料は、よくできていた。	**Ms. Okura's documents were really well done.** ＊well done＝よくできた

会議

10 時から会議があった。	**There was a meeting starting at 10:00.**
明日は 9 時から会議だ。	**There's a meeting tomorrow at 9:00.**
新規事業の方向性について話し合った。	**We talked about the direction of the new business.**
活発に意見が交わされた。	**Everyone actively traded their opinions.** ＊trade＝～を交換する
厳しい意見も出た。	**There were some pretty harsh opinions, too.** ＊harsh＝厳しい
結論は次回に持ち越された。	**The conclusion was carried over to the next meeting.** ＊carry over ～＝～を持ち越す
難しい問題だった。	**It was a difficult issue.** ＊issue＝議題、問題
少し考える時間が必要だ。	**We need time to think.**
前向きに検討したい。	**I want to give it a positive consideration.** ＊consideration＝検討、熟考
有意義な会議だった。	**That was a worthwhile meeting.** ＊worthwhile＝価値のある
意味のない会議だった。	**That was a meaningless meeting.**
会議中、ウトウトしてしまった。	**I dozed off during the meeting.** ＊doze off＝ウトウトする

うちの会社、会議が多過ぎるよ。	**We have too many meetings at work.**
うちの会議は長過ぎる！ うんざり。	**Our meetings are too long! I'm sick and tired of them.**
会議が多くて、仕事が全然はかどらない。	**We have so many meetings that I can't get any work done.**

オンライン会議

明日は14時からオンライン会議だ。	**I have an online meeting from 2:00 p.m. tomorrow.**
今日はオンライン会議が2つあった。	**I had two online meetings today.**
オンライン会議の前は緊張する。	**I feel nervous before online meetings.**
オンライン会議は発言のタイミングがつかみにくい。	**It's hard to get the right time to speak during online meetings.**
画面共有に手間取った。	**It took me a while to share my screen with others.**
画面共有のやり方を覚えないと。	**I need to learn how to share my screen.**
Zoom会議があるから、上半身だけは着替えた。	**I have a Zoom meeting, so I just changed my shirt.**
下はジャージを着ていた。	**My bottom half was sweat pants.**
ビデオオンだったから、サボれなかった。	**It was a meeting with video, so I couldn't be lazy.**
ビデオオンで参加するように言われた。	**We were told to participate with our videos on.**
ビデオオフで参加した。	**I participated with my video off.**
ビデオオフだったから、部長の話をあまり聞いていなかった。	**It was a meeting without video, so I didn't really listen to what my boss was saying.**
音声をオンにするのを忘れていた。	**I forgot to turn on my mic.**

＊**mic**［マイク］

オンライン会議だと、部屋の様子も映っちゃう。	**They can see my room in online meetings.**
背景を変えた。	**I changed my background.**
ビデオ会議にタマが乱入!	**Tama interrupted my video meeting!**
みんなに「可愛い」と言われていた。	**Everyone said she was cute.**
途中で夫が映り込んでしまった。	**My husband accidentally appeared in the video.**
子どもたちの騒ぐ声が入ってしまった。	**They could hear my kids running around.**
ネット接続が悪くて、何度もフリーズしちゃった。	**My connection was bad and it kept freezing.**
ネット接続のトラブルがなくて、ひと安心。	**I'm glad there weren't any connection problems.**

プレゼンテーション

プレゼンの準備をしなきゃ。	**I have to prepare for my presentation.**
プレゼンの準備をした。	**I prepared for my presentation.**
午後、新規プロジェクトについてのプレゼンをした。	**I made a presentation about our new project this afternoon.**
プレゼンはうまくいった。	**The presentation went well.** ＊go well＝うまくいく
プレゼンの出来は、あまりよくなかった。	**The presentation wasn't done so well.**
緊張したけど、何とか乗り切った。	**I was nervous, but I made it through somehow.** ＊make it through＝何とかやり遂げる
最初、声が震えた。	**My voice got shaky in the beginning.**
もっと堂々と話せるようになりたい。	**I want to be able to speak more confidently.**

質問がたくさん出た。	**There were a lot of questions.**
質問にちゃんと答えられてよかった。	**I'm glad I could answer the questions properly.**
時間が足りなかった。	**There wasn't enough time.**

外回り

午後はずっと外回りだった。	**I was visiting clients all afternoon.**
道に迷って、B社との約束に遅れてしまった。	**I got lost on my way and was late for my appointment at B Company.**
時間が空いたので、喫茶店で休んだ。	**I had some free time, so I relaxed at a café.**

契約・ノルマ・売上

契約を結んだ！ やった！	**I sealed a deal! All right!** ＊seal a deal＝取引をまとめる
どうにか契約にこぎ着けた。	**I somehow managed to get a contract done.** ＊manage to 〜＝何とか〜する
大口の契約を取り付けた。	**I got a big contract.**
今月はノルマを達成できそうだ。	**It looks like I'll be able to fill my quota this month.** ＊fill＝〜（要求など）を満たす quota［クウォウタ］＝割り当て、ノルマ
今月はノルマを達成できないかもしれない。	**I might not be able to fill my quota this month.**
何とかしてノルマを達成したい。	**I want to fill my quota somehow.**
無事にノルマを達成できて、ほっとした。	**I was relieved that I was able to fill my quota okay.** ＊okay＝うまく、ちゃんと
ノルマを達成できなかった。	**I couldn't fill my quota.**
売上がなかなか伸びない。	**Sales aren't really increasing.**
今月の売上目標を達成した。	**We achieved our sales target for this month.**

セガワさんが今期のトップセールスだった。	**Segawa-san was this period's top seller.**

パソコン（→ p. 592「パソコン・ネット」参照）

オフィス機器

新しい複合機の使い方が、よくわからない。	**I don't really know how to use the new MFP.** ＊MFP＝複合機。multifunction peripheralの略
スキャナーを導入してほしい。	**We need a scanner.**
コピー機の調子が悪かった。	**The copier was acting up.** ＊act up＝(機械などが)不調である
またプリンターの調子が悪くなった。	**The printer was on the blink again.** ＊on the blink＝(機械などの)調子が悪くて
プリンターが紙詰まりを起こした。	**The printer got jammed.** ＊get jammed＝(紙が)詰まる。getの過去形はgot
ファクスの紙がなくなった。	**The fax ran out of paper.** ＊run out of ～＝～を使い果たす。runの過去形はran
替えのインクを買っておかなきゃ。	**I need to buy replacement ink.**

名刺

A 社の人たちと名刺を交換した。	**I exchanged business cards with people from A Company.**
あいにく名刺を切らしていた。	**Unfortunately, I was all out of business cards.** ＊be out of ～＝～を切らしている
名刺を 200 枚注文した。	**I ordered 200 business cards.**
最近、名刺交換する機会が減った。	**I have less opportunities to exchange business cards these days.**

オフィスの掃除・整理整頓

事務所の掃除当番だった。	**It was my turn to clean the office.** ＊turn＝順番
事務所に掃除機をかけた。	**I vacuumed the office.** ＊vacuum［ヴァキューム］＝～に掃除機をかける
給湯室を片付けた。	**I cleaned the office kitchen.**

清掃員さんが掃除してくれた。	**The cleaner cleaned the office.**
会社の大掃除があった。	**We had major cleaning at work.**
不用品がたくさん出てきた。	**There were a lot of things that weren't being used.**
机の上に資料が山積みだった。	**Documents were piled up on my desk.** ＊piled up＝積み重なった
机周りを整理した。	**I organized my desk.** ＊organize＝～を整理する
古い書類をシュレッダーにかけた。	**I shredded some old documents.**
いらない資料をごみに出した。	**I threw out some old materials.**
すっきりした気分で、仕事もはかどった。	**I felt refreshed and got a lot of work done.**

残業

今日も残業だった。	**I had to work overtime again today.** ＊work overtime＝残業をする
今日は２時間残業した。	**I worked overtime for two hours today.**
徹夜で仕事をした。	**I worked throughout the night.**
ここのところ、残業続きだ。	**Recently, I've been working overtime regularly.**
今日はノー残業デーだった。	**There was no overtime allowed today.** ＊overtime＝残業
今日は残業しなくてすんだ。	**I managed to finish today without having to work overtime.** ＊manage to ～＝何とか～する
先月の残業時間は、30時間。	**I worked 30 hours of overtime last month.**
今日もサービス残業だった。	**I worked off the clock again today.** ＊work off the clock＝サービス残業をする
家に仕事を持ち帰った。	**I brought my work home with me.**

明日こそは定時で帰るぞ！	**Tomorrow I'm definitely leaving the office on time!**
残業代が出るのは助かる。	**Overtime pay helps.**
残業代がつくのが、せめてもの救いだ。	**Thankfully, I at least get paid for overtime.**
管理職になったから、残業代がつかない。	**Now that I'm a manager, I'm not getting paid for overtime.**

接待

A 社の人を接待した。	**We wined and dined the people from A Company.** ＊wine and dine ～＝～を高級な酒と食事でもてなす
なかなか有意義な会だった。	**We had a very worthwhile meeting.** ＊worthwhile＝価値のある
A 社の人と腹を割って話せてよかった。	**I was glad we were able to talk openly and freely with the people from A Company.**
アンドウ部長は酒癖が悪かった。	**Mr. Ando drank too much and caused problems.** ＊直訳は「アンドウ部長は飲み過ぎて面倒を起こした」
今日は接待ゴルフだった。	**I went golfing with some customers today.**
たまの休みぐらい、寝ていたいよ。	**I wish I could at least get some sleep on these rare days off.** ＊rare＝めったにない　day off＝非番の日、休日
打ちっ放しの成果を発揮するチャンス！	**This is a chance to show what I've been doing on the driving range!** ＊driving range＝(打ちっ放しの)練習場

出張 (→ p. 177「特急・新幹線」、p. 464「飛行機」も参照)

明日は福岡に出張だ。	**I'm going on a business trip to Fukuoka tomorrow.**
2 年ぶりの大阪出張だ。	**I'm going on a business trip to Osaka for the first time in two years.**

駅前のビジネスホテルを予約した。	**I made a reservation at an economy hotel right by the station.**
ここのところ出張続きだ。	**I've been making a lot of business trips.**
最近は以前ほど出張がない。	**I don't make as many business trips as I used to.**
今日は名古屋に日帰り出張だった。	**I had a one-day business trip to Nagoya today.**
1泊2日で青森に出張した。	**I made an overnight business trip to Aomori.**
たまには出張もいいな。	**I like a business trip every once in a while.**
今回は飛行機で行った。	**I flew there this time.** ＊**fly**＝飛行機で行く。過去形は**flew**［フルー］
出張の醍醐味（だいごみ）は、ご当地名物を食べられることだ。	**The best part of business trips is trying out the local cuisine.** ＊**try out** 〜＝〜を試食する **cuisine**［クィズィーン］＝料理
来月は広州に出張だ。	**Next month I have a business trip to Guangzhou.** ＊**Guangzhou**［グワンジョウ］＝広州
久しぶりの海外出張でワクワクする。	**I'm excited about my first overseas business trip in a while.**

研修・セミナー

今日はIT研修だった。	**We had IT training today.**
来週は新人研修だ。	**We have new employee training next week.**
ビジネス英語の研修があった。	**There was a training session for business English.**
私はオンラインで参加した。	**I attended it online.**
新しい税制度について、オンラインセミナーを受講した。	**I attended an online seminar about the new tax system.**

11 仕事

現場研修で販売店に行った。	**We went to a store for on-site training.** ＊on-site＝現場の
著作権についてのセミナーがあった。	**There was a seminar on copyrights.** ＊copyright＝著作権
すごく役立った。	**It was really useful.**
講師がよかった。	**The lecturer was really good.**
たいした内容じゃなかった。	**There wasn't much to learn.**
途中で眠くなってしまった。	**I got sleepy during the seminar.**
チャットで講師に質問した。	**I asked the lecturer a question in the chat.**

グローバル化

来月から会議を英語でやるんだって！	**Starting next month, we're going to have our meetings in English!**
みんな、英語話せるのかな？	**I wonder if everyone speaks English.**
英語で会議なんて、できるわけない。	**There's no way we'll be able to hold a meeting in English.**
英語でプレゼンすることになった。どうしよう！	**I have to give a presentation in English. What am I going to do?**
来年から、TOEIC の受験が必須になった。	**Starting next year, taking the TOEIC test will become a requirement.** ＊requirement＝必要条件
スコアが査定に関わるらしい。	**It seems the scores will reflect on our employee assessments.** ＊reflect on ～＝～に反映する　assessment＝評価
うちの社では、外国人スタッフが増えてきている。	**Our company is hiring more employees from other countries.** ＊hire＝～を雇う
うちの社では、グローバル化が進んでいる。	**Our company is globalizing more and more.**
うちの社も、もっとグローバル化を進める必要があるだろう。	**Our company needs to become more global.**

外国人スタッフと英語で話すのは楽しい。	**It's fun to speak English with employees from other countries.**
アヅマさんは英語のほかに中国語とスペイン語ができるらしい。	**I heard Azuma-san can speak Chinese and Spanish as well as English.**

会社の行事

今日はヤマダさんの歓迎会だった。	**We had Mr. Yamada's welcoming party today.** ＊welcome partyとも言う
新人歓迎会だった。	**We had a welcome party for our new employees.**
金曜日はタシロさんの送別会だ。	**This Friday we're going to have Ms. Tashiro's farewell party.** ＊「送別会」は、going-away partyやsend-offとも言う
歓送迎会をした。	**We had a welcome and going-away party.**
入社式だった。	**We had a new-employee ceremony.**
明日から社員旅行だ。	**We're going on a company trip tomorrow.**
社員旅行で伊豆に行った。	**We went to Izu on a company trip.**
会社のボウリング大会があった。	**We had a company bowling event.**
会社の健康診断があった。	**We had a company physical check-up.**
社屋の引っ越しがあった。	**We moved to a new office building.**
創立50周年記念パーティーだった。	**Our company had a 50th anniversary party.**

ランチ・同僚と一杯

ランチ（→ p. 365「外食」も参照）

今日は社食で食べた。	**I ate at the company cafeteria today.** ＊company cafeteria＝社員食堂

11 仕事

うちの会社は社食がおいしくてうれしい。	**I'm glad our company cafeteria serves such good food.**
社食のご飯は、味がイマイチ。	**The food at our company cafeteria is just okay.**
社食は安いので助かる。	**It's great that our company cafeteria has reasonable prices.**
コンビニでおにぎりを買ってきた。	**I bought rice balls at a convenience store.**
仕事をしながらパンをかじった。	**I ate some bread while working.**
弁当の出前を取った。	**I had a bento delivered.** ＊deliver＝～を配達する
ランチはUber Eatsで配達を頼んだ。	**I ordered lunch from Uber Eats.**
幕の内弁当を食べた。	**I had a makunouchi bento.**
弁当を持っていった。	**I brought my own lunch.**
会議室で弁当を食べた。	**I ate my lunch in the meeting room.**
妻が作ってくれた弁当を食べた。	**I ate the lunch my wife made for me.**
昼食をササッと済ませ、仕事に戻った。	**I had a quick lunch and went back to work.**
クロベさんとランチミーティングをした。	**I had a lunch meeting with Kurobe-san.**
忙しくて、お昼を食べる暇がなかった。	**I was so busy that I didn't have time to eat lunch.**
4時ごろ、ようやくお昼を食べた。	**I finally got to eat lunch at around 4:00.**

同僚と一杯 （→ p. 379「お酒」も参照）

仕事の後、ホソイさんと一杯やった。	**I had a drink with Hosoi-san after work.**
いつもの店に行った。	**We went to the usual spot.**

五反田のABCバーに行った。	**We went to ABC Bar in Gotanda.**
部長の行きつけの店に連れていってもらった。	**My manager took me to her favorite restaurant.** ＊「店」は、状況によりrestaurantやbarなどを使い分ける
ヤマモトさんがおごってくれた。	**Mr. Yamamoto treated me.** ＊treat＝～におごる
若手の分も私が払った。	**I footed the bill for the younger guys.** ＊foot the bill＝勘定を持つ
今日は打ち上げだった。	**We had a good-job party today.**
みんなでカラオケに行った。	**We all went to karaoke together.**
朝までコースだった。	**We were out until morning.**
1次会で帰った。	**I went home after the first party.**
たまにはパーッとやるのもいいな。	**It's good to cut loose every now and then.** ＊cut loose＝羽目を外す　every now and then＝たまに
会社の飲み会はあまり行きたくないな。	**I don't really want to go to the company drinking party.**
部長は酔うとウザ絡みしてくる。	**The boss becomes a nuisance when he's drunk.** ＊nuisance［ニューサンス］＝迷惑な人
酔うと説教くさくなるのがイヤ。	**I don't like how he gets preachy when he's drunk.** ＊preachy＝説教じみた

11 仕事

人事・給与・休暇

人事

営業部に異動の希望を出した。	**I submitted a transfer request to the sales department.** ＊transfer＝異動
明日は人事異動の発表だ。	**Changes in personnel will be announced tomorrow.** ＊personnel＝人事
来週から企画部に異動だ。	**I'll be moving to the planning department next week.**
来週から、ナリタさんのチームに異動だ。	**I'll be transferring to Mr. Narita's team next week.** ＊transfer to ～＝～に異動する

ようやく、広報部に異動になった。	**Finally, I got transferred to the PR department.** ＊get transferred to 〜＝〜に異動になる PRはpublic relationsの略
異動の希望が通ってうれしい。	**I'm happy my transfer request went through.**
今回の異動は不服だ。	**I'm not happy with my new post.**
タムラさん、総務部に異動するらしい。	**Rumor has it that Ms. Tamura will be transferring to the general affairs department.** ＊rumor has it that 〜＝〜というううわさである
キタノさん、子会社に出向だって。	**Kitano-san is being temporarily transferred to our subsidiary.** ＊temporarily＝一時的に　subsidiary＝子会社

昇進

課長に昇進した。	**I've been promoted to department manager.** ＊promote＝〜を昇進させる
早く昇進したいな。	**I hope I get promoted soon.**
やったー、来月から昇進だ！	**Yeees! I've got a promotion coming next month!** ＊promotion＝昇進
年収が 50 万円くらい上がる。	**My annual income will go up by about 500,000 yen.**
昇進にはあまり興味がない。	**I'm not really interested in a promotion.**
昇進しても、責任が重くなるだけ。	**Being promoted just means more responsibility.**

転勤

4 月から、大阪に転勤が決まった。	**They decided to transfer me to Osaka in April.** ＊transfer＝〜を転勤させる
転勤はおそらく 2 年くらいだろう。	**My transfer will probably last about two years.** ＊transfer＝転勤

向こうに何年いることになるのか、わからない。	**I don't know how long I'll be over there.**
単身赴任することになりそうだ。	**It looks like I won't be able to take my family with me.**
家族も一緒に行く予定だ。	**I'm planning on bringing my family with me.**
転勤の多い仕事だから、仕方ない。	**This job calls for a lot of transfers, so it can't be helped.** ＊call for ～＝～を必要とする

リストラ・解雇

リストラされるのは怖い。	**Restructuring sounds scary.** ＊restructuring＝リストラ
うちの会社もリストラを考えているらしい。	**Rumor has it that our company is thinking about restructuring.** ＊rumor has it that ～＝～といううわさである
肩たたきされた。	**I was told I was no longer needed.**
リストラされてしまった。	**I got laid off due to the restructuring.** ＊lay off ～＝～を一時解雇する。layの過去分詞はlaid
クビになった。	**I got fired.** ＊fire＝～をクビにする
アカサカさんが解雇された。何があったんだろう。	**Akasaka-san was dismissed. I wonder what happened.** ＊be dismissed＝解雇される

退職・休職

上司に退職の意向を伝えた。	**I told my supervisor about my intention to quit.** ＊supervisor＝上司　quit［クイット］＝辞める
上司に退職願を出した。	**I submitted a letter of resignation to my supervisor.** ＊resignation＝退職
会社が早期退職希望者を募集している。	**My company is asking everyone if they want to retire early.**
早期退職も悪くないかもしれないな。	**Early retirement might not be so bad.**
キノシタさんに引き留められた。	**Mr. Kinoshita tried to make me stay.**

彼は退職について理解してくれた。	**He was understanding about my leaving.**
「新しい職場でも頑張って」と言われた。	**He wished me good luck at my new job.**
仕事はしっかり引き継ごう。	**I'm going to give my replacement a proper handover.** ＊replacement＝後任者　proper＝適切な　handover＝引き継ぎ
スダさんが仕事を引き継いだ。	**Ms. Suda took over my old post.** ＊take over ～＝～を引き継ぐ。takeの過去形はtook
退職前に、有休を消化したい。	**I want to use all of my paid vacation days before I leave my job.**
今日はいよいよ退職の日だった。	**Today was the day that I finally left the company.**
今日は最後の出社日だった。	**Today was my last day at work.**
部下がパーティーを開いてくれた。	**My workers threw me a party.** ＊throw ～ a party＝～のためにパーティーを開く
しばらくはのんびりするつもりだ。	**I'm going to relax for a while.**
しばらくは子育てに専念しよう。	**I'm going to dedicate my time to raising my child.** ＊dedicate ～ to ...＝…に～をささげる
復帰は来年９月の予定だ。	**I'm planning to return to work next September.**
半年間、休職することにした。	**I'll take a leave of absence for half a year.** ＊leave of absence＝休職
ヨシノさんは休職中だ。	**Ms. Yoshino is taking a leave of absence.**
オダさんが今月で辞める。寂しくなるな。	**Mr. Oda is quitting this month. I'll miss him.**
ヤマザキさんが退職した。	**Yamazaki-san retired.**
彼は退職代行サービスを使って離職願いを出した。	**He used a resignation agency service to submit his resignation.** ＊resignation＝退職、辞職
彼の仕事は誰が引き継ぐんだろう？	**I wonder who will take over his job.**

彼女はみんなに丁寧にあいさつして回っていた。	**She went around and greeted everyone politely.**
彼は誰にもあいさつしないで辞めちゃった。	**He quit without greeting anyone.**
彼はABC社に転職するらしい。	**I hear he's moving to ABC Company.**
彼女は介護離職したらしい。	**She quit her job to take care of her sick family member.**
夫は今年で定年だ。	**It's the year for my husband's mandatory retirement.** ＊mandatory＝(法律・規則によって)必須の
うちの会社は定年退職がない。	**Our company doesn't have mandatory retirement.**

給料

やった！ 今日は給料日！	**All right! Today is payday!** ＊payday＝給料日
今の給料には満足している。	**I'm happy with my current salary.** ＊current＝現在の　salary＝給料
今の給料には不満だ。	**I'm not happy with my current salary.**
今月も給料が少ないなぁ。	**This month's salary is low, as always.**
給料、もっと上がらないかなぁ。	**I wish I could get paid more.**
手取りで20万円未満では苦しい。	**A salary of less than 200,000 yen after taxes isn't enough at all.**
出来高制ではキツイ。	**Being paid by the job is tough.** ＊pay ～ by the job＝～に出来高制で支払う
夫の給料だけでは生活できない。	**We can't live on my husband's salary alone.**
給料は少ないけれど、やりがいのある仕事だ。	**The pay is low, but it's a rewarding job.** ＊rewarding＝やりがいのある
家賃補助が出るのはありがたい。	**I'm glad I get rent allowance.** ＊allowance＝手当て

特定の資格を取ると、手当てが加算される。	**I will get extra pay if I get a certain qualification.**

ボーナス

ボーナス出るかな？	**I wonder if I'll get a bonus.** ＊アメリカではボーナスは業績などに応じて支払われ、日本のように定期的に支給されるわけではない
やった！ ボーナスが出た！	**Yes! I got a bonus!**
ボーナスは、手取りで 45 万円だった。	**I got a 450,000-yen bonus after taxes.**
2 カ月分のボーナスが支給された。	**I got a bonus of two month's pay.**
ボーナス、ほんの少しだった。	**The bonus was really small.**
まぁ、ないよりマシか。	**Well, it's better than nothing.**
今年はボーナスが増えた。	**My bonus increased this year.**
ボーナスで何を買おうかな？	**What should I buy with my bonus?**
ボーナスは全部貯金に回そう。	**I should put all of my bonus into my savings.** ＊savings＝預金口座
あーあ、ボーナスなしか。	**Darn, no bonus.** ＊darnは、不満や怒りなどを表す

休暇

今日は会社を休んだ。	**I took a day off from work.** ＊take a day off＝1日休暇を取る
具合が悪くて会社を休んだ。	**I felt sick so I took the day off.**
来週、代休を取ろうっと。	**I'm going to take a make-up day off next week.** ＊make-upは、「埋め合わせの」という意味
午前半休にした。	**I took the morning off.**
半休を取って病院に行った。	**I took a half day off and went to the hospital.**
有休がだいぶたまっている。	**I have a lot of paid vacation days saved up.** ＊save up ～＝～をためる　paid vacation＝有給休暇

今日は有休を取った。	**I took a paid vacation day today.**
会社を休んでゆずのコンサートに行った。	**I took a day off to go to Yuzu's concert.**
長期休暇を取りたいなぁ。	**I want to take a long vacation.**
ゴールデンウイークは、９日間も休める。	**I have nine days off for Golden Week.**
夏休みは取れそうにないな。	**I don't think I'll be able to get a summer vacation.**
10月に、遅めの夏休みを取ることにした。	**I decided to take a late summer vacation in October.**
年末年始はゆっくりできそうだ。	**It looks like I'll be able to relax over the New Year's holiday.**
来月から産休に入る。	**I'm taking maternity leave from next month.** ＊maternity leave＝産休
キムラさんが産休に入った。	**Ms. Kimura is now on maternity leave.**
育休を取ることにした。	**I decided to be on childcare leave.** ＊childcare leave＝育児休暇
うちの会社でも、育休を取る男性が増えてきた。	**More and more guys are taking childcare leave at my company.**
育休を取る男性がもっと増えるといいな。	**It would be good if more guys take childcare leave.**
ササキさんは今、介護休暇を取っている。	**Sasaki-san is on caregiving leave now.** ＊caregiving leave＝介護休暇
今年は勤続25年で、１週間のリフレッシュ休暇が取れる。	**This year is my 25th year working, so I can take a week off to refresh.**

ワークライフバランス

仕事に追われるだけの生活は嫌だ。	**A lifestyle that's just work isn't for me.**

11 仕事

家族と過ごす時間は削れない。	I don't want to miss out on family time. ＊miss out on ～＝～を逃す
趣味を楽しむ時間も確保したい。	I want to keep enough time to enjoy my hobbies.
今の働き方は自分にぴったりだ。	This work style is perfect for me.
仕事と趣味のバランスがちょうどいい。	My work-hobbies balance is just right.
もう少しのんびり働ける会社に転職したい。	I want to move to a more relaxed company.
子どもが小さいうちは、時短勤務も仕方ない。	I can only work short hours while the kids are young.

上司・同僚・部下

上司のこと

オクムラさんは、尊敬できる上司だ。	Mr. Okumura is a boss I can look up to. ＊look up to ～＝～を尊敬する
彼はいつでも親身になって相談に乗ってくれる。	He's always really nice and ready to give advice.
彼女には何でも相談できる。	I can talk to her about anything.
彼は部下に信頼されている。	He's well trusted by his people. ＊one's peopleで「～の部下」の意味
メグロさんに、仕事について相談した。	I went to Mr. Meguro for advice about my job.
的確なアドバイスをもらった。	He gave me appropriate advice.
カワハラさんにこっぴどく叱られた。	Ms. Kawahara bawled me out. ＊bawl ～ out＝～をひどく叱る
彼女は部下に厳し過ぎると思う。	I think she's too strict with her people. ＊strict＝厳しい
オダ部長とはそりが合わない。	I don't get along with my manager, Mr. Oda. ＊get along with ～＝～と気が合う

同僚のこと

同僚には本当に恵まれている。	**I'm blessed to have such great co-workers.** ＊be blessed＝恵まれている　co-worker＝同僚
信頼できる同僚がいるって、幸せだな。	**I'm so glad to have co-workers I can trust.**
うちの課はチームワークがいい。	**My department works together well.**
ヨシダさんと組むことになった。	**I got paired with Yoshida-san.**
同期のイシイさんとは馬が合う。	**I get on well with my colleague Ishii-san.** ＊get on well with ～＝～と気が合う
タバタさん、来月結婚するらしい。	**I hear Mr. Tabata is getting married next month.**
オグラさんは１年先輩だからって威張り過ぎ！	**Ogura-san is too bossy just because he's one year senior!** ＊bossy＝偉そうな　senior＝年上の

部下のこと

クロキさんは、頼もしい部下だ。	**Ms. Kuroki is a reliable subordinate.** ＊subordinate＝部下
頼んだ仕事をどんどん片付けてくれる。	**She always quickly finishes what she's asked to do.**
彼は本当に手際がいい。	**He really is efficient.**
タカハシくんは、やる気満々だ。	**Mr. Takahashi is really motivated.** ＊motivated＝やる気のある
ササキさんには期待している。	**I'm counting on Ms. Sasaki.** ＊count on ～＝～を頼りにする
ヨシノくんは、ちょっと頼りないなぁ。	**I can't really count on Yoshino-kun.**
新人のヒライくんは要領が悪いなぁ。	**The newcomer, Mr. Hirai, isn't very efficient.** ＊efficient＝有能な

自営業・自由業

自営業

今月は売り上げがよかった。	**Sales were good this month.**
今月は売り上げが悪かった。	**Sales were bad this month.**
今日はお客さんが多かった。	**We had a lot of customers today.**
今日はトマトの売れ行きが悪かった。	**Tomatoes didn't sell very well today.**
先月より 10%落ちた。	**It's down 10% from last month.** ＊売り上げや客数などさまざまな事柄に使える
去年より 20%上がった。	**It's up 20% from last year.**
明日は棚卸しだ。	**We have to take stock tomorrow.** ＊take stock＝在庫調査をする
バイトさんを増やそうかな。	**Maybe I should hire more part-time workers.**
店の改装をしようかな。	**Maybe I should remodel the store.** ＊remodel＝～を改装する・リフォームする
もっと宣伝しよう。	**I need to advertise more.** ＊advertise＝宣伝する

自由業

原稿の締切に間に合わないよ～！	**I'm not going to have the manuscript ready by the deadline!** ＊manuscript＝原稿
タカノさんから、原稿催促の電話がかかってきた。	**Ms. Takano called me to tell me to turn in my manuscript.** ＊turn in ～＝～を提出する
居留守を使った。	**I pretended not to be home.** ＊pretend to ～＝～のふりをする
ギリギリの生活だ。	**I'm barely making ends meet.** ＊barely ＝かろうじて～する make ends meet＝帳尻を合わせる、赤字を出さない
もっと仕事を増やさなきゃ。	**I need to get more work.**
新しい取引先を開拓しなきゃ。	**I need to get some new clients.**
仕事がだいぶ込み合ってきた。	**I've got a lot of work piled up.** ＊piled up＝積み重なった

昨夜は遅くまで仕事をした。	I burned the midnight oil last night. *burn the midnight oil＝夜遅くまで働く・勉強する
今日は徹夜だ。	I'll need to work through the night today.
明日は休みにしちゃおうかな。	Maybe I should take tomorrow off. *take 〜 off＝〜を休みにする

経理・確定申告（→ p. 331「税金」も参照）

帳簿を付けた。	I made an entry into the account book. *make an entry＝記入する account book＝会計帳簿
オンラインソフトで帳簿管理をしている。	I'm using online software to figure the accounts. *figure＝〜を計算する
クレジットカードの利用情報を自動で取り込めるので、便利。	I can automatically import the credit card transactions, so it's convenient. *transaction＝取引
そろそろ確定申告しなきゃ。	I need to file my income taxes soon. *file＝〜(書類など)を提出する
領収書の整理が面倒くさい。	Sorting receipts is such a hassle. *sort＝〜を分類する hassle＝面倒なこと
毎月やっていればラクだったのに…。	It would've been easier if I'd done it every month. *would've＝would have I'd＝I had
去年も同じことを思ったな。	I thought the same thing last year.
何度やっても数字が合わない！	The figures just don't add up, no matter how many times I try. *figure＝数字 add up=計算が合う
税理士さんに来てもらった。	I had a tax accountant come over. *tax accountant＝税理士
税理士さんに領収書を渡した。	I gave my receipts to my tax accountant.
確定申告が終わった。	I finished filing my income taxes.
e-tax で確定申告した。	I filed my income tax return online.
税務署に書類を提出した。	I submitted the documents to the tax office.

11 仕事

期限に間に合った！	**I made it in time!** ＊make it＝無事にやり遂げる
期限を少し過ぎちゃった。	**I didn't quite make it in time.**
来年から、青色申告にしようかな？	**Maybe I should file a blue return from next year.** ＊blue return＝青色申告
青色申告用のソフトを買った。	**I bought software for the blue return.**

アルバイト・パート

バイトを見つけなきゃ。	**I need to find a part-time job.** ＊欧米では特に「正社員」「パート」「アルバイト」を区別しないので、find a jobとしてもOK
夜勤のバイトを探そう。	**I should look for a job working the night shift.**
ネットでバイトを探した。	**I looked for part-time job information on the Internet.**
近所のコンビニでバイトを募集していた。	**A nearby convenience store was hiring part-timers.**
その会社に電話してみた。	**I called that company.**
明日、面接を受けることになった。	**I managed to get an interview for tomorrow.** ＊manage to ～＝何とか～する
担当はツカダさんだ。	**The person in charge is Tsukada-san.**
採用された。	**I got hired.**
不採用だった。	**I didn't get hired.**
早速、明日から働くことになった。	**I start working tomorrow.**
レストランで働くことにした。	**I'm going to work at a restaurant.**
週３日、働くことにした。	**I decided to work three days a week.**
土日だけ働くことにした。	**I decided to work only on Saturdays and Sundays.**

時給は1200円。	**I get 1,200 yen an hour.**
時給、もう少し上がらないかな。	**It would be nice if I could get a raise.** ＊raise［レイズ］＝昇給
やったぁ！ 時給が50円上がった！	**Great! My hourly wage went up 50 yen!**
もっと時給の高いパートに変えようかな。	**I wonder if it's better to look for a job with a higher hourly wage.**
今月のバイト代は6万5000円。	**I got 65,000 yen from my part-time job this month.**
来月はもう少し、シフトを増やそうかな。	**Maybe I should take more shifts next month.**
バイト仲間はいい人ばかり。	**All my co-workers at my part-time job are great people.**
先輩たちは親切に仕事を教えてくれた。	**My seniors all kindly taught me the job.**
社員のオガワさんがちょっと怖い。	**One of the full-time workers, Mr. Ogawa, is a little scary.**
立ちっぱなしで足がむくんだ。	**My legs swelled up from all the standing.** ＊swell up＝（手足が）はれる
バイトを辞めた。	**I quit my part-time job.** ＊quit［クイット］＝～を辞める。過去形もquit
時給が安過ぎた。	**My hourly wage was too low.** ＊wage＝時間給、賃金
大学とバイトの両立は難しい。	**Attending university and working part-time is tough.**

就職・転職

就職活動

そろそろ就職活動の時期だ。	**It's about time I started looking for a job.**
大学のキャリアセンターに相談に行った。	**I went to the career center at my college for advice.**

就活サイトに登録した。	**I registered for a job-hunting site.** ＊job-hunting＝就職活動
エージェントから連絡があった。	**I was contacted by an agent.**
リクルートスーツを買った。	**I bought a job-hunting suit.**
リクルートスーツには慣れないな。	**I'm not used to this job-hunting suit.** ＊be used to ～＝～に慣れている
ネクタイがうまく結べない。	**I can't tie a necktie well.**
本当に就職できるのかな。	**I really wonder if I can get a job.**
狭き門だけど、夢をあきらめたくない。	**The odds are against me, but I don't want to give up on my dream.** ＊odds are against ～＝～にとって勝ち目がない・見込みが薄い
地元で就職しようか、東京に残ろうか迷う。	**I wonder if I should get a job in my hometown or stay here in Tokyo.**
会社の規模にはこだわらない。	**The size of the company doesn't matter to me.**
自分の夢をかなえられる会社がいい。	**I want to work at a company where I can make my dreams come true.**
D 社は通年採用を始めたらしい。	**I heard that D Company started a year-round recruitment policy.** ＊year-round＝通年の　recruitment＝採用
まずは志望業界を決めないと。	**First, I need to decide what industry I want to work in.** ＊industry＝産業
業界研究をしてみよう。	**I'll do some industry research.**
早く働きたい。	**I want to start working as soon as possible.**
就職したくないな。	**I don't want to start working.**
一生、学生でいられたらいいのに。	**I wish I could be a student forever.**

転職活動

転職したい。	**I want to change jobs.**
転職しようかな。	**Maybe I should change jobs.**

転職することに決めた。	**I decided to change jobs.**
もっと給料のいい仕事に就きたい。	**I want a job that pays better.**
やりたい仕事をさせてくれる会社に行きたい。	**I want to work at a company that lets me do the work I want to do.**
今までの経験を生かせる仕事を探そう。	**I'll look for a job that lets me make the most of my experience.** ＊make the most of ～＝～を最大限に活用する
転職サイトに登録した。	**I registered on a career change site.**
なかなか希望の求人が見つからない。	**I'm struggling to find jobs I like.** ＊struggle＝悪戦苦闘する、取り組む
いい求人が出ないかなぁ。	**I hope there will be some good job offers.** ＊job offer＝求人、仕事の申し出
やっと希望の求人が見つかった！	**I finally found the job opening I was hoping for!** ＊job opening＝求人、空きポスト
B 社が中途採用の募集をしている。	**B Company is looking for experienced employees.** ＊experienced＝経験のある　employee＝従業員
応募締切は 13 日だ。	**The application deadline is the 13th.** ＊application＝応募　deadline＝締切

就職説明会・OB/OG 訪問

明日は 10 時から梅田で G 社の就職説明会がある。	**G Company is having a job fair tomorrow at 10:00 in Umeda.**
企業の合同説明会に参加した。	**I attended a joint job fair.**
TM 社の就職説明会に参加した。	**I attended TM Company's job orientation.**
オンラインの就職説明会に出席した。	**I attended an online job orientation.**
Zoom で会社説明会に参加した。	**I attended a company information session on Zoom.**
IT 企業の合同説明会に参加した。	**I attended a joint job fair by IT companies.**

説明会に行くのに道に迷ってしまった。	**I got lost on the way to the job fair.**
説明会に参加して、ますますこの会社で働きたくなった。	**The job fair made me even more sure that I wanted to work there.**
思っていた企業とちょっと違うかも。	**I think the company is a little different from what I had in mind.**
募集人数が少なそうだ。	**The number of positions seems small.**
A 銀行のゴトウさんを OB 訪問した。	**I spoke to Mr. Goto from A Bank.** ＊「OB/OG訪問」は、英語ではこのように具体的に表す
仕事内容を具体的にイメージできた。	**I was able to get a clear picture of what the job is about.** ＊clear picture＝明確なイメージ
大変だけど、やりがいのありそうな仕事だ。	**The job sounds tough, but it also sounds fulfilling.** ＊tough［タフ］＝きつい、大変な　fulfilling＝充実した

応募書類・エントリーシート

今週末までに、A 社の応募書類を出さなきゃ。	**I've got to hand in my application to A Company by this weekend.** ＊hand in ～＝～を提出する　application＝応募（書類）
証明写真を撮りに行った。	**I got my ID photo taken.**
B 社のエントリーシートを書いた。	**I filled out the entry sheet for B Company.** ＊fill out ～＝～に書き込む　「エントリーシート」は英語にはないが、日記にはentry sheetと書いてOK。またはapplication form（応募書類）としてもよい
D 社のエントリーシートを書くのに、3 時間かかった。	**It took me three hours to fill in the entry sheet for D Company.** ＊fill in ～＝～に必要事項を記入する
自己分析から始めることにしよう。	**I'll start with a self analysis.** ＊analysis［アナラスィス］＝分析
私の強みって何だろう？	**What are my strengths?** ＊strength［ストレングス］＝強み、長所
私の長所は、協調性があるところかな。	**I think one of my strengths is that I'm cooperative.**
エントリーシートをモリ先輩に見てもらった。	**I asked Mori-senpai to take a look at my entry sheet.** ＊take a look at ～＝～を見る

オンラインでエントリーシートを提出した。	**I submitted my entry sheet online.**

入社試験・面接

やったぁ！ 筆記試験合格！	**Yes! I passed the written test!** ＊pass＝〜に合格する
あ〜あ！ 書類で落ちちゃった。	**Oh no! I failed the application screening.** ＊application screening＝応募審査、書類選考
来週はB社の面接だ。	**I have an interview with B Company next week.**
B社の事業内容を調べておこう。	**I should look up B Company's business beforehand.** ＊beforehand＝前もって
模擬面接を受けた。	**I had a mock interview.** ＊mock interview＝模擬面接
A社の一次面接だった。	**I had the first round interview with A Company.**
Skypeで面接を受けた。	**I had an interview on Skype.**
初めての面接で、すごく緊張した。	**It was my first interview, so I was really nervous.**
自分の考えをきちんと言えたと思う。	**I think I expressed myself well.**
ちゃんと自己PRできた。	**I was able to promote myself well.** ＊promote＝〜を売り込む
面接官と話が盛り上がった。	**The interviewer and I had a great conversation.**
合格してるといいな。	**I hope I passed.**
圧迫面接を受けた。	**I had a stress interview.**
緊張して、うまく答えられなかった。	**I was so nervous that I couldn't answer the questions very well.**
自己PRで失敗した。	**I failed at self-promotion.**

内定

なるべく早く就職先を決めたい。	**I want to get a job as soon as possible.**

まだ内定が出ない。どうしよう。	**I haven't received any job offers yet. What should I do?** ＊job offer＝採用通知。厳密には、「内定」はunofficial job offer（非公式の採用通知）
とりあえず1社は決まってるから安心だ。	**I'm relieved that I got an offer from at least one company.**
やったぁ！ A社から内定が出た！	**Yes! I got a job offer from A Company!**
B社はあきらめていたので、すごくうれしかった。	**I had already given up hope on B Company, so I was thrilled.** ＊thrilled［スリォド］＝興奮した
ヒロは、もう2社から内定をもらったんだって。	**Hiro has already received two job offers.**
アヤも内定が出た。本当によかった！	**Aya also got a job offer. That's really good for her!**
第一志望のG社も受かるといいな。	**It would be great if I also got a job offer from my first choice, G Company.**
周りの人に内定が出始めていて、焦る。	**I'm worried because everyone else is getting job offers.**
またお祈りメールか…。	**Another rejection email ...** ＊rejection＝不合格、却下
最悪、就職浪人も考えよう。	**In the worst case, maybe I should spend another year at university.** ＊in the worst case＝最悪の場合
コネで内定を手に入れた。	**I used connections to get the job.**
大学院に進学することに決め、就活をやめた。	**I decided to go to grad school, so I stopped job hunting.** ＊grad school＝大学院
お世話になった人にお礼と内定の報告をした。	**I thanked the people who helped me and told them about my getting a job.**
みんなすごく喜んでくれた。	**They were all really happy for me.**

Memo

仕事に関することを、メモしておきましょう。

仕事について 英語日記を書いてみよう

仕事にまつわることについて、英語で書いてみましょう。

接待ゴルフ

I'm playing golf with clients tomorrow. I need to get up early and keep pleasing them ... Oh, I wish I didn't have to.

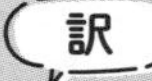

明日は接待ゴルフ。朝は早いし、気を遣うし……。あ～、行かなくて済むならなぁ。

「接待ゴルフ」を表す英単語はないので、play golf with clients（顧客とゴルフをする）としました。「気を遣う」は「顧客を喜ばせ続ける」と考えて、(I need to) keep pleasing them に。英語にしづらい言い回しは、臨機応変に考えてみましょう。

寝に帰るだけの日々

I've been extremely busy. No matter how hard I work, I can't get my work done. All I do at home is just sleep.

ここのところ多忙を極めている。どんなに頑張っても仕事が終わらない。家に帰って寝るだけの日々だ。

「このところ」のニュアンスは、「継続」の意味を表す現在完了形 I've been で表せます。「多忙を極める」は super busy でも OK。No matter how hard I work は「どんなに頑張って働いても」。get ～（人・物事）...で「～を…の状態にする」、done は「終わった」です。

新しい上司

My new boss came to our office today. I heard he was really stern, but actually, he seemed like an ideal boss with a good balance of strictness and kindness. (Whew)

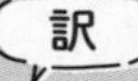

今日から新しい上司がうちの支社に配属になった。かなり厳しい人だと聞いていたけど、厳しさと優しさを持ち合わせた理想の上司という印象だった。（ホッ）

sternは「温かみがなく、取りつく島もない厳格な様子」を、strictは「しつけや規律を守らせようとする厳しい様子」を指す形容詞。「厳しさ」は、sternness/strictnessで表します。「印象だった」はseemed like ～（～のように思われた）とすればOK。

なかなか内定が出ない

I've had 11 job interviews, but I haven't received any job offers yet. I'm getting really worried, depressed and tired.

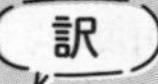

これまでに採用面接を11社受けたけど、まだ1つも内定が出ていない。すごく焦るし、落ち込むし、もう疲れてきた。

「採用面接」はjob interview。「内定が出る」はreceive a job offer（仕事の申し出を受ける）と表します。worried（焦った、不安な）、depressed（落ち込んだ）、tired（疲れた）をbe gettingと一緒に用いると、「そういう状態になりつつある」ことを表せます。

12
学校生活

学校生活全般

小・中・高の学年を表す単語

※ grade は「学年」を表す。
大学の学年の表し方は、p. 290 参照。

小学1年生	the first grade	中学1年生	the seventh grade
小学2年生	the second grade	中学2年生	the eighth grade
小学3年生	the third grade	中学3年生	the ninth grade
小学4年生	the fourth grade	高校1年生	freshman
小学5年生	the fifth grade	高校2年生	junior
小学6年生	the sixth grade	高校3年生	senior［スィーニア］

入学・進級

もうすぐ中学2年生だ。
I'll be in the eighth grade pretty soon.

息子は高校3年生だ。
My son is a senior in high school.

時のたつのは早い。
Time flies.

期待と不安が半々だ。
I have a lot of expectations and worries.
＊expectation＝期待

娘は小学校に通うのを楽しみにしている。
My daughter is looking forward to going to elementary school.

入学準備

母が娘にランドセルを買ってくれた。
My mother bought my daughter a school backpack.
＊school backpackは、「学校用のリュック」の意味

息子は水色のランドセルを選んだ。	**My son chose a light blue school backpack.**
息子にはまだランドセルが大き過ぎる。	**Right now the school backpack looks too big for him.**
入学準備が大変。	**Getting ready to enter school is tough.**
息子の体操服や上履きを買った。	**I bought gym clothes and indoor shoes for my son.** ＊gym clothes［クロウズ］＝体操服
布を買ってきてランチョンマットを作った。	**I bought material and made a place mat.** ＊place mat＝ランチョンマット
息子にとって初めての電車通学だ。	**It's his first time to go to school by train.**
通学のために定期券を買った。	**We bought a commuter pass for him to use when traveling to and from school.** ＊commuter pass＝定期券

制服

制服の採寸に行った。	**I had my measurements taken for my school uniform.** ＊measurement＝計測、採寸　uniform＝制服
ABC 高校って、制服がおしゃれだな。	**ABC High School's uniform looks awesome.** ＊awesome［オーサム］＝とてもよい
XYZ 高校の制服って、イマイチ。	**XYZ High School's uniform doesn't look so good.**
うちの学校は夏服がかわいい。	**Our summer uniforms are cute.**
スカートの丈が長過ぎるよ。	**The skirt is too long.**
スカートの丈をもっと短くしたいな。	**I want to shorten my skirt.** ＊shorten＝～を短くする
制服がキツくなった。	**My uniform has gotten too tight.**
ユキの制服を新調した。	**We had Yuki's new uniform made.**

クラス分け

私は5組だ。
I'm in Class 5.

トモちゃんと同じクラスだった。やった！
I got in the same class as Tomo-chan. Great!

タカハシくんと別のクラスになっちゃった。
Takahashi-kun and I are in different classes.

楽しそうなクラスだ。
The class looks like a lot of fun.

クラスのみんなと仲良くやっていけるといいな。
I hope I can get along with everyone in the class.
＊get along with ～＝～(人)とうまくやる

前のクラスに戻りたいな。
I miss my previous class.
＊previous＝以前の

通学（→ p. 162「通勤・通学」を参照）

出席・欠席

今年は今のところ一度も休んでない。
I haven't missed a day of school this year so far.
＊miss＝～を欠席する　so far＝今までのところ

皆勤を目指すぞ！
I'm aiming for the perfect attendance!
＊aim for ～＝～を目指す　attendance＝出席

今日は学校を休んだ。
I stayed home from school today.

ケンジが学校をサボった。
Kenji cut class. ＊cut class＝授業をサボる

サリは風邪で学校を休んだ。
Sari stayed home with a cold.

ヌマタくんが最近、学校に来ていない。
Numata-kun hasn't been coming to school recently.

出席日数が足りないと、進級できないかも。
If his attendance isn't good enough, he might not be able to move up to the next grade.

インフルエンザで学級閉鎖中だ。
Classes are suspended due to the flu.
＊suspend＝～を一時停止する　flu＝インフルエンザ

12日まで学校が休みになった。
Our school is closed until the 12th.

遅刻・早退

また遅刻しちゃった。 **I was late again.**

危うく遅刻しそうになった。 **I was almost late.**

明日こそ、遅刻しないようにしよう。 **I'm going to be careful not to be late tomorrow.**

サチはまた遅刻したみたい。 **It looks like Sachi was late again.**

2時間目の後、早退した。 **I came home after the second class.**

シュウくんが早退した。 **Shu-kun left school early.**

保健室で休んだ。 **I took a rest in the nurse's office.**

＊nurse's office＝保健室

学校が好き・嫌い

学校は楽しい。 **I enjoy school.**

学校は嫌い。 **I don't like school.**

学校、行きたくないなぁ。 **I don't want to go to school.**

息子は学校が楽しいみたい。 **It looks like my son enjoys his school life.**

先生のこと

息子の担任が、またイシイ先生でよかった。 **I'm glad Mr. Ishii is my son's homeroom teacher again.**

＊homeroom teacher＝担任の先生

前の担任のほうがよかったな。 **I liked my previous homeroom teacher better.**

イシハラ先生、好きだな。 **I like Mr. Ishihara.**

イシハラ先生って、苦手。 **I don't like Mr. Ishihara.**

シライ先生、怖過ぎ。 **Mr. Shirai is too strict.**

ヨシダ先生の授業は楽しい。 **Ms. Yoshida's class is fun.**

ノムラ先生は教え方がうまい。	**Ms. Nomura's teaching is great.**
ムラカミ先生の授業は眠くなる。	**I get sleepy in Mr. Murakami's class.**
オオタ先生に、もう遅刻しないように注意された。	**Ms. Ota warned me not to be late again.** ＊warn［ウォーン］＝～に警告する
職員室に呼び出された。	**I was called to the teacher's room.**
クボノ先生が転任してしまう。	**Ms. Kubono is going to transfer to another school.**
来年度も教わりたかったな。	**I wanted to take her class again next year.**
スズキ先生は、来月から産休だ。	**Ms. Suzuki is taking maternity leave from next month.** ＊maternity leave＝産休
教育実習の先生が来た。	**A student teacher came to our class.**

給食・弁当

今日の弁当は、ハンバーグと野菜炒めだった。	**Today's lunch was hamburger steak and stir-fried vegetables.**
給食はカレーだった。	**We had curry for school lunch.**
購買部でパンを買った。	**I bought some bread rolls at the school shop.**
2時間目の後、早弁した。	**I had an early lunch during my second recess.** ＊recess［リセス］＝休み時間
授業中におなかが鳴って恥ずかしかった。	**I was embarrassed my stomach was growling in class.** ＊growl［グラオゥ］＝（おなかなどが）ゴロゴロ鳴る
今日の弁当には、ユキの好物のコロッケを入れた。	**I put Yuki's favorite croquettes in her lunch box today.** ＊croquette［クロケット］＝コロッケ
ミッキーのキャラ弁を作った。	**I made a lunch box with a Mickey Mouse character on it.**

部活動

部活動を表す単語

～部	～ club
野球	baseball
ソフトボール	softball
サッカー	soccer（米）/ football（英）
アメフト	American football
ラグビー	rugby
陸上	track-and-field
体操	gymnastics
水泳	swimming
テニス	tennis
バトミントン	badminton
卓球	table tennis
バレーボール	volleyball
バスケットボール	basketball
スキー	skiing
スケート	ice skating
ホッケー	hockey
剣道	kendo
柔道	judo
相撲	sumo
フェンシング	fencing
アーチェリー	archery
弓道	Kyudo / Japanese archery
ラクロス	lacrosse
レスリング	wrestling
ボクシング	boxing
登山	mountain climbing
ダンス	dance
軽音楽	pop music
吹奏楽	brass band
オーケストラ	orchestra
合唱	chorus
美術	art
演劇	drama
書道	calligraphy
俳句	haiku
茶道	tea ceremony
華道	flower arranging
写真	photography
鉄道	train
新聞	school newspaper
料理	cooking
将棋	shogi
囲碁	go
映画	movie
文芸	literature
漫画	cartoon / manga
クイズ	quiz
科学	science
プログラミング	programming
ロボット工学	robot engineering

何部に入ろうかな。
I wonder what club I should join.

テニス部か写真部かで迷ってる。
I'm torn between the tennis club and the photography club.

＊be torn between ～ and ...＝～か…かの選択で悩む

どんな雰囲気なんだろう。
I wonder what the atmosphere is like.

体験入部してみようかな。	**I think I'll join the club for a trial period.**
バスケ部に入部した。	**I joined the basketball club.**
今年は新入部員がたくさん入った。	**Lots of people joined the club this year.**
今年は新入部員が1人もいない！	**We didn't even get one new club member this year.**
廃部の危機!?	**Is the club in danger of being disbanded!?** ＊disband＝～を解散する
うちの学校、部活の選択肢が少ないな。	**Our school doesn't have many clubs to choose from.**
毎日、朝練がある。	**We have to practice every morning.**
走り込みや筋トレはつらい。	**The running and muscle training are tough.** ＊muscle［マッソォ］＝筋肉
土日も部活がある。	**There's practice on the weekends, too.**
今日は部活が休みだった。	**There was no club practice today.**
インターハイまで、あと1カ月。	**There's just one month before the interscholastic meet.** ＊interscholastic meet＝インターハイ
もうすぐ、吹奏楽コンクール。	**The brass band contest is coming up soon.**
とりあえず予選突破を目指そう。	**I want to at least pass the preliminaries.** ＊preliminary＝予選
大会では、金賞を狙うぞ！	**I'm going for the gold in the tournament!**
目指せ、関西大会進出！	**I'm going to make it to the Kansai tournament!** ＊make it to ～＝～に到達する
悔いのないように頑張ろう。	**I want to do my best and have no regrets.** ＊regret＝後悔

うちの高校が甲子園に出る！	**Our school is going to Koshien!**
応援に行こう！	**I'll go and cheer them on!**
残念だったけど、また来年がある。	**It's too bad, but there's always next year.**
娘は吹奏楽部で楽しそうにやっている。	**It looks like she's having a good time in the brass band club.**
野球部の練習、ハードみたい。	**It looks like the baseball practice is really hard.**

休日・休暇

明日は学校が休みだ。	**I don't have any classes tomorrow.**
来週の水曜は、学校の創立記念日でお休み。	**Next Wednesday is a holiday because it's the school's foundation anniversary.**
明日学校に行けば、三連休だ。	**If I go to school tomorrow, then I'll have a three-day holiday.** ＊週末を含む三連休は、three-day weekend
明日から春休みだ！	**Spring break starts tomorrow!**
夏休みはダラダラ過ごしている。	**I'm not doing anything during the summer vacation.**
夏休みもあと少しで終わり。	**Summer vacation is almost over.**
冬休みもあと１日で終わりかぁ。	**There's only one day left in the winter break.**
みんなに会えるのが楽しみだな。	**I can't wait to see my friends.**
冬休みは、冬季講習くらいしか予定がない。	**My only plans for the winter break are a winter session class.**
もうすぐ受験だから、冬休みなんてないよ。	**Entrance exams are coming soon, so I don't really have a winter vacation.**
休み中は、子どもたちがうるさくて大変だ。	**During vacations, it's really crazy with the kids around all the time.**

生徒会

生徒会選挙があった。
There was a student council election.
＊student council＝生徒会

マスダくんが生徒会長に立候補した。
Masuda-kun ran for student council president.
＊run for ～＝～に立候補する。runの過去形はran
president＝長

誰に投票しようかな。
I wonder who I should vote for.

カガワさんは演説が上手だった。
Kagawa-san's speech was great.

生徒会長はコモダさんに決まった。
Komoda-san was chosen as the student council president.

そのほかの学校生活

彼は停学になった。
He got suspended from school.
＊suspend＝～を停学にする

彼は退学させられた。
He was kicked out of school.
＊kick out ～＝～を退学させる

彼は自主退学した。
He withdrew himself from school.
＊withdraw＝～(人など)を退かせる。過去形はwithdrew

うちの学校、校則が厳し過ぎる。
The rules at my school are too strict.
＊strict＝厳しい

うちの学校は生徒の自主性を大切にしている。
Our school values students' initiative.

席替えがあった。
We changed seats.

クラス替えがあった。
We changed classes.

掃除当番だ。面倒くさいな。
I have the cleaning assignment. It's such a pain.
＊assignment＝割り当て、任務

エミは忘れ物が多い。
Emi is always forgetting things.

学校行事

学校行事を表す単語

入学式	entrance ceremony
始業式	opening ceremony
身体検査	physical checkup
朝礼	morning assembly
全校集会	school assembly
遠足	school outing
校外学習	field trip
修学旅行	school trip
林間学校	school camp
臨海学校	seaside summer camp
スキー教室	ski trip
運動会・体育祭	sports festival / field day
スポーツ大会	sports competition
学芸会	school play
文化祭	cultural festival / school festival
観劇	theatre visit
合唱コンクール	choir [クワィア] contest
マラソン大会	marathon
卒業式	graduation ceremony
終業式	closing ceremony
謝恩会	thank-you party for the teachers
保護者会	parents meeting
授業参観	parents' day
三者面談	parent-teacher-student meeting
部活動	club activities
練習試合	practice game / practice match
（部活などの）合宿	training camp

入学式

今日は入学式だった。

We had our entrance ceremony today.

今日はハヤトの入学式だった。

Today was Hayato's entrance ceremony.

入学式は緊張した。

I got nervous at the entrance ceremony.

校長先生の話が長過ぎた。

The speech by the principal was too long.

12 学校生活

合唱コンクール

うちのクラスの曲は「大地讃頌（さんしょう）」に決まった。
We decided to sing “Daichi Sansho” in the choir contest.

好きな曲になってうれしい。
I’m glad we chose a song I like.

かなり難易度の高い曲だ。
It’s a really hard song.

ピアノ伴奏をすることになった。
I will do the piano accompaniment.
＊accompaniment＝伴奏

指揮者はトクダくんだ。
Tokuda-kun will be the conductor.

明日はいよいよ本番！
Tomorrow is the big show!

頑張ったかいあって、優勝した！
Our hard work paid off. We won!
＊pay off＝報われる

あんなに頑張ったのに、3位だった。
We practiced really hard, but we just got third place.

スポーツ大会

今日はクラス対抗スポーツ大会だった。
We had an inter-class sports competition today.

授業がなくてラッキー！
I was so glad there weren’t any classes!

私はバレーボールに参加した。
I played volleyball.

サカキさんは大活躍だった。
Sakaki-san was the star.

うちのクラスは学年2位だった。
Our class was second in our grade.
＊ここでのgradeは「学年」

運動会・体育祭

100m走と障害物競走に出ることになった。
I’m going to be in the 100-meter race and the obstacle race.
＊obstacle＝障害物

リレーのメンバーに選ばれた。
I was chosen to be a member of the relay team.

応援のし過ぎで声がかれちゃった。
I cheered so much that my voice went hoarse.
＊hoarse［ホーァ］＝しわがれた、かすれた

今日は体育祭だった。　**Today we had the sports festival.**
＊アメリカには、体育祭や運動会がない学校もある。sports festivalは、field dayと言うことも

雨で来週に延期になった。　**It was postponed until next week because of the rain.**
＊postpone＝～を延期する

お母さんが応援に来てくれた。　**My mom came to cheer for me.**
＊cheer for ～＝～を応援する

玉入れと二人三脚に出場した。　**I was in the put-the-balls-in-the-basket and the three-legged race.**

３年生の綱引きは、迫力満点だった。　**The third grade's tug-of-war was really exciting.**

早起きして、体育祭の弁当を作った。　**I got up early and made lunch for the sports festival.**

お弁当を持って、運動会の応援に出かけた。　**I took our lunch and went for the sports festival.**

文化祭

うちのクラスの出し物は、カフェに決まった。　**Our class decided to set up a café.**

放課後、文化祭の準備をした。　**We prepared for the cultural festival after school.**
＊「文化祭」は、school festivalとも言う

クラスでおそろいのＴシャツを作った。　**We made identical T-shirts for the class.**
＊identical＝同一の

校門の近くで呼び込みをした。　**I called out near the school gate.**
＊call out＝（人に）呼びかける

写真部で作品を展示した。　**We exhibited our photos at the photography club.**
＊exhibit［イグズィビット］＝～を展示する

たこ焼きの模擬店を出した。　**We opened a takoyaki stall.**
＊stall＝売店、屋台

うちのクラスはお化け屋敷をやった。　**Our class did a haunted house.**
＊haunted＝幽霊のよく出る

予想外の大盛況だった。　**Surprisingly, it was a big success.**

SEKAI NO OWARI の曲を演奏した。　**We played SEKAI NO OWARI songs.**

サトウくんたちのバンド演奏がかっこよかった。	**Sato-kun's band was really cool.**
ABC 高校の文化祭に行ってきた。	**I went to the school festival at ABC High.**

遠足・校外学習

今日は遠足だった。	**We went on a school outing today.**
校外学習だった。	**We had a field trip today.** ＊field trip＝校外学習
高尾山に登った。	**We climbed Mt. Takao.** ＊climb［クライム］
オリエンテーリングをした。	**We went orienteering.**
工場見学をした。	**We went on a factory tour.**
ピアノの製造過程を見学した。	**We saw how they make pianos.**
陶製の湯飲み作りに参加した。	**We got to try to make our own ceramic teacup.** ＊ceramic＝陶器

修学旅行

明日から修学旅行だ。	**We're going on a school trip tomorrow.** ＊school trip＝修学旅行
マリコは今日から修学旅行。	**Mariko is leaving on her school trip today.** ＊すでに出かけたなら、Mariko left ...と過去形にする
行き先は京都と奈良。	**We're going to Kyoto and Nara.**
修学旅行で台湾に行く。	**We're going to Taiwan on a school trip.**
旅行中のスケジュールを組んだ。	**We planned our school trip itinerary.** ＊itinerary［アイティネラリィ］＝旅程
ガイドさんの解説は興味深かった。	**The guide's comments were really interesting.**
午後は班ごとに自由行動だった。	**In the afternoon, each group could do what they wanted.**

夜はみんなで恋バナをした。 | **At night, we shared our love stories.**

先生が見回りに来ないか、ヒヤヒヤした。 | **We were worried that our teacher would come by.**

楽しくて、なかなか寝付けなかった。 | **I had so much fun that I could hardly sleep.**

林間学校・合宿

8月2日から6日まで、林間学校だった。 | **We went to a school camp from August 2 to 6.**

蓼科に行った。 | **We went to Tateshina.**

自然を満喫した。 | **We enjoyed nature to the fullest.**
＊to the fullest＝最大限に

山登りはキツかった。 | **The mountain climbing was tough.**

初めて海で泳いだ。 | **I swam in the ocean for the first time.**

夜はキャンプファイアーをした。 | **We made a camp fire at night.**

飯ごう炊さんが楽しかった。 | **It was fun to cook rice on a fire.**

スキー合宿から帰ってきた。 | **I came back from the ski camp.**

授業参観・面談

今日は授業参観だった。 | **We had parents' day today.**

お母さんが授業を見に来た。 | **My mom came to see the class.**

子どもの授業参観に行った。 | **I went for parents' day.**

マサは頑張って発言していた。 | **Masa did his best to speak up.**

トモはあまり先生の話を聞いていなかった。もう！ | **Tomo wasn't really listening to the teacher. That kid!**

活気のある授業だった。 | **That was a lively class.**
＊lively［ライヴリィ］＝元気いっぱいの

保護者会があった。 | **There was a parent-teacher assembly.**
＊assembly＝集会、集まり

ミキちゃんのママとおしゃべりした。	**I chatted with Miki-chan's mom.**
いろいろなお母さん、お父さんと話せて面白かった。	**It was interesting to talk with other moms and dads.**
三者面談があった。	**There was a parent-student-teacher meeting.** ＊「個人面談」なら、parent-teacher meeting

PTA

PTA 役員をすることになった。	**I became a PTA board member.** ＊board member＝役員
ほかに誰もやる人がいなかった。	**There wasn't anyone else who volunteered to do it.**
キクチさんが役員をやることになった。	**Kikuchi-san became a board member.**
PTA の仕事でイベントの手伝いをした。	**I helped out at an event as PTA work.**
PTA の仕事、もっと簡素化したらいいのに。	**I really think the PTA work should be simplified.** ＊simplify＝～を簡単にする

修業式・卒業式

今日は修業式だった。	**We had the closing ceremony today.**
あと 3 カ月で卒業かぁ。	**I'll be graduating in three months.**
あっという間の 3 年間だった。	**These three years went by like a flash.** ＊like a flash＝あっという間に
高校生活、楽しかったな。	**I really had a good time in high school.**
卒業したくないな。	**I don't want to graduate.**
友達と離ればなれになるの、嫌だな。	**I don't want to say goodbye to my friends.**
今日は卒業式だった。	**Today we had our graduation ceremony.**
涙が止まらなかった。	**I couldn't stop crying.**

ハラ先生も泣いていた。	**Even Mr. Hara cried.**
友達と抱き合って泣いた。	**We cried as we hugged.**
連絡を取り合おうね、と約束した。	**We promised to keep in touch.** ＊keep in touch＝連絡を取る
卒業アルバムと卒業文集が配られた。	**The year book and graduation composition collection were handed out.** ＊year book＝卒業アルバム　hand out ～＝～を配る
卒業アルバムに寄せ書きをした。	**We wrote messages in each other's year books.**
みんなでたくさん写真を撮った。	**We took lots of pictures together.**
後輩に色紙をもらった。	**I got a message card from my juniors.**

転校

２学期いっぱいで転校することになった。	**I'll have to transfer schools after the second semester.** ＊transfer schools＝転校する
離れても友だちでいられますように。	**Even if we're far apart, I hope we can still be friends.**　＊far apart=遠く離れて
新しい学校で友だちができるといいな。	**I hope I can make friends at my new school.**
今日が転校初日だった。	**Today was my first day at my new school.**
クラスの何人かと話した。	**I talked with several people in my class.**
アベさんとは気が合いそう。	**I think I'll get along with Abe-san.** ＊get along with ～＝～と仲良くする
早くクラスになじめるといいな。	**I hope I can adjust to my class quickly.**　＊adjust＝慣れる
転校生が来た。	**A new student came to our school.**
彼は緊張しているみたいだった。	**He looked nervous.**
明日、彼に話しかけてみよう。	**I'll try talking to him tomorrow.**

12 学校生活

勉強・成績

授業

授業・教科を表す単語

～の授業	～ class
国語	Japanese
現代文	contemporary Japanese
古文	classical literature
漢文	Chinese classics
英語	English
外国語	foreign language
算数	arithmetic
数学	math
社会科	social studies
歴史	history
世界史	world history
日本史	Japanese history
地理	geography
政治・経済	politics and economics
公民	civics
理科	science
物理	physics [フィズィクス]
生物	biology
化学	chemistry
科学	science
地学	earth science
体育	physical education / PE
保健体育	health and physical education
音楽	music
図画工作	arts and crafts
美術	art
書道	calligraphy
技術	industrial arts / technical arts
情報	information
家庭科	home economics
道徳／倫理	ethics [エシックス]
宗教	religion
総合	integrated studies
生活科	life environment studies

英語は得意。 **I'm good at English.**

化学は苦手。 **I'm not good at chemistry.**

体育は好きじゃない。 **I don't like PE.**

今日は４時間授業だった。 **I had four classes today.**

３時間目は体育だった。 **Our third class was PE.**

＊PE（体育）は、physical educationの略

世界史の授業は面白かった。 **World history class was interesting.**

数学の授業はつまらなかった。	**Math class was boring.**
古文の授業は長く感じた。	**The classical literature class felt long.**
今日の授業はオンラインだった。	**Today's class was online.**
うまくつながらなくて焦った。	**I panicked because I had trouble connecting.**
理科で実験をした。	**We did an experiment in science class.** ＊experiment＝実験
調理実習でハンバーグとサラダを作った。	**I made hamburger steak and salad in cooking class.**
水泳の授業は寒かった。	**It was cold during the swimming lesson.**
物理の教科書を忘れてしまった。	**I forgot my physics textbook.**
アヤに教科書を見せてもらった。	**I asked Aya to share her textbook with me.**
娘の学校は紙の教科書をやめてデジタル教科書になった。	**My daughter's school has switched from paper textbooks to digital ones.**
持ち物はタブレットだけだから、荷物が軽くなった。	**She only has to take a tablet, so her bag is much lighter now.**
体操服を忘れてしまった。	**I forgot my gym clothes.**
ナオに借りた。	**I had to borrow Nao's.**
授業で当てられた。	**The teacher called on me in class.** ＊call on ～＝～に発言を求める
予習をしていたのでバッチリだった。	**I was prepared, so it went perfectly.**
授業についていけない。	**I can't keep up with the class.** ＊keep up with ～＝～についていく
授業中、居眠りしちゃった。	**I dozed off during class.** ＊doze off＝ウトウトする
授業中に内職をした。	**I was working on another subject during class.**

宿題・課題

生物で宿題がたくさん出た。	I have a lot of biology homework to do.
今日は宿題なし。ひゃっほう！	No homework today. Hurray!
夏休みの宿題がたくさん出た。	I got a lot of summer homework.
春休みは宿題がないからうれしい。	I like spring break because I don't have homework.
まだ宿題に手を付けてない！	I haven't even started my homework!
そろそろ宿題をやり始めないとマズい。	I'd better start doing my homework now.
何とか宿題を終わらせた。	I somehow managed to finish my homework. ＊manage to ～＝何とか～する
ユキと一緒に宿題をやった。	I did my homework with Yuki.
古文の宿題を提出した。	I turned in my classical literature homework. ＊turn in ～＝～を提出する
世界史のレポートを提出した。	I turned in my world history report. ＊turn in ～＝～を提出する
作文を書いた。	I wrote an essay.
読書感想文を書いた。	I wrote a book report.
自由研究のテーマ、何にしようかな。	What should I do for my independent study project? ＊independent＝自主的な
生物の課題をやらなきゃ。	I have to do my biology homework.
来週の発表に備えて準備しなきゃ。	I have to get ready for the presentation next week.
タイチのアサガオの観察日記を手伝った。	I helped Taichi with his morning glory observation diary. ＊observation＝観察、観測
ミキは絵日記を書いていた。	Miki was writing a picture diary.

ハナはちゃんと宿題をやったのかな。	**I wonder if Hana did her homework.**

勉強

高校の勉強って難しい。	**High school studies are difficult.**
最近、勉強が楽しい。	**I've come to enjoy studying recently.**
何のために勉強するんだろう？	**I wonder why I have to study.**
やる気が出ない。	**I can't get motivated.**
やる気が出てきた。	**I'm really motivated.**
英単語のつづりは得意だ。	**I'm good at spelling English words.**
公式がどうしても覚えられない。	**I simply can't remember the formulas.** ＊simply＝（否定語の前に置いて）どうしても　formula＝公式
最近、勉強をサボってる。	**I've been slacking off at studying lately.** ＊slack off＝サボる
最近、勉強を頑張ってる。	**These days, I'm really studying hard.**
昨日は徹夜で勉強した。	**I stayed up studying last night.** ＊stay up＝徹夜する
今日は４時間、試験勉強をした。	**I crammed for exams for four hours today.** ＊cram＝詰め込み勉強をする
家では集中できないので、図書館に行った。	**I can't concentrate at home, so I went to the library.**
部活で忙しくて、テスト勉強をする時間がない。	**I'm busy with club activities and don't have time to study for exams.**
息子は最近、勉強を頑張っている。	**He's studying hard these days.**
娘は全然勉強していないみたい。	**She doesn't seem to be studying at all.**
息子はテスト前になって、勉強に励んでいるようだ。	**He's studying hard now because exams are coming up.**
来週はテストだというのに、娘は全然勉強している様子がない。	**She has exams next week, but she hasn't even started to study.**

テスト

テストにまつわる表現

入学試験	entrance exam
(大学入学)共通テスト	the common test (for university admissions)
模擬テスト	mock exam / practice test
小テスト	quiz
抜き打ちテスト	pop quiz
中間テスト	mid-term (exam)
期末テスト	final (exam)
学力テスト	academic aptitude test
追試	make-up exam
満点	perfect score
平均点	average score
落第点	fail mark / failing grade
偏差値	deviation value / T-score
合格する	pass
落第する	fail
単位	credit
～の単位を落とす	fail in ～
～でカンニングをする	cheat on ～

抜き打ち小テストがあった。 **We had a pop quiz.**

＊pop quiz＝抜き打ちテスト

明日から期末テストだ。 **The finals start tomorrow.**

今日からテスト期間だ。 **Exam week starts today.**

テスト、嫌だなぁ。 **I hate exams.**

英語は自信がある。 **I'm confident in English.**

社会と化学が心配。 **I'm worried about social studies and chemistry.**

暗記科目は苦手だ。 **I'm bad at memorizing subjects.**

明日でテストが終わる。わ～い！ **Tomorrow is the last day of exams. Whoopee!**

やっとテストが終わった！ **My exams are finally over!**

やっと解放された気分！ **I finally feel free!**

今日は思い切り寝るぞ！ **I'm going to get a good sleep tonight!**

明日は遊びに行くぞ！ **I'm going to have fun tomorrow!**

テストの出来

すごく難しかった。	**It was really hard.**
思ったほど難しくなかった。	**It wasn't as hard as I thought.**
最後まで解けなかった。	**I couldn't answer all the questions.**
余裕だった！	**It was a piece of cake!** ＊a piece of cake＝簡単なこと
歴史で93点取った。	**I got 93 on my history exam.**
英語は、なんと満点だった。	**I couldn't believe it, but I got a perfect score in English.**
中間テストより20点も上がった。	**My score went up 20 points from the mid-terms.** ＊mid-terms＝mid-term exams（中間テスト）
前回より30点も下がった。	**My score dropped by 30 points from the previous exam.** ＊drop＝落ちる、下がる　previous＝前の
英語の平均点は、68点。	**The average score on the English exam was 68.** ＊average score＝平均点
平均点に満たない科目がいくつかあった。	**There were a few classes that I scored lower than average in.**
数学は追試になっちゃった。	**I need to take a make-up exam in math.** ＊make-up exam＝追試
ギリギリ赤点を免れた。	**I was really close to failing.** ＊close to 〜＝〜に近い　failing＝落第
赤点が3つもある。	**I've failed three tests.** ＊fail＝〜（試験）に落ちる
学年で83番だった。	**I was 83rd in my grade.** ＊ここでのgradeは「学年」
徹夜したかいあって、いい点が取れた。	**I crammed all night, so I got a pretty good score.** ＊cram＝詰め込み勉強をする
一夜漬けじゃ、やっぱりダメだった。	**I crammed for the test the night before, but it didn't help.**
次こそは、早めにテスト勉強を始めよう。	**Next time, I'm going to start studying sooner.**

成績

数学の成績が上がった。	**My math grade improved.** *「下がった」なら、improvedをdroppedに
塾に行っている成果だな。	**This is the result of going to a cram school.** *cram school＝塾
家庭教師のサトウ先生のおかげだ。	**It's all thanks to my tutor, Ms. Sato.** *tutor［テューター］＝家庭教師
1学期よりも成績が下がった。	**My grades dropped from the first term.** *grade＝成績　term＝学期
成績表をお母さんに見せた。	**I showed my grades to my mom.**
成績が上がって、褒められた。	**She praised me because my grades went up.** *praise＝～を褒める
成績が下がって、ぐちぐち言われた。	**She nagged me because my grades went down.** *nag＝～に文句を言う
最近、娘の成績が落ちている。	**Her grades have fallen recently.** *fall＝落ちる。過去分詞はfallen
塾に通わせるべき？	**Should I send her to a cram school?** *cram school＝塾
息子に家庭教師を頼んでみようか。	**Maybe I should hire a tutor for him.**
息子の成績が下がったら、小遣いを減らそう。	**If his grades go down, I'll cut his allowance.** *allowance＝小遣い
1学期の通知表が渡された。	**I got my first term report card.**
「5」は3つあった。	**There were three A's.** *Aは、「5」「優」など最も良い成績を表す
「1」はなかった。	**There weren't any F's.** *Fはfail（落第）の頭文字で、「不可」を表す

塾・家庭教師・予備校

どの塾に通おうかな？	**Which cram school should I go?**
塾に通い始めた。	**I started going to cram school.** *cram school＝塾
週3日、通うことになった。	**I'll go three times a week.**
週に8クラスある。	**I take eight classes a week.**

塾の冬期講習を受けた。	**I took the winter course at the cram school.**
塾通いもなかなか大変だ。	**It's not easy to go to cram school.**
塾の自習室で勉強した。	**I studied in the study room at the cram school.**
予備校の授業はすごくハード。	**Preparatory school classes are really hard.** ＊preparatory school＝予備校
家庭教師の先生に来てもらうことになった。	**I'm going to have a tutor come and teach me.** ＊tutor［テューター］＝家庭教師
今日は初めての授業だった。	**I had my first lesson today.**
トミタ先生の教え方は、わかりやすい。	**Ms. Tomita's teaching is easy to follow.** ＊follow＝～を理解する
スズキ先生はABC大出身だ。	**Mr. Suzuki went to ABC University.**
オンラインの授業は、聞き逃しても巻き戻せるから便利。	**Online lessons are convenient because I can rewind if I missed something.** ＊rewind＝巻き戻す

進路・受験

進路について

英語の先生になりたい。	**I want to be an English teacher.**
卒業後は、カナダに留学したい。	**After graduating, I hope to study in Canada.**
専門学校でグラフィックデザインを学びたい。	**I want to learn graphic design at a vocational school.** ＊vocational school＝専門学校
大学で法律を学びたい。	**I want to study law at university.**
とりあえず大学に行きたい。	**I want to go on to college first.**
高校を卒業したら就職する。	**I'll get a job after I graduate high school.**

まだ進路が決められない。	**I haven't decided what I want to do yet.**
将来、何がしたいのかわからない。	**I don't know what I want to do in the future.**
進路について、両親と話をした。	**I talked to my parents about what I'm going to do.**
私の好きにすればいいと言ってくれた。	**They told me to do what I want.**
息子の進路について話した。	**We talked about his future.**
彼の進みたい道に進むのが一番だ。	**I think he should do what he wants to do.**
大学へ行かせてあげたいけど、そんな余裕はない。	**I wish we could let him go to college, but we can't afford it.**
奨学金を申し込もうかな？	**Should I apply for a student loan?** ＊student loan＝貸与型奨学金
奨学金を返済できるか心配。	**I don't know if I can pay back my student loan.**
奨学金で大学に行けたらいいのに。	**I wish I could go to college on a scholarship.** ＊scholarship＝給付型奨学金

就職 (→ p. 251「就職・転職」を参照)

志望校

そろそろ志望校を決めなきゃ。	**I really need to decide which school I want to go to.**
どうしても ABC 大学に行きたい。	**I really want to go to ABC University.**
母は、XYZ 大学のほうがいいと言っている。	**My mom says XYZ University is better.**
滑り止めに、EFG 大学も受けようかな。	**Just to be on the safe side, maybe I'll also take the EFG University exams.** ＊be on the safe side＝安全を期する
ABC 大学のオープンキャンパスに行ってきた。	**I went to an open-campus event at ABC University.**

あの大学に行きたい気持ちがますます高まった。	**I started to feel more and more like going to that university.**
娘はABC大学に進学したいと言っている。	**She says she wants to go on to ABC University.**
できれば国公立大学に行ってほしい。	**I want her to go to a national university if possible.**
私立でも家から通えるならOK。	**Private universities are okay as long as she can commute from home.** ＊commute＝通学する、通勤する
現役合格してもらいたい。	**I hope she can go to college right out of high school.**
浪人しないでほしいなぁ。	**I hope she doesn't have to spend another year in cram school.** ＊cram school＝塾、予備校

受験対策

今日は模試だった。	**I had a mock exam today.**
模試の結果が出た。	**I got the results of the mock exam.**
英語の偏差値が50だった。	**My T-score for English was 50.** ＊T-score＝偏差値
ABC大学の基準点には、10足りない。	**My score is 10 points lower than ABC University's standard score.**
これなら第一志望校に入れそうだ。	**I think I can get in my first choice school with this score.**
ABC大学の入試の過去問を買った。	**I bought a book with previous exam questions from the ABC University entrance exam.** ＊previous＝以前の
ABC大学はA判定。やった！	**I was ranked A for ABC University. Yay!** ＊rank ～ ...＝～を…にランク付けする
XYZ大学はD判定のままだ。	**I'm still ranked D for XYZ University.**
このままじゃマズい！	**I'm not going to make it!** ＊make it＝成功する、やり遂げる

12 学校生活

最後の追い込みだ。	**It's my last chance to study.**
あと少しだ。頑張るぞ!	**Just a little longer. I can do it!**
試験当日まで体調管理に気を付けよう。	**I'll take care of my health until exam day.**
総合型選抜に向けて、面接の練習をしている。	**I'm practicing for the interview for the comprehensive selection.** ＊comprehensive＝総合的な
小論文対策をしている。	**I'm practicing for the short essay.**
英検2級は取っておきたい。	**I want to get EIKEN level 2.**

受験

ABC大学の願書を取り寄せた。	**I requested an application form from ABC University.** ＊application form＝応募書類
XYZ大学に願書を提出した。	**I submitted an application to XYZ University.** ＊submit＝～を提出する
ABC大学にオンラインで出願した。	**I applied for ABC University online.**
前期日程は2月25日・26日。	**The first round is on February 25 and 26.** ＊first round＝第1回。「後期日程」ならsecond roundに
試験日は3月10日。	**The exam is on March 10.**
今日はABC大学の受験日だった。	**I had the entrance exam for ABC University today.**
今日は共通テストだった。	**We had the common test today.**
試験会場はABC大学だった。	**We took the exams at ABC University.**
落ち着いて試験に臨んだ。	**I took the exams with a calm mind.** ＊calm[カーム]＝落ち着いた
緊張で震えた。	**I was nervous and shaking.** ＊nervous＝緊張している
まあ、やれるだけのことはやった。	**Well, I did all I could.**
解答速報を見て、答え合わせをした。	**I looked at the preliminary answers and checked my own answers.** ＊preliminary＝予備の、仮の

思ったよりできた。	**I did better than I expected.**
どの教科も平均点より下だ。	**I got a below-average score in every subject.**
ABC 大学の二次試験に進んだ。	**I got through to ABC University's second exam.**
トモは推薦入学が早々に決まっている。	**Tomo got admitted early on recommendation.** ＊recommendation＝推薦
もう受験しなくていいのはうらやましい。	**I'm jealous of him not having any more exams.**

合格・不合格

ABC 大学に合格した！	**I got accepted to ABC University!** ＊get accepted＝入学を許可される
XYZ 大学は不合格だった。	**I didn't get into XYZ University.**
これで浪人確定だな。	**So now I'll have to spend another year studying.**
ABC 大学は補欠合格だ。	**I'm on the waiting list for ABC University.**
どうかマモルが合格していますように。	**I hope Mamoru gets accepted to the school.**
マモルが ABC 大学に合格した！ よかった！	**Mamoru got accepted to ABC University! Good for him!**
息子は本当によく頑張った。	**He really did the best he could.**
残念ながら、娘は XYZ 大学に落ちてしまった。	**Unfortunately, my daughter didn't get into XYZ University.**
アヤは ABC 大学に行くことに決めた。	**Aya decided to go to ABC University.**
友だちには合否を聞きにくい。	**I hesitate to ask friends whether they passed or failed.** ＊hasitate to ～＝～するのをためらう

学校生活について
英語日記を書いてみよう

学校生活について、英語で書いてみましょう。

調理実習の時間

We cooked sweet-and-sour pork in cooking class today. It was delicious and surprisingly easy. I love cooking class!

今日、調理実習の時間に酢豚を作った。すごくおいしくて、しかも、意外と簡単だった。調理実習って大好き！

「酢豚」は sweet-and-sour pork、「調理実習」は cooking class。「家庭科」は home economics ですが、cooking class のほか、sewing class（被服）、parenting class（育児）などと具体的に表しても OK。「意外と」は surprisingly（驚くほど）で表せます。

このままだと推薦入試が…

Mr. Sato said if I'm late again, he won't write a recommendation to the college I want to go to. I MUST get to school on time from now on.

サトウ先生に「今度遅刻したら、もう大学の推薦状は書かない」と言われた。これからは遅刻しないようにしないとマズい。

ここでの「大学」は「私が行きたい大学」と考えて、the college I want to go to とします。「遅刻しない」は get to school in time（学校に時間内に着く）で表せますね。「マズい」は must（～しなければならない）を大文字にして、意味を強調してみました。

部活の仲間とカラオケ

My club members are going to karaoke this Sunday. Uh-oh, there isn't a recent song I can sing. Maybe I'll go and practice by myself tommorow.

日曜日は部活の仲間とカラオケ。ヤバい、最近の曲は歌えないよ。明日、1人カラオケに行って練習しようかな。

ほぼ確実に実行する予定は〈現在進行形＋近未来の時〉で表せます。「ヤバい」「大変だ」という気持ちは uh-oh（おっと）で表しました。「1人カラオケに行く」は go (to karaoke) by myself ですが、流れから to karaoke は明白なので省略しています。

進路を決めないと

There was a parent-student-teacher meeting today. I still can't decide what I want to do after I graduate. I've started feeling really worried.

今日、三者面談があった。進路がまだ決まってない。マジで焦ってきた。

「三者面談」は parent-student-teacher meeting。「進路」は「卒業後にしたいこと」と具体的に考えて、what I want to do after I graduate としました。「マジで焦ってきた」は I've started feeling ～（～と感じ始めている）を使って表してみました。

13 大学・専門学校

学部・学科・学年などを表す単語

～学部・～学科	the ～ department / the department of ～
～専攻	～ major
文学	literature
(日本の) 国文学	Japanese literature
英文学	English literature
外国語	foreign languages
英語	English
韓国語	Korean
中国語	Chinese
フランス語	French
スペイン語	Spanish
ドイツ語	German
言語学	linguistics
社会学	sociology
文化人類学	cultural anthropology
法学	law
商学	commerce
経営学	business administration
哲学	philosophy
史学	history
政治学	politics
経済学	economics
政治経済学	politics and economics
国際関係学	international studies
教育学	education
体育学	physical education
スポーツ科学	sports science
医学	medicine
薬学	pharmacy
歯学	dentistry
理工学	science and technology
工学	engineering
数学	mathematics / math
理学	science
物理学	physics [フィジクス]
化学	chemistry
科学	science
建築学	architecture
機械学	mechanics
農学	agriculture
生物学	biology
環境学	environmentology
異文化コミュニケーション	cross-cultural communication
情報科学	computer science
神学	theology [セオロジー]
キャンパス	campus
図書館	library
講堂	auditorium
学食	cafeteria
運動場	sports field
大学1年生	freshman
大学2年生	sophomore [サフォモー]
大学3年生	junior
大学4年生	senior [スィーニア]
修士課程	master's course
博士課程	doctoral course

専門学校の分野を表す単語

専門学校	vocational school
美術	art
彫刻	sculpture
写真	photography
デザイン	design
ウェブデザイン	web design
CG デザイン	CG design
IT エンジニア	IT engineer
プログラミング	programming
アニメ	animation
アニメーター	animator
漫画家	cartoonist
声優	voice actor
アナウンサー	announcer / anchor
インテリア	interior design
美容師	hairstylist / hairdresser
理容師	barber
トリマー	groomer / trimmer
調理	cooking
製菓	confectionery
看護師	nurse
保育士	nursery teacher
介護士	care worker
針灸師（しんきゅう）	acupuncturist and moxa-cauterizer
栄養	nutrition
建築	architecture
秘書	secretary
歯科衛生	dental hygiene
簿記	bookkeeping
法律	law
税務	tax accounting
会計	accounting
医療事務	medical coding
翻訳	translation
通訳	interpretation
ウエディングプランナー	wedding planner
客室乗務員	flight attendant

入学

今日は入学式だった。
We had the entrance ceremony today.

初めてスーツを着た。
It was my first time to wear a suit.

講堂が大きくて圧倒された。
I was overwhelmed by the size of the auditorium.
＊overwhelmed＝圧倒されて　auditorium＝講堂

文学部だけで 2000 人の学生がいる。
The literature department alone has 2,000 students.
＊literature＝文学

新入生向けのガイダンスがあった。
There was a guidance session for new students.
＊guidance＝学生指導、ガイダンス

キャンパスには学生があふれていた。
The campus was full of students.

キャンパスで迷子になった。 **I got lost on campus.**

クラスがないから、友達ができるか不安。 **We don't have fixed classes, so I don't know if I'll be able to make friends.**
＊fixed＝固定の、決まった

隣に座ったキタジマさんという女の子と話した。 **I talked to Kitajima-san, a girl who sat next to me.**

サークルの勧誘がすごかった。 **The clubs were trying really hard to attract new members.**
＊attract＝～を呼び寄せる

講義・ゼミ

履修科目をなかなか決められない。 **I still haven't decided what classes to take.**

履修登録の仕方がよくわからない。 **I don't quite understand how to register for classes.**
＊not quite ～＝あまり～でない　register＝登録する

ウェブで履修登録をした。 **I registered for classes online.**

必修は週に 15 コマだ。 **I have 15 required classes a week.**
＊required＝必須の

国際関係論は必ず履修しよう。 **I'm definitely taking International Relations.**
＊definitely＝絶対に

文化人類学って面白そう。 **Cultural Anthropology sounds interesting.**
＊anthropology［アンスロポロジィ］＝人類学

第二外国語はフランス語を取ろう。 **I'll take French for my second foreign language.**

楽に単位を取れる講義はないかな。 **I wonder if there are any classes with easy credits.**
＊credit＝単位

あの講義は、出席していれば単位をもらえるらしい。 **I heard that you can earn credits for that class by just attending.**
＊earn＝～を得る　attend＝出席する

寝坊して、1 限に間に合わなかった。 **I overslept, so I couldn't make it to the first class.**
＊make it to ～＝～に間に合う

ミキに代返を頼んだ。 **I asked Miki to take attendance for me.**
＊attendance＝出席

今日の哲学の講義はオンラインだった。	**Today's philosophy class was online.**
対面授業のほうがいいな。	**I prefer in-person classes.**
オンライン授業ばかりだから、なかなか友達ができない。	**All my classes are online so I can't really make friends.**
スペイン語は休講だった。	**My Spanish class was cancelled.**
来週からちゃんと講義に出よう。	**I'll make sure to start attending lectures next week.** ＊lecture＝講義
必修の講義はなかなか難しい。	**Required classes are kind of difficult.** ＊required＝必須の
今日の講義はすごく面白かった。	**Today's lecture was really interesting.**
毎回、予習の量が多くて大変。	**It's tough because there's always so much studying to do before the class.**
休んだ講義のノートをカオルに見せてもらった。	**Kaoru showed me her notes from the class I missed.**
ソウタのノートを写真に撮らせてもらった。	**I took some photos of Sota's notebook.**
セイラに資料を共有してもらった。	**Seila shared her materials with me.**
ゼミの志望書を提出した。	**I submitted an application letter for the seminar class.**
ゼミ訪問をした。	**I visited a seminar class.**
ゼミの発表があった。	**I gave a presentation for my seminar class.**
発表の準備をしなきゃ。	**I have to prepare my presentation.**
ゼミでディスカッションをした。	**We had an open-discussion in my seminar class.**

課題・実習

金曜までに、製図の課題を仕上げなきゃ。
I have to complete the draft assignment by Friday.
＊draft＝図案、設計図　assignment＝課題

図面を元に、模型を作成した。
I created a model based on the drawing.

なかなかの完成度だ。
I managed to do quite a good job.
＊manage to ～＝何とか～する　quite a ～＝本当に～

イラストのポートフォリオを作った。
I made a portfolio with my illustrations.

キャラクターデザインの課題に取り組んでいる。
I'm working on a character design assignment.

キャラクターのモーション制作に手こずっている。
I'm having a hard time animating the characters.
＊have a hard time ～ing＝～するのに苦労する

プログラミングの課題、余裕だった。
The programming assignment was easy.

制作課題のテーマが決まらない。
I can't decide on the production theme.
＊theme[スィーム]＝テーマ

今日も引き続き、ワンピース制作に取り組んだ。
I continued to work on the dress design today.

カネダさんの作品の出来栄えがすごくよかった。
Ms. Kaneda's creation turned out really well.
＊creation＝創作物　turn out ～＝～の結果になる

今日の実習では、野菜の飾り切りをした。
I practiced carving vegetables today.
＊carve＝～を彫る

アニメのアテレコ実習をした。
I practiced doing animation voice-over.
＊voice-over＝ボイスオーバー、ナレーション

実習で、犬のトリミングをした。
I practiced trimming a dog.
＊trim＝～の毛を刈り込んで形を整える

今日から病院での看護実習が始まった。
I started my nursing practice at the hospital today.

明日から、保育園での実習。楽しみだな。
I'm going to start my training at the nursery school tomorrow. I'm looking forward to it.
＊nursery (school)＝保育園

実習での反省点を書き留めておこう。	**I'm going to write down my self-evaluation at training.** ＊self-evaluation＝自己評価
実習をすると、教科書だけではわからないことに気付く。	**Practical training helps me realize that you can't learn some things just from the textbook.** ＊realize＝～に気付く
グループワークのリーダーになった。	**I became the leader of our group project.**
グループワークのメンバーが決まった。	**The members for the group work have been decided.**
グループのみんなと、発表の準備をした。	**Our group worked together to prepare a presentation.**

テスト・レポート

もうすぐテスト期間だ。	**Exam week is coming up.**
心理学のテストは範囲が広い。	**The psychology exam covers a lot of topics.** ＊psychology［サイカラジー］＝心理学
教育学は持ち込み可だった。	**The education exam was open-book.** ＊open-book＝教科書持ち込み可の
社会学は持ち込み不可だった。	**The sociology exam was closed-book.** ＊closed-book＝教科書持ち込み不可の
大学の図書館で勉強した。	**I studied in the college library.**
文学の講義は、レポート提出のみ。	**We only need to submit a report for the literature class.** ＊submit＝～を提出する
レポートは 1000 字以上だ。	**My report needs to be at least 1,000 words.**
来週までにレポートを書かなきゃ。	**I have to write a report by next week.**
金曜日に締切のレポートが 3 つもある。	**I have three reports to turn in by Friday.** ＊turn in ～＝～を提出する
サイトのコピペはダメだ。	**You shouldn't copy and paste straight from a website.**

13 大学・専門学校

スゴい！　Chat GPTのほうがうまく書けてる。
Oh my! Chat GPT writes better.

明け方、何とかレポートを書き上げた。
I barely managed to finish writing the report at dawn.
＊barely＝かろうじて　manage to 〜＝何とか〜する

まだ手を付けていない。ヤバい！
I haven't even touched it yet. I'm screwed!
＊screwed［スクルード］＝まずい状態にある

テストの出来 （→ p. 281「テストの出来」を参照）

成績・単位

成績通知表が届いた。
My report card arrived.

成績がオンラインで公開された。
Our grades were posted online.
＊post＝掲示する

無事、全講義の単位が取れた。
Thankfully, I got full credits for all my classes.
＊credit＝単位

オールAだった。
I got straight A's.

AとBが半分ずつくらいだった。
About half my scores were A's and the rest were B's.

卒業分の単位を取り終えてホッとした。
I'm relieved that I received all of my graduation credits.

必修の授業を1つ、落としちゃった！
I failed one required class!
＊required＝必須の　fail＝〜に落第する・落ちる

留年決定だ。どうしよう。
I have to repeat one year. What am I going to do?

教授に泣きついてみよう。
Maybe I should beg the professor.
＊beg＝〜に懇願する

単位が足りていた。
I had enough credits.

無事に進級できてホッとした。
I'm glad I made it to the next grade.
＊make it to 〜＝〜に達する

学食・カフェテリア

お昼は学食で食べた。
I had lunch at the cafeteria.
＊cafeteria＝（学校などの）食堂

安くてありがたい。 It's great that they have reasonable prices.

学食は混んでいた。 The cafeteria was packed.
＊packed＝混んだ、すし詰めの

うちの学食はおいしくてうれしい。 I'm glad we have good food at our cafeteria.

人気のメニューはカレーピラフだ。 The most popular dish is curry pilaf.

うちの学食はイマイチだ。 Our cafeteria food is not so good.

３限終了後、カフェテリアでリオとおしゃべりした。 After the third period, I chatted with Rio at the cafeteria.

お昼は大学生協で買った。 I bought lunch at the university co-op.
＊co-op［コウオプ］＝生活協同組合

サークル活動

どのサークルに入ろうか迷う。 I'm wondering what club to join.
＊「サークル」は、circleとは言わないので注意

サークルを２つ掛け持ちしようかな。 Maybe I'll join two clubs.

テニスサークルの見学に行った。 I checked out the tennis club.
＊check out ～＝～をチェックする

軽音部に入ることにした。 I decided to join the pop music club.

チャラチャラしたサークルには入りたくないな。 I don't want to join a club that just messes around.
＊mess around＝ふざける、騒ぐ

サークルの年会費がかなり高い。 The annual club dues are quite expensive.
＊annual ＝毎年の　dues＝会費、料金

サークルの新歓があった。 There was a welcome party for new club members.
＊welcome party＝歓迎会

サークルの幹事をすることになった。 I'm going to be the leader of the club.

マチダ先輩が夕飯をおごってくれた。 Machida-senpai bought me dinner.
＊buy ～ ... ＝～（人）に…をおごる

午後はずっと部室にいた。 I was in the club room all afternoon.

サークルの打ち上げでオールした。 Our club party lasted all night.
＊last＝続く

週に１度の、サークルの会合だった。 **We had a weekly club meeting.**

サークル合宿に行った。 **I went to a club camp.**

卒業生や他大生とも話せて視野が広がる。 **Talking to alumni and students from other universities helps me widen my world view.**

＊alumni［アラムナィ］＝alumnus（卒業生）の複数形
widen＝～を広げる

このサークルに入って本当によかった。 **I'm really glad I joined this club.**

学園祭

サークルでおでん屋台を出すことになった。 **Our club decided to set up an oden stall.**

＊stall＝屋台

有志でたこ焼き屋をやることになった。 **Some of us got together and decided to set up a takoyaki stall.**

美術部で展示をする。 **The art club will have an exhibition.**

英語劇を上演する。 **We're going to perform an English play.**

学園祭での展示に向けて、準備が追い込みだ。 **We're working really hard on our display for the campus festival.**

呼び込みのチラシを作った。 **We made information fliers.**

＊flier（チラシ）は、flyerともつづる

予想以上にたくさんのお客さんが来た。 **There were more visitors than we expected.**

雨だったので、お客さんの入りがイマイチだった。 **It was rainy, so there weren't so many people.**

売り上げは目標額に届かず。 **We didn't reach our sales target.**

途中で食材を切らしてしまって焦った。 **We panicked when we ran out of ingredients too soon.**

＊run out of ～＝～を切らす　ingredient＝材料、食材

から揚げは３時までに売り切れてしまった。 **The deep-fried chicken sold out by 3:00.**

いろいろな屋台で、あれこれつまんだ。 **I ate a little bit of everything from the stalls.**

＊a little bit＝少し、ちょっと

お笑いコンビのライブがあった。 **A comedy duo came to perform.**

すごく盛り上がった。 **The audience was really fired up.**
＊fired up＝はしゃいだ、興奮した

お金・バイト

給付型奨学金の申請をした。 **I applied for a scholarship.**
＊apply for ～＝～を申し込む
scholarship＝給付型奨学金

給付型奨学金を得られることになった。 **I got a scholarship.**

奨学金を借りることにした。 **I took out a student loan.**
＊take out ～＝～(ローンなど)を組む

教科書代でお金が飛んだ。 **I spent a lot on textbooks.**

塾講師のバイトをしようかな。 **I wonder if I should work at a cram school.**
＊cram school＝塾

時給のいいバイトを探そう。 **I'll look for a part-time job that pays well.**

バイト代をためて旅行に行きたい。 **I want to save my part-time job money and go on a trip.**

最近、バイトのし過ぎで講義をサボりがち。 **I've been working too much lately, so I've been missing classes.**
＊miss＝～を欠席する

今月はあまり稼げなかった。 **I didn't earn much this month.**

次の仕送りまでピンチ！ **I'm in a tough spot until my next allowance comes!**
＊tough spot＝困った状況、地点　allowance＝小遣い、手当て

長期休暇

2カ月の夏休みって、結構長い。 **A two-month summer vacation is pretty long.**

夏休み、やることないよ～！ **There's nothing to do during summer vacation!**

夏休みの間に、運転免許を取ろう。 **I'm going to get my driver's license during summer vacation.**

合宿免許に行こう。	**I'll attend a driving school camp.**
夏休みを利用して、カナダに短期留学したい。	**I want to use my summer vacation to study in Canada for a short time.**
旅行に行きたいけど、お金がないな。	**I want to travel, but I don't have enough money.**
夏休みといっても、バイトばかり。	**I'm on summer vacation, but all I do is work part time.**
実家に帰ってのんびり過ごそうかな。	**I'm thinking about going back home and taking it easy.** ＊take it easy＝休む、くつろぐ
久しぶりに帰省した。	**I went back home for the first time in ages.** ＊for the first time in ages＝久しぶりに
お母さんは私の顔を見てすごく喜んでいた。	**My mom was really happy to see me.**

就職活動（→ p. 251「就職・転職」を参照）

卒論

卒論のテーマが決まらない。	**I haven't decided what my graduation thesis should be about.** ＊thesis［スィースィス］＝論文
ようやく卒論のテーマが決まった。	**I've finally decided what my graduation thesis should be about.**
指導教官はタナベ先生だ。	**My instructor is Mr. Tanabe.**
卒論の締切が近い。	**My thesis deadline is coming up.**
卒論、間に合うかな？	**I wonder if I'll be able to finish my thesis on time.** ＊on time＝時間通りに

卒業

もうすぐ卒業。	**I'm graduating soon.**
今日は卒業式だった。	**We had the graduation ceremony today.**
卒業証書をもらった。	**I got my diploma.** ＊diploma＝卒業証書

卒業式で泣いてしまった。	**I cried at the graduation ceremony.** ＊「卒業式」は、graduationだけでもOK
あっという間の4年間だった。	**The four years went by so fast.**
4年で卒業できてよかった。	**I'm glad I was able to graduate in four years.**
卒業式ではかまを着たい。	**I want to wear hakama to my graduation.**
卒業式に着るはかまを予約した。	**I reserved the hakama I'll wear to my graduation.**
はかまを何着か試着した。	**I tried on some hakama.**
赤いはかまが気に入った。	**I liked the red hakama.**
卒業式用のスーツ、買いに行かないとな。	**I have to go buy a suit for graduation.**
卒業式に着るスーツを母と買いに行った。	**I went to buy a graduation suit with my mom.**
卒業式の後、後輩が追いコンを開いてくれた。	**After the graduation ceremony, my juniors held a farewell party for me.** ＊junior＝後輩　farewell party＝送別会
卒業式の後、みんなで飲みに行った。	**We went drinking after the graduation ceremony.**
働き始めたら、なかなか集まれなくなるだろうな。	**After we start working, we probably won't be able to meet up so often.**
社会人になっても、時々は集まりたいな。	**Even after we start working, I want to meet up with them every once in a while.**
卒業旅行でオーストラリアに行く。	**We're going to Australia for our graduation trip.**

大学・専門学校について英語日記を書いてみよう

大学や専門学校での出来事について、英語で書いてみましょう。

大学生活スタート

This is my sixth day in Tokyo, and I'm a little homesick. We have the entrance ceremony the day after tomorrow. Hope I can make friends soon.

今日で東京に来て６日目。ちょっぴりホームシック。あさっては入学式。早く友達ができるといいな。

「今日で東京に来て６日目」は、It's been six days since I moved to Tokyo. と現在完了形でも表現できます。「あさって」は the day after tomorrow（明日の翌日）と表します。「～だといいな」は I hope ～ですが、くだけて Hope ～とすることも多いです。

方言っていいな

I've become good friends with Keiko and Norika. Keiko's Kumamoto accent is cute and Norika's Kyoto dialect is kind of relaxing. I love the way they talk.

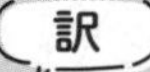

ケイコとノリカと仲良くなった。ケイコの熊本なまりはかわいいし、ノリカの京都弁はなんだか落ち着く。ああいう方言っていいな。

「仲良くなる」は「いい友達になる」と考えて、become good friends とします。accent は「なまり」、dialect は「方言」のこと。最後の文は、the way they talk（彼女たちの話し方）とすれば、「ああいう方言」のニュアンスを出すことができます。

学園祭で大成功！

We had a college festival today. Our class ran a Korean food stall. Our food was so popular that we ran out of ingredients by 3:00!

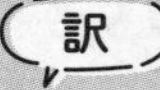

今日は学園祭だった。うちのクラスは韓国料理の屋台を出した。料理はすごく好評で、3時には材料がなくなってしまうほどだった！

「屋台を出す」は run（過去形は ran）を使います。この run は「～（店など）を切り盛りする」という意味です。so ～ that … は「とても～で、…するほどだ」の意。「～がなくなる、～を切らす」は run out of ～。このように、run にはいろいろな使い方があります。

バイトを減らそうかな

Oh no, I failed one required class ... Maybe I should cut down on the amount of time I work. I don't want to do another year.

あ～あ、必修の授業を1つ落としちゃった……。バイトを少し減らしたほうがいいかな。留年なんて、したくないよ～。

「必修の授業」は required class。「～したほうがいいかな」は Maybe I should ～（動詞の原形）で表します。「バイトを減らす」は「働く時間量を減らす」と考えて、cut down on the amount of time (that) I work としましょう。「バイトする」は work で OK です。

14 買い物

買い物をする

買い物に行く

渋谷に買い物に行った。	**I went shopping in Shibuya.**
いろいろな店を見て回った。	**I went around the stores.**
ウインドーショッピングをした。	**I went window-shopping.**
アウトレットモールで買い物をした。	**I did some shopping at the outlet mall.**
スーツを買いに行った。	**I went shopping for a suit.** ＊go shopping for ～＝～を買いに行く
3 階の子ども服売り場に行った。	**I went to the children's clothing section on the third floor.**
1 時間ほど買い物をした。	**I shopped for about an hour.**
買い物に時間がかかった。	**I spent a lot of time shopping.**
夫は私の買い物にイライラしていた。	**My husband was impatient with my shopping.**
欲しい物がたくさんあった。	**There were a lot of things that I wanted.**

買った

シャツなど 4 着も買ってしまった。	**I bought four items, including shirts.** ＊item＝品目
懐中電灯と電池を買った。	**I bought a flashlight and some batteries.** ＊flashlight＝懐中電灯

衝動買いをしてしまった。	I did some impulse buying. ＊impulse buying＝衝動買い
バッグを衝動買いしてしまった。	I bought a bag on impulse. ＊on impulse＝衝動的に
冬物をまとめ買いした。	I bought winter clothes in bulk. ＊in bulk＝大量に
最近、買い物し過ぎだ。	I've been shopping too much lately.
3万円くらい使ってしまった。	I spent about 30,000 yen.

買わなかった

欲しい物が見つからなかった。	I couldn't find what I wanted.
買いたい物がなかった。	There wasn't anything I wanted.
欲しかったけど買えなかった。	I wanted it, but I couldn't afford it.
さんざん悩んだけど、買うのをやめた。	I thought about it a lot, and I decided not to buy it. ＊buyをgetにしてもOK
買うかどうか、もう少し考えよう。	I'll think a little more about whether to buy it.
買わなくて正解だった。	I was right not to buy it.

買った物の感想

買ってよかった。	I'm glad I bought it.
掘り出し物だった。	It was a real bargain. ＊bargain＝お買い得品、掘り出し物
いい物を買った。	It was a good buy.
すごく満足。	I'm totally satisfied.
早く友達に自慢したい。	I can't wait to show it off to my friends. ＊show ～ off＝～を（自慢げに）見せびらかす
買わなきゃよかった。	I shouldn't have bought it.
とんだ散財だ。	I ended up spending too much money. ＊end up ～ing＝結局～してしまう
なんでこんな物、買ったんだろう？	Why did I buy something like this?

安物買いの銭失いだ。	**It was penny-wise and pound-foolish.**

値段・支払い

値段について

安かった。	**It was cheap.** ＊cheapは、「安くて品質が悪い」という意味で使うことも
高かった。	**It was expensive.**
手ごろな値段だった。	**It was a reasonable price.**
手の届く値段だった。	**It was an affordable price.**
（品質の割に）高くなかった。	**It was inexpensive.**
特価だった。	**It was a bargain.** ＊bargain＝お買い得品、掘り出し物
会員価格だった。	**It was a members' price.**
かなりお買い得だった。	**It was a steal.** ＊steal＝格安品、掘り出し物
まけてもらった。	**I got a discount.**
クーポンで割引された。	**I got a discount with a coupon.**
値引きしてもらえなかった。	**I couldn't get a discount.**
2つで9800円だった。	**It was 9,800 yen for two.**
2個買うと、もう1つ無料になった。	**It was buy-two-get-one-free.**
配送料が高かった。	**The shipping fee was high.**
配送料が無料だった。	**It was free shipping.**

セール

店内全品、5割引だった。	**Everything in the store was 50% off.**
タイムセールで、さらに2割引になっていた。	**There was a limited-time discount, so I got an additional 20% off.** ＊additional＝追加の

いよいよ夏のセール。 **The summer sale is starting soon.**

セールの時期に、まとめ買いしておかなきゃ。 **I should do most of my shopping during the sale season.**

会員限定のセールだった。 **The sale was for members only.**

セールで靴を買った。 **I bought a pair of shoes at a sale.**

在庫一掃セールをやっていた。 **They were having a clearance sale.**

あそこの閉店セール、絶対に行かなきゃ。 **I really should go to their going-out-of-business sale.**

＊going-out-of-business＝店じまい

レジ

レジには行列ができていた。 **There was a long line at the checkout counter.**

＊checkout counter＝レジ

レジの人の手際がよかった。 **The cashier was really speedy.**

＊cashier＝レジ係

セルフレジを使った。 **I used the self-checkout.**

配送にしてもらった。 **I asked them to deliver my purchase.**

＊purchase＝買った物、購入品

支払い

現金で払った。 **I paid in cash.**

1万円札で支払った。 **I paid with a 10,000-yen bill.**

＊bill＝紙幣

おつりが間違っていた。 **I got the wrong change.**

＊change＝つり銭

クレジットカードで支払った。 **I paid with a credit card.**

一括払いで買った。 **I paid in one payment.**

分割払いで買った。 **I paid in installments.**

＊installment＝分割払いの1回分。「3回払い」なら、three installments

リボ払いで支払った。 **I paid in monthly installments.**

キャッシュレス決済

Suicaで支払った。	**I paid with Suica.**
キャッシュレス決済の仕方を店員さんに教えてもらった。	**The shop staff showed me how to do cashless payment.**
支払い時にアプリがうまく動作しなくて焦った。	**I panicked because the app wouldn't work when I went to pay.**
バーコードをうまく読み取れなかった。	**I had trouble reading the barcode properly.**
残高不足だったので、1万円チャージした。	**My balance was low, so I charged my card with 10,000 yen.** ＊balance＝残高
今月の明細書を見たら、意外と多く使っていた。	**When I looked at this month's statement, I saw I'd used it more than I expected.** ＊I'd＝I had
キャッシュレス決済がずいぶん普及したな。	**Cashless payments have really spread.** ＊spread＝広がる
キャッシュレス決済だと、現金を持たなくていいから便利。	**Cashless payments are convenient because I don't need to carry cash.**
キャッシュレス決済だと、つい余計な買い物をしちゃう。	**Cashless payments make me buy too much stuff.** ＊stuff＝物

ポイントカード

ポイントカードを作った。	**I got a point card.**
100円で1ポイントたまる。	**You get one point for every 100 yen you spend.**
購入金額の10パーセントがポイントとしてたまる。	**Ten percent of the price you pay is converted to points.** ＊convert ～ to ...＝～を…に変換する
500ポイントたまったら、500円割引される。	**You get a 500-yen discount for 500 points.**
スタンプが15個たまったら、プレゼントがもらえる。	**You can get a present after collecting 15 stamps.**

ポイント2倍デーだった。	**Today was double-point day.** ＊「ポイント3倍デー」なら、doubleをtripleに
ポイント5倍デーだった。	**Today was quintuple-point day.** ＊quintuple［クウィントゥーポゥ］＝5倍の
ポイントで1000円分を支払った。	**I paid 1,000 yen in points.**
ポイントで全額、支払った。	**I paid for everything with my points.**
ポイントカードって、どんどん増えて困る。	**I have too many point cards. They're becoming a bother.** ＊bother＝厄介な物
アプリのポイントカードが増えて便利。	**It's convenient that there are more app-based point cards now.**

店で

店・店員

店は混んでいた。	**The store was crowded.**
入場制限で15分待った。	**I had to wait for 15 minutes due to an entry limit.**
店はガラガラだった。	**The store was empty.**
店員が親切だった。	**The clerk was kind.**
おすすめのコーデを教えてくれた。	**She recommended an outfit.** ＊outfit＝衣服、洋服
店員の態度が悪かった。	**The clerk was rude.** ＊rude＝失礼な
店員がちょっとしつこかった。	**The clerk was a bit pushy.** ＊pushy＝強引な、しつこい
店員とおしゃべりするのは楽しい。	**It's fun to chat with clerks.**
店員に話しかけられるのって、どうも苦手。	**I don't really like it when clerks come to talk to me.**

品切れ・在庫

品切れだった。悔しい！	**It was sold out. Too bad!**
欲しい色の在庫がなかった。	**The color I wanted was out of stock.** ＊out of stock=品切れで

14 買い物

自分のサイズだけ売り切れていた。 **Just my size was sold out.**

ずっと品切れが続いている。 **It's still out of stock.**
It's been sold out for a long time.

限定品なので、あっという間に完売。 **It was a limited item, so it sold out in a flash.** ＊in a flash＝一瞬で

転売のために買っている人がいるのかな？ **I wonder if some people are buying it for resale.**

フリマサイトで高値で売られてた！ **It was sold for a high price on a flea market site!**

次回入荷は来週だという。 **They said that the new stock will arrive next week.** ＊stock＝在庫

次回入荷は未定だって。 **They don't know when they have more coming in.**

入荷したら連絡をもらう予定だ。 **They'll call me when it comes in.**

取り寄せてもらうことにした。 **I back-ordered it.** ＊back-order＝〜を取り寄せ注文する

注文した。 **I ordered it.**

返品・交換

ズボンを返品した。 **I returned the pair of pants.**

サイズが合わないから、返品したいな。 **I want to return it because it doesn't fit me.** ＊fit＝〜に合う・フィットする

返品できるか、店に問い合わせた。 **I asked the store if I could return it.**

不良品だったので、店に返品した。 **I took it back to the store because it was defective.** ＊defective＝欠陥がある

セール品だから、返品できない。 **It was a sale item, so I can't return it.**

返品期限を過ぎてしまった。 **I missed the return deadline.**

送料元払いで返品した。 **I returned the item and paid for shipping myself.** ＊shipping＝送料

送料着払いで返品した。 I returned the item and sent it by COD.
＊COD＝cash on delivery（着払い）の略

9号サイズと交換してもらった。 I had it exchanged for a size 9.

服・服飾雑貨を買う （→ p. 474「ファッション」を参照）

電化製品を買う

パソコン （→ p. 592「パソコン」を参照）

デジカメ

デジタル一眼レフが欲しいな。 I want a DSLR camera.
＊DSLR＝digital single-lens reflexの略

コンパクトなデジカメが欲しい。 I want a compact digital camera.
＊cameraだけで「デジカメ」を指すことも多い

いろんなデジカメを見せてもらった。 The clerk showed me several digital cameras.

あのデジカメ、小さくて使いやすそうだった。 That digital camera looked small and easy to use.

とても人気のある機種らしい。 I heard that it's a really popular model.

古いカメラを5000円で下取りしてもらえるらしい。 They said I can trade in my old camera for 5,000 yen.
＊trade in ～＝～を下取りに出す

家電製品を表す単語

テレビ	television / TV
4K テレビ	4K TV
DVD レコーダー	DVD recorder
ブルーレイレコーダー	blu-ray recorder
ゲーム機	game console
洗濯機	washing machine / washer
洗濯乾燥機	washer-dryer
ドラム式洗濯乾燥機	drum-type washer-dryer
乾燥機	dryer / drying machine
掃除機	vacuum cleaner
ロボット掃除機	robot vacuum / cleaning robot
加湿器	humidifier
除湿機	dehumidifier
空気清浄機	air cleaner
冷蔵庫	fridge / refrigerator
食洗機	dishwasher
炊飯器	rice cooker
圧力鍋	pressure pot
電子レンジ	microwave (oven)
オーブン	oven
ガスレンジ	gas cooker / stove
IH 調理台	electoric stove / IH cooker
トースター	toaster
コーヒーメーカー	coffee machine
ホームベーカリー	bread maker
ホットプレート	hot plate
ミキサー	blender
エアコン	air conditioner
扇風機	(electric) fan
電気ストーブ	electric heater
オイルヒーター	oil heater
石油ファンヒーター	oil fan heater
ホットカーペット	electric carpet
こたつ	kotatsu
電話	telephone / phone
スマートフォン	smartphone
スマートウォッチ	smart watch
スマートスピーカー	smart speaker
ファクス	fax (machine)
電子辞書	electronic dictionary
デジタルカメラ	(digital) camera
ビデオカメラ	camcorder
CD プレーヤー	CD player
ラジオ	radio
マッサージチェア	massage chair
ドライヤー	hairdryer
アイロン	iron
シェーバー	electric shaver
電動歯ブラシ	electric toothbrush
美顔器	facial care device
体重計	scale

電子レンジを買い替えた。 **I bought a new microwave.**

＊「電子レンジ」は、microwave ovenとも言う

食洗機が欲しいな。 **I want a dishwasher.**

最近の食洗機は、小さくなったなぁ。 **Dishwashers are smaller these days.**

静かな洗濯機が欲しいな。	**I want a noiseless washing machine.**
ドラム式の洗濯乾燥機を買った。	**I bought a drum-type washer-dryer.**
新しく買った洗濯機、静かだな。	**The washing machine I recently bought is quiet.**
妻が、洗濯機を買い替えたいと言っている。	**My wife says she wants to buy a new washing machine.**
まだ十分使えるのに。	**We can still use it.**
音の静かな掃除機が欲しい。	**I want a noiseless vacuum cleaner.**
もっと軽い掃除機が欲しい。	**I want a lighter vacuum cleaner.**
ロボット掃除機って、使い勝手はどうなんだろう？	**I wonder how handy cleaning robots are.**
10 畳用のエアコンを買った。	**I bought an air conditioner for a 10-tatami room.**
省エネナンバーワンを受賞したらしい。	**It got first prize for energy saving.**
ひと回り大きいテレビを買った。	**I bought a TV one size larger.**
冷凍室の大きな冷蔵庫を買った。	**I bought a fridge with a large freezer space.**
マッサージチェアが欲しいけど、置くところがないな。	**I want a massage chair, but I don't have a place to put it.**
災害時用に、懐中電灯付きラジオを買った。	**I bought a radio with a flashlight for emergencies.** ＊flashlight＝懐中電灯
最新の家電を見ているだけで楽しい。	**It's fun to just look at the latest household appliances.** ＊household appliance＝家電

インテリア用品を買う （→ p. 336「インテリア」を参照）

食料品・日用品を買う

食料品を買う

食料品を表す単語

野菜	vegetable
キャベツ	cabbage
レタス	lettuce
ホウレンソウ	spinach
小松菜	Japanese mustard spinach
白菜	Chinese cabbage
ニンジン	carrot
ジャガイモ	potato
サツマイモ	sweet potato
かぼちゃ	pumpkin
大根	daikon radish
レンコン	lotus root
トマト	tomato
ミニトマト	cherry tomato
きゅうり	cucumber
なす	eggplant
ピーマン	green pepper
しいたけ	shiitake mushroom
玉ねぎ	onion
長ねぎ	leek
肉	meat
牛肉	beef
豚肉	pork
鶏肉	chicken
ひき肉	ground meat
魚	fish
刺身	raw fish / sashimi
サケ	salmon
アジ	horse mackerel
サバ	mackerel
ブリ	yellow tail
サンマ	saury [ソーリー]
マグロ	tuna [トゥーナ]

イカ	squid [スクイッド]
タコ	octopus
エビ	shrimp
貝類	shellfish
アサリ	littleneck clam
ハマグリ	clam
ワカメ	wakame seaweed
ニンニク	garlic
ショウガ	ginger
ミカン	tangerine
バナナ	banana
オレンジ	orange
イチゴ	strawberry
メロン	melon
スイカ	watermelon
ブドウ	grape
キウイ	kiwi fruit
パイナップル	pineapple
卵	egg
牛乳	milk
生クリーム	fresh cream
バター	butter
チーズ	cheese
ヨーグルト	yogurt [ヨゥガート]
米	rice
酒	sake / rice wine
しょうゆ	soy sauce
砂糖	sugar
塩	salt
小麦粉	flour [フラウァ]
みそ	miso
マヨネーズ	mayonnaise
ケチャップ	ketchup

食料品の買い出しに行った。	I went grocery shopping. ＊grocery shopping＝食料品の買い出し
夕方、スーパーに行った。	I went to the supermarket in the evening. ＊「スーパー」はgrocery storeとも言う
夕飯の食材を買ってきた。	I bought some food for dinner. ＊「明日のお弁当の(食材)」なら、for tomorrow's lunch
野菜の特売の日だった。	It was a bargain day for vegetables.
ミカンを１袋買った。	I bought one bag of tangerines.
豚肉を 300 グラム買った。	I bought 300g of pork.
今日は卵がすごく安かった。	Eggs were really cheap today.
多くの食品が値上がりしていた。	A lot of grocery prices have gone up.
そんなに買っていないのに、7000 円もした。	I didn't buy that much, but it came to 7,000 yen.
バターが売り切れていた。	Butter was sold out.
特売のイチゴに人だかりができていた。	A crowd of people went to the special sale on strawberries.
エコバッグを持っていった。	I took my own bag with me. ＊「エコバッグ」は、eco bagとしてもOK
エコバッグを持っていくのを忘れた。	I forgot to take my own bag.
B スーパーのほうが、食材が新鮮。	B Store has fresher food.
C スーパーのほうが、ちょっと安い。	C Store is a little less expensive.
スーパーを３軒ハシゴした。	I shopped at three supermarkets.
ネットスーパーで買い物した。	I shopped at an online supermarket.
最近はネットスーパーをよく使う。	I've been using the online supermarket a lot lately.
重い物も玄関まで持ってきてもらえるから助かる。	They deliver heavy items to the door so it's helpful.

日用品を表す単語

ごみ袋	garbage bag
ラップ	plastic wrap
アルミホイル	aluminum foil
クッキングシート	cooking sheet
キッチンペーパー	paper towel
食器用洗剤	dishwashing detergent
スポンジ	sponge
洗濯洗剤	laundry detergent
柔軟剤	fabric softener
洗濯ばさみ	clothespin
ハンガー	(clothes) hanger
歯ブラシ	toothbrush
歯磨き粉	toothpaste
シャンプー	shampoo
コンディショナー	conditioner
ボディソープ	body wash
石けん	soap
トイレットペーパー	toilet paper
ティッシュ	Kleenex / tissue
生理用品	sanitary items
綿棒	Q-tip / cotton swab
電池	battery
電球	light bulb

ドラッグストアで日用品を買った。
I bought some daily necessities at the drugstore.
*daily necessities＝生活必需品

100ワットの電球を2個買った。
I bought two 100-watt light bulbs.
*light bulb＝電球

トイレットペーパーがもうすぐなくなりそう。
It looks like I'm running out of toilet paper.
*run out of 〜＝〜を使い果たす

箱ティッシュは1人につき1パックまでだった。
There was a limit of one pack of tissue boxes per person.

明日、忘れずに買いに行こう。
I'll make sure to buy some tomorrow.

来客用の歯ブラシを買った。
I bought toothbrushes for guests.

歯ブラシの替えを買っておいた。
I bought some spare toothbrushes.

災害時用の非常食を買った。
I bought emergency food for a disaster.
*「非常食」はemergency rationsとも言う

帰宅途中にアルミホイルを買った。
I picked up aluminum foil on the way home.
*pick up 〜＝(ついでに)〜を買う

花屋さんでガーベラの花束を買ってきた。
I bought a bouquet of gerberas from the florist's.
*bouquet［ボウケィ］＝花束、ブーケ

綿棒を買い忘れた！	I forgot to get Q-tips! ＊Q-tip（綿棒）は、商標が一般名詞化したもの

プレゼントを買う

ミサキへの誕生日プレゼント、何がいいだろう。	What should I get Misaki for her birthday?
彼女、財布なら喜んでくれるかも。	I think a wallet would make her happy.
お母さん、ああいう色好きかな？	I wonder if my mom likes that kind of color.
気に入ってもらえるといいな。	I hope she likes it.
プレゼント選びって、難しい。	It's hard to select presents.
プレゼントを選ぶのって、ワクワクする。	I get excited when choosing presents.
プレゼント用に、スカーフを買いに行った。	I went to buy a scarf for a present.
プレゼント用に包んでもらった。	I had it gift wrapped. ＊gift wrap＝～をプレゼント用に包む
赤い包装紙と黄色のリボンを選んだ。	I picked out red wrapping paper and a yellow ribbon. ＊pick out ～＝～を選ぶ
のしを付けて包装してもらった。	I had the gift wrapped with a noshi.
カードを付けてもらった。	I asked for a message card.
結婚祝いに、ペアのカップ＆ソーサーを買ってあげた。	I bought them a cup-and-saucer set for a wedding present. ＊saucer［ソーサー］＝受け皿、ソーサー
新築祝いだから、観葉植物がいいかな？	I guess a house plant would be a good housewarming present. ＊housewarming present＝新築祝い
あまり高価なものだと、かえって気を遣わせちゃうかも。	If my present is too expensive, it might make them uncomfortable.

通販・ネットショッピング

通販カタログを見るのは楽しい。	I like looking at mail-order catalogs.
通販でロールケーキをお取り寄せした。	I mail-ordered a roll cake. ＊roll cakeは、Swiss rollとしてもOK
テレビの通販で掃除機を買った。	I bought a vacuum cleaner from a TV shopping show.
ネットでリュックサックを買った。	I bought a backpack online.
深夜のテンションでポチッてしまった。	I was midnight high and clicked "order."
ネットショッピングって、すごく便利。	Online shopping is really convenient.
届くのが楽しみ。	I'm looking forward to getting the package.
注文した翌日に、もう届いた。早っ！	I received the package the day after I ordered it. That's fast!
思ったとおりのステキな財布だった。	The wallet was just as nice as I expected.
実物はイメージとちょっと違った。	The actual item was a little different from the picture.
色味が思っていたのと違った。	It wasn't the color I expected.
サイトで見たのより安っぽい感じ。	It looked cheaper than it did on the site.
ネットでの買い物で、いつも失敗しちゃう。	I always fail when I shop online. ＊fail＝失敗する

Memo

買い物に関することを、メモしておきましょう。

買い物について 英語日記を書いてみよう

日々の買い物について、英語で書いてみましょう。

どっちにしようかな

I went to check out some washing machines. I couldn't decide which to buy, a regular type or a drum type.

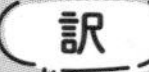

洗濯機を見に行ったものの、普通のタイプかドラム型か、どちらを買おうか迷ってしまった。

check out ～は「～を調べる・見てみる」の意で、値段や機能性を確認したり、複数の商品を比較したりするニュアンスになります。ここでの「迷った」は「決められなかった」と考えて、I couldn't decide としました。which to buy は「どちらを買うべきか」の意。

見なければよかった

In a newspaper insert, I saw the same down jacket as mine, but it was 5,000 yen cheaper. I was disappointed! I wish I hadn't seen it.

新聞の折り込み広告に自分のと同じダウンジャケットが載っていた。5000円も安くなっててガッカリ！見なければよかったなぁ。

insert は「(新聞などの) 折り込み広告」のこと。ちなみに、flier/flyer は「チラシ、ビラ」、ad/advertisement は「広告（全般）」を指します。I wish I hadn't seen it は、「(実際は見てしまったけれど) 見なければよかった」というニュアンスです。

早く驚く顔が見たいな

I found the very necklace Chie always wanted! I got it for her birthday without thinking twice. I can hardly wait to see her look of surprise.

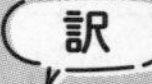

チエがずっと欲しがっていたネックレスを発見！　迷わず、誕生日プレゼントに買った。早く驚く顔が見たいな。

「チエがずっと欲しがっていたネックレス」は、the very necklace (that) Chie always wanted のように、関係代名詞で表します。この very は「まさにその」という強調の意味。「迷わず」は without ～（～なしで）と think twice（よく考える）を組み合わせました。

我慢できずに…

Aya and I went to the outlet mall. When I saw a pair of Cazal sunglasses at 50% off, I couldn't resist them. I ended up spending quite a bit of money. But I'm happy!

アヤとアウトレットへ行った。カザールのサングラスが半額になっているのを見たら、どうしても我慢できなくて。結局、かなりお金を使ってしまった。でも、うれしい！

「サングラス」は、a pair of sunglasses、two pairs of sunglasses のように数えます。resist は「～を我慢する・抑える」の意。end up ～ing は「結局～することになる」という意味で、ここでは、予定外の高い買い物に対する反省のニュアンスも表しています。

15 お金

家計

支払い

いろいろな料金を表す単語

食費	food expenses
固定費	fixed costs
交通費	transportation expenses
医療費	medical expenses
教育費	education expenses
臨時出費	unexpected expenses
公共料金	utility bills
電気代	electric bill
水道代	water bill
ガス代	gas bill
インターネット代	Internet bill
新聞代	newspaper bill
電話代	phone bill
（国民）健康保険料	(national) health insurance fee
保険料	insurance premium
年金保険料	pension premium
入学金	admission fee
給食費	school lunch fee
（学校の）授業料	tuition
月謝	tuition / lesson fee
家賃	rent
交通費	transportation fee
宿泊費	accommodation fee
駐車場代	parking fee
駐輪場代	bicycle parking fee
運賃	fare
片道料金	one-way fare
往復料金	round-trip fare
航空券代	air fare
バス代	bus fare
タクシー代	taxi fare
病院代	medical bill
入院費	hospital charges
入場料	entrance fee
送料	shipping fee
取り扱い手数料	handling fee

電話代を払った。 **I paid my phone bill.**

コンビニで水道料金を支払った。 **I paid the water bill at a convenience store.**

電気代の支払い期限が過ぎていた。 **The electric bill was past due.**
＊due［デュー］＝期限

毎日、届くのは請求書ばかり。 **All I get every day is bills.**

健康保険料の支払い、高いなぁ。 **The health insurance payment is really high.**

家賃の振込をした。 **I paid my rent by bank transfer.**
＊bank transfer＝銀行振込

家賃の振込を忘れてた。 **I forgot to transfer my rent.**
＊transfer＝〜を送金する・振り込む

家賃は毎月自動で引き落とされる。 **The rent is automatically withdrawn from my account each month.**
＊withdraw＝〜を引き落とす

口座引き落としは便利でいい。 **Payment by direct debit is really convenient.**

息子の入学金の振込をした。 **I transferred my son's school admission fee.**

ネットで振込をした。 **I transferred money online.**

ほとんどの支払いを電子決済にしている。 **I pay digitally for most things.**

家計の管理

夕飯の後、家計簿を付けた。 **After dinner, I did my household accounts.**
＊household accounts＝家計簿

今月から家計簿を付け始めた。 **I started keeping my household accounts this month.**

パソコンで家計簿を付けることにした。 **I decided to keep my household accounts on my PC.**

家計簿アプリを使い始めた。 **I started using a household accounting app.**
＊household accounting＝家計

固定費をなるべく安くしたい。 **I want to keep my fixed costs as low as possible.**
＊fixed＝固定された

発泡酒は家計に優しい。 **Low-malt beer is easy on the household budget.**
＊malt＝麦芽、モルト

今月は赤字だ。 **We're in the red this month.**
＊in the red＝赤字で

今月は少し余裕がありそう。 **We have a little extra money this month.**
＊extra＝余分な

この調子なら貯金できそう。 **At this rate, I'll be able to save money.**
＊at this rate＝この調子なら

うちの家計は火の車。 **We're very hard up.**
＊hard up＝金に困っている

これ以上どうやって出費を削れというの！ **How can I cut back on more expenses?**

光熱費はうなぎ上りだ。 **Utility costs are skyrocketing.**
＊skyrocket＝急上昇する

浪費・散財

最近、お金を使い過ぎだ。 **I've been spending too much money lately.**

気付かない間に、カードを使い過ぎていた。 **I had overused my credit card before I knew it.**

散財しちゃった。 **I spent too much money.**

すっからかんだ。 **I'm broke.**
＊broke＝無一文の、金欠の

懐が寂しい。 **I'm low on cash.**
＊cash＝お金、現金

今月も金欠だ。 **I'm short of cash again this month.**

浪費癖を何とかしないと。 **I ought to do something about my spending habits.**
＊ought to 〜＝〜しないといけない　habit＝癖、習慣

節約

少し節約しなきゃなぁ。 **I ought to save some money.**

食費を減らそう。 **I'll cut down on my food expenses.**
＊expense＝支出、費用

外食を控えよう。 **I'll try to eat out less.**
＊eat out＝外食する

電気代を節約したい。 **I want to reduce my electric bill.**
＊reduce＝〜を減らす

省エネタイプのエアコンを買った。	**I bought an energy-saving air conditioner.**
なるべく扇風機を使おう。	**I'll try to use the fan as much as possible.**
今月は電気代が 2000 円安くなった。	**The electric bill is 2,000 yen cheaper than the last month.** ＊cheaperをlowerとしてもOK

貯金

100 万円ためたいな。	**I want to save up one million yen.**
貯金ゼロは、さすがにまずい！	**Having no savings is bad, seriously!**
毎月 3 万円ずつ貯金するぞ。	**I'm going to save 30,000 yen every month.**
半年で 50 万円ためるぞ！	**I will save 500,000 yen in six months!**
留学費用として 200 万円ためよう。	**I'm going to save two million yen to study abroad.**
とりあえず、将来に備えたい。	**I just want to put money away for the future.** ＊put money away＝貯蓄する、お金を取っておく
老後の蓄えをしておきたい。	**I want to put some money away for my retirement.**
年金だって少ししかもらえないし。	**Pension is next to nothing.** ＊next to＝（通例否定語の前で）ほとんど
少しずつでも着実にためていこう。	**I'll save steadily even just a little bit at a time.**
500 円玉貯金を始めた。	**I've started to save 500-yen coins.**
今日から「つもり貯金」を始めるぞ。	**I'm going to start my "tsumori" savings today.**
「飲みに行ったつもり」で、3000 円貯金した。	**I set aside 3,000 yen which I would have spent drinking.** ＊set aside ～＝～（お金など）を別に取っておく

15
お金

順調にお金がたまってきたぞ。	**I'm doing pretty well on saving money.**
なかなかお金がたまらない。	**It's hard to save up money.**
ドル建ての外貨預金を始めた。	**I started a dollar-based currency savings plan.** ＊dollar-based＝ドル建ての　currency＝通貨、貨幣
円高の今がチャンスだ。	**The yen is strong, so now is my chance.**
今はかなりの円安だ。	**The yen is so weak now.**
金利、低過ぎ！	**Interest rates are too low!**
50万円を定期預金にした。	**I made a time deposit of 500,000 yen.** ＊time deposit＝定期預金、積立預金
定期預金を中途解約した。	**I withdrew the time deposit before maturity.** ＊withdraw＝～を引き落とす。過去形はwithdrew。withdrewはcanceledにしてもOK　maturity＝満期
今の給料では貯蓄ができない。	**With my current salary, I don't have enough for any savings.**
いろんな物が値上げされて、貯金どころではない。	**Many things are getting more expensive, so I can't save money at all.**

お金の貸し借り

手持ちが2000円しかなかった。	**I only had 2,000 yen with me.**
マサに5000円借りた。	**I borrowed 5,000 yen from Masa.**
お父さんに1万円返した。	**I paid back 10,000 yen to my dad.**
オノさんにお金を返すのを忘れてた！	**I forgot to pay Ono-san back!** ＊pay ～ back＝～(人)にお金を返す
明日、必ず返さなきゃ。	**I must pay her back tomorrow.**
次に会ったときに返そう。	**I'll pay her back next time I see her.**

ハルキが、この間貸した5000円を返してくれた。
Haruki paid me back the 5,000 yen I lent him the other day.
＊lend ～ ...＝～に…を貸す。過去形はlent

サトコがお金を返してくれない。
Satoko won't pay me back.

ヒロくん、いつになったらお金を返してくれるのかな？
I wonder when Hiro-kun is going to pay me back.

借用書を書いた。
I wrote an IOU.
＊IOU＝借用証書。I owe you.（あなたに借りがある）から

お金の貸し借りは、なるべくしたくない。
I don't want to borrow or lend money if I don't have to.

銀行

銀行口座

A銀行で口座を開設した。
I opened an account in A Bank.
＊account＝口座

定期預金のほうがいいかな？
I wonder if the time deposit is better for me.
＊time deposit＝定期預金、積立預金

普通口座だとほとんど利息がつかない。
A regular account gains almost no interest at all.
＊interest＝利息、金利

ネット銀行で、口座開設の申し込みをした。
I applied for an account with an online bank.
＊apply for ～＝～を申し込む

B銀行の口座を解約した。
I canceled my account with B Bank.

口座の残高

残高を確認した。
I checked my balance.

給料が振り込まれていた。やった！
My salary was deposited into my bank account. Great!
＊deposit＝～を預け入れる

残高が3万円しかない。
I only have 30,000 yen in my bank account.

クレジットカードの引き落としが痛いなぁ。
My credit card payment is a real pain.
＊pain＝苦悩、苦しみ

通帳記入をした。
I updated my bank book.
＊update＝～の内容を最新のものにする

ATM・口座取引

コンビニの ATM でお金を下ろした。	**I withdrew some money from a convenience store ATM.** ＊「銀行のATM」なら、bank ATM
10 万円、預け入れをした。	**I deposited 100,000 yen.** ＊deposit＝〜を預け入れる
220 円の手数料がかかった。	**The fee was 220 yen.** ＊fee＝手数料
最近は手数料が高過ぎる。	**Handling fees are really high these days.** ＊handling fee＝取扱手数料
ATM コーナーに行列ができていた。	**There was a line at the ATM corner.**
連休前だからだろう。	**It's probably because it's right before the holidays.**
ああ、今日は給料日か。	**Ah, today's payday.**
近くに ATM がなくて困った。	**There weren't any ATMs nearby, so I was at a loss.** ＊at a loss＝困って、途方に暮れて
ネットバンキングだと窓口や ATM に行く必要がない。	**With internet banking, you don't need to go to the counter or ATM.**
銀行のアプリで送金手続きをした。	**I transferred the money using my bank app.** ＊transfer＝〜を振り込む

株・投資

株・投資

銀行に株式口座を開設した。	**I opened a bank account for trading stocks.** ＊trade＝〜を売買する　stock＝株
アライさんは、株で 200 万円もうけたらしい。	**I heard that Arai-san made two million yen in the stock market.** ＊stock market＝株式市場。このinはonでもOK
XYZ 株を 1000 株購入した。	**I bought 1,000 XYZ shares.** ＊share＝株
XYZ 株を売却した。	**I sold my XYZ shares.**
銀行で投資信託を勧められた。	**The bank advised me to invest in a mutual fund.** ＊invest in 〜＝〜に投資する　mutual fund＝投資信託

給料が上がらないから、投資で資産を作るしかない。
I'm not getting a raise, so I have to build my assets through investment.
＊raise＝昇給　build＝〜を築く　assets＝資産

株価上昇

XYZの株価が上がっている。
The value of XYZ is rising.
＊value＝価値、額面

XYZの株価が急騰している。
The value of XYZ is skyrocketing.
＊skyrocket［スカイラケット］＝急騰する

昨日買っておけばよかった。
I wish I had bought it yesterday.

XYZ株が20円上がった！
The value of XYZ rose by 20 yen!

XYZ株は、買値から30パーセント値上がりした。
The value of XYZ has increased by 30% since I bought it.

手持ちの株が、軒並み値上がりした。
All my stocks went up. ＊stock＝株

含み益は100万円を超えた。
My unrealized capital gains are over a million yen.
＊unrealized＝未回収の　capital gain＝資本利得

株価下落

ABCの株価が急落している。
The value of ABC is plummeting.
＊plummet＝急落する

ABCは大幅値下げでストップ安。
The value of ABC dropped sharply and hit the limit.
＊hit the limit＝限界に達する

昨日売っておけばよかった。
I should've sold it yesterday.

今が買い時かも。
Maybe now is a good time to buy.

ABC株の含み損が膨らんでいる。
The unrealized capital losses on ABC are increasing.
＊unrealized＝未回収の　capital loss＝資本損失

塩漬けにするしかないか…。
I guess I'll have to keep these shares for the long-term ...

為替・両替

外国為替

このところ円安だ。	**The yen has been weak for a while.**
円高が進んでいる。	**The yen is getting stronger.** ＊円安の場合はstrongerをweakerに
円が1ドル＝130円まで値上がりした。	**The yen has risen to 130 yen to the dollar.** ＊値下がりした場合はrisenをdroppedに
1ユーロは今、140円だ。	**The current exchange rate is 140 yen to the euro.**
人民元は、日本円に対して下落している。	**The yuan is falling against Japanese yen.** ＊yuan［ユアン］＝人民元、中国元
旅行するなら今がチャンスだ。	**If you're going to travel, now is a good time.**
この円安じゃ、海外旅行は当分お預けだな。	**I guess we can't go overseas for now due to the weak yen.** ＊due to ～＝～が原因で
製造業への影響が心配だ。	**I'm worried about the impact on the manufacturing industry.**
円安の影響でいろいろな物が値上がりしてる。	**The prices of a lot of things are going up due to the weak yen.**

両替

新札の1万円札に替えてもらった。	**I exchanged my 10,000-yen bills for crisp ones.** ＊crisp＝新品の、パリッとした
1万円を1000円札に両替してもらった。	**I exchanged the 10,000-yen bill for 1,000-yen bills.**
1000円札を崩してもらった。	**I asked to change a 1,000-yen bill to coins.**
5万円分、米ドルに両替した。	**I exchanged 50,000 yen for US dollars.**

空港でユーロに両替した。	**I exchanged money for euros at the airport.**
1万円で72ドルになった。	**I got 72 dollars for 10,000 yen.**
レートは1ドル＝139円だった。	**The rate was 139 yen to the dollar.**
手数料が2ドルかかった。	**The fee was two dollars.**
なんだか損した気分。	**I feel I've wasted some money.**

税金 （→ p. 249「経理・確定申告」も参照）

税金を表す単語

所得税	income tax
住民税	resident tax
県民税／都民税／府民税	prefectural tax
市民税／町民税／村民税	municipal tax
区民税	ward tax
消費税	consumption tax
固定資産税	property tax
法人税	corporation tax
事業税	business tax
たばこ税	tobacco tax
酒税	liquor tax
贈与税	gift tax
相続税	inheritance tax
自動車税	automobile tax
軽自動車税	light vehicle tax
ガソリン税	gasoline tax
地方税	local tax
入湯税	bathing tax

税金を支払わなきゃ。	**I have to pay my taxes.**
税金の支払いを済ませた。	**I paid my taxes.**
天童市にふるさと納税をした。	**I paid my hometown tax to Tendo City.**
ふるさと納税で牛肉を申し込んだ。	**I applied for beef with my hometown tax.**
ふるさと納税した分、住民税が安くなる。	**The hometown tax portion will make my resident tax cheaper.**
固定資産税が、家計に重くのしかかる。	**The property tax is a big burden on my household budget.**

＊burden＝負担、重荷　household budget＝家計

15 お金

確定申告の時期がやってきた。 It's time to file my income taxes.
*file=～を提出する

医療費控除を申請しなくちゃ。 I have to apply for a medical expenses tax deduction.
*expense=費用　deduction=控除

所得税の還付金が振り込まれていた。 The tax refund was deposited into my account.
*refund=払い戻し　deposit=～を預け入れる

税金の無駄遣いだけはやめてほしい。 I just wish they would stop wasting tax money.

保険

保険を見直そう。 I'm going to reconsider my insurance.
*reconsider=～を考え直す

保険料が高過ぎて、家計が苦しい。 The insurance premium is too high, and it's hurting the household budget.
*premium=保険料　hurt=～に打撃を与える

自動車保険が高過ぎる。 The car insurance is too high.

医療保険に入らなきゃ。 I need to get medical insurance.

保険の営業担当者が説明をしてくれた。 An insurance salesperson gave me an explanation.

どの保険がいいのか、さっぱりわからない。 I have no idea which insurance is good for me.

ムトウさんは、A社の保険がお薦めだと言っていた。 Muto-san recommended A Company's insurance.

いくつかの保険会社に資料請求をした。 I requested some brochures from several insurance companies.
*brochure[ブロウシュア]=パンフレット、案内書

医療保険のパンフレットをもらってきた。 I got a brochure for medical insurance.

どの保険に入るべきか、ファイナンシャルプランナーに相談した。 I talked with a financial planner about what insurance I should buy.

生命保険を解約しようか迷う。 I'm wondering if I should cancel my life insurance.

独り身だから生命保険は必要ないかな。	**I don't need life insurance as I'm single.**

ローン（→ p. 352「住宅ローン」も参照）

頭金は500万円くらいで考えている。	**I'm thinking about making a deposit of about five million yen.** ＊deposit＝頭金、手付金
ローン返済のシミュレーションをした。	**I made a simulation for loan repayment.** ＊repayment＝返済、払い戻し
ボーナスは、ローンの繰り上げ返済に充てよう。	**I'm going to use my bonus to pay back my loan early.**
やった！ ローンの審査に通った！	**Great! My loan has gotten approved!** ＊approve＝～を承認する
ローンの審査に通らなかった。	**My loan didn't get approved.**
ついにローン完済！	**I've finally paid off my loan!** ＊pay off ～＝～を完済する
ローンで車を買った。	**I bought a car with a loan.**
20年ローンを組んだ。	**We took out a 20-year loan.** ＊take out ～＝（申請して）～を受ける・得る
夫とペアローンを組んだ。	**I got a pair loan with my husband.**
変動金利と固定金利、どちらがいいの？	**Which one is better, an adjustable rate or a fixed rate?** ＊adjustable＝調節可能な　fixed＝固定した
ローンを組むなら、低金利の今がチャンスだ。	**Now is a good time to take out a loan because of the low interest rate.** ＊low interest rate＝低金利
給料が、家や車のローンでほとんど消えちゃうよ。	**Most of my salary goes to my mortgage and car payments.** ＊mortgage［モーギッジ］＝住宅ローン

お金について
英語日記を書いてみよう

お金にまつわるあれこれを、英語で書いてみましょう。

1万円発見！

I came across 10,000 yen in my old wallet when I was cleaning my room! Lucky me!

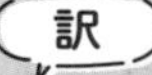

部屋の掃除をしていたら、古い財布の中に1万円を見つけた！ ラッキー！

come across ～は、直後に物を続けると「ふと～を見つける」、人を続けると「偶然～に会う」という意味になります。「ラッキー！」は、Lucky! でなく、Lucky me! とするのが英語らしい表現。I was lucky! や How lucky! などと表すこともできます。

めでたいけれど懐が…

I've been invited to two weddings this month. They're happy events, but my wallet feels light.

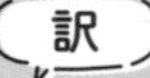

今月は2つの結婚式に招待されている。めでたいことだけど、懐が寂しいなぁ。

「2つの結婚式に招待されている」は、I have two weddings to attend（出席する結婚式が2つある）としても OK です。「懐が寂しい」は my wallet feels light（財布が軽い）としましたが、I'm short of money（金欠だ）などと表してもよいでしょう。

お小遣いを前借りしたい

I'm dying to go to the YOASOBI concert, but I don't have enough money ... I'll ask my mom if I can get next month's allowance in advance.

YOASOBIのライブに行きたくてたまらない。でも、お金が足りない……。来月のお小遣いを前借りできるか、お母さんにお願いしてみようっと。

「～したくてたまらない」は、be dying to ～(動詞の原形) で表してみました。dyingはdie(死ぬ)の -ing形で、全体で「死ぬほど～したい」という意味。ask ～ if ... は「…してくれるよう～に頼む」、allowanceは「お小遣い」、in advanceは「前もって」。

大学へ行かせてやりたい

My son said he wants to go on to college. I'll need at least two million yen. OK, I'll cancel the time deposit.

息子が大学に進学したいと言い出した。少なくとも200万円はいる。よし、定期預金を解約しよう。

「～に進学する」はgo (on) to ～でOK。「少なくとも、最低でも」はat least、「定期預金」はtime depositと表します。cancelは「～を取り消す」で、cancel the time depositで「定期預金を解約する」という意味になります。

16 住まい

住まいについて

インテリア

インテリア用品を表す単語

家具	**furniture**
棚	shelf
食器棚	**cupboard** [カッバード]
クローゼット	closet
たんす	**dresser**
テーブル	table
ダイニングテーブル	**dining table**
折りたたみ式のテーブル	folding table
サイドテーブル	**side table**
コーヒーテーブル	coffee table
机	**desk**
いす	chair
ロッキングチェア	**rocking chair**
リクライニングチェア	reclining chair
スツール	**stool**
ソファ	sofa / couch
2人用ソファ	**love seat**
クッション	cushion
ベッド	**bed**
シングルベッド	single bed
ダブルベッド	**double bed**
ソファベッド	sofa bed
カーペット	**carpet**
ラグ	rug
カーテン	**curtain**
ロールスクリーン	shade
パーティション	**partition**
壁紙	wallpaper
照明	**lighting**
スタンドライト	(floor) lamp
ランプ	**lamp**
鏡台	dressing table
姿見	**full-length mirror**
時計	clock
額絵	**framed painting**
観葉植物	(house) plant

シンプルなインテリアでまとめたい。 **I want simple décor.**

＊décor＝装飾。decorとも書く

ドラマに出てくるようなおしゃれな部屋にしたいな。 **I want a stylish room like one in a drama.**

サチの家みたいなインテリアにしたい。	**I want to decorate my house like Sachi's.** ＊decorate ＝～を飾る
この部屋をもっとかわいい感じにしたい。	**I want to redo this room and make it cuter.** ＊redo［リドゥー］＝～をやり直す・改装する
アジアンテイストの部屋が理想だ。	**An Asian-style room would be ideal.** ＊ideal［アイディーゥ］＝理想的な
遮光カーテンを買った。	**I bought blackout curtains.**
アンティークの鏡台を買った。	**I bought an antique dressing table.**
カーペットをセミオーダーした。	**I placed an order for a semi-custom-made carpet.** ＊place an order for ～＝～を注文する
中古家具店を回った。	**I looked around used furniture stores.** ＊used＝中古の　furniture＝家具
リサイクルショップでダイニングテーブルを買った。	**I bought a dining table at a secondhand shop.** ＊secondhand＝中古の
あのコーヒーテーブル、うちのソファに合うと思う。	**I'm sure that coffee table would match my sofa.**
あのスタンドライト、おしゃれだった！	**That floor lamp was so stylish!**
あんなソファが家にあったら、すてきだろうな。	**I think that sofa would make my house look really nice.**
安いのはいいけど、自分で組み立てなきゃいけないんだよね。	**It's nice that it's cheap, but I have to put it together myself.** ＊put ～ together＝～を組み立てる
組み立てが難しそう。	**It looks difficult to assemble.** ＊assemble＝～を組み立てる
私にも組み立てられるかな？	**I wonder if I can assemble it myself.**
夫が上手に組み立ててくれた。	**My husband did a good job putting it together.**
観葉植物が欲しいけど、どうせすぐ枯れちゃうだろうな。	**I want some plants, but they'll probably wither quickly.** ＊wither＝枯れる

模様替え

部屋を模様替えしたい。
I want to rearrange my room.
＊rearrangeは、家具などを配置し直すこと

リビングの模様替えをした。
I redecorated my living room.
＊壁紙などを変えて模様替えするときは、redecorate

畳が古くなってきた。
The tatami mats are getting old.

カーペットを新しくしたい。
I want to get new carpet.

うちは物が多過ぎるんだよね。
We have too many things.

家具の配置を変えた。
I moved the furniture around.
＊move ～ around＝～を動かす　furniture＝家具

配置を変えるだけでも、ずいぶん印象が変わる。
Just moving the furniture around really creates a different feel.
＊feel＝感じ、雰囲気

カーテンをクールな感じのものに替えた。
I changed my curtains to ones that make the room look cool.

部屋の隅に観葉植物を置いた。
I put a house plant in the corner of the room.
＊「観葉植物」は、foliage plantやleafy plantとも言う

住まいのトラブル

トイレが詰まっちゃった。
The toilet got clogged.
＊clog＝～を詰まらせる

トイレの水が流れなくなった。
The toilet wouldn't flush.
＊flush＝（トイレの水が）流れる

シンクの下から水漏れしている。
There's water leaking from under the sink.
＊leak＝漏れる

お風呂場の換気が悪い。
The ventilation in the bathroom isn't very good.
＊ventilation＝換気

給湯器の調子が悪い。
The water heater isn't working very well.

リビングのドアの建て付けが悪い。
The living room door won't open smoothly.

トイレのドアがキーキーいう。
The bathroom door is squeaky.
＊squeaky＝キーキーいう

油を差したほうがいいかな？
Maybe I should oil it.
＊oil＝～に油を差す

寝室の天井が雨漏りしている。 **The bedroom ceiling has a leak.**
＊ceiling［スィーリング］＝天井　leak＝水漏れ

修理を依頼しないと。 **I'd better have someone fix it.**
＊fix＝～を修理する

屋根の修理をしてもらわなきゃ。 **I have to have the roof repaired.**
＊repair＝～を修理する

壁の施工不良を見つけた。 **I found a defect in the wall.**
＊defect＝欠陥、不良

壁が薄くて、隣の部屋の音が聞こえる。 **The walls are thin and I can hear noises from the room next door.**

鍵をなくしちゃった。 **I've lost my keys.**

ブレーカーが落ちちゃった。 **The breaker blew a fuse.**
＊blow＝～（ヒューズ）を飛ばす。過去形はblew［ブルー］

マンションが建ってから、日当たりが悪くなった。 **We don't get much sunlight because of the new apartment building.**

リフォーム

キッチンをリフォームしたい。 **I want to remodel my kitchen.**
＊remodel＝～をリフォームする

シャワートイレを付けたい。 **I want to get an electric bidet toilet.**
＊bidet［ビーデイ］＝ビデ

壁紙を貼り替えたいなぁ。 **I feel like changing the wallpaper.**

壁を塗り替えたい。 **I want to repaint the walls.**

階段に手すりを付けたい。 **I want to install a handrail for the stairs.**
＊install＝～を取り付ける　handrail＝手すり

台所にABC社のシステムキッチンを入れたい。 **I want to get an ABC integrated kitchen installed.**
＊integrated＝統合した　install＝～を取り付ける

床暖房にしたいな。 **I want floor heating.**

浴室乾燥機付きのユニットバスにしたいなぁ。 **I want to make it a modular bathroom with a room dryer.**
＊modular bathroom＝ユニットバス

外壁をきれいにしたい。 **I want to clean the exterior walls.**
＊exterior＝外側の

収納を増やしたい。 **I want more storage space.**

バリアフリーの家にしたい。	**I want to make our house barrier-free.**
お風呂場の段差をなくしたほうがよさそうだ。	**We should get the bathroom floor evened out.** ＊even out ～＝～を平らにする
お父さんのために、玄関にスロープを付けようかな。	**I'm thinking about making the entrance ramped for my father.** ＊ramped＝スロープになった
太陽光パネルを付けようかな。	**I'm thinking about getting solar panels.**
オール電化にしようかな。	**Maybe we'll make our house completely electric.**
耐震強度が不安だ。	**I'm worried about earthquake resistance.** ＊earthquake＝地震　resistance＝抵抗
耐震補強を検討している。	**I'm considering having our house reinforced for earthquakes.** ＊reinforce＝～を強化する・補強する
工務店に工事の見積もりを依頼した。	**I asked the builder for an estimate.** ＊builder＝建築業者　estimate＝見積もり
3社から見積もりを取った。	**I got estimates from three companies.**
予算オーバーだ。	**It went over our budget.** ＊budget＝予算
プランを変更するしかないか。	**We have no choice but to change our plans.** ＊have no choice but to ～＝～するより仕方がない
どうせリフォームするなら一気にきれいにしたい。	**Since we're renovating our house, I want to make everything new.**

友人の住まいについて

友人の住まい

彼、どこに住んでいるんだろう。	**I wonder where he lives.**
彼はうちの近所に住んでいる。	**He lives in my neighborhood.** ＊neighborhood＝近隣
彼は同じ町内に住んでいる。	**He lives in the same town.**
彼は神奈川県横浜市に住んでいる。	**He lives in Yokohama, Kanagawa.**

彼女は琵琶湖のほとりに別荘を持っている。	She has a vacation home by Lake Biwa.
彼女は一軒家に住んでいる。	She lives in a house.
彼女は賃貸マンションに住んでいる。	She lives in an apartment. ＊分譲マンションなら、apartmentをcondoに。mansionは「洋館、豪邸」の意味なので注意
彼女は豪華なマンションに住んでいる。	She lives in a gorgeous apartment.
彼女はタワマンの27階に住んでいる。	She lives on the 27th floor of a high-rise apartment building. ＊high-rise apartment building＝タワマン
彼は3階建てのアパートに住んでいる。	He lives in a three-story apartment. ＊story＝階
彼女は学生寮に住んでいる。	She lives in a student dormitory. ＊dormitory＝寮、寄宿舎
彼のところは二世帯住宅だ。	He lives in a two-family home.
彼は郊外に家を買ったそうだ。	I heard he bought a house in the suburbs. ＊suburb＝郊外の住宅地
彼女は故郷に戻ろうか迷っている。	She's seriously thinking about moving back to her hometown.

住まいの印象

豪邸だった。	It was a big, luxurious house. ＊luxurious＝豪華な、ぜいたくな
昔ながらの日本家屋だった。	It was a traditional Japanese house.
趣のある家だった。	It was a nice house with a great atmosphere. ＊atmosphere［アトモスフィア］＝雰囲気
広々とした家だった。	It was a spacious house. ＊spacious［スペイシャス］＝広々とした
こぢんまりとした家だった。	It was a small but comfortable house.
割と狭かった。	It was pretty small.
おしゃれなマンションだった。	It was a stylish apartment.

「映(ば)える」インテリアだった。 The interior décor was very photogenic. ＊décor＝装飾。decorとも書く

ドラマに出てきそうな部屋だった。 It was like a room in a drama.

家具が高そうだった。 The furniture looked expensive.
＊furniture＝家具

書斎がハイテクだった。 It was a high-tech home office.

キッチンがすごく機能的だった。 The kitchen was really functional.

くつろげる部屋だった。 It was a cozy room.
＊cozy（居心地のよい）は、snug［スナッグ］としてもOK

あんなすてきな家に住めたらいいな。 I wish I could live in such a great house.

片付いていた。 It was neat and tidy.
＊neat＝小ぎれいな　tidy［タイディ］＝整とんされた

散らかっていた。 It was messy. ＊messy＝散らかった

殺風景な部屋だった。 It was a very bare room.
＊bare［ベァ］＝家具のない

住まいの条件

立地

通勤が楽な場所がいいな。 I want a place that's convenient for my commute.
＊このplaceは、「（住まいとしての）部屋」の意味
commute＝通勤

中央線の中野駅近辺にしよう。 I'll get a place near Nakano Station on the Chuo Line.

東西線の沿線がよさそう。 A place on the Tozai Line would be nice.

駅から歩いてすぐだ。 It's a short walk from the station.

駅まで歩いて６分ほどだ。 It's about six minutes on foot to the station.

駅からは少し距離がある。 It's a little ways away from the station. ＊a (little) ways away＝（少し）距離がある

駅からバスで15分くらいだ。 It's about 15 minutes by bus from the station.

駅からずっと上り坂だ。 It's uphill all the way from the station.
＊uphill＝上り坂の

車の通りが多い。 The traffic is heavy on that road.
＊traffic＝交通量

見晴らしがいい。 It has a nice view.

住めば都だ。 Anywhere can be your home once you get used to it.

間取り

2DKがいいな。 I want two bedrooms, a dining room and a kitchen.
＊正式な英語ではないが、日記では「2DK」としてもOK

3LDKだ。 It has three bedrooms, a living room, a dining room and a kitchen.
＊日記では「3LDK」としてもOK

ワンルームだ。 It's a studio apartment.

メゾネットだ。 It's a duplex apartment.
＊duplex＝メゾネット

6畳の和室と、洋室がある。 It has a 6-tatami Japanese-style room and a Western-style room.

6畳と4.5畳の洋室がある。 It has a 6-tatami and a 4.5-tatami Western-style room.

LDKは10畳だ。 The living room, dining room and kitchen are 10 tatami mats altogether.
＊日記では「LDK」としてもOK

ロフト付きだ。 It has a loft.

住みやすそうな間取りだ。 That floor plan looks really convenient.

リビングの日当たりがよさそう。 The living room seems to get a lot of sunshine.

南向きの角部屋だ。 It's a corner room facing the south.

設備

バス・トイレ別がいいな。	**I want a separate toilet and bathroom.**
広いベランダがあるといいな。	**A large balcony would be nice.** ＊balcony＝(2階以上にある)ベランダ
セキュリティーシステムは必要。	**I need to have a security system.**
管理人さんが常駐しているマンションがいいな。	**I want an apartment with a full-time building manager.**
エントランスはオートロックだ。	**The entrance is auto-locking.**
宅配ボックスは絶対に必要。	**A package delivery box is a must.**
駐車場が必要だ。	**I need a parking space.** ＊parking spaceは、parking lotとしてもOK
駐輪場が広くていい感じ。	**I like the spacious bike parking lot.**
エレベーターはない。	**There's no elevator.**
すごく小さいけれど、庭がある。	**It's really small, but there is a yard.**
庭に物置がある。	**There's a garden shed.** ＊garden shed＝庭の物置
ネットが無料で使えるみたい。	**It seems like there's free Internet.**
リビングの床暖房は必須だ。	**The living room has to have floor heating.** ＊floor heating＝床暖房
ウォークインクローゼットがあるといいな。	**It would be nice to have a walk-in closet.**
理想はアイランド型のキッチン。	**A kitchen with an island counter would be ideal.** ＊ideal［アイディーゥ］＝理想的な

建物の階数・築年数

10 階建てのマンションだ。	**It's a ten-story apartment building.** ＊story＝階
2 階建てのアパートだ。	**It's a two-story apartment building.**
2 階建ての一軒家だ。	**It's a two-story house.**

5階建ての3階だ。	**It's on the third floor of a five-story building.**
1階なので、防犯が心配。	**It's on the first floor, so I'm worried about security.**
2階以上の部屋がいい。	**A room on the second floor or above would be best.**
築15年だ。	**It's a 15-year-old building.**
新築マンションだ。	**It's a new apartment building.**
中古マンションだ。	**It's a used apartment building.**

周辺環境

静かな環境がいいな。	**I want a quiet place.**
便利な場所がいいな。	**I want a place in a convenient location.**
静かでいい環境だ。	**It's in a nice and quiet environment.**
閑静な住宅街だ。	**It's a quiet residential area.** ＊residential＝居住の
公園が目の前だ。	**There's a park right in front of it.** ＊right＝ちょうど
コンビニが目と鼻の先だ。	**It's really close to a convenience store.**
近所にスーパーが3つもある。	**There are three supermarkets in the neighborhood.** ＊「スーパー」は、grocery storeとも言う
家の周りに店が何もないな。	**There aren't any shops nearby the house.**
図書館まで自転車で5分だ。	**It takes five minutes to get to the library by bicycle.** ＊bicycleは、bikeとしてもOK
幼稚園と小学校が近くにある。	**There is a preschool and an elementary school nearby.** ＊a(n) ～ and a(n) ...という形の場合、There are ...ではなく、くだけてThere is ...とすることが多い

繁華街に近くてにぎやかだ。 It's close to a shopping area, so it's busy. ＊busy＝にぎわっている

大通りに面しているので、騒音が気になる。 It faces a main street, so the noise bothers me. ＊bother＝～を悩ます

大通りから1本入ったところがいいな。 A place off the main street would be nice. ＊off ～＝～から離れた

線路に近いので、電車の音が聞こえる。 It's near the railroad tracks, so I can hear the trains. ＊track＝線路

交通量が多いので、ちょっと危ないかな。 The traffic is quite heavy, so it's kind of dangerous.

周囲に街灯が少ないのが気になる。 There aren't many streetlights around, which worries me. ＊worry＝～を心配させる

夜道は暗いかもしれない。 It might be too dark at night.

部屋を借りる

賃貸の希望条件

新しい部屋を探している。 I'm looking for a new place.

どんな部屋がいいかな？ What kind of place should I get?

希望の条件を書き出してみよう。 I'm going to write down everything I want.

通勤に便利な場所なら、条件にはこだわらない。 I don't mind the details as long as the commute is convenient. ＊detail＝細かい点　commute＝通勤

ペットが飼える部屋じゃなきゃ。 I need a place that allows pets.

賃貸のほうが、身軽で好き。 I prefer renting because it's less of a commitment. ＊commitment＝責任、義務

物件探し

ネットで賃貸物件を探した。 I looked for a place to rent on the Internet.

不動産会社のアプリに希望条件を登録した。	**I registered my desired conditions on the real estate agency's app.** ＊desired＝望ましい　real estate agency＝不動産会社
アプリで物件を検索した。	**I searched for places on an app.**
不動産会社に行った。	**I went to a real estate agency.**
いくつか物件を紹介してもらった。	**They showed me several places.**
間取り図を見せてもらった。	**They showed me some room layouts.** ＊room layout＝間取り、間取り図
ちょうどいい物件があった。	**I found the perfect place.**
条件に合った物件が見つからなかった。	**I couldn't find a place that met my conditions.** ＊meet＝～(希望など)を満たす　condition＝条件
もう少し広い部屋がないか、聞いてみよう。	**I'm going to ask if there's a bigger place.**
ほかの不動産会社も当たってみよう。	**I'm going to try another real estate agency.**

家賃・初期費用

家賃は5、6万円で考えている。	**I'm thinking of somewhere between 50,000 and 60,000 yen for rent.**
家賃は10万円以内がいいな。	**I want to stay under 100,000 yen for rent.** ＊stay ～＝～のままでいる
家賃は15万円だ。	**The rent is 150,000 yen.**
あの部屋であの値段なら、安いと思う。	**That's a great price for such a nice place.**
管理費が高い。	**The management fees are expensive.**
初期費用をなるべく抑えたい。	**I want to keep the initial costs as low as possible.** ＊initial cost＝初期費用
敷金2カ月分と礼金2カ月分がかかる。	**I'll need to pay two months as deposit and two months as key money.** ＊deposit＝敷金　key money＝礼金

手数料は1カ月分だ。	**The commission is one month's rent.** ＊commission＝委託手数料
保証料は家賃の0.5カ月分。	**The guarantee fee is half a month's rent.** ＊guarantee＝保証
鍵交換に2万6500円かかる。	**It costs 26,500 yen to change the locks.**
なんだかんだで、引っ越しに100万円近くかかっちゃう。	**It'll end up costing about a million yen for the move.** ＊move＝引っ越し
更新料は1カ月分だ。	**The contract renewal fee is one month's rent.** ＊contract＝契約　renewal＝更新

内見

今日、内見してきた。	**I went to check out the inside today.**
2つの部屋を内見した。	**I looked at two places.**
VRを使って内見した。	**I used VR to check out the inside.** ＊VR＝virtual reality（仮想現実）
新しくてきれいな部屋だった。	**It was a beautiful new place.**
古い感じの部屋だった。	**It felt old.**
築40年だった。	**It was 40 years old.**
日当たりがいい。	**It gets a lot of sunshine.**
日当たりが悪い。	**It doesn't get much sunshine.**
西日が強いかも？	**The late afternoon sun might be too bright.**
風通しがよかった。	**It was well-ventilated.** ＊ventilated＝換気された
風通しが悪かった。	**It was poorly ventilated.**
収納がたっぷりあった。	**It had plenty of storage space.** ＊storage＝収納
収納が少なかった。	**It didn't have enough storage space.**

キッチンはリフォームされたばかりで、きれいだった。	**The kitchen was just remodeled and looked really nice.** ＊remodel＝～をリフォームする
リビングが広々としていた。	**The living room was spacious.** ＊spacious＝広々とした
壁が薄そうなのが気になった。	**I was worried the walls might be a little thin.**
なかなかいい部屋だった。	**It was a pretty good place.**
思ったよりよかった。	**It was better than I expected.**
まさに理想の物件だった。	**It was exactly what I wanted.**
ちょっとボロかった。	**It was a little run-down.** ＊run-down＝老朽化した
期待外れだった。	**It was disappointing.**
あの部屋にしよう。	**I'm going to decide on that place.**
もう少し検討しよう。	**I'm going to look a little longer.** ＊look＝探す、調べる
いい部屋が見つかってよかった。	**I'm glad I found a good place.**
なかなか理想の部屋が見つからない。	**It's hard to find the perfect place.**

賃貸契約

不動産会社で契約してきた。	**I signed a contract at the real estate office.** ＊sign a contract＝契約書に署名する
担当者が親切だった。	**My agent was really nice.** ＊agent＝仲介者
大家さんにあいさつした。	**I said hi to my landlord.** ＊say hi to ～＝～にあいさつをする landlord＝(男性の)大家。女性の場合はlandlady
引っ越しが楽しみ。	**I can't wait to move in.** ＊move in＝入居する

住宅の購入

購入物件を探す

タワーマンションにあこがれる。	**Living in a high-rise condo is my dream.** ＊condoは、condominium（分譲マンション）の略
庭付きの一戸建てに住みたい。	**I hope to live in a house with a yard.**
不動産会社のサイトで中古住宅を探した。	**I looked for a used house on a real estate agency's website.** ＊real estate agency＝不動産会社
会社まで50分以内で通えるところで、新築の分譲マンションを探そう。	**I'm going to look for a new condo within 50 minutes from my workplace.**
もう少し頑張って、3LDKにしようかな。	**Maybe I'll spend a little more and get a 3LDK place.** ＊正式な英語ではないが、日記では「3LDK」としてOK
2LDK、55m² で2500万円だ。	**It's 25 million yen for a 55m² 2LDK.** ＊m^2＝square meter（平方メートル）

モデルルーム見学

住宅展示場へ行った。	**I went to a show home exhibition.** ＊show home＝モデルハウス　exhibition＝展示
チラシの新築分譲マンションを見に行った。	**I went to see the new condo I saw in the flyer.** ＊flyer＝チラシ
B社のモデルハウスを見学した。	**I took a tour of a show home made by B Company.**
営業さんに説明を聞いた。	**We talked to the real estate agent.**
立地は申し分ない。	**The location is perfect.**
周辺環境が気に入った。	**I like the surrounding environment.**
来年2月に完成予定の新築だ。	**It's scheduled to be completed next February.**
中古マンションだけど、新築同様にきれいだ。	**It's a used condo, but it's just as good as new.** ＊as good as new＝新品同様の

間取りと採光のよさが気に入った。	**I really liked the layout and the daylighting.** ＊layout＝設計、配置
広々としたキッチンにうっとりした。	**I was enchanted by the spacious kitchen.** ＊enchanted＝うっとりして
防音、断熱性に優れた高気密住宅だ。	**It's a well-sealed place with nice soundproofing and insulation.** ＊well-sealed＝高気密の soundproofing＝防音性 insulation＝断熱性
エコ性能に優れている。	**It's really eco-friendly.**

購入物件の比較・検討

B社のマンションのほうが間取りがいいな。	**B Company's condo has a nicer layout.** ＊condoは、condominium（分譲マンション）の略
A社のマンションなら、将来的に値が下がりにくそう。	**Maybe the value of A Company's condos won't drop in the future.**
高級過ぎて、私には向かないかも。	**It's a little too luxurious, so maybe it's not for me.** ＊luxurious［ラグジュリアス］＝ぜいたくな、豪華な
あんなに広くなくていいんだけどな。	**It doesn't have to be that spacious.**
B社の家は、坪単価が高過ぎ。	**B Company's house is too expensive per tsubo.** ＊per 〜＝〜につき
C社の家は、ちょっとチープかな。	**C Company's house is a little too cheap.** ＊cheap＝安っぽい
明日、見積もりを取ることにした。	**I'm going to ask for an estimate tomorrow.** ＊estimate＝見積もり
両親とも相談して、B社の家にしようと決めた。	**I talked with my parents and decided to go with B Company's house.** ＊go with 〜＝〜を選択する
将来の間取り変更を考えると、浦和のマンションがよさそう。	**I might want to change the floor plan someday, so I'll go with the condo in Urawa.**
気に入った物件が出てくるまで気長に待とう。	**I should wait patiently until I find something I really like.** ＊patiently＝我慢強く

住宅ローン

週末、ローン相談会に参加した。
I went to a housing loan consultation on the weekend.

30年ローンだと、月々10万円の支払いになる。
With a 30-year loan, I'll be paying back 100,000 yen a month.

35年ローンを組んだ。
I took out a 35-year loan.
*take out ～＝～(申請してローンなど)を受ける

頑張って15年で返すぞ！
I'm going to try hard to repay it in 15 years.
*repay＝～を返済する

ボーナス払いにしたほうがいいかな？
I wonder if I should make bonus payments.

元利均等、35年の夫婦ペアローンを組んだ。
I got a 35-year couple loan with principal and interest equal repayment.
*principal＝元金　interest＝利息

頭金が150万円必要だ。
I need to put a 1.5-million-yen down payment.
*down payment＝頭金

銀行にローンの審査書類一式を提出した。
I submitted the loan application to the bank.
*submit＝～を提出する

兄に連帯保証人を依頼した。
I asked my brother to cosign the loan.
*cosign[コウサイン]＝～に連署する

ローン審査に通るといいな。
I hope my loan gets approved.
*approve＝～を承認する

A銀行は「融資不可」だった。
I got a rejection notice from A Bank.
*rejection＝拒否　notice＝通知

ローン審査に通った！ やった！
My loan has gotten approved! Great!

ローンのプレッシャーはかなり大きい。
The loan is a lot of pressure.

身が震える思いだ。
It makes me shiver just to think about it.
*shiver＝震える

これまで以上に稼がないとな。
I have to make more money from now on.

ローンが払えなければ、売るまでだ。
If I can't pay back the loan, I'll just sell the place.

ボーナスは全部、住宅ローンの繰り上げ返済に充てよう。
I should put my entire bonus towards paying some of my mortgage in advance.
＊mortgage［モーギッジ］＝住宅ローン

住宅購入の契約

A社に契約の意向を伝えた。
I told A Company that I was going to go with them.
＊go with ～＝～を選択する

契約書に実印を押してきた。
I put my official seal on the contract.
＊seal＝印鑑、はんこ

不動産会社に10万円の手付け金を支払った。
I paid the real estate agency a 100,000-yen deposit.

不動産会社に購入申込書を送付した。
We sent a written intent-to-buy notification to the real estate agency.
＊intent-to-buy＝購入意思、購入申込書

住民票と印鑑証明を準備しなきゃ。
I need to prepare a proof-of-residence document and a seal certificate.
＊proof-of-residence＝住民票　certificate＝証明書

ついに一国一城の主になった。
I finally got a house of my own.

家を建てる

土地探し

まずは土地探しから。
I should find land first.

最低50坪は欲しいかな。
I need at least 50 tsubos.

坪50万円かぁ。高いな。
500,000 yen per tsubo is expensive.
＊per ～＝～につき

この土地で坪22万円ならよさそう。
220,000 yen a tsubo for this place looks all right.

70坪の土地を買った。
I bought a plot of 70 tsubos.
＊plot＝地所、区画地

広さを取るか、立地のよさを取るか迷う。
I don’t know if I should go for size or location.
＊go for ～＝～を支持する、～に賛成する

土地を2カ所、見に行った。
I checked out two plots of land.

ここは岩盤だから、地盤がしっかりしていてうれしい。	**I'm glad the ground here is really stable since it's bedrock.** ＊stable＝しっかりした、安定した　bedrock＝岩盤
活断層がないことがわかって安心。	**I'm relieved it's not on an active fault.** ＊active fault＝活断層
傾斜地ですてきだけど、地震のことを考えると心配。	**It's nice that it's on a slope, but I'm worried about earthquakes.** ＊slope＝斜面
地盤調査をしてもらったほうがよさそう。	**Maybe I should have the land inspected.** ＊inspect＝～を検査する
商業用地だから、住むのには向いていないかも？	**Since it's a commercial area, it might not be a good place to live.**
旗ざお地だ。	**It's a flagpole-shaped lot.** ＊lot＝土地、敷地
角地のいい物件が見つかった。	**I found a corner lot with the right conditions.** ＊conditions＝条件
ここならL字に家を建てられる。	**Here, I can build an L-shaped house.**

建築プラン

今日は建築業者と打ち合わせをした。	**I had a meeting with the builders today.** ＊builder＝建築業者
建ぺい率は 50%かぁ。	**The building-to-land ratio is 50%.** ＊building-to-land ratio＝建ぺい率
建ぺい率の制限がないから、好きなように使えそう。	**Since there's no limit on the building-to-land ratio, it looks like I'll be able to use it however I like.**
日本家屋が理想だ。	**A Japanese-style house would be ideal.** ＊ideal［アイディーゥ］＝理想的な
ぜいたくに平屋建てにしようかな。	**Maybe I should pamper myself and build a one-story house.** ＊pamper oneself＝欲望を思う存分満たす　story＝階
3 階建てにしたいけど、延べ面積が大きくなっちゃう。	**I want to make it three stories, but that would increase the total area.** ＊increase＝増える
容積率 200%なら大丈夫そう。	**The 200% floor-area ratio should be fine.** ＊floor-area ratio＝容積率

カナディアンハウスにも興味がある。	**I'm also interested in the Canadian house design.**
耐火性を考えて、鉄筋コンクリートにしようかな。	**I'm thinking about reinforced concrete because it's fire resistant.** ＊reinforced concrete＝鉄筋コンクリート fire resistant＝耐火性の
木造が暖かくてよさそう。	**It would be nice and warm if it was made out of wood.** ＊made (out) of ～＝～で作られた
ルーフテラスがあったらすてき。	**It would be great to have a rooftop terrace.**
車２台分の車庫が欲しいな。	**I want a two-car garage.**
絶対に床暖房にしよう。	**I'm definitely getting floor heating.**
書斎は２階にしようかな。	**Maybe I should put the home office on the second floor.** ＊(home) office＝書斎
屋根裏部屋を作ったら、孫が喜びそうだ。	**I think my grandchildren would be happy if we had an attic made.** ＊attic＝屋根裏部屋
ヒノキ風呂に決定だ。	**I've decided to go with a hinoki bathtub.** ＊go with ～＝～を選択する
ミストサウナってよさそう。	**A mist sauna sounds nice.**
予算的に全部は無理だな。	**I can't afford everything I want.**

建築工事

解体工事が終わった。	**The demolition work was completed.** ＊demolition＝取り壊し、解体
ようやく基礎工事が完了した。	**The foundation has finally been finished.** ＊foundation＝土台、基礎
これから本体工事に取りかかる。	**Now we're about to start the main construction.**
明日は上棟式。	**We have the ridgepole-raising ceremony tomorrow.** ＊ridgepole＝棟木
だんだん形になってきた。	**It's gradually starting to take shape.** ＊gradually＝徐々に　take shape＝形になる

完成が待ち遠しいな。	**I can't wait for it to be finished.**
雨続きで工事が長引いている。	**Construction is taking a while due to the continuous rain.** ＊due to ～＝～のせいで
いよいよ来月、新居完成！	**My new place is finally going to be finished next month!**

引っ越し

引っ越し準備

4月29日に引っ越すことにした。	**I've decided to move on April 29.**
これで引っ越しは5回目だ。	**This is my fifth move.**
引っ越し貧乏だ。	**Moving all the time has made me poor.**
荷物が少ないので、自分でできそうだ。	**I don't have many things, so I think I can do it myself.**
ガス・水道・電気の移転手続きをしなきゃ。	**I have to transfer all the utilities to my new place.** ＊utilities＝（ガス・水道・電気を含む）公共サービス
郵便物の転送手続きをしなきゃ。	**I need to have my mail forwarded.** ＊forward＝～を転送する
友だちに新しい住所を知らせなきゃ。	**I need to let my friends know my new address.**
長年住み慣れた家を離れるのは、寂しい。	**It's sad to say good-bye to this place where I've lived so long.**
マサシは転校しなきゃならないから、かわいそうだな。	**Poor Masashi has to transfer to another school.** ＊transfer＝転校する
友達と別れるのは寂しいだろう。	**I'm sure he's sad that he has to say good-bye to all his friends.**

引っ越し費用

ネットで複数の業者に見積もりを取った。	**I got estimates from several companies online.** ＊estimate＝見積もり

A 社に見積もりを依頼した。 **I asked A Company for an estimate.**

B 社と C 社に、見積もりに来てもらった。 **I had B Company and C Company come and give me their estimates.**

B 社は 8 万 5000 円、C 社は 10 万円だった。 **B Company said 85,000 yen and C Company said 100,000 yen.**

C 社のほうが信頼できそう。 **I feel C Company is more reliable.**
＊reliable＝信頼できる

C 社に決めた。 **I chose C Company.**

荷造り

荷造りは自分たちでやろう。 **We're trying to do our own packing.**

荷物が全部でダンボール 70 箱にもなった！ **We've got 70 boxes of stuff to move.**
＊stuff＝物

荷物が多過ぎる。 **That's too much stuff.**

これを機に、物を減らそう。 **I should take this opportunity to get rid of some of my stuff.**
＊get rid of ～＝～を処分する

今から少しずつ荷造りしていこう。 **I'm going to do the packing little by little starting now.**
＊little by little＝少しずつ

全部、引っ越し業者に任せよう。 **I'm going to have the movers take care of everything.** ＊mover＝引っ越し業者

荷造りって、結構大変。 **Packing isn't so easy.**

夫ももっと荷造りを手伝ってくれればいいのに。 **I wish my husband would help more with the packing.**

引っ越し当日

9 時ごろ、引っ越し業者が来た。 **The movers came at around 9:00.**

夕方には引っ越しが完了した。 **We finished moving in the early evening.**

さすが業者さん、手際がよかった！ **The movers were great! They were really efficient.** ＊efficient＝手際がよい

引っ越し先は階段なので、業者さんたちは大変そうだった。	**We had to climb the stairs to my new place, so it was hard for the movers.** ＊climb［クライム］ mover＝引っ越し業者
荷運びを手伝った。	**I helped carry things.**
腰が痛くなった。	**My lower back got sore.** ＊sore＝痛い
ご近所に引っ越しのあいさつをした。	**I went and greeted my new neighbors.** ＊greet＝（丁寧に）あいさつする

荷解き

新しい家は、ダンボール箱の山だ。	**My new place is full of cardboard boxes.** ＊cardboard box＝ダンボール箱
荷解きをするのも、一苦労だな。	**Unpacking is a pain.** ＊unpacking＝荷解き a pain＝面倒で嫌なこと
本を全部、本棚にしまった。	**I put all the books on the bookshelf.**
食器を全部、食器棚にしまった。	**I put away all the dishes in the cupboard.** ＊put away ～＝～を片付ける
洗濯機の設置をした。	**I set up the washing machine.**
服をクローゼットにしまった。	**I put the clothes in the closet.**
どの箱に何が入っているか、わからなくなってしまった。	**I don't remember what I put in each box.**
全然片付かなくて、嫌になる！	**It's taking forever to organize my room. What a pain!**
いまだに開けてないダンボール箱がある。	**There are still some boxes I haven't opened yet.**

Memo

住まいに関することを、メモしておきましょう。

住まいについて 英語日記を書いてみよう

住まいにまつわるあれこれを、英語で書いてみましょう。

部屋探しをしよう

I have too many things and my apartment is getting too small for them. I want a bigger place. OK, I'll go see a real estate agency tomorrow.

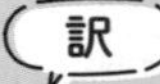

訳

物が多過ぎて、この部屋が手狭になってきた。もっと大きな部屋がいいな。よし、明日は不動産屋さんに行ってこよう。

ポイント

「物が多過ぎる」は have too much stuff とも表します。thing は数えられる名詞、stuff は数えられない名詞です。「部屋」は、マンションなら apartment で表しますが、place（住まい）でも OK。「手狭」は small で。「（道路など細長いものが）狭い」場合は narrow です。

バスルームをリフォーム

We remodeled our bathroom. A bigger bathtub with a Jacuzzi, a tiled floor and walls ... It looks totally different. We love it!

訳

バスルームをリフォームした。ジャグジー付きの大きな浴槽に、タイル張りの床と壁……。雰囲気ががらりと変わった。すごくいい感じ！

ポイント

「〜（家）をリフォームする」は、remodel で表します。reform は「〜を革新する、〜に改心させる」という意味なので注意。「雰囲気ががらりと変わった」は「（以前とは）まったく違って見える」と考えて、It looks totally different. とすれば簡単に表現できます。

マイホーム購入を決意

We've decided to buy a house! We want a new house if we can afford one. If not, a used one is OK. We're really excited to own a house in the near future!

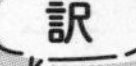

マイホームを購入することにした！　金銭的に可能なら新築がいいけど、無理なら中古でも構わない。近い将来、マイホームを手に入れられるなんて、すごくワクワクする！

「マイホーム」は、単に a house か a home で OK。明確に表したいなら、a house of one's own（～所有の家）とします。can afford ～は「（金銭的に、時間的に）～の余裕がある」。「～」に to ～（動詞の原形）を入れると、「～する余裕がある」という意味になります。

部屋の模様替え

I rearranged my room for a change. I wiped the windows and furniture, too. It feels really refreshing! Maybe I should change the curtains as well.

気分転換に、部屋の模様替えをした。窓や家具もふいて、気分さっぱり！　ついでにカーテンも替えようかな。

「部屋の模様替えをする」は rearrange my room や redecorate my room と言います。「気分転換に」は for a change、「気分さっぱり」は refreshing で。「ついでに」はぴったりな英語がありませんが、as well（その上、～も）でニュアンスを出しています。

17

食べる・飲む

食べる

食べ物を表す単語

ハンバーグ	hamburger steak
スパゲティ	spaghetti
カルボナーラ	carbonara
ペペロンチーノ	peperoncino
ピザ	pizza
パエリヤ	paella［パエーラ］
ブイヤベース	bouillabaisse［ブージャベス］
グラタン	gratin［グラートゥン］
コロッケ	croquette［クロウケット］
オムライス	rice omelet
ロールキャベツ	stuffed cabbage
エビフライ	fried shrimp
ローストビーフ	roast beef
シチュー	stew［ストゥー］
カレーライス	curry and rice
ご飯	rice
玄米	brown rice
チャーハン	fried rice
もち	rice cake
みそ汁	miso soup
納豆	natto
漬け物	pickles
焼き魚	grilled fish
うなぎのかば焼き	broiled eel
鶏のから揚げ	fried chicken
肉じゃが	stewed meat and potatoes
お好み焼き	okonomiyaki
鍋	hot pot
牛丼	beef bowl
冷奴	cold tofu
焼きギョウザ	potsticker
春巻き	spring roll
マーボー豆腐	mabo-dofu
ホイコーロウ	twice cooked pork
パッタイ	pad thai
フォー	pho
トムヤムクン	tom yam kung
ラーメン	ramen
焼きそば	fried noodles
パン	bread
食パン１斤	a loaf of bread
食パン１枚	a slice of bread
トースト	toast
菓子パン	sweet bread
フランスパン	baguette
クロワッサン	croissant［クラサーント］
サンドイッチ	sandwich
ベーグル	bagel
あんパン	red bean bun
カレーパン	curry bun

食欲（→ p. 51「食欲がある・ない」を参照）

おなかがいっぱい・すいた

おなかがペコペコだった。 **I was starving.**

おなかが減って死にそうだった。 **I felt like I was starving to death.**

あまりおなかがすいていなかった。 **I wasn't too hungry.**

満腹になった。 **I was full.**
＊「今おなかがいっぱい」なら、I'm full.に

おなかがはちきれそうだった。 **My stomach felt like it was about to burst.**
＊burst＝破裂する

おなかいっぱいになった。 **I was stuffed.**
＊stuffed＝いっぱいになった、満腹の

腹八分目がちょうどいい。 **Eating moderately is the best.**
＊moderately＝ほどほどに、控えめに

「デザートは別腹」って本当だな。 **It's really true that you always have room for dessert.**
＊room＝余裕、余地

食べた

食べ過ぎた。 **I ate too much.**

食べ過ぎて動けなかった。 **I ate too much and couldn't move.**

少しだけ食べた。 **I only ate a little.**

たらふく食べた。 **I ate my fill.**
＊eat one's fill＝たらふく食べる

もう一口も食べられなかった。 **I wasn't able to have another bite.**
＊bite＝一口

彼女は少ししか食べなかった。 **She ate like a bird.**

彼はモリモリ食べていた。 **He ate like a horse.**

栄養バランス

栄養が偏り気味だ。 **My diet is out of balance.**
＊diet＝食生活、食習慣

栄養バランスに気を付けよう。 **I need to be careful to have a balanced diet.**

栄養バランスの取れた昼食だった。	**I had a well-balanced lunch.**
今日の夕飯の栄養バランスは完璧だった。	**Tonight's dinner was a perfectly balanced meal.**
野菜が足りていない。	**I'm not getting enough veggies.** ＊veggies＝vegetables（野菜）
野菜ばかりじゃなくて、肉も食べなきゃ。	**I need to eat meat, not just vegetables.**
貧血気味だから、ホウレンソウを食べよう。	**I have slight anemia, so I'd better eat spinach.** ＊slight＝わずかな　anemia［アニーミァ］＝貧血
ビタミン不足だ。	**I don't get enough vitamins.** ＊vitamin［ヴァイタミン］
炭水化物を取り過ぎかも。	**I may be eating too many carbs.** ＊carbs＝炭水化物
カロリーを取り過ぎたかも。	**I might have eaten too many calories.**

食べ物の好き嫌い・アレルギー

タイ料理、大好き。	**I love Thai food.**
夫はラーメンに目がない。	**My husband loves ramen more than anything.**
子どもたちはトマトが苦手だ。	**The kids don't like tomatoes.**
セロリだけは、どうしても食べられない。	**Celery is the only thing I just can't eat.** ＊celery［セレリ］
豚肉が入っていたので、食べられなかった。	**It had pork in it, so I couldn't eat it.**
食べ物の好き嫌いが変わってきた。	**My likes and dislikes about food are changing.** ＊likes and dislikes＝好き嫌い
最近、肉料理が重くなってきた。	**Meat feels really heavy in my stomach these days.**
パクチーが食べられるようになった。	**Now I can eat cilantro.** ＊cilantroはcorianderでもOK
年のせいかも。	**Maybe it's because I'm getting old.**
彼女は食べ物の好き嫌いが多い。	**She's really picky about food.** ＊picky＝好き嫌いが激しい

うちの子たちはあまり好き嫌いがなくて、ありがたい。 **I'm glad my kids aren't too picky about food.**

ミホは乳製品アレルギーだ。 **Miho is allergic to dairy products.**
＊allergic［アラージック］to 〜＝〜にアレルギーのある

そばを食べると湿疹が出てしまう。 **I get a rash when I eat soba.**
＊rash＝湿疹、吹き出物

外食

店の予約

土曜の夜7時に、2人で席を予約した。 **I booked a table for two at 7:00 on Saturday evening.**
＊book＝〜を予約する

今週の土曜は満席だったので、来週の土曜に予約した。 **This Saturday was full, so I made a reservation for next Saturday.**
＊full＝満席で

3カ月先まで満席だ。びっくり！ **They're booked for the next three months. What a surprise!**

ネットで予約した。 **I made a reservation online.**

窓際の席を予約した。 **I reserved a table by the window.**
＊reserve＝〜を予約する

個室を予約した。 **I reserved a private room.**

5000円のコースにした。 **We ordered 5,000-yen course meals.**

予約は受け付けていないらしい。 **They don't accept reservations.**

外食・テイクアウト

週末は外食でもしようかな。 **Maybe I'll eat out on the weekend.**
＊eat out＝外食する

久しぶりに外食をした。 **I ate out for the first time in a while.**

ママ友たちとランチした。 **I had lunch with my mom friends.**

雑誌に載っていたレストランに行ってみた。 **I went to the restaurant I saw in a magazine.**

ヨネダさんとイタリアンのお店に行った。	**I went to an Italian restaurant with Mr. Yoneda.**
ヨシキさんが高級レストランに連れて行ってくれた。	**Yoshiki-san took me to an upscale restaurant.** ＊upscale＝高級な
いつものそば屋で、お一人様ランチした。	**I had lunch by myself at my usual soba restaurant.**
昼はフードコートで済ませた。	**We had a quick lunch at the food court.**
通りがかりのラーメン屋に入った。	**I ate at a ramen shop I passed by.** ＊pass by＝そばを通りかかる
天気がいいので、テイクアウトして公園で食べた。	**The weather was nice, so I got takeout and ate in the park.**
テイクアウトできる店が増えてうれしいな。	**I'm happy that more stores offer takeout now.**
最近、外食がちでよくないな。	**I've been eating out too often lately, which isn't good.**
外食続きで太ってしまった。	**I've gained weight from eating out so much.** ＊gain weight＝太る
しばらく外食していないな。	**I haven't eaten out in a while.**
以前ほど外食しなくなった。	**Now I don't eat out as often as I used to.**

飲食店にて

雰囲気のいいレストランだった。	**The restaurant had a nice atmosphere.** ＊atmosphere［アトモスフィア］＝雰囲気
さすが、ミシュラン2つ星のレストランだな。	**It is indeed a two-Michelin-star restaurant.** ＊indeed＝本当に、確かに
カジュアルなレストランだった。	**It was a casual restaurant.**
待たずに店に入れた。	**We got a table without waiting.**
30分も並んだ。	**We had to stand in line for as long as 30 minutes.** ＊stand in line＝列に並ぶ

混んでいたので、別の店に行った。 **It was crowded, so we went to another restaurant.**

テレビで紹介されて人気が出たらしい。 **It was featured on a TV show and became really popular.**
＊feature＝～を特集する

禁煙席にしてもらった。 **We asked for a non-smoking table.**

テラス席に座った。 **We sat on the terrace.**

畳の個室だった。 **We had a private room with tatami.**

注文する

メニューが豊富だった。 **There were a lot of dishes on the menu.**

店員におすすめを聞いた。 **We asked the server what they recommend.**

彼と同じ物を注文した。 **I ordered the same thing he did.**

モバイルオーダーができる店だった。 **They had a mobile ordering system.**

スマホで注文した。 **We ordered from the phone.**

タブレットで注文した。 **We ordered from the tablet.**

それぞれ食べたい物を注文した。 **Each of us ordered what we wanted to eat.**

食べきれないほど注文しちゃった。 **Our eyes were bigger than our stomachs.**
＊直訳は「胃より目のほうが大きかった」

会計

1万2000円だった。 **The bill was 12,000 yen.** ＊bill＝勘定書

サービス料込みだった。 **It included a service charge.**

あの料理であの金額なら、かなりコスパがいいと思う。 **That price for that food is a pretty good deal.** ＊good deal＝お得な買い物

お得なセットだった。 **It was a great combo meal.**

高かったのに、量は少なかった。	**It was expensive, but the portions were small.** ＊portion＝(食べ物の)1人前
高かったのに、味は普通だった。	**It was expensive, but the taste was average.** ＊average＝平均的な
会計が間違っていた。危なかった！	**The bill was wrong. I'm glad I noticed!**
残った料理を持ち帰った。	**I took home the leftovers.** ＊leftovers＝残り物

クーポン

クーポンで会計から10パーセント引きになった。	**I got 10% off with a coupon.**
クーポンで最初の1杯が無料になった。	**I had a coupon, so the first drink was free.**
クーポンでハンバーガーが200円になった。	**I bought a hamburger for 200 yen with a coupon.**
次回の会計が2000円引きになるクーポンをもらった。	**I got a coupon for 2,000 yen off the next time I go there.**
クーポンを持っていくのを忘れた。	**I forgot to bring the coupon.**
スタンプがたまったので、ドリンクが1杯無料になった。	**I saved up some stamps, so I got a free drink.** ＊save up ～＝～をためる

洋食

スパゲッティ・カルボナーラを食べた。	**I had spaghetti carbonara.**
前菜、スープ、メインを1つずつ選んだ。	**We chose an appetizer, a soup and a main dish.** ＊appetizer＝前菜
アラカルトで注文した。	**I ordered à la carte.** ＊à la carte＝アラカルトで
アラカルトだと、好きなものをいろいろ頼める。	**With à la carte, I can order all my favorite dishes.**
コースにした。	**We chose a course meal.**

ボリュームたっぷりのコースだった。 **It was a course with plenty of food.**

サラダとかぼちゃのスープを頼んだ。 **I ordered a salad and pumpkin soup.**

ブイヤベースをシェアした。 **We shared a bouillabaisse.**

食後にデザートを頼んだ。 **After the meal, I ordered a dessert.**

コーヒーを２つ頼んだ。 **We ordered two coffees.**
＊two coffees＝two cups of coffee

和食

本日のおすすめ定食を頼んだ。 **I ordered the recommended combo meal of the day.**

サンマ定食にした。 **I had a saury combo meal.**
＊saury［ソーリー］＝サンマ

ご飯は大盛りにした。 **I had a large serving of rice.**
＊serving＝1人分。「小盛り」なら、small serving

きつねうどんを食べた。 **I had a kitsune udon.**

揚げたての天ぷらは最高だった。 **The crispy tempura was the best.**
＊crispy＝サクサクした

中トロが口の中でとろけた！ **The fatty tuna melted in my mouth!**
＊fatty＝脂ののった　melt＝溶ける

霜降り和牛が滑らかな舌触りだった。 **The marbled Japanese beef had a smooth texture.**

刺身がすごく新鮮だった。 **Their sashimi was very fresh.**
＊刺身はraw fishとも言う

和食ってヘルシー。 **Japanese food is really healthy.**

お好み焼きが鉄板の上でジュージューいっていた。 **The okonomiyaki was sizzling on the iron plate.**
＊sizzle＝ジュージューいう

食後に日本茶を飲んだ。 **After eating, I had Japanese tea.**

エスニック・中華

ギョウザの皮がパリパリでおいしかった。 **The potsticker skins were nice and crispy.**

辛くないマーボー豆腐なんて、マーボー豆腐じゃない！ **If mabo-dofu isn't spicy, it isn't mabo-dofu!**

パクチーって、やっぱり苦手。	**I really don't like cilantro.** ＊cilantro＝コリアンダー、香菜、パクチー。corianderでもOK
パクチー抜きにしてもらった。	**I asked for it without cilantro.**
トムヤムクンは何度食べても飽きない。	**I never get tired of tom yam kung.** ＊get tired of ～＝～に飽きる
期間限定のインドカレーを食べた。	**I had the limited-time-only Indian curry.**
カレーもナンもおいしかった。	**Both the curry and the naan were good.**
スパイスが効いていた。	**It was really spicy.**
思ったより辛かった。	**It was hotter than I expected.**
ベトナム料理って、ヘルシーで大好き。	**Vietnamese food is so healthy. I love it.**

ラーメン

屋台でラーメンを食べた。	**I ate ramen at a stall.**
麺にコシがあった。	**The noodles were nice and chewy.** ＊chewy＝(麺などが)コシのある
スープが本格的だった。	**The broth was authentic.** ＊authentic＝本物の
スープにコクがあった。	**The broth had a really rich taste.**
トッピングに味玉を載せてもらった。	**I got a flavored egg on top.** ＊flavored＝味付けされた
トッピング全部載せにした。	**I got all the toppings.**

ファミレス

「本日のランチ」を頼んだ。	**I ordered the lunch-of-the-day.**
コウスケはお子様セットを食べた。	**Kosuke had the kid's plate.**
チョコレートパフェを食べた。	**I had a chocolate parfait.**
ドリンクバーを２人分、注文した。	**We ordered self-serve soft drinks for two.** ＊self-serve＝セルフサービス方式の

だいぶ長居してしまった。	**We stayed there for a long time.**

ファストフード

昼食は ABC バーガーで食べた。	**I had lunch at ABC Burger.**
ファストフード店でささっと昼食を取った。	**I had a quick lunch at a fast-food restaurant.**
持ち帰りにした。	**I took it home.**
店内で食べた。	**We ate in the restaurant.**
チーズバーガーのポテトセットを頼んだ。	**I ordered a cheese burger with French fries.** ＊「フライドポテト」は、friesと表すことも多い
飲み物はコーラにした。	**I had a Coke.**
新発売のサーモンバーガーがおいしそうだった。	**The new salmon burger looked really delicious.**
今度はあれにしてみよう。	**I'll try it next time.**
フライドポテトって時々、無性に食べたくなる。	**Sometimes, I just crave French fries.** ＊crave ～＝無性に～が欲しい
ドライブスルーでハンバーガーとフライドポテトを買った。	**I got a hamburger and French fries at a drive-through.**
ファストフードばかりじゃ体に悪いよね。	**I know eating fast food often isn't good for me.**

出前・デリバリー

ピザを注文した。	**I ordered a pizza.**
マルゲリータの M サイズを 1 枚注文した。	**I ordered a medium-sized Margherita pizza.**
トッピングでコーンを追加した。	**I got corn topping.**
30 分以内に届けてくれた。	**They delivered it within 30 minutes.**
2 時間待ちだった。	**I waited for two hours.**

たぬきうどんと親子丼を頼んだ。	**I ordered a tanuki udon and an oyako-don.**
中華弁当を３人前頼んだ。	**I ordered Chinese bento boxes for three people.**
Uber Eats でタイ料理を頼んだ。	**I ordered Thai food from Uber Eats.**
最近は、いろいろなデリバリーサービスがあって便利だな。	**It's convenient that there are lots of different delivery services now.**

弁当・総菜

弁当を買って帰った。	**I bought a boxed meal before going home.**
今日もコンビニ弁当を食べた。	**I had a convenience store bento today again.**
あの店の弁当は結構イケる。	**Their bentos are pretty good.**
最近のコンビニ弁当はクオリティーが高い。	**Convenience store bentos are good-quality these days.**
デパートで総菜を買った。	**I got some ready-made dishes from the department store deli.** ＊deli＝delicatessen（デリカテッセン）の略
総菜がすべて半額になっていた。	**All the ready-made dishes were half price.** ＊ready-made＝あらかじめ作られた
家で作るより、弁当を買うほうが安いかも。	**It might be cheaper to buy a bento than to cook at home.**
冷凍のスパゲティを買って食べた。	**I bought frozen spaghetti to eat.**
最近の冷凍食品はホントおいしい。	**Frozen food these days is really tasty.**

デザート・カフェ

デザートを表す単語

ショートケーキ	strawberry and cream sponge cake
チョコレートケーキ	chocolate cake
チーズケーキ	cheesecake
レアチーズケーキ	rare cheesecake
シフォンケーキ	chiffon cake
ロールケーキ	roll cake / Swiss roll
モンブラン	Mont Blanc / chestnut cream cake
アップルパイ	apple pie
タルト	tart［ター ト］
タルトタタン	tarte tatin
カヌレ	canelé
マカロン	macaroon
マドレーヌ	madeleine
クッキー	cookie
シュークリーム	cream puff
ゼリー	jelly / Jell-o
プリン	pudding

飲み物を表す単語

ホットの	hot
アイスの	iced
コーヒー	coffee
アメリカンコーヒー	mild coffee
アイスコーヒー	iced coffee
エスプレッソ	espresso
カフェオレ	café au lait
カフェラテ	café latte
カプチーノ	cappuccino
ココア	hot chocolate
アイスココア	chocolate milk
紅茶	tea
ミルクティー	tea with milk
レモンティー	tea with lemon
アールグレイ	Earl Grey
ウーロン茶	oolong tea
緑茶	green tea
ハーブティー	herbal tea
ルイボスティー	Rooibos tea
タピオカミルクティー	bubble tea / boba
炭酸飲料	pop / soda / soda pop
コーラ	cola / Coke
ジンジャーエール	ginger ale
オレンジジュース	orange juice / OJ
リンゴジュース	apple juice

ケーキセットを注文した。 **I ordered a cake set.**

「本日のケーキ」はガトーショコラだった。 **The cake-of-the-day was gateau chocolat.**

ケーキはどれもおいしそうだった。 **All the cakes looked really good.**

どのケーキにするか、なかなか決められなかった。	**I had a hard time deciding which cake I wanted.**
シフォンケーキがすごくおいしかった。	**The chiffon cake was so good.**
ラテアートがすごくかわいかった。	**The latte art was really cute.**
期間限定のゆずスカッシュを飲んだ。	**I had the limited-time yuzu squash.**

おやつ・お菓子

おやつ・お菓子を表す単語

スナック菓子	snacks
ポテトチップス	potato chips
せんべい	rice cracker
クラッカー	cracker
チョコレート	chocolate
クッキー	cookie
ガム	gum
あめ	hard candy
グミ	gummy candy
キャラメル	caramel candy
プリン	pudding
ヨーグルト	yogurt [ヨウガート]
ゼリー	jelly / Jell-o
杏仁豆腐	almond jelly
アイスクリーム	ice cream
シャーベット	sherbet
シュークリーム	cream puff
エクレア	éclair
まんじゅう	steamed bean-jam bun
大学いも	toffee sweet potatoes
わらびもち	bracken-starch chewy jelly
ぜんざい	sweet red bean soup
おはぎ	bean cake

おやつにプリンを食べた。	**I had pudding for a snack.** ＊snack＝軽食、間食
ああ、おやつにケーキを2つも食べちゃった！	**Oh no, I had two pieces of cake for a snack!**
あの店のシュークリームって、大きくて大好き。	**Their cream puffs are big. I love them.** ＊cream puff＝シュークリーム
あの店のエクレアは最高！	**That place has the best éclairs!**
駅前にできたケーキ屋のモンブラン、驚くほどおいしかった。	**The Mont Blanc at the new pastry shop near the station was surprisingly good.** ＊pastry＝焼き菓子

あそこのケーキは人工甘味料不使用だ。	**No artificial sweeteners are used in their cakes.**
ポテトチップスを半袋食べた。	**I ate half a bag of potato chips.**
コンビニで新作のチョコを見つけた。	**I found a new kind of chocolate at the convenience store.**
コンビニのロールケーキが、すごくおいしかった。	**The convenience store roll cake was delicious.** ＊「ロールケーキ」は、Swiss rollとも言う
最近は、コンビニのデザートも本格的。	**The desserts at convenience stores these days are like those made by pastry chefs.**
お菓子をどか食いしてしまった。	**I binged on snacks.** ＊binge［ビンジ］on ～＝～をどか食いする
我慢できず、夜中にお菓子を食べてしまった。	**I couldn't help eating snacks in the middle of the night.** ＊can't help ～ing＝～せずにいられない

料理する

料理方法を表す表現

～（料理）を出す	**serve ～**
～（料理）を作る	cook ～ / fix ～
～を切る	**cut ～**
～をさいの目に切る	dice ～
～をみじん切りにする	**chop ～**
～を千切りにする	shred ～
～を短冊切りにする	**cut ～ into rectangles**
～の皮をむく	peel ～
～（大根など）をおろす	**grate ～**
～を煮る・ゆでる	boil ～
～をぐつぐつ煮る	**simmer ～**
～を焼く・炒める	fry ～
～を揚げる	**deep-fry ～**
～を蒸す	steam ～
～を（オーブン・焼き網で）焼く	**broil ～**
～を（バーベキューで）焼く	grill ～
～（パンなど）を焼く	**bake ～**
～と…を混ぜる	mix ～ and ...
～を泡立てる	**whip ～**
～を冷やす・冷ます	cool ～
～を冷凍する	**freeze ～**
～を解凍する	thaw［ソー］～
～を…で包む	**wrap ～ in ...**
～を…で味つけする	**season ～ with ...**
～を電子レンジにかける	microwave ～ / nuke［ヌーク］～

自炊する

もう少し自炊しなきゃ。 I need to cook for myself a little more often.

今週は毎晩自炊した。 I cooked for myself every night this week.

家に帰ってから、急いで夕飯を作った。 After getting home, I hurried and cooked dinner.

料理キットはすごく助かる。 Home cooking kits are very helpful.

自炊していたら、2キロやせた。 I lost 2kg after I started cooking for myself.

卵焼きがうまくできた。 I made a Japanese omelet just right.

家族にも好評だった。 My family really liked it.

肉じゃがを作り過ぎてしまった。 I made too much nikujaga.

グラタン、あまりおいしくできなかった。 My gratin wasn't that good.

手順を間違えたみたい。 I guess I made a mistake somewhere.

レイコの手料理は、本当においしい。 Reiko's homemade dishes are really tasty.

彼は料理がうまい。 He's a great cook.

彼は、私が作ったものは何でも食べてくれる。 He eats just about anything I cook for him.

＊just about＝(強調して)まさに

料理本・レシピ

有名シェフの料理本を買った。 I bought a recipe book by a famous chef.

ネットでレシピを検索した。 I looked for a recipe on the Internet.

動画で料理の手順を見ながら作った。 I made the dish while watching a video on how to do it.

電子レンジだけで作れるレシピだった。 It was a recipe that you can make with just a microwave.

最近、SNSでバズってるレシピだ。 It's a recipe that's going viral on social media. ＊go viral［ヴァイラゥ］＝バズる

簡単なのに、本格的な味になった。 It was simple and easy, but it tasted like a pro made it. ＊pro＝professional

得意料理が増えた。 Now I've learned another good recipe.

お菓子作り

クッキーを焼いた。 I baked some cookies.

レアチーズケーキに挑戦した。 I tried making rare cheesecake.

混ぜて焼くだけの簡単レシピだった。 It was an easy recipe — just stir and bake. ＊stir［ステァ］＝混ぜる

サトミの誕生日ケーキを焼いた。 I baked a birthday cake for Satomi.

きれいにデコレーションできた。 I decorated it beautifully.

「売り物みたい」と褒められた。 She said it was like something you would get at a pastry shop. ＊pastry shop＝焼き菓子店

おやつは手作りが一番。 Homemade snacks are the best.

素朴な味でおいしかった。 It had a nice and simple flavor.

ちょっと焦げてしまった。 It was a little overcooked. ＊overcooked＝焼き過ぎた、焦げた

硬くなってしまった。 It turned out hard.

生焼けだった。 It was half-baked.

パサパサになっちゃった。 It was all dried out.

スポンジがうまく膨らまなかった。なんで？ The sponge cake didn't rise like it was supposed to. How come? ＊rise＝膨らむ

パン作り

パン作りに挑戦した。	**I tried my hand at making bread.** ＊try one's hand at ～＝～に挑戦する
ロールパンを焼いた。	**I baked some rolls.**
天然酵母のパンを焼いた。	**I baked bread using natural yeast.** ＊yeast［イースト］＝酵母
焼きたての手作りパンって、本当においしい！	**Hot and fresh home-baked bread tastes so good!**
あまり膨らまなかった。	**It didn't rise very much.**
一次発酵が足りなかったのかも。	**Maybe the first fermentation wasn't enough.** ＊fermentation＝発酵
パン作りって難しい。	**It's not easy to make bread.**
ホームベーカリーでパンを焼いた。	**I baked bread using a bread machine.** ＊「ホームベーカリー」は、bread makerとも言う
材料を入れてセットするだけで、おいしいパンが焼けちゃう。	**All I need to do to make good bread is put in the ingredients and press the start button.** ＊ingredient＝材料

お酒

お酒を表す単語

ビール	beer
クラフトビール	craft beer
発泡酒	low-malt beer
日本酒	sake
吟醸酒	ginjo-shu
純米酒	junmai-shu
赤ワイン	red wine
白ワイン	white wine
スパークリングワイン	sparkling wine
ボルドー	Bordeaux wine
シャルドネ	Chardonnay
シャンパン	champagne
蒸留酒	distilled spirit
焼酎	shochu
ウオッカ	vodka［ヴァードカ］
ラム酒	rum
マッコリ	makkoli
カクテル	cocktail
ハイボール	highball
ウイスキーの水割り	whiskey and water
オンザロックの	on the rocks
モスコミュール	Moscow mule
ブラッディマリー	bloody Mary
スクリュードライバー	screwdriver
ドライマティーニ	dry martini
ソルティードッグ	salty dog
マルガリータ	margarita
ジントニック	gin and tonic
カシスソーダ	cassis and soda
カンパリソーダ	Campari and soda
ブルーハワイ	blue Hawaii
ピニャコラーダ	pina colada
モヒート	mojito
テキーラ	tequila
ダイキリ	daiquiri
バカルディ	Bacardi
ギムレット	gimlet
ノンアルコールの	non-alcoholic

飲みに行く

仕事帰りにタナカくんと１杯飲んだ。
I went for a drink with Tanaka-kun after work. ＊go for a drink＝飲みに行く

行きつけの店で１杯飲んで帰った。
I went to my regular place for one drink and then went home.

仕事終わりの１杯は最高！
Having a drink after work is the best!

仲間と楽しくお酒を飲んだ。
I had fun drinking with my friends.

ここのところ、飲みに行ってないなぁ。 **I haven't been out for a drink lately.**

お酒を飲んだので、運転代行を頼んだ。 **I had some drinks, so I asked for a designated driver service.**

＊designated［デジグネイテッド］driver＝運転手役の人

お酒に酔う

今日はすぐにお酒が回ってしまった。 **I got drunk pretty quickly today.**

すきっ腹に飲んだせいかな。 **Maybe it was because I drank on an empty stomach.**

彼女、本当にお酒に強いなぁ。 **She can really hold her alcohol.**

＊hold one's alcohol＝～(人)が酒に強い

私ってお酒に弱いなぁ。 **I can't handle much alcohol.**

＊handle＝～を扱う

今夜は酔っ払った。 **I got drunk tonight.**

ほろ酔い気分になった。 **I felt a little tipsy.**

酔って気分が悪くなった。 **I got drunk and felt awful.**

＊awful［オーフォ］＝ひどい

彼、明日は絶対に二日酔いだな。 **I bet he'll have a hangover tomorrow.**

＊I bet ～＝～に違いない　hangover＝二日酔い

彼は酒癖が悪い。 **He's a nasty drunk.**

＊nasty drunk＝酒癖の悪い人

夫は酒臭かった！ **My husband reeked of alcohol!**

＊reek of ～＝～の嫌なにおいがする

夫がぐでんぐでんに酔っ払って帰ってきた。 **My husband came home dead drunk.**

＊dead drunk＝泥酔状態で

最近、飲み過ぎだな。 **I've been drinking too much lately.**

お酒は週2回までにしよう。 **I'm not going to drink more than twice a week.**

ビール・発泡酒

とりあえずビールを頼んだ。 **We ordered beers to start off with.**

＊start off with ～＝～から始める

ビールに枝豆って最高！ **Edamame goes great with beer!**

＊go great with ～＝～とよく合う

やっぱり生ビールが最高！ **Draft beer is the best of all!**

家で缶ビールを飲んだ。 **I had canned beer at home.**

最近は発泡酒ばかりだ。 **I've been drinking only low-malt beer lately.**

ノンアルコールビールを頼んだ。 **I ordered a NAB.**
＊nabは、non-alcoholic beerの略

最近のノンアルコールビールっておいしい。 **Recent NABs taste pretty good.**

ワイン

赤ワインを飲んだ。 **I had red wine.**

おすすめのワインを聞いた。 **I asked them to recommend a wine.**

白ワインをグラス２杯飲んだ。 **I had two glasses of white wine.**

食前にスパークリングワインを飲んだ。 **I had some sparkling wine before eating.**

フルーティーでおいしかった。 **It was nice and fruity.**

ちょっと甘みが強過ぎた。 **It was a little too sweet.**

すっきりした味わいだった。 **It had a refreshing taste.**

ボトルを２本空けてしまった。 **We drank two bottles.**

明日はボジョレー・ヌーボーの解禁日！ **Beaujolais Nouveau goes on sale tomorrow!**
＊go on sale＝販売される

日本酒

日本酒を１合飲んだ。 **I had one cup of sake.**
＊グラスで飲んだ場合は、one glass of sake

「越後武士（さむらい）」という新潟の地酒を飲んだ。 **I tried a local sake from Niigata called Echigosamurai.**

かなり辛口の酒だった。 **The sake was really dry.**

甘口で飲みやすい酒だった。 **The sake had a mild sweet flavor and it was easy to drink.**

すっきりした後味の酒だった。 **The sake left a clean aftertaste.**
＊clean＝純粋な、異物のない

そのほかのお酒

焼酎のお湯割りを飲んだ。 I had shochu with hot water.

梅酒のソーダ割りを飲んだ。 I had plum wine with soda.

ウイスキーをロックで飲んだ。 I had whiskey on the rocks.

カクテルを何杯か飲んだ。 I had a couple of cocktails.

居酒屋・バー

みんなで居酒屋に行った。 We all went to an izakaya.

初めてホテルのバーで飲んだ。 It was my first time to drink at a hotel bar.

オリジナルカクテルがたくさんあった。 They had a lot of original cocktails.

夜景がきれいなバーだった。 The bar had a beautiful night view.

バーテンダーの手際が見事だった。 The bartender's tricks were amazing.

＊trick＝芸、技

2000円の飲み放題コースにした。 We got the all-you-can-drink course for 2,000 yen.

＊all-you-can-drink＝飲み放題の

飲み物が全品半額だった。 All drinks were half price.

つまみを何品か頼んだ。 I ordered a couple of bar snacks.

Memo

お酒にまつわることを、メモしておきましょう。

食べる・飲むについて英語日記を書いてみよう

食べたり飲んだりしたことについて、英語で書いてみましょう。

このままだと太る…

I've been eating too many snacks lately. I'd better stop it, or I'm going to gain weight for sure ...

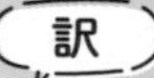

最近、私、お菓子を食べ過ぎ。やめないと確実に太る……。

「お菓子を食べる」は eat snacks、または eat snack foods。このところ続いている事柄は、I've been eating のように現在完了進行形で表しましょう。2 文目の or ～は「さもないと～、そうでなければ～」という意味。「確実に」は for sure で表します。

焼きたてのパンは最高！

I got a bread machine today and tried baking bread right away. It tasted so good! I'll bake bread for breakfast from now on.

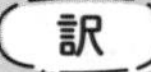

今日、ホームベーカリーをゲット。早速、パンを焼いてみた。とてもおいしかった！　これからは朝食にパンを焼こうっと。

「ホームベーカリー」は bread machine。「早速」は、right away（すぐに）でニュアンスを出してみました。「これから」が「今後ずっと」を表すときは、from now on。「これから（＝今から）勉強する」という場合は、now だけで OK です。

慣れない高級レストラン

Yoshiki-san took me to an upscale restaurant. Everything was delicious, but I feel more comfortable in casual restaurants.

ヨシキさんが高級レストランに連れていってくれた。どれもすごくおいしかったけど、カジュアルなレストランのほうが気楽でいいな。

upscale は「上流階級向けの、高級志向の」。「とてもおいしい」は delicious で表し、さらに強調したい場合は really や so を加えます。very delicious とは言わないので注意。but 以降は、casual restaurants are just fine with me としても OK です。

つい欲張ってしまう食べ放題

We went to an all-you-can-eat restaurant. We were already full, but we went back to get some more just to get our money's worth. We're always so greedy.

家族で食べ放題に行った。おなかがいっぱいにもかかわらず、元を取るために、追加で取りに行った。わが家はホント、いつもガツガツしてるなぁ。

「食べ放題の」は all-you-can-eat、「飲み放題の」なら all-you-can-drink で表します。「元を取る」は get one's money's worth（～が払った分の価値を得る）。「ガツガツしてる」は greedy がぴったり。「食い意地の張った、欲張りな」という意味です。

18 見る・読む・聞く

映画

映画にまつわる単語

外国映画	foreign movie
邦画	Japanese movie
アクション映画	action movie
恋愛もの	love story
サスペンス	suspense
ホラー	horror
SF	science fiction / sci-fi
コメディー	comedy
戦争映画	war movie
フィクション	fiction
ノンフィクション	nonfiction
ドキュメンタリー	documentary
ミュージカル	musical
アニメ	cartoon / anime
怪獣映画	monster movie
西部劇	Western movie
吹き替えの	dubbed
字幕の	subtitled

映画館に行く

映画館で『ラスト・サマー』を見た。
I saw “Last Summer” at the movie theater. ＊映画館で見る場合は一般的にseeを使う

1人で映画を見に行った。
I went to the movies by myself.
＊go to the movies＝映画を見に行く

彼女と映画を見に行った。
My girlfriend and I went to see a movie.

ネットで前売り券を買った。
I bought an advance ticket online.
＊advance ticket＝前売り券

事前に席を予約して行った。
I reserved my seat in advance.
＊in advance＝事前に、前もって

サービスデーで1200円だった。ラッキー！
It was service day, so it was just 1,200 yen. Lucky me!

後ろのほうの席に座った。
I sat in the back.

映画館はすごく混んでいた。 **The movie theater was packed.**
＊packed＝ぎっしり詰まった、満員の

映画館はすいていた。 **The movie theater wasn't crowded.**

やっぱり、映画館ではポップコーンとコーラだね。 **You can't watch a movie at a theater without popcorn and a cola.**
＊cola＝コーラ

あの映画館は、音響がいい。 **That theater has great acoustics.**
＊acoustics＝音響効果

大画面で見ると迫力が違う。 **Watching it on a big screen gives it more of an impact.**
＊impact＝衝撃、影響

3D 映画を見た。 **I saw a movie in 3D.**

画面が飛び出してきて、大迫力！ **It was really impressive the way the images jump out at you!**
＊impressive＝見事な

3D 眼鏡がちょっと落ちつかなかった。 **The 3D glasses were a little uncomfortable.**

映画の感想

面白くて、長さを感じなかった。 **It was really good, so it didn't feel so long.**

退屈で、すごく長く感じられた。 **It was so boring that it felt really long.**
＊boring＝退屈な

途中でウトウトしちゃった。 **I nodded off during the movie.**
＊nod off＝ウトウトする

アン・ハサウェイの演技がよかった。 **Anne Hathaway's performance was great.**

吹き替えの声が合っていた。 **The dubbed-in voices suited the characters.**
＊dubbed-in voice＝吹き替え音声　suit＝～に合う

吹き替えの声が合っていなかった。 **The dubbed-in voices didn't suit the characters.**

評判通りのいい映画だった。 **It was as good as the review said.**
＊review＝批評

ネットのレビューはよかったのにな。 **The online reviews were good, but ...**

手に汗握る映画だった。 **It was such an exciting movie.**

展開が速かった。 **The story developed very quickly.**

最後にどんでん返しがあった。	**It had an unexpected twist at the end.** ＊twist＝（話の）意外な展開
もう少し意外な展開があってもよかったかな。	**I think it needed a little more of a twist.**
見る前にネタバレを目にしちゃってたのは残念。	**Too bad I saw the spoilers before I saw the movie.** ＊spoiler＝ネタバレ
見る前に情報を入れないよう気を付けた。	**I was careful not to see any spoilers before watching it.**
お涙ちょうだいものだった。	**It was a tearjerker.** ＊tearjerker＝お涙ちょうだいもの
映画より小説のほうがよかった。	**I liked the novel better than the movie.**

家での映画鑑賞

韓国映画を配信で見た。	**I streamed a Korean movie.** ＊stream＝～を配信で見る（聞く）
スマホのアプリで映画を見た。	**I watched a movie on a smartphone app.**
『ローマの休日』を DVD で見た。	**I saw "Roman Holiday" on DVD.** ＊sawは、watchedでもOK
特典映像が充実していた。	**It had a variety of bonus features.**
映画のメイキング映像が面白かった。	**The "making of" was really fascinating.** ＊"making of"は、making of ～（～のメイキング）の略で、メイキング映像全般を指す　fascinating＝魅了する
制作陣のコメンタリーが興味深かった。	**The commentary by the production team was interesting.** ＊commentary＝解説
監督のインタビューが見られてよかった。	**I'm glad I was able to see the interview with the director.**

動画配信・テレビ

番組を表す単語

ニュース	news
ドラマ	drama
クイズ番組	quiz show
昼メロ	soap opera
ドキュメンタリー	documentary
ワイドショー	variety show
お笑い番組	comedy show
スポーツ番組	sports program
インタビュー番組	interview program
トーク番組	talk show
音楽番組	music program
語学番組	language program
教育番組	educational program
料理番組	cooking show
グルメ番組	gourmet program
映画	movie
アニメ	cartoon / anime

動画を見る （→ p. 603「動画共有サービス」も参照）

ネットフリックスで韓国ドラマを見た。
I watched a Korean drama on Netflix.

アマゾンプライムでアニメを見た。
I watched an anime on Amazon Prime.

見逃し配信でお笑い番組を見た。
I watched a catch-up broadcast of a comedy show.
＊catch-up＝遅れを取り戻すための　broadcast＝放送

『マンダロリアン』の配信が今日から始まった。
"The Mandalorian" starts streaming today.
＊stream＝～を配信する

あのドラマ、もう配信期間が終わっちゃった！
That drama isn't available to stream anymore!

最近、韓国ドラマを見まくってる。
Recently I've been watching Korean dramas all the time.

新作映画も配信で見られる時代だ。
This is an age where we can watch new releases via streaming.
＊via ～＝～によって

配信サービスなら、いつでもどこでも見られる。
With a streaming service, you can watch whenever and wherever.

テレビ番組を録画する必要がなくなった。	**I don't need to record TV programs anymore.**
1人加入すれば、ほかの家族もアカウントを利用できる。	**If one person subscribes, the whole family can share the account.** ＊subscribe＝加入する
週末にシリーズを一気見してしまった。	**I binge-watched the series over the weekend.** ＊binge-watch＝～を一気に見る
せっかく加入しているのに、ドラマを見る時間がない。	**I subscribed to the streaming service, but I have no time to watch dramas.**
見たい作品が多過ぎて、時間が足りないよ～。	**There are too many things I want to watch and I don't have enough time.**
配信サービスに加入し過ぎて、お金がかかる。	**I subscribed to too many streaming services and it's getting expensive.**
サブスクは今月で解約しよう。	**I'm going to cancel my subscription this month.**
最近、テレビを見なくなったなぁ。	**I haven't watched TV recently.**

テレビを見る

2時間ほどテレビを見た。	**I watched TV for about two hours.**
身支度しながら朝の番組を見た。	**I watched a morning show while getting dressed.**
面白そうなドラマをやっていたので、見てみた。	**There was a drama that looked interesting, so I watched it.**
最終回だった。	**It was the final episode.**
最終回を見逃しちゃった。	**I missed the final episode.**
9時からクイズ番組を見た。	**I watched a quiz show from 9:00.**
録画していたNHKのドキュメンタリー番組を見た。	**I watched an NHK documentary I had recorded.**
『映像の世紀』を録画しておいた。	**I recorded "Eizo no Seiki."**

今日のゲストはドリカムだった。	**Today's guest was Dreams Come True.**
たまたま見ていた番組に、MISIAが出ていた。	**I saw MISIA on a TV show I just happened to be watching.** ＊happen to ～＝偶然～する
見たい番組が重なっていた。	**The shows I wanted to watch were on at the same time.**
今日は見たい番組がなかった。	**There were no shows I wanted to watch today.**
どの番組も、お笑い芸人ばかりだなぁ。	**There's nothing but comedians on TV.** ＊nothing but ～＝～ばかり・だけ
夫はテレビばかり見ている。	**All my husband does is watch TV.**
帰ってから、録画しておいたドラマを見た。	**After I got home, I watched the TV show I had recorded.**
忙しくて、録画した番組を見る時間がない。	**I'm so busy that I don't have time to watch the TV shows I've recorded.**
録画した番組が、だいぶたまってきちゃった。	**All the TV shows I've recorded are starting to pile up.** ＊pile up＝たまる、山積する
録画に失敗してた。あー、もう！	**I didn't record it right. Darn it!**

番組の感想

切ない話だった。	**It was a heartrending story.** ＊heartrending＝胸が張り裂けるような
心温まるドラマだった。	**It was a heartwarming drama.**
爆笑した。	**I laughed hard.**
思ったより怖かった。	**It was scarier than I expected.** ＊scary＝怖い
ハラハラした。	**It kept me in suspense.** ＊in suspense＝ハラハラして
後味が悪かった。	**It left a bad aftertaste.**
イタリアに行ってみたくなった。	**It made me want to go to Italy.**

このドラマは、期待していたほど面白くないな。	**This series isn't as good as I thought it would be.** ＊series＝連続物
続きが気になる！	**I can't wait to see what happens next!**
最終回、見逃しちゃった。最悪！	**I missed the final episode. This sucks!** ＊suck＝ひどい、最悪である
脚本が上手だと思う。	**I think it has a good script.** ＊script＝脚本
俳優陣の演技が素晴らしい。	**They're amazing actors.**
豪華キャストのドラマだ。	**The drama has a star-studded cast.** ＊star-studded＝スター勢ぞろいの　cast＝配役
ミユちゃんってホント、天才子役だ。	**Miyu-chan is such a talented child actor.** ＊talented＝才能のある
あの俳優、ホントに大根だなぁ。	**She really is a ham actor.** ＊ham actor＝大根役者

DVD レンタル

ツタヤで DVD を 3 本借りてきた。	**I rented three DVDs at Tsutaya.**
5 本で 1000 円だった。	**It was 1,000 yen for five movies.**
新作は、安くなってから借りよう。	**I'll rent the new ones when they get cheaper.**
『タイタニック』が見たかったけど、置いてなかった。	**I wanted to see "Titanic" but they didn't have it in stock.** ＊have ～ in stock＝～の在庫がある
『スーツ』の DVD は、全部借りられちゃってた。	**All the copies of "Suits" had already been rented.**
返却予定日は、土曜日だ。	**I need to return them by Saturday.**
まずい！ 今日は DVD の返却予定日だった！	**Oh no! The DVD is due back today!** ＊be due back＝戻ることになっている
DVD を延滞しちゃった。あ～あ。	**The DVD is overdue. Oh, shoot.** ＊overdue＝期日を過ぎた　shoot＝しまった！

ラジオ・ポッドキャスト

ラジオ

ラジオの英語講座を聞いた。	**I listened to an English language program on the radio.**
英会話の講座を聞き逃してしまった。	**I missed the English conversation program.**
伊集院光のラジオ番組を聞いた。	**I listened to the Hikaru Ijuin radio show.**
聞き逃し配信で番組を聞いた。	**I listened to the show I missed on a catch-up broadcast.** ＊catch-up＝遅れを取り戻すための　broadcast＝放送
ラジオでかかった曲が気に入って、検索した。	**I liked a song I heard on the radio, so I looked it up.** ＊look ～ up＝～を調べる
ラジオで思い出の曲がかかって、高校時代が懐かしくなった。	**An oldie came on the radio and it took me back to my high school days.** ＊oldie＝懐メロ　take ～ back to ...＝～に…を思い出させる
ラジオ番組に投稿した。	**I sent my comments to the radio show.**
投稿が読まれた。やった！	**My comment was read out. Yay!**
大好きなラジオ番組が終わって悲しい。	**I'm sad because my favorite radio show has ended.**
新しいラジオ番組が始まった。	**A new radio show has started.**
たまには違う番組も聞いてみよう。	**I should try listening to different shows sometimes.**

ポッドキャスト

英語学習系のポッドキャストで、何かいいのはないかな？	**I wonder if there are any good English learning podcasts.**
ヤマキさんが薦めてくれたポッドキャスト番組を聞いた。	**I listened to a podcast that Yamaki-san recommended.**

iTunes Storeの「語学」ジャンルで1位のポッドキャストだった。	**It was the most popular podcast in the language section on iTunes.**
電車の中で、BBCのポッドキャストを聞いた。	**I listened to a BBC podcast on the train.**
ポッドキャストは、いつでも好きな時に聞けるのがうれしい。	**The good thing about podcasts is you can listen to them whenever you want.**

本・雑誌

本にまつわる単語

フィクション	fiction
ノンフィクション	nonfiction
文庫本	pocket edition / paperback
ハードカバー	hardcover
ペーパーバック	paperback
小説	novel
短編小説	short story
歴史小説	historical novel
恋愛もの	love story
ミステリー	mystery
エッセイ、随筆	essay
ビジネス書	business book
自己啓発書	self-improvement book
伝記	biography
自叙伝	autobiography / memoir
絵本	picture book
英語学習書	English textbook
～の対策本	～ book / book about ～
～の問題集	workbook for ～
写真集	photo collection
展覧会の図録	exhibition catalog
～のガイドブック	guidebook for ～ / ～ guidebook
旅行本	travel book
電子書籍	e-book

本

京極夏彦の新刊を買った。	**I bought Natsuhiko Kyogoku's new book.**
『三国志』を読み始めた。	**I started reading "Sangokushi."**
スピルバーグの伝記を読んでいる。	**I'm reading Spielberg's biography.** ＊biography＝伝記
川上未映子の新刊、早く出ないかな。	**I hope Mieko Kawakami's new book comes out soon.**

いつかアガサ・クリスティの原作を読めるようになりたいな。	**Someday, I want to be able to read Agatha Christie in the original English.**
今月は６冊、本を読んだ。	**I read six books this month.**

電子書籍

タブレットで電子書籍をダウンロードした。	**I downloaded an e-book on my tablet.** ＊e-book＝電子書籍
電子書籍って、一度に何冊も持ち歩けるから便利。	**E-books are convenient because you can carry a lot of books at once.** ＊at once＝一度に
キンドルって使いやすいのかな？	**I wonder if the Kindle is easy to use.**
電子書籍もいいけど、やっぱり紙で読みたい。	**E-books are okay, but I would rather read printed books.** ＊would rather ～＝むしろ～したい
父は画面上で本を読むと目が疲れると言っている。	**My father says that reading books on a screen makes his eyes tired.**
紙で読むほうが、内容を理解しやすいらしい。	**He says it's easier to understand books when reading hard copies.**

マンガ

明日は『ジャンプ』の発売日だ。	**The new "JUMP" goes on sale tomorrow.** ＊go on sale＝販売される
『SPY × FAMILY』の最新刊を買った。	**I bought the latest issue of "SPY× FAMILY."** ＊latest issue＝最新号
『キングダム』がすごく面白い。	**"Kingdom" is really good.**
昔の名作マンガを読みたい気分。	**I'm in the mood to read old manga masterpieces.** ＊in the mood to ～＝～する気分で
今日の新聞の４コママンガが面白かった。	**Today's newspaper comic strip was funny.** ＊comic strip＝4コママンガ
アプリで漫画を読んだ。	**I read manga via an app.** ＊via ～＝～によって

読書と感想

まだ読み始めたばかりだ。	**I just started reading it.**
まだ読み始めていない。	**I haven't started reading it yet.**
ヤバい、「積ん読」状態だ。	**Uh-oh, my un-read books are piling up.** ＊pile up＝たまる、山積する
今、半分くらい。	**I'm halfway through it now.** ＊halfway through ～＝～の半ばで
いよいよクライマックス。	**I'm finally at the climax of the book.**
もう少しで読み終わりそう。	**I'm almost done reading it.** ＊be done ～ing＝～し終える
夢中になって読んだ。	**I couldn't put it down.** ＊put ～ down＝～を下へ置く
朝まで読むのをやめられなかった。	**I couldn't stop reading until morning.**
今のところ、今年読んだ中で一番いい小説だ。	**It's the best novel I've read so far this year.** ＊so far＝今までのところ
号泣してしまった。	**It had me in tears.** ＊have ～ in tears＝～を泣かせる
彼の文章はわかりづらい。	**His writing is hard to understand.**
難し過ぎて、挫折した。	**It was way too hard, so I gave up.** ＊way＝ずっと、はるかに
つまらなくて、途中でやめた。	**It was boring, so I put it down.**
トモくんに貸してあげよう。	**I should lend it to Tomo.**
これ、だんだん面白くなくなってきたなぁ。	**It has gotten less and less interesting.**

雑誌

雑誌を表す単語

月刊誌	monthly magazine	芸能誌	show-biz magazine
週刊誌	weekly magazine	文芸誌	literary magazine
ファッション誌	fashion magazine	マンガ雑誌	comic magazine
スポーツ誌	sports magazine	科学雑誌	science magazine
ビジネス誌	business magazine	釣り雑誌	fishing magazine
エンタメ誌	entertainment magazine	ゴルフ雑誌	golf magazine
映画雑誌	movie magazine		

『Hanako』の最新号は温泉特集。
The latest "Hanako" is a special issue on hot springs.
＊latest＝最新の　hot spring＝温泉

『AERA』の今月号の特集、すごく面白そう。
This month's "AERA" feature looks really interesting.
＊feature＝特集

今月の『Oggi』、いつもより厚い気がする。
I feel this month's "Oggi" seems a little thicker than usual.
＊thick＝厚い

今月の特集はイマイチ。
This month's feature didn't really impress me.
＊impress＝～を感心させる、～によい印象を与える

この雑誌、定期購読しようかな。
Maybe I should subscribe to this magazine.
＊subscribe to ～＝～を購読する

付録のポーチは、すごくかわいかった。
The pouch that came with it was really cute.

最近の女性誌は、付録の充実ぶりがすごい。
Women's magazines these days sure do come with amazing extras.
＊extra＝おまけ

書店

G 書店に行った。
I went to G Bookstore.

中古書店に行った。
I went to a used bookstore.

古本屋さんを巡るのは楽しい。
Walking around used bookstores is fun.

10 分ほど立ち読みをした。	**I thumbed through books in the bookstore for about 10 minutes.**
	*thumb[サム] through ～＝～をパラパラめくる
小説を 2 冊と、雑誌を 1 冊買った。	**I bought two novels and a magazine.**
730 円の文庫を 2 冊買った。	**I bought two 730-yen paperbacks.**
洋書が半額になっていた。	**All foreign books were half price.**
	*foreign＝外国の
著者のサイン本を買った。	**I bought a book signed by the author.**
角田光代のサイン会に行った。	**I went to Mitsuyo Kakuta's signing.**
あこがれの著者に会えて感激！	**I was so excited to meet the author I admire!**
	*admire＝～を崇拝する・素晴らしいと思う
翻訳者のトークショーに行った。	**I went to a translator's talk show.**

図書館

東野圭吾の新刊を予約した。	**I reserved a copy of Keigo Higashino's new book.**
	*reserve＝～を予約する
予約は 200 人待ちだった。	**There's a waiting list of 200 people.**
いつになったら読めるんだろう？	**I wonder how long I'll have to wait to read it.**
スペインのガイドブックを借りた。	**I borrowed a Spain guidebook.**
雑誌の最新号を何冊か読んだ。	**I read a few of the latest magazines.**
	*latest＝最新の
本を 5 冊借りた。	**I borrowed five books.**
予約していた本を取りに行った。	**I went to pick up the book I had reserved.**
借りていた本を返却した。	**I returned the book I had borrowed.**
返却期限を過ぎていた。	**My book was overdue.**
	*overdue＝期日を過ぎた
今日は休館日だってこと、すっかり忘れてた。	**I totally forgot it was closed today.**

返却ボックスに本を返した。	**I returned the books to the drop box.**
早く本を返しに行かなきゃ。	**I have to return the books soon.**

マンガ喫茶

マンガ喫茶に行った。	**I went to a manga café.**
4時間いた。	**I was there for four hours.**
3時間パックにした。	**I got the three-hour pack.**
禁煙席にした。	**I sat in the non-smoking section.**
ソファ席にした。	**I sat on a sofa.**
『ワンピース』を15巻まで一気に読んだ。	**I read up to volume 15 of "One Piece" in one sitting.** ＊up to ～＝～に至るまで in one sitting＝一気に。at one sittingとも言う
結局、全部は読めずじまいだった。	**It turned out that I didn't have time to read them.** ＊turn out ～＝結局～になる
ソフトクリームが無料だった。	**The ice cream cones were free.** ＊「ソフトクリーム」を正確に表すなら、soft serve ice cream
一部のマンガ喫茶にはシャワーもあってすごい。	**I'm amazed that some manga cafés have showers.**

音楽

音楽を表す単語

クラシック	classical	ヒップホップ	hip-hop
ロック	rock	ラップ	rap
ポップス	pop	テクノ	techno
演歌	enka	ボサノヴァ	bossa nova
ジャズ	jazz	カントリー	country
ソウル	soul	リズム・アンド・ブルース	rhythm and blues / R&B
ゴスペル	gospel	童謡	nursery rhyme / children's song
ブルース	blues		
レゲエ	reggae		

音楽全般

クイーンの曲を聞いた。	**I listened to Queen songs.**
iPhone で音楽を聞いた。	**I listened to music on my iPhone.**
ジャズ喫茶に行った。	**I went to a jazz café.**
アリシア・キーズのニューアルバムを買った。	**I bought Alicia Keys' new album.**
SEKAI NO OWARI の新譜を、iTunes でダウンロードした。	**I downloaded SEKAI NO OWARI's new release from iTunes.**
米津玄師のニューシングル、300 万ダウンロード突破だって。	**Yonezu Kenshi's new song has reached over three million downloads.**
MV がすごくかっこよかった。	**The music video was really cool.**
この曲は本当に泣ける。	**This song really makes me cry.**
この曲を聞くと、大学時代を思い出す。	**This song reminds me of my college days.** ＊remind ～ of ...＝～に…を思い出させる
この曲の振り付けを完璧に踊れるようになりたい！	**I want to be able to dance the choreography for this song perfectly!** ＊choreography＝振り付け
やっぱり、秋の夜長はクラシック。	**Classical music is just right for long autumn nights.**

ライブ・コンサート

King Gnu のライブ、チケットが取れなかった。	**I couldn't get a ticket for the King Gnu concert.**
今週末は、待ちに待った EXILE のライブだ。	**This weekend is the EXILE concert I've been waiting for.**
すごく見やすい席が取れた。ラッキー！	**I got a seat with a great view. I was so lucky!**
2階席の最前列だった。	**My seat was in the front row of the second floor.** ＊row＝列

ステージの真ん前に陣取った。	**I got a spot in front of the stage.** ＊spot＝場所、地点
後方席でよく見えなかった。	**My seat was in the back, so I could hardly see them.**
双眼鏡を持っていってよかった。	**I'm glad I brought my binoculars.** ＊binoculars＝双眼鏡
今日のライブも最高だった。	**Today's concert was also awesome.** ＊awesome［オーサム］＝すごい、素晴らしい
みんなで合唱して、すごく盛り上がった。	**We all sang together. It was really exciting.**
クラシックコンサートに行った。	**I went to a classical concert.**
素晴らしい演奏だった。	**It was an amazing performance.**
最後はスタンディングオベーションだった。	**There was a standing ovation at the end.**
ジャズ・クラブに行った。	**I went to a jazz club.**
いつかニューヨークのブルーノートに行ってみたい。	**Someday, I want to go to the Blue Note in New York.**
川井郁子のバイオリンを聞きに行った。	**I went to Ikuko Kawai's violin concert.**
小林香織のサックスは、パワフルで素晴らしかった。	**Kaori Kobayashi's sax performance was powerful and fantastic.**
今週末は、フジロックに行く。	**I'm going to the Fuji Rock Festival this weekend.**
レッチリとレディオヘッドの時間帯が重なってる！	**The Red Hot Chili Peppers and Radiohead are playing at the same time!**
どっちを見るべきか !?	**Which should I see?**
外でビールを飲みながら聞く音楽は最高だ。	**Nothing beats listening to music while drinking beer outdoors.** ＊beat＝～に勝る
ライブは配信で見た。	**I watched the concert via streaming.** ＊via ～＝～によって

現地に行きたかったな。	**I wish I could've been there in person.** ＊in person＝直接自分で

美術館・博物館

美術館・博物館に行く

山梨県立美術館でミレーの絵画を見てきた。	**I saw Millet's paintings at the Yamanashi Prefectural Museum of Art.** ＊painting＝絵画　prefectural＝県の
今、大阪でルノワール展をやっている。	**There's a Renoir exhibit in Osaka.** ＊exhibit＝展覧会、展示
葛飾北斎の浮世絵を見た。	**I saw Hokusai Katsushika's ukiyoe prints.**
恐竜の展示を見に、子どもたちを科学博物館に連れていった。	**I took my kids to the dinosaur exhibit at the science museum.** ＊dinosaur＝恐竜
オザキさんの写真展を見に行った。	**I went to see Mr. Ozaki's photo exhibit.**
入場料は1500円だった。	**The admission was 1,500 yen.** ＊admission＝入場料
入場するまで1時間も待った。	**I had to wait for an hour to get in.**
作品集を買った。	**I bought an art book.**
写真撮影OKだった。	**We were allowed to take pictures.** ＊allow ～ to ...＝～に…することを許す
フラッシュなしなら、写真撮影OKだった。	**We were allowed to take pictures as long as we didn't use flash.** ＊as long as ～＝～である限りは

美術館・博物館の感想

とてもよかった。	**It was really good.**
やっぱり本物はいいなぁ。	**There's nothing like the real thing.** ＊there's nothing like ～＝～ほどよいものはない
息をのむほど素晴らしかった。	**It was breathtaking.** ＊breathtaking＝息をのむような
作品のよさがあまりわからなかった。	**I didn't really understand what was so good about it.**

本物だったのかな？	**I wonder if they were the real McCoys.** *the real McCoy＝正真正銘の本物
現代アートは理解しがたい。	**Contemporary art is hard to appreciate.** *contemporary＝現代の appreciate＝～の価値がわかる・よさがわかる
アジサイを描いた絵が、一番印象に残った。	**A painting of hydrangeas left the biggest impression on me.** *hydrangea＝アジサイ　impression＝印象
「バベルの塔」に魅了された。	**I was fascinated by "the Tower of Babel."**
原画を見られて感激した。	**I was thrilled to see the original drawings.**
歌川国芳の展示を見に行った。	**I went to see the Kuniyoshi Utagawa exhibition.**
浮世絵がこんなに面白いとは思いもしなかった。	**I never thought ukiyoe art was this fascinating.** *this＝これほど
どうしたら、あんなに深い色合いが出せるんだろう。	**I wonder how they get such deep hues.** *hue［ヒュー］＝色調、色合い
戦争の悲惨さが写真によく表れていた。	**Those photos really conveyed the tragedy of war.** *convey＝～を伝える　tragedy＝悲劇
彫刻が生き生きとしていた。	**The sculptures looked real.** *sculpture＝彫刻
展示の仕方が工夫されていた。	**The way the exhibition was presented was ingenious.** *ingenious＝工夫に富む
子どもたちも興味を持っていた。	**Even children were interested in it.**
ワークショップが面白かった。	**The workshop was interesting.**
ガイドさんの説明がわかりやすかった。	**The guide's explanation was easy to follow.**

舞台・お笑い

演劇

三谷幸喜の新作舞台を見に行った。
I went to see Koki Mitani's new play.
＊went to seeは、sawとしてもOK

劇団四季の『ライオン・キング』を見に行った。
I went and saw the Shiki Theater Company's "Lion King."

主人公の俳優の歌がすごくよかった。
The leading actor's singing was fascinating.
＊fascinating＝素晴らしい

いい声だった。
He had a great voice.

主演女優の演技は、とても迫力があった。
The female lead's performance was really powerful.
＊lead＝主役

一度、宝塚歌劇団を見に行きたい。
Someday, I want to see the Takarazuka Revue.

この劇団は、今注目の劇団だ。
This theater company is currently in the limelight.
＊in the limelight＝脚光を浴びて

彼らの次回の公演もぜひ見てみたい。
I would love to see their next performance.
＊would love to ～＝ぜひ～したい

バレエ

ロイヤル・バレエ団の公演を見に行った。
I went to see a public performance of the Royal Ballet.

演目は「白鳥の湖」だった。
They performed "Swan Lake."

彼女の踊りは、すごく気品があった。
Her dancing was really elegant.
＊elegant＝気品のある、優雅な

優雅な動きに魅せられた。
I was enchanted by their graceful dancing.
＊enchanted＝魅了されて　graceful＝優雅な

後半の群舞は圧巻だった。
The group dance in the second half was the highlight of the performance.
＊highlight＝ハイライト、圧巻

スピード感があった。
We could feel the speed.

高いリフトがとても美しかった。	**The high lifts were really beautiful.** ＊lift＝(バレエの)リフト

落語

浅草に寄席を見に行った。	**I saw a vaudeville show in Asakusa.** ＊vaudeville［ヴォードヴィゥ］＝寄席演芸
柳家喬太郎の落語を見に行った。	**I went to see a rakugo performance by Kyotaro Yanagiya.**
今日のネタは「芝浜」だった。	**Today's story was "Shibahama."**
心温まる話だった。	**It was a heartwarming story.**
大笑いした。	**I laughed so hard.**
登場人物の演じ分けが見事だった。	**He played a lot of characters skillfully.** ＊skillfully＝巧みに、器用に
立川志の輔の新作落語が面白かった。	**Shinosuke Tatekawa's new rakugo performance was really funny.**

お笑い

なんばグランド花月に、吉本新喜劇を見に行った。	**I went to see the Yoshimoto Shinkigeki at Namba Grand Kagetsu.**
かまいたちのライブを見に行った。	**I went to see the Kamaitachi comedy show.**
中川家の漫才を見た。	**I saw Nakagawake's manzai.**
おなかがよじれるほど笑った。	**I laughed so hard that my stomach hurt.**
正直、ちょっとスベり気味だった。	**Honestly, they were kind of lame.** ＊lame＝つまらない、盛り上がらない
新ネタをやっていた。	**They performed some new jokes.**
前に見たことのあるネタだった。	**I had seen it before.**

見る・読む・聞くについて 英語日記を書いてみよう

ドラマや本、音楽などについて、英語で書いてみましょう。

人気の新刊

I went to the library to borrow Keigo Higashino's latest book. I was surprised that there was a waiting list of 107 people! I've decided to buy a copy instead.

東野圭吾の新刊を借りに図書館へ行った。予約待ちの人が107人もいるなんてビックリ！ 自分で買うことにした。

「〜を借りる」は、無料で借りるときはborrow、お金を払って借りる場合はrentを使います。「予約待ちの人が107人もいる」は、I was surprisedの時制（過去）に合わせてthere was 〜とします。insteadは「その代わりに」の意味。

息子が書いた作文

I read a composition Sosuke wrote in class for Mother's Day. He wrote that he thanked me and loved me. It brought tears to my eyes.

ソウスケが学校の授業で母の日のために書いたという作文を読んだ。私に感謝しているということと、私が大好きということが書かれていた。涙があふれてきちゃった。

「学校の授業で」は、in class。2文目はHe wrote 〜と過去形の文になっているので、he thankedと(he) loved meの下線部は、時制を一致させて過去形にしています。「〜が涙を誘う、〜に涙があふれ出す」は、〜 bring tears to my eyesで。

最近の映画館

Aki asked me out to the movies, so we went. I didn't know that theaters nowadays have wide, comfortable reclining seats and great acoustics.

アキに誘われて、一緒に映画を見に行った。最近の映画館って、ゆったりとして気持ちいいリクライニングシートだし、音響も素晴らしいんだなぁ。

「アキに誘われて」は「アキが私を誘った」と考えて、Aki asked me (out) と表します。「映画に」なら to the movies、「食事に」なら to dinner か for dinner を続けましょう。nowadays は「(昔と比較して)最近では」という意味。「音響」は acoustics で表します。

ラジオでメールが読まれた！

I e-mailed a request for a Toni Braxton song, and it was read on the radio today! I was so excited that I couldn't help telling Kanae about it.

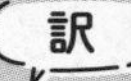

今日、トニー・ブラクストンの曲をリクエストしたメールがラジオで読まれた！　めっちゃ興奮して、カナエに話さずにはいられなかった。

「～のリクエスト」は request for ～。e-mailed (～をメールで送った) は、sent (～を送った。現在形は send) としても OK です。so ～ that ... は、「とても～なので…する、…するほど～だ」。can't help ～ing は「～せずにはいられない」という意味です。

19 趣味・習いごと

習いごと・趣味全般

習いごとを表す単語

語学	language study
楽器	musical instrument
カラオケ	karaoke
ダンス	dance
バレエ	ballet
フラメンコ	flamenco
ジャズダンス	jazz dance
ヒップホップダンス	hip-hop dance
社交ダンス	social dance
日本舞踊	classical Japanese dance
絵画	drawing / painting
油絵	oil painting
水彩画	watercolor painting
風景画	landscape painting
水墨画	ink-wash painting
写真	photography
和装、着付け	kimono dressing
茶道	tea ceremony
華道	flower arranging
書道	calligraphy
料理	cooking
剣道	kendo
柔道	judo
そろばん	abacus
囲碁	go / igo
将棋	shogi
チェス	chess

何か新しいことを習いたい気分だ。 **I feel like learning something new.**

来週から茶道教室に通うことにした。 **I've decided to start taking tea ceremony lessons next week.**

月謝は1万5000円だ。 **The tuition is 15,000 yen per month.**

＊tuition［トゥイション］＝授業料

場所は、市のコミュニティーセンターだ。 **It's at the city's community center.**

今日はハシモト先生だった。 **Ms. Hashimoto taught us today.**

先生の授業は楽しい。 **Her classes are fun.**

生徒は６人だった。	**There were six students.**
おけいこ仲間とお茶をした。	**I went to a café with my classmates.**
ミエコさんは多趣味だなぁ。	**Mieko has a lot of hobbies.**
ミユは乗馬をしているらしい。	**I hear Miyu is taking horseback riding lessons.**
アイコさんの影響を受けて、私も野菜作りを始めた。	**Aiko influenced me to start growing vegetables.** ＊influence＝～に影響を与える
下手の横好きだけど、気にしない。	**I'm not good at it, but I don't care.**
忙しくてレッスンに行けてない。	**I've been too busy to take lessons.**
習いごとをしたいけど、金銭的な余裕がない。	**I want to take up something, but I can't afford it.** ＊take up ～＝（趣味として）～を始める
みんなについていけるかな？	**I wonder if I can keep up with my classmates.** ＊keep up with ～＝～に遅れずについていく
ちゃんと続けられるかな？	**I wonder if I can keep it up.** ＊keep ～ up＝～を継続する
私、三日坊主だからなぁ。	**I'm the type of person who never sticks to anything.** ＊stick to ～＝～をやり通す

語学

語学にまつわる単語

英語	English	ロシア語	Russian
韓国語	Korean	タイ語	Thai
中国語	Chinese	ベトナム語	Vietnamese
フランス語	French	会話	conversation
ドイツ語	German	作文	composition
スペイン語	Spanish	リスニング	listening comprehension
イタリア語	Italian	文法	grammar
ポルトガル語	Portuguese		

英語

英会話の授業に行った。	**I attended an English conversation class.** ＊attend＝～に出席する
ソフィア先生とフリートークをした。	**I had a free-conversation session with Sophia.**
カフェでブラウン先生のレッスンを受けた。	**I had a lesson with Mr. Brown at a café.**
オンラインで 25 分間、レッスンを受けた。	**I had a 25-minute online lesson.**
みんなの前で、英作文を発表した。	**I presented my English composition in front of the class.** ＊present＝～を発表する composition＝作文
“We had a ball.”という表現を習った。	**I learned the expression, “We had a ball.”** ＊have a ball＝大いに楽しむ
言語交換のパートナーが見つかった。	**I found a language exchange partner.**
カフェで 2 時間、おしゃべりした。	**We talked for two hours in a café.**
アリーが私の英語を、私がアリーの日本語を添削した。	**Allie checked my English and I checked her Japanese.**
冠詞って難しい。	**Articles are difficult.** ＊article＝冠詞
今日は 2 時間、TOEIC の勉強をした。	**I studied for TOEIC for two hours today.**
英語の絵本を読んでみた。	**I tried reading an English picture book.**
最後まで読めた！	**I was able to read the whole book!** ＊whole＝全体の、全部の
今日から英語で日記を書くことにした。	**I've decided to write in my diary in English starting today.**
英語でブログを書くことにした。	**I've decided to write my blog in English.**

（ツイッターで）英語でつぶやくことにした。	I've decided to tweet in English. ＊tweet＝（ツイッターで）つぶやく
インスタの写真に英語で説明を付け始めた。	I've started posting pictures with captions in English on my Instagram.
ケイゴの英語はネイティブ・スピーカーみたいだ。	Keigo speaks English like a native speaker.

英語学習の目標

英語がペラペラになりたい。	I want to be fluent in English. ＊fluent［フルーエント］＝流ちょうな
海外旅行に行っても困らないくらい、英語が話せるようになりたい。	I want to speak enough English to get by when I travel abroad. ＊abroad＝海外へ　get by＝何とかやっていく
外国人とおしゃべりできるようになりたい。	I want to be able to enjoy talking with people from other countries.
字幕なしで映画を見られるようになりたい。	I hope to be able to enjoy movies without relying on subtitles. ＊rely on ～＝～に頼る　subtitles＝字幕
英語の資料を苦労せず読めるようになりたい。	I want to be able to read English materials easily. ＊material＝資料
ハナみたいにきれいな英語を話せるようになりたいな。	I want to be able to speak beautiful English like Hana.
いつか留学したいな。	I want to study abroad someday.
まずは1年間、英語日記を続けるぞ！	I will keep a diary in English at least for a year! ＊at least＝とにかく、せめて
英検2級に合格するよう、頑張るぞ！	I will do my best to pass the Eiken grade 2 test!
TOEICのスコアを200点上げたい。	I want to increase my TOEIC score by 200 points. ＊increase＝～を上げる・増やす
半年以内にTOEICで700点を超えるぞ！	I will get over 700 on the TOEIC test within six months!
目指せ800点！	Go for 800 points! ＊go for ～＝～を目指す

英語が上達する・しない

英会話を習い始めて３年。	**It has been three years since I started taking English conversation lessons.**
英語で日記を書き始めて３カ月。	**It has been three months since I started keeping a diary in English.**
英語は上達してるのかな？	**I wonder if my English is getting better.**
少しずつ上達している気がする。	**I feel that I'm improving little by little.** ＊improve＝上達する
前より話せるようになった。	**I've become better at speaking English than I was before.** ＊become better at ～＝～がより上手になる
今日はたくさん発言できた。満足！	**I was able to speak a lot today. I'm satisfied!**
耳が英語に慣れてきた。	**I'm getting used to listening to English.**
なかなか上達しない。	**My progress is slow.** ＊progress＝進歩
上達しなくても、楽しければいいや。	**I don't care if my English isn't improving as long as I enjoy myself.** ＊as long as ～＝～である限りは
スランプに陥っている。	**I'm in a slump.** ＊slump＝スランプ
スランプから抜け出したい。	**I want to pull myself out of my slump.**
発音がなかなかうまくできない。	**I have a hard time pronouncing English words.** ＊pronounce＝～を発音する
相変わらずリスニングが苦手。	**I'm still not good at listening.**
言いたいことがうまく言えなくて、もどかしかった。	**I was frustrated because I couldn't express my thoughts well.** ＊frustrated＝もどかしい　thought[ソート]＝考え
英語がパッと口をついて出てこない。	**When I speak English, words don't come easily to me.**

なかなか単語が覚えられない。 I have a hard time memorizing English words.

そのほかの外国語

韓国語の勉強を始めた。 I started studying Korean.

中国語を勉強しようかな。 Maybe I'll study Chinese.

今日からラジオで中国語の勉強を始めた。 I started studying Chinese on the radio today.

ハングル文字が覚えられないよ〜。 I can't remember the hangul characters.
＊character＝文字

覚えた韓国語を使ってみたい。 I want to use the Korean I've learned.

字幕なしで韓ドラを見たい。 I want to watch Korean dramas without subtitles.
＊subtitle＝字幕

フランス語が話せたら、かっこいいだろうな。 I would look so cool if I could speak French.

ドイツ語って発音が難しそう。 German seems hard to pronounce.

スペイン語の響きが好き。 I like the way Spanish sounds.

言語を学ぶのは面白い。 It's fun to study languages.

推し活

最近、宝塚にハマってる。 I've been obsessed with Takarazuka recently.
＊be obsessed with 〜＝〜に夢中である

沼に沈むのは一瞬だ。 You get obsessed with it in no time.

ファンになってもうすぐ2年。 It has been almost two years since I became their fan.

推しは今日も尊かった。 My fave was precious today, just as always.
＊fave［フェイヴ］＝お気に入り、推し

今日も推し活がはかどった。	**I did a lot of things for my fave today as well.**
オフ会に参加した。	**I attended an offline meet-up.**
みんなで推しの誕生日を祝った。	**We celebrated our fave's birthday together.**
イベントのため札幌まで遠征してきた。	**I traveled all the way to Sapporo for the event.**
聖地巡礼してきた。	**I went on a pilgrimage.** ＊pilgrimage＝巡礼
応援用にうちわを自作した。	**I made a paper fan for cheering my fave.** ＊paper fan＝うちわ。uchiwaとしてもOK
ペンラの振り過ぎで腕が痛い。	**My arms hurt from shaking my light stick too much.**
トラジャのアクキー買っちゃった♪	**I got Travis Japan's acrylic key chain!**
鑑賞・保存・布教用に3冊買った。	**I bought one for watching, one for preserving, and one for promoting.**
最近、推しに課金し過ぎてる。	**Recently I've been spending too much on my fave.**
夜中までリアタイ視聴した。	**I watched it live until late at night.**
神回だった。	**The episode was just incredible.** ＊incredible＝信じられないほど素晴らしい、すごい
控えめに言って最高だった。	**It was the best, to say the least.**
ダンスがキレッキレだった。	**Their dancing was so crisp.** ＊crisp＝キビキビした
推しの笑顔を見るだけで幸せ。	**I'm happy just to see my fave's smile.**
Tommyが脱退するって。ウソでしょ!?	**I hear Tommy is going to leave the group. Seriously?**
推しなしでどうやって生きていけばいいの？	**How am I going to live without my fave?**

楽器

楽器を表す単語

ピアノ	piano	チェロ	cello
ギター	guitar	フルート	flute
ウクレレ	ukulele［ユークレイリ］	トランペット	trumpet
エレキギター	electric guitar	トロンボーン	trombone
アコースティックギター	acoustic guitar	サックス	saxophone / sax
クラシックギター	classical guitar	アコーディオン	accordion
フォークギター	folk guitar	クラリネット	clarinet
ドラム	drum	三味線	shamisen
バイオリン	violin	二胡	erhu［アーフー］
ビオラ	viola		

楽器を習う

何か楽器を弾けるようになりたいな。 **I want to be able to play a musical instrument.**
＊musical instrument＝楽器

電子オルガンを習いたい。 **I want to learn to play the electronic organ.**

バイオリンを弾いてみたい。 **I want to try the violin.**

ギターを習い始めた。 **I took up guitar lessons.**
＊take up ～＝(趣味として)～を始める

お琴のおけいこに行った。 **I took a koto lesson.**
＊tookをhadにしてもOK

きれいな音が出せた。 **I was able to make a nice sound.**

ようやくコツがつかめてきた。 **I'm finally getting it.**
＊get it＝コツがつかめる

みんなでセッションをした。 **We had a session.**

きれいな音がなかなか出せない。 **I'm having a hard time making a nice sound.**

楽譜を読むのは難しい。 **It's difficult to read music.**
＊read music＝楽譜を読む

弦をうまく押さえられない。 **I can't hold the strings down well.**
＊hold＝～を押さえる　string＝弦

発表会・コンクール

来月、ウクレレの発表会がある。 **I have a ukulele recital next month.**
＊recital＝リサイタル、発表会

初めての発表会で緊張する。 **I'm nervous about my first recital.**

ピアノのコンクールに出場した。 **I played in a piano contest.**

すっごく緊張した。 **I was so nervous.**

緊張して手が震えた。 **I was nervous and my hands were shaking.**

最後まで間違えずに弾けた！ **I played to the end without any mistakes!**

何度か間違えちゃった。 **I made several mistakes.**

コンクールで最優秀賞を受賞した。 **I won the highest award in the contest.**
＊win＝～を獲得する。過去形はwon［ワン］

コンクールで2位だった。 **I placed 2nd in the contest.**

人前で演奏するのは気持ちいい。 **It feels great to perform before an audience.**
＊audience＝観客、聴衆

みんなで演奏するのは楽しい。 **It's fun to play with other people.**

カラオケ

アヤちゃんとカラオケに行った。 **Aya and I went to a karaoke place.**

3時間ぶっ通しで歌った。 **We sang for three hours non-stop.**

「ひとカラ」してきた。 **I went for karaoke alone.**
＊「ひとカラ」は、「1人カラオケ」の略

竹内まりやの曲ばかり歌っちゃった。 **I sang mostly Mariya Takeuchi songs.**

懐かしい曲をたくさん歌った。 **I sang a lot of old songs.**
＊「最近の曲」なら、new songs

最近の曲は、あまりわからない。 **I don't really know many new songs.**

ヒロくんのGLAY、超うまかった。	**Hiro did a good job singing GLAY songs.**
やっぱり80年代の曲はサイコー！	**Songs from the 80's are the best!**
ドリカムの曲は、すごく難しい。	**Dreams Come True songs are so hard.**
歌って踊って、ストレス発散！	**I destressed by singing and dancing!** ＊destress＝ストレスを解消する
今日はのどの調子がよかった。	**I sounded good today.**
今日はうまく歌えなかった。	**I couldn't sing well today.**
採点機能で100点ゲット！	**I got 100 points on the scoring system!**
採点結果はイマイチだった。	**My score wasn't so good.**

ダンス

ジャズダンスを習ってみたい。	**I want to learn jazz dance.**
フラダンスって、見た目よりキツい！	**The hula is harder than it looks!**
先生の動きに、なかなかついていけない。	**I have a hard time following the teacher.**
まずは体を柔らかくすることから始めなきゃ。	**I need to limber up first.** ＊limber up＝(体を)柔軟にする
今日は指先に意識を向けて踊った。	**I focused on my finger tips when dancing today.** ＊focus on ～＝～に集中する　tip＝先、先端
1時間踊って、気分爽快(そうかい)！	**I danced for an hour, and it felt great!**
フラメンコの発表会があった。	**I had a flamenco dance recital.**
衣装を着て踊ると、プロのダンサーになった気分。	**When I dance in a costume, I feel like a professional dancer.**

絵画

絵画教室に行った。	**I went to a painting class.**
水彩画を始めた。	**I took up watercolor painting.** ＊take up ～＝（趣味として）～を始める
油絵に挑戦したい。	**I want to try oil painting.**
水墨画を習い始めた。	**I started studying ink-wash painting.** ＊ink-wash painting＝水墨画
人物のデッサンをした。	**I drew a portrait.** ＊draw［ドゥロー］＝～を線で描く。過去形はdrew［ドゥルー］ portrait＝肖像画
公園でスケッチをした。	**I did some sketching in the park.**
風景画を何枚か描いた。	**I painted a few landscapes.** ＊landscape＝風景画
娘の肖像画を描いている。	**I'm painting a portrait of my daughter.**
なかなか思うように描けない。	**I'm having a hard time painting what I want.**
少し上手になってきたかな。	**Maybe I'm getting better.**
何度も描き直した。	**I drew it over and over again.**
絵はほぼ完成した。	**My painting is nearly done.** ＊done＝済んだ、終了した
絵画教室の展覧会に絵を出品する予定だ。	**I'm going to show my painting at the painting class exhibition.**
県の絵画コンテストで佳作を取った。	**I received an honorable mention in a prefectural painting contest.** ＊honorable mentuon＝佳作、特別賞　prefectural＝県の

写真

写真を撮る

写真教室に通い始めた。	**I started taking a photography class.**

風景写真の撮り方を学びたい。	**I want to learn how to take landscape photos.** ＊landscape＝風景
高尾山に春の野草を撮りに行った。	**I went to Mt. Takao to photograph wild spring flowers.** ＊photograph＝～を撮影する
写真サークルの仲間と撮影に出かけた。	**I went out to take photos with some friends from the photo club.**
街歩きをしながら写真を撮った。	**I took some pictures as I walked around town.**
モデルの撮影会に行った。	**I went to a photo shoot with some models.** ＊photo shoot＝写真撮影会
富士山の写真を撮った。	**I took pictures of Mt. Fuji.**
新宿の夜景を撮った。	**I took pictures of the night views in Shinjuku.**
絶景スポットで列車の写真を撮った。	**I took photos of trains in a picturesque spot.** ＊picturesque＝絵のように美しい

写真の出来

いい写真が何枚か撮れた。	**I was able to take a few nice pictures.**
いい表情が撮れた。	**I was able to capture some great expressions.** ＊capture＝～をとらえる　expression＝表情
満足のいく写真が撮れなかった。	**I wasn't happy with the pictures I took.**
どうしても平凡な写真になってしまう。	**My pictures always look so ordinary.** ＊ordinary＝普通の、ありふれた
逆光になっていて撮影が難しかった。	**It was hard to take photos against the sun.**
写真がブレていた。	**The picture came out blurred.** ＊blurred＝ぼやけた
ピントが合っていなかった。	**It was out of focus.** ＊out of focus＝焦点が外れて
写真コンテストに応募してみよう。	**I'm going to enter a photo contest.**

着付け

着付けのレッスンを受けた。 I took a kimono dressing lesson.

1人で着付けができるようになりたいな。 I want to be able to wear a kimono on my own.

鏡を見ながら着付けの練習をした。 I practiced putting on a kimono in front of a mirror.

きれいに着られた。 I wore it nicely.

帯を結ぶのが難しい。 It's difficult to tie an obi. ＊tie＝～を結ぶ

訪問着で出かけた。 I went out in a semi-formal kimono.

コウタの卒業式に着物で出席した。 I wore a kimono for Kota's graduation.

ライリーに着付けをしてあげた。 I helped Riley get dressed in a kimono.

着物を新調した。 I bought a new kimono.

そろそろ留め袖をそろえたほうがいいかな？ Maybe it's about time to get a formal kimono.

茶道

今日は茶道教室だった。 I had a tea ceremony class today.

流派は裏千家だ。 My school is Urasenke. ＊school＝流派

お抹茶をたてて飲んだ。 I made green tea and drank it.

とてもおいしかった。 It was great.

お茶菓子がおいしかった。 The tea sweets were good.

干菓子をいただいた。 I had dried sweets.

水菓子をいただいた。 I had jelly sweets.
＊「水菓子」が果物なら、jelly sweetsをfruitsに

今日のお茶菓子は、桜をかたどったものだった。 **Today's tea sweets looked like cherry blossoms.**
＊cherry blossom＝桜の花

お手前を覚えるのが難しい。 **It's hard to remember the proper tea ceremony etiquette.**

足がしびれた。 **My feet went numb.**
＊go numb［ナム］＝しびれる。go to sleepとも言う

書道

書道教室に行った。 **I went to a calligraphy class.**

上手に書けた。 **I made some great brush strokes.**
＊brush stroke＝筆さばき、筆遣い

今日はあまり上手に書けなかった。 **My brush strokes weren't very good today.**

いい筆を使うと、いい字が書けるものだ。 **Good brushes sure help me write nice characters.**
＊character＝文字

先生に「生き生きとした字だね」と褒められた。 **The teacher complimented me on my vibrant characters.**
＊compliment＝～を褒める　vibrant＝活気のある

囲碁・将棋・チェス

囲碁のレッスンを受けた。 **I had a go lesson.**

オンラインで将棋の指導対局を受けた。 **I played a learning game of shogi online.**

プロ棋士に直接教われるなんて最高。 **Being taught by a pro is great.**

攻め方のコツを教わった。 **I learned how to attack.**

受け方のコツを教わった。 **I learned how to defend.**
＊defend＝防御する

ほかの生徒さんたちと対局した。 **I played against the other students.**

２勝１敗だった。 **I won twice and lost once.**

初めてフカウラさんに勝てた。	**I won against Fukaura-san for the first time.**
前より強くなっている気がする！	**I feel like I'm getting better!**
アオシマさんには全然勝てないなぁ。	**I just can't win against Aoshima-san.**
ちっとも強くなっている気がしない。	**I don't feel like I'm improving at all.** ＊improve＝上達する
やった！　ついに初段になった！	**Yay! I finally got to the first rank!** ＊「初段」は、shodanや1-danとしてもOK
大会、Bクラスで準優勝だった。	**I was runner-up in the B class in the tournament.** ＊runner-up＝準優勝者
次はもっと上を目指そう。	**I want to aim for a higher result next time.** ＊aim＝目指す

ガーデニング

草花を表す単語

アサガオ	**morning glory**
キキョウ	balloon flower / bellflower
キク	**chrysanthemum**
シクラメン	cyclamen
スイートピー	**sweet pea**
スイセン	narcissus
スズラン	**lily of the valley**
スミレ	violet
タンポポ	**dandelion**
チューリップ	tulip
ナデシコ	**dianthus** ［ダイアンサス］
バラ	rose
パンジー	**pansy**
ヒマワリ	sunflower
ヒャクニチソウ	**zinnia** ［ズィニア］
ヒヤシンス	hyacinth ［ハイアスィンス］
マリーゴールド	**marigold**
ユリ	lily
ラベンダー	**lavender**
ハーブ	herb
バジル	**basil**
ミント	mint
クレソン	**watercress**
タイム	thyme

種・球根を植える

チューリップの球根を植えた。	**I planted tulip bulbs.** ＊bulb＝球根

ゴーヤの苗を植えた。 **I planted goya seedlings.**
＊seedling＝苗。「ゴーヤ」はbitter gourdだが、日記ではgoyaでもOK

ハーブを何種類か植えた。 **I planted several herbs.**

鉢に寄せ植えしてみた。 **I planted various plants together in a pot.**

クレマチスの植え替えをした。 **I transplanted the clematis.**
＊transplant＝～(植物)を移植する

芽が出るのが楽しみ。 **I'm looking forward to the budding.**
＊budding＝発芽

きれいな花が咲くといいな。 **I hope that there will be beautiful flowers.**

今年はトマトを栽培してみよう。 **I'm going to try growing tomatoes this year.**

草花の世話

ビオラをプランターに移した。 **I transplanted the violas into a planter.** ＊transplant＝～(植物)を移植する

ラベンダーの刈り込みをした。 **I trimmed the lavender.** ＊trim＝～を刈る

芝生に水をまいた。 **I watered the lawn.**
＊water＝～に水をやる　lawn[ローン]＝芝生

菜園の土を耕した。 **I plowed the vegetable patch.**
＊plow＝すきで耕す　patch＝小さな畑

土を替えた。 **I changed the soil.** ＊soil＝土

庭に肥料をまいた。 **I put fertilizer in the garden.**
＊fertilizer[ファーティライザー]＝肥料

殺虫剤を散布した。 **I sprayed pesticide.**
＊pesticide[ペスティサイド]＝殺虫剤、農薬

庭の雑草を取った。 **I weeded the garden.**
＊weed＝～の雑草を除く

庭木がだいぶ茂ってきた。 **The garden was really overgrown.**
＊overgrown＝(葉などが)生い茂った

枝切りをした。 **I pruned the tree.**
＊prune[プルーン]＝～(枝など)を刈り取る

庭師さんに来てもらった。 **I had the gardener come.**

庭の木を剪定(せんてい)してもらった。 **I had the trees in the garden trimmed.**

草花の生長

シャクヤクの芽が出ていた！ **The peonies are budding!**
＊peony［ピーアニー］＝シャクヤク　bud＝芽が出る

バラのつぼみが膨らんできた。 **The rose buds are getting bigger.**
＊bud＝つぼみ、芽

もう少しで花が咲きそう。 **The flowers are nearly out.**

ルピナスの苗が大きくなってきた。 **The lupine seedlings are growing.**
＊lupine［ルーピン］＝ルピナス　seedling＝苗

シャコバサボテンの花がきれいに咲いた。 **The Christmas cactuses are blooming beautifully.**
＊Christmas cactus＝シャコバサボテン　bloom＝花が咲く

車・バイク （→ p. 458「ドライブ」も参照）

そろそろ車を買い替えよう。 **I guess it's time to change cars.**

次は、トヨタの車にしようかな。 **I'm thinking about getting a Toyota next.**

72 年式のアルファロメオを買った。 **I bought a 1972 Alfa Romeo.**

BMW に乗るのが夢。 **My dream is to own a BMW.**
＊own＝～を所有する

キャンピングカーが欲しい。 **I want a camper van.**
＊camper vanは、camperとも言う

ホイールを替えたいな。 **I want to get new wheel covers.**

ドライブレコーダーを付けようかな。 **Maybe I should get a dashcam.**
＊dashcam＝ドライブレコーダー

サスペンションが硬い。 **The suspension feels stiff.** ＊stiff＝硬い

洗車した。 **I washed my car.**
I had my car washed.
＊上は自分で洗った場合。下は人に洗ってもらった場合

来月は車検だ！ **The car inspection is coming up next month!** ＊inspection＝検査

テツシとバイクでツーリングに出かけた。 **Tetsushi and I went on a motorcycle ride.**
＊go on a motorcycle ride＝バイクでツーリングに出かける

彼のバイクに二人乗りした。 **We rode his motorcycle together.**
＊ride（～に乗る）の過去形はrode

釣り

宇和島沖に釣りに行ってきた。	**We went fishing off Uwajima Island.** ＊off 〜＝〜沖に
天竜川へハゼ釣りに出かけた。	**We went goby fishing on the Tenryu River.** ＊goby＝ハゼ
渓流釣りを楽しんだ。	**We enjoyed mountain stream fishing.** ＊stream＝小川、流れ
8時半ごろ、釣り場に到着した。	**We arrived at the fishing spot at around 8:30.**
水深は5メートルくらい。	**The water was about five meters deep.**
メバルを狙った。	**I went mostly for black rockfish.** ＊go for 〜＝〜を得ようとする　mostly＝主に
小型の魚をリリースした。	**I released the small fish back into the water.**
残念ながら、大型の魚には出合えなかった。	**Unfortunately, I couldn't get a big fish.**
45センチの大物が釣れた！	**I caught a big one measuring 45cm!** ＊measure＝〜の大きさがある
帰宅後、さばいて刺身にした。	**I made it into sashimi after I got home.**
海がしけていたので、釣りはあきらめた。	**We gave up fishing because the sea was rough.** ＊rough［ラフ］＝荒れた

趣味・習いごとについて 英語日記を書いてみよう

趣味や習いごとについて、英語で書いてみましょう。

 手作りケーキ

Naoko and Ayako came over, so I served them my homemade earl grey chiffon cake. They both said it was delicious. I was so happy.

ナオコとアヤコが遊びに来たので、手作りのアールグレイ・シフォンケーキでもてなした。2人においしいと褒められて、とてもうれしかった。

「遊びに来た」は came over (to my house) や came to see me で。「Aを～でもてなす」は serve A ～や、entertain A with ～で表します。「手作りの」は homemade。「褒められた」は、They both said ～（2人とも～と言った）で表せます。

 編み物が上達

I used to be able to knit only scarves, but now I can knit caps and socks. I want to be able to knit sweaters soon.

以前はマフラーしか編めなかったのが、今ではニット帽や靴下も編めるようになった。早くセーターが編めるようになりたいな。

「以前はマフラーしか編めなかった」は、「以前はマフラーだけ編めた」と表現するのが自然です。used to ～（動詞の原形）は「以前は～した」、be able to ～（動詞の原形）は「～できる」という意味。「マフラー」は scarf と表します。scarves は複数形です。

新しい英会話の先生

We had a lesson with our new teacher, David, today. His English was very clear and his way of teaching was easy to understand. We had a great lesson.

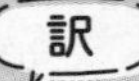

今日からデイビッド先生に変わった。とても聞きやすい英語で、教え方もわかりやすかった。すごく楽しい授業だった。

「今日からデイビッド先生に変わった」は、「今日は新しい先生、デイビッドの授業だった」と表すと自然な英語に。「～先生」はMr./Ms.＋名字ですが、Davidのようにファーストネームを用いる場合はMr./Ms.は不要です。「わかりやすい」はeasy to understand。

カリグラフィーの体験レッスン

I had a one-time calligraphy lesson at the culture hall today. I wrote pretty well. I'm thinking of taking lessons regularly.

今日、文化会館でカリグラフィーの１日体験レッスンを受けた。結構うまく書けた。本格的に習おうか検討中。

「１日体験レッスン」はone-time lesson（１回のレッスン）としましたが、trial lessonでもOK。「検討中」はI'm thinking of ～ing（～しようかと考えている）、「本格的に習う」はtake lessons regularly（定期的にレッスンを受ける）で表しました。

20 スポーツ

運動全般

最近、体がなまってる。	**I'm out of shape these days.** ＊be out of shape＝体がなまっている
運動不足で、このままだとヤバイ。	**I don't get enough exercise. I really have to do something.**
体が硬い。	**My body is stiff.**
きれいな姿勢になりたい。	**I want to have nice posture.** ＊posture＝姿勢
インナーマッスルを鍛えたい。	**I want to train my inner muscles.**
体幹を鍛えなきゃ。	**I need to train my body's core muscles.** ＊core＝中心部、核
汗を流して、気分爽快（そうかい）だった。	**It felt refreshing to work up a sweat.** ＊work up a sweat＝ひと汗かく
汗びっしょりになった。	**I was covered in sweat.** ＊covered in 〜＝〜に覆われて
100キロカロリーは消費したかな？	**I guess I burned at least 100kcal.** ＊burn＝〜を燃やす・燃焼する
明日も運動するぞ。	**I'm going to work out again tomorrow.** ＊work out＝トレーニングをする
明日は筋肉痛になりそう。	**I'm going to have sore muscles tomorrow.** ＊sore［ソァ］＝痛む
少しはぜい肉が落ちてるといいけど。	**Hopefully I've lost a little flab.** ＊flab＝脂肪、ぜい肉
こんなに運動してるのに、どうして体重が減らないんだろう。	**I'm doing so much exercise, but I don't know why I can't lose weight.** ＊lose weight＝体重を減らす
筋肉量がアップしていた。やった！	**My muscle mass has increased. Great!** ＊muscle mass＝筋肉量

パーソナルインストラクターについてもらうと、違うんだなぁ。	**It seems having a personal trainer really makes a difference.**

軽い運動

何か軽い運動を始めようかな。	**Maybe I should do some light exercise.**
駅や会社では、階段を使うようにしている。	**I try to use the stairs at the train station and at work.** ＊stairs＝階段
今朝は一駅分歩いた。	**I walked from one station to another this morning.**
新宿から原宿まで歩いた。	**I walked from Shinjuku to Harajuku.**
電車を待つときは、つま先立ち。	**I stand on tiptoe while waiting for the train.** ＊tiptoe［ティップトゥ］＝つま先
自転車通勤を始めた。	**I've started to commute by bike.** ＊commute＝通勤する　bike＝自転車
自転車通勤を始めて、今日で１週間。	**It has been a week since I started to bike to work.** ＊bike＝自転車に乗る
犬の散歩は私にとってもいい運動。	**Walking the dog is good exercise for me, too.** ＊walk＝～を散歩させる
音楽に合わせて体を動かすだけでもいい運動になる。	**Just moving my body to the music is good exercise.**

ウォーキング

今朝は30分間ウォーキングをした。	**I walked for 30 minutes this morning.**
iPhoneで音楽を聞きながら、ウォーキングをした。	**I listened to music on my iPhone as I walked.**
川沿いの道を歩いた。	**I walked along the side of the river.**
公園まで行って戻ってきた。	**I went as far as the park and came back.**

早朝のウォーキングは気持ちがいい。	**It feels good to go for a walk early in the morning.** ＊go for a walk＝散歩に行く
毎日１万歩以上歩くようにしている。	**I try to walk more than 10,000 steps a day.** ＊step＝1歩、歩み
5000歩歩くのって、結構大変。	**It's not easy to walk 5,000 steps.**
歩数計を買おうかな。	**Maybe I should buy a pedometer.** ＊pedometer［ピダーミター］＝歩数計
雨だったので、ウォーキングはやめた。	**It was raining, so I didn't go walking.**

ジョギング・マラソン

ジョギング

ジョギングする前に、公園でストレッチをした。	**I stretched in the park before jogging.**
30分間、ジョギングをした。	**I jogged for 30 minutes.**
5時に起きて、約10キロ走った。	**I woke up at 5:00 and ran for about 10km.**
皇居の周りを走った。	**I ran around the Imperial Palace.**
1キロ約7分のペースで走った。	**I ran at a pace of about seven minutes per kilometer.** ＊per ～＝～につき
多摩川まで走って往復した。	**I ran to and from the Tama River.**
皇居でのランニング会に参加した。	**I joined a running event at the Imperial Palace.**
ヤマグチさんと近所をジョギングした。	**I went jogging around the neighborhood with Yamaguchi-san.**
久々のジョギングで、息切れした。	**I went jogging for the first time in a while and I got out of breath.** ＊get out of breath＝息切れする
ジョギング後の銭湯って最高！	**Going to the public bath after jogging feels great!**
5キロを30分で走れた。まずまずだ。	**I ran 5km in 30 minutes. Not bad.** ＊Not bad.＝なかなかよい。

最近、タイムが落ちてきた。	**My running speed has been dropping recently.** ＊drop＝低下する
もっとタイムを上げたい。	**I want to increase my running speed.** ＊increase＝～を上げる
ランニングフォームを見直したほうがいいな。	**I need to reconsider my running form.** ＊reconsider＝～を考え直す・再考する
ジョギングでひざを痛めてしまった。	**I hurt my knees from jogging.** ＊hurt＝～を痛める。過去形もhurt　knee［ニー］＝ひざ
しばらくお休みしよう。	**I'll give it up for a while.**
体が引き締まってきた気がする。	**My body feels firmer.** ＊firm＝引き締まった

マラソン

来年は東京マラソンにチャレンジしたい。	**I want to run the Tokyo Marathon next year.**
東京マラソンの抽選に外れてしまった。	**I didn't win the lottery to participate in the Tokyo Marathon.** ＊participate in ～＝～に参加する
福岡国際マラソンの応援に行った。	**I went to cheer for the runners at the Fukuoka International Marathon.**
マラソン選手はやっぱり速い！	**Marathon runners are just as fast as I thought they were!**
市民マラソンに出た。	**I ran in a city marathon.**
フルマラソンなんて絶対ムリ。	**A full marathon is absolutely impossible for me.**
ハーフマラソンなら、完走できるかも。	**Maybe I can manage to complete a half marathon.** ＊manage to ～＝何とか～する
レースまであと４日！	**Four more days until the race!**
５時間以内での完走が目標だ。	**My goal is to finish within five hours.** ＊goal＝目標
４時間 26 分で完走！ 目標達成！	**I finished in 4 hours and 26 minutes! I achieved my goal!** ＊achieve＝～を達成する

5時間切りの目標は達成できなかった。	**I couldn't achieve my goal of finishing within five hours.**
制限時間オーバーで、失格になってしまった。	**I was disqualified because I didn't finish within the time limit.** ＊disqualify＝～の資格を奪う
何とか完走できた。	**I managed to finish.**
沿道ではたくさんの人が応援していた。	**Lots of people were cheering along the way.**
ゴールした瞬間は感動した。	**I was so moved the moment I reached the finish line.**
走り終えた後は、大きな達成感があった。	**After finishing, I had a great feeling of accomplishment.** ＊accomplishment＝達成
足首が痛くなって、30キロ地点でリタイアした。	**Because of the pain in my ankle, I had to give up at 30km.** ＊pain＝痛み　ankle＝足首
途中、あきらめて歩いてしまった。	**I gave up partway through and just walked.** ＊partway through＝途中で

ウエア・シューズ

新しいランニングウエアが欲しい。	**I want some new running clothes.** ＊clothes［クロウズ］＝衣類
新しいランニングウエアを着て、気持ちよく走れた。	**I enjoyed running in my new running clothes.**
シューズが合わなくて足が痛くなった。	**My shoes don't fit, so my feet hurt.** ＊feet＝foot（足先）の複数形　hurt＝痛む。過去形もhurt
新しいシューズは、走りが軽い。	**My new shoes feel really light to run in.**
ランニングタイツを新調した。	**I got new running tights.**
かわいいランスカを発見！	**I found a cute running skirt!** ＊「ランスカ」は、「ランニングスカート」の略
ランニング用にスマートウォッチを買った。	**I bought a smartwatch for running.**

駅伝

今年の箱根駅伝は、どの大学が優勝するかな？
I wonder which university will win this year's Hakone Ekiden.

沿道で選手たちを応援した。
I cheered for the runners from the side of the road.

かなりの接戦だった。
It was a really close race.
＊close［クロウス］＝接戦の、きわどい

往路は青山学院大が新記録で優勝。
In the first half of the race, Aoyama Gakuin University won and set a new record.
＊win＝勝つ。過去形はwon［ワン］　set＝～(新記録)を出す

9区では区間新記録が出た。
A new record was set in the ninth section.

6区で国学院が追いついた。
Kokugakuin caught up in the sixth section of the race.
＊catch up＝追いつく。catchの過去形はcaught［コート］

東海大がトップに躍り出た。
Tokai University moved into the lead.
＊lead＝先頭

ヤマモトの走りは圧巻だった。
Yamamoto's running was just incredible.
＊incredible＝素晴らしい

駒澤大学が逆転優勝を果たした。
Komazawa University had a come-from-behind victory.
＊come-from-behind＝逆転の

ジム・トレーニング

ジム・筋トレにまつわる表現

インストラクター	instructor
パーソナルトレーナー	personal trainer
運動をする	work out
準備運動をする	do a warm-up
ランニングマシンで走る	run on a treadmill
腹筋をする	do sit-ups
腕立て伏せをする	do push-ups
懸垂をする	do chin-ups
スクワットをする	do squats
～のストレッチをする	stretch ～
～を鍛える	strengthen ～
上腕二頭筋	biceps［バイセプス］
大たい筋	thigh［サイ］muscle
肩甲骨	shoulder blade
筋肉痛になる	have sore muscles

ジム・筋トレ

ジムに通い始めた。	I started going to the gym.
仕事帰りにジムに行った。	I went to the gym after work.
ランニングマシンで1時間走った。	I ran for an hour on a treadmill.
腹筋20回を3セットやった。	I did three sets of 20 sit-ups.
20回、腕立て伏せをした。	I did 20 push-ups.
レッグカールを65キロ×10回×3セットやった。	I did three sets of 10 leg curls with 65kg weights.
ダンベルで二の腕を鍛えた。	I gave my arms a workout using dumbbells.
中高年女性専用のジムに通い始めた。	I started going to a gym for middle-aged and older women.
メイクしなくていいし、気軽に通える。	I don't need to wear makeup, so it feels easy to go there.
ジムで友達ができた。	I made a friend at the gym.

エクササイズ

動画を見ながら30分、エクササイズをした。	**I exercised for 30 minutes to a video.** ＊このtoは「～に合わせて」の意
結構キツかった！	**It was pretty tough!**
テレビでヒップアップに効く運動をやっていた。	**A TV program showed an exercise for firmer buttocks.** ＊firm＝引き締まった　buttock＝尻
バランスボールを買った。	**I bought an exercise ball.**
また新しいダイエット器具を買っちゃった。まぁ、いいか。	**I bought more fitness equipment again. Oh well.** ＊equipment＝用具
前に買ったダイエット器具、全然使ってないな。	**I haven't used the fitness equipment I bought a while ago.**
加圧トレーニングに行ってきた。	**I went for Kaatsu training.**
午前中、エアロビのクラスに出た。	**I joined an aerobics class in the morning.**
アクアビクスのレッスンを受けた。	**I took an aqua-aerobics lesson.**
ボクササイズの体験レッスンを受けた。	**I took a trial lesson for boxercise.**
アンチエイジングに効果大と聞いた。	**I hear it's very effective for anti-aging.** ＊effective for ～＝～に効果的な
このエクササイズをすると、体が軽くなる。	**This exercise makes my body feel light.**
確実に体が引き締まった。	**It definitely helped tone up my body.** ＊definitely＝確実に　tone up ～＝～(体・筋肉など)を鍛える・引き締める
このエクササイズのおかげで、体年齢が10歳若返った。	**Thanks to this exercise, my body feels ten years younger.**
今日のトレーナーさんとは気が合った。	**I got along great with my trainer today.** ＊get along with ～＝～とうまが合う
次も彼を指名しよう。	**I'm going to choose him again the next time.**

30分で4200円だった。	**It was 4,200 yen for 30 minutes.**

ダンス（→ p. 417「ダンス」を参照）

ヨガ・ピラティス

最近、ヨガを始めた。	**I've started doing yoga recently.** ＊do yoga（ヨガをする）は、practice yogaとも言う
駅前のヨガスタジオで、体験レッスンを受けた。	**I took a trial lesson at the yoga studio in front of the train station.**
最近、ピラティスにはまってる。	**I've been hooked on Pilates recently.** ＊be hooked on ～＝～にはまる
動画を見ながら家でピラティスをした。	**I did Pilates at home to a video.**
ヨガをしていると、心が落ち着く。	**While doing yoga, my mind is calm.** ＊calm［カーム］＝落ち着いた
ヨガでは、ゆったりした呼吸が大切。	**In yoga, breathing slowly is important.** ＊breathe［ブリーズ］＝呼吸する
ヨガの呼吸法が、少しずつ身についてきた。	**I'm slowly starting to learn how to do yoga breathing.**
ヨガのポーズ、なかなかうまくできない。	**I have a hard time doing yoga poses.**
ピラティスで骨格のゆがみが直った。	**Doing Pilates helped straighten my frame.** ＊straighten［ストゥレイトゥン］＝～のゆがみを取る
サーフヨガ、やってみたいな。	**I want to try surf yoga.**

水泳・プール

プールで400メートル泳いだ。	**I swam 400m in the pool.**
クロールで500メートル泳いだ。	**I swam the crawl for 500m.** ＊crawl＝クロール
背泳ぎで200メートル泳いだ。	**I swam the backstroke for 200m.** ＊backstroke＝背泳ぎ
バタフライのフォームがきれいにできない。	**I can't make good butterfly form.**

ビート板を使ってバタ足をした。 | **I practiced doing flutter kicks on the kickboard.**
＊flutter kick＝バタ足

25メートル泳ぐのが精いっぱいだ。 | **I can swim 25m at the most.**
＊at the most＝多くて、せいぜい

100メートル泳げるようになりたい。 | **I want to be able to swim 100m.**

平泳ぎだと、なかなか前に進まない。 | **When swimming the breaststroke, I hardly go forward.**
＊breaststroke＝平泳ぎ

300メートル、水中ウォーキングをした。 | **I walked in the swimming pool for 300m.**

泳いだ後、サウナに入った。 | **I got in a sauna after swimming.**

野球

プロ野球

巨人対阪神の試合をテレビで見た。 | **I watched the Giants and Tigers game on TV.**

神宮球場で、楽天対ヤクルトの試合を見た。 | **I went to Jingu Stadium and saw a game between Rakuten and Yakult.**

3対2で阪神が負けた。 | **The Tigers lost 3-2.**
＊3-2は、three to twoと読む

5対2で西武が勝った。 | **Seibu won 5-2.**

完封勝利だ！ | **It's a shutout victory!**
＊shutout＝完封

延長11回で、ようやく勝負がついた。 | **The game went into the 11th inning before being decided.**
＊inning＝（野球の）回

延長12回で引き分けとなった。 | **The game went into the 12th inning and ended in a draw.**
＊draw［ドゥロー］＝引き分け

ドラゴンズ、今日も点が取れなかった。 | **The Dragons didn't get a point today, either.**

ムラカミがサヨナラホームランを打った。 | **Murakami got a game-winning homerun.**
＊「サヨナラホームラン」はgame-ending homerunとも言う

20 スポーツ

今シーズンのオカモトは不調だ。 **Okamoto isn't having a good season.**

今日はササキが好投した。 **Sasaki pitched really well today.**

＊pitch＝投げる

イシイ監督の采配には納得できない。 **I can't agree with Manager Ishii's strategy.**

＊strategy＝戦略、作戦

ハラ監督の采配は素晴らしい。 **Manager Hara's strategy is great.**

センガもメジャーに移籍しちゃった。 **Senga moved to the Majors, too.**

高校野球

春の高校野球が始まった。 **The spring high school baseball tournament has started.**

選手宣誓に胸が熱くなった。 **The reading of the player's oath gave me a warm feeling inside.**

＊oath［オウス］＝宣誓

長崎の海星高校が、兵庫の社（やしろ）高校と対戦した。 **Nagasaki's Kaisei High played against Hyogo's Yashiro High.**

＊high＝high school（高校）

2対0で山梨学院が勝った。おめでとう！ **Yamanashi Gakuin won 2-0. Congratulations!**

＊2-0は、two to zeroと読む

東北高校、頑張れ！ **Go for it, Tohoku High School!**

沖縄尚学高校のエースが好投した。 **Okinawa Shogaku's ace pitched really well.**

すごくいい試合だった。 **It was a great game.**

大阪桐蔭のナインは試合後、号泣していた。 **The Osaka Toin players all broke down in tears after the game.**

＊break down in tears＝感情を抑えきれず泣く

東海大相模のナインは、抱き合って喜んでいた。 **The Tokaidai Sagami players all embraced in joy.**

＊embrace＝抱き合う　joy＝喜び、歓喜

思わず、私ももらい泣き。 **Just watching them made me cry, too.**

高校野球はアツい！ **High school baseball is full of passion!**

高校野球は、何が起きるかわからない。 **You never know what will happen with high school baseball.**

球児たちのひたむきな姿に胸を打たれる。	**The dedication of the high school players is inspiring.**

＊dedication＝熱心さ　inspiring＝感激させる

草野球・少年野球

市営グラウンドで草野球の試合をした。	**We had an amateur baseball game on the city field.** ＊amateur＝アマチュア、素人
会社の草野球チームで練習した。	**I practiced with my company's amateur baseball team.**
T 印刷のチームと対戦した。	**We played against T Printing.**
明日は草野球のリーグ戦！	**We have an amateur league championship tomorrow!**
見事リーグ優勝。やった！	**We won the league championship. Yes!**
A グループ 2 位だった。	**We were second in the A Group.**
最下位だった。あ〜あ。	**We were at the bottom. Too bad.**

＊Too bad.＝残念だ。

明日はハルトの野球の試合だ。	**Haruto has a baseball game tomorrow.**
ハルトがホームランを打った！	**Haruto hit a homerun!**
今日のハルトはエラーが多かった。	**Haruto made a lot of mistakes today.**

サッカー

サッカー観戦

グランパス対アルビレックスの試合を見に行った。	**I went to see a game between Grampus and Albirex.**
柏レイソルの練習を見学した。	**I went and saw Kashiwa Reysol's practice.**
2 対 1 で大宮アルディージャが勝った。	**Omiya Ardija won 2-1.**

＊2-1は、two to oneと読む

アルビレックス新潟がJ1に昇格。やった!	**Albirex Niigata got promoted to J1. Excellent!** *get promoted to 〜=〜に格上げされる
清水エスパルスがJ2に降格。あ〜あ…。	**Shimizu S-Pulse got demoted to J2. Too bad ...** *get demoted to 〜=〜に格下げされる
明日はウズベキスタン戦。	**There's a game against Uzbekistan tomorrow.**
W杯アジア2次予選、日本はC組だ。	**Japan is in Group C of the World Cup Asian second round qualifier.** *qualifier=予選
やった! 日本がアジア予選を突破した!	**Great! Japan passed the AFC Asian Qualifiers!**
次の相手は強豪ブラジル。	**Our next opponent is the powerhouse, Brazil.** *opponent=対戦相手、敵　powerhouse=最強チーム
オマーンは手強いな。	**Oman is formidable.** *formidable=(敵などが)手強い
ゴール!!	**Goal!**
キーパー、よく止めた!	**The goalie did a good job!** *goalie=ゴールキーパー
彼は日本の守護神だ!	**He's the savior of the Japanese team!** *savior=救世主、救い主
2対0から巻き返した!	**They came back from being behind 2-0!** *2-0は、two to zeroと読む
2対1で日本が勝った。	**Japan won 2-1.**
PK戦にもつれ込んだ。	**It came down to a penalty shoot-out.** *come down to 〜=〜に及ぶ
ドウアンのアシストは見事だった。	**Doan's assist was incredible.** *incredible=素晴らしい
ミトマがすごかった!	**Mitoma was awesome!**
シバサキが退場になった。	**Shibasaki got ejected.** *get ejected=退場させられる
勝てる試合だったのに。	**We could have won that game.**
最後の最後で油断しちゃったな。	**They let down their guard at the last moment.** *let down one's guard=油断する

相手チームの反則が目立った。	**The other team made a lot of fouls.**
今回のワールドカップは番狂わせが多い。	**This World Cup had quite a few upsets.** ＊upset＝予期せぬ結果、番狂わせ
私ってにわかファン。	**I'm a bandwagon fan.**

少年サッカー

アオの少年サッカーの試合を見に行った。	**I went and saw Ao's boys' soccer game.**
アオがシュートを決めた！	**Ao's shot went in!** ＊go in＝入る
ドリブルがうまくなった。	**His dribbling has improved.**
パスがうまく回っていなかった。	**They didn't pass well today.**
フジミノ FC が地区大会で優勝！	**Fujimino FC won the district tournament!** ＊district＝地区、地域

ゴルフ

会社帰りに打ちっ放しに寄った。	**I stopped at a driving range on my way home from work.** ＊driving range＝（打ちっ放しの）ゴルフ練習場
ゴルフのコンペだった。	**I had a golf competition.**
クライアントと接待ゴルフだった。	**I played golf with some clients.**
7 時ごろ、ゴルフ場に着いた。	**I got to the golf course at around 7:00.**
ナイスショット！	**Nice shot!**
ホールインワン！	**Hole in one!**
バンカーにつかまった。	**I got caught in a bunker.** ＊get caught in ～＝～にひっかかる・はまり込む
池ポチャだった。	**I hit it into the pond.** ＊pond＝池
2 番ホールはボギーだった。	**I bogeyed the second hole.** ＊bogey＝～をボギーで終える
なんと、バーディーを 3 つ取った！	**Oh wow, I got three birdies!** ＊birdie＝バーディー

ハーフが終わって、スコアは53。	**At the halfway point, my score was 53.**
スコアは53 + 50 = 103。	**My score was 53+50=103.**
自己ベストが出た！	**It was my personal best!**
なかなか上達しない。	**I'm not improving much.** ＊improve＝上達する
フォームが悪いのかも。	**Maybe there's something wrong with my form.**
全米オープンをテレビ観戦した。	**I watched the U.S. Open on TV.**
マツヤマ、頑張れ！	**Go, Matsuyama!**
3アンダーで予選通過だ。	**He qualified with 3-under-par.** ＊qualify＝資格を得る
今年の賞金女王は山下美夢有だ。	**This year's top female earner was Miyuu Yamashita.** ＊earner＝稼ぐ人、稼ぎ手

スキー・スノーボード

5時間ほど滑った。	**I skied for about five hours.**
初心者コースで練習した。	**I practiced on the beginners' course.**
何度も転んだ。	**I fell a lot of times.** ＊fall＝転ぶ。過去形はfell
ミナに滑り方を教えてあげた。	**I taught Mina how to ski.**
ボーゲンはできるようになった。	**I learned how to do a snowplow turn.** ＊snowplow＝ボーゲン　turn＝ターン、方向転換
ターンできるようになった。	**I learned how to turn.**
リフトに乗るのが怖かった。	**It was scary to ride the lift.** ＊scary＝(物事が)怖い、おそろしい
リフトからの眺めは絶景だった。	**The view from the lift was fantastic.**
かなり急な斜面だった。	**The slope was really steep.** ＊steep＝急な
パウダースノーって最高！	**Powder snow is the best!** ＊powder snowは、単にpowderとも言う
アイスバーンが結構あった。	**There were a lot of icy spots.** ＊icy＝凍って滑りやすい

今年は雪が少ないみたい。	**It looks like there isn't much snow this year.**
ナイターもすごく楽しかった。	**Night skiing was also great fun.** ＊スノーボードの場合は、skiingをsnow boardingに
スノボの後の温泉は最高！	**Nothing beats taking a hot-spring bath after snowboarding!** ＊nothing beats ～＝～に勝るものはない、～は最高だ

登山

今日は筑波山に登った。	**I climbed Mt. Tsukuba today.** ＊climb［クライム］
来週は高尾山に行く。	**I'm going to climb Mt. Takao next week.**
いつか槍ヶ岳に登ってみたい。	**I want to climb Yarigatake someday.**
これで今年の登山は10回目だ。	**I've climbed ten mountains so far this year.** ＊so far＝今までのところ
絶好の登山日和だった。	**It was a perfect day for mountain climbing.**
空気がおいしかった。	**The air was great.**
頂上を目指して登った。	**We climbed towards the summit.** ＊summit＝頂上
ストックを使いながら、慎重に登った。	**We took our time climbing while using climbing sticks.** ＊take one's time ～ing＝（慌てず）ゆっくり～をやる
8合目あたりで、少し頭が痛くなってきた。	**My head started to hurt at about 80 percent up the mountain.** ＊hurt＝痛む。過去形もhurt
高山病になったようだった。	**It seems I got altitude sickness.** ＊altitude sickness＝高山病
山小屋で少し休憩した。	**We took a little break in a mountain hut.** ＊hut＝小屋
やっと頂上に着いた！	**We finally reached the top!**
最高の眺めだった！	**The view was spectacular!** ＊spectacular＝見事な、壮観な

上りより、下りのほうがキツかった。 Coming down was harder than going up.

足にまめができてしまった。 I got some blisters on my feet.
＊blister＝(足の)まめ

高山植物をたくさん見ることができた。 I enjoyed seeing various kinds of alpine plants.
＊various＝さまざまな　alpine＝高山の

新しい登山ウェアを買った。 I bought new mountain climbing clothes.
＊clothes[クロウズ]＝服

かっこいいザックが欲しい。 I want a cool backpack.

ボクシング・格闘技

横浜アリーナに格闘技を見に行った。 I went to see a martial arts contest at Yokohama Arena.
＊martial art＝武術、格闘技　contest＝競技、大会

イノウエ対バトラーの試合を観戦した。 I saw the match between Inoue and Butler.

4度目の防衛戦だ。 It was his fourth defense of his title.
＊defense＝防衛

右ストレートが決まった。 He got in a right-straight punch.
＊get in 〜＝〜(パンチなど)を入れる

パンチにキレがなかった。 His punches were a little weak.
＊weak＝(力などが)弱い

試合終了のゴングが鳴った。 The bell rang and the game ended.

3ラウンドTKO勝ち！ It was a three-round TKO!

2ラウンドKO負けだった。 He lost in a two-round KO.

判定でイオカの勝ちだった。 Ioka got a decision win.
＊decision win＝判定勝ち

3-0でソノダの判定負けだった。 Sonoda lost by a 3-0 decision.
＊3-0は、three to zeroと読む

あの判定には納得がいかない。 I can't agree with that decision.

彼は5度目の防衛に成功した。 He successfully retained his title for the fifth time.
＊retain＝〜を持ち続ける

新チャンピオンの誕生だ。 A new champion was born.

オリンピック・パラリンピック

パリオリンピックが楽しみだ。	**I'm looking forward to the Paris Olympics.** ＊「冬季オリンピック」は、Winter Olympics
オリンピックが始まった。	**The Olympics have started.**
開会式は生中継で見た。	**I watched a live broadcast of the opening ceremony.**
開会式の演出が面白かった。	**The performances at the opening ceremony were interesting.**
どの国の衣装もすてきだった。	**All the countries' costumes looked great.**
サトウが金メダルを取った！	**Sato got a gold medal!**
コミネは惜しくもメダルならず。	**Unfortunately Komine didn't get a medal.**
マツザキは絶好調だ。	**Matsuzaki is in perfect form.** ＊form＝調子
トヤマは調子が悪そうだ。	**Toyama doesn't look so good.**
日本、15 個目のメダル獲得！	**Japan got its 15th medal!**
今日は男子 200m 平泳ぎの決勝がある。	**Today is the final of the men's 200m breaststroke.**
柔道女子、アベが金メダル！	**Abe got gold in the women's judo!**
卓球女子団体、日本は準優勝！	**Japan was the runner-up in the women's team table tennis!** ＊runner-up＝準優勝者
日本は５位だった。	**Japan came in fifth place.**
カーリングが面白くなってきた。	**Curling is getting more and more exciting.**
スキージャンプは息をのんで見守った。	**I watched the ski jumping with a gasp.** ＊gasp＝はっと息をのむこと

女子フィギュア、フリーで逆転できますように！	I hope we can turn it around in the free skate of the women's figure skating! ＊turn around＝好転させる
車いすバスケはすごい迫力だった。	The wheelchair basketball game was intense. ＊intense＝強烈な、すごい
車いすテニス、選手たちの動きが本当にすごかった。	The movements of the athletes in the wheelchair tennis match were really amazing.
ボッチャをやってみたくなった。	Now I want to try boccia.
生で観戦してみたいな。	I want to watch it live sometime.

そのほかのスポーツ

テニス教室に通い始めた。	I started taking tennis lessons.
バドミントンをした。	I played badminton.
サノさんと卓球をした。	I played table tennis with Sano-san.
同僚とフットサルをした。	I played futsal with some co-workers.
市のスポーツ大会に参加した。	I participated in a city sports event. ＊participate in ～＝～に参加する
乗馬をやってみた。	I tried horseback riding.
公園でスケートボードの練習をした。	I practiced skateboarding in the park.
ボルダリングに挑戦してみたい。	I want to try bouldering.

Memo

スポーツに関することを、メモしておきましょう。

スポーツについて 英語日記を書いてみよう

体を動かしたことについて、英語で書いてみましょう。

ウォーキングを開始

I installed a pedometer app on my smartphone. Now, I'm ready to take up walking tomorrow. I will stick to it!

スマホに歩数計のアプリを入れた。これで、明日からウォーキングを始める準備はできた。三日坊主にはならないぞ！

このNow, は、「これで」「さぁ」というニュアンスです。take up ～は「～（趣味など）を始める」。「三日坊主にはならないぞ」は、I will stick to it（それを続けるぞ）で表現しました。stick to ～は「～（挫折せずに決心したことなど）を続ける」という意味です。

ホノルルマラソン

Naoto completed the Honolulu Marathon and came back to Japan today. He said his legs were killing him, but he wanted to try a triathlon next. He's amazing!

ナオトがホノルルマラソンを完走し、今日、日本に戻ってきた。足が死ぬほど痛いと言いながらも、次はトライアスロンにチャレンジしたいんだって。スゴイ！

「マラソンを完走する」はcomplete a marathon、「マラソンに出る」はrun a marathon。このkillは「（痛さや驚きなどが）～を我慢できなくする」という意味で、通常、his legs were killing himのように進行形で表します。「～にチャレンジする」はtryで。

久しぶりのバドミントン

I found the badminton set in the storeroom while cleaning. So, my sister and I played badminton for the first time in about 15 years. We both worked up a sweat.

物置を掃除していたら、バドミントンセットを発見。約 15 年ぶりにお姉ちゃんとバドミントンをした。2 人とも汗をかいた。

「物置」は storeroom、「約 15 年ぶりに」は for the first time in about 15 years、「汗をかく」は work up a sweat で表します。work up a good sweat（いい汗をかく）、work up a sweat all over one's body（体中に汗をかく）を使ってもいいですね。

高校野球に感動！

Sendai Ikuei and Keio played a close game. They went into extra innings and Sendai Ikuei won 2-1. The players' tears made me cry, too. I love high school baseball!

仙台育英対慶応は接戦だった。延長戦にもつれ込み、仙台育英が 2 対 1 で勝利。選手たちの涙にもらい泣きしてしまった。高校野球っていいなぁ！

試合の「対」は and のほか、vs. で表しても OK。「接戦」は close［クロウ ス］game と表します。「（野球で）延長戦に入る」は go into extra inning(s)。「もらい泣きした」は、〜 made me cry, too（〜が私のことも泣かせた）と表現してみました。

21 レジャー・旅行

娯楽施設

遊園地

東京ディズニーランドに行った。	**I went to Tokyo Disneyland.**
これで5回目だ。	**It was my 5th visit.**
初めてUSJに行った。	**I went to USJ for the first time.**
地元の遊園地へ行った。	**I went to a local amusement park.**
入園料は3000円で、ワンデーパスは5000円だった。	**It cost 3,000 yen to get in, and a one-day pass was 5,000 yen.**
1日たっぷり遊んだ。	**We enjoyed the whole day there.**
ジェットコースターに乗った。	**I rode a roller coaster.** ＊roller coaster＝ジェットコースター
すごいスピードだった。	**It was really fast.**
すごく怖くて、絶叫してしまった。	**I was so scared that I screamed.** ＊scared＝(人が)怖がった
FUJIYAMAは強烈だった。	**FUJIYAMA was really scary.** ＊scary＝(物事が)怖い
ナツとミナは、コーヒーカップに乗って楽しんでいた。	**Natsu and Mina enjoyed the teacup ride.**
子どもたちはメリーゴーランドに乗った。	**The kids rode the merry-go-round.** ＊メリーゴーランドはcarouselとも言う
観覧車はかなりの高さだった。	**The Ferris wheel was quite high.** ＊Ferris wheel＝観覧車
風があったので、結構揺れた。	**It was swaying a lot because of the wind.** ＊sway＝揺れる

お化け屋敷に入った。	**We entered the haunted house.** ＊haunted house＝お化け屋敷
かなり本格的で、怖かった。	**It was quite realistic and scary.**
ジェットコースターは2時間待ちだった。	**We had to wait for two hours to ride the roller coaster.**
すごく混んでて疲れちゃった。	**It was so crowded and I felt tired.**
案外すいていて、それほど並ばなかった。	**It wasn't so crowded, so we didn't have to wait long.**
ミッキーと一緒に写真を撮った。	**We took some pictures with Mickey Mouse.**
たくさん写真を撮った。	**We took lots of pictures.** ＊lots of＝a lot of（たくさんの）
ハナはミニーに会えて、とてもうれしそうだった。	**Hana looked really happy to meet Minnie Mouse.**
キャラクターの限定スイーツを食べた♪	**I ate some limited-edition character sweets.**
ギフトショップは激混みだった。	**People were packed into the gift shops.**
たくさんお土産を買った。	**I bought lots of souvenirs.**
夜のパレードは最高だった。	**The night parade was stunning.** ＊stunning＝素晴らしい、驚くべき
夕方ごろから場所取りをした。	**We saved a place to sit in the late afternoon.** ＊save＝～（席など）を取っておく
結構いい場所で見られた。	**We had a pretty good spot with a nice view.**
少し見づらかったけど、それでも十分に楽しめた。	**It was a little hard to see, but we still enjoyed it.**
夢のような光景だった。	**It was a dreamlike scene.**

動物園

動物を表す単語

パンダ	panda
クマ	bear
ホッキョクグマ	polar bear
キリン	giraffe
ゾウ	elephant
サイ	rhinoceros［ライノサラス］/ rhino［ライノゥ］
カバ	hippopotamus［ヒパパタマス］/ hippo
シマウマ	zebra［ズィーブラ］
シカ	deer
ヒツジ	sheep
ヤギ	goat
ライオン	lion
トラ	tiger
サル	monkey
ゴリラ	gorilla
チンパンジー	chimpanzee
オランウータン	orangutan
ナマケモノ	sloth
コアラ	koala［コウアーラ］
カンガルー	kangaroo
カピバラ	capybara
アライグマ	raccoon
ミーアキャット	meerkat
クジャク	peacock
ワニ	alligator / crocodile

上野動物園に行った。
We went to Ueno Zoo.

クマの赤ちゃんを見た。
We saw a bear cub.
＊cub［カブ］=（クマなどの）赤ちゃん、子ども

すごくかわいかった。
It was really cute.
＊動物の性別が不明なときは、itでOK

寝ていた。
It was sleeping.

ササを食べていた。
It was eating bamboo leaves.
＊leaf＝葉。複数形はleaves

遠くてよく見えなかった。
It was too far to see clearly.

息子はゾウを見て喜んでいた。
My son was excited to see an elephant.

シマウマの赤ちゃんがかわいかった。
The baby zebra was cute.

ウサギを抱っこした。
I held a rabbit.
＊hold＝～を抱く。過去形はheld

カピバラにえさをあげた。
I fed a capybara.
＊feed＝～に食物を与える。fedは過去形

ペンギンの散歩を見た。
We watched the penguins walking.

ホッキョクグマが見られてラッキー。
We were lucky to see polar bears.

ライオンはおりの中で寝ていた。	**The lions were sleeping in the cage.** ＊cage＝おり
だるそうだった。	**They looked sluggish.**

水族館

水族館にまつわる単語

イルカ	dolphin
アザラシ、オットセイ	seal
アシカ、トド	sea lion
ラッコ	sea otter
カワウソ	otter
シャチ	killer whale
ペンギン	penguin
エイ	ray
サメ	shark
ジンベイザメ	whale shark
サンショウウオ	salamander
タツノオトシゴ	sea horse
チンアナゴ	spotted garden eel
クリオネ	clione / sea angel
クラゲ	jellyfish
ヒトデ	starfish
カメ	turtle / tortoise［トータス］
熱帯魚	tropical fish
深海魚	deep-sea fish

美(ちゅ)ら海水族館に行った。	**We went to Churaumi Aquarium.**
海遊館のライトアップがよかった。	**The illuminations at Kaiyukan Aquarium were really nice.**
熱帯魚がきれいだった。	**The tropical fish were beautiful.** ＊fishは、複数形もfish
ジンベエザメは迫力があった。	**The whale shark was impressive.** ＊whale shark＝ジンベエザメ
深海魚って不思議な形をしてる。	**Deep-sea fish have strange shapes.**
クリオネがかわいかった。	**The cliones were cute.** ＊「クリオネ」は、sea angelとも言う
カワウソの泳ぐ速さに驚いた。	**I was surprised how fast the otters swam.** ＊otter＝カワウソ
水槽のトンネルを通った。	**We walked through a water tunnel.**
ペンギンの泳ぐ様子を下から眺めた。	**We watched the penguins swimming from below.**
イルカのショーは面白かった。	**The dolphin show was fun.**

しぶきがかかった。	We were caught in the spray. *caught in ～＝～に巻き込まれて
レオはびっくりしていた。	Reo was startled. *startled＝驚いて
イルカって、すごく頭がいいんだな。	Dolphins are really smart.
どうしてあんなに高く跳べるんだろう？	How do they jump so high?

プール・海

プール・海へ行く

よみうりランドのプールに行った。	We went to the swimming pool at Yomiuri Land.
市民プールに泳ぎに行った。	I went swimming in the public swimming pool.
流れるプールで泳いだ。	We swam in the lazy river. *lazy river＝流れるプール
ウォータースライダーで遊んだ。	We got on the water slide.
プールは大混雑だった。	The swimming pool was way too packed.
逗子海岸に海水浴に行った。	I went to Zushi Beach for a swim.
海で泳ぐのは久しぶりだった。	I hadn't swum in the sea in a long time. *swim（泳ぐ）の過去分詞は、swum
浮き輪に乗って、ぷかぷか浮かんだ。	I floated in the water on my float. *float＝浮かぶ／浮き輪
大きな空の下で海に浮かぶのは、すごく気持ちいい。	It felt great to float in the sea under the big sky.
水が透明だった。	The water was so clear.
魚が泳いでいるのが見えた。	I could see fish swimming around.
水が濁っていたのはちょっと残念。	Unfortunately, the water was a bit murky. *murky＝濁った、よどんだ
久しぶりに泳いで楽しかった。	I had a good time swimming for the first time in ages.

泳ぎ疲れて、今晩はよく眠れそう。	**I got exhausted from swimming. I'm sure I'll sleep like a log tonight.** *sleep like a log＝ぐっすり眠る

ビーチで

白砂のビーチがすごくきれいだった。	**The white sand beach was so beautiful.**
ビーチに寝そべった。	**I lay down on the beach.** *lie down＝横になる。lie［ライ］の過去形はlay［レイ］
ビーチで飲むビールは最高！	**Nothing beats a beer on the beach!** *beat 〜＝〜に勝る
ビーチバレーをした。	**We played beach volleyball.**
スイカ割りをした。	**We played a game of split-the-watermelon.** *split＝〜を割る　watermelon＝スイカ
パラソルの下で読書をした。	**I read a book under a parasol.**
海の家で焼きそばを食べて、ビールを飲んだ。	**We had yakisoba and some beers at a beach shop.**
子どもたちと磯遊びをした。	**We played on the rocky shore with the children.** *rocky shore＝磯
カニやヤドカリを見つけた。	**We found some crabs and hermit crabs.** *hermit crab＝ヤドカリ

日焼け

日焼け止めを塗った。	**I put on sunscreen.** *sunscreen＝日焼け止め
日焼け止めを塗り忘れた。	**I forgot to put on sunscreen.**
サンオイルを塗った。	**I put on suntan lotion.** *suntan＝日焼け
(健康的に) 日焼けした。	**I got suntanned.** *get suntanned＝日焼けする
(過度に) 日焼けした。	**I got sunburned.**
日焼けしたくない。	**I don't want to get a tan.**
体中がひりひりする。	**My body is stinging all over.** *sting＝(体の部分が)刺すように痛む

21 レジャー・旅行

日焼けで顔が真っ赤。	**My face is sunburned red.**
シミにならないといいけど。	**I hope I won't get spots.**
いい具合に日焼けできた。	**I got a nice suntan.**
あこがれの黄金色。	**My skin has a golden color, just the way I like it.**

潮干狩り

潮干狩りに行った。	**We went clamming.** ＊clam＝潮干狩りをする
たくさんアサリが取れた。	**We got a lot of littleneck clams.** ＊littleneck clam＝アサリ
最初に掘ったところは、あまり出てこなかった。	**There weren't many in the first spot we dug.** ＊dig＝～を掘る。過去形はdug
何度か場所を変えたら、ハマグリがたくさん出てきた。	**We got a lot of clams when we tried different spots.** ＊clam＝ハマグリなどの二枚貝
成果は 6 キロ！	**We gathered 6kg in total!** ＊gather＝～を集める
ハマグリが 20 個取れた。	**We gathered 20 clams.**
ハマグリを家で酒蒸しにした。	**I steamed the clams in sake at home.** ＊steam＝～を蒸す

アウトドア・ドライブ

川・湖

大学時代の友達と、川辺でバーベキューをした。	**I had a BBQ at the riverside with friends from college.** ＊BBQ＝barbeque（バーベキュー）
川に魚釣りに行った。	**We went fishing in the river.**
鬼怒川でライン下りをした。	**We went on a boat ride down the Kinu River.**
信濃川でラフティングに挑戦した。	**I tried rafting on the Shinano River.**
カヌーで川を下った。	**I canoed down the river.** ＊canoe＝カヌーをこぐ

遊覧船で湖を回った。	**We went around the lake on a sightseeing boat.**

ピクニック

六甲山にピクニックに行った。	**We went for a picnic on Mt. Rokko.**
お弁当を持っていった。	**We brought packed lunches.**
フジノさん、ヤマダさんの家族と一緒に行った。	**We went with the Fujinos and the Yamadas.** ＊the＋名字s＝～家の人たち
食べ物や飲み物を持ち寄った。	**We had a potluck lunch.** ＊potluck＝持ち寄りの
レジャーシートの上でご飯を食べた。	**We sat and ate on a picnic blanket.** ＊picnic blanket＝ピクニック用の敷物
外で食べるご飯って、なんであんなにおいしいんだろう？	**Why does food taste so good outside?**
子どもたちは芝生を駆け回っていた。	**The children ran around on the grass.**
花がたくさん咲いていた。	**There were a lot of flowers.**

キャンプ

三連休は家族でキャンプに行った。	**On the three-day weekend, I went camping with my family.** ＊three-day weekend＝週末を含む三連休
週末にソロキャンプデビューした。	**I went solo camping for the first time on the weekend.**
まずは日帰りのデイキャンプからチャレンジ。	**I tried doing a camping day trip first.**
テントを張った。	**We set up a tent.**
テントを張るのにちょっと苦労した。	**Putting up the tent was a little tough.**
グランピングは、自分では何もしなくてもキャンプ気分が味わえる。	**Glamping gives you the feeling of camping without actually having to do anything.**
バーベキューをした。	**We had a barbecue.** ＊barbecueは、BBQとも書く

21 レジャー・旅行

カレーがおいしくできた。	**The curry turned out to be so good.**
マシュマロを焼いた。	**We toasted marshmallows.** ＊toastedはroastedでもOK
薪の火は見ているだけで心が落ち着く。	**I feel calm just by watching the burning firewood.** ＊calm[カーム]＝落ち着いた
寝袋で寝た。	**We slept in sleeping bags.**
夜は結構冷えた。	**It got pretty cold at night.**
星空がきれいだった。	**The stars were beautiful.**

ドライブ

家族でドライブに行った。	**I went for a drive with my family.**
絶好のドライブ日和だった。	**It was a perfect day for a drive.**
ポチも車に乗せていった。	**We took Pochi with us.**
瀬戸大橋を渡った。	**We crossed the Seto Bridge.**
帰りの車の中で、子どもたちはぐっすり眠っていた。	**The kids were fast asleep on the drive back.** ＊fast asleep＝ぐっすり眠って
渋滞につかまって、大変だった。	**We got caught in a traffic jam. It was terrible.** ＊traffic jam＝交通渋滞
ヒマリが「トイレに行きたい」というので、困った。	**We didn't know what to do when Himari said she wanted to go to the restroom.**
サービスエリアまで我慢させた。	**I had her wait until we got to a rest area.** ＊rest area＝(高速道路の)サービスエリア
ギリギリセーフ！	**We made it just in time!** ＊make it＝間に合う、たどり着く

そのほかのレジャー

植物園へ行った。	**I went to the botanical garden.** ＊botanical garden＝植物園
公園を散策した。	**I strolled in the park.** ＊stroll＝散策する

息子と公園でキャッチボールをした。	**I played catch with my son in the park.** ＊play catch＝キャッチボールをする
尾瀬にハイキングに行った。	**We went hiking in Oze.**
日帰りバスツアーでブドウ狩りを満喫した。	**We fully enjoyed the one day bus tour to go pick grapes.** ＊pick＝～を摘む
イチゴ狩りをした。	**We went strawberry picking.**
鍾乳洞を見に行った。	**We went to see some limestone caves.** ＊limestone cave＝鍾乳洞
洞穴の中はひんやりとしていた。	**It was nice and cool inside the cave.**
千鳥ヶ淵で花見を楽しんだ。	**I enjoyed looking at beautiful cherry blossoms at Chidorigafuchi.** ＊cherry blossom＝桜の花
スキューバダイビング体験をした。	**I tried scuba diving.**
友達と高遠へ紅葉を見に行った。	**I went to see autumn colored leaves at Takato with my friends.** ＊leaf＝葉。複数形はleaves

温泉

温泉に行く

2泊3日で白浜温泉に行った。	**We went to Shirahama Hot Spring for two nights and three days.** ＊hot spring＝温泉
立ち寄り温泉に行った。	**We went to a "stop-by-hot-spring."** ＊stop by＝立ち寄る
いくつもお風呂があった。	**There were several different baths.**
家族で貸切風呂に入った。	**We soaked in a private bath as a family.** ＊soak in ～＝(風呂に)漬かる
雪を見ながらお風呂に入った。	**We looked at the snow as we soaked in the bath.**
いくつかのお風呂を巡った。	**We went around to several baths.**
その日は3回、温泉に入った。	**We took three hot spring baths that day.**

露天風呂ってホントに気持ちいい！	**Open-air baths really feel great!**
体が芯から温まった。	**My body was warmed to the core.** ＊core＝芯、核
お肌がつるつるになった！	**My skin became so smooth!**
のんびり漬かり過ぎて、のぼせちゃった。	**I got dizzy from staying in the water too long.** ＊get dizzy＝目が回る、めまいがする
湯あたりを起こしてしまった。	**I got tired from staying too long in the water.** ＊get tired＝疲れる

お湯について

お湯の温度はちょうどよかった。	**The water temperature was just right.**
お湯の温度が熱過ぎた。	**The water temperature was too hot.** ＊「ぬるかった」なら、wasn't hot enoughに
かけ流し式の温泉だった。	**The hot spring water was flowing from the source.** ＊source＝水源、源
炭酸泉だった。	**It was a carbonated spring.** ＊carbonated＝炭酸ガスを含んだ
ちょっと刺激のあるお湯だった。	**The water was a little irritating to the skin.** ＊irritating＝刺激のある
滑らかなお湯だった。	**The water felt really soft.**
その温泉は神経痛に効くらしい。	**They say that hot spring is good for neuralgia.** ＊neuralgia［ニューラウジャ］＝神経痛

温泉街で

浴衣で温泉街を散歩した。	**We walked around the town in yukatas.**
通りのいたるところに足湯があった。	**There were footbaths everywhere on the street.**
硫黄のにおいがした。	**It smelled of sulfur.** ＊sulfur［サゥファー］＝硫黄
温泉卵を食べた。	**We ate hot spring eggs.**
温泉まんじゅうを食べた。	**We ate hot spring manju.**

旅行

旅行の計画（→ p. 108「国・地域名を表す単語」、p. 109「都市名を表す単語」も参照）

どこかに旅行に行きたいな。	**I want to go somewhere.**
温泉巡りをしたい。	**I want to enjoy many different hot springs.**
御朱印を3つゲットしよう！	**I will get three shrine or temple stamps!**
「ななつ星」に乗りたいな。	**I want to ride the Nanatsuboshi.**
海外旅行に出かけたいな。	**I want to travel abroad.**
スイスに行きたい。	**I want to visit Switzerland.**
明日から、カナエとシンガポール旅行。	**Kanae and I are going on a trip to Singapore tomorrow.**
初めてのアメリカ旅行だ。	**It's my first trip to America.**
来週の今ごろはロンドンを満喫中。	**I'll be enjoying myself in London this time next week.**
両親をどこか旅行にでも連れていってあげようかな。	**Maybe I should take my parents on a trip somewhere.**
今年の夏休みは海外に行きたいな。	**I want to travel abroad during this summer vacation.**
自分の目でナイアガラの滝を見てみたい。	**I want to see Niagara Falls with my own eyes.**
自分の英語が通じるか試してみたい。	**I want to see if I can make myself understood in English.**

旅行の準備

旅行代理店でパンフレットをもらってきた。	**I got some brochures at a travel agency.**

＊brochure［ブロウシュァ］＝パンフレット
travel agency＝旅行代理店

代理店で旅行に申し込んだ。	**I booked a trip at a travel agency.** ＊book＝～を予約する
3泊4日の台湾ツアーに申し込んだ。	**We signed up for a 4-day tour of Taiwan.**
ネットで飛行機のチケットを買った。	**I bought plane tickets online.**
やっと飛行機のチケットが取れた！	**I finally got plane tickets!**
LCCを予約した。	**I booked a flight with an LCC.**
すごく安くチケットが買えた。	**I got a really cheap ticket.**
直行便にした。	**I got a direct flight.**
乗り継ぎ便にした。	**I got a connecting flight.** ＊connecting＝乗り継ぎの
途中、ソウルで乗り継ぎがある。	**I have a transfer in Seoul.** ＊transfer＝乗り換え
トータルで23時間かかる。	**It takes 23 hours altogether.**
夜中に出発して、明け方に現地に着く。	**I leave late at night and then arrive there in the early morning.**
窓側の席にした。	**I got a window seat.**
通路側の席しか空いてなかった。	**Only aisle seats were available.** ＊aisle［アイゥ］＝通路側の　available＝空いている
旅行の日程表が届いた。	**I received my itinerary.** ＊itinerary［アイティネラリー］＝旅程表
荷造りをした。	**I did my packing.**
スーツケースがいっぱいになった。	**My suitcase is full.**
バックパックで行くことにした。	**I decided to take just my backpack.**
足りない物は、現地で調達しよう。	**If there's something I need, I'll get it when I'm there.**

パスポート・ビザ

パスポートの申請をした。	**I applied for a passport.** ＊apply for ～＝～を申請する
パスポートの更新をしなきゃ。	**I have to renew my passport.** ＊renew＝～を更新する

パスポートの更新手続きに行った。	**I went to renew my passport.**
申請窓口にはたくさんの人が来ていた。	**There were many people at the passport center.**
パスポートがようやくできた。	**My passport is finally ready.**
パスポートを受け取りに行った。	**I went to receive my passport.**
大使館に行ってビザをもらってきた。	**I went to the embassy and got a visa.** ＊embassy＝大使館
代理店にビザを取ってもらった。	**I had the travel agency get my visa.**

空港で

空港にまつわる単語

空港	airport	搭乗時刻	boarding time
チェックインカウンター	check-in counter	免税店	duty-free shop
手荷物検査	baggage inspection	税関	customs
セキュリティーチェック	security checks	検疫	quarantine
出入国審査	immigration	展望デッキ	viewing deck
コンコース	concourse	両替所	currency exchange counter
搭乗口	boarding gate	土産売り場	souvenir shop / gift shop
搭乗券	boarding pass	フードコート	food court

空港に着くのが早過ぎた。	**I got to the airport too early.**
遅れそうだったので、焦った。	**I was worried because I was almost late.**
空港はすごくきれいだった。	**The airport was really nice.**
空港でラーメンを食べた。	**I ate ramen at the airport.**
スマホでチェックインした。	**I checked in with my phone.**
チェックインカウンターには、たくさんの人が並んでいた。	**There were a lot of people in line at the check-in counter.**

荷物が重量オーバーだった！ ショック！	**My baggage was over the weight limit! What a shock!** ＊baggage＝荷物
両替をした。	**I exchanged my money.**
出国審査に時間がかかった。	**It took a long time to get through immigration.** ＊immigration＝出入国管理
免税店でお母さんに化粧品を買った。	**I bought some cosmetics for my mother at a duty-free shop.**
スマホで出国審査をしたのでスピーディーだった。	**I got through the immigration with my phone, so it was quick.**
入国審査は緊張した。	**I got nervous at the immigration check.**
乗り継ぎで４時間待った。	**I had a four-hour layover.** ＊layover＝乗り継ぎ時間

飛行機

飛行機にまつわる単語

国際線	international flight
国内線	domestic flight
直行便	direct flight
乗り継ぎ便	connecting flight
離陸する	take off
着陸する	land
現地時刻	local time
エコノミークラス	economy class
ビジネスクラス	business class
ファーストクラス	first class
通路側の座席	aisle［アイゥ］seat
窓側の座席	window seat
機内販売	in-flight shopping
機内食	in-flight meal
乱気流	turbulence
機長	captain
客室乗務員	flight attendant
非常口	escape hatch / emergency exit

飛行機が１時間遅れた。	**The plane was an hour late.**
乗り継ぎ便に遅れそうで焦った。	**I panicked because I thought I would miss my connecting flight.** ＊connecting＝乗り継ぎの
飛行機は満席だった。	**My flight was full.**

飛行機はガラガラだった。	**My flight was almost empty.**
乱気流ですごく揺れた。	**The plane shook a lot due to turbulence.** ＊turbulence［タービュランス］＝乱気流
気分が悪くなってしまった。	**I got airsick.** ＊get airsick＝飛行機に酔う
東京からロンドンまで約 13 時間だった。	**It took about 13 hours from Tokyo to London.**
すごく長く感じられた。	**The flight felt really long.**
あっという間だった。	**The flight was over before I knew it.** ＊before ～ know it＝～が気付く間もなく、あっという間に
座席がきゅうくつだった。	**The seat was cramped.** ＊cramped＝狭苦しい
ビジネスクラスは快適だった。	**Business class was really comfortable.**
一度でいいから、ファーストクラスに乗ってみたいなぁ。	**I want to travel in first class even just once.**
機内食はおいしかった。	**The in-flight meal was good.** ＊in-flight meal＝機内食
機内食はあまりおいしくなかった。	**The in-flight meal wasn't very good.**
ワインを飲んだ。	**I had wine.**
客室乗務員が親切だった。	**The flight attendants were kind.**
機内販売で香水を買った。	**I bought some perfume on the plane.**
現地の情報を調べた。	**I gathered a lot of information about the destination.** ＊destination＝目的地
隣の席の人と話した。	**I talked to the person next to me.**
映画を 2 本見た。	**I watched two movies.**
ゲームをして遊んだ。	**I played computer games.**
ぐっすり眠ってしまった。	**I fell fast asleep.** ＊fall fast asleep＝ぐっすり眠る
ほとんど眠れなかった。	**I could hardly sleep.** ＊can hardly ～＝ほとんど～できない

現地時間の夜8時に到着した。	**We arrived at 8:00 at night, local time.**
飛行機は1時間遅れで到着した。	**The flight arrived an hour late.**
現地の気温は23℃だった。	**The local temperature was 23℃.**
飛行機を降りたら独特なにおいがした。	**There was a peculiar smell when I got off the plane.**

ホテル・旅館

ホテルはきれいでよかった。	**I'm glad the hotel was nice and clean.**
ホテルの部屋は狭かった。	**My hotel room was small.**
広くはなかったけど、十分。	**It wasn't very spacious, but it wasn't a problem.**
広々として快適だった。	**It was really spacious and comfortable.**
スイートルームに泊まった。	**We stayed in a suite.**
趣のある旅館だった。	**It was a nice and quaint inn.** ＊quaint＝古風で趣のある　inn＝宿屋
また行きたいと思える旅館だった。	**It was the kind of inn I want to stay at again.**
露天風呂付きの部屋だった。	**It was a room with an open-air bath.**
すごくすてきな部屋で、入ったとたん歓声を上げた。	**It was such a nice room that I let out a shout of joy as I walked in.** ＊let out ～＝～(声)を出す
窓からの景色がきれいだった。	**The view from the window was great.**
川のせせらぎが心地よかった。	**The sound of the river was really relaxing.**
女将さんは上品ですてきな人だった。	**The landlady was nice and elegant.** ＊landladyは「宿の女主人」。「(女性の)大家」の意味もある
ウェルカムドリンクがシャンパンだった!	**The welcome drink was champagne!**

好きな柄の浴衣を無料で借りられた。 **We could borrow a yukata, and even chose the pattern we liked.**

夜10時にホテルにチェックインした。 **I checked in to the hotel at 10 p.m.**

9時ごろチェックアウトした。 **We checked out at around 9:00.**

夕方まで荷物を預かってもらった。 **I asked them to keep my bags until evening.**

またあそこに泊まりたい。 **I want to stay there again.**

ホテル・旅館でのトラブル

シャワーが出なかった。 **The shower didn't work.**
＊work＝正常に動く

バスルームのお湯が出なかった。 **There was no hot water in the bathroom.**

トイレが詰まってしまった。 **The toilet got clogged.**
＊clog＝～を詰まらせる

隣の部屋がうるさかった。 **The people in the next room were noisy.**

観光する

犬山城を訪れた。 **We visited Inuyama Castle.**

観光案内所で街の地図をもらった。 **I got a map of the city at the tourist information center.**

おすすめのレストランを尋ねた。 **I asked them to recommend a restaurant.**

おすすめのミュージカルを尋ねた。 **I asked them to recommend a musical.**

ニューヨークは本当に刺激的な街だ。 **New York is a really exciting city.**

アンコールワットを見て、感動した。 **I was moved when I saw Angkor Wat.**
＊move＝～を感動させる

雄大な景色だった。 **It was a magnificent sight.**
＊magnificent＝雄大な

旅先での移動

地下鉄の路線図をもらった。	**I got a subway map.**
タクシーで美術館に向かった。	**I took a taxi to the art museum.**
シンガポールでは常にGrabを利用した。	**We always used Grab in Singapore.** ＊Grab＝タクシー配車サービス
初めての蒸気機関車だった。	**It was my first steam train ride.**
寝台列車はまさに「動くホテル」だった。	**The sleeper train was just like a "moving hotel."**
フェリーからの眺めは最高だった。	**The view from the ferry was amazing.**

旅先での食事

朝食は、ホテルでパンケーキとフルーツを食べた。	**I had pancakes and fruit at the hotel for breakfast.**
人気のベーカリーで買ったパンを食べた。	**I ate some bread from a popular bakery.**
朝食は広間で食べた。	**We ate breakfast in the dining hall.**
部屋で会席料理を食べた。	**We had a kaiseki dinner in our room.**
旅館の食事は豪華だった。	**The meal at the inn was incredible.**
旅館の朝ご飯がすごくよかった！	**I loved the breakfast at the inn!**
評判のレストランで食事をした。	**We ate at a popular restaurant.**
地元の人が行くような食堂でご飯を食べた。	**We ate at the kind of restaurant that locals go to.** ＊local＝地元の人
地元の食材を生かした料理だった。	**The meal was made using local ingredients.** ＊ingredient＝材料、食材
下関といえば、やっぱりフグ！	**You can't leave Shimonoseki without eating blowfish!** ＊blowfish＝フグ
市場でカニを食べた。	**I had crab at the market.**

お土産を買う

途中でお土産を見た。	**I checked out some souvenirs on the way.** ＊souvenir［スーヴェニァ］＝土産物
免税店で買い物をした。	**I shopped at a duty-free shop.** ＊shop＝買い物をする
日本で買うより安かった。	**It was less expensive there than it was in Japan.**
マリにかわいいキーホルダーを買った。	**I got Mari a cute key ring.**
お母さんに、すてきなネックレスを買った。	**I bought a beautiful necklace for my mother.**
現地の伝統工芸品なんだって。	**I was told that it's a traditional handicraft.** ＊handicraft＝手工芸品
相場より高かったみたい。	**It looks like it was higher than the market price.**
もしかしてボラれた!?	**Was I overcharged!?** ＊overcharge＝～に通常より高い値を要求する
スーパーで現地のお菓子をたくさん買った。	**I bought a lot of local snacks at the supermarket.**
会社のみんなにお土産を買った。	**I bought some things for all my co-workers.** ＊co-worker＝同僚

記念写真を撮る

近くにいた人に写真を撮ってもらった。	**I asked someone near me to take our picture.**
カップルの写真を撮ってあげた。	**I took a photo for a couple.**
滝の前で自撮りした。	**I took a selfie in front of the waterfall.**
みんなで自撮りした。	**We all took a selfie together.**
写真を撮りまくった。	**I took a lot of pictures.**
いい写真がたくさん撮れた。	**I took a lot of nice photos.**

旅先での交流

韓国からの旅行者と友達になった。	I made friends with a Korean tourist. ＊make friends with ～＝～と友達になる
ペンションのオーナーと仲良くなった。	I made friends with the inn owner.
隣の席の人に日本語で話しかけられた。	The person sitting next to me spoke to me in Japanese.
彼女は日本語が上手だった。	Her Japanese was really good.
一緒に夕飯を食べた。	We had dinner together.
一緒に写真を撮った。	We took some pictures together.
メールアドレスを交換した。	We exchanged e-mail addresses.
彼女が日本に来ることがあったら会おうと約束した。	We promised to meet if she ever visits Japan. ＊ever＝いつか

旅から戻って

あっという間の１週間だった。	The week was over before I knew it. ＊before ～ know it＝～が気付く間もなく、あっという間に
楽しい旅はあっという間に終わってしまった。	The fun trip was over in an instant. ＊in an instant＝一瞬のうちに
すごく楽しかった。	I had a great time.
移動が多くて疲れた。	We had to move around a lot, which was tiring. ＊tiring＝疲れさせる、疲れた
キムラさんと旅行先で大げんか。最悪。	I had a big fight with Kimura-san during the trip. It was terrible.
写真の整理をしよう。	I'll sort out the pictures. ＊sort out ～＝～を分類する
いい思い出になった。	It's a nice memory.
一生忘れない。	I'll never forget it.
また行きたい。	I want to go there again.
次はどこに行こうかな。	Where should I go next?

Memo

レジャーや旅行のことを、メモしておきましょう。

レジャー・旅行について 英語日記を書いてみよう

遊びや旅行に出かけたときのことを、英語で書いてみましょう。

旅行の計画

I'm making plans for a trip to Hiraizumi. There are many places I want to visit, like Chuson-ji, Motsu-ji, Jodo Pure Land Garden, Mt. Kinkeizan, etc. I'm getting excited.

平泉旅行を計画中。中尊寺や毛越寺、浄土庭園や金鶏山など、行きたいところがたくさん。ワクワクしてきた。

「～を計画中」は be making plans for ～(名詞)、「～することを計画中」は be making plans to ～(動詞の原形)で表します。「行きたいところ」は places (that) I want to visit。I'm getting excited. は、徐々にワクワクしてきている状態を表します。

子どもの視点

We went to the zoo. When Daigo saw a giraffe, he said, "Wow, long legs!" We adults would say "a long neck." Kids have a pretty interesting point of view.

家族で動物園へ行った。キリンを見てダイゴが「すごーい、長い脚!」と言った。俺たち大人なら「長い首」と言うだろう。子どもの視点は面白いなぁ。

「俺たち大人なら～するだろう」は We adults would ～(動詞の原形)と表します。このwould は、「もし…なら～するだろう」という仮定のニュアンスを含んでいます。「視点」は、point of view で表しましょう。ここでの pretty は「かなり、なかなか」の意味。

美容ざんまいの韓国旅行

Yukiko, Ikumi and I went to Korea. We indulged in authentic Korean food, facials, body scrubs, etc. and bought a load of Korean cosmetics. We had a great trip!

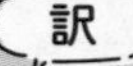

ユキコとイクミと私の３人で韓国へ行ってきた。本場の韓国料理にエステ、あかすり、韓国コスメの大量買い……と美容ざんまい。すっごく楽しい旅だった！

「〜ざんまい」はピッタリな英語がないため、indulge in 〜（〜にふける）で表しました。「本場の」は authentic、（Korean）body scrub は「（韓国式の）あかすり」。a load of 〜は「たくさんの〜」で、loads of 〜でも同じ意味になります。

バイクでツーリング

My girlfriend and I went on a motorcycle ride to Ashinoko Skyline. We rode my motorcycle together for the first time in ages. It was refreshing!

ガールフレンドと芦ノ湖スカイラインへツーリングに出かけた。久しぶりの２人乗り。リフレッシュできた！

バイクでツーリングに出かけるときは、go on a motorcycle ride や go on a motorcycle trip〈tour〉と言います。「バイクに２人乗りする」は ride one's motorcycle together で OK。for the first time in ages は「久しぶりに」という意味です。

22 ファッション

ファッション全般

服

春物のカーディガンが欲しい。	**I want a spring cardigan.**
そろそろスーツを新調したいな。	**Maybe it's about time I got a new suit.**
雑誌で見たシャツが欲しい。	**I want the shirt I saw in the magazine.**
ワンピースを着て出かけた。	**I went out in a dress.** ＊dress＝ワンピース
いつも同じような服を買っちゃう。	**I always end up buying clothes similar to what I already have.** ＊end up ～ing＝結局～する　similar to ～＝～に似た
マネキンが着ている服をセットで買った。	**I bought the whole outfit that the mannequin was wearing.** ＊outfitは、「コーディネートされた衣装一式」を表す
買ったばかりのジャケットを着た。	**I wore my brand-new jacket.** ＊brand-new＝買ったばかりの、新品の
ストライプのシャツにベージュのパンツを合わせた。	**I chose a striped shirt and beige pants.**
グレーのカットソーにピンクのスカーフを合わせた。	**I chose a gray top and a pink scarf.**
クローゼットの中は、グレーや黒系の服が多い。	**I have a lot of gray and black clothes in my closet.**
明るい色の服も着てみようかな。	**Maybe I'll try wearing clothes with brighter colors.** ＊bright＝(色が)鮮やかな
今日買った服を着て、早くお出かけしたい。	**I can't wait to go out in the outfit I bought today.**

服・下着を表す単語

日本語	英語
シャツ	shirt
ワイシャツ	business shirt
Tシャツ	T-shirt
タンクトップ	tank top
ポロシャツ	polo shirt
ブラウス	blouse
トップス	top
セーター	sweater
ニット	knitwear
カーディガン	cardigan
トレーナー	sweatshirt
パーカー	parka / hoodie
スーツ	suit
タキシード	tuxedo / tux
ジャケット	jacket
ウィンドブレーカー	windbreaker
ズボン	pants
ジーンズ	jeans
短パン	shorts
スカート	skirt
キュロット	culottes
ワンピース、ドレス	dress
カクテルドレス	cocktail dress
パジャマ	pajamas / PJ's
ネグリジェ	nightie［ナイティ］
下着	underwear
ブラジャー	bra
ブリーフ	briefs
トランクス	boxer shorts
半袖の	short-sleeved
長袖の	long-sleeved
ノースリーブの	sleeveless
タートルネックの	turtleneck

模様・素材を表す単語

日本語	英語
無地の	plain
チェックの	checkered
タータンチェックの	tartan / tartan-checkered
ギンガムチェックの	gingham / gingham-checkered
ストライプの	striped
ボーダーの	horizontal-striped
水玉模様の	polka-dot
花柄の	floral-print
ヒョウ柄の	leopard-print
幾何学模様の	geometric-pattern
レースの	lacy
綿	cotton
麻	linen
ウール、毛	wool
絹	silk
ナイロン	nylon
アクリル	acrylic
ポリエステル	polyester
ポリウレタン	polyurethane
レーヨン	rayon
コーデュロイ	corduroy
フリース	fleece
ベルベット、ビロード	velvet
デニム	denim

試着する

鏡の前で合わせてみた。
I checked myself out in the mirror.
＊check ～ out＝～を確かめる・よく見る

試着してみた。
I tried it on.
＊try ～ on＝～を試着する。tryの過去形はtried

バーチャル試着してみた。
I had a virtual try-on. ＊try-on＝試着

シャツとズボンを試着した。
I tried on a shirt and a pair of pants.

気になったジャケットを羽織ってみた。
I tried on a jacket I was interested in.

3着、試着した。
I tried on three pieces of clothing.

試着室が空くまで少し待った。
I had to wait a little to use the fitting room. ＊fitting room＝試着室

妻に見てもらった。
I asked my wife how I looked.

スカートがキツくて、がっかり。
I was disappointed that the skirt was too tight for me. ＊tight＝きつい

太って見えたから買うのをやめた。
It made me look fat, so I decided not to get it.

試着って面倒くさい。
It's a bother to try clothes on.
＊bother＝面倒、やっかいなこと

試着せずに買っちゃった。
I bought it without trying it on.

似合う・似合わない

エルメスのスカーフ、私に似合うかな？
I wonder if an Hermès scarf would look good on me.
＊Hermèsは、[ハーミーズ]や[エルメズ]のように発音

予想以上に似合って、うれしかった。
I was happy because it looked surprisingly good on me.

あまり似合わなかった。
It didn't look so good on me.

色が似合わなかった。
The color didn't suit me.
＊suit＝～に似合う

夫に似合わないって言われた。
My husband told me that it wasn't for me.

私は似合うと思ったんだけどな。	I thought I looked good in it.
私って、赤系の服が似合わない。	I don't look good in red.
厚めの素材は私には似合わない。	Heavy material isn't for me.
骨格診断によると、私は小花柄が似合うらしい。	According to the skeletal diagnosis, small floral patterns look good on me. ＊skeletal＝骨格の diagnosis＝診断
はやりの服よりも、自分に似合う服を買いたい。	Rather than buying what's in fashion, I want to buy clothes that suit me. ＊in fashion＝はやって suit＝～に似合う

サイズ

サイズが合わなかった。	The size was wrong. ＊wrong＝妥当でない、間違った
小さ過ぎた。	It was too small.
大き過ぎた。	It was too big.
ぴったりだった。	It was the right size for me.
ちょっとキツかった。	It was a bit too tight.
思ったよりブカブカだった。	It was bigger than I thought.
二の腕のあたりがキツかった。	It was tight around my upper arms. ＊upper arm＝二の腕
大きいサイズを出してもらった。	I asked for a larger size.
小さいサイズを出してもらった。	I asked for a smaller size.
大きいサイズは在庫切れだった。	The larger size was out of stock. ＊out of stock＝品切れで
9号にするべきだったかなぁ。	Maybe I should've gotten a size 9.
3キロ痩せたら着られるかなぁ？	Will I fit into it if I lose 3kg?

デザイン

とてもかわいかった。	It was really cute.

すごくかっこよかった。	**It was really cool.**
派手過ぎるかも。	**Maybe it's too flashy.** ＊flashy＝派手な、けばけばしい
地味過ぎるかな？	**I wonder if it's too plain.** ＊plain＝地味な
太って見えるかな？	**I wonder if it makes me look fat.**
シンプルなデザインが一番だ。	**A basic design would be best.** ＊basicをsimpleにしてもOK
タータンチェックは冬の定番だ。	**Tartan is standard in winter.**
着回ししやすいデザインだ。	**It's a design that's easy to mix-and-match.** ＊mix-and-match＝～を着回しする
最近、ああいうデザインがはやってるんだな。	**It seems such designs are popular these days.**
体のラインがはっきり出るワンピースだ。	**It's the kind of dress that shows my body shape.**
着る人を選ぶ服だ。	**This design of clothes isn't for everyone.**
このワンピースを着ると、イメージががらっと変わる。	**This dress could give me a whole new look.**
そのスーツは、体のラインが細く見えてすてきだった。	**That suit was great because it made me look slim.**

素材

やっぱり綿は着心地がいい。	**Cotton is really comfortable.**
麻の手触りが好き。	**I like the feel of linen.** ＊linen＝麻
デリケートな素材でできている。	**It's made from delicate material.** ＊material＝(服などの)生地
高級感のある素材だ。	**It seems like high-quality material.**
さらりとした生地で気持ちよかった。	**The material was silky and smooth.** ＊silky＝肌ざわりのよい　smooth＝滑らかな
すてきだけど、洗濯が大変そう。	**It's beautiful, but it looks like it would be a pain to wash.** ＊pain＝苦労、面倒

ストレッチ素材のパンツが一番楽。 **Pants made from a stretchy material are the most comfortable.**

セーターが少しチクチクした。 **The sweater was a little scratchy.**

＊scratchy＝チクチクする

色

色を表す単語

白	white		
オフホワイト	off-white		
黒	black	オレンジ	orange
赤	red	山吹色	golden yellow
青	blue	カーキ	khaki
黄	yellow	黄緑	yellow green
緑	green	こげ茶	dark brown
茶色	brown	紫	purple
ベージュ	beige	薄紫	lilac［ライラック］
グレー	gray	紺	navy
水色	light blue	金	gold
ピンク	pink	銀	silver

いい色だった。 **It was a nice color.**

白だと汚れが目立ちそう。 **I think spots will stand out more on white.**

＊spot＝シミ、汚れ　stand out＝目立つ

水色とオレンジで迷ってしまった。 **I couldn't choose between light blue and orange.**

私に合う色じゃなかった。 **It wasn't my color.**

緑は私に合わない。 **Green isn't my color.**

ピンクは売り切れだった。 **Pink was sold out.**

ほかにピンク、ベージュ、グレーもあった。 **There were other colors too — pink, beige and gray.**

パステルカラーのセーターが欲しい。 **I want a pastel-colored sweater.**

色違いを買った。	**I bought one in a different color.**
お姉ちゃんと色違いだ。	**It's the same design as my sister's, but in a different color.**

流行

今年はシフォンスカートがはやってるみたい。	**Chiffon skirts seem to be in fashion this year.** ＊in fashion＝はやって
この春はパステルカラーがはやってる。	**Pastel colors are in fashion this spring.**
このパンツ、もう流行遅れかな？	**I wonder if these pants are already out of fashion.** ＊out of fashion＝流行遅れの
クロップトパンツがはやってるみたい。	**It looks like cropped pants are in fashion.**
このデザイン、来年もはやってるかどうかは微妙だな。	**I don't know if this design will still be popular next year.**
30年前にはやった服が、今またはやってる。	**Clothes that were fashionable 30 years ago are back in style again.**
はやりの服より定番の服を買いたい。	**I would rather buy standard clothes than fashionable clothes.** ＊would rather ～ than ...＝…するよりむしろ～したい
はやりに流されず、好きな服を着よう。	**Don't be influenced by trends, just wear what you like.**
若い子は流行に敏感だなぁ。	**Young people are sensitive to trends.** ＊sensitive to ～＝～に敏感な
年相応の格好をしようっと。	**I'll dress in clothes suitable for my age.** ＊dress in ～＝～を着る suitable for ～＝～に合った

コーディネート・おしゃれ

何を着ていくか迷ってしまった。	**It took a long time for me to decide what to wear.**
鏡の前で、1時間ほどコーディネートに頭を悩ませた。	**I spent an hour trying out clothes in front of the mirror.** ＊try out ～＝～を試す

この時期って、何を着ていいのかわからない。	I don't know what I should wear during this season.
私の格好って、どうもあか抜けない気がする。	I don't think my fashion is chic enough. ＊chic［シーク］＝しゃれた、あか抜けた
タナカくんって、いつもおしゃれだな。	Tanaka-kun really has style. ＊have style＝洗練されている、あか抜けている
おしゃれのコツが知りたい。	I want to know how to be stylish.
今日の服、いろんな人に褒められた。	Quite a few friends complimented me on my outfit today. ＊compliment＝～を褒める
今日のコーディネート、ちょっと変だった。	My outfit today looked kind of funny.
この前買ったセーター、マリちゃんとかぶってた！	The sweater I bought the other day was the same as Mari's!
マチダさんに、靴がすてきと言われた。	Mr. Machida liked my shoes.

衣類の手入れ

セーターに穴があいていた。	There was a hole in my sweater.
カーディガンの穴を繕った。	I fixed the hole in my cardigan. ＊fix＝～を修繕する
ジーンズがすり切れてきた。	My jeans are getting worn out. ＊worn out＝すり切れた
裏から当て布をして縫った。	I sewed on a patch from the inside. ＊sew［ソウ］on ～＝～を縫い付ける
ジーンズの丈詰めをした。	I shortened my jeans. ＊shorten＝～を縮める
スカートの丈を5センチ詰めてもらった。	I had the hem of the skirt taken up 5cm. ＊hem＝（スカートやパンツの）裾
お店でパンツの丈詰めをしてもらった。	I got my pants shortened at the store.
30分ほどで仕上がった。	It took about 30 minutes.
シャツのボタンが取れそうだった。	A button on my shirt was loose. ＊loose［ルース］＝しっかり止まっていない
カーディガンのボタンが取れた。	A button on my cardigan came off. ＊come off＝取れる、外れる

ボタンを付け直した。	I sewed a button back on.
ワンピースをクリーニングに出した。	I took my dress to the cleaners. ＊cleaners＝クリーニング店
セーターを手洗いした。	I handwashed a sweater.
カットソーのシミ抜きをした。	I removed a stain from my top. ＊stain＝シミ　英語には「カットソー」という表現がないため、topでOK
ブーツに防水スプレーをかけた。	I sprayed my boots with water repellent. ＊water repellent＝防水剤
セーターの毛玉取りをした。	I removed the fuzz balls from my sweater. ＊remove＝～を取り除く　fuzz ball＝毛玉
ジャケットにブラシをかけた。	I brushed the jacket.
コートを風通しのいい所に掛けた。	I aired the coat out.

カバン・財布

カバン・財布を表す単語

ハンドバッグ	purse	ポシェット	pochette
トートバッグ	tote bag	スーツケース	suitcase
クラッチバッグ	clutch bag	キャリーバッグ	roller bag
ボストンバッグ	Boston bag	ブリーフケース	briefcase
ショルダーバッグ	shoulder bag	財布	wallet
リュックサック	backpack	革の財布	leather wallet
ウエストポーチ	fanny pack	小銭入れ	coin purse
サコッシュ	shoulder bag		

すてきなカバンだった。	It was a nice bag.
使いやすそうだった。	It looked easy to use.
大きいから荷物がたくさん入る。	It's big, so I can carry a lot of things in it.
ポケットがたくさん付いてて便利そうだった。	It looked handy because it had a lot of pockets. ＊handy＝便利な、扱いやすい

かわいかったけど、あまり物が入らないかも。	**It was cute, but I don't think it can carry very many things in it.**
通勤カバンによさそうだ。	**It would make a good commuting bag.** ＊commuting＝通勤
長財布が欲しい。	**I want a long wallet.** ＊「二つ折り〈三つ折り〉財布」ならbi-fold〈tri-fold〉wallet
あのブランドの財布、一度は持ってみたいなあ。	**It would be nice to own a wallet from that brand.** ＊own＝～を所有する
この財布、カードがたくさん入る。	**I can fit a lot of cards in this wallet.** ＊fit＝～に納める・入れる
革の色味がよかった。	**The leather had a nice color.**
使えば使うほど、いい味が出そう。	**The more you use it, the better it feels.**
コードバンの革を使っているらしい。	**They say it's cordovan.**

靴

靴を表す単語

パンプス	pumps		
ローファー	loafers		
ハイヒール	high heels	ミュール	mules
ローヒール	kitten heels	運動靴	sports shoes
ブーツ	boots	スニーカー	sneakers
革靴	leather shoes	ウォーキングシューズ	walking shoes
サンダル	sandals	ランニングシューズ	running shoes
ビーチサンダル	flip flops	登山靴	hiking boots
スリッパ、上履き	slippers	長靴	rain boots
厚底靴	platform shoes	靴ひも	shoelace

靴の種類

ランニングシューズが欲しい。	**I want running shoes.**
このスニーカー、欲しかったんだ。	**I really wanted these sneakers.**
あの靴、かわいかったな。	**Those shoes were really cute.**

最新モデルだ。	**It's the latest design.** ＊latest＝最新の
冬はブーツを履くのが好き。	**I like wearing boots in the winter.**
暑くなってきたから、サンダルが欲しいな。	**Now that it's getting hot, I want sandals.**
今年はああいうサンダルがはやってるみたい。	**Those sandals are in fashion this year.** ＊in fashion＝流行して
イタリア製の靴っておしゃれだな。	**Italian shoes are really stylish.**
ブラウンのほうが、いろんな服に合わせやすそう。	**Brown is probably easier to match with various clothes.** ＊match ～ with …＝～を…と合わせる
ヒールがちょっと高過ぎるかな？	**These heels might be a bit too high.** ＊a bit＝少し
ローヒールの靴が欲しい。	**I want kitten heels.** ＊kitten heels＝ローヒールの靴
靴磨きも買った。	**I bought shoe polish, too.** ＊shoe polish＝靴磨き

靴の手入れ

靴を洗った。	**I washed my shoes.**
靴を磨いた。	**I shined my shoes.** ＊shine＝～を磨く
ヒールの修理をしてもらった。	**I had the heel fixed.** ＊fix＝～を修理する
穴の開いたブーツを修理に出した。	**I went to get the hole in my boot fixed.**
ヒールの革の張り替えをしてもらった。	**I had the leather on my heels replaced.** ＊replace＝～を替える

靴の試着

履いてみた。	**I tried them on.** ＊try ～ on＝～を試着する
少し緩かった。	**They were a bit loose.** ＊loose［ルース］＝緩い
少しきつかった。	**They were a bit tight.** ＊tight＝きつい
足にぴったりだった。	**They fit my feet just right.**

つま先のところが余っていた。	**There was space at the toes.** ＊toe＝つま先
つま先のところがきつかった。	**They were tight around the toes.**
つま先が少し痛かった。	**My toes hurt a little.** ＊hurt＝痛む。過去形もhurt
かかとのあたりが痛かった。	**They hurt around my heels.** ＊heel＝かかと
外反母趾で履けなかった。	**The shoes didn't fit because of my bunions.** ＊bunion［バニオン］＝外反母趾
すごく歩きやすい。	**These are super easy to walk in.**
ちょっと歩きにくかった。	**The shoes were a bit difficult to walk in.**
靴擦れしちゃうかも。	**They might give me blisters.** ＊blister＝まめ、靴擦れ
履き心地がすごくよかった。	**They were really comfortable to wear.**
ひと回り小さいサイズを出してもらった。	**I asked for one size smaller.**
家に帰って中敷きを敷いた。	**I added an insole when I got home.**

服飾雑貨

服飾雑貨を表す単語

傘	umbrella
日傘	parasol
折り畳み傘	folding umbrella
腕時計	watch
スマートウォッチ	smartwatch
帽子	hat
麦わら帽子	straw hat
野球帽	baseball cap
ニット帽	knit cap
サングラス	sunglasses
手袋	gloves
耳あて	earmuffs
靴下	socks
ストッキング	pantyhose
レギンス	leggings
マフラー	scarf
スカーフ	scarf
ストール	stole
ハンカチ	handkerchief / hanky
ベルト	belt
ネクタイ	necktie / tie
ネクタイピン	tiepin

夏らしい帽子が欲しい。	I want a summer hat.
つばの広い帽子がいいな。	A hat with a wide brim would be nice. ＊brim＝つば
麻のストールが欲しい。	I want a linen stole. ＊linen＝麻
自分へのご褒美に、シャネルのスカーフを買っちゃおうかな。	Maybe I should just treat myself and buy a Chanel scarf. ＊treat＝〜をもてなす
このスカーフはコーディネートのアクセントになる。	This scarf will be a nice accent when coordinating my clothes.
あの腕時計、かっこよかったな。	That watch was cool.
今年の冬は手袋を新調しよう。	I should get new gloves this winter.
このサングラスをかけると映画スターみたい。	These sunglasses make me look like a movie star.
3足1000円の靴下を買った。	I bought three pairs of socks for 1,000 yen.

アクセサリー

アクセサリーを表す単語

指輪	ring	アンクレット	anklet
ネックレス	necklace	ブローチ	brooch / pin
ペンダント	pendant	コサージュ	corsage
イヤリング	earrings	シュシュ	scrunchie［スクランチー］
ピアス	(pierced) earrings	バレッタ	barrette / hair clip
ブレスレット	bracelet	カフス	cufflinks

ペンダントを買った。	I bought a pendant.
真珠のネックレスを買った。	I bought a pearl necklace.
小ぶりのピアスがかわいかった。	The little earrings were cute.
ネックレスとおそろいの指輪を買った。	I bought a necklace and a matching ring. ＊matching＝そろいの

その指輪は、デザインがすごく凝っていた。
The ring had a really elaborate design.
＊elaborate＝凝った

天然のパールらしい。
The clerk said they're natural pearls.
＊clerk＝店員

あのダイヤ、何カラットだろう。
I wonder how many carats that diamond is.

1.38 カラットもあるらしい！
The clerk said that it's 1.38 carats!

指輪をクリーニングしてもらった。
I had my ring cleaned.

指輪のサイズを測ってもらった。
I had my ring size measured.
＊measure＝～を測る

指輪のサイズ直しをしてもらった。
I had the ring size adjusted.
＊adjust＝～を調節する

5 日後にできる予定だ。
It should be done in five days.
＊done＝済んだ、終了した

ファッションについて英語日記を書いてみよう

服装やおしゃれについて、英語で書いてみましょう。

電熱ベストを買ってみようかな

I'm interested in a heated vest. Kayo and Tomo said it was light but really warm. Maybe I should buy one.

電熱ベストが気になる。カヨちゃんもトモちゃんも軽いのにスゴク暖かいって言ってたし。1着買ってみようかな。

ここでの「気になる」は interested in ～（～に興味がある）がぴったり。「電熱」は electric heated で、electric は省略できます。「～してみようかな」は Maybe I should ～を使って表します。buy one の one は、ここでは a heated vest を指しています。

服装にもっと気を遣わなきゃ

I bumped into Misa-san at Omotesando Hills. She looked really sophisticated. I mean, she always dresses nicely. I should pay more attention to what I wear.

表参道ヒルズで偶然、ミサさんに会った。とても洗練されたファッションだった。というか、ミサさんはいつもすてきな格好をしている。私ももっと服装に気を遣わなきゃ。

bump into ～は「～に偶然会う」、look sophisticated は「洗練されて見える＝洗練された格好をしている」という意味です。I mean, は直前の発言に補足したり、訂正したりするときの表現で、「というか」「つまり」「じゃなくて」といったニュアンスです。

セールでの戦利品

I went shopping in Umeda. They were having a summer sale, so it was really crowded. I got the dress that I had always wanted at half price. Lucky me ♪

梅田へ買い物に行った。夏物のセールをやっていたので、すごい人だった。前から狙っていたワンピースを半額でゲット。ラッキー♪

「〜へ買い物に行った」は went shopping in 〜（地名）または went shopping at 〜（店名）で表します。at half price は「半額で」。「3 割引きで」なら、at a 30% discount とします。Lucky me.（私ってラッキー）は、会話でもよく使われる表現です。

クールビズ

It's "Cool Biz" season again. It feels comfortable without a jacket. Seeing Mr. Matsui in a Hawaiian shirt took everyone in the office by surprise.

またクールビズの季節が来た。ジャケットなしだと、やっぱり快適だ。アロハシャツを着たマツイさんを見て、みんな面食らっていた。

「クールビズ」はぴったりな英語表現がないので、そのまま "Cool Biz" で OK。Mr. Matsui in a Hawaiian shirt は「アロハシャツを着たマツイさん」。take 〜 by surprise は「〜を面食らわせる」という意味のフレーズです。

23 美容・ボディケア

ダイエット

ダイエットの決意

おなかまわりにぜい肉がついてきた。	**I'm putting on some flab around the waist.** ＊put on 〜＝〜(脂肪など)を増す　flab＝ぜい肉
ダイエットしなきゃ。	**I must go on a diet.** ＊英語のdietは「食事制限」の意味
今度こそ頑張るぞ！	**I will do it this time!**
二の腕とおなかの脂肪、何とかしなきゃ。	**I have to do something about the fat on my upper arms and belly.** ＊fat＝脂肪　belly＝腹
体重を 5 キロ落としたい。	**I want to lose 5kg.**
目指せ、マイナス 3 キロ！	**I will try to lose 3kg!**
3 カ月で 4 キロ減らしたい。	**I want to lose 4kg in three months.**
ウエストをあと 5 センチ細くしたい。	**I want to lose five more centimeters off my waist.**
体脂肪率を 20 パーセント以下にしたい。	**I want to have less than 20% body fat.**
9 号のスカートがはけるようになりたい。	**I want to be able to fit into a size 9 skirt.** ＊fit into 〜＝〜に合う・収まる
ビキニを着られる体になるぞ！	**I'm going to have a bikini body!**
あのズボンが入るようになるまで頑張るぞ。	**I'm going to keep at it until I can fit into those pants.** ＊keep at 〜＝〜を根気よく続けてやる
毎日 3 キロ歩くぞ。	**I'm going to walk 3km every day.**

週に何日か30分、ジョギングしよう。 **I'll jog for 30 minutes a few days a week.**

自転車通勤をしよう。 **I'll bike to work.** ＊bike＝自転車に乗る

徒歩通勤をしよう。 **I'll walk to work.**

ダイエット法

あのダイエット食品、効果あるのかな？ **I wonder if that weight-loss food really works.**
＊weight-loss food＝ダイエット食品
work＝効果がある

試してみるのもいいかな。 **I might as well try it.**
＊might as well ～＝～するのも悪くない・するのがよさそう

レコーディングダイエットを始めた。 **I started a "recording diet."**

朝と晩、体重を測って記録するだけでいい。 **All you need to do is weigh yourself and record your weight in the morning and at night.**
＊weigh＝～を測る　weight＝体重

白米の代わりに玄米を食べることにした。 **I've decided to eat brown rice instead of white rice.**

テレビでオートミールダイエットが紹介されていた。 **I learned about an oatmeal diet on TV.**

私には効果があるみたい。 **It seems to be working for me.**

この方法でやせた人がたくさんいるらしい。 **This method has apparently worked for a lot of people.**
＊apparently＝どうやら～らしい

サプリメントに頼り過ぎるのはよくない。 **It's not good to rely on supplements too much.** ＊rely on ～＝～に頼る

やっぱり、適度な食事と適度な運動が一番！ **The best way is definitely moderate meals and moderate exercise!**
＊definitely＝確実に　moderate＝適度な

野菜を先に食べるのがいいらしい。 **They say it's better to eat vegetables first.**

食べ物をしっかりかむことが大事。 **It's important to chew food well.**

食事制限

腹八分目を心がけよう。	**I'll try to eat moderately.** ＊moderately＝適度に
30回はかむようにしよう。	**I'll try to chew at least 30 times.** ＊chew＝かむ
油ものは厳禁！	**No oily foods for me!**
スナック菓子は厳禁！	**No snacks for me!**
今日から甘いもの断ち！	**No more sweets from now on!**
バランスのいい食事を心がけよう。	**I'll try eating a balanced diet.** ＊diet＝日常の食事、食生活
夜は食べ過ぎないようにしよう。	**I'll try not to eat too much at night.**
寝る2時間前以降は食べないようにしよう。	**I won't eat anything two hours before bed.**
夕飯は8時までに食べるようにしよう。	**I'll try to finish my dinner before 8:00.**
夜はダイエット食品だけにした。	**I only had diet food for dinner.**
あれだけじゃ足りない。	**That wasn't enough.**
おなかがすいて死にそう。	**I'm starving.** ＊starvingは、starvedでもOK
おなかがすいたけど、我慢、我慢。	**I'm hungry, but I have to control myself.**
ストレスがたまる。	**It's stressing me out.**
寝る前にお菓子を食べてしまった…。	**I ate some snacks before bed, but I shouldn't have ...**
ちょっとぐらい、いいか。	**Just a little should be fine.**
どうしても甘いものが食べたくなる。	**I can't resist sweets.** ＊resist＝〜に抵抗する

エクササイズ （→ p. 435「エクササイズ」を参照）

ダイエット・成功

ダイエットは順調。	**My diet is going well.** ＊go well＝うまくいく
やった、2キロやせた！	**Yes! I've lost 2kg!**
2カ月前と比べて3キロやせた。	**I weigh 3kg less than I did two months ago.** ＊weigh＝〜の重さがある
ウエストは4センチのサイズダウン。	**My waist is smaller by 4cm.**
胃が小さくなった気がする。	**I think my stomach has shrunk.** ＊shrink＝小さくなる、縮む。過去分詞はshrunk
体が締まってきた気がする。	**My body feels firmer.** ＊firm＝引き締まった
ズボンが緩くなった。	**My pants have gotten loose.** ＊loose［ルース］＝緩い
昔の服がまた着られるようになった。	**I can now wear my old clothes again.**
顔が小さくなった気がする。	**I think my face has gotten smaller.**
友達に「やせたね」と驚かれた。	**My friends were surprised that I had lost weight.**
サトシに「きれいになったね」と褒められた。	**Satoshi told me that I looked more beautiful.**

ダイエット・失敗

ダイエット、失敗！	**The diet didn't work!** ＊work＝うまくいく
三日坊主なんだよね。	**I can't stick to anything.** ＊stick to 〜＝〜（決心したことなど）を続ける
リバウンドしちゃった。	**I've gained weight again.** ＊gain＝〜を増す
せっかく減量したのに…。	**After losing all that weight ...**
1キロ太っちゃった。なんで!?	**I gained 1kg. Why?!**
何をしてもやせない。	**No matter what I do, I can't lose weight.** ＊no matter 〜＝たとえ〜であろうとも
ダイエット法が間違っているのかも。	**Maybe I'm using the wrong weight-loss method.** ＊method＝方法

昔よりやせにくくなった。	**It's harder to lose weight now than it was before.**
新陳代謝が落ちているんだと思う。	**I suppose my metabolism is slower.** ＊metabolism＝新陳代謝
在宅ワークばかりで体を動かさないからなぁ。	**It's because I work from home and never really move around.**
運動すると食欲がわいて食べ過ぎちゃう。	**Exercise makes me hungry and I eat more than I should.**
運動する時間がない。	**I don't have time to exercise.**
間食をやめられない。	**I just can't stop eating snacks.**
単純にカロリーオーバーなんだよね。	**I simply eat too many calories.**

肌

肌の調子

最近、肌の調子がいい。	**My skin is in good condition these days.**
最近、肌の調子がよくなってきた。	**My skin is in better condition these days.**
肌年齢をチェックしてもらった。	**I had a skin age test.**
やった！ 肌年齢は 25 歳！	**Yes! I have the skin of a 25-year-old!**
肌年齢は 42 歳だった。	**My skin age was 42 years old.**
実年齢より 5 歳も上だなんて！	**That's five years older than my actual age!** ＊actual＝実際の
実年齢より 5 歳も若かった。	**That's five years younger than my actual age.**
実年齢とほぼ同じだった。	**It's about the same as my actual age.**
肌がきれいだと褒められた。	**I was told that I have beautiful skin.**

リョウコさんの肌ってハリがある。	**Ryoko has youthful skin.** ＊youthful＝若々しい
エリコさんは肌がきれいでうらやましい。	**I envy Eriko's beautiful skin.** ＊envy＝～をうらやむ
マツダさんみたいに肌がきれいだったらなぁ。	**I wish I had beautiful skin like Ms. Matsuda's.**

肌の悩み

最近、肌の調子がよくない。	**My skin condition isn't so good these days.**
今日は化粧ののりが悪かった。	**I had a bad makeup day today.** ＊makeup＝化粧
最近、肌が荒れている。	**My skin is rough these days.** ＊rough＝荒れた
最近、肌が乾燥している。	**My skin is dry these days.**
T ゾーンが脂っぽい。	**My T-zone is oily.**
肌を明るくしたい。	**I want to lighten my skin.** ＊lighten＝～を明るくする
肌のキメを整えたい。	**I want to improve my skin texture.** ＊texture＝手触り
もっと若々しい肌になりたい。	**I want to make my skin look younger.**
目尻のシワが気になる。	**I don't like my crow's feet.** ＊crow's feet＝目尻のシワ
ファンデーションが小じわにたまる。	**My foundation collects in the fine wrinkles.**
ほうれい線をなくしたい。	**I want to get rid of my smile lines.** ＊get rid of ～＝～を取り除く 「ほうれい線」はlaugh linesとも言う
シミ、消えてくれないかなぁ。	**I hope I can get rid of these spots.** ＊spot＝シミ
フェイスラインのたるみが気になる。	**I'm worried about my sagging face lines.** ＊sagging＝たるんだ
顔にニキビができた。	**I got pimples on my face.** ＊pimple＝ニキビ
ニキビが治った。	**The pimples cleared up.** ＊clear up＝きれいになる、消える
ニキビをつぶしちゃった。	**I popped the pimple.** ＊pop＝～を破裂させる・はじけさせる

顔にブツブツができちゃった。	**A rash broke out on my face.** ＊rash＝発疹
肌のお手入れを念入りにしよう。	**I should take better care of my skin.**
基礎化粧品を変えたほうがいいかな？	**I wonder if I should change the skin care products I use.**

肌のお手入れ

お風呂上がりにパックをした。	**I put on a facial mask after my bath.** ＊put on 〜＝〜を付ける・塗る
寝る前に美白パックをしようっと。	**I'll wear a skin lightening facial mask before going to bed.** ＊lightening＝明るくする　facial＝顔の
話題のフェイスマッサージをやってみた。	**I tried the face massage everyone's raving about.** ＊rave about 〜＝〜を絶賛する、〜について夢中で話す
毎晩、続けてみよう。	**I'll try to do it every night.**
小顔になるといいな。	**I hope my face gets smaller.**
血行がよくなった気がする。	**I feel like my blood circulation has improved.** ＊circulation＝循環、流れ　improve＝〜を改善する
美顔器でホームエステをした。	**I used a facial massager to give myself a facial.** ＊give oneself a facial＝〜に美顔術を施す
肌がすべすべになった。	**My skin is smoother now.** ＊smooth＝滑らかな、すべすべした
小顔ローラーって、ホントに効くのかなぁ？	**Will this roller really make my face smaller?**
顔の産毛をそった。	**I shaved my facial hair.** ＊shave＝〜をそる
レーザーでシミを取ってもらった。	**I got some spots lasered off.**
洗顔以外、特に何も肌のお手入れをしていない。	**I don't do anything for my skin. I just wash my face.**
最近は男性も肌のお手入れをしているらしい。	**I hear men also take care of their skin these days.**

紫外線対策

日焼けしたかも。	**I think I got tanned.** ＊get tanned＝日焼けする。get suntannedとも言う

日焼けしちゃった。	**I got tanned.**
紫外線対策をしっかりしなきゃ。	**I have to protect myself from UV rays.** ＊protect＝～を守る　UV ray＝紫外線
紫外線対策はバッチリ。	**I've done all I need to do for protection from the sun.** ＊protection＝保護
SPF50の日焼け止めを買った。	**I bought some SPF 50 sunblock.** ＊sunblock＝日焼け止め
日焼け止めを塗り忘れた。	**I forgot to put on the sunscreen.** ＊put on ～＝～を付ける・塗る　sunscreen＝日焼け止め
日焼け止めを塗るべきだった。	**I should've put on some sunscreen.**
日焼け止めを塗ったのに、日焼けしちゃった。	**I put on sunscreen, but I still got tanned.**
帽子をかぶるべきだった。	**I should've worn my hat.**
両腕にアームカバーを着けた。	**I wore arm covers on both arms.**
長い時間、日なたにい過ぎた。	**I spent too long out in the sun.**

身だしなみ

身だしなみ全般

耳掃除をした。	**I cleaned my ears.**
鼻毛を抜いた。	**I pulled out my nose hairs.**
鼻毛を切った。	**I cut my nose hairs.**

ムダ毛処理

脇のレーザー脱毛をした。	**I got laser hair removal on my underarms.** ＊removal＝除去
ムダ毛処理をした。	**I removed my unwanted hair.** ＊remove＝～を除去する　unwanted＝無用の
すね毛をそった。	**I shaved my legs.** ＊shave＝～をそる

メイク

化粧品を表す単語

ファンデーション	foundation
リキッドファンデ	liquid foundation
パウダリーファンデ	powder foundation
クッションファンデ	cushion foundation
コンシーラー	concealer
チーク	blush / blusher
マスカラ	mascara
ビューラー	eyelash curler
付けまつ毛	false eyelashes
アイライナー	eyeliner
ペンシルアイライナー	pencil eyeliner
リキッドアイライナー	liquid eyeliner
アイシャドウ	eye shadow
アイブロウ	eyebrow pencil / eyebrow brush
口紅	lipstick
リップクリーム	lip balm
リップグロス	lip gloss
基礎化粧品	skin care products
化粧水	skin lotion / toner
乳液	milky lotion
美容液	beauty essence
マニキュア	nail polish
ペディキュア	pedicure
日焼け止め	sunscreen / sunblock
脂取り紙	face oil blotting paper

メイクをする

ばっちりメイクした。
I did my makeup perfectly.
＊makeup＝化粧

デートの前にメイクを直した。
I fixed my makeup before my date.
＊fix＝〜を直す

メイクが濃くなってしまった。
My makeup was a bit heavy.
＊a bit＝少し　heavy＝濃い

ファンデーションののりが悪かった。
My foundation didn't stay on well.
＊stay on＝くっついたままでいる

ナチュラルメイクのコツが知りたい。
I want to know how to put on makeup for a natural look.

ノーメイクで外出した。
I went out without makeup.

まつげパーマをしよう。
I'll get my eyelashes permed.
＊eyelash＝まつげ　perm[パーム]＝〜にパーマをかける

まつげエクステをしてみようかな。
Maybe I should try those eyelash extensions.

私のメイク、古くさい感じがする。
My makeup seems old fashioned.

今風のメイクを覚えたいな。	I want to learn some current makeup. ＊current＝最新の
メイクアップセミナーに行こうかな。	Maybe I'll go to a makeup seminar.
今風のメイクのコツを教えてもらった。	I learned some tricks for doing up-to-date makeup. ＊trick＝コツ、秘けつ
プロのメイクさんって、やっぱりすごい。	Professional makeup artists really are amazing.

化粧品

雑誌に、ランコムの新しいマスカラが載っていた。	I saw the new Lancôme mascara in a magazine.
このアイシャドウは発色がいい。	This eyeshadow has good color payoff. ＊color payoff＝発色
春の新色リップ、どれもかわいい！	All the new lipstick colors this spring are so cute!
シミが消える、いいコンシーラーはないかな。	I wonder if there's a good concealer that can hide my spots. ＊concealer＝コンシーラー　spot＝シミ
無添加の化粧品を使いたい。	I want to use makeup that doesn't have additives. ＊additive＝添加物
また新しい化粧品を買っちゃった。	I bought new makeup again.
ドラッグストアでマスカラを買った。	I bought mascara at the drugstore.
プチプラコスメだけど、いい仕事するんだよね。	It's cheap, but it works well.
かわいい色のマニキュアを買った。	I bought nail polish in a cute color.
コエンザイム Q10 配合の美容液を買った。	I bought beauty essence with coenzyme Q10.
デパートの化粧品売り場に行った。	I went to the cosmetics counter in the department store.
BA さんにいろいろなアイシャドウを試してもらった。	The beauty advisor tried various eyeshadows on me.

BAさんおすすめの化粧下地を買っちゃった。	**I bought the makeup base recommended by the beauty advisor.**

ネイル

つめのお手入れ

つめを切った。	**I clipped my nails.** ＊clip＝～（つめなど）を切る
足のつめを切った。	**I clipped my toenails.**
やすりでつめを整えた。	**I filed my nails.** ＊file＝～にやすりをかける
深づめしちゃった。	**I cut my nails too short.**
甘皮の処理をした。	**I removed my cuticles.** ＊cuticle＝甘皮
マニキュアを塗った。	**I painted my nails.**
ペディキュアを塗った。	**I painted my toenails.**
自分でしたネイルが、きれいにできた。	**I did my nails myself and they turned out well.** ＊turn out ～＝結果的に～となる
このマニキュア、色がきれい。	**This nail polish has a beautiful color.** ＊nail polish＝マニキュア
マニキュアがはがれてきた。	**My nail polish started to peel.** ＊peel＝はがれる
マニキュアを落とした。	**I removed my nail polish.** ＊remove＝～を取り除く

ネイルサロン

今日、ネイルをしてもらった。	**I had my nails done today.**
両手で8400円だった。	**It cost 8,400 yen for both hands.**
すごくかわいかったので、大満足。	**I'm totally satisfied with how pretty they are.**
花柄のネイルアートをしてもらった。	**I asked the nail artist to put flower designs on my nails.**

ピンクベースのフレンチネイルにしてもらった。 **I got a French manicure with a pink base coat.**

着物に合わせてツバキのネイルアートにしてもらった。 **I got camellia nail art to go with my kimono.**

＊camellia＝ツバキ go with ～＝～に合う

ラインストーンを付けてもらった。 **I got rhinestones on my nails.**

ジェルがはがれてきた。 **The gel is peeling off.**

＊peel off＝はがれる

ジェルオフをしてもらった。 **I had the gel removed.**

美容院

髪型を表す単語

ショートヘア	short hair	三つ編み	braids
セミロング	shoulder-length hair	編み込み	French braid
ロングヘア	long hair	ポニーテール	ponytail
ボブ	bob	まとめ髪	updo
角刈り	crew cut	ストレートの	straight
丸刈り	shaven head	パーマのかかった	permed
アフロ	Afro	染めた	colored / dyed［ダイド］
モヒカン	Mohawk［モゥホーク］		

美容院の予約

髪がずいぶん伸びてきちゃった。 **My hair has grown too long.**

＊grow＝（髪やつめが）長くなる、伸びる。過去分詞はgrown

明日こそ美容院の予約をしなきゃ。 **I definitely need to make an appointment at the hair salon tomorrow.**

＊hair salon＝美容院

ネットで美容院の予約をした。 **I made an appointment at the hair salon online.**

8月12日の10時に、美容院の予約をした。 **I made an appointment at the hair salon for 10:00 on August 12.**

今週末は空きがないみたいで残念。 **It looks like there aren't any appointments available this weekend. Too bad.**

新しい美容院を予約した。	**I made a booking at a new hair salon.**
いい美容師さんだといいな。	**I hope the hairdresser is good.**
もう4カ月も美容院に行ってない!	**I haven't been to the hair salon for four months!**

美容院で

美容院に行った。	**I went to the hair salon.** ＊hair salon＝美容院
なりたいヘアスタイルの画像を見せた。	**I showed them the kind of hairstyle I wanted.**
カットとカラーをした。	**I got a haircut and had my hair dyed.** ＊dye[ダイ]＝～を染める
角刈りにした。	**I got a crew cut.** ＊crew cut＝角刈り
長さをそろえた。	**I had my hair trimmed.** ＊trim＝～を刈り整える
そろえてもらうだけにした。	**I just got a trim.** ＊trim＝調髪
すいて軽くしてもらった。	**I had my hair thinned and lightened.** ＊thin＝～を薄くする　lighten＝～を軽くする
ばっさり切ってもらった。	**I told them to just cut off my hair.**
パーマをかけた。	**I got a perm.**
ストレートパーマをかけた。	**I got a straight perm.**
縮毛矯正をした。	**I had my hair straightened.** ＊straighten＝～をまっすぐにする
シャンプーが気持ちよかった。	**It felt nice when my hair was being shampooed.**
ヘッドスパもしてもらった。	**I got the head spa, too.**
すごく気持ちよかった!	**It felt awesome!** ＊awesome[オーサム]＝すごい
カットとパーマで1万6500円だった。	**It was 16,500 yen for a haircut and a perm.**
コバヤシさんのカットは本当に上手。	**Ms. Kobayashi is really good at giving haircuts.**

今の美容院は、あまり上手じゃない。	**The hair salon I go to isn't very good.**
美容院を変えようかな。	**Maybe I should find another hair salon.**
美容院に行ったのに、誰も気付いてくれなかった。	**No one noticed that I had been to the hair salon.**

髪型

イメチェンしたいな。	**I want a makeover.** ＊makeover＝イメージチェンジ
春らしい髪型にしたい。	**I want a hairstyle that's good for spring.**
綾瀬はるかみたいな髪型にしたい。	**I want a hairstyle like Haruka Ayase's.**
手入れのラクな髪型がいい。	**I want a hairstyle that's easy to maintain.** ＊maintain＝～を維持する
髪を伸ばしたいな。	**I want to grow my hair.** ＊grow＝～（髪など）を伸ばす
ストレートロングが好き。	**I like my hair long and straight.**
パーマをかけようか迷う。	**I can't decide whether or not I should get a perm.** ＊whether or not ～＝～かどうか
ボブにしたい。	**I want to cut my hair into a bob.**
角刈りが一番ラクだ。	**A crew cut is the easiest to take care of.** ＊take care of ～＝～の手入れをする
新しい髪型、いい感じ。	**I like my new hairstyle.**
新しい髪型、気に入らない。	**I don't like my new hairstyle.**
自分で前髪を切った。	**I trimmed my bangs.** ＊trim＝～を刈り整える　bang＝前髪
新しい髪型に、まだ慣れない。	**I'm not used to my new hairstyle yet.** ＊used to ～＝～に慣れて
ちょっと切り過ぎちゃったかな。	**I feel my hair was cut a bit too short.**
このパーマ、大失敗！	**This permed hair doesn't look good on me at all!**

カラー・白髪染め

今年の秋は、マロンブラウンがはやってるみたい。	**Chestnut brown seems to be a popular color this fall.**
アッシュ系の髪色にあこがれる。	**I really admire ash-based hair colors.** ＊admire＝～に見とれる
髪の色をもっと明るくしたい。	**I want to dye my hair a lighter color.** ＊dye[ダイ]＝～を染める
髪の色、ちょっと明るくし過ぎたかな。	**I think I dyed my hair too light.**
ダークブラウンにしてもらった。	**I had my hair dyed dark brown.**
パープルのメッシュを入れてもらった。	**I got purple highlights.**
インナーカラーを入れてみたいな。	**I want to get hidden highlights.**
グリーンのインナーカラーを入れた。	**I got green hidden highlights.**
黒髪に戻した。	**I went back to having black hair.**
白髪が増えてきた。	**My hair is going gray.** ＊go gray＝白髪になる
白髪染めをしなきゃ。	**I need to dye my gray hair.** ＊gray hair＝白髪
白髪染めをしてもらった。	**I had my gray hair dyed.**
自分で白髪染めをした。	**I dyed my gray hair myself.**
カラーリング専門店で白髪染めをした。	**I had my gray hair dyed at a salon that specialized in hair color.**
お父さんの髪が真っ白になった。	**Dad's hair has turned white.**

ヘアアレンジ

髪を後ろで結んだ。	**I tied my hair back.** ＊tie＝～を結ぶ
今日は髪を下ろした。	**I let my hair down today.** ＊let one's hair down＝髪を下ろす
髪をアップにした。	**I put my hair up.**
ウェブ記事に載っていたヘアスタイルを試してみた。	**I tried that hairstyle from the online article.** ＊「ヘアアレンジ」の場合もhairstyleでOK

ヘアピンを付けた。	**I put a hairpin in my hair.**
バレッタを付けた。	**I put a clip in my hair.**
ヘアアイロンで巻いた。	**I used a curling iron.**
三つ編みにした。	**I braided my hair.** ＊braid［ブレイド］＝～（髪など）を編む
ポンパドールにした。	**I made a pompadour.**
夜会巻きにした。	**I wore my hair in French twist.**

髪の悩み

最近、髪がパサつく。	**My hair is dry these days.**
髪がまとまらない。	**My hair won't stay put.** ＊stay put＝一つにまとまる
雨の日には髪が爆発しちゃう。	**My hair gets frizzy on rainy days.** ＊frizzy＝（髪が）細かく縮れた
髪が多くてイヤだ。	**I don't like my thick hair.**
髪がペチャンコになる。	**I have flat hair.**
髪の分け目を変えようかな。	**Maybe I should change my hair parting.**
毎朝、寝癖がひどい。	**I get terrible bed hair in the morning.** ＊bed hair＝寝癖
今日の髪型、最悪だった。	**I had a bad hair day.**
枝毛がひどい。	**I have a lot of split ends.** ＊split end＝枝毛
髪にコシがなくなってきた。	**My hair is getting limp.** ＊limp＝柔軟な、弱々しい
髪に弾力が欲しい。	**I want to give my hair some bounce.** ＊bounce＝弾力
髪が薄くなってきた。	**My hair is thinning.** ＊thin＝薄くなる
増毛すべきかな。	**Maybe I need to get hair implants.** ＊implant＝移植
カツラを着けるのは抵抗があるなぁ。	**I'm reluctant to wear a wig.** ＊reluctant＝気の進まない　wig＝かつら

23 美容・ボディケア

エステ・マッサージ

エステに行く

エステに行きたいな。	I want to go to a beauty treatment salon.
エステに行った。	I went to the beauty treatment salon.
フェイシャル 60 分コースを受けた。	I got a 60-minute facial. ＊facial＝美顔術
痩身エステを受けた。	I got a slimming treatment.
全身 90 分コースを受けた。	I got a 90-minute full-body treatment.
ダイエット 6 回コースを契約した。	I signed on for a six-session weight loss course. ＊sign on＝契約する

マッサージに行く

会社帰りにマッサージに行った。	I saw a massage therapist after work. ＊see a massage therapist＝マッサージを受ける
腰痛がひどいので、マッサージに行った。	I had a terrible backache, so I saw a massage therapist. ＊backache＝背中・腰の痛み
全身マッサージを受けた。	I got a full-body massage.
足ツボマッサージを受けた。	I got an acupressure massage on my feet. ＊acupressure＝ツボ押し、指圧
タイ古式マッサージを受けた。	I got a traditional Thai massage.
骨盤マッサージを受けた。	I got a pelvic massage. ＊pelvic＝骨盤の
アロマオイルを使ったマッサージだった。	They used aroma oil for the massage.
60 分 6000 円のコースにした。	The course was 6,000 yen for 60 minutes.
全身をもんでもらった。	They massaged my whole body.

肩がだいぶ凝っていると言われた。	They said I had a really stiff lower neck.
	＊stiff＝凝った　lower neckは、neckとしてもOK
15分延長した。	I extended the massage for 15 minutes. ＊extend＝延長する
マッサージチェアを買おうかな。	It might be a good idea to get a massage chair.

エステ・マッサージの感想

とても気持ちよかった。	It felt really good.
気持ちよくて寝てしまった。	It felt really good, so I fell asleep.
少し痛かった。	It hurt a little.
かえって体が痛くなった気がする。	It seems like my body actually hurts more now.
すごくリラックスできた。	It was very relaxing.
体が軽くなった。	My body feels lighter.
ぜいたくな気分だった。	It felt really luxurious.
	＊luxurious＝ぜいたくな
たまにはエステもいいね。	It's nice to go to a beauty treatment salon once in a while.
	＊once in a while＝時には
ふくらはぎが引き締まった。	My calves have gotten firmer.
	＊calf＝ふくらはぎ。複数形はcalves　firm＝引き締まった
小顔になった気がする。	I feel my face has gotten a bit smaller. ＊a bit＝少し
肌がぷるぷるになった。	My skin has gotten softer.
ウエストがサイズダウンしていて、びっくり。	I was surprised that my waist got smaller.
セラピストが上手だった。	The therapist was really good.
	＊「マッサージ師」にも使える表現
セラピストが下手だった。	The therapist wasn't very good.

サウナ・健康ランド・銭湯

近所の銭湯に行った。	**I went to a public bath near my house.** ＊public bath＝公共浴場
近所の健康ランドに行った。	**I went to a health spa nearby.**
お風呂が 10 種類もあった。	**There were 10 different types of baths.**
ちょっとお湯が熱過ぎた。	**The water was a bit too hot.**
銭湯は混んでいた。	**The bath house was crowded.**
番台で入浴セットを買った。	**I bought a bath set at the entrance.**
ミルク風呂が好き。	**I like milk baths.**
水風呂に入った。	**I took a cold-water bath.**
露天風呂が気持ちよかった。	**The open-air bath felt so good.**
しょうぶ湯の日だった。	**There were sweet flags in the bath.** ＊sweet flag＝しょうぶの葉
冬至なので、ゆず湯をやっていた。	**They put yuzu in the bath because it's the winter solstice.** ＊the winter solstice[サールスティス]＝冬至
やっぱり広いお風呂って気持ちいい。	**For sure, big baths feel really good.** ＊for sure＝確かに
サウナに入った。	**I got in a sauna.**
サウナと水風呂に交互に入って、整った。	**I felt relaxed to switch between the sauna and the cold bath.**
アカスリをしてもらった。	**I got Korean-style body scrub.**
岩盤浴に行った。	**I took a bedrock bath.** ＊bedrock＝岩盤
たくさん汗をかいてスッキリした。	**I felt refreshed after all that sweating.** ＊all that ～＝あれほどの～　sweat＝汗をかく
湯上がりのコーヒー牛乳は最高！	**Coffee milk after a bath is the best!**

Memo

美容やボディケアについて、メモしておきましょう。

美容・ボディケアについて英語日記を書いてみよう

美容やボディケアなどについて、英語で書いてみましょう。

体重が減らない

I've been eating less, avoiding sweets and fatty foods, but I'm not losing weight at all. How come?

食べる量を減らして、甘いものや脂っこいものを控えているのに、全然やせない。どうして？

eat less は「食べる量を減らす」、avoid は「～を避ける」。I've been eating less や（I've been）avoiding と現在完了進行形にして、「ずっと～し続けている」という動作の継続を表しています。How come? は Why?（どうして？）のくだけた言い方です。

顔のくすみ

I've been worried about the dullness of my skin, so I splurged on a bottle of expensive beauty essence. I feel my skin tone is getting lighter. Is it my imagination?

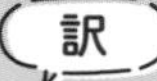

ここのところ顔のくすみが気になっていたので、奮発して高い美容液を買った。肌の色が明るくなってきた気がする。気のせいかな？

ここでの「気になる」は worried about ～（～が心配で）がよいでしょう。「ここのところ気になっている」という継続した状況は、現在完了形で表します。「くすみ」は dullness。「奮発して～を買う」は splurge on ～、「気のせい」は imagination（想像）で表しました。

マッサージでリラックス

I went and got a massage. I was told my neck and lower back were very stiff. The therapist was really good and now my neck and lower back have loosened!

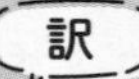

マッサージに行った。肩と腰がだいぶ凝っていると言われた。マッサージしてくれた人がとても上手で、肩と腰がほぐれた！

「～だと言われた」はI was told (that) ～（文）で表し、言われた内容を～に入れましょう。「肩が凝っている」と言うときの「肩」は、首に近い部分であればneck（首）で表します。shoulderは「（肩甲骨を含む背中の上部の）肩」というイメージです。

新しい髪型

I went to the beauty salon today. I asked my hairdresser for advice and decided on a lightly permed short bob. I'm happy that I look pretty good! ☺

今日は美容院に行った。美容師さんと相談して、ゆるいパーマのかかったショートボブにした。かなり似合っててうれしい！☺

asked my hairdresser for adviceは「美容師にアドバイスを求めた」が直訳で、これで「相談した」というニュアンスになります。decided on ～は「（いろいろある選択肢の中から）～に決めた」という意味です。permed［パームド］は「パーマのかかった」。

24

恋愛

出会い

出会い全般

ハラダさんがタザワさんを紹介してくれた。	**Harada-san introduced me to Tazawa-san.** ＊introduce ～ to ...＝～を…に紹介する
異業種交流会で、タニグチさんと知り合った。	**I met Taniguchi-san at the cross-industry get-together.** ＊cross-industry＝異業種間の　get-together＝集まり
今日の集まりで、すてきな出会いがあった。	**I met some nice people at the get-together today.**
セミナーで、たまたま彼と隣の席になった。	**I happened to sit next to him at the seminar.** ＊happen to ～＝偶然～する
高校の同窓会がきっかけで、２人で会うようになった。	**After our high school reunion, we started to see each other.**
明日はブラインドデート。	**I have a blind date tomorrow.** ＊blind date＝会ったことのない人とのデート
マッチングアプリで出会った。	**We met on a dating app.**
オンラインでデートした。	**We had an online date.**
最初から気が合った。	**We hit it off from the beginning.** ＊hit it off＝うまが合う
出会った瞬間に、彼は運命の人だと感じた。	**As soon as I met him, I felt that he was the man for me.**

ナンパする

みんなで（女性を）ナンパに出かけた。	**We went out looking for girls.** ＊「男性を」なら、girlsをguysに

バーで隣の席の男性たちに声をかけた。	**We spoke to a couple of guys sitting next to us at the bar.**
思い切って彼女に声をかけた。	**I got up my courage and talked to her.** ＊get up one's courage［カーリッジ］＝思い切る
収穫ナシ。	**I didn't have any luck.**
1人の女の子が、電話番号を教えてくれた。ラッキー！	**One girl gave me her number. Lucky me!** ＊(phone) number＝電話番号
ナンパする勇気がなかった。	**I didn't have the courage to talk to anyone.** ＊courage＝勇気

ナンパされる

駅前でナンパされた。	**Someone tried to pick me up in front of the train station.** ＊pick ～ up＝～をナンパする
無視して通り過ぎた。	**I ignored him and moved on.** ＊ignore＝～を無視する
彼にLINEを教えた。	**I gave him my LINE info.**
最近、ナンパされなくなったなぁ。	**No one tries to pick me up these days.**
たまにはナンパされたい。	**I wish someone would try to pick me up sometimes.**
ナンパされてもウザいだけ。	**Being hit on is just annoying.** ＊hit on ～＝～をナンパする annoying＝［アノィイング］＝気に障る、迷惑な

合コン

合コンに行った。	**I went to a mixer.** ＊mixer＝合コン
男性4人、女性4人だった。	**There were four men and four women.**
かわいい子が多かった。	**Most of the girls were cute.**
みんなかっこよかった。	**They were all cute guys.** ＊cuteは男性に対して「かっこいい」という意味でも使う
右から2番目の人がかっこよかった。	**The second guy from the right was good-looking.**

24 恋愛

一番左の男性がタイプだった。	**The guy on the far left was my type.** ＊far left＝一番左の
今日の合コンはイマイチだった。	**Today's mixer was not so good.**
タイプの人がいなかった。	**No one there was my type.**
二次会はカラオケに行った。	**We went to karaoke for the after-party.**
もちろん、一次会だけで解散。	**Of course, we parted after the first party.** ＊part＝分かれる
イダさんが駅まで送ってくれた。	**Ida-san walked me to the station.** ＊walk 〜 to ...＝〜を…まで歩いて送る

好みのタイプ

彼、タイプだな。	**He's my type.**
彼女は好みのタイプじゃない。	**She's not my type.**
彼の顔が好みじゃない。	**His face is not my type.**
自分のタイプがよくわからない。	**I don't know what my type is.**
好きになった人がタイプ。	**The person I fall in love with is my type.**
浜辺美波みたいな女性、どこかにいないかな。	**I wonder where I can find a woman like Minami Hamabe.**
玉木宏と付き合えたらいいのに！	**I wish I could go out with Hiroshi Tamaki.** ＊go out with 〜＝〜と付き合う
私の理想は現実離れしてるのかな？	**Is my ideal too unrealistic?** ＊ideal［アイディーゥ］＝理想

相手の印象

彼はシャイでかわいかった。	**He was shy and sweet.**
彼女は経済力がありそう。	**She seems well off.** ＊well off＝裕福な
彼女はさっぱりとした人だった。	**She was a frank person.**

彼はクールに見えて、結構おっちょこちょいだった。	**He seemed cool, but he was pretty careless.** ＊pretty＝かなり
彼は見た目と実際のギャップがいい。	**I like the gap between how he looks and how he really is.**
彼女の第一印象は、笑顔のすてきな子。	**My first impression was that she had a beautiful smile.**
彼女は自分のことをよくわかっている感じだった。	**She seemed self-aware.**
彼女は北川景子に似てる。	**She looks like Keiko Kitagawa.**
彼は、吉沢亮と佐藤健を足して２で割った感じ。	**He looks like Ryo Yoshizawa and Takeru Sato combined and divided in half.** ＊combine＝～を組み合わせる　divide＝～を分ける
彼、私に興味がありそう。	**He seemed interested in me.**
私たちは気が合わなかった。	**We didn't hit it off.** ＊hit it off＝うまが合う
私たちは話が合わなかった。	**We spoke a different language.** ＊speak a different language＝話が合わない
彼女とは話が盛り上がらなかった。	**The conversation with her was kind of boring.** ＊boring＝退屈な
彼女、きれいだけど気が強そう。	**She's good-looking, but she seems to have a strong personality.** ＊good-looking＝美形の
彼、遊んでそうな感じ。	**He looks like he's a player.** ＊player＝遊び人（の男性）
彼、オクテな感じ。	**He seems like he's a late bloomer.** ＊late bloomer＝遅咲きの人
彼女、自意識過剰な感じ。	**She's a self-conscious type.**
彼、自分のことばかり話してた。	**He only talked about himself.**
食べ方の汚い人って苦手。	**I can't stand people with piggish table manners.** ＊stand＝～を我慢する　piggish table manners＝品のない食べ方
彼、バツイチらしい。	**I heard he has been divorced once.** ＊divorced＝離婚した
別に気にしないけど。	**It doesn't matter to me, though.** ＊matter＝重要である

24
恋愛

連絡先の交換

タバタさんに電話番号を聞いた。	I asked Ms. Tabata for her number. ＊(phone) number＝電話番号
タカハシさんに電話番号を聞かれた。	Takahashi-san asked me for my number.
みんなで LINE を交換し合った。	We exchanged LINE info.
彼とツイッターでフォローし合った。	We followed each other on Twitter.
彼にインスタのアカウントを教えた。	I gave him my Instagram account info.
今度ヨシダさんに会ったら、タシロ君の連絡先を聞いてみよう。	I'm going to ask Yoshida-san for Tashiro-kun's contact info the next time we meet.

また会いたい

彼女にまた会いたい。	I want to see her again.
今度は 2 人で会おうと約束した。	We agreed to meet just the two of us next time.
彼女のこと、もっとよく知りたい。	I want to know her better.
彼にまた会いたいと言われた。	He told me he wanted to see me again.
すごくうれしい！	I'm so happy!
ついさっき、彼から LINE が来た。	He LINE'd me a few minutes ago. ＊このLINEは「〜にLINEする」という動詞の意味
「また会える？」と書いてあった。	It said, "Can I see you again?"
彼女の LINE にすぐに返信した。	I LINE'd her back right away. ＊right away＝すぐに
彼に OK のメッセージを送った。	I texted him my okay. ＊text＝〜に(スマホで)メッセージを送る
彼女にメッセージを送ってみようかな。	Maybe I'll text her.
彼から電話がかかってくるといいな。	I hope he'll call me.

もう会いたくない

もう彼女に会う気はしない。	**I don't feel like seeing her again.**
次はないかな。	**I don't think there will be a next time.**
彼から電話がかかってきたら最悪。	**If he called, it would be the worst thing.** ＊worst thing＝最悪な事態
ゲッ！ 彼からLINEが来た。	**Ugh! He LINE'd me.** ＊ugh［ウア］＝うわっ、ゲッ
彼女のメッセージは無視しよう。	**I'll ignore her message.** ＊ignore＝〜を無視する
彼から食事に誘われた。	**He asked me out for dinner.** ＊ask 〜 out＝〜を誘う
返事に困るな。	**I don't know what to reply.**
彼にお断りのメッセージを送った。	**I sent him a message and turned down the invitation.** ＊turn down 〜＝〜を断る invitation＝誘い

告白する

好き

彼女が気になる。	**She's on my mind.** ＊be on one's mind＝〜の気にかかっている
彼を好きなのかな？	**Do I like him?**
彼を好きになりかけてる。	**I'm starting to like him.**
彼女を好きになっちゃったかも。	**Maybe I'm falling for her.** ＊fall for 〜＝〜を好きになる
彼女が好きだ。	**I like her.**
彼が大好き。	**I really like him.**
彼のすべてが好き。	**I like everything about him.**
彼女のことで頭がいっぱい。	**I can't take my mind off her.**
一目ぼれだった。	**It was love at first sight.** ＊love at first sight＝一目ぼれ

初めて会ったときから、ずっと彼女が好きだった。	**I've always liked her since I first met her.**
学生時代から、ずっと彼が好きだった。	**I've been in love with him since we were students.**
彼を思うと胸が苦しくなる。	**My heart aches when I think of him.** ＊ache[エイク]＝痛む
毎日でも彼女に会いたい。	**I want to see her every day.**
彼のことが好き過ぎて、ほかのことが何も手に付かない。	**I like him so much that I can't think of anything else.**
彼といると落ち着く。	**I feel so comfortable when I'm with him.** ＊feel comfortable＝安心していられる
彼女といると、素の自分でいられる。	**I can be myself when I'm with her.** ＊be oneself＝本来の自分である
彼女も僕のことが好きだといいな。	**I hope she likes me, too.**
私の思いが彼に届きますように。	**I hope my thoughts reach him.** ＊thought[ソート]＝思い

かなわぬ恋

私の片思いだ。	**My love is one-sided.** ＊one-sided＝一方的な
片思いって苦しい。	**One-way love is painful.** ＊one-way＝一方通行の
片思いで終わった。	**My love was never returned.**
チエの彼氏を好きになっちゃった。どうしよう。	**I have a crush on Chie's boyfriend. What should I do?** ＊have a crush on ～＝～を好きになる、～に気がある
ダメダメ、彼は好きになってはいけない人。	**No, I mustn't fall in love with him.** ＊mustn't[マスント]
彼女が独身ならよかったのに。	**I wish she weren't married.**

告白前のドキドキ

彼と付き合いたい。	**I want to go out with him.** ＊go out with ～＝～と付き合う
彼女は僕をどう思ってるんだろう？	**I wonder what she thinks about me.**

お互い同じ気持ちだといいな。	**I hope we feel the same way.**
ほかに好きな人がいるのかな？	**I wonder if she likes someone else.**
彼、付き合ってる人はいるのかな？	**I wonder if he's seeing someone.** ＊see＝～と付き合う
彼女にふられたら嫌だなあ。	**I don't want her to reject me.** ＊reject＝～を拒絶する
告白する勇気が出ない。	**I don't have the courage to confess my love.** ＊courage［カーリッジ］＝勇気　confess＝～を告白する
思い切って、彼女に告白してみようか。	**I should pluck up the courage and tell her that I like her.** ＊pluck up the courage［カーリッジ］＝思い切る
よし、彼に告白しよう！	**Okay, I'm going to tell him that I like him!** ＊愛する気持ちが強いときは、likeをloveに
「当たって砕けろ」だ！	**Just go for broke!** ＊go for broke＝当たって砕けろ

告白する

ノダさんに告白された。	**Noda-san told me that he liked me.**
帰り道で彼女に告白した。	**I told her on our way back that I liked her.** ＊on one's way back＝～(人)の帰り道で
ずっと好きだったと彼に伝えた。	**I told him that I had always liked him.**
彼女にLINEで告白された。	**She LINE'd me to say she liked me.** ＊このLINEは「～にLINEする」という動詞の意味
彼に付き合ってほしいと言われた。	**He told me that he wanted to date me.** ＊date＝～と付き合う
彼から真剣に交際を申し込まれた。	**He said he wanted to go out with me and that he was serious.** ＊go out with ～＝～と付き合う

告白の返事・OK

もちろんOKした！	**Of course I said okay!**
私も好きだと彼に伝えた。	**I told him that I liked him, too.**

彼女、OK してくれた。やったー！	**She said yes. Hooray!**
絶対、彼に断られると思ってた。	**I didn't think he would say yes.**
ついに彼女の心をものにできた。	**I finally managed to win her heart.**

告白の返事・NO

彼女にふられた。	**She turned me down.** **I was turned down.** ＊turn down 〜＝〜を断る
彼にきっぱりふられちゃった。	**He rejected me.** **I was rejected.** ＊reject＝〜を拒絶する
予想はしてたけど、やっぱりショック。	**I expected it, but it was still a shock.** ＊expect＝〜を予想する
ほかに好きな人がいると彼に言われた。	**He told me he liked someone else.**
彼女、付き合ってる人がいるんだって。	**She says she's seeing someone.**
彼、今は恋愛する気持ちになれないらしい。	**He says he doesn't feel like seeing anyone now.** ＊see＝〜と付き合う
彼女、今は資格試験の勉強に集中したいって。	**She says she wants to focus on studying for her certification exam now.** ＊focus on 〜＝〜に集中する certification exam＝資格試験
彼とは友達のままでいたい。	**I just want to stay friends with him.**
彼女を恋愛対象としては意識できない。	**I can't imagine being in a relationship with her.** ＊be in a relationship with 〜＝〜と付き合う
なんだ、彼って結婚してたんだ。ショック！	**Oh, I didn't know he was married. What a shock!**

付き合う

付き合う

昨日から彼と付き合い始めた。	**I started dating him yesterday.** ＊date＝～と付き合う
今日で、付き合い始めて１カ月。	**It has been a month today since we started going out.** ＊go out＝付き合う
毎日 LINE してる。	**We LINE each other every day.**
夜、彼に電話した。	**I called him at night.**

デートの計画

週末はどこへ行こうかな。	**Where should we go this weekend?**
彼女、どこに行きたいだろう？	**I wonder where she wants to go.**
彼となら、どこに行っても楽しい。	**I'm happy wherever I go as long as I'm with him.** ＊as long as ～＝～である限りは
見たい映画があったので、彼を誘った。	**There was a movie I wanted to see, so I asked him along.**
遊園地か美術館に行こう。	**Maybe we'll go to an amusement park or an art museum.** ＊amusement park＝遊園地
公園でのんびりしたいな。	**I'd like to hang out in the park.** ＊hang out＝ブラブラして時を過ごす
一緒に買い物に行きたい。	**I want to go shopping together.**
おうちデートもいいかも。	**Just chilling at home would also be nice.** ＊chill＝まったりする
家で彼とドラマを見まくりたい。	**I want to stay home and binge-watch dramas with him.** ＊binge-watch＝～を一気に見る
夜はどこで食べようかな。	**Where should we go for dinner?**
明日はデート。ルンルン♪	**I have a date tomorrow. What a great feeling!**
何を着ていこうかな。	**What should I wear?**

24 恋愛

おしゃれして行こうっと。	**I'm going to dress up for my date.**
彼女と1泊で出かけたい。	**I want to go on an overnight trip with her.**

デート

ドライブに行った。	**We went for a drive.**
手をつないで歩いた。	**We walked holding hands.** ＊hold hands＝手をつなぐ
近所を散歩した。	**We walked around the neighborhood.** ＊neighborhood＝近所
夜景がきれいだった。	**The night view was beautiful.**
彼女の家に行った。	**I went to her house.**
彼に家に上がってもらった。	**I invited him in.** ＊invite ～ in＝～を家に入るように誘う
家でまったりして楽しかった。	**It was nice to hang out at home.** ＊hang out＝ブラブラする
帰りたくなかった。	**I didn't want to go home.**
彼女を帰したくなかった。	**I didn't want her to leave.**
終電がなくなってしまった。	**I missed the last train.** ＊miss＝～を逃す
わざと終電を逃した。（エヘッ）	**I missed the last train on purpose. (hehe)** ＊on purpose＝わざと、意図的に
また彼とデートしたいな。	**I want to go out with him again.** ＊go out with ～＝～とデートする

愛し合う

彼とホテルに行った。	**I went to a hotel with him.**
彼女と初めて愛し合った。	**I made love to her for the first time.** ＊make love＝愛し合う、セックスをする
すごく緊張した。	**I was very nervous.**
久しぶりだったので、盛り上がった。	**It had been a while, so we were really excited.**
彼の車でイチャイチャした。	**We were making out in his car.** ＊make out＝互いに首に抱きついて熱烈なキスをする

会うたびにエッチしちゃう♡	**We make love every time we see each other.**
彼女とは体の相性が合う。	**We seem to be compatible in bed.** ＊compatible＝相性のよい
彼、ちょっと下手かも。	**He's not so great in bed.**
彼、私の体だけが目当てなのかな。	**Maybe he's only interested in my body.**
彼女、あんまりエッチが好きじゃないんだろうな。	**Maybe she doesn't like making love.**
今日はしたい気分じゃなかった。	**I didn't feel like making love today.**
コンドームは必ず着けてもらってる。	**I always make sure that he uses a condom.**
コンドームなしでしちゃった。ちょっと心配。	**We made love without a rubber. I'm a little worried.** ＊rubber（コンドーム）は、condomでもOK
生理だったので、今日はエッチなし。	**I was on my period today, so we didn't make love.** ＊period＝生理

愛してる

彼女を愛してる。	**I love her.**
彼女とずっと一緒にいたい。	**I want to be with her for the rest of my life.** ＊the rest of ～＝残りの～
彼なしでは生きていけない。	**I can't live without him.**
こんな気持ち、初めて。	**I've never felt like this before.**
こんなに人を愛したことはない。	**I've never loved anyone as much as I love her.**
彼女とは運命を感じた。	**I felt like she was my destiny.** ＊destiny＝運命
彼といる時間は、すごく幸せ。	**I'm really happy when I'm with him.**
彼と一緒にいるだけで毎日がバラ色。	**Just being with him makes every day seem rose-colored.**

彼女が喜ぶことなら何でもしてあげたい。 **I would do anything to make her happy.**

彼を悲しませたくない。 **I wouldn't do anything to make him sad.**

一緒に年を重ねたい。 **I want to grow old with her.**

年を取っても手をつないで出かけたい。 **I want to walk with him hand-in-hand even when we're old.**

*hand-in-hand＝手をつないで

うまくいく

私たち、ラブラブ♡ **We're lovey-dovey with each other.**

*lovey-dovey［ラヴィダヴィ］＝ラブラブの

毎日が楽しくてたまらない。 **Every day is so much fun.**

毎日彼に会いたいくらい。 **I want to see him every day.**

信じられないくらい幸せ。 **I can't believe how happy I am.**

私たち、仲良しカップルだ。 **We're lovebirds.**

*lovebird＝仲のいいカップル

私たち、お似合いかも。 **We make a great couple.**

私たち、全然けんかをしない。 **We never fight.**

私たち、相性ぴったりだと思う。 **We have great chemistry with each other.**

*have great chemistry［ケミストリー］＝相性が合う

彼はまさに運命の人。 **He's the one.** *the one＝唯一無二の人・もの

私たち、一緒になる運命だ。 **We're meant to be together.**

うまくいかない

最近、彼とうまくいってない。 **He and I haven't been getting along very well lately.**

*get along well＝うまくいく

彼女とぎくしゃくしている。 **Things haven't been going so smoothly with her.**

*smoothly［スムーズリィ］＝順調に

彼の気持ちが冷めてきているのを感じる。 **I sense that he's growing colder toward me.** *grow ～＝徐々に～の状態になる

彼、もう私に飽きちゃったのかな。	**I wonder if he's tired of me.** ＊tired of ～＝～に飽きて
彼、本当に私のこと好きなのかな？	**Does he really love me?**
彼女の態度が素っ気ない。	**She has been kind of cold.**
彼女のことがわからない。	**I don't understand her.**
彼のワガママに振り回されてる。	**He's so selfish. It drives me crazy.** ＊drive ～ crazy＝～をひどくイライラさせる
彼女、すごく嫉妬深い。	**She's really jealous.** ＊jealous［ジェラス］＝嫉妬深い
私たち、合わないのかも。	**Maybe we're not made for each other.** ＊be made for each other＝似合いのカップルである
彼への気持ちが冷めてきたのかな。	**Maybe I don't love him so much anymore.**
彼女の存在が重荷になってきた。	**She's too much for me.**
だんだん彼に飽きてきた。	**I'm getting bored with him.** ＊bored with ～＝～に飽きて・退屈して

けんか

彼女とけんかした。	**I had a fight with her.**
彼と口論になった。	**We had an argument.** ＊argument＝議論、口論
彼が在宅勤務になってから、けんかばかり。	**We've been fighting a lot since he started working from home.**
彼って本当にむかつく！	**I'm really upset with him!** ＊be upset with ～＝～に対して腹を立てる
しばらく彼女には会いたくない。	**I don't want to see her for a while.**
彼の顔なんて見たくもない。	**I don't even want to see his face.**
彼の LINE は無視している。	**I'm ignoring his LINE messages.** ＊ignore＝～を無視する
彼からの電話に出ていない。	**I'm ignoring his calls.**
けんかなんかしたくないのに。	**I really don't want to fight with him.**

最近、ささいなことでよくぶつかる。	**We've been fighting over little things lately.**
会うたびにけんかする。	**We have a fight every time we see each other.**
彼が私のスマホを勝手に見たなんて、あり得ない。	**I can't believe that he actually looked at my phone.** ＊actually＝実際に
彼女、完全に誤解してる。	**She's got it all wrong.** ＊get ～ wrong＝～を誤解する
彼女、なんで僕を信じてくれないんだ。	**Why doesn't she believe me?**
うそだけは嫌だ。	**I hate lies.** ＊lie［ライ］＝うそ
言い訳しないでほしい。	**I don't want to hear any excuses.** ＊excuse＝言い訳
彼に出ていってほしい。	**I want him to leave.**
「もうここに来ないで」と彼に言った。	**I told him not to come back.**

仲直り

僕から謝った。	**I apologized first.** ＊apologize＝謝る、謝罪する
彼に謝られた。	**He apologized to me.**
気付けば仲直りしていた。	**We found ourselves getting back together.** ＊find oneself ～＝（自分の意思と関係なく）～している自分に気付く　get back together＝よりを戻す
うやむやになってしまった。	**We never dealt with the issue.** ＊deal with ～＝～に対処する。過去形はdealt［デゥト］　issue＝論点、争点
仲直りできて、本当によかった。	**I'm so glad we got back together.**
もう絶対にうそはつかないと約束した。	**I promised him that I would never lie again.** ＊lie［ライ］＝うそをつく
けんかして、よりいっそう仲が深まった。	**After the fight, we became closer than ever.**
もうけんかはしたくないな。	**I don't want to fight anymore.**

遠距離恋愛

彼がアメリカに1年間、留学することになった。	**He's going to be away for a year while he studies in America.**
彼女が福岡に転勤になった。	**She's going to be transferred to Fukuoka.** ＊be transferred to ～＝～に転勤する
4月からは遠距離恋愛だ。	**We'll be starting a long-distance relationship in April.** ＊long-distance relationship＝遠距離恋愛
遠距離恋愛は、やっぱり不安。	**I feel uneasy about this long-distance relationship.** ＊uneasy＝不安な
うまくやっていけるか自信がない。	**I'm not all that confident.** ＊all that＝それほど　confident＝自信のある
私たちなら、きっと乗り越えられるはず。	**I know we can overcome the challenge.** ＊overcome＝～に打ち勝つ、～を乗り越える
なかなか会えないのは、やっぱりつらい。	**It's hard not to be able to see each other that often.**
もっと頻繁に会えたらいいのに。	**I wish we could see each other more often.**
もっと近くにいられたらいいのに。	**I wish we were a little closer.**
あと2週間で彼に会える！	**I can see him in two weeks!**
たまにしか会えないと、新鮮な気持ちを保てる。	**We don't see each other that often, so our relationship always seems fresh.**

同せい

そろそろ一緒に暮らそうかな。	**Maybe we should move in together.** ＊move in＝(人と)住むようになる
結婚を前提に、彼と一緒に暮らしたい。	**I want to move in with him with marriage in mind.** ＊with ～ in mind＝～を念頭に置いて
結婚前に同せいするほうがいいよね？	**It's better to live together before getting married, isn't it?**
一緒に住む家を探すことにした。	**We've decided to look for a place to live together.**

24 恋愛

彼女の両親が同せいに反対してる。	**Her parents are against us moving in together.**
彼と同せいして初めてわかった部分もある。	**There are things that I've learned about him since we started living together.**

浮気する

彼女に浮気がバレた。	**She knows I'm cheating.** **She found out I was cheating on her.** ＊cheat (on 〜)＝(〜を裏切って)浮気をする
ネットで知り合った人と浮気しちゃった。	**I cheated on him with someone I met online.**
マッチングアプリを使ってるのがバレた。	**I got caught out using a dating app.** ＊catch out＝不正を見破る
レンくんとミナトくんが鉢合わせしてしまった。	**Ren and Minato ran into each other.** ＊run into 〜＝〜と鉢合わせする。runの過去形はran
彼に、ほかの人とのLINEのやりとりを見られてしまった。	**He saw some LINE messages I exchanged with someone else.**
ほんの出来心だった。	**It was just a whim.** ＊whim［ホイム］＝出来心、気まぐれ
どっちを選ぶのかと彼女に迫られた。	**She told me I had to make a choice.**
修羅場だった。	**It was a mess.** ＊mess＝混乱、修羅場
もう絶対に浮気はしない。	**I will never cheat again.**
僕って浮気性なのかなぁ。	**Am I a flirt by nature?** ＊flirt［フラート］＝浮気者　by nature＝生まれつき

浮気される

彼、ほかに女がいる気がする。	**I have a feeling he's seeing someone else.** ＊see＝〜と付き合う
女の直感。	**It's a woman's intuition.** ＊intuition＝直感
彼女が浮気をしてたことがわかった。	**I know now that she was cheating on me.**

彼が女性と歩いていたと、人づてに聞いた。	**I heard that he was walking with another woman.**
彼女が浮気してたなんて。	**I can't believe she's having an affair.** ＊have an affair＝浮気をする
二股かけてたなんて、信じられない！	**I can't believe he was two-timing me!** ＊two-time＝～に隠れて浮気をする
あいつ、サイテー！	**That jerk!** ＊jerk［ジャーク］＝ばか、ムカつくやつ
絶対に許せない！	**I'll never forgive him!**
最近、何かおかしいと思ったんだ。	**I felt like something wasn't right recently.**
浮気するような人は、こっちから願い下げ。	**I would rather dump someone unfaithful.** ＊have no business with ～＝～とは関係がない unfaithful＝不貞な、浮気をする

不倫

不倫はよくないとわかってるけど、どうしようもない。	**I know having an affair is wrong, but I can't help it.** ＊can't help it＝どうにもできない
早く終わらせなきゃ。	**I had better end this right away.**
ダブル不倫はリスクが高過ぎる。	**Having a double affair is too much of a risk.**
妻と彼女は比べられない。	**I can't compare my wife with her.** ＊compare ～ with ...＝～を…と比べる
夫は安心できるけど、レンくんといるとドキドキする。	**I feel comfortable with my husband, but being with Ren is so exciting.**
結婚しても、一生恋愛していたい。	**I want to be in love, even after I get married.**
なんだかんだ言って、家庭が一番大事だ。	**No matter what happens, my family is the most important thing to me.** ＊no matter what happens＝何があっても

別れ

彼とはもうやっていけない。	**I can't be with him any longer.**

もう別れたほうがいいよね。	It's better that we go separate ways. ＊go separate ways＝別々の道を行く、別れる
彼と別れたくない。	I don't want to break up with him. ＊break up (with ～)＝(～と)別れる
もう一度やり直したい。	I want to try one more time.
別れたい。	I want to break up.
私たちは別れた。	We broke up.
彼に別れを切り出された。	He suggested that we break up. ＊suggest (that) ～＝～と提案する
彼女にふられた。	She left me. ＊leave＝～を見捨てる。過去形はleft
私からふってやった。	I dumped him. ＊dump［ダンプ］＝～をふる
私は別れたいのに、彼が別れてくれない。	I want to end it, but he won't let me.
私たち、いい友達になれるかな。	I wonder if we can remain good friends. ＊remain＝～のままでいる
時間が解決してくれる。	Time will solve this. ＊solve＝～を解決する
時が心の傷を癒やしてくれる。	Time is a great healer. ＊healer＝治すもの、薬
彼女のことが忘れられない。	I can't forget her.
彼がどれだけ大事かわかった。	I realized how important he was in my life.
いつまでも彼のことを待つつもり。	I'm going to wait for him no matter how long it will take.
もう彼女と会えないなんて、つら過ぎる。	Not being able to see her is too hard.
次はもっと優しい人と出会いたい。	I hope to meet someone kinder next time.
彼女によりを戻したいと言われた。	She told me that she wanted to start over. ＊start over＝最初からやり直す
もう恋愛は当分したくない。	I don't want to be in love again for a while. ＊for a while＝しばらくの間

楽しい時間をくれた彼に感謝。	**I'm grateful to him for the good times.** ＊grateful＝感謝している
独り身は寂しい。	**Being single is lonely.**
やっぱり１人は楽だ。	**It's so much easier being on my own.** ＊on one's own＝1人で
未練なんてない。	**I have no regrets.** ＊regret＝後悔
ほかに男〈女〉はいくらでもいる！	**There are plenty more fish in the sea!** ＊plenty＝たくさんの
次行こ、次！	**On to the next one!**

恋愛について 英語日記を書いてみよう

恋愛や好きな人について、英語で書いてみましょう。

今年のクリスマス

I've decided to work on Christmas since I have no exciting plans. In a way, it's good not to have a date because I can avoid spending money.

クリスマスは特に予定がないのでバイトを入れることにした。恋人がいないと出費を抑えられて、ある意味よし。

「〜することにした」は I('ve) decided to 〜と表します。「バイトを入れる」は work で OK。英語では、正社員やアルバイトなどをあまり区別しません。in a way は「ある意味」、date は「デートの相手、恋人」のこと。「出費を抑える」は「お金を使うのを避ける」と表しました。

家電量販店デートもいいけれど

Yusuke always takes me to electrical appliance shops when we go out. To tell the truth, it's no fun. I want to go to an outlet mall or an amusement park.

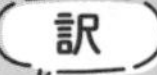

デートといえば、ユウスケが連れていってくれるのは家電量販店ばかり。正直、楽しくない。アウトレットとか遊園地に行きたいよ。

「家電量販店」は electrical appliance shop〈store〉。「家電量販店ばかり」は、when we go out（私たちがデートするときは）と always（いつも）を組み合わせて表してみました。to tell the truth は「本音を言うと」という意味の、前置き表現です。

別れたほうがいいかも

Rina and I have been fighting over little things lately. She gets angry easily and always argues just for the sake of arguing. Maybe it's better we just end it.

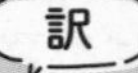

最近、どうでもいいことでリナとけんかになる。リナはすぐにキレるし、へりくつばかり。別れたほうがいいかな。

「どうでもいいことで」は「ささいなことで」と考えて、over little things とします。「へりくつを言う」は argue just for the sake of arguing（議論のための議論をする）と表しました。for the sake of ～は、「（ただ）～のためだけに」。arguing は it としても OK です。

付き合って今日で3年

It's been three years today since Tim and I started seeing each other. He's really sweet and fun to be with. I'm really happy he's my partner.

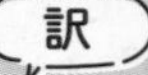

ティムと付き合って、今日で３年になる。優しくて思いやりがあるし、一緒にいて楽しい。ティムがパートナーで本当によかった。

「～して…年になる」は It's been ...（数字）years since ～（過去形の文）で表します。「～と付き合う」は see ～や go out with ～で。sweet は「優しくて思いやりがある」といったニュアンスで、fun to be with は「一緒にいて楽しい」という意味です。

25

結婚・離婚

結婚準備

結婚全般

トガシさんは恋愛結婚らしい。	**I hear Togashi-san has a love-based marriage.**
彼らはお見合い結婚らしい。	**I hear theirs is an arranged marriage.**
イクちゃんは授かり婚らしい。	**I hear that Iku-chan had a shotgun wedding.** ＊shotgun wedding＝授かり婚
ユカさん、寿退社だって。	**I hear Yuka-san is quitting her job to get married.** ＊quit［クイット］＝～を辞める
友達が次々に結婚して、取り残された気分。	**I feel left behind as my friends get married one after another.**
結婚したいな。	**I want to get married.**
結婚資金をためなきゃ。	**I have to save money for my wedding.**
焦って結婚したくない。	**I don't want to rush into marriage.**
結婚しない人生もありだよね。	**Remaining single is also a choice.** ＊remain ～＝～のままでいる
結婚がすべてじゃない。	**Marriage isn't everything.**
ソロウエディングの写真を撮るだけで十分。	**I'll be satisfied to wear a wedding dress and have some pictures taken solo at a studio.**

国際結婚がいいな。	**An international marriage would be nice.**
事実婚がいいな。	**I prefer de facto marriage.** ＊de facto＝事実上の、内縁の
破談になってしまった。	**We broke off our engagement.** ＊break off ～＝～(婚約)を解消する・破談にする。breakの過去形はbroke

婚活

今、婚活中。	**I'm looking for a spouse.** ＊spouse[スパウズ]＝配偶者
婚活しようかな。	**Maybe I should start spouse hunting.** ＊spouse hunting＝配偶者探し
お見合いサービスに登録しよう。	**I'll register with a dating service.** ＊register with ～＝～に登録する
お見合いパーティーに参加した。	**I attended a match-making party.** ＊match-making＝お見合い、結婚仲介
マッチングアプリに登録した。	**I signed up for a dating app.**
希望の条件を登録した。	**I registered my preferences.** ＊preference＝好み
何人かのプロフィールが送られてきた。	**I got sent some profiles.**
1人、気になる人がいた。	**There's one person I'm interested in.**
みんなイマイチだった。	**None of them was quite right.**
35歳までに結婚したいな。	**I want to get married by the time I'm 35.**
いいなと思う男性は、みんな結婚してる。	**The men I'm interested in are all married.** ＊「女性は」なら、menをwomenに
お母さんが結婚しろとうるさい。	**Mom keeps bugging me to get married.** ＊bug ～ to ...＝…するよう～にうるさく言う
誰かうちの娘と結婚してくれないかしら。	**I wish someone would marry my daughter.**
うちの息子はいつになったら結婚するんだろう。	**I wonder when my son is going to get married.**

25 結婚・離婚

結婚したい

彼女と結婚したい。	**I want to marry her.**
彼とずっと一緒にいたい。	**I want to be with him forever.**
私たちなら幸せな家庭を築けると思う。	**I think we can make a happy home together.** ＊homeは、familyとしてもOK
彼こそが運命の人だ。	**He's my destiny.** **He's my Mr. Right.** **He's the one.** ＊destiny＝運命。Mr. Rightは、相手が女性の場合はMs. Rightに
彼女とは相性がいい。	**She and I have good chemistry.** ＊chemistry＝相性
彼女のこと、絶対幸せにする。	**I'm going to make her happy no matter what.** ＊no matter what＝何があっても
2人で協力して、幸せな家庭を築くぞ。	**We're going to work together to build a happy home.**

プロポーズ

彼、なかなかプロポーズしてくれない。	**I've been waiting a long time for him to propose.**
待ってるのにな。	**I've been waiting.**
私からプロポーズしちゃおうかな。	**Maybe I should propose instead.** ＊instead＝その代わりに
明日、プロポーズするぞ。	**I'm going to propose tomorrow.**
彼女にプロポーズした。	**I proposed to her.**
結婚を申し込んだ。	**I popped the question.** ＊pop the question＝プロポーズする
彼にプロポーズされた。	**He proposed.**
やっと彼がプロポーズしてくれた。	**He finally proposed.**
彼のプロポーズを受け入れた。	**I said yes.** **I accepted his proposal.**

彼のプロポーズを断った。 I said no.
I turned down his proposal.
＊turn down ～＝～を断る

彼からのプロポーズの言葉は「結婚しよう」だった。 His proposal was, "Let's get married."

「ずっと一緒にいてほしい」と彼に言われた。 He said that he wants to spend the rest of his life with me.
＊spend＝～を過ごす　the rest of ～＝残りの～

「結婚してくれませんか」って、シンプルだけどベストかも。 "Will you marry me?" is simple but the best, I think.

婚約指輪・結婚指輪

指輪をもらって、最高にうれしい。 I got an engagement ring and I couldn't be happier.
＊engagement ring＝婚約指輪

2人で結婚指輪を見に行った。 We went to check out wedding rings together.

いくつか指輪を試着した。 We tried on a couple of rings.

私に似合う指輪があった。 There was a ring that suited me.
＊suit＝～に似合う

2人ともプラチナの指輪にした。 We decided to get platinum rings.

小さなダイヤがちりばめられた指輪が気に入った。 I liked the pavé diamond ring.
＊pavé［パヴェイ］ring＝小粒の宝石を敷き詰めた指輪

名入れをしてもらうことにした。 We decided to have our names engraved.
＊engrave＝～を彫り込む

裏側にサファイアの石留めをしてもらった。 We had them embed sapphire on the inside.
＊embed＝～を埋め込む

婚約指輪と結婚指輪を合わせると、結構お金がかかる。 The engagement ring and wedding ring together cost quite a lot.

彼女は豪華な指輪が欲しいらしい。 She apparently wants a lavish ring.
＊apparently＝～のようだ　lavish＝ぜいたくな、豪華な

そんなに高い指輪はいらない。 We don't need such expensive rings.

婚約指輪をやめて、ペアの腕時計にした。 We decided to get matching watches instead of engagement rings.
＊matching＝おそろいの

そのお金を節約して、新婚旅行に使うことにした。	**We decided to save the money and use it for our honeymoon.**

実家へのあいさつ

彼女の実家にあいさつに行った。	**I went to her home to meet her parents.**
彼を両親に会わせた。	**I introduced him to my parents.** ＊introduce ～ to ...＝～を…に紹介する
アミと結婚したい気持ちを伝えた。	**I told them I want to marry Ami.**
「娘をよろしく頼む」と言われた。	**They told me to take good care of her.**
とても緊張した。	**I had butterflies in my stomach.** ＊have butterflies in one's stomach＝ひどく緊張する
緊張し過ぎて、何を言ったか覚えていない。	**I was so nervous that I don't remember what I said.**
彼、とても緊張しているようだった。	**He looked really nervous.**
リラックスした雰囲気だった。	**The atmosphere was relaxing.** ＊atmosphere［アトモスフィア］＝雰囲気
彼女のご両親は厳格そうだった。	**Her parents looked stern.** ＊stern＝厳格な、厳しい
彼女のご両親とは気が合いそうだ。	**I think her parents and I can get along.** ＊get along＝仲良くやっていく
夫は落ち着かない様子だった。	**My husband looked restless.** ＊娘・息子が婚約者を連れてきた場合
彼のご両親に気に入ってもらえますように。	**I hope his parents liked me.** ＊会った後の表現。会う前ならwill like meとする
彼のご家族は皆、いい人そうだった。	**His family all seemed nice.**
両親に、彼との結婚を反対されている。	**My parents are against me marrying him.** ＊be against ～ ...ing＝～が…するのを反対する
両親には祝福してもらいたい。	**I want my parents to be happy for us.**
お父さん、彼と一言も話さなかった。	**My dad didn't say a word to him.**

両家の顔合わせ・結納

両家の顔合わせの食事会をした。 We went out to dinner so the parents on both sides could get to know each other.

ホテルのレストランを予約した。 We made a reservation at a hotel restaurant.

料亭の個室を予約した。 We booked a private room at a Japanese-style restaurant.

＊book＝～を予約する

和やかな雰囲気で進んだ。 It was a relaxed atmosphere.

＊atmosphere＝雰囲気

会食はつつがなく終わった。 The dinner went smoothly.

＊smoothlyは、wellにしてもOK

互いの両親は話が盛り上がっていた。 Our parents all enjoyed the conversation.

結納を取り交わした。 We exchanged marriage gifts.

シホの着物姿がきれいだった。 Shiho looked beautiful in a kimono.

結納は交わさないことにした。 We decided not to exchange marriage gifts.

婚姻届

明日、婚姻届を出しに行く。 We are registering our marriage tomorrow.

＊register＝～を届け出る

市役所に婚姻届を出した。 We registered our marriage at the city hall.

私たち、ついに夫婦になったんだ。 We finally became husband and wife.

婚姻届にサインした。 We signed our marriage registration form.

書類に不備があって、受理されなかった。 They didn't accept our documents because they weren't complete.

もう一度、市役所に行かなきゃ。 We need to go to the city hall again.

結婚式の準備

結婚式は来年４月にすることにした。	**We've decided to have our wedding in April next year.**
式はどこで挙げようかな？	**Where should we hold our ceremony?** ＊hold＝～(式)を挙げる
神前式がいい。	**I want a Shinto wedding.**
教会式にあこがれる。	**I have a longing for a church wedding.** ＊longing＝あこがれ
人前式にしたい。	**I want a civil wedding.**
レストランウエディングがいいな。	**I'd like a wedding at a restaurant.**
2人の思い出の場所で式を挙げたい。	**I want to have the wedding ceremony somewhere we both share memories of.**
海外ウエディングってすてき！	**It would be nice to get married abroad!**
ハワイで式を挙げたい。	**I want to get married in Hawaii.**
式は挙げずに、記念写真だけでいい。	**I don't want a ceremony. I just want to take pictures.**
誰を招待しようかな？	**Who should I invite?** ＊「自分の招待客」でなく「2人の招待客」なら、Iをweに
部長を招待したほうがいいかな？	**Should I invite my manager?**
何人ぐらい招待すればいいだろう。	**How many people should we invite?**
200人くらい招待して盛大にやりたい。	**I want to invite about 200 people and have a big wedding.**
身内や親しい友人だけを招いて、こぢんまりとやりたい。	**I want a small wedding with our families and close friends.** ＊close［クロウス］＝親しい
Aホテルの式場を見学した。	**We went to check out the venue at A Hotel.** ＊venue＝会場、開催場所
Bホテルに資料請求をした。	**I asked B Hotel for some brochures.** ＊brochure［ブロウシュア］＝パンフレット

教会の雰囲気がすてきだった。 **The atmosphere at the church was wonderful.**

私はAホテルが好きだけど、彼はBホテルを気に入っている。 **I like A Hotel, but he prefers B Hotel.**
＊prefer＝～のほうを好む

ようやく式場を決めた。 **We finally decided on the venue.**
＊venue＝会場、開催場所

結婚式の準備って、すごく大変。 **It's really hard to prepare for a wedding.**

テーブルフラワーを決めた。 **We decided on the flowers for the tables.**

招待状を準備しなきゃ。 **We have to prepare the invitations.**

招待客の席順をどうするか、悩む！ **I can't decide what to do about the seating arrangements!**
＊arrangement＝配置

お料理は中くらいのコースにした。 **We went for the medium-priced food.**

一番豪華なコース料理にした。 **We chose the fanciest food.**

ミクちゃんにスピーチを頼んだ。 **I asked Miku-chan to make a speech.**

高校の友人たちが演奏してくれる。 **My friends from high school are going to play some music.**

会社の同僚がみんなで踊るらしい。 **I hear my coworkers are going to perform a dance.**

結婚

自分の結婚式

いよいよ結婚式の日を迎えた。 **We're finally having our wedding today.**
＊1日の終わりに書くなら、We finally had ...に

メイクや着付けに時間がかかった。 **It took a long time to do makeup and get dressed.**

体中を締め付けるので、苦しかった。	My clothes were tight, so it was really uncomfortable.
転ばないか心配だった。	I was worried about tripping. ＊trip＝つまずく
ウエディングドレスを着られて、うれしかった。	I was so happy that I got to wear a wedding dress.
タキシード姿の彼、かっこよかった。	He looked fabulous in his tux. ＊tux＝tuxedo（タキシード）の略
彼女の着物姿は、なかなかサマになっていた。	She looked really nice in her kimono.
彼がきれいだと言ってくれた。	He told me I looked beautiful.
指輪を交換したとき、夫婦になったのだと実感した。	When we exchanged rings, it felt real to me that we had become husband and wife.
結婚式では、泣いてしまった。	I cried at the wedding.
みんなが祝福してくれた。	Everybody congratulated us.
披露宴はつつがなく終わった。	The reception went smoothly. ＊reception＝レセプション、披露宴
マイコのスピーチに泣いてしまった。	Maiko's speech made me cry.
お母さんへの手紙を読んでいて、泣いてしまった。	I cried as I read the letter to my mother.
おばあちゃんにウエディングドレス姿を見せたかったな。	I wish my grandma had seen me in my wedding dress.
二次会も盛り上がった。	The after-party was also really fun. ＊after-party＝二次会
ビンゴゲームで盛り上がった。	Everybody got excited playing the bingo game.
いい結婚式になってよかった。	I'm glad the wedding turned out great. ＊turn out ～＝結果的に～となる

家族・友人の結婚式

アツコの結婚式だった。	Today was Atsuko's wedding.

いい式だった。	**It was a nice ceremony.**
感動的な式だった。	**It was a moving ceremony.** ＊moving＝人を感動させる
彼女の晴れ姿に、思わず泣いてしまった。	**I found myself crying when I saw her in her beautiful wedding dress.** ＊find oneself doing＝～している自分に気付く
エミの白無垢(むく)姿、きれいだった。	**Emi was beautiful in her white wedding kimono.**
ウエディングドレス姿もすてきだった。	**She looked great in her wedding dress, too.**
私も結婚したくなっちゃった。	**She made me want to get married, too.**
豪華な披露宴だった。	**It was a lavish reception.** ＊lavish＝ぜいたくな、豪華な
料理がとてもおいしかった。	**The food was really good.**
ご祝儀に３万円包んだ。	**I gave them 30,000 yen as a gift.**
スピーチでは、とても緊張した。	**I was really nervous when giving my speech.**
（ブーケトスで）ブーケをキャッチした。	**I caught the bouquet.** ＊bouquet［ボウケィ］＝ブーケ
次は私の番かな？	**Will I be next to marry?**
引き出物はティーセットだった。	**We got a tea set as a wedding souvenir.** ＊souvenir［スーヴェニァ］＝記念品
二次会にも参加した。	**I went to the after-party, too.** ＊after-party＝二次会
二次会から参加した。	**I only went to the after-party.**
ビンゴゲームで掃除ロボットを当てた！	**I won a robot vacuum from the bingo game!**

新婚旅行

新婚旅行はどこに行こう？	**Where should we go for our honeymoon?** ＊forは、onにしてもOK

25 結婚・離婚

パリに行きたいな。	**I want to go to Paris.**
彼女はドバイに行きたいようだ。	**She says she wants to go to Dubai.**
新婚旅行はスペイン・イタリアを周遊することにした。	**We decided to tour Spain and Italy on our honeymoon.**
新婚旅行でモルディブに行った。	**We went to the Maldives for our honeymoon.** ＊forは、onにしてもOK
新婚旅行でお金を使い過ぎた。	**We spent too much on our honeymoon.**
新婚旅行はしばらく行けそうにないな。	**I don't think we can go for our honeymoon anytime soon.**
新婚旅行は国内でいい。	**We'll just go somewhere in Japan for our honeymoon.**

結婚生活

彼と結婚してよかった。	**I'm so happy I married him.**
結婚生活は楽しい。	**Married life is fun.**
同せいが長かったから、新婚って感じがしない。	**We lived together for a long time before marriage, so we don't feel like newlyweds.** ＊newlyweds＝新婚夫婦
明日は３回目の結婚記念日。	**Tomorrow is our third wedding anniversary.**
一緒に料理した。	**We cooked together.**
家事を分担してもらおう。	**I'll ask him to share the housework.**
皿洗いは彼、洗濯は私の担当。	**He does the dishes and I do the laundry.**
彼にもっと家事をしてほしい。	**I want him to do more housework.**
家事はなるべく分担している。	**We're trying to share the housework.**
お互いに協力しないとね。	**Yeah, we have to cooperate.**

彼、亭主関白なんだよね。	**He's domineering.** ＊domineering＝いばり散らす
うちはカカア天下だ。	**My wife wears the pants in our house.** ＊wear the pants＝(妻が)主導権を握る houseは、familyとしてもOK
彼女の尻に敷かれている。	**She bosses me around.** ＊boss ～ around＝～をこき使う
あの２人はおしどり夫婦だ。	**They're lovebirds.** ＊lovebird＝おしどり夫婦
うちは週末婚だからうまくいってる。	**Our married life is going well because we spend time together only on the weekends.**

離婚・再婚

結婚生活への不満

彼と結婚しなきゃよかった。	**I shouldn't have married him.**
結婚前は、彼がこんな人だと思わなかった。	**Before I married him, I didn't know he was like this.**
彼女、結婚前は優しかったのに。	**She used to be kind before we got married.** ＊used to ～＝昔は～であった
子育てのことで意見が合わない。	**We aren't on the same page about raising kids.** ＊on the same page＝意見が同じで raise＝～を育てる
夫の暴力には我慢できない。	**I can't take my husband's abuse anymore.** ＊abuse［アビュース］＝虐待、暴行
妻の怒鳴り声に耐えられない。	**I can't stand my wife's shouting.** ＊stand＝～を我慢する shout＝怒鳴る
夫のモラハラがひどい。	**My husband's moral harassment is terrible.**
お互い、性格が合わない。	**Our personalities don't match.**
彼のことが信じられなくなった。	**I don't trust him anymore.**
けんかばかりの毎日。	**We fight all the time.**
彼はいつだって仕事優先。	**He always puts his work first.**

家のことは何もしてくれない。	**He doesn't do anything to help around the house.**
お義母さんの世話だって、私に任せきり。	**He doesn't help me take care of his own mother.**
今はもう会話もなくなった。	**We don't even talk anymore.**
彼女は実家に帰ってばかりだ。	**She's always going to her parents' home.**
義両親との同居は絶対に嫌。	**I absolutely do not want to live with my in-laws.** ＊in-law＝姻戚

不倫（→ p. 529「不倫」を参照）

家庭内別居

家庭内別居状態が続いている。	**We have separate lives under the same roof.**
私たちは仮面夫婦だ。	**We're only together for appearances.** ＊appearance＝見せかけ、体裁
1週間、口をきいていない。	**We haven't spoken in a week.** ＊inは、forとしてもOK
家の中に険悪なムードが漂っている。	**The atmosphere in the house is awkward.** ＊awkward［オークワード］＝ぎこちない
実家に帰ってやる！	**I'm going to my parents' home!**
「勝手にしろ」と彼に言われた。	**He told me to suit myself.** ＊suit［スート］ oneself＝自分の好き勝手にする
「今すぐ出ていって！」と言われた。	**I was told to leave immediately.**

離婚を考える

離婚したい。	**I want a divorce.** ＊divorce＝離婚
離婚してほしい。	**I want him to divorce me.** ＊このdivorceは、「〜と離婚する」という意味の動詞
離婚しようかと考えている。	**I'm thinking about getting a divorce.**
一度別居して考えたい。	**I want to live apart and think about a divorce.**

これ以上一緒にやっていくのは無理。	**We can't live together anymore.**
別れたほうが、お互いのためだ。	**I think a divorce would be best for both of us.**
私は離婚したいけど彼は嫌がっている。	**I want a divorce, but he doesn't.**
なかなか彼女と離婚できない。	**I'm having a hard time getting a divorce from her.**

やり直したい

もう一度話し合いたい。	**I want us to talk about it one more time.**
もう一度やり直したい。	**I want us to start over.** ＊start over＝最初からやり直す
じっくり話し合う必要がある。	**I think we really need to sit down and talk.** ＊sit down and talk＝じっくり話し合う
お互い頭を冷やしたほうがいい。	**I think we should both cool off.**
私が悪かった。	**I was wrong.**
やり直せるならやり直したい。	**I want to try again if there's a chance.**
私は家庭をないがしろにしていた。	**I've been neglecting our family.** ＊neglect＝放置する
妻への感謝の気持ちを忘れていた。	**I've forgotten how grateful I am to her.**

離婚する

妻に突然、離婚を切り出された。	**My wife suddenly asked for a divorce.** ＊ask for ～＝～を求める
家庭を顧みなかった僕が悪い。	**It was my fault for not taking good care of my family.** ＊fault［フォールト］＝責任、落ち度
私のわがままが原因だ。	**It's because of my selfishness.**
2人で決めたことだ。	**It was a mutual decision.** ＊mutual＝相互の
夫と別れた。	**I divorced my husband.** ＊「妻と」なら、husbandをwifeに

今日、離婚届を出した。	**I filed divorce papers today.** ＊file＝～(書類など)を提出する
ようやく離婚が成立した。	**We finally got a divorce.**
結婚15年で離婚した。	**We split after 15 years of marriage.** ＊split＝別れる。過去形もsplit
いわゆる「熟年離婚」だ。	**It's a so-called late-life divorce.** ＊so-called＝いわゆる　late-life divorce＝熟年離婚
これでやっと1人になれる。	**I can finally be alone.**
結婚はもうこりごり。	**I've had enough of marriage.** ＊have enough of ～＝～はもうたくさん
今になって家族のありがたみがわかる。	**Now I know how good it is to have a family.**
離婚訴訟を起こそうかと考えている。	**I'm thinking about filing for divorce.** ＊file for ～＝(法的に)～を申し立てる
慰謝料を払ってもらうつもりだ。	**I'm going to make him pay alimony.** ＊alimony[アリモゥニ]＝離婚の慰謝料
慰謝料として200万円を払うことになった。	**I was ordered to pay two million yen in alimony.**

子どものこと

子どもたちはどうしよう？	**What do we do about the kids?**
子どもたちも、うすうす気付いているようだ。	**I think the kids have an idea of what's happening.**
両親がいがみ合っている姿を見せたくない。	**I don't want them to see their parents fighting.**
子どもたちの親権についてもめている。	**We're arguing about custody of the kids.** ＊custody＝親権
親権を手放したくない。	**I don't want to give up custody.**
私1人で子どもを育てよう。	**I'll raise the kids myself.** ＊raise[レイズ]＝～を育てる
幸い、蓄えはある。	**Luckily, I have some savings.**
1人で子どもを育てる自信がない。	**I'm not confident that I can raise the children alone.**

子どものことを考えると離婚できない。	**When I think of the kids, I can't decide on a divorce.**
別れても、彼女は子どもたちの母親だ。	**Even if we split, she's still their mother.** ＊split＝別れる
子どもたちにはいつでも会えるようにしたい。	**I want to make sure I can see the kids whenever I want.**
たまにしか子どもに会えないのがつらい。	**I can only meet my kids sometimes. That's tough.**
夫に毎月、養育費を払ってもらうことになった。	**He's going to pay child support every month.** ＊child support＝子どもの養育費
今月の養育費がまだ振り込まれていない。	**He hasn't paid this month's child support yet.**

再婚

再婚したい。	**I want to get married again.**
いい再婚相手を見つけたい。	**I want to meet a good person to remarry.** ＊remarry＝～と再婚する
しばらく再婚は考えられない。	**It'll be a while before I start thinking of remarrying.**
スズキさんに女性を紹介された。	**Suzuki-san introduced me to a lady.** ＊introduce ～ to ...＝～を…に紹介する
彼女もバツイチらしい。	**She's also divorced.**
彼は奥さんと死別したらしい。	**I heard that his wife passed away.** ＊pass away＝亡くなる
彼、子どもはいないみたい。	**He doesn't have any kids.**
子どもたちは再婚に賛成してくれるだろうか。	**I wonder if my kids will agree to my remarriage.** ＊remarriage＝再婚
再婚することにした。	**I'm getting married again.**
今度こそ、幸せな結婚生活を送りたい。	**This time for sure, I want to have a happy marriage.** ＊for sure＝確かに

結婚・離婚について
英語日記を書いてみよう

結婚や離婚について、英語で書いてみましょう。

寿退社

Mari told me that she's quitting her job at the end of April to get married. I'm happy for her, but I'll miss her.

マリが4月末で寿退社するとのこと。私もうれしい。でも、さみしくなるなぁ。

「寿退社」は一言で表す語がないので、quit one's job to get married（結婚するために仕事を辞める）と説明的に表しました。「～とのこと」は、～ told me ...（～が…と教えてくれた）やI heard ～（…と聞いた）でOK。「4月末」はat the end of Aprilです。

結婚の準備

I followed several Instagram accounts to get some wedding ideas. Just imagining our wedding makes me smile from ear to ear. I couldn't be happier!

ウエディングの参考用に、インスタのアカウントをいくつかフォローした。結婚式の想像をするだけで、にっこり笑顔になれる。私、最高に幸せ！

Just ～ingは「ただ～すること」。ここではimagine（～を想像する）と組み合わせて「ただ～を想像するだけで」と表しました。smile from ear to earは「満面の笑みを浮かべる」。両耳の位置まで頬をつり上げて笑うイメージからできた表現です。

ずっと独身もいいかも

I find my job rewarding. I don't want to take a career break for pregnancy and raising children. Staying single might be a choice for me.

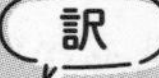

仕事にやりがいを感じている。妊娠や育児でキャリアを中断するのは嫌だな。ずっと独身っていうのも一つの選択肢かも。

find ～ ... は「～を…だと感じる」という意味。特に、経験によって感じたことを表します。「やりがいのある」は rewarding のほか、challenging や fulfilling なども使えます。career break は、家庭の事情や療養、学び直しやスキルアップなどの理由による一時的な離職のことです。

離婚すべき？

My husband and I keep arguing. I want to get a divorce, but when I think about the kids, I know I shouldn't make the decision lightly. What should I do?

相変わらず、夫と口論ばかり。離婚したいけど、子どもたちのことを考えると、簡単に決断するわけにもいかない。どうしたらいいの？

keep arguing は「口論の状態が続いている」という意味。これで「相変わらず、口論ばかり」のニュアンスを表せます。「～するわけにもいかない」は、「～すべきでない」と考えて shouldn't ～で表しても、「～できない」と考えて can't ～で表してもいいですね。

26

出産・育児

妊娠・出産

妊娠

そろそろ子どもが欲しい。	**I want to start a family.** ＊start a family＝子ども（第一子）をつくる
子どもは 2 人欲しいな。	**I want two kids.**
基礎体温を付けたほうがいいかな。	**Maybe I should take my basal body temperature.** ＊basal＝基礎の
生理が遅れてる。	**My period is late.** ＊period＝生理
妊娠してるかも？	**Maybe I'm pregnant.** ＊pregnant＝妊娠している
妊娠検査薬でチェックしようかな。	**Should I do a home pregnancy test?** ＊pregnancy＝妊娠
気のせいだった。	**It was just my imagination.**
妊娠していなかった。	**I wasn't pregnant.**
病院で検査してもらった。	**I went to the hospital for a pregnancy test.**
赤ちゃんができた。	**I'm pregnant.** **I'm expecting.** ＊be expecting＝妊娠している
最高にうれしい。	**I couldn't be happier.**
両親はとても喜んでいた。	**My parents were really happy.**
授かり婚になった。	**Now we're having a shotgun marriage.** ＊shotgun marriage＝できちゃった婚、授かり婚
今、妊娠 10 週目。	**I'm ten weeks pregnant.** ＊「妊娠4カ月」なら、four months pregnant

安定期に入った。 **I'm in my stable period.**
＊stable period＝安定期

おなかが目立ってきた。 **My bump is starting to show.**
＊bump＝ふくらみ

出産間近だ。 **My baby is due soon.**
＊due＝(子どもが)生まれる予定で

臨月だ。 **I'm in my last month of pregnancy.**

予定日は来年の1月5日。 **I'm due January 5 next year.**
My baby is due January 5 next year.

12月から産休を取ることにした。 **I've decided to take maternity leave from December.**
＊maternity leave＝産休

男の子かな、女の子かな。 **Is it a boy or a girl?**

女の子がいいな。 **I want a girl.**

性別はどちらでも構わない。 **It doesn't matter whether it's a boy or a girl.**
＊matter＝重要である

妊娠中の体調管理

つわりがひどい。 **I have awful morning sickness.**
＊awful[オーフォ]＝ひどい　morning sickness＝つわり

つわりはほとんどない。 **I don't really have morning sickness.**

明日は定期健診。 **I'm having a routine checkup tomorrow.**
＊routine[ルーティーン]＝決まった、定期的な

母子共に順調だって。 **Both the baby and I are doing fine.**

エコー写真を見た。 **I saw the ultrasound photo.**
＊ultrasound＝超音波

腕がはっきり見えた。 **I could clearly see an arm.**

動いていた。 **The baby was moving.**

おなかを蹴っていた。 **The baby was kicking.**

体調管理に気を付けよう。 **I'm going to take care of my health.**

体重が増え過ぎだと言われた。 **I was told I've gained too much weight.**

体重が減ってしまっている。	**I'm losing weight.**
血圧が高めだった。	**My blood pressure was high.**
血糖値が高めだった。	**My blood sugar level was high.**

出産

安産でありますように。	**I'm hoping for a safe delivery.** ＊delivery＝出産
無痛分娩にしたい。	**I want to have a painless delivery.** ＊painless＝痛みのない、無痛の
自然分娩がいいな。	**I'd like to have a natural delivery.**
出産予定日が近づいてきた。	**The due date is getting closer.** ＊delivery＝出産
5 時ごろ、陣痛が始まった。	**I went into labor at around 5:00.** ＊go into labor＝陣痛が始まる
分娩室に入って 10 時間後に生まれた。	**The baby was born ten hours after I went into the delivery room.**
安産だった。	**It was a smooth delivery.** ＊It wasは、I hadとしてもOK
難産だった。	**I had a difficult delivery.** ＊I hadは、It wasとしてもOK
帝王切開で産んだ。	**I had a C-section.** ＊C-section＝Caesarean section（帝王切開）の略
予定日より 3 週間早かった。	**The baby was three weeks earlier than my due date.** ＊「3週間遅い」なら、three weeks late
死ぬほど痛かった。	**I thought I would die of pain.** ＊die of ～＝～のために死ぬ
大声で叫んじゃった。	**I screamed out.**
3275 グラムだった。	**He weighed 3,275g.** ＊weigh［ウェイ］＝～の重さがある
元気な男の子だ。	**He's a healthy boy.** ＊「女の子」なら、HeをShe、boyをgirlに
夫が出産に立ち会った。	**My husband attended the birth.**
夫は出産に立ち会えなかった。	**My husband couldn't attend the birth.**
（自分が）出産に立ち会った。	**I was there for the birth.**

出産に間に合わなかった。	**I couldn't make it for the delivery.** ＊make it for ～＝～に間に合う
立ち会って、出産がいかに大変かがわかった。	**Attending the birth made me realize how tough it is.**
ユキコが無事に出産できてよかった。	**I'm glad Yukiko gave birth without any problems.**
ミサキ、頑張ってくれてありがとう。	**Thank you for all your effort, Misaki.**
ついに俺も父親になった。	**I'm finally a father.**
初孫は本当にかわいい。	**Our first grandchild is so adorable.** ＊adorable＝愛らしい
生まれた瞬間は、感動した。	**The moment my baby was born, I was moved.** ＊moved＝感動して
初めて抱いたとき、涙が出た。	**I cried the first time I held him.** ＊hold＝～を抱く。過去形はheld
生まれてきてくれてありがとう。	**Thank you for being our child.**
名前はまだ決めていない。	**We haven't decided on a name yet.**
名前はサクラに決めた。	**We decided to name her Sakura.**

日々の育児

あやす

ミホを抱いてあやした。	**I cradled Miho in my arms.** ＊cradled＝～を揺すってあやす
息子は縦抱っこが好きみたい。	**He seems to like being held upright.** ＊upright＝直立の
眠るまで、ひたすらスクワット。	**I kept on squatting until he finally fell asleep.**
娘の背中をトントンしてあげた。	**I patted her on the back.** ＊pat＝～を軽くたたく
息子の髪をなでてあげた。	**I stroked his hair.** ＊stroke＝～をなでる
娘にガラガラを振って見せたら喜んでいた。	**She loved it when she saw me shake her rattle.** ＊rattle＝ガラガラ

娘に「いないいないばあ！」をしたら、すごく笑った。
She really laughed when I played peekaboo with her.
＊play peekaboo＝いないいないばあをする

アイルは高い高いが大好きみたい。
Airu seems to love it when I hold her up in the air.

ソラが泣くのであやした。
I hushed Sora when he cried.
＊hush＝～をなだめる

娘をおんぶした。
I gave my daughter a piggyback ride.
＊piggyback ride＝おんぶ。rideは省略してもOK

パパが息子に肩車をしてあげた。
Daddy carried him on his shoulders.

授乳

娘におっぱいをあげた。
I breast-fed her.
＊breast-feed＝～に母乳を飲ませる。過去形はbreast-fed

息子に粉ミルクをあげた。
I gave him formula. ＊formula＝粉ミルク

手早くミルクを作るコツをつかんだ。
I got the hang of making formula quickly.
＊get the hang of ～ing＝～するコツをつかむ

パパが娘にミルクを作ってあげた。
Daddy prepared some formula for her. ＊prepare＝～を作る・用意する

息子はミルクをたっぷり飲んだ。
He drank a lot of formula.

娘は今日、あまりミルクを飲まなかった。
She didn't drink much formula today.

娘はおっぱいを飲みながら寝ちゃった。
She fell asleep while being breast-fed. ＊fall asleep＝眠りにつく

最近、娘はおっぱいがないと寝てくれない。
Lately, she doesn't sleep unless she's breast-fed.

ミルクの後、娘にげっぷを出させた。
I burped her after she had formula.
＊burp＝～にげっぷをさせる

息子はなかなかげっぷが出なかった。
He wouldn't burp. ＊burp＝げっぷをする

ほ乳瓶を消毒した。
We sterilized the baby bottle.
＊sterilize＝～を殺菌する　baby bottle＝ほ乳瓶

息子もそろそろ卒乳の時期かな？
I think it's time I stopped breast-feeding him.

息子の断乳３日目。
It has been three days since I stopped breast-feeding him.

おっぱいが張ってつらいよ〜。	**It hurts when my breasts are tight.**
搾乳した。	**I pumped some breast milk.** ＊pump＝〜をポンプでくみ上げる

離乳食・食事

そろそろ娘の離乳食を始めなきゃ。	**I have to start giving her solids soon.** ＊solids＝固形物、離乳食
今日は離乳食デビュー！	**We started with baby food today!**
娘の離乳食を作った。	**I made her baby food.**
離乳食の作り置きをしておいた。	**I prepared extra baby food.** ＊prepare＝〜を作る・用意する　extra＝余分の
離乳食６日目。	**It has been six days since I started giving her solids.**
娘に初めてチーズを食べさせた。	**I fed her cheese for the first time.** ＊feed＝〜に食べ物を与える。過去形はfed
かぼちゃペーストを作った。	**I made pumpkin paste.**
にんじんケーキを作った。	**I made carrot cake.**
息子は好き嫌いが多くて困っちゃう。	**His fussy eating is a problem.** ＊fussy eating＝偏食
娘は好き嫌いがほとんどない。	**She's not a picky eater.** ＊picky eater＝食べ物のえり好みが激しい人
息子にもっと野菜も食べてもらいたいんだけどな。	**I wish he would eat more vegetables.**
パンダ型のおにぎりを作ったら、子どもたちに大好評だった。	**The kids loved the panda-shaped rice balls I made.**
娘はおなかがすいてたみたい。	**It looks like she was hungry.**
息子は食べる量が少ない。	**He doesn't eat much.**
娘は小さい体なのに、よく食べる！	**She's small, but she eats a lot!**
息子には、なるべくスナック菓子や甘いものを与えないようにしたい。	**I'm trying not to give him snacks or sweets.**

おむつ・トイレ

娘のおむつを替えた。	I changed her diaper. ＊diaper［ダイァパー］＝おむつ
パパが娘のおむつを替えた。	Daddy changed her diaper.
娘はいっぱいおしっこをしていた。	She had peed a lot. ＊pee＝おしっこをする
息子はやっぱりウンチをしていた。	Just as I thought, he had pooped. ＊poop＝ウンチをする
ウンチが背中に漏れていた。	His poop went all up his back. ＊poop＝ウンチ
娘のウンチが前より固くなってきた。	Her poop is getting more solid than it was before. ＊solid＝固い
おむつを開けた途端に、息子がおしっこしちゃった（泣）。	He peed the moment I opened his diaper. (Oh no)
トイレトレーニング、なかなか大変。	Toilet training is quite a challenge.
娘はおまるがお気に入り。	She likes her potty.
息子は１人でおしっこできるようになった。	Now he can pee on his own. ＊on one's own＝自力で
なぜかウンチだけはおむつでしたがる。	For some reason she'll only poop in her diaper.
娘のおむつが取れた。	She's out of diapers.
春になるまでに娘のおむつが取れるといいな。	I hope she can be out of diapers before spring.

お風呂・歯磨き

エマをお風呂に入れた。	I gave Ema a bath.
パパがユイをお風呂に入れた。	Daddy gave Yui a bath.
外遊びの後、息子をお風呂に入れた。	I gave him a bath after he played outside.
たまには１人でゆっくりお風呂に入りたいな。	It would be nice to have a leisurely bath by myself once in a while. ＊leisurely＝ゆったりとした、のんびりとした

息子の歯を磨いた。	**I brushed his teeth.**
娘に仕上げ磨きをしてあげた。	**I helped her finish brushing.**
息子が自分で歯磨きできるようになった！	**He can brush his teeth on his own now!** ＊on one's own＝自力で

寝かし付け

9時ごろ、子どもたちを寝かし付けた。	**I put the kids to bed at around 9:00.** ＊put ～ to bed＝～を寝かし付ける
マーくんが寝付くまで、2時間格闘した。	**I struggled to get Ma-kun to sleep for two hours.** ＊struggle＝格闘する
子どもたちを寝かし付けていて、いつの間にか私も寝てしまった。	**I fell asleep while putting the kids to bed.** ＊fall asleep＝寝入る。fallの過去形はfell
息子は夜中に3回起きた。	**He woke up three times in the night.**
娘は11時ごろ寝て、そのまま朝の8時まで寝てくれた。	**She went to sleep at around 11:00 and didn't wake up till 8:00 in the morning.**
娘の寝付きがあまりよくなかった。	**She had a hard time falling asleep.**
チビちゃん、やっとお昼寝してくれた！	**The little one finally took a nap!** ＊nap＝昼寝
ターくんが珍しく昼寝した。	**Ta-kun slept during the day, which is unusual for him.** ＊unusual＝まれな
息子は遊び疲れたのかな？	**Maybe he was tired out from playing.** ＊tired out＝疲れ果てた
娘はあくびしていた。	**She was yawning.** ＊yawn［ヨーン］＝あくびをする
娘がパパにおやすみのキスをした。	**She kissed her dad good night.**

子どもの体調・けが （→ p. 44「体調」も参照）

今日は息子を1カ月健診に連れていった。	**I took him for his one-month checkup today.** ＊checkup＝健康診断
娘がインフルエンザの予防接種を受けた。	**She got a flu shot.** ＊flu［フルー］＝インフルエンザ　shot＝注射
息子は鼻水がひどい。	**He has a terrible runny nose.** ＊runny nose＝鼻水

今日になって娘がせきをしている。 She just started coughing roday.

息子は夜になって急に熱が出た。 At night, he suddenly came down with a fever.
＊come down with ～＝～(病気など)にかかる

娘に熱があるようだったので、病院に駆け込んだ。 It seemed like she had a fever, so I took her to the hospital in a rush.
＊in a rush＝急いで

すぐに息子を診てもらえた。 I was able to get a doctor to see him right away.
＊get ～ to ...＝(掛け合って)～に…してもらう

娘は胃腸炎にかかったみたい。 It seems she caught the stomach flu.
＊stomach flu＝胃腸炎

ユウタが床ですべって転んだ。 Yuta slipped and fell on the floor.

頭を打ったので、慌ててしまった。 He hit his head, so I was a little panicked.

大丈夫そうだけど、心配。 He seems OK, but I'm still worried.

心配で胸がはりさけそうだった。 I was so worried that I thought my heart was going to break.

娘は少し下痢気味だけど、熱もないし食欲もある。 My daughter seems to have diarrhea, but she has no fever and she still has an appetite.
＊diarrhea[ダイアリーァ]＝下痢　appetite＝食欲

胸の辺りに湿疹が出ている。 She has a rash on her chest.
＊rash＝発疹

もう少し様子を見てみよう。 I'll wait and see.

子どものこと

子どもの性格

ヨウタは私にベッタリだ。 Yota is always clinging to me.
＊cling to ～＝～にまとわり付く

娘は最近、だいぶお利口さんになった。 She's quite well behaved these days.
＊well behaved＝行儀のいい

息子はお利口さんで手がかからない。 He's a bright child. I don't have any trouble with him.
＊bright＝頭のいい

ユリは、本当にいい子。 Yuri is such a good girl.

娘は思いやりのある優しい子。	**She's a thoughtful, kind child.** ＊thoughtful＝思いやりのある
ケイタはいつも元気いっぱい。	**Keita is always full of energy.**
息子はわがままだ。	**He's selfish.**
サキは自己主張が激しい。	**Saki is quite assertive.** ＊assertive＝しっかり自己主張する
娘は人見知りが始まったみたい。	**She has started being afraid of strangers.** ＊stranger＝見知らぬ人、他人
トウマはすごくおしゃべりだ。	**Toma is very talkative.**
息子は、今日はお行儀が悪かった。	**He behaved badly today.** ＊behave＝ふるまう

似てる・似てない

目はママ似で、口元は僕似だ。	**Her eyes are like her mother's, and her mouth looks like mine.**
パパの子どものときの写真を見たら、ハヤトにそっくり！	**I saw a picture of Daddy when he was a baby — he looked just like Hayato!**
だんだんママに似てきたな。	**She's looking more and more like her mom.**
髪が天然パーマなのは、父親似だ。	**She has naturally curly hair like her dad.**

子どもへの愛情

コウタ、大好き。	**I love Kota.**
うちの子って、本当にかわいい！	**Our kids are so cute!**
やっぱり、うちの子が一番かわいい！	**Our kids are definitely the cutest!** ＊definitely＝間違いなく
食べちゃいたいくらいかわいい。	**He's the apple of my eye.** ＊apple of one's eye＝大切なもの、自慢の種
親バカかな？	**Am I too much of a doting parent?** ＊doting parent＝子煩悩の親
息子のほっぺたは柔らかくて、すべすべ。	**His cheeks are so soft and smooth.** ＊smooth［スムーズ］＝すべすべした

天使のような寝顔だ。	**He has an angelic sleeping face.** ＊angelic＝天使のような
うちの子って、もしかして天才かも？	**My child just might be a genius.**
娘には絵の才能があるのかもしれない。	**My daughter might have a gift for drawing.** ＊gift＝才能

きょうだい

息子は、生まれたばかりの妹に興味津々みたい。	**He seems to be really curious about his newborn little sister.** ＊curious＝好奇心の強い
娘は弟の頭を優しくなでてあげていた。	**She gently stroked her little brother on the head.** ＊stroke＝～をなでる
マリちゃんが生まれてから、マーくんはちょっと寂しそう。	**Ever since Mari-chan was born, Ma-kun seems a little lonely.**
マーくんのことも、もっと構ってあげなきゃ。	**I should show Ma-kun a little more affection.** ＊affection＝愛情
ミーちゃんがタイキの面倒を見てくれるから、本当に助かる。	**Mi-chan has been a big help taking care of Taiki.**
またきょうだいげんかをしていた。	**The kids fought again.** ＊fight＝けんかをする。過去形はfought［フォート］
うちの子たちは、いつも仲良く遊んでる。	**Our kids always play nicely together.**
トモは、お兄ちゃんのことを尊敬してるみたい。	**It looks like Tomo looks up to his big brother.** ＊look up to ～＝～を尊敬する

成長の記録

体の成長

息子は今日で生後１カ月。	**He's one month old today.**
息子の体重は 7.4 キロ。	**He weighs 7.4kg.** ＊weigh＝～の重さがある
娘の身長は 80.3 センチ。	**She's 80.3cm tall.**
息子は大きくなったなぁ。	**He has gotten so big.**

もう娘を片手で抱えるのは無理！	**I can't hold her in one arm anymore!** ＊hold＝〜を抱く
息子の首がすわった。	**He can now hold his head up.** ＊hold＝〜を支える
息子の首がしっかりしてきた。	**He can finally hold his head up steadily.** ＊steadily＝しっかりと
息子の歯が生えてきてる。	**His teeth are starting to grow.** ＊grow＝発達する　tooth＝歯。複数形はteeth
息子の乳歯が生えそろった。	**He has all his baby teeth now.** ＊baby tooth＝乳歯

できること

娘が初めて寝返りをうった。	**She rolled over for the first time.** ＊rolled over＝寝返りをうつ
娘が１人でお座りできるようになった。	**She can sit on her own now.** ＊on one's own＝自力で
息子は頑張ってハイハイしようとしていた。	**He tried his best to crawl.** ＊crawl＝はう
ユイトはすっかりハイハイができるようになった。	**Yuito is now able to crawl with no problem.**
ミホがつかまり立ちをした！	**Miho grabbed onto something and stood up!**
今日、ターくんが歩いた！ すごい！	**Ta-kun walked today! It was amazing!**
娘は１人遊びができるようになった。	**She can play on her own now.**
息子は「アー」とか「ウー」とか声を出すようになった。	**He can say "aah" and "ooh."**
息子は今日初めて「ママ」って言った。	**He said "mama" for the first time today.**
娘に「お名前は？」と聞くと「ちーちゃん！」と答えるようになった。	**When we ask her, "What's your name?" she can now answer, "Chi-chan!"**
リオは言葉を覚えるのが早い。	**Rio learns new words quickly.**
息子は簡単な会話ができるようになった。	**He can have a simple conversation.**

娘は自分でボタンを留められるようになった。	**She can do up her buttons on her own now.** ＊do up ～＝～(服のボタン)を留める on one's own＝自力で
息子は自分でボタンを外せるようになった。	**He can undo his buttons on his own now.** ＊undo＝～(服のボタン)を外す
娘は三輪車に乗れるようになった。	**She can ride a tricycle now.**
ナミちゃん、もう少しで自転車に乗れるようになりそう。	**I think Nami-chan will be able to ride her bike soon.** ＊bike＝自転車
子どもって、日々成長してるんだなぁ。	**Children grow a little every day.** ＊grow＝成長する
子どもたちの成長の速さに驚かされる。	**I'm surprised by how fast children grow.**
あっという間に大きくなってしまいそうだ。	**I feel like they'll be grown before we know it.** ＊grow(成長する)の過去分詞はgrown before we know it＝あっという間に

子どもの誕生日

今日はアヤナの１歳の誕生日。	**Today is Ayana's first birthday.**
みんなで集まってお祝いした。	**We all got together to celebrate.**
息子は一升餅を背負った。	**Our son carried the "isshou mochi" on his back.**
友達を呼んで誕生会をした。	**We invited friends over for his birthday party.** ＊invite ～ over＝～をこちらに招く
誕生日ケーキを焼いた。	**I baked a birthday cake for him.**
近所のケーキ屋さんに誕生日ケーキを注文した。	**I ordered a birthday cake at the nearby cake shop.** ＊nearby＝近くの　cake shop＝ケーキ店
ターくん、ろうそくの火を吹き消すのに苦労してた。	**Ta-kun was struggling to blow out the candles.** ＊blow out ～＝～を吹き消す
みんなで「ハッピーバースデー」を歌った。	**We sang "Happy Birthday" together.**
息子に誕生日カードをあげた。	**We gave him a birthday card.**

娘の誕生日プレゼントに、プリキュアのおもちゃをあげた。	**We gave her a Precure toy as a birthday gift.**
保育園で娘の誕生会をしてくれた。	**They threw her a birthday party at nursery school.** ＊throw a party＝パーティーを開く。throwの過去形はthrew［スルー］

写真・動画

公園でソウスケの写真をたくさん撮った。	**I took many pictures of Sosuke at the park.**
今日1日で100枚は撮ったかな。	**I probably took at least 100 pictures today.**
たくさんの写真を写真プリント機でプリントした。	**I printed out lots of photos with a photo printing machine.**
アプリで写真をプリント注文した。	**I ordered some photo prints with an app.**
マキは自分の写真を見るのが大好き。	**Maki likes looking at pictures of herself.**
カメラを向けると、すました顔になる。	**She puts on a straight face when she faces the camera.** ＊straight face＝まじめな顔　face＝～のほうを向く
1人目の子だから、つい写真をたくさん撮ってしまう。	**We just keep taking photos because she's our first child.**
写真スタジオで娘の写真を撮ってもらった。	**We had her pictures taken at the photo studio.**
娘はエルサの衣装を着た。	**She dressed up as Elsa.**
すごくかわいかった。	**She looked adorable.** ＊adorable［アドーラボゥ］＝かわいい、愛らしい
息子の動画を撮った。	**I took a video of him.**
息子のあんよを動画にとって両親に送った。	**I took a video of him toddling and sent it to my parents.** ＊toddle=よちよち歩く
卒園式のアルバムを作ろう。	**I'll make an album of her graduation.** ＊graduation＝卒業、卒園

26 出産・育児

ベビー用品・服

ベビー用品を表す単語

ほ乳瓶	**feeding bottle**
粉ミルク	formula
おしゃぶり	**pacifier** [パスィファイアー]
スタイ	bib
ガラガラ	**rattle**
ベビーベッド	crib
おむつ	**diaper** [ダイァパー]
紙おむつ	disposable diaper
布おむつ	**cloth diaper**
おしりふき	baby wipe
ベビーカー	**stroller**
スリング	baby sling
抱っこひも	**baby carrier**
ベビー服	baby wear / baby clothes
ベビー用品	**baby goods**
離乳食	baby food

子ども服

マキの服を何着か買った。
I bought some clothes for Maki.

去年の服は、もう入らない。
She doesn't fit her clothes from last year anymore.

リョウの好きそうな恐竜柄の服を買った。
I bought clothes with a dinosaur print that I thought Ryo would like.

あのブランドの子ども服は高くて、なかなか手が出ない。
We can't afford children's clothes from that brand.
＊can afford ～＝～(高価な物など)を持つ余裕がある

子ども服は安いもので十分。
As for children, cheap clothes do just fine.
＊as for ～＝～に関しては　do＝用を足す、間に合う

子どもはどうせすぐに大きくなっちゃうし。
They'll grow out of them soon anyway.

すぐにサイズアウトしちゃう。
The clothes will be too small before you know it.
＊before we know it＝あっという間に

マリコが子ども服のお下がりをくれた。
Mariko gave me some hand-me-down children's clothes.
＊hand-me-down＝(衣服の)お下がり

ヤマシタさんに、ミキのお下がりをあげた。
I gave Yamashita-san Miki's old clothes.

フリマアプリで中古のトレーナーを買った。	**I bought a secondhand sweatshirt on a flea market app.**
リサイクルショップで息子の服を買った。	**I bought some clothes for my son at the thrift shop.** ＊thrift［スリフト］shop＝リサイクルショップ
最近、昼間は暑くなるので息子に何を着せるか悩む。	**It gets really warm during the day these days, so it's hard to decide what to put on him.**
アサコはおばあちゃんにもらった長靴がお気に入りみたい。	**Asako seems to love the rain boots Grandma gave her.**

ベビーカー

義兄からベビーカーを譲ってもらった。	**My brother-in-law gave us their stroller.** ＊stroller＝ベビーカー
AとB、どっちのベビーカーがいいかな。	**Which stroller should we choose, A or B?**
娘はベビーカーに乗っている間はおとなしくしているので、助かる。	**I'm glad the baby stays quiet when she's in the stroller.**
ベビーカーで電車に乗るのは、気を遣っちゃう。	**I don't feel comfortable taking a train with the stroller.**
ケンはベビーカーが好きじゃないみたい。	**Ken doesn't seem to like to be on his stroller.**
ベビーカーに乗せると泣き始める。	**He starts crying when I put him in the stroller.**
雨カバーを付けるとギャン泣きする。	**When I put on the rain cover, he starts wailing.** ＊wail＝泣き叫ぶ
ベビーカーで足をバタバタするの、やめてほしい。	**I want him to stop kicking his feet in the stroller.**

絵本

寝る前に絵本を読んであげた。	**I read him a picture book at bedtime.** ＊read 〜 ...＝〜に…を読んで聞かせる
絵本を読んだら楽しそうに聞いていた。	**She was happy to listen to me read the picture book.**

好きな絵本を 2 冊選ばせてあげた。 **I let him choose two picture books.**

ルイくんは『ぐりとぐら』と『ノンタン おはよう』を選んだ。 **Rui-kun chose “Guri to Gura” and “Nontan Ohayo.”**

息子に同じ絵本を何度も読んでとせがまれる。 **He pesters me to read him the same picture book over and over again.**
＊pester ～ to ...＝～に…してとせがむ

お姉ちゃんに、お古の絵本を 10 冊もらった。 **My sister gave me ten old picture books.**

子どもとお出かけ

お出かけ

市の育児学級に参加した。 **I participated in the parenting class held by the city.** ＊hold＝～(会など)を催す

ベビーヨガの教室に参加した。 **We took a class on baby yoga.**

マモルを母に任せて外出した。 **I left Mamoru with my mother and went out.**

ママ友たちとビュッフェランチ♪ **I had a buffet lunch with my mom friends.**

息子と近所を散歩した。 **My son and I walked around the neighborhood.**

ハツネをナオコおばさんの家に連れて行った。 **I took Hatsune to Auntie Naoko’s house.**
＊auntieは、aunt(おば)の親しみを込めた言い方

サカタさん家族とキャンプに行った。 **We went camping with the Sakatas.**
＊the＋名字s＝～家の人たち

姉家族と一緒に、お弁当を持って近くの公園に行った。 **We brought our lunch to the nearby park with my older sister’s family.**

ららぽーとに子ども服を買いに行った。 **I went shopping for kids’ wear at the LaLaport.**

店員さんが息子と遊んでくれた。 **The shop staff played with him.**

ベビーチェアを用意してくれて、ありがたかった。 **I appreciated them bringing him a high chair.** ＊appreciate＝～に感謝する

電車で席を譲ってもらって、うれしかった。	**I was glad that someone offered us a seat on the train.** ＊offer ～ …＝～に…を勧める

公園デビュー

ユイと公園デビューした。	**I went to the park with Yui for the first time.**
公園にいたママさんたちと仲良くなった。	**I became friends with some playground moms.**
ママさんたちの輪に入りづらかった。	**It wasn't easy getting into the group of moms.**
ベビーカーのママさんが近くを通ったので、話しかけてみた。	**A mother with a stroller passed by, so I spoke to her.** ＊stroller＝ベビーカー　pass by＝そばを通り過ぎる
マーくんにお友達ができた。	**Ma-kun made a friend.**
小学生たちが息子をかわいがってくれた。	**The elementary school kids adored my son.** ＊adore＝～が大好きである

遊び

遊具・遊びを表す表現

ボール	**ball**
ブランコ	swing
すべり台	**slide**
シーソー	teeter-totter
登り棒	**climbing bar**
鉄棒	horizontal bar
うんてい	**monkey bars**
砂場	sandbox
ジャングルジム	**jungle gym**
かくれんぼをする	play hide-and-seek
鬼ごっこをする	**play tag**
かけっこをする	run around
キャッチボールをする	**play catch**
フリスビーをする	play frisbee
縄跳びをする	**skip rope / jump rope**
ままごと遊びをする	play house
ごっこ遊びをする	**play make-believe**
砂遊びをする	play in the sand
遊具で遊ぶ	**play on the equipment**
ブランコに乗る	play on the swing
紙飛行機を飛ばす	**fly a paper plane**
たこ揚げをする	fly a kite
しゃぼん玉を飛ばす	**blow bubbles**

外遊び

公園に遊びに行った。	**We went to the park to play.**
娘は午後、パパと公園で遊んでいた。	**She spent the afternoon playing with Daddy in the park.**
小学校の校庭開放に遊びに行った。	**The elementary school's playground was open, so we went to play.** ＊public＝一般の人々
娘はすべり台が楽しかったみたい。	**Our daughter seemed to enjoy the slide.**
ジャングルジムで遊んだ。	**We played on the jungle gym.**
アスレチックで遊んだ。	**We played on the obstacle course.** ＊obstacle［アブスタクゥ］course＝アスレチックコース
ミキちゃんとアサくんは、２人で自転車を乗り回していた。	**Miki-chan and Asa-kun were riding around on their bicycles together.**
息子は家の前で縄跳びをしていた。	**He was jumping rope in front of the house.**
娘は落ち葉をたくさん拾っていた。	**She picked up so many fallen leaves.**
また服をどろんこにした。	**Their clothes got all muddy again.** ＊muddy＝泥だらけの
ま、仕方ないか。子どもは遊ぶのが仕事だもんね。	**Oh well. A child's job is to have fun.**

家遊び

娘はたくさんお絵描きしていた。	**She drew lots of pictures.** ＊draw＝～を描く。drew［ドルー］は過去形
息子は粘土遊びをしていた。	**He played with clay.**
子どもたちと一緒に工作をした。	**I did some crafts with the kids.**
お絵描きしてもいいけど、服を汚さないでほしいな。	**Drawing is fine, but I wish she wouldn't dirty her clothes.** ＊dirty＝～を汚す
息子が私の口紅で絵を描いていた！	**He was drawing with my lipstick!**

最近、子どもたちはテレビゲームばかり。	**The kids are always playing video games these days.**
もっと外で遊んで欲しい。	**I want them to play outside more often.**
娘が私のスマホで遊んでばかりで困る。	**My daughter keeps playing with my phone. It's a little annoying.** ＊annoying＝困った
最近、私の iPhone で写真を撮るのが息子のお気に入り。	**My son enjoys taking pictures with my iPhone these days.**
息子は結構いい写真を撮るんだよなぁ。	**He actually takes pretty nice photos.**
息子にタブレットを触らせてみたら、すぐに操作に慣れてびっくり！	**I let him use my tablet and was amazed by how fast he got used to it!** ＊get used to 〜＝〜に慣れる

おもちゃ

息子に新しいおもちゃを買った。	**I bought him new toys.**
息子はトミカが大のお気に入り。	**His favorite toy is Tomica.**
娘はメルちゃんといつも一緒。	**She always has her Mell-chan doll.**
新しく買ったおもちゃ、もう飽きちゃったみたい。	**He seems to already be sick of the new toy I bought him.** ＊sick of 〜＝〜が嫌になって
せっかく買ったのに！	**I bought it specially!** ＊specially＝わざわざ
おもちゃが多過ぎて家が片付かない！	**I can't clean the house because he has so many toys!** ＊clean＝〜を片付ける
もう遊ばないおもちゃは誰かにあげよう。	**I'll give away his old toys.** ＊give away 〜＝〜を人にあげる
息子は高いおもちゃを買っても遊んでくれないんだよね。	**He won't even play with the expensive toys we buy.**
娘は手作りのおもちゃが一番楽しいみたい。	**Handmade toys seem to amuse her the most.** ＊amuse＝〜を楽しませる

息子はおばあちゃんにもらったトーマスのおもちゃが一番のお気に入り。 His favorite is the Thomas toy he got from his grandmother.

子育ての大変さ

夜泣き

最近、娘の夜泣きがひどい。 She has been crying a lot at night lately.

息子の連日の夜泣きで睡眠不足。 He cries every night, so I haven't been getting enough sleep.

昨日はナオキが夜泣きしなかったから、ぐっすり眠れた。 I slept well last night because Naoki didn't cry.

不機嫌・ぐずる

今日は息子がご機嫌ななめだった。 He wasn't in a good mood today.
＊good mood＝ご機嫌

どうあやしても、息子の機嫌は直らなかった。 No matter how hard I tried to make him happy, he was stuck in a bad mood.
＊stuck in ～＝～から抜け出せなくて　bad mood＝不機嫌

「歩きたくない」とぐずった。 He got cranky and kept saying, "I don't want to walk." ＊cranky＝気難しい

娘が電車の中でぐずって、大変だった。 It was tough that she made a terrible fuss on the train. ＊make a fuss＝ぐずる

幼稚園からの帰り道、息子は道路に寝そべってだだをこね始めた。 On the way home from preschool, he got very crabby and lay on the ground.
＊crabby＝不機嫌な
lie［ライ］＝寝そべる、横たわる。過去形はlay［レイ］

暴れるサトシを抱えて家まで戻った。 Satoshi tried to wriggle out of my arms while I carried him home.
＊wriggle＝のたうつ、もがく

娘が大泣きして大変だった。 She cried a lot. It was terrible.

息子はなかなか泣きやまなかった。 It took a long time for him to stop crying.

抱っこしたら、息子は泣きやんだ。	**I held him in my arms and he stopped crying.** ＊hold＝～を抱く。過去形はheld

イヤイヤ期・反抗期

ケンタはイヤイヤ期の真っ最中だ。	**Kenta is right in the middle of his terrible twos.** ＊in the middle of ～＝～のさなかで terrible twos＝魔の2歳（児）、イヤイヤ期
最近、ケンタがイヤイヤばかり言う。	**Kenta always says "no" these days.**
何をしても「イヤ」と言う。	**He says "no" to everything.**
娘は最近、わがままばかり。	**She has been so selfish lately.**
何を聞いても「別に」としか言わない。	**No matter what I ask, she just says "whatever."**
「クソババア」と言われた。	**He called me a "stupid hag."** ＊hag＝老婆
反抗期かな？	**I wonder if this is her rebellious phase.** ＊rebellious［レベリアス］phase＝反抗期
早く反抗期が終わってほしい。	**I hope this rebellious phase will end soon.**

育児の悩み

子育てしていると、自分の時間がほとんどない。	**When you are raising a child, you don't get much time for yourself.** ＊raise＝～を育てる
ちょっと育児疲れがたまってるかも。	**I might be getting a bit tired from parenting.** ＊parenting＝子育て
育児と仕事の両立って大変。	**It's not easy to raise a child and have a job at the same time.**
ストレスがたまりまくり。	**I'm stressed out.**
またケンに怒鳴ってしまった。反省。	**I yelled at Ken again. I shouldn't have done that.** ＊yell at ～＝～に向かって怒鳴る
イライラしない！	**I should quit being frustrated!** ＊quit＝～をやめる

できないことより、できることを数えてあげよう。	**Instead of focusing on what he can't do, I'll focus on what he can do.** ＊focus on 〜＝〜に集中する・注目する
育児ノイローゼになりそう。	**I'm going to have a nervous breakdown over child-raising.** ＊nervous breakdown＝ノイローゼ
母に育児の悩みを相談した。	**I talked to my mom about my parenting problems.**

保育園・幼稚園・おけいこ

入園準備

息子が４月から、無事に保育園に入れるといいけど。	**I hope my son can get into nursery school in April.** ＊nursery (school)＝保育園
今、近所の保育園に空きがないみたい。	**It doesn't look like the neighborhood nursery has any openings.** ＊opening＝空き、空席
保育園の待機児童問題を解決してほしい。	**I hope something is done about the waiting-list problem for nurseries.**
A 保育園は、待機児童が 20 人。	**There are 20 children on the waiting list for A Nursery School.**
B 保育園は、歩いて行くにはちょっと遠いな。	**It's a little too far to walk to B Nursery School.**
C 保育園に入れますように。	**I hope we can get into C Nursery School.**
A 幼稚園はかなり人気らしい。	**I hear A Preschool is really popular.** ＊preschool＝幼稚園
B 幼稚園は教育プログラムが充実している。	**B Preschool has an excellent education program.**
C 幼稚園に願書を提出した。	**I submitted an application for admission to C Preschool.** ＊submit＝〜を提出する
幼稚園の面接、緊張するなぁ。	**I'm really nervous about the preschool interview.**
マモルはちゃんと話せるかな。	**I wonder if Mamoru can speak properly.**

息子が希望の保育園に通えることになった！	**He got a place at the nursery school we wanted!**
C幼稚園に入れた。よかった！	**We got into C Preschool. Thank goodness!**
息子が喜んで通園してくれるといいな。	**I hope he'll enjoy going there.**
近所の保育園なのでうれしい。	**I'm glad that the nursery school is close to our house.**
入園グッズを準備しなきゃ。	**I have to get all the things he needs to start nursery school ready.** ＊幼稚園なら、nursery schoolをpreschoolに
布団カバーを手作りするのが大変！	**It's tough to make the futon cover!**
入園式に何を着ようかな。	**What should I wear to the entrance ceremony?**

保育園・幼稚園

5時ごろ、保育園のお迎えに行った。	**I picked her up from nursery school at around 5:00.** ＊pick up＝迎えに行く
ばあばがサチを幼稚園に送っていってくれた。	**Granny took Sachi to preschool.** ＊granny＝おばあちゃん
娘のお迎え時間に遅れてしまった。	**I was late picking up my daughter.**
保育園は楽しかったみたい。	**I think she had a good time at nursery school.**
いい先生たちでよかった。	**I'm glad the teachers are nice.**
6時まで預かってくれるので、本当に助かる。	**They look after children until 6 p.m., so it's a big help.** ＊look after ～＝～の世話をする
先生たちには感謝しかない。	**I can't thank the teachers enough.** ＊直訳は「先生たちに感謝しきれない」
連絡ノートを見ると、今日はいい子にしてたみたい。	**According to the daily report, he was a good boy today.**
ユウタはミキちゃんのことが好きみたい。	**It seems that Yuta likes Miki-chan.**

26 出産・育児

息子はまたマホちゃんに意地悪してた。 **He was mean to Maho-chan again.**
＊mean to ～＝～に対して意地悪い

今日は幼稚園のお遊戯会だった。 **The preschool children put on a performance today.**
＊put on ～＝～（劇など）を上演する

子どもたちは、アンパンマンの歌を歌って踊っていた。 **The kids sang and danced to an Anpanman song.**
＊to ～＝～に合わせて

みんな、ダンスが上手でびっくり。 **I was surprised by how well they danced.**

ミーちゃんは歌手になりたいんだって。 **Mi-chan said she wants to be a singer.**

おけいこ

息子にピアノを習わせてみようかな？ **I wonder if I should have him take piano lessons.**

娘に何か楽器を習わせたい。 **I want her to learn a musical instrument.**
＊musical instrument＝楽器

息子が空手を習いたいって。 **My son says he wants to learn karate.**

英語は早いうちに習わせたい。 **I want him to start learning English early on.**
＊early on＝早くから

娘をプログラミング教室に通わせることにした。 **I've decided to let her take a programming class.**
＊let ～ ...＝～に…をさせてあげる

月謝にびっくり。 **I was surprised at the lesson fee.**
＊「高い」ときにも「安い」ときにも使える

息子を水泳教室に通わせることにした。 **I've decided to have him take swimming lessons.**
＊make ～ ...＝～に（無理矢理）…させる

息子が水泳大会で１位を取った！すごい！ **He came in first place in the swimming competition! Amazing!**

水泳教室が楽しいみたいで、よかった。 **I'm glad he's enjoying swimming class.**

娘が習字教室にもう通いたくないと言い出した。 **She said that she doesn't want to go to calligraphy class anymore.**
＊calligraphy＝習字、書道

娘はピアノの練習を全然しない。 She doesn't practice playing the piano at all.

ちっとも上達しない。 She's not getting any better.
＊get better＝よりうまくなる

近ごろ、ぐんと上達してきた。 She suddenly started getting better recently.

明日は娘のピアノの発表会！ She has a piano recital tomorrow!

複数の習いごとに通っていると忙しい。 Taking several kinds of lessons at once makes us busy.

土日は習いごとで終わっちゃう。 Weekends are so busy with lessons.

興味がなさそうな習いごとはやめることにしよう。 We've decided to let her quit the lessons she isn't interested in.

就学準備

娘に受験させるべきかなぁ。 I wonder if we should have her take entrance exams.

ヨシちゃんは名門小学校を受験する。 Yoshi-chan is going to try to get into a prestigious elementary school.
＊prestigious［プリスティージャス］＝名声のある、一流の

ABC小学校は自由な教育方針だ。 ABC Elementary School has a liberal education policy.
＊liberal＝自由な

小学校は地元の公立で十分。 In my opinion, a local public elementary school is good enough.

もう小学生だなんて信じられない。 I can't believe he's already an elementary school student.

入学前に準備するものがたくさんある！ There are so many things I need to prepare before he starts school!

そろそろラン活を始めよう。 We should start researching her school backpacks.

息子のランドセルは、ばあばが買ってくれるって。 Granny says she will buy a school backpack for him.
＊granny＝おばあちゃん

出産・育児について 英語日記を書いてみよう

妊娠・出産や子育てについて、英語で書いてみましょう。

念願のおめでた！

I found out I'm pregnant! I've been waiting for this moment for a long time. I'm so happy! I couldn't help but LINE my husband about it. He sounded happy, too.

妊娠していることが判明！ずっとこの瞬間を待っていたから、本当にうれしい！思わず夫にLINEしちゃった。彼も喜んでいるようだった。

found out ～は find out ～（～だということがわかる）の過去形。I've been waiting と現在完了進行形にすることで、「ずっと～してきた」という状態の継続を表します。can't help but ～(動詞の原形)は「～せずにはいられない」という意味です。

夜泣きでクタクタ

Marina cries and wakes up every couple of hours almost every night. I'm exhausted ☹ Just sleep all night, for Pete's sake!

マリナが毎晩のように2、3時間おきに夜泣きするから、もうクタクタ☹お願いだから朝まで寝て～！

「数時間おきに」は every couple of hours、または、every few hours とします。exhausted は「クタクタの、疲れ切った」という意味。イライラしているときの「お願いだから」や「頼むから」は、for Pete's［ピーツ］sake や for Heaven's sake などと表します。

すくすく成長

I took Reika to her three-month checkup. Her doctor said she was perfectly healthy. What a relief!

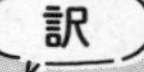

レイカを3カ月検診に連れていった。先生に健康そのものだと言われた。ホッ、よかった！

「3カ月検診」は three-month checkup。通常、「3カ月」は three months と month を複数形にしますが、「3カ月の（検診）」のように形容詞にするときは、単数形のまま three-month とハイフンでつなげます。What a relief! は「ホッとした、安心した」。

ニンジンのパンケーキ

I tried making pancakes with grated carrots mixed in. Saki said it was yummy, and she wanted another one. YEEEES!

すりおろしたニンジンを入れたパンケーキを作ってみた。サキは「おいしい、もっと」だって。大成功！

「試しに〜してみる」は try 〜ing で表します。「作ってみた」は tried baking でも OK。grated carrots の grated は「すりおろされた」、yummy は「とてもおいしい」という意味です。「大成功！」は YEEEES! と大文字で書いて、うれしい気持ちを表してみました。

27
ペット

ペット全般

ペットを表す単語

犬	**dog**	**トカゲ**	**lizard**
子犬	puppy	ヘビ	snake
猫	**cat**	**イグアナ**	**iguana**
子猫	kitten	カメレオン	chameleon
ハムスター	**hamster**	**ウーパールーパー**	**axolotl** [アクサラトォ]
モルモット	guinea [ギニ] pig	金魚	goldfish
ハリネズミ	**hedgehog**	**メダカ**	**killifish**
フェレット	ferret	グッピー	guppy
ウサギ	**rabbit**	**熱帯魚**	**tropical fish**
インコ	parakeet	クラゲ	jellyfish
文鳥	**Java sparrow**	**ヒトデ**	**star fish**
九官鳥	mynah [マイナ]	ザリガニ	crayfish
カナリア	**canary**	**クワガタ**	**stag beetle**
ジュウシマツ	Bengalese finch	カブトムシ	beetle
ヒヨコ	**chick**	**カマキリ**	**mantis**
ニワトリ	chicken	スズムシ	bell cricket
カメ	**tortoise** [トータス]	**コオロギ**	**cricket**
カエル	frog	カタツムリ	snail

ペットを飼う

何かペットを飼いたいな。 **I want to have a pet.**

犬を飼いたいな。 **I want a dog.**

公園で捨て猫を見つけた。 **I saw an abandoned cat in the park.**

＊abandoned＝捨てられた

飼いたいなぁ。	**I want to get it.**
夫を説得しなきゃ。	**I need to convince my husband.** ＊convince＝～を説得する
うちのマンションは、ペットの飼育禁止なんだよね。	**We can't keep pets in our apartment building.**
ペット飼育可の部屋に引っ越したい。	**I want to move to an apartment where I can keep pets.**
ペット可の物件は少ない。	**There aren't a lot of places that allow pets.**
週末にペットショップへ行こうっと。	**I'll go to a pet shop this weekend.**
動物病院で子犬の里親を募集していた。	**The vet was looking for a home for a puppy.** ＊vet［ヴェット］＝veterinarian（獣医）の略
カワノさんの家で子猫が生まれた。	**Kawano-san's cat had kittens.** ＊kitten＝子猫
もらい手を探しているそうだ。	**They're looking for people to adopt the kittens.** ＊adopt＝～の養い親になる
1匹譲ってもらいたいな。	**I want to get one.**
子猫を見に行ってきた。	**I went to see the kittens.**
子どもたちが保護犬を飼いたいと言っている。	**The kids say they want to get a rescue dog.** ＊rescue dog＝保護犬
市の動物保護施設へ行ってきた。	**We went to the city's animal shelter.**
週末、みんなで保護犬譲渡会に行く。	**We're going to the rescue dog adoption event this weekend.**
保護猫カフェに行った。	**I went to a rescue cat café.**
すごくかわいい猫がいた。	**There was a super cute cat there.**
出会った瞬間、運命を感じた。	**I felt it was fate from the moment we met.**

ペットの世話

ちゃんと世話できるかな?	**I wonder if I can take care of it.**
しっかり世話するぞ。	**I will take good care of it.**
かわいいけど、世話は結構大変だ。	**It's cute, but it's also a lot of work.**
コタロウを散歩に連れていった。	**I walked Kotaro.**
雨で愛犬の散歩ができなかった。	**I couldn't walk my dog because of the rain.**
コタロウを庭に出してやった。	**I let Kotaro out in the yard.**
コタロウをお風呂に入れた。	**I gave Kotaro a bath.**
モモのつめを切った。	**I clipped Momo's nails.** ＊clip one's nails＝～のつめを切る
コタロウを犬の美容室に連れていった。	**I took Kotaro to the grooming salon.** ＊grooming＝グルーミング、ペットの手入れ
コタロウのグルーミングをしてもらった。	**I had Kotaro groomed.** ＊「ブラッシング」ならgroomedをbrushedに
家じゅう毛だらけだ!	**The house is covered in fur!**
6時に夕飯をあげた。	**I gave him his dinner at 6:00.**
コタロウは喜んで食べていた。	**Kotaro was happy with his food.**
新しいえさは、あまり好きじゃないみたい。	**He doesn't seem to like the new food.**
モモにおやつをあげた。	**I gave Momo a snack.**
袋を開けるやいなや、駆け寄ってきた。	**As soon as I opened the bag, she came running.**
無我夢中で食べていた。	**She lost herself in eating.** ＊lose oneself in ～ing＝夢中で～する
あのおやつが大好物みたい。	**It looks like she loves that snack.**

ペットのしつけ

しっかりしつけなきゃ。	**I have to train him well.** ＊train＝～をしつける

どうしたら、うまくしつけられるかな。	**How should I train him?**
コタロウはまだ粗相が多い。	**Kotaro still has a lot of toilet accidents.** ＊toilet accident＝粗相
早くトイレを覚えてほしい。	**I hope he's toilet trained soon.** ＊toilet train＝～にトイレのしつけをする
もう少しでトイレを覚えてくれそう。	**He's almost fully toilet trained.**
トイレのしつけはバッチリ。	**He's fully toilet trained.**
人間をかまないように教えなきゃ。	**I have to teach him not to bite people.** ＊bite＝～をかむ

ペットとの生活

モモは今日で３歳になった。	**Momo turned three today.** ＊turn＝～になる
コタロウも今年で10歳か。	**Kotaro is turning ten this year.**
モモは家族の一員だ。	**Momo is a member of our family.**
コタロウといると癒やされるなぁ。	**Being with Kotaro relaxes me.**
私は断然、猫派。	**I'm definitely a cat person.** ＊「犬派」なら、dog personに
モモが熟睡していた。	**Momo was deep asleep.** ＊deep asleep＝熟睡して
モモが寝言を言っていた。	**Momo was talking in her sleep.**
猫も寝言を言うんだなぁ。	**I didn't know cats talk in their sleep, too.**
コタロウはドライブが好きだ。	**Kotaro likes riding in the car.**
犬と一緒に泊まれるホテルを見つけた。	**I found a dog-friendly hotel.**
留守中はペットシッターに来てもらった。	**I had a pet sitter come while I was out.**
ペット見守りカメラを買おうかな。	**I'm thinking about getting a pet camera.**
遠隔カメラで留守中のモモの様子を見た。	**I used a remote camera to see how Momo was doing.**

ぐっすり寝ていた。 **She was sound asleep.**
＊sound asleep＝よく眠って

ペットの出産

今朝、リコが５匹子犬を産んだ。 **Riko had five puppies this morning.**

出産は感動的だった。 **The birth was really moving.**
＊moving＝感動的な

出産は大変だった。 **The birth was really difficult.**

頑張ったね、リコ！ **Good job, Riko!**

子猫って、すごくかわいい。 **Kittens are so cute.**

まだ目が見えていないみたい。 **They still can't see.**

よちよち歩きをしていた。 **They toddled along.** ＊toddle＝よちよち歩く

子犬のもらい手を探さなきゃ。 **We have to look for people to adopt the puppies.** ＊adopt＝～の養い親になる

オオタニさんが１匹もらってくれることになった。 **Ms. Otani told me that she wants one.**

ペットの病気・トラブル

最近、元気がない。 **He doesn't seem energetic these days.** ＊energetic＝元気いっぱいの

病気かな？ **I wonder if he's sick.**

最近、食欲がない。 **He doesn't have an appetite these days.** ＊appetite［アパタイト］＝食欲

最近、脚が弱ってきたようだ。 **His legs seem weaker these days.**

最近、寝てばかりいる。 **She sleeps all day these days.**

視力が落ちてきたみたい。 **His eyesight has declined.**
＊eyesight＝視力　decline＝衰える、低下する

元気になってきた。 **She's getting better.**

食欲が出てきた。 **She's eating well now.**

早くよくなるといいけど。 **I hope he gets better soon.**

モモががんになった。 **Momo got cancer.** ＊cancer＝がん

痛がっているのがわかる。 **I can tell she's in pain.**
＊can tell ～＝～がわかる　in pain＝痛む

見ていてつらい。 **I can't bear seeing it.** ＊bear＝～に耐える

交通事故に遭ってしまった。 **He was involved in a car accident.**
＊involved in ～＝～に巻き込まれる

左の後ろ脚を骨折した。 **His left hind leg got broken.**
＊hind leg＝後ろ脚

行方不明になった。 **We don't know where she is.**

もう5日も経つのにまだ見つからない。 **It's already been 5 days and we still haven't found him.**

近所に迷い猫の貼り紙をした。 **I put up lost cat posters around the neighborhood.**

無事に戻ってきた！ よかった！ **She's back safe and sound! Thank goodness!**
＊safe and sound＝無事に
Thank goodness!＝やれやれ助かった、ありがたい

動物病院

動物病院に連れていったほうがいいかなぁ。 **Maybe I should take him to the vet's.**
＊vet［ヴェット］＝veterinarian（獣医）の略。vet'sはvet's officeを表す

そろそろ去勢手術をしないと。 **It's time we had him neutered.**
＊have ～ neutered＝～に去勢手術をする

そろそろ避妊手術をしないと。 **It's time we had her spayed.**
＊have ～ spayed＝～に避妊手術をする

ワクチンを受けさせなきゃ。 **We have to take her for her shot.**
＊shot＝注射

午後、モモを動物病院へ連れていった。 **I took Momo to the vet's in the afternoon.**

コタロウはおとなしくしていた。 **Kotaro was a good boy.**

かなり暴れて大変だった。 **He was restless and hard to handle.**
＊restless＝絶えず動いている　handle＝～を扱う

３人がかりでモモを押さえた。 **Three people had to hold Momo down.**

コタロウに健康診断を受けさせた。	**We had a physical exam done on Kotaro.** ＊physical exam＝身体検査
血液検査をした。	**They did a blood test.**
注射を打ってもらった。	**He got an injection.** ＊injection＝注射
薬をもらってきた。	**He got some medicine.**
保険がきかないので、かなり高くついた。	**Our insurance doesn't cover it, so it was quite expensive.** ＊cover＝～をまかなう
ペット保険に入っておこう。	**We should sign up for pet insurance.**

ペットとの別れ

今日、モモが息を引き取った。	**Momo died today.** ＊動物にはdie（死ぬ）を、人にはpass away（亡くなる、他界する）を用いることが多い
ペットの葬儀社さんに来てもらった。	**We called a pet funeral director.** ＊funeral director＝葬儀社の人
お寺で埋葬してもらった。	**The temple buried her for us.** ＊bury［ベリー］＝～を埋葬する
棺おけに、好きだったおもちゃを入れた。	**We put her favorite toy in her casket.** ＊casket＝棺、ひつぎ
モモといた日々は、本当に楽しかった。	**We really enjoyed the time we shared with Momo.**
ありがとう、モモ。	**Thank you, Momo.**
モモがいないなんて、信じられない。	**I can't believe that Momo is not around anymore.** ＊around＝存在して
つらくて耐えられない。	**It's so hard to take it.** ＊take it＝耐える
気を落とさずに、頑張らなきゃ。	**I have to take heart and be strong.** ＊take heart＝気を取り直す、元気を出す
モモのことはずっと忘れない。	**I'll never forget Momo.**
リビングにモモの写真を飾った。	**We put Momo's picture in the living room.**

犬

犬の種類を表す単語

秋田犬	Akita dog
アフガンハウンド	Afghan Hound
コーギー	Corgi
ゴールデンリトリーバー	Golden Retriever
コリー	Collie
シーズー	Shih Tzu
シェパード	German Shepherd
柴犬	Shiba (Inu)
シベリアンハスキー	Siberian Husky
スピッツ	Spitz
セントバーナード	Saint Bernard
ダックスフント	Dachshund
ダルメシアン	Dalmatian
チワワ	Chihuahua
土佐犬	Tosa dog
ドーベルマン	Doberman
パグ	Pug
パピヨン	Papillion
ビーグル	Beagle
プードル	Poodle
トイプードル	Toy Poodle
ブルドッグ	Bulldog
ポメラニアン	Pomeranian
マルチーズ	Maltese (dog)
ヨークシャーテリア	Yorkshire Terrier
ラブラドールリトリーバー	Labrador Retriever
雑種	mixed breed

トイプードルを飼いたい。 **I want a Toy poodle.**

やっぱり柴犬が一番！ **Shiba dogs are the best!**

ジョニーと名付けた。 **I named him Johnny.**

雑種だ。 **He's a mixed breed.** ＊mixed breed＝雑種

血統書付きだ。 **He's a pedigree dog.**
＊pedigree＝証明書付きの

犬小屋を作った。 **I made a dog house for him.**

犬って、人なつこいから好き。 **I like dogs because they're friendly.**

ジョニーはしっぽを振っていた。 **Johnny was wagging his tail.**
＊wag＝～(しっぽ)を振る　tail＝しっぽ

ジョニーを散歩に連れていった。 **I walked Johnny.**
＊walk＝～(犬など)を散歩させる

ドッグランで遊ばせた。 **We let him play in the dog run.**

うれしそうに走り回っていた。 **He was running around happily.**

ボール遊びをした。	**We played with a ball.**
ジョニーがよくほえるので困った。	**Johnny's barking was a big problem.** ＊bark＝ほえる
ムダぼえをやめさせたい。	**I want to teach him not to bark so much.**
ジョニーに「お手」を教えた。	**I taught Johnny to shake hands.** ＊shake hands＝握手する、お手をする
ジョニーは「おすわり」ができるようになった。	**Johnny has learned to sit.**
まだ「伏せ」ができない。	**He still can't lie down on command.** ＊on command＝命令で

猫

猫の種類を表す単語

アメリカンショートヘア	**American Shorthair**
アビシニアン	Abyssinian
アンゴラ	**Angora**
シャム	Siamese
スコティッシュフォールド	**Scottish Fold**
バーミーズ	Burmese
バリニーズ	**Balinese**
ヒマラヤン	Himalayan
ブリティッシュショートヘア	**British Shorthair**
ペルシャ	Persian
ベンガル	**Bengal**
マンクス	Manx
マンチカン	**Munchkin**
メインクーン	Maine Coon
ロシアンブルー	**Russian Blue**
三毛猫	calico［キャリコゥ］
黒猫	**black cat**
トラ猫	tabby
キジ猫	**brown tabby**
サバ猫	gray tabby
雑種	**mixed breed**

猫って本当に気まぐれだ。	**Cats are really moody.** ＊moody＝気まぐれな
猫は自由きままなところが好き。	**I like the way cats are free-spirited.** ＊free-spirited＝自由気ままな
ネズミのおもちゃが好きみたい。	**She seems to like her mouse toy.**
キャットフードがなくなりそうだ。	**I'm running out of cat food.** ＊run out of ～＝～がなくなる、～を切らす

かつお節を少しあげた。 **I gave her some bonito shavings.**
＊bonito shavings＝かつお節

魚を料理していたら、モモが寄ってきた。 **Momo came into the kitchen when I was cooking fish.**

明日はトイレの砂を買ってこよう。 **I'll get her litter tomorrow.**
＊litter＝(猫のトイレの)砂

ちゃんとつめとぎ器でつめをとぐから感心。 **I'm impressed that she uses the claw sharpener.**
＊claw sharpener＝つめとぎ器

カーテンをボロボロにされた（泣）。 **My cat tore up my curtains. (Boo-hoo)**
＊tear[テァ] up ～＝～を破る。tearの過去形はtore

あんなに高い場所に上れるなんて。 **How does she get up so high?**

ゆうべはモモがベッドの中に入ってきた。 **Momo climbed into my bed last night.**
＊climb into ～＝～にもぐり込む

そのほかのペット

今日からハムスターを飼い始めた。 **I got a hamster today.**

滑車をぐるぐる回していた。 **It was turning its wheel round and round.**
＊round and round＝ぐるぐると

えさを食べる様子がかわいらしい。 **It looks cute when it's eating.**

インコって飼いやすいのかな？ **I wonder if parakeets are easy to take care of.**
＊parakeet[パラキート]＝インコ

縁日の金魚すくいで、金魚を取ってきた。 **I got a goldfish when I tried goldfish scooping at the fair.**
＊scoop＝～をすくう　fair＝縁日

大きな水槽が欲しいな。 **I want a big aquarium.**
＊aquarium[アクウェアリアム]＝水槽

すっかり熱帯魚にはまってしまった。 **I'm really into tropical fish.**
＊be into ～＝～に熱中する・はまる

ザリガニを２匹捕ってきた。 **We caught two crayfish.**
＊crayfish＝ザリガニ

コウタがカブトムシを捕ってきた。 **Kouta caught a beetle.**
＊beetle＝カブトムシ

ペットについて

英語日記を書いてみよう

ペットとの生活について、英語で書いてみましょう。

子犬をもらってきた

Emi's dog, Maru-chan, had five puppies. I got one of them and named her Pon-chan. She's so cuddly!

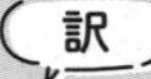

エミさん家のマルちゃんが子犬を5匹産んだので、1匹もらってきてポンちゃんと名付けた。抱き締めたいくらい、かわいい！

puppy は「子犬」のこと。ちなみに、「子猫」は kitten です。「～を…と名付ける」は、name ～ ... で表しましょう。cuddly は「抱き締めたいほどかわいい」。She's so cute. や She's so adorable. としてもいいですね。adorable は「愛らしい」の意味です。

捨て猫

I found an abandoned cat on the way home from school. As soon as I got home, I asked my mom if we could keep it. As I expected, she said no.

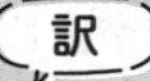

学校の帰りに捨て猫を見つけた。家に帰ってすぐ、お母さんに飼ってもいいか聞いてみたけど、やっぱりダメだって。

「捨て猫」は abandoned cat。on the way home from school は「学校の帰りに」。ask ～（人）if ...（文）は、「…かどうか～に尋ねる」という意味の表現です。As I expected は「予想していた通り」が直訳で、ここでは「やっぱり」といったニュアンスです。

ハムスターのハムちゃん

Hamu-chan is getting used to playing with me. He likes turning the wheel round and round. He's really fun to watch.

ハムちゃんは、私と遊ぶのにだいぶ慣れてきた。滑車の上でぐるぐる回るのが好きみたい。見ていて飽きない。

get used to ～は「～（すること）に慣れる」。すでに慣れている場合は、be used to ～（～に慣れている）を使います。いずれも、「～」には名詞または動詞の -ing 形が入ります。「見ていて飽きない」は、fun to watch（見るのが楽しい）と表しました。

リキとの別れ

Riki died of old age today. It's too sad. I still can't stop crying. His last weak howl sounded like he was saying thank you. No, thank YOU, Riki.

今日、リキが老衰で息を引き取った。悲し過ぎて、今でも涙が止まらない。最後の弱々しい遠吠えは、「ありがとう」と言っているかのようだった。ううん、お礼を言うのは私だよ、リキ。

「老衰で死ぬ」は die of old age。「（犬やオオカミの）遠吠え」は howl［ハウォ］と言います。thank YOU と YOU を大文字で強調することで、「お礼を言うのはこちらのほうだ」や「こちらこそ、ありがとう」というニュアンスになります。

28 パソコン・ネット

パソコン

パソコン・ネットにまつわる表現

パソコン	computer / PC	USB	USB
デスクトップパソコン	desktop computer / desktop PC	USB ドライブ	USB drive
ノートパソコン	laptop	電源アダプター	power adapter
タブレット	tablet	～を圧縮する	compress
iPad	iPad	～を解凍する	decompress
スマートフォン	smartphone	ウイルス	virus［ヴァイラス］
フリーズする	freeze	ウイルスソフト	antivirus software
～を再起動する	restart ～ / reboot ～	ウイルスに感染する	have a virus
～をインストールする	install ～	ソフトをバージョンアップする	upgrade the software
～をアンインストールする	uninstall ～	インターネット	the Internet
ログインする	log in	オンラインで	online
ログアウトする	log out	サーバー	server
～を終了する	shut down ～	LAN ケーブル	LAN cable
～を強制終了する	force ～ to shutdown	Wi-Fi	Wi-Fi
モニター	monitor	ウェブサイト	website
マウス	mouse	ブログ	blog
キーボード	keyboard	SNS	social media
テンキー	numerical keypad	アプリ	app
外付け HDD	external HDD		

パソコンを買う

新しいパソコンを買った。　**I bought a new computer.**

＊computerは、PCとしてもOK

パソコンを買い替えたい。　**I want to get a new computer.**

NEC か富士通のどちらかを買おうと思う。	**I think I'll buy either an NEC or a Fujitsu.**
昔に比べると、パソコンはずいぶん安くなった。	**Computers are much cheaper now than they were in the past.**
最近のパソコンは小さいなぁ。	**Computers are really small these days.**
デスクトップとノートパソコン、どちらにしよう？	**Which should I get, a desktop or a laptop?** ＊laptop＝ノートパソコン
ノートパソコンがあれば、どこでも仕事ができる。	**If I have a laptop, I can work anywhere.**
持ち歩かないから、デスクトップでいいのかも。	**I think I should get a desktop because I don't need to carry it around.**
タブレットを買うことにした。	**I decided to buy a tablet.**
iPad があれば十分。	**An iPad will do for me.**
新しいパソコンは、とても使いやすい。	**My new PC is really easy to use.**
軽いので、持ち運びが苦にならない。	**It's light, so carrying it won't be a problem.**
バッテリーが長時間もつのはうれしい！	**This long-lasting battery is great!** ＊long-lasting＝長持ちする
大きめのモニターを買った。	**I bought a large monitor.**

設定・カスタマイズ

前のパソコンからデータを移行した。	**I transferred data from my old computer.** ＊transfer＝～(データ)を転送する・移す
パソコンの設定に時間がかかった。	**It took a lot of time to set up my computer.**
パソコンの設定に苦労した。	**I struggled with the computer settings.** ＊struggle with ～＝～と格闘する
設定は一瞬で終わった。	**I finished setting it up in an instant.** ＊in an instant＝一瞬のうちに

オンラインのマニュアルに従ったら、簡単に設定できた。	**It was easy to set up my computer when I followed the online manual.**
カスタマーサービスの人が来て、パソコンの設定をしてくれた。	**A customer service employee came to set up my computer.** ＊employee＝従業員

パソコンを使う

起動した。	**I turned it on.**
初期化した。	**I initialized it.** ＊initialize＝〜を初期化する
終了した。	**I shut it down.**
強制終了した。	**I forced it to shutdown.** ＊force 〜 to shutdown＝〜を強制終了する
ソフトをインストールした。	**I installed software.** ＊アプリの場合は、softwareをappに
ウイルスソフトを入れた。	**I installed antivirus software.** ＊antivirus［アンタイヴァイラス］＝ウイルス対策の
念のため、データのバックアップを取っておいた。	**I backed up my data just in case.** ＊just in case＝念のため
3時間ほど、パソコンで作業した。	**I worked on my computer for about three hours.**
やっとエクセルを使えるようになってきた。	**I'm finally getting used to Excel.** ＊get used to 〜＝〜に慣れる
パワーポイントって苦手。	**I'm not good at using PowerPoint.**
ファイルを圧縮した。	**I compressed the file.** ＊compress＝〜を圧縮する
お父さんがパソコン教室に通い始めた。	**Dad started taking PC lessons.**

印刷・スキャン

レストランまでの地図を印刷した。	**I printed out the map to the restaurant.**
そろそろインクを買っておかなきゃ。	**I'll have to buy ink soon.**

年賀状を印刷した。	I printed out my New Year's greeting cards.
宛名を印刷した。	I printed out the addresses.
箱根で撮った写真を印刷した。	I printed out the pictures I took in Hakone.
プリンターがまた紙詰まりした。	My printer got jammed again. *get jammed＝詰まる
マサシが描いた絵をスキャンした。	I scanned Masashi's drawing. *drawing＝絵、線画

パソコンのトラブル

最近、パソコンの調子が悪い。	My computer has been acting up lately. *act up＝(機械などが)調子が狂う
動作が遅い。	It's slow.
頻繁にフリーズするようになった。	It has been freezing a lot. *freeze＝フリーズする
フリーズしてしまった。	It's frozen. *frozen＝フリーズした
最近、パソコンの立ち上がりが遅い。	It takes a long time to boot these days. *boot＝起動する
起動しなくなってしまった。	It won't start.
買ったばかりなのに、壊れるなんて。	How can it be broken when I've just bought it?
買ってから4年だから、仕方ないか。	I bought it four years ago, so I guess it can't be helped.
HDDの容量がいっぱいだ。	My HDD is full.
パソコンにコーヒーをこぼしちゃった！	I spilled coffee on my computer!
大事なデータが消えてしまった。	I lost important data. *lose[ルーズ]＝～を失う。過去形はlost
データが全部消えちゃった。最悪！	I've lost all my data! This is terrible!
2時間作業したデータが消えた。	Two hours' worth of data disappeared. *worth＝価値

なんでバックアップを取っておかなかったんだ！	**Why didn't I back it up!**
バックアップを取っておいたから、セーフ！	**I backed it up, so it's okay!**
クラウド上にデータを保存しておいて、よかった。	**I'm glad I saved it to the cloud.**
ウイルスに感染したかも。	**It might have a virus.** ＊virus［ヴァイラス］＝ウイルス

パソコンの修理

修理に出そう。	**I'll take it to be fixed.** ＊fix＝～を修理する
パソコンを修理に出した。	**I took my computer for repairs.** ＊repair＝修理
初期不良だった。	**It had an initial defect.** ＊defect＝欠陥
修理には2週間ほどかかるらしい。	**They said it would take about two weeks to fix it.**
パソコンが修理から戻ってきた。	**My computer is back from being repaired.**
部品を交換する必要があったらしい。	**They said they had to replace the parts.** ＊replace＝～を交換する
修理センターの対応がよかった。	**The repair center staff were nice and helpful.**
保証期間中だったので、修理代は無料だった。	**It was within the warranty period, so it was free.** ＊warranty＝保証　period＝期間
新品と交換してくれた。	**They exchanged it for a new one.**
修理は有償だった。	**I had to pay for repairs.**
修理に最大5万円かかるらしい。	**They said that it would cost up to 50,000 yen for repairs.** ＊up to ～＝～に至るまで
それなら新しいのに買い替えようっと。	**If that's the case, I might as well buy a new one.** ＊might as well ～＝～するのがよさそうだ

インターネット

インターネット全般

1時間ほどネットした。	**I was online for about an hour.**
ニュースサイトをざっとチェックした。	**I skimmed through the news websites.** ＊skim＝～をざっと読む
海外のニュースサイトを読んで、英語の勉強をした。	**I practiced my English by reading foreign news websites.**
オンラインで本を注文した。	**I ordered a book online.**
ネットでYOASOBIの新曲を聞いた。	**I listened to YOASOBI's new song online.**
夫はネット中毒だ。	**My husband is addicted to the Internet.** ＊addicted to ～＝～中毒で
ケンジは、暇さえあればネットを見ている。	**Kenji surfs the Internet whenever he has free time.** ＊surf＝～(ウェブサイト)を次々と見て回る
Wi-Fiにしてよかった。	**I'm glad I have Wi-Fi now.**
ネット環境がよくない。	**I have a bad Internet connection.**
ネットにつながらなくなってしまった。	**I lost my Internet connection.** ＊connection＝接続
原因がわからなかった。	**I couldn't figure out why.** ＊figure out ～＝～がわかる

ネット検索

ネットで調べ物をした。	**I did some research online.**
英単語をググった。	**I googled an English word.** ＊google＝グーグルで～を検索する
例文を検索した。	**I searched for some example sentences.**
ネットでイタリアンのお店を検索した。	**I looked up Italian restaurants on the Internet.** ＊look up ～＝～を調べる

口コミを見て、評判のいいお店を探した。	**I looked for restaurants with good reviews.**
グーグルマップって便利だな。	**Google Maps is really useful.**
自分の家の画像が見えちゃうのは、ちょっと怖い。	**It's a little scary that everyone can see an image of my house.**
ネットで、あのロボット掃除機の最安値がいくらか調べた。	**I checked online to find the lowest price of that robot vacuum.**

AI

DeepLでドイツ語から日本語に翻訳した。	**I used DeepL to translate from German to Japanese.**
だいたいの意味がわかった。	**I understood most of it.**
AI翻訳の性能、どんどん上がってる。	**The performance of AI translation is getting better and better.**
チャットGPTに自分のことを質問したら、笑える回答だった。	**I asked Chat GPT about myself and the answer was funny.**
チャットGPTに観光PR文を考えてもらったら、素晴らしいのができた。	**I had Chat GPT write a tourism promotion. It turned out great.**

ネットショッピング （→ p. 318「通販・ネットショッピング」を参照）

フリマアプリ・ネットオークション

もう着ない服をフリマアプリに出した。	**I put the clothes I don't wear anymore on a flea market app.**
高値では売れないけど、捨てるよりはいい。	**I won't get much money for them, but it's better than throwing them out.** ＊throw out ～＝～を処分する
4000円で売れた。	**I sold it for 4,000 yen.**
値下げ交渉をされた。ま、いっか。	**They asked for a lower price. Oh well.** ＊相手が1人でも、Theyを使ってよい
売れたお金で何か買おうっと。	**I'll buy something with the money I made.**

フリマアプリでバッグを買った。	**I bought a bag on a flea market app.**
値下げしてもらえた。やった！	**They lowered the price for me. Yay!**
ネットオークションでカバンを買った。	**I bought a bag in an online auction.**
落札金額は 9200 円。	**The highest bid was 9,200 yen.** ＊bid＝入札
ライバルが多くて落札できなかった。	**There were many bidders, so I couldn't bid successfully.** ＊bidder＝入札者
2 人掛けソファをネットオークションに出した。	**I put my love seat up for auction online.** ＊put up 〜＝〜を売りに出す　love seat＝2人掛けソファ
高値で売れるといいな。	**I hope it goes for a high price.** ＊go for 〜＝〜（の値）で売れる
やった！ 1 万 3000 円で売れた！	**Yay! I sold it for 13,000 yen!**
買い手がつかなかった。ちぇっ！	**I couldn't get a buyer. Darn it!** ＊Darn it!＝ちぇっ！、もう！

ブログ

彼女のブログは本当に面白い。	**Her blog is really interesting.**
留学している人のブログを見て回った。	**I looked at blogs written by people studying abroad.**
ブログを始めようかな？	**I'm thinking of starting a blog.**
ブログを開設した。	**I set up a blog.**
英語で書こう。	**I'll write it in English.**
長く続けるように頑張ろう。	**I'll do my best to stick with it for a long time.** ＊stick with 〜＝〜を続ける
なるべく毎日、投稿しよう。	**I'll try to post something new every day.** ＊post＝〜を投稿する
ブログを更新した。	**I updated my blog.**
温泉に行ったときのことをブログに書いた。	**I blogged about my trip to a hot spring.** ＊ここでのblogは、「ブログを書く」という意味の動詞

写真を何枚かアップした。	**I posted several photos.**
ブログにコメントが付いていた。	**There were comments on my blog.**
彼のブログにコメントを書いた。	**I posted a comment on his blog.**
コメントにレスを付けた。	**I responded to the comment.**
ブログにネガティブなコメントがたくさん来た。	**My blog got a lot of negative comments.** ＊negative＝否定の、反対の
ブログを閉鎖した。	**I shut down my blog.** ＊shut down ～＝～を閉鎖する。shutは過去形もshut

ビデオ通話 （→ p. 197「ビデオ通話」を参照）

SNS

SNSにまつわる表現

～のアカウントを作成する	open a/an ～ account	ダイレクトメッセージを送る	DM ～ / send a DM to ～
～を投稿する	post ～	～をブロックする	block ～
～にリプライする	reply to ～	～をリストに加える	add ～ to the list
～をリツイートする	retweet ～ / RT ～	～をブックマークする	bookmark ～
～をリポストする	repost ～	～に「いいね」する	like ～
フォロワー	follower	「いいね」の数	the number of likes
フォロワー数	the number of followers	ハッシュタグ	hashtag
～をフォローする	follow ～	認証マーク	verification badge
～にフォローされる	～ follow me		
～のフォローを外す	unfollow ～		

X（ツイッター）

ツイッターに登録した。	**I signed up for Twitter.** ＊sign up for ～＝～に登録する　TwitterはXでもOK
最近、ツイッターにハマってる。	**I'm into Twitter these days.** ＊into ～＝～に夢中になって
ツイッターをやっている人は多い。	**Lots of people are using Twitter.**
電車の中でツイッターをチェックした。	**I checked Twitter on the train.**

ツイッターは見るだけで、自分ではつぶやかない。	**I just look at Twitter; I don't tweet anything myself.**
災害や事故の情報は、テレビのニュースよりツイッターが速いかも。	**It's probably faster to get information about disasters or incidents via Twitter rather than TV news.** ＊via〜＝〜を用いて
ジュンさんのツイートはいつも面白い。	**Jun's tweets are always interesting.** ＊tweetsはposts（投稿）としてもOK
ツイッターでシャキーラをフォローしている。	**I'm following Shakira on Twitter.**
アリヨシさんからリプライをもらって興奮！	**I was so excited when Ariyoshi-san replied to me!**
私のつぶやきが100回以上RTされた。	**One of my tweets has been retweeted over 100 times.**
今日はたくさんリプライが来た。	**I had many replies today.**
loveEngさんにダイレクトメッセージを送った。	**I DM-ed loveEng.** ＊DM＝DM（ダイレクトメッセージ）を送る
Allieさんからダイレクトメッセージが届いた。	**I got a DM from Allie.**
1日1回は英語でツイートしよう。	**I'll tweet in English at least once a day.** ＊tweetはpost（投稿する）としてもOK
英語の280字って、結構少ないんだなぁ。	**280 characters in English really aren't much.** ＊character＝文字
海外の人と英語でやりとりするのは楽しいな。	**Tweeting in English with people from other countries is fun.**
海外の友達ができた！	**I made foreign friends!**
Craigさんの英語ツイートってわかりやすい。	**Craig's tweets in English are easy to understand.**

そのほかのSNS

話題のパフェ、食べる前にインスタ用の写真を撮ろう。
I'll make sure to take a photo of the famous parfait for Instagram before I eat it.

アキちゃん、すごく映(ば)える画像をアップしてた。
Aki-chan posted a really nice photo.

ミラの写真はいつもおしゃれだな〜。
Mila's photos are always so stylish.

インスタをコーデの参考にしてる。
I use Instagram for outfit inspiration. ＊inspiration＝ひらめき、発想の源

アプリで加工した写真をアップした。
I uploaded a photo I edited with an app. ＊edit＝編集する

インスタでつながってる人が増えてきた。
I'm connected with more people via Instagram. ＊via 〜＝〜によって

SNS で知り合った人とリアルで会った。
I met someone from online in person. ＊in person＝直接

最初は緊張したけど、いい人だった。
I was nervous at first, but she was nice.

推しの話で盛り上がった。
We had fun talking about our faves. ＊fave［フェイヴ］＝お気に入り、推し

京都旅行の写真をフェイスブックにアップした。
I uploaded photos from my trip to Kyoto on Facebook. ＊upload＝〜をアップロードする

小学校時代の同級生とフェイスブックでつながった。
I reconnected with an elementary school classmate on Facebook. ＊reconnect with 〜＝〜と再びつながる

フェイスブックを通じて、昔の友人たちとどんどんつながっていく。
I've gotten in touch with many old friends on Facebook. ＊get in touch with 〜＝〜と連絡を取る

久しぶりに連絡が取れて、うれしいな。
I'm happy that I could get in touch with them after so long.

旅先で知り合った人とフェイスブックでつながった。
I became Facebook friends with someone I met on a trip.

友達の近況がわかるのは楽しい。
It's fun knowing what your friends are up to. ＊up to 〜＝〜をして

フェイスブックに登録したものの、使い方がよくわからない。	**I got a Facebook account, but I don't know how to use it.**
上司からフェイスブックの友達リクエストがきた。どうしよう？	**My boss sent me a friend request on Facebook. What should I do?**

動画共有サービス

YouTube で BTS の動画を見た。	**I watched BTS videos on YouTube.**
ヒカキンの YouTube 動画を見まくった。	**I watched so many Hikakin videos on YouTube.**
ポメロンは、最近人気の YouTuber。	**Pomeron is a recent popular YouTuber.**
ユウキにオススメされた。	**Yuuki recommended it to me.**
ロンの YouTube、英語の発音の参考になる。	**I can learn a lot about English pronunciation from Ron's YouTube.**
YouTube を見ていると時間があっという間だ。	**Time flies by when you watch YouTube.**
電車の中でずっと TikTok の動画を見てた。	**I kept watching TikTok videos on the train.**
子犬の動画がめちゃくちゃかわいかった。	**The puppy video was so cute.**
ヒカルの「踊ってみた」動画、すごいクオリティーだった！	**Hikaru's copy dance video was really good!**
キャッチャーズの動画、いつも面白過ぎる。	**Catchers' videos are always so funny.**
TikTok 用にみんなで踊って動画を撮った。	**We took a video of us dancing for TikTok.**
TikTok に動画をアップした。	**I uploaded a video to TikTok.**
たくさんコメントが付いてうれしい。	**I'm happy it got so many comments.**
YouTube で生配信した。	**I did a livestream on YouTube.**

息子が将来 YouTuber になりたいらしい。	**My son seems to want to be a YouTuber in the future.**

SNS のトラブル

彼とツイッター上で口論になった。	**I got into a fight with him on Twitter.**
文字でのやりとりって難しい。	**It's difficult to communicate with just text.**
ツイートが炎上しちゃった。	**My tweet blew up.** ＊blow up＝(ネット上で)炎上する。blewはblowの過去形
私の書き方がまずかったかも。	**Maybe I worded it badly.** ＊word＝～を言葉で表す
誤解を招く書き方だった。	**The way I wrote it invited misunderstandings.**
見当違いなリプライばかり来て、うんざり。	**I'm sick of all these off-topic replies.** ＊off-topic＝話題から外れた
変な DM が来て、嫌な気分になった。	**I got a weird DM that made me uncomfortable.** ＊weird[ウィアード]＝奇妙な
性的な DM が来た。最悪。	**I got a sexual DM. Gross.** ＊gross[グロウス]＝気持ち悪い
彼のフォローを外した。	**I unfollowed him.**
彼女をブロックした。	**I blocked her.**
フェイクニュースをリツイートしちゃった。	**I accidentally retweeted some fake news.**
ちゃんと事実を調べる癖をつけよう。	**I need to get into the habit of fact checking things.** ＊habit＝癖、習慣
デマやフェイクニュースには気を付けなくちゃ。	**We have to be careful of misinformation and fake news.**

E メール (→ p. 201「LINE」も参照)

Eメールにまつわる表現

メールをチェックする	check one's e-mail	迷惑メール	spam
メールを受け取る	receive an e-mail / get an e-mail	メールアドレス	e-mail address
～にメールを送る	e-mail ～	文字化けした	garbled
～に返信する	reply to ～ / e-mail ～ back	添付ファイル	attachment / attached file
～に携帯メールを送る	text ～	絵文字	emoji
～を添付する	attach ～	顔文字	emoticon / smiley

サイトウくんにメールした。 **I e-mailed Saito-kun.**
＊e-mail＝～にEメールを送る

お姉ちゃんにも cc した。 **I Cc'd my sister.**
＊Cc＝～にccメールを送る。過去形はCc'd

シノダさんに返信した。 **I replied to Shinoda-san.**

タカヤマさんからメールが来た。 **I got an e-mail from Takayama-san.**

英語でメールを書けるようになりたい。 **I want to be able to write e-mails in English.**

誕生会の写真を添付した。 **I attached a photo from the birthday party.**
＊attach＝～を添付する

旅行会社に問い合わせのメールを送った。 **I e-mailed an inquiry to the travel agency.**
＊inquiry＝問い合わせ

メールアドレスを変更した。 **I changed my e-mail address.**

メールアドレスの変更を、みんなに知らせた。 **I let everyone know that I changed my e-mail address.**

マキちゃんにメールアドレスを教えてもらった。 **Maki gave me her e-mail address.**

最近、友達からのメールが減ったなぁ。 **I don't receive many e-mails from my friends these days.**

地図をPDFで送ってもらった。	**I received a PDF map.**
メールが文字化けしていて、読めなかった。	**The e-mail was garbled, so I couldn't read it.** *garbled＝文字化けした
容量が大き過ぎて、エラーになってしまった。	**The file was too big, so I got an error message.**
迷惑メールが多すぎる。アドレスを変えようかな？	**I get so much spam. Maybe I should change my e-mail address.** *spam＝迷惑メール
メールを送ったら不達通知が来た。	**I sent an e-mail, but got a bounce message.** *bounce message＝不達通知メール

Memo

パソコン・ネットに関することを、メモしておきましょう。

パソコン・ネットについて 英語日記を書いてみよう

パソコンやインターネットについて、英語で書いてみましょう。

タブレットの買い替え

My tablet is acting up. Come to think of it, I've been using it for five years now. Maybe it's about time to get a new one.

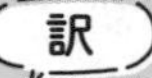

訳

タブレットの調子が悪い。思えば、もう5年も使っている。そろそろ買い替え時かな。

ポイント

act up は「(機械などが)うまく動かない」、come to think of it は「気が付けば、よく考えると」という意味です。「そろそろ〜し時かな」は Maybe it's about time to 〜という表現がぴったり。「〜」には動詞の原形を入れましょう。

英語でつぶやく

Starting today, I've decided to tweet in English at least once a day. 280 characters isn't much, so I think I can do it. I'm going to continue doing it!

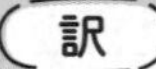

訳

今日から、1日1回は英語でつぶやくことにした。280字って意外と短いから、何とかなるかも。続けるぞ！

ポイント

「〜することにした」は、I've decided to 〜または I decided to 〜で表し、「〜」には動詞の原形を入れます。tweet は「(ツイッターで)つぶやく」。「何とかなるかも」は I think I can do it.(自分はできると思う)と表現するとよいでしょう。

複雑な気持ち

I found Yamashita-senpai on Facebook. I got mixed feelings when I looked at his pictures. He looked a lot older ...

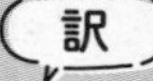

フェイスブックでヤマシタ先輩を見つけた。だいぶ老けた写真を見て、複雑な気持ちになった……。

「フェイスブックで」は、on Facebookと言います。「インスタグラムで」ならon Instagram、「ネットで」ならonlineかon the Internet。「複雑な気持ちになった」はgot mixed feelings、「老けた」はlooked older（年を取ったように見えた）で表します。

オーストラリアからのメッセージ

I got a WhatsApp message from Cathie in Australia. She sent me a picture of her family. Her son is very cute! I want to visit her during the summer vacation.

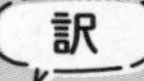

オーストラリアのキャシーからWhatsAppのメッセージが来た。家族の写真を送ってくれた。息子さんがとてもかわいい！　夏休みに遊びに行きたいな。

got a message from ～で「～からメッセージが来た」という意味。messageの前にWhatsAppとアプリの名前を入れれば、「WhatsAppのメッセージが来た」と表せます。gotの代わりにreceived（受け取った）としてもOKです。

29 災害・事件・事故

自然災害

災害・警報にまつわる単語

地震	earthquake
余震	aftershock
震度	intensity
マグニチュード	magnitude
震源	epicenter
稲光、稲妻	lightning
台風	typhoon
洪水	flood
(川の)氾濫	overflow
津波	tsunami
豪雨	downpour
線状降水帯	training
豪雪	heavy snow
吹雪	snow storm
雪崩	avalanche
竜巻	tornado
土砂崩れ	landslide
山火事	forest fire
噴火	eruption
緊急地震速報	earthquake early warning
暴風波浪警報	severe storm and high surf warning

防災対策

災害時に備えておかなくちゃ。
I need to get ready for a disaster.
＊disaster＝災害

防災用品の見直しをした。
I checked my emergency supplies.
＊emergency supplies＝防災用品

非常食と水を３日分、用意した。
I got three days worth of emergency food and water.
＊～ worth of ...＝～(ある期間)分の…

これで足りるかな？
Will it be enough?

懐中電灯の電池が切れていた。
The flashlight batteries needed replacing.
＊flashlight＝懐中電灯　replacing＝取り換え、交換

電池を買い置きしておこう。
I'll stock up on batteries.
＊stock up on ～＝～を買い置きする

浴槽にはいつも水をためておこう。	**I'll keep the bathtub filled with water.**
家具をしっかり壁に固定した。	**I've secured the furniture to the walls.** ＊secure＝～を固定する
家の耐震工事をしよう。	**I'll make my house earthquake-proof.** ＊earthquake-proof＝耐震の
地域の避難訓練に参加した。	**I participated in an emergency drill in our neighborhood.** ＊participate in ～＝～に参加する emergency drill＝避難訓練
災害時の避難場所を確認した。	**I checked the evacuation site in our area.** ＊evacuation site＝避難場所
緊急時の連絡方法を家族で話し合った。	**My family talked about how to contact one another in emergency situations.** ＊contact＝～に連絡する
ハザードマップ、どこにあるっけ？	**Where did I put the hazard map?**
あの川が氾濫すると、この辺りは浸水するみたい。	**If that river overflows, then this area might get flooded.**

地震

午後３時半ごろ、地震があった。	**There was an earthquake at about 3:30 this afternoon.**
夜中に地震があったらしい。	**I hear that there was an earthquake in the middle of the night.**
かなり大きかった。	**It was a pretty big one.**
揺れが長かった。	**It shook for a long time.** ＊shake＝揺れる。過去形はshook[シュック]
外にいたので、全然気付かなかった。	**I didn't notice it at all because I was outside.** ＊notice＝～に気付く
寝ていたので、気付かなかった。	**I didn't notice it because I was asleep.**
ビルの25階にいたので、かなり揺れた。	**It shook a lot on the 25th floor of the building where I was.**
震度５弱の地震があった。	**There was an earthquake of intensity 5 lower.** ＊intensity＝強度。「震度5強」はintensity 5 upperと表す

久しぶりに震度3の地震があった。	**That was the first earthquake of intensity 3 in a while.**
震源地は千葉県沖。	**The epicenter was in the ocean off the coast of Chiba.** ＊epicenter＝震源地　off the coast of ～＝～沖に・の
震源地がどこか、テレビの地震速報で確認した。	**I checked the epicenter of the earthquake on the TV earthquake news.**
マグニチュードは4.5だった。	**The magnitude was 4.5.**
実家の辺りがすごく揺れたみたいだ。	**It seems like the shaking was really strong near my parents' home.**
実家と電話がつながらない。心配。	**I can't get a hold of my parents. I'm worried.** ＊get a hold of ～＝～に連絡する
最近、地震が多い。	**There have been a number of earthquakes lately.** ＊a number of ～＝たくさんの～
日本は地震大国だからなぁ。	**Japan is an earthquake-prone country.** ＊earthquake-prone＝地震が多発の
今日も余震があった。	**We had another aftershock today.** ＊aftershock＝余震
すごく怖かった。	**I was really scared.**
緊急地震速報が流れると怖くなる。	**I'm scared when I hear the earthquake early warning.**
いつか巨大地震が起きると思うと怖い。	**I feel scared that there will be a massive earthquake someday.**

津波

津波の心配はないとのことだった。	**They said there was no danger of a tsunami.** ＊danger＝危険性
20センチの津波が観測された。	**A 20cm tsunami was reported.**
津波のときの避難ルートを確認した。	**We checked the escape route in case of a tsunami.**

津波に備えて新しい防潮壁が作られた。	**New seawalls were built to protect us from tsunamis.** ＊seawall＝防潮壁
小さな津波だからといって侮ってはいけない。	**We shouldn't take tsunamis lightly, even small ones.** ＊take＝〜を受け止める
津波が予想以上に早く到達した。	**The tsunami arrived earlier than expected.**

台風・豪雨

台風15号が近づいてきている。	**Typhoon No.15 is approaching.** ＊approach＝近づく
台風15号が明日、東海地方に上陸するらしい。	**It looks like Typhoon No.15 is going to hit the Tokai area tomorrow.** ＊hit＝(台風などが)〜を襲う
台風がそれてよかった。	**I'm relieved the typhoon turned away.**
台風がこの付近を直撃した。	**This area got hit directly by the typhoon.**
歩けないほどだった。	**It was hard to walk.**
店の看板が飛んでいた。	**I saw a store sign being blown away.** ＊blow away 〜＝〜を吹き飛ばす
傘が折れちゃった。	**My umbrella broke.**
雨戸をしっかりと閉めた。	**I closed the shutters tight.**
屋根が雨漏りしてしまった。	**The roof leaked.** ＊leak＝漏れる
ゲリラ豪雨に見舞われた。	**We were caught in a sudden downpour.** ＊downpour＝どしゃ降り、豪雨
市内に大雨警報が出た。	**There was a heavy rain warning for the city.**

雷

雷が響いた。	**I heard thunder.**
さっきから雷がすごい。	**It has been thundering a lot.**
昨夜はひどい雷だった。	**It thundered a lot last night.**

すごい稲光だった。 There was a bright bolt of lightning.
*bright=光っている a bolt of lightning=(一光りの)稲妻

近所に落ちた。 It hit somewhere near my house.

停電に備えて、パソコンのデータを保存しておいた。 I saved the data in my PC in case the lights went out.
*go out=(明かりが)消える。goの過去形はwent

落雷で停電した。 Lightning caused a blackout.
*blackout=停電

大雪

今日だけで 40cm も積もった。 It snowed 40cm just today.

タナカさんが雪下ろしで屋根から落ちて、けがをしてしまった。 Tanaka-san got hurt when he fell from the roof while clearing snow.
*get hurt=けがをする clear=〜を取り除く

ニュースによると、雪崩に巻き込まれて５人が亡くなったそうだ。 According to the news, five people were killed in an avalanche.
*be killed=(事故などで)死ぬ avalanche=雪崩

洪水・浸水

川が氾濫した。 The river overflowed.
*overflow=氾濫する

洪水で橋が流された。 The flood washed the bridge away.
*flood=洪水

浸水で、ほとんどの家具が使い物にならなくなった。 Most of the furniture got ruined by the flood and was totally useless.
*ruin=〜を台無しにする useless=役に立たない

神田川の水位がすごく上がってる。 The water level of the Kandagawa River has risen a lot.
*rise=上昇する。過去分詞はrisen

洪水で多くの家屋が水に漬かった。 A lot of houses got flooded.
*flood=〜(土地や家屋など)を水浸しにする

タイヤは半分くらい水に漬かっていた。 Water came up to the middle of the wheels.

洪水で川が増水していた。 The river was flood-swollen.
*flood-swollen=洪水で増水した

異常気象

記録的な寒波がヨーロッパを襲っているらしい。 I hear Europe is having a record-breaking cold front.
*record-breaking=記録的な

冷夏で農作物に大きな影響が出ている。	**The cool summer is having a huge impact on crops.** ＊impact＝影響　crops＝作物、収穫物
干ばつの影響で作物の価格が高騰しそうだ。	**Crop prices are likely to go up because of the drought.** ＊drought［ドゥラウト］＝干ばつ
日照りによる水不足が深刻だ。	**The water shortage caused by the long dry spell is serious.** ＊shortage＝不足　spell＝（しばらく続く）期間
地球温暖化が心配だ。	**I'm concerned about global warming.**

そのほかの災害

土砂崩れで県道が寸断された。	**The prefectural highway got cut off by landslides.** ＊prefectural＝県の　landslide＝土砂崩れ
土砂崩れで、村が孤立化している。	**The village is isolated because of landslides.** ＊isolated＝孤立化した
市内で竜巻が発生した。	**There was a tornado in the city.**
新燃岳が噴火した。	**Mt. Shinmoe erupted.** ＊erupt＝噴火する

交通機関への影響

落雷で電車が３時間も止まった。	**The trains stopped for three hours due to the lightning.** ＊due to ～＝～のために、～が原因で
３時間後、電車が動き出した。	**The trains started to move again after three hours.**
新幹線の中に２時間も閉じ込められた。	**We were stuck in the Shinkansen for two hours.** ＊stuck＝立ち往生して
会社から家まで歩いて３時間かかった。	**It took me three hours to walk home from work.**
歩いて帰る人で道が混雑していた。	**The streets were crowded with people walking home.**
会社に泊まった。	**I spent the night at the office.** ＊spend＝～を過ごす。過去形はspent
バスターミナルには長い行列ができていた。	**There were long lines of people at the bus terminal.**

タクシーは、もちろんつかまらなかった。	**Of course, there were no taxis available.** ＊available＝利用できる
吹雪で高速道路が閉鎖された。	**The expressway was closed due to a blizzard.** ＊blizzard＝猛吹雪、ブリザード
大雪で交通がまひした。	**The heavy snow paralyzed traffic.** ＊paralyze＝～をまひさせる
大雪で高速道路の車が立ち往生してる。	**Cars on the expressway have been stranded because of the heavy snow.**
車の中にいて動けない人たちが気の毒だ。	**I feel sorry for people stuck inside the cars.**
飛行機は軒並み欠航したようだ。	**Most flights seem to have been cancelled.**
全便が欠航となった。	**All flights were canceled.**

事件・事故

ニュースを見て

ひどい事件だ！	**What a terrible incident!** ＊incident＝事件
痛ましい事故だ！	**What a harrowing accident!** ＊harrowing＝悲痛な
何て残酷なんだ！	**How cruel!** ＊cruel＝残酷な、むごい
ひどいことをする人がいるものだ。	**Some people do terrible things.**
犯人が許せない。	**That criminal is unforgivable.** ＊criminal＝犯罪者　unforgivable＝許すことのできない
容疑者が逮捕された。	**The suspect has been arrested.** ＊suspect＝容疑者　arrest＝～を逮捕する
容疑者が捕まってよかった。	**I'm glad they caught the suspect.**
物騒な世の中だ。	**It's a rough world out there.** ＊rough［ラフ］＝騒々しい、物騒な　out there＝外は
自分も気を付けよう。	**I should be careful, too.**
この裁判の行方が気になる。	**I want to know how the trial goes.** ＊trial＝裁判

判決は無罪だった。 **The verdict was "not guilty."**
＊verdict＝判決　guilty＝有罪の

懲役1年、執行猶予3年の判決が言い渡された。 **He was sentenced to one year in prison, with three years of probation.**
＊be sentenced to ～＝～という判決を下される　probation＝執行猶予

通報・警察

110番通報した。 **I called 110.**

119番通報した。 **I called 119.**

救急車を呼んだ。 **I called for an ambulance.**
＊ambulance＝救急車

一応、警察に通報しておいた。 **I reported it to the police just in case.**
＊just in case＝念のため

近所の交番に相談した。 **I went to the local police box.**

すぐに警察官が来てくれた。 **A police officer came right away.**

見回りを強化してくれるらしい。 **They said they're going to increase patrols.**
＊increase＝～を増やす・拡大する

盗難の被害届を出した。 **I turned in a theft report.**
＊turn in ～＝～を提出する　theft[セフト]＝盗難

強盗・盗難

サトウさんの家に空き巣が入ったらしい。 **I hear Sato-san's house was broken into.**
＊break into ～＝～に押し入る。breakの過去分詞はbroken

置いておいた現金が盗まれたらしい。 **I hear the money he kept in his house was stolen.**
＊steal＝～を盗む。過去分詞はstolen

特に盗まれた物はなかったらしい。 **It seems nothing was actually stolen.**

2丁目のコンビニに強盗が入ったらしい。 **I hear there was a robbery at the convenience store in the second block.**
＊robbery＝強盗

最近、この辺りで車上荒らしが相次いでいる。	**Lately, car break-ins have been happening one after another in this area.** ＊car break-in＝車上荒らし
ひったくりに気を付けよう。	**I need to watch out for purse snatchers.** ＊purse＝ハンドバッグ snatcher＝ひったくり
スリに遭ったかもしれない。	**I may have been pickpocketed.** ＊pickpocket＝〜(人から金など)をする

火事

駅の近くで火事があった。	**There was a fire near the station.**
隣町で放火が3件あった。	**There were three cases of arson in a nearby town.** ＊arson［アースン］＝放火
黒い煙が上がっていた。	**There was black smoke rising.**
すごい野次馬だった。	**There were a lot of onlookers.** ＊onlooker＝見物人
消防車が何台も来ていた。	**There were several fire trucks there.** ＊fire trucksは、fire enginesでもOK
民家が全焼した。	**A house completely burned down.** ＊burn down＝全焼する
火はなかなか消えなかった。	**The fire wouldn't die down easily.** ＊die down＝(火などの勢いが)弱まる
全員無事だった。	**Everyone was all right.**
ぼやで済んでよかった。	**I'm relieved it ended in a small fire.**
火の元に注意しなきゃ。	**We have to be careful to prevent fires.** ＊prevent＝〜を防ぐ

詐欺

オガワさんちのおばあちゃん、振り込め詐欺に引っかかったらしい。	**I hear Mrs. Ogawa fell for a money transfer scam.** ＊fall for 〜＝〜にだまされる。fallの過去形はfell transfer＝振り込み scam＝詐欺
500万円を振り込んでしまったんだって。	**I hear she transferred five million yen.** ＊transfer＝〜を振り込む
友達が結婚詐欺に引っかかった。	**My friend fell for a marriage fraud.** ＊fall for 〜＝〜にだまされる fraud［フロード］＝詐欺

タダさん、印鑑を18万円で買わされたって。	**Mr. Tada was forced to buy a name seal for 180,000 yen.** ＊force ～ to ...＝～に…するよう強制する name seal＝印鑑
彼、どうやら投資話に引っかかってしまったらしい。	**It looks like he has been conned in an investment fraud.** ＊con＝～をだます　investment＝投資
みんな、どうして簡単に引っかかるんだろう？	**I wonder why people get tricked by these scams so easily.** ＊scam＝詐欺
そんなにうまい話があるわけないよね。	**There's no such thing as a free lunch.** ＊「ただほど高いものはない」という意味のことわざ
ワンクリック詐欺にやられた。	**I got tricked by one-click fraud.** ＊get tricked＝だまされる
自分だけは引っかからないと思ってた。	**I never thought I would fall for something like this.**

交通事故

近所で交通事故があった。	**There was a car crash in my neighborhood.**
単独事故だった。	**It was a single-car accident.**
玉突き事故だった。	**It was a pile-up.**
自動車がガードレールにぶつかった。	**A car hit the guardrail.**
霧のため、9台を巻き込む玉突き事故が発生した。	**Due to the fog, there was a nine-car collision.** ＊due to ～＝～のために、～が原因で collision［カリジョン］＝衝突
交差点で自動車とオートバイの出合い頭の事故があったようだ。	**It seems there was a collision at a crossing between a car and a motorcycle.**
自転車と自動車がぶつかるところを目撃した。	**I saw a bike run into a car.** ＊run into ～＝～に衝突する
自転車が高齢の男性にぶつかった。	**A bike ran into an elderly man.**
交通事故を起こしてしまった。	**I had a car accident.**
当て逃げされた！	**I was in a hit-and-run accident!** ＊hit-and-run＝当て逃げの

後ろから追突された。	**My car got rear-ended.** ＊get rear-ended＝(車に)追突される
相手の車は雨でスリップしたらしい。	**The other person's car seems to have slid because of the rain.** ＊slide＝滑る。過去分詞はslid
運転手いわく、居眠り運転をしていたらしい。	**The driver said he dozed off at the wheel.** ＊doze off＝ウトウトする　at the wheel＝運転して
信号無視をしたらしい。	**It seems the driver ran a red light.** ＊run＝～を突破する
運転手の前方不注意が原因だ。	**It was caused by the driver not paying attention to where he was going.** ＊pay attention to ～＝～に注意を払う
運転手はスマホに気を取られていたらしい。	**It seems the driver was distracted by his smartphone.** ＊distracted＝注意が散漫な
バンパーがへこんでしまった。	**My bumper was dented.** ＊dent＝～をへこませる
修理代に８万円かかる。痛いなぁ…。	**It'll cost 80,000 yen for repairs. This is terrible ...** ＊repair＝修理
逆走車がいて焦った。	**I almost panicked when a wrong-way driver was coming toward me.**
あおり運転をしている車を見た。	**I saw a car tailgating.** ＊tailgate＝前方の車にぴったり付く
あおり運転されて怖かった。	**I was scared someone was tailgating me.**
あわや、大事故に巻き込まれるところだった。	**I was nearly in a major accident.**
すんでのところで事故を免れた。	**I just barely avoided an accident.** ＊barely＝何とか、かろうじて　avoid＝～を回避する
ドライブレコーダーを付けようかな。	**Maybe I should get a dashcam.** ＊dashcam＝ドライブレコーダー
事故で高速道路が通行止めになった。	**The expressway was closed due to a car accident.**
けが人が出なくて何よりだ。	**Good thing no one was hurt.** ＊hurt＝～にけがをさせる。過去分詞もhurt

そのほかの事件・事故

通勤電車で痴漢にあった。	**I was groped on the commuter train.** ＊grope＝〜の体をまさぐる　commuter＝通勤者
この辺りに露出魔が出るらしい。	**I hear there's a flasher around here.** ＊flasher＝露出魔
この近くで女性が通り魔に襲われた。	**A woman was attacked by a random attacker in the neighborhood.** ＊random attacker＝通り魔
子どもたちが男に盗撮されたらしい。	**It seems the children were being sneakily photographed by a man.** ＊sneakily＝こっそりと
電話が盗聴されていた。	**My phone was being tapped.** ＊tap＝〜を盗聴する
ストーカーにつけられている気がする。	**I feel like I'm being stalked.** ＊stalk＝〜をこっそり追跡する
市内で強盗殺人事件が起きた。	**There was a robbery and murder case in my city.**
隣町で発砲事件が起きた。	**There was a shooting incident in a nearby town.** ＊incident＝事件
虐待を受けた子たちを思うと、胸が痛む。	**My heart aches for those abused children.** ＊ache［エイク］＝痛む　abused＝虐待を受けた
一家心中のニュースに、胸がつぶれる思いだ。	**The family suicide news crushed me.** ＊suicide＝自殺　crush＝〜をつぶす

災害・事件・事故について 英語日記を書いてみよう

災害・事件・事故について、英語で書いてみましょう。

台風が来た

Typhoon No. 7 will close in tomorrow afternoon. I hope it doesn't cause a lot of damage ...

台風7号が明日の午後、接近してくるようだ。大きな被害にならないといいけど……。

close[クロウズ] in は「迫ってくる、襲ってくる」という意味の表現です。「～だといいけど」はI hope ～(文)で。後に「これから起きること」を続ける場合、現在時制(it doesn't ～)と未来を表す表現(it won't ～)のどちらも使えます。

余震が続く

There have been aftershocks almost every day. With so many earthquakes, I got used to them. Intensity three doesn't scare me anymore, which ins't good, I know.

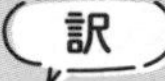

ここのところ、ほとんど毎日余震が続いている。あまりに地震が多くて体が慣れちゃった。震度3程度では驚かない。それはよくないとわかってるけど。

「地震」は earthquake で、口語では shake や quake とも言います。「余震」は aftershock。get used to ～は「～に慣れる」という意味で、「～」には名詞または動詞の -ing 形が入ります。scare は「～を驚かせる・怖がらせる」の意味です。

車をこすっちゃった

I scraped my car on a telephone pole. I feel terrible.

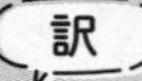

電柱に車をこすっちゃった。最悪。

「車をこする」は scrape a car、「電柱」は（telephone）pole と表します。「電柱に車をぶつけた」なら、I crashed my car into a pole. や I hit a pole with my car. と表しましょう。terrible は「ひどく不快な、嫌な」という意味です。

スリに遭った

I went shopping, and when I was ready to pay, I realized that my wallet was gone. I must've been pickpocketed. How shocking! I should've been more careful.

買い物に行って支払いを済ませようとしたとき、財布がなくなっていることに気付いた。スリに遭ったに違いない。すごくショック！もっと気を付けるべきだった。

gone は「なくなっている」、be pickpocketed は「スリに遭う」。must've ～（動詞の過去分詞）は過去の事柄について「～だったに違いない」、should've ～（動詞の過去分詞）は「～しておくべきだった」と書くときの構文です。～'ve は have の短縮形。

30 ボランティア

いろいろなボランティア

ボランティアに参加する

ボランティアに参加したい。	**I want to do some volunteer work.**
ネットでボランティアの募集を探した。	**I searched for volunteering opportunities online.**
英語を使ったボランティアがしたいな。	**I want to try volunteering where I can use English.**
ボランティアで街の観光ガイドをしてみたい。	**I want to try doing volunteer tour guiding in my town.**
区のイベントでボランティアしたいな。	**I want to volunteer at a ward event.** ＊ward＝区
ボランティアの募集が出ていた。	**I saw a volunteer recruitment ad.**
ボランティアに申し込んだ。	**I applied to be a volunteer.** ＊apply＝申し込む
ボランティア保険に加入した。	**I bought volunteer insurance.**
ボランティアの説明会があった。	**There was an orientation for volunteer staff.**
街のボランティア活動に参加した。	**I joined in the volunteer activities in the town.**
ボランティアに参加した人が大勢いた。	**Many people came to volunteer.**

環境美化

町内のごみ拾いに参加した。	**I participated in the city cleanup.** ＊participate in 〜＝〜に参加する

公園の清掃をした。 **We cleaned up the park.**

荒川の河川敷で、空き缶拾いをした。 **We picked up cans along the Arakawa River.**

公園の花壇に花を植えた。 **I planted flowers in the park's flower bed.**
＊plant＝～を植える flower bed＝花壇

ブナ植樹のボランティアに参加した。 **I helped plant a beech tree.**
＊beech tree＝ブナ

近所の緑道の草取りをした。 **I did some weeding along the neighborhood pedestrian path.**
＊weeding＝草取り pedestrian path＝歩道

商店街のシャッターの落書きを消す手伝いをした。 **I helped clean up the graffiti-covered shutters on the shopping street.**
＊graffiti＝落書き

福祉

介護施設を慰問した。 **I visited a nursing home.**
＊nursing home＝介護施設

みんなで歌を歌った。 **We all sang together.**

私はウクレレを演奏した。 **I played the ukulele.**
＊ukulele［ユークレイリ］＝ウクレレ

みんなに散髪してあげた。 **I gave them haircuts.**

喜んでもらえてうれしかった。 **I was happy that they were happy.**

お年寄りと話すのは楽しかった。 **It was fun to talk with the elderly people.**
＊elderly＝年配の

皆さんの笑顔に心が癒された。 **Their smiles made me feel comforted.**
＊comforted＝ほっとした

自分の孫のようにかわいがってくれた。 **They treated me like their own grandchild.**
＊treat＝～を扱う

お手玉を教えてもらった。 **They taught me otedama.**

みんなで塗り絵をした。 **We did coloring together.**
＊do coloring＝塗り絵をする

みんなで体操をした。 **We did exercises together.**

一緒に折り紙をした。 **We folded origami together.**
＊fold＝～を折り畳む

みんな童謡を歌うのが好きなようだ。	**It seems they all like to sing children's songs.**
美空ひばりの歌をリクエストされた。	**They asked me to sing a Hibari Misora song.**

献血・ドナー

外に移動献血車が止まっていた。	**There was a bloodmobile outside.** ＊bloodmobile＝採血車、献血車
献血しに行った。	**I went to donate blood.** ＊donate＝〜を寄付する
新宿の献血ルームで献血をした。	**I gave blood at a blood donation center in Shinjuku.**
400ml、献血した。	**I gave 400ml of blood.**
血圧が低過ぎて、献血できなかった。	**I couldn't donate blood because I had low blood pressure.** ＊donate＝〜を寄付する　blood pressure＝血圧
献血をしたら特典のグッズをもらった。	**I got a special item for donating blood.**
骨髄バンクにドナー登録をした。	**I registered as a bone marrow donor.** ＊bone marrow donor＝骨髄ドナー

募金・寄付

駅前で募金活動をしていた。	**There was a fund-raising campaign in front of the train station.** ＊fund-raising＝募金運動
募金活動に参加した。	**I helped with fund-raising.**
歳末助け合いの募金に寄付した。	**I donated to a year-end charity drive.** ＊charity drive＝慈善活動。driveは「(慈善などの)運動」
1000円、募金した。	**I donated 1,000 yen.** ＊donate＝〜を寄付する
NPOに5000円、寄付をした。	**I donated 5,000 yen to an NPO.**
地震被害への支援金として1万円寄付した。	**I donated 10,000 yen to support the earthquake victims.**
書き損じはがきを寄付した。	**I donated spoiled postcards.**

おもちゃを寄付した。	**I donated some toys.**
町の児童福祉施設にランドセルを2つ寄贈した。	**I donated two school backpacks to the children's institution in town.** ＊school backpack＝ランドセル　institution＝施設
母校に10万円分のスポーツ用品を寄贈した。	**I donated sporting goods worth 100,000 yen to my alma mater.** ＊worth ～＝～の価値がある alma mater［アールマ マーター］＝母校、出身校
本を20冊ほど児童館に寄付した。	**I donated about 20 books to the children's center.**
会社で寄付金を募った。	**We raised money at work.** ＊raise＝～（寄付など）を集める
今のところ、9万2300円集まった。	**We've collected 92,300 yen so far.**
彼らのクラウドファンディングに5000円を寄付した。	**I donated 5,000 yen to their crowdfunding project.**
ヘアドネーションに興味がある。	**I'm interested in hair donation.**

国際交流

国際交流イベントの手伝いをした。	**I helped with an international event.**
国際交流クラブに入ってみようかな。	**Maybe I should join the international club.**
通訳ボランティアに登録した。	**I registered as a volunteer interpreter.**
家で外国人の受け入れをすることにした。	**I decided to open my house to people from abroad.**
彼らを家に招いて和食をふるまった。	**I invited them to my house and served them Japanese food.** ＊serve＝～（飲食物）を出す
外国人向けの茶道体験イベントを手伝った。	**I helped at a tea ceremony event for non-Japanese.**
外国人に日本語を教えた。	**I taught Japanese to people from abroad.**
外国人と日本語でおしゃべりした。	**I talked with people from abroad in Japanese.**

日本語での書類の記入を手伝った。	**I helped them to fill out forms in Japanese.** ＊fill out ～＝～に記入する
和食の作り方を教えた。	**I taught them how to make some Japanese dishes.**
折り紙を教えた。	**I taught origami.**
ボランティアで観光ガイドをすることになった。	**I've been assigned to be a volunteer tour guide.** ＊be assigned to ～＝～するよう任命される
英語で東京を案内した。	**I gave a guided tour of Tokyo in English.**

そのほかのボランティア

被災地にボランティアに行った。	**I went to volunteer in the disaster-affected area.** ＊disaster-affected＝被災した
被災者のために炊き出しボランティアをした。	**I helped cook food for disaster victims.** ＊disaster＝災害　victim＝被災者、被害者
泥かきをした。	**I shoveled mud.** ＊shovel＝～をシャベルですくう　mud＝泥、土
雪かきをした。	**I shoveled snow.**
データの入力をした。	**I entered data.** ＊enter＝～を入力する
広報誌を作った。	**I made a brochure.** ＊brochure［ブロウシュァ］＝パンフレット
町のお祭りの運営ボランティアに参加した。	**I volunteered to help run the town festival.** ＊run＝～を運営する
イベントの受付を手伝った。	**I helped at the reception desk of the event.** ＊reception＝受付
地域の見回りをした。	**I helped make community rounds.** ＊round＝巡回
小学生の子たちの勉強を見てあげた。	**I watched the elementary school students study.**
子どもたちに絵本の読み聞かせをした。	**I read picture books to children.**

夏休みのキャンプボランティアに参加した。
I participated as a summer camp volunteer.

子ども食堂でボランティアをした。
I volunteered at the children's cafeteria.

手話通訳をした。
I interpreted sign language.
＊interpret＝～を通訳する　sign language＝手話

子猫のミルクボランティアに興味がある。
I'm interested in volunteering to bottle-feed kittens.
＊bottle-feed ～＝～にほ乳びんでミルクを与える

ボランティアについて 英語日記を書いてみよう

ボランティア活動について、英語で書いてみましょう。

地元の夏祭りでお手伝い

We had a local summer festival today. I was in charge of bingo. Some kids looked excited, and some looked disappointed. It was a lot of fun.

今日は地元の夏祭りだった。私はビンゴゲームの担当。うれしそうな子もいれば、ガッカリしている子もいた。とても楽しかった。

local は「地元の」、be in charge of 〜は「〜を担当する、〜の係である」。excited は「ワクワクした」、disappointed は「ガッカリした」、be a lot of fun は「すごく楽しい」という意味です。後に名詞が続かない fun は名詞で、very fun とは言いません。

川の掃除

We cleaned up the river a week ago, but it was already littered with some plastic bags and cans. Whoever did it must have no conscience!

1週間前にみんなで川をきれいにしたばかりなのに、もうビニール袋や空き缶が捨てられていた。そんなことをする人はきっと良心がとがめないんだろうな！

litter は「(ごみを)散らかす」という意味で、ここでは it was littered with 〜（川が〜で散らかされていた）と受け身で表しています。whoever did it は「それをした人は誰であれ」が直訳で、「誰がやったか知らないけど、その人は」というニュアンスです。

料理で国際交流

At the International Center, we invited some people from overseas and taught them how to make temakizushi. We were happy they enjoyed it.

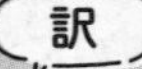

国際センターに外国人を招いて、手巻きずしの作り方を教えてあげた。楽しんでもらえて、うれしかった。

「外国人＝ foreigner」と覚えている人も多いと思いますが、これは「よそ者」というニュアンスに響くことがあるので、people from overseas や people from abroad といった表現がベターです。enjoyed it（楽しかった）の it を忘れないように注意しましょう。

歳末助け合い募金

There were people working for a year-end charity drive in front of the train station. I donated 5,000 yen. I was thankful I had a healthy and happy year.

駅前で、歳末助け合い運動をしていた。5千円募金した。今年一年、健康で幸せに過ごせたことに感謝。

there were people 〜ing は「〜している人たちがいた」という意味。「歳末助け合い運動」は year-end charity drive と表します。この drive は「（ある目的のためにする）運動、キャンペーン」のこと。「〜を寄付する・募金する」は、donate で表します。

31 書き留めたい言葉

夢・目標

夢

いつかアメリカに留学したい。	**I hope to study in the U.S. someday.**
英語が上手に話せるようになりたい。	**I want to be able to speak English fluently.** ＊fluently＝流ちょうに
海外に移住したい。	**I want to move overseas.**
大きな家に住みたい。	**I want to live in a big house.**
宝くじで３億円当てたい。	**I want to win 300 million yen in the lottery.** ＊win＝〜を得る　lottery＝宝くじ
お金に不自由なく暮らしたい。	**I want to be well-off.**
伊豆に別荘が持てたらいいな。	**It would be nice to have a vacation house in Izu.** ＊vacation house＝別荘
幸せな家庭を築きたい。	**I want to build a happy home.**
美容師になりたい。	**I want to be a hairdresser.**
レストランを経営したい。	**I hope to run a restaurant.** ＊run＝〜を経営する
旅行者のためのホステルを運営したい。	**I want to run a hostel for travelers.**
起業したい。	**I want to start a business.**
農業を始めたい。	**I want to start a farm.**
健康で長生きしたい。	**I hope to live a long healthy life.**

世界遺産を回りたい。	I want to go around visiting world heritage sites. ＊world heritage＝世界遺産　site＝場所
退職したらマレーシアに住みたい。	I want to live in Malaysia after I retire.
一度でいいから、ブラッド・ピットに会いたい。	I really want to meet Brad Pitt just once.

目標

英語日記を1年続けるぞ。	I will keep a diary in English for one year.
TOEIC テストで 700 点を取るぞ！	I will score 700 points on the TOEIC test! ＊score＝～の点を取る
英検2級に合格するぞ！	I will pass the Eiken Grade 2 exam!
週に3回、ジムに通おう。	I will go to the gym three times a week.
3キロやせるぞ！	I will lose 3kg!
フラメンコを始める！	I will take up flamenco! ＊take up ～＝～(趣味など)を始める
少なくとも週に3回は自炊しよう。	I will cook for myself at least three times a week.
今度こそタバコをやめるぞ！	I will quit smoking this time for sure! ＊quit[クイット]＝～をやめる　for sure＝確実に
もっといい仕事に就くぞ！	I'm going to get a better job!
昇進試験に合格するぞ！	I'll pass the promotion test!
教員資格を取るぞ！	I'm going to get a teaching qualification!
車を買うぞ！	I'm going to buy a car!
100万円ためる！	I'm going to save one million yen!
すてきな彼氏を見つけるぞ！	I'll find an amazing boyfriend!

子どもたちとの時間を増やすように努力しよう。	**I will try to spend more time with the kids.**
毎週１冊、本を読もう。	**I will read one book a week.**
スマホを見る時間を減らそう。	**I will spend less time on my smartphone.**
一日一善しよう。	**I will do a good deed every day.** ＊good deed＝善行

心に響く言葉

自分を励ます

大丈夫、私ならできる。	**Don't worry. I can do it.**
簡単にあきらめちゃダメ。	**Don't give up too easily.**
元気を出して！	**Cheer up!**
あなたは頑張ってるよ。	**You're doing your best.**
次はうまくいくさ。	**Better luck next time.**
可能性はあるさ。	**There's a chance.**
ダメでもともとだ。	**It won't hurt to try.** ＊直訳は「やってみて困ることはない」
奇跡は起こると信じよう。	**Believe in miracles.**
幸せは必ずやってくる。	**Happiness will surely come your way.**
待っているだけじゃダメ。自分の幸せは自分で探そう。	**Don't just wait; search for your own happiness.**
ナンバーワンでなくても、オンリーワンになればいいんだよ。	**You don't need to be No.1; just be the only one.**
自分に自信を持とう。	**Be confident in yourself.** ＊be confident in ～＝～に自信を持つ
自分に誇りを持って。	**Be proud of yourself.**

自分の気持ちに素直にね。	**Follow your heart.** ＊follow＝～に従う
自分の直感に従おう。	**Follow your instincts.** ＊instinct＝直感、本能
自分の考えを信じよう。	**Trust your own point of view.** ＊own＝自分自身の　point of view＝見方、考え方
失敗なんて笑い飛ばそう。	**Laugh off your failure.** ＊laugh off ～＝～を笑い飛ばす　failure＝失敗
失敗あってこそ成功がある。	**Success comes after much failure.**
失敗したっていい。何度でも挑戦しよう。	**It's OK to fail. Just keep on trying.** ＊fail＝失敗する
人生に無駄な経験なんてない。	**No experience is useless in life.** ＊useless＝役に立たない
どんな経験も自分の糧となる。	**Every single experience helps us grow.** ＊grow＝成長する

自分に活を入れる

今やらずにいつやる？	**If you don't do it now, when will you do it?**
今日できることは今日のうちに。	**Don't put off what you can do today.** ＊put off ～＝～を先延ばしにする・延期する
「でも」の前に、まずトライ。	**No "buts." Just try it.**
困難から逃げ出すのは簡単だけど、それじゃ成長できないよ。	**Running away from my troubles is easy, but I know it won't help me mature.** ＊mature＝成長する
人生をよくするも苦しくするも、自分次第。	**Whether life is better or bitter, it's totally up to you.** ＊up to ～＝～の責任で
自分を幸せにできるのは自分自身。	**No one can make you happy except you.** ＊except ～＝～以外は
やり直すのに遅い時期はない。	**It's never too late to start over.** ＊start over＝最初からやり直す

夢をかなえる

夢はきっとかなう。	**Dreams will come true.**
夢は追い続けるもの。	**Keep pursuing your dreams.** ＊pursue[パースー]＝～を追い求める

成功に近道はない。	**There is no shortcut to success.**
成功への鍵は、決してあきらめないこと。	**The key to success is to never quit.** ＊quit[クイット]＝やめる
夢を実現できるかどうかは、自分の努力次第。	**Whether or not your dream comes true depends on your efforts.** ＊depend on 〜＝〜次第である
肝心なのは「成功できる」と信じること。	**The most important step toward success is to believe that you can succeed.** ＊succeed＝成功する
成功者の努力に終わりはない。	**Successful people never cease to strive.** ＊cease to 〜＝〜するのをやめる　strive＝努力する
成功するためには、まず自分の仕事をこよなく愛すること。	**To be successful, the first thing to do is love your work.**

つらいときに

あまり無理し過ぎないで。	**Don't push yourself too hard.** ＊push oneself＝無理をする
少し自分に厳し過ぎるんじゃない?	**Aren't you a bit too tough on yourself?** ＊tough[タフ]＝厳しい
冬が終われば必ず春がくる。	**Spring always follows winter.** ＊follow＝〜に続く
明けない夜がないように、つらい状況もいつか終わる。	**There are no dawnless nights; your darkness will end, too.** ＊dawnless＝朝のない　darkness＝暗さ、闇
まぁ、人生こんなときもあるさ。	**Well, life isn't always easy.**
いい時もあれば悪い時もある、それが人生。	**We all have our ups and downs. That's life.** ＊ups and downs＝浮き沈み、いい時と悪い時
他人と比べて自分の人生を評価するのはやめよう。	**Don't measure your success in life by comparing yourself with others.** ＊measure＝〜を判断する・評価する
不運なことも、人生で役に立つときがある。	**Misfortune can sometimes be useful in life.** ＊misfortune＝不運
そんなに悲しまないで。世界の終わりじゃないんだから。	**Don't be so sad. It's not the end of the world.**

大丈夫。出口のないトンネルなんてないよ。	**Don't worry. Every tunnel has an exit.**
時間がかかるときだってあるよ。	**It just takes time sometimes.**

前向きになろう

人生をプラスに考えよう。	**Be positive about your life.** ＊positive＝肯定的な
「できない」ではなく「できる」と言おう。	**Learn to say "I can," instead of "I can't."** ＊learn to ～＝～できるようになる
過去は振り返らず、先を見よう。	**Don't look back on the past; look toward the future.** ＊past＝過去
悪いことよりも、いいことのほうに目を向けよう。	**Focus on the good things in life, not on the bad.** ＊focus on ～＝～に集中する
人生は短い。毎日を前向きに過ごさなきゃ。	**Life is short. Why not spend every day positively?**
過去は変えられないけど、未来はいくらでも変えられる。	**The past is over and it can't be changed, but the future can be altered.** ＊alter＝～を変える・改める
扉を開けてごらん。新しい自分が見つかるかもしれないよ。	**Open the door. You may find a new you.**
ため息をつく人に幸せはやってこないよ。	**Sighing just keeps happiness away.** ＊sigh［サィ］＝ため息をつく

友情・友達への感謝

いつも支えてくれてありがとう。	**Thank you for your continuous support.** ＊continuous＝絶え間ない
友達でいられてよかった。	**I'm so glad we are friends.**
あなたのような友達がいることが自慢。	**I'm proud of having a friend like you.**
あなたの幸せは私の幸せ。	**Your happiness is my happiness.**
幸せを分けてくれてありがとう。	**Thank you for sharing your happiness with me.**

君への感謝の気持ちを表す言葉が見つからない。	**It's hard to find words to express my gratitude to you.** ＊gratitude＝感謝
自分を刺激してくれる友達がいるのはありがたいこと。	**I'm grateful for having friends who inspire me.** ＊grateful for ～＝～に感謝して　inspire＝～を刺激する
あなたに出会えたことが、何よりの宝物。	**Meeting you is the best thing that ever happened to me.**
真の友情ほど大切なものはない。	**Nothing is more priceless than true friendship.** ＊priceless＝非常に貴重な
うわべだけの友達100人より、真の友達1人のほうがいい。	**I would rather have one true friend than 100 superficial friends.** ＊would rather ～＝むしろ～したい　superficial＝外見上の、見せかけの
なかなか会えなくても、あなたは本当の友達。	**Even if we can't see each other often, we're true friends.**

愛の言葉

あなたがすべて。	**You're my one and only.**
愛してる、これからもずっと。	**I love you and I always will.**
あなたといるときは、何もかもが特別。	**With you around, everything is special.**
あなたのそばにいられるだけで幸せ。	**I'm happy just to be with you.**
あなたがいるから、私の人生に意義がある。	**You make my life meaningful.**
私たち、離れていても気持ちは一緒だよ。	**We're physically apart but emotionally together.** ＊physically＝身体上、物理的に　emotionally＝感情的に
私たち、一緒になる運命なんだ。	**We're meant to be together.** ＊meant［メント］to ～＝～する運命で
一緒に年を重ねたい。	**I want to grow old with you.**
生まれ変わってもあなたと一緒になりたい。	**Even if I'm reborn, I want to be with you in my next life.**
愛に勝るものはない。	**Love is more powerful than anything.**

ことわざ・信条

当たり前の生活が送れることに感謝しよう。	**Be thankful for the ordinary life that you have.** ＊ordinary＝普通の
幸福とは、あるがままを受け入れ感謝すること。	**Happiness is accepting and appreciating what is.** ＊accept＝～を受け入れる appreciate＝～に感謝する
努力は裏切らない。	**Your efforts won't betray you.** ＊betray＝～を裏切る
継続は力なり。	**Perseverance pays off.** ＊perseverance＝粘り強さ pay off＝実を結ぶ
笑顔は最高の化粧。	**A smile is the best makeup.**
遅くてもしないよりはまし。	**Better late than never.**
学問に近道なし。	**There are no shortcuts to learning.** ＊shortcut＝近道
陰で支えてくれている人への感謝の気持ちを忘れずに。	**Don't forget to thank those who've supported you behind the scenes.** ＊behind the scenes＝陰で
過去のことは水に流そう。	**Forgive and forget.** ＊forgive＝許す
感情を選ぶことはできないけど、対処の仕方には選択があるよ。	**I can't choose how I feel, but I can choose what I do about it.**
苦労なくして得るものなし。	**No pain, no gain.** ＊pain＝骨折り、苦労
経験は最良の師。	**Experience is the best teacher.**
行動は言葉よりも雄弁に語る。	**Actions speak louder than words.**
歳月は人を待たず。	**Time and tide wait for no man.** ＊tide＝潮
幸せを広めれば、自分にも返ってくる。	**If you spread happiness, you will receive it back.**
情けは人のためならず。	**Your kindness will be rewarded in the end.**
失敗は成功のもと。	**Every failure is a stepping-stone to success.** ＊failure＝失敗 stepping-stone＝足がかり、踏み石
正直は最良の策。	**Honesty is the best policy.** ＊policy＝方策、手段

初心忘れるべからず。	**Always maintain a beginner's first-time enthusiasm and humility.** ＊maintain＝～を維持する　enthusiasm＝熱中、熱狂　humility＝謙そん、謙虚
信用を得るには年月がかかるけれど、失うときは一瞬。	**It takes time to earn trust, but it can be lost in an instant.** ＊in an instant＝一瞬で
出会いを大切に。	**Treasure each encounter.** ＊treasure＝～を大切にする　encounter＝出会い
できると思えばできるし、できないと思えばできない。	**If you think you can, you can. If you think you can't, you can't.**
努力し続けることも才能のうち。	**Continuous effort is a talent, too.** ＊continuous＝継続的な
ちりも積もれば山となる。	**Many a little makes a mickle.** ＊mickle＝たくさん
どんな達人だって、最初は初心者。	**All experts were beginners at one time.** ＊at one time＝かつては、ある時は
悩みは話せば半減する。幸せは話すと２倍になる。	**A trouble shared is halved, and a joy shared is doubled.** ＊halve[ハァヴ]＝～を半分にする　double＝～を倍にする
半分入ったグラスと半分空のグラス、基本的には同じこと。それをどう捉えるかが違うだけ。	**A half-full glass and a half-empty glass are basically the same. It just depends on how you look at it.**
人のふり見てわがふり直せ。	**Gain wisdom from the follies of others.** ＊wisdom＝賢明、知恵　folly＝愚行
覆水盆に返らず。	**It is no use crying over spilt milk.** ＊no use ～ing＝～しても役に立たない　spilt[スピルト]＝こぼれた
用心するに越したことはない。	**Better safe than sorry.**
毎日を精一杯生きよう。	**Live every day to the fullest.** ＊to the fullest＝十分に、心ゆくまで
まさかの友は、真の友。	**A friend in need is a friend indeed.**
勇敢になれるまで、勇敢に振る舞っていよう。	**Act bravely until you really feel brave.** ＊bravely＝勇敢に　brave＝勇敢な
意志があれば道は開ける。	**Where there's a will, there's a way.** ＊will＝意志

Memo

心に留めておきたい言葉を、メモしておきましょう。

書き留めたい言葉を使って 英語日記を書いてみよう

心に残る言葉やことわざを交えて、英語で書いてみましょう。

自分を信じよう

I'm not confident in myself these days. Running away from my troubles is easy, but I know it won't help me mature. I need to believe in myself.

最近、自分に自信がない。困難から逃げ出すのは簡単だけど、それじゃ成長できないこともわかってる。自分を信じなきゃ。

confidentは「自信がある」という意味の形容詞で、「自分に自信がある」はconfident in myselfと表します。running away from ～は「～から逃げ出すこと」、matureは「成長する」、believe in myselfは「自分を信じる」という意味です。

成功者の共通点

I read an article about successful people. Basically, successful people never give up and never cease to strive.

成功者の記事を読んだ。基本的に成功者は決してあきらめないし、努力をやめることもない。

successfulは「成功した、好結果を収めた」という意味の形容詞です。ちなみに、名詞はsuccess（成功、成功者）、動詞はsucceed（成功する、うまくいく）。cease to ～（動詞の原形）は「～するのをやめる」、striveは「努力する」の意味です。

口先だけの人

That guy is all talk, but no action. I wanna teach him the saying, "Actions speak louder than words."

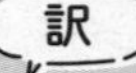

あの人、口では偉そうなことを言うくせに、実際は何もしない。「行動は言葉よりも雄弁に語る」ということわざを教えてやりたい。

That guy is all talk, but no action. は「あの人は口先だけの男で、実行はしない」というニュアンス。wanna［ワナ］は want to のカジュアルな形です。「ことわざ」は saying や proverb と言います。

親友のありがたみ

Something unpleasant happened to me. Kanae came to comfort me even though it was late at night and she was tired. I realized nothing is more priceless than true friendship.

イヤなことがあった。夜遅く、疲れていたのにもかかわらず、カナエが慰めに来てくれた。真の友情ほど大切なものはないと感じた。

something unpleasant は「イヤなこと」。このように、something ～（形容詞）で「～なこと」という意味を表します。「～にもかかわらず」は even though ～または although ～で。comfort は「～を慰める」、priceless は「（値段がつけられないほど）貴重な」の意味。

2章

英語日記に役立つ文法

英文を書く上で知っておきたい基本的な文法を、詳しく解説。
ルールを押さえておけば、英語日記もラクに書けるようになります。

文法 1
名詞の複数形

two oranges（2 個のオレンジ）や 20 students（20 人の生徒）のように、数えられるものが 2 つ以上あるとき、その名詞の最後が -s や -es などに変化します（複数形）。変化のパターンにはいくつかあるので、以下の表で確認してみましょう。複数形の多くは単語の末尾に -s を付けますが、それ以外の変化のパターンもあります。

複数形のつくり方に迷うこともあるかもしれませんが、間違いを気にし過ぎず、少しずつ慣れていきましょう。また、辞書で名詞を引くと、見出し語の近くに複数形が載っているので、迷ったら確認してみるのもいいですね。

■複数形をつくるときのパターン

● -s を付けるパターン

大部分の名詞は、語尾に -s を付けます。

book（本）→ **books**
DVD（DVD）→ **DVDs**
month（[暦の]月）→ **months**
idea（考え）→ **ideas**
orange（オレンジ）→ **oranges**
place（場所）→ **places**

● -es を付けるパターン

つづり字が -s、-x、-ch、-sh で終わる名詞と、-o で終わる名詞の一部は、語尾に -es を付けます。

bus（バス）→ **buses**
box（箱）→ **boxes**
watch（腕時計）→ **watches**
dish（皿）→ **dishes**
tomato（トマト）→ **tomatoes**

● -y → -ies になるパターン

つづり字が〈子音字 + y〉で終わる名詞は、-y を -i に変えて es を付けます。

例
city（都市）→ cities
country（国）→ countries
story（物語）→ stories
dictionary（辞書）→ dictionaries

● -f / -fe → -ves になるパターン

つづり字が -f または -fe で終わる名詞の一部は、語尾を -ves に変えます。

例
leaf（葉）→ leaves
half（半分）→ halves
knife（ナイフ）→ knives
wife（妻）→ wives

●不規則に変化するものと単複同形のもの

これまでのパターン以外に、不規則に変化する名詞や、単数形と複数形が同じ名詞もあります。

例
man（男）→ men
woman（女）→ women
child（子ども）→ children
foot（足）→ feet
deer（シカ）→ deer
fish（魚）→ fish

two oranges

文法2 冠詞

英語では多くの場合、名詞の前に冠詞を付けます。冠詞とは、a、an、the のこと。a は、a dog（1 匹の犬）や a pencil（1 本の鉛筆）のように、数えられる名詞のものが 1 つのときに使います。

an は a と同じ働きをしますが、an apple（1 つのリンゴ）の apple のように、単語が母音（アイウエオに近い音）で始まるときに使います。hour（[アゥア] と発音）のように、スペルは子音で始まっていても発音が母音で始まる場合は、an hour（1 時間）のように an を用います。

a/an と the の使い分け

a や an は、主に「不特定のもの、一般的なもの」について書くときに付けます。これに対して、「特定のもの」について書くときは the を使います。例えば、「（家の近所の）あのカフェ」なら the café、「（昨日読んだ）その本」なら the book となります。the は、その後に続く名詞が 1 つ（単数）でも 2 つ以上（複数）でも使うことができます。

■冠詞の基本ルール

本を１冊買いました。その本はマザー・テレサに関するものです。

I bought a book. The book is about Mother Teresa.

ここでは、「(書店にある、たくさんの本の中の) １冊」を指している(不特定)。

前に出てきた「(書店で買った) その本」を指している (特定)。

私は本が好きです。

I like books.

一般的なさまざまな本を指しているので複数形になり、冠詞は付かない。

図書館に (複数の) 本を返却し、英語の本を１冊借りた。

I returned the books to the library and borrowed an English book.

返却したのは「(借りていた) その本」と特定しているので、theを付ける。

新しく借りたのは図書館に数ある英語の本のうちの１冊であり、English bookは母音で始まるので、冠詞はanになる。

a/an、theはこのほかにもさまざまな使い方があります。完ぺきに覚えるのは難しいので、まずは、ここで紹介した基本ルールに慣れていきましょう。冠詞が合っているか間違っているかにとらわれ過ぎず、楽しく英語日記を書いてくださいね。

文法 3 前置詞

英文に、「いつ」「どこで」「誰と」などの要素を補うときに便利なのが前置詞です。前置詞は、〈前置詞＋名詞〉のセットで使われます。まずは、英語日記を書くときによく使う前置詞を押さえておきましょう。

■場所を表す前置詞

前置詞	例文
at ～ 【～（店や駅といった具体的な場所など）で】	私はカフェで彼に会った。 I met him at the café.
in ～ 【～（国名、地名、建物や部屋の中など）で】	彼は岩手で育った。 He grew up in Iwate.
to ～ 【～（到着点）へ】	カオリはバンクーバーへ行った。 Kaori went to Vancouver.
for ～ 【～（方向・目的地）へ】	私は香港へ向かった。 I left for Hong Kong.
into ～ 【～の中へ】	彼女は試着室の中に入っていった。 She went into the fitting room.
from ～ 【～から】	昨日、和歌山から帰った。 I came back from Wakayama yesterday.
near ～ 【～の近くに】	そのレストランは駅の近くにある。 The restaurant is near the station.
by ～ 【～のすぐそばに】	彼は入口のすぐそばに立っていた。 He was standing by the entrance.
in front of ～ 【～の前に・前で（位置関係を表す）】	市役所の前で交通事故があった。 There was a car accident in front of the City Hall.
behind ～ 【～の後ろに・後ろで（位置関係を表す）】	ポチはソファの後ろに隠れた。 Pochi hid himself behind the sofa.

■時を表す前置詞

at ～ 【～（時刻・時）に】	午後7時にオフィスを出た。 **I left the office at 7 p.m.**
on ～ 【～（日付・曜日・特定の日時）に】	ペギーは3月7日に日本に着く。 **Peggy arrives in Japan on March 7.**
in ～ 【～（年・月・季節・午前・午後など）に】	7月にシンガポールに行く予定だ。 **I'm going to go to Singapore in July.**
from ～ 【～（時の起点）から】	来週から新しいオフィスで働く。 **I'm going to work in the new office from next week.**
from ～ to ... 【～から…まで】	明日は朝9時から夜7時まで働かなくてはいけない。 **I have to work from 9 a.m. to 7 p.m. tomorrow.**
until ～ / till ～ 【～（終点）までずっと】	今朝の4時までプレゼンテーションの準備をした。 **I prepared for the presentation until 4:00 this morning.**
by ～ 【～（期限）までに】	金曜日までにレポートを提出しなければならない。 **I have to hand in the report by Friday.**
for ～ 【～（動作や状態が継続する時間）の間】	今日は2時間、英語を勉強した。 **I studied English for two hours today.**
during ～ 【～（特定の期間）の間】	夏休みの期間中、タイに滞在した。 **I stayed in Thailand during the summer vacation.**
in ～ 【今から～後に】	2日後にミカに会える！ **I can see Mika in two days!**
within ～ 【～以内に】	3日以内に決断しなければならない。 **I have to make the decision within three days.**
before ～ 【～の前に】	明日、夜8時前には家に帰りたい。 **I want to get back home before 8 p.m. tomorrow.**
after ～ 【～の後に】	私たちは仕事の後、飲みに行った。 **We went for a drink after work.**

■そのほかの前置詞

with ～ 【～と一緒に】	ショウコと夕飯を食べた。 **I had dinner with Shoko.**
for ～ 【～（目的・理由）のために】	そのプレゼンテーションのために頑張った。 **I worked hard for the presentation.**
by ～ 【～（交通や通信の手段）で】	バスでおばの家に行った。 **I went to my aunt's house by bus.**
from ～ 【～（物事の起点）から】	リョウタからメールをもらった。 **I got an e-mail from Ryota.**

■前置詞がいらない語句

場所や時を表す語句の中には、前置詞がいらないものもあります。下に、よく使う語句をまとめました。これらは、副詞（副詞句）と呼ばれます。

【場所を表す語句】

here　ここで、ここへ
there　そこで、そこへ
home　家で、家へ
abroad / overseas　海外で、海外へ
upstairs　上の階で、上の階へ
downtown　繁華街で、繁華街へ

いつかそこに行けたらいいな。
I want to go there someday.

※ here、there、home は意味をはっきりさせるために前置詞と共に使うこともあります。
例：It was hot in there.（そこは［＝その中は］暑かった）

【時を表す語句】

today　今日
yesterday　昨日
tomorrow　明日
tomorrow が付く語
（tomorrow evening［明日の夕方］など）
this が付く語　（this morning［今朝］など）
that が付く語
（that afternoon［その日の午後］など）
last が付く語　（last night［昨夜］など）
next が付く語　（next year［来年］など）

明日、買い物に行きたいな。
I want to go shopping tomorrow.

文法4 動詞の語形変化

動詞は、主語が誰（何）なのか、時制が現在なのか過去なのかなどによって、**形を変化させる**必要があります。

例えば「東京に住んでいる」のように現在のことを表す文の場合、日本語では主語が「私」でも「彼」でも「住んでいる」の形は変化しません。ところが英語では、主語によって動詞の形が変わります。

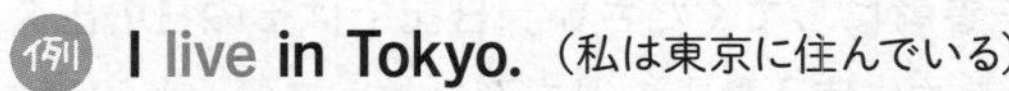

例 **I live in Tokyo.**（私は東京に住んでいる）

He lives in Tokyo.（彼は東京に住んでいる）

動詞の３人称単数現在形

主語がhe、she、it（３人称の代名詞）や名詞の単数形で、時制が現在の場合、**動詞の語尾に -s や -es を付けます**。どのように動詞を変化させるかは、次の通りです。

■３人称単数現在形のルール

動詞	ルール	例
下記以外の動詞	-sを付ける	**live**（住む）→ **lives** **work**（働く）→ **works**
語尾が -s、-x、-ch、-sh の動詞	-esを付ける	**pass**（通り過ぎる）→ **passes** **wash**（洗う）→ **washes**
語尾が〈子音字＋y〉の動詞	yをiに変えて -esを付ける	**try**（試みる）→ **tries** **study**（勉強する）→ **studies**
語尾が〈子音字＋o〉の動詞	-esを付ける	**go**（行く）→ **goes** **echo**（反響する）→ **echoes**

過去形のつくり方

過去を表す文の場合は、**動詞に -d または -ed を付けます（不規則に変化するものもあります）**。また、動詞の過去形は、どんな主語でも同じ形を用います。例えば、「5 キロ歩いた」という場合、「私は 5 キロ歩いた」「母は 5 キロ歩いた」のどちらでも、動詞の過去形は同じ walked です。

 **I walked 5km.**（私は 5 キロ歩いた）

My mother walked 5km.（母は 5 キロ歩いた）

過去形のつくり方は、下の表を参考にしてください。日記ではその日の出来事を過去形で表すことが多いので、日常的に使う動詞の過去形を覚えておくと便利です。

■過去形をつくるときのルール

動詞	ルール	例
下記以外の動詞	-ed を付ける	**walk**（歩く）→ **walked** **work**（働く）→ **worked**
語尾が -e の動詞	-d を付ける	**live**（住む）→ **lived** **like**（好む）→ **liked**
語尾が〈1 母音字＋ 1 子音字〉の動詞	語尾の子音字を重ねて -ed を付ける	**stop**（止まる）→ **stopped** **plan**（計画する）→ **planned**
語尾が〈子音字＋ y〉の動詞	y を i に変えて -ed を付ける	**cry**（泣く）→ **cried** **study**（勉強する）→ **studied**
一部の動詞	不規則	**make**（作る）→ **made** **take**（手に取る）→ **took** **see**（見る）→ **saw** **write**（書く）→ **wrote** **cut**（切る）→ **cut** **put**（置く）→ **put**

過去分詞のつくり方

過去分詞は、現在完了形（p. 676 参照）や受け身の文（p. 681 参照）で使う動詞の形です。過去分詞は過去形と同じ形に変化することも多いのですが、動詞によっては過去形とまったく異なる形に不規則に変化するものもあります。例えば、see–saw–seen（見る）や write–wrote–written（書く）といった具合です。

p. 656 〜 663 の「日記で使える動詞ミニ辞典」や辞書などを参考にして、よく使う動詞の過去分詞を覚えておくと便利ですよ。

-ing 形のつくり方

動詞に -ing を付けた形（-ing 形）で、「〜している」という意味の進行形をつくったり、「〜すること」という意味を表したりすることができます。例えば、Yoko is cooking.（ヨウコは料理している）や、I like driving.（運転することが好きだ）という具合です。-ing 形のつくり方は次の通りです。

■ -ing 形をつくるときのルール

動詞	ルール	例
下記以外の動詞	-ing を付ける	**play**（遊ぶ）→ **playing** **cook**（料理する）→ **cooking**
語尾が〈子音字+ e〉の動詞	-e を取って -ing を付ける	**make**（作る）→ **making** **drive**（運転する）→ **driving**
語尾が〈1 母音字＋ 1 子音字〉の動詞	子音字を重ねて -ing を付ける	**run**（走る）→ **running** **get**（得る）→ **getting**
語尾が -ie で終わる動詞	-ie を y に変えて -ing を付ける	**die**（死ぬ）→ **dying** **tie**（結ぶ）→ **tying** **lie**（横たわる）→ **lying**

動詞の変化形は、「ルールが細かい上に例外も多くて、覚えるのが大変」と思うかもしれません。でも、焦らずに少しずつ覚えていけば大丈夫です。次ページからの「日記で使える動詞ミニ辞典」を参照しながら日記を書き続けるうちに、自然と頭に定着していきますよ。

■日記で使える動詞ミニ辞典

日記でよく使う動詞の変化形をまとめました。迷ったら、この「ミニ辞典」を参考にしてみてくださいね。

	意味	現在形
あ	アイロンがけをする	do the ironing
	～に会う	meet
	…に～をあげる	give ... ～
	朝寝坊する	sleep in
	～に謝る	apologize to ～
	歩く	walk
い	～と言う	say
	家を出る	leave home
	～へ行く	go to ～
	医者に診てもらう	see a doctor
	犬の散歩をする	walk my dog
う	～を歌う	sing
	～を打ち負かす	beat
	運動する	exercise
え	映画を見に行く	go to the movies
お	～を終える	finish
	起きる	get up
	…に～を教える	teach ... ～
	おしゃべりする	have a chat
	～だと思う	think (that) ～
	泳ぐ	swim
	～を（車から）降ろす	drop off
か	外食する	eat out
	買い物に行く	go shopping
	～を買う	buy
	～を返す	return
	～を書く	write
	～を貸す	lend

※句動詞の変化形は、変化した動詞部分のみ記載しています。

主語が he、she などのとき	過去形	過去分詞	-ing 形
does	did	done	doing
meets	met	met	meeting
gives	gave	given	giving
sleeps	slept	slept	sleeping
apologizes	apologized	apologized	apologizing
walks	walked	walked	walking
says	said	said	saying
leaves	left	left	leaving
goes	went	gone	going
sees	saw	seen	seeing
walks	walked	walked	walking
sings	sang	sung	singing
beats	beat	beat, beaten	beating
exercises	exercised	exercised	exercising
goes	went	gone	going
finishes	finished	finished	finishing
gets	got	got, gotten	getting
teaches	taught	taught	teaching
has	had	had	having
thinks	thought	thought	thinking
swims	swam	swum	swimming
drops	dropped	dropped	dropping
eats	ate	eaten	eating
goes	went	gone	going
buys	bought	bought	buying
returns	returned	returned	returning
writes	wrote	written	writing
lends	lent	lent	lending

	意味	現在形
か	～に勝つ	win
	髪を切る	get a haircut
	～を借りる（無料）	borrow
	～を借りる（有料）	rent
き	～を聞く	listen to ～
	～が聞こえる	hear
	帰宅する	get (back) home
	～を気に入る	like
	～を着る	wear
く	来る	come
け	化粧を落とす	take off my makeup
	化粧をする	do my makeup
こ	ごみを出す	take out the garbage
さ	サービス残業する	work off the clock
	～を探す	look for ～
	皿洗いをする	do the dishes
	～に参加する	take part in ～
	残業する	work overtime
し	～を試着する	try on ～ / try ～ on
	～を修理する	fix
	出産する	have a baby
	～の準備をする、～を用意する	prepare
	ジョギングをする	jog
	（自宅で）食事する	dine (at home)
	食料品を買いに行く	go grocery shopping
す	～（時）を過ごす	spend
	～をする	do
せ	洗濯をする	do the laundry
そ	～に掃除機をかける	vacuum
	～を掃除する	clean

主語が he、she などのとき	過去形	過去分詞	-ing 形
wins	won	won	winning
gets	got	got, gotten	getting
borrows	borrowed	borrowed	borrowing
rents	rented	rented	renting
listens	listened	listened	listening
hears	heard	heard	hearing
gets	got	got, gotten	getting
likes	liked	liked	liking
wears	wore	worn	wearing
comes	came	come	coming
takes	took	taken	taking
does	did	done	doing
takes	took	taken	taking
works	worked	worked	working
looks	looked	looked	looking
does	did	done	doing
takes	took	taken	taking
works	worked	worked	working
tries	tried	tried	trying
fixes	fixed	fixed	fixing
has	had	had	having
prepares	prepared	prepared	preparing
jogs	jogged	jogged	jogging
dines	dined	dined	dining
goes	went	gone	going
spends	spent	spent	spending
does	did	done	doing
does	did	done	doing
vacuums	vacuumed	vacuumed	vacuuming
cleans	cleaned	cleaned	cleaning

	意味	現在形
た	退院する	get out of the hospital
	滞在する、泊まる	stay
	立ち寄る	stop by
	楽しい時を過ごす	have a good time
	～を楽しみにする	look forward to ～
	～を楽しむ	enjoy
	～を頼む	ask
	食べ過ぎる	overeat
	～を食べる	eat
ち	…から～を注文する・取り寄せる	order ～ from ...
つ	～に着く	get to ～
	～を作る	make
て	～を提出する	hand in ～
	～に手紙を書く	write to ～
	～を手伝う	help
	～に電話をする	call
な	～になる	become
に	入院する	go into the hospital
ね	ネットサーフィンする	surf the Internet
	眠る、寝る	sleep
	寝る、床につく	go to bed
の	飲みに行く	go (out) for a drink
は	パーマをかける	get a perm
	～を始める	begin
	走る	run
	働き過ぎる	overwork
	働く	work
	～と話をする	talk with ～
	～を話す・伝える	tell
ひ	昼寝する	take a nap

主語が he、she などのとき	過去形	過去分詞	-ing 形
gets	got	got, gotten	getting
stays	stayed	stayed	staying
stops	stopped	stopped	stopping
has	had	had	having
looks	looked	looked	looking
enjoys	enjoyed	enjoyed	enjoying
asks	asked	asked	asking
overeats	overate	overeaten	overeating
eats	ate	eaten	eating
orders	ordered	ordered	ordering
gets	got	got, gotten	getting
makes	made	made	making
hands	handed	handed	handing
writes	wrote	written	writing
helps	helped	helped	helping
calls	called	called	calling
becomes	became	become	becoming
goes	went	gone	going
surfs	surfed	surfed	surfing
sleeps	slept	slept	sleeping
goes	went	gone	going
goes	went	gone	going
gets	got	got, gotten	getting
begins	began	begun	beginning
runs	ran	run	running
overworks	overworked	overworked	overworking
works	worked	worked	working
talks	talked	talked	talking
tells	told	told	telling
takes	took	taken	taking

	意味	現在形
ふ	～を復習する	review
	風呂に入る	take a bath
へ	～を勉強する	study
	～に返信する	reply to ～
ま	～に負ける	lose to ～
	～を待つ	wait for ～
み	～を見送る	see off ～ / see ～ off
	～を磨く	polish
	～を見つける	find
	～を見る	see
む	～を（車で）迎えに行く	pick ～ up
め	～にメールする	e-mail
	目を覚ます	wake up
	～の面倒をみる	take care of ～
も	～を申し込む	apply for ～
	～を持っていく・連れていく	take
	～を持っている	have
	～を持ってくる・連れてくる	bring
	～をもらう・得る	get
や	～を辞める	quit
よ	ヨガをする	practice yoga
	（病気や体調が）よくなる	get better
	横になる	lie down
	予習する	prepare (for) my lesson
	～を読む	read
	～を予約する	book
り	料理する	cook
	（～へ）旅行に出かける	go on a trip (to ～)
れ	～を練習する	practice
	～から連絡がある	hear from ～

主語が he、she などのとき	過去形	過去分詞	-ing 形
reviews	reviewed	reviewed	reviewing
takes	took	taken	taking
studies	studied	studied	studying
replies	replied	replied	replying
loses	lost	lost	losing
waits	waited	waited	waiting
sees	saw	seen	seeing
polishes	polished	polished	polishing
finds	found	found	finding
sees	saw	seen	seeing
picks	picked	picked	picking
e-mails	e-mailed	e-mailed	e-mailing
wakes	waked, woke	waked, woken	waking
takes	took	taken	taking
applies	applied	applied	applying
takes	took	taken	taking
has	had	had	having
brings	brought	brought	bringing
gets	got	got, gotten	getting
quits	quit	quit	quitting
practices	practiced	practiced	practicing
gets	got	got, gotten	getting
lies	lay	lain	lying
prepares	prepared	prepared	preparing
reads	read［レッド］	read［レッド］	reading
books	booked	booked	booking
cooks	cooked	cooked	cooking
goes	went	gone	going
practices	practiced	practiced	practicing
hears	heard	heard	hearing

文法 5 文のつながりをよくする言葉

ただ文を並べるだけでは淡々としてしまいがちな日記も、下で紹介している「つなぎの言葉」を使うことで、全体がなめらかになります。右ページの例を参考にしながら使ってみましょう。

■文のつながりをよくする言葉

first	初めに、まず
at first	最初のうちは、最初は
then	それから
after that	その後
in the end	最後に、結局
but	でも、だけど
and yet	それなのに、けれども、それでも
still	とはいえ、それでもやはり
on the other hand	その一方で
also	その上
besides	おまけに、しかも
actually	実際には、こともあろうに
anyway	とにかく、いずれにしても
come to think of it	そういえば、考えてみると
as I thought	思った通り、やはり
as A said	Aが言っていたように
surprisingly	驚いたことに、意外にも
or	でないと、そうでなきゃ
if possible	できたら、可能なら
I don't know why, but	なぜだかわからないけれど
as a result	結果として、結果的に

例えばこう書く！

I had a busy day today. First, I went to the dentist. Then, I visited my uncle in the hospital. After that, I went to a department store to look for a present for Miyuki. At first, I didn't know what to buy, but in the end I found a pretty pearl necklace. It was a bit expensive. Anyway, I hope she'll like it.

First：まず
Then：それから
After that：その後
At first：最初は
in the end：最後には
Anyway：とにかく

今日は忙しい日だった。まず歯医者に行った。それから入院中のおじのお見舞いに行った。その後デパートに行って、ミユキへのプレゼントを探した。最初は何を買えばいいかわからなかったけど、最後にはかわいい真珠のネックレスを見つけた。ちょっと高かった。とにかく、彼女に気に入ってもらえるといいな。

文法6 現在のことを書く［現在形］

次のようなことについて日記を書くときは、動詞を現在形にします。

❶現在の気持ちや状態
❷現在の習慣
❸ことわざ

❶現在の気持ちや状態

「現在の気持ちや状態を表す文」とは、例えば次のような文のことです。

【現在の気持ちを表す文】

例 **I want a car.**（車が欲しいな）
I feel lonely.（寂しい［と感じる］）
I'm happy.（うれしいな／幸せだ）

【現在の状態を表す文】

例 **I know he's right.**（彼が正しいことはわかっている）
My son lives in Kyoto.（息子は京都に住んでいる）
It's cold today.（今日は寒い）

上の例文の中で、want（～が欲しい）、feel（～のように感じる）などは「現在の気持ち」を表しています。一方、know（～だとわかっている・知っている）、live（住んでいる）などは「現在の状態」です。

am や is などの be 動詞は、I'm happy. / It's cold today. のように、「気持ち」を述べるとき、「状態」を説明するときの両方で、よく使われます。I'm は I am の、It's は It is の短縮形です。

例えばこう書く！

My computer is slow. I want a new one.

パソコンの動きが遅い。新しいのが欲しいな。

It's cold every day. I don't want to get out of bed in the morning.

毎日寒い。朝は布団から出たくない。

❷現在の習慣

習慣的あるいは反復的に起こっている現在の事柄について書くときにも、現在形を使います。

例 **Mika always dresses beautifully.**

（ミカはいつもすてきな服装をしている）

Kayo brings her lunch to work every day.

（カヨは毎日会社にお弁当を持ってくる）

I don't cook so often.

（私はあまり料理をしない）

人に関することに限らず、物に関すること（例：The bus is usually on time. =そのバスはたいてい時間通りだ）も、習慣的な事柄であれば動詞を現在形にします。

また、どのぐらいの頻度でしているのかを表すために、次ページにあるような、頻度を表す語句を加えることがよくあります。

●頻度を表す語句の例

always	いつも	every day	毎日
often	よく	every other day	1日おきに
usually	たいてい、普通は	every ～(曜日)	毎週～曜日に
sometimes	時々	every year	毎年
rarely	めったに～ない	once a week	週に1度
never	まったく～ない	a few times a month	月に数回

例えばこう書く！

Rie takes English lessons every Sunday. She really is hardworking.

リエは毎週日曜日に英語のレッスンを受けている。彼女は本当に頑張り屋だ。

Seiya is always five minutes late. Why doesn't he get up a little early?

セイヤはいつも5分遅刻する。どうして少し早く起きないのかな。

❸ことわざ

ことわざや格言などを書くときにも、動詞を現在形で表します。また、文中でことわざや格言を引用するときは、文全体が過去形であっても、ことわざや格言は過去形にせず現在形のままでOKです。時制の一致（p. 693参照）というルールには当てはまりません。

例 **He said actions speak louder than words.**

主となる動詞（過去形）→ ことわざ内の動詞（現在形のまま）

時制の一致を受けない

（彼は、言葉より行動のほうが大切だと言った）

●英語のことわざ

Time is money.（時は金なり）

Birds of a feather flock together.（類は友を呼ぶ） ＊a feather＝同じ種類　flock＝集まる

When in Rome, do as the Romans do.（郷に入っては郷に従え）

Two heads are better than one.
（三人寄れば文殊の知恵／二人で考えたほうがよい案が出る）

No pain, no gain.（苦労なくして得るものなし） ＊gain＝得るもの

Where there's smoke, there's fire.（火のないところに煙は立たぬ）

No news is good news.（便りのないのはよい便り）

Even Homer sometimes nods.
（弘法にも筆の誤り） ＊Homer＝ホメロス　nod＝うとうとする

A cheap purchase is money lost.（安物買いの銭失い）

Failure teaches success.（失敗は成功のもと）

Practice makes perfect.（習うより慣れよ）

The early bird catches the worm.（早起きは三文の徳） ＊worm＝虫

Slow and〈but〉steady wins the race.（急がば回れ／遅くても着実なほうが勝つ）

例えばこう書く！

I woke up around 5:00 and saw Hugh Jackman on TV! As the saying goes, the early bird catches the worm.

5時ごろ起きたら、テレビにヒュー・ジャックマンが出ていた！　ことわざにある通り、早起きは三文の徳だ。　＊saying＝ことわざ

文法7 過去のことを書く［過去形］

次のようなことについて日記を書くときは、動詞を過去形（p. 654 参照）にします。その日に「したこと」や「あったこと」をよく書く日記では、使用頻度の高い時制です。

❶したこと

例 **I weeded my yard today.**（今日、庭の草取りをした）

I called my father.（父に電話した）

❷あったこと

例 **My mother sent me some apples.**
（母がリンゴを送ってきてくれた）

There was a car accident near the office today.
（今日、会社の近くで交通事故があった）

❸過去のある時点での感情

例 **I was happy.**（うれしかった）

It was a shame.（残念だった）

❹（1日を振り返って）今日の天気や自分の状態

例 **It was really hot today.**（今日はとても暑かった）

I was very busy.（とても忙しかった）

例えばこう書く！

I had a job interview today. I was very nervous.
今日、就職面接があった。すごく緊張した。

文法8 未来のことを書く［be going to、willなど］

日記には、予定や計画、それに対する気持ちなど、未来のことについて書くこともありますね。未来のことを表す形にはいくつかのパターンがあり、「実現の可能性がどのくらいか」や、「いつ決めた予定か」などによって使い分けます。

■未来のことを表すパターンの例

表すこと	英語での表し方
❶日時が決まっている行事や、時刻表などによって確定している予定	**動詞の現在形**
❷すでに決めてある予定や、状況から判断してそうなると思われること	**be going to ＋動詞の原形** **be ＋動詞の –ing 形**
❸日記を書きながら決めたこと	**〜 'll ＋動詞の原形**
❹「〜するぞ」という、未来に対する強い意志	**will ＋動詞の原形** **be going to ＋動詞の原形** **be ＋動詞の –ing 形**

※❷❸❹の「動詞の原形」とは、動詞が変化していない「元の形」です。be 動詞（is、am、are など）の原形は be です。❸の「〜'll」は、will の短縮形です。

❶日時が決まっている行事や、時刻表などで確定している予定

年間行事などの日時が決まっていることや、時刻表などで確定している交通機関の発着などは、未来のことであっても現在形で表します。自分が決めた個人的な予定ではなく、公的な行事・イベントなどについて表現するときによく使われます。

例 **The new term starts next Monday.**
（来週の月曜日から新学期が始まる）

My flight leaves at 9:10 tomorrow.
（私が乗る飛行機は、明日の 9 時 10 分に出発する）

●未来のことでも現在形で表すことが多い動詞

【行事の開始や終了を表す動詞】

start 始まる

begin 始まる

finish 終わる

end 終わる

open 始まる、開店する

close 終わる、閉店する

【交通機関の発着を表す動詞】

go 行く

come 来る

leave 出発する

depart 出発する、離陸する

arrive 到着する

get 着く

例えばこう書く！

The winter sale starts tomorrow. I'm so excited!

明日から冬のバーゲンが始まる。すごく楽しみ！

❷すでに決まっている予定

日時や場所などが決まっていて、自分がこれからそうするつもりである予定（例：I'm going to write my New Year's greeting cards this weekend. ＝今週末は年賀状を書く）や、状況から判断してそうなるだろうと思われる事柄（例：It's going to snow. ＝雪が降りそうだ）などは、〈be going to ＋動詞の原形〉を使って表します。

前者のように、「いつ・どこで・誰と・何を」するのかという具体的なことが決まっている個人的な予定は、〈be ＋動詞の -ing 形〉を使って表すこともできます（例：I'm writing my New Year's greeting cards this weekend. ＝今週末は年賀状を書く）。また、状況や人によっては、〈～'ll be ＋動詞の -ing 形〉で、すでに決まっている予定を表すこともあります。

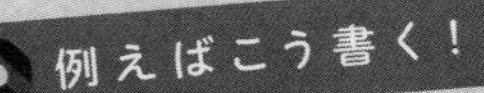

I'm going to visit my sister's family the day after tomorrow. What should I take?

あさって、姉家族の家に遊びに行く。何を持っていこうかな？

❸日記を書きながら決めたこと

すでに決まっている予定とは違い、「～しようっと」「～しようかな」のように、その場で思い付いて決めたことは、will の短縮形を使って〈～'ll＋動詞の原形〉で表します。例えば、庭に生えた雑草を見て、I'll weed my yard tomorrow.（明日は草取りをしようかな）と思い立ったり、明日は雨になると天気予報で聞いて、I'll stay home tomorrow.（明日は家にいようっと）と決めたりしたときなどに使います。

〈be going to＋動詞の原形〉と〈～'ll＋動詞の原形〉の違いを理解するために、次の2つの例文を比較してみましょう。

We're going to have Hiro's birthday party on Saturday.（土曜日にヒロの誕生日パーティーを開く予定だ）

Oh, tomorrow is Hiro's birthday! I'll give him a present.（あっ、明日はヒロの誕生日だ！　プレゼントをあげようっと）

例えばこう書く！

My room is so messy. OK, I'll clean it this Sunday.

部屋が汚いなぁ。よし、今度の日曜日は部屋を掃除しようっと。

＊ messy ＝散らかった

❹「〜するぞ」という強い意志

will は強い意志を表すことができ、この場合は、「〜'll」と短縮せずに will と書きます。例えば、試験の不合格通知を受けて、I will study harder to pass the exam next time.（今度こそ合格できるように、もっと勉強を頑張るぞ）と誓ったり、I will absolutely invite you to my new house.（あなたを新居に必ずご招待しますよ）と強い意志を示したりするときには、will を使うのがぴったりです。日記では、自分自身のことについての意気込みを述べたり、新年の抱負などの決意を書いたりするときに使ってみましょう。

強い意志は、このほかに、〈be going to ＋動詞の原形〉や〈be ＋動詞の -ing 形〉で表すこともできます。これらの表現は、あらかじめ決まっている事柄について用いることから、「〜するぞ」とすでに心に決めている意志や意気込みを表せるのです。

例えばこう書く！

I failed the exam again. Next time I will absolutely pass it!

また不合格だった。次は絶対に合格するぞ！　＊ fail ＝〜（試験など）に落ちる

will のそのほかの用法

will は強い意志のほかにも、次のような事柄を表すときに使います。

●「～だろう」という、話し手の確信度が高い推量

例 **She will probably be late.**（たぶん彼女は遅れるだろう）
※ she will は、she'll と表しても OK。

●「～するものだ」という、習性や傾向、必然性

例 **Accidents will happen.**（事故は起こるものだ）

●「何が何でも～しようとする」「どうしても～しようとしない」という強い固執

例 **My boss will go his own way.**
（上司は、何が何でも自分の思い通りにしようとする）

My daughter won't listen to me.
（娘は私の言うことを聞こうとしない） ※ won't は will not の短縮形

●疑問文で、勧誘・依頼

例 **Will you join us?**（一緒に来ませんか）

Will you wait for me here?（ここで待っていてくれますか）

現在までに起きたことを書く［現在完了形］

現在完了形は〈have/has ＋動詞の過去分詞〉で表し、主に次の 3 つの用法があります（動詞の過去分詞については、p. 655 を参照）。また、I have は I've と短縮して表すこともよくあります。

❶継続　「ずっと～している」
❷完了　「～し終えた」
❸経験　「～したことがある」

❶「継続」の用法

「…の間ずっと～している」「…からずっと～している」という、過去のある時から今まで続いている状態について表す場合は、〈have/has ＋動詞の過去分詞〉を使います。「…の間ずっと～していない」や「…からずっと～していない」という否定文は、〈haven't/hasn't ＋動詞の過去分詞〉で表します。また、be busy（忙しい）のように be 動詞を用いる文は、〈have/has been ～〉とします。

「継続」を表す現在完了形の文では、〈for ＋期間〉で「どのくらいの期間、その状態にあるのか」（例：for five years ＝ 5 年間）を表したり、〈since ＋起点〉で「いつからその状態にあるのか」（例：since yesterday ＝昨日から）を表したりすることがよくあります。

【〈for ＋期間〉の例】		【〈since ＋起点〉の例】	
for three days	3 日間	**since yesterday**	昨日からずっと
for a week	1 週間	**since last Sunday**	この前の日曜日からずっと
for a few months	数カ月間	**since last week**	先週からずっと
for ten years	10 年間	**since this morning**	今朝からずっと
for a long time	長い間	**since I was in high school**	高校の時からずっと
for ages	長い間	**since then**	それからずっと
for years	何年も	**since 2020**	2020 年からずっと

since と ago は一緒に使わない

「4日前から（〜している）」と言いたいとき、since four days ago（×）としてしまいがちですが、since と ago は一緒に使わないのが基本ルールです。この場合は、期間に置き替えて for four days（この4日間）のように表しましょう。

for や since を用いた語句のほか、all day（1日中ずっと）や all afternoon（午後ずっと）など、時間的な幅を持つ語句を用いることもあります。

例えばこう書く！

Aiko has been absent from school for three days.

アイコはこの3日間、学校を欠席している。

Kanae and I have known each other for almost eight years.

カナエと知り合って、もうすぐ8年になる。

It has been raining since last week.

先週からずっと雨だ。

It has been over 20 years since I started writing in my diary in English.

英語で日記を書き始めて20年以上になる。 ＊write in one's diary ＝日記を書く

❷「完了」の用法

「完了」を表す現在完了形は、過去の出来事について述べつつ、その結果が現在に結び付いていることを表します。過去形との区別が難しいと感じる人が多いようですが、現在完了形は、いわば過去と現在の橋渡しのような役割を果たす用法なのです。

例えば、I lost my wallet. は「財布をなくした」という過去の出来事そのものを表した文で、その財布が今も紛失したままなのか、見つかったのかについてはわかりません。一方、現在完了形を使って I've lost my wallet. とすると、「財布をなくし、今もその状態が続いている」→「早く見つかってほしいな、困ったな」という心境まで暗示することができます。

現在完了形が「完了」を表す場合、よく次のような副詞と一緒に使います。

●「完了」の用法でよく使われる副詞

just　ちょうど～したばかり、今～したところだ
already　すでに、もう（～した）
yet　〈否定文で〉まだ（～ない）

注意したいのは、「過去の一時点を表す語句を用いる場合は、現在完了形は使えない」ということです。～ ago（～前に）や yesterday（昨日）のように「過去の一時点を表す語句」が付くと、過去の出来事のほうに焦点が移ってしまいます。現在完了形は、「（過去の出来事の結果）現在の状況や気持ちがどうであるか」ということに意識が向けられているため、違和感が生じてしまうのです。

例えば、「今朝、財布をなくした」なら、I lost my wallet this morning. のように過去形で表します。this morning（今朝）という過去の一時点を表す語句を使っているので、現在完了形は使えません。

実際は、現在完了形を用いるのがふさわしい場合でも、くだけて過去形で表すネイティブ・スピーカーもいます。現在完了形が難しいと感じるうちは過去形で表してもかまいませんが、現在完了形にすべきところは、やはり現在完了形で表現するのが理想的です。

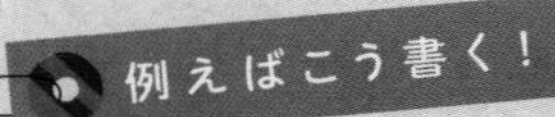

The plates that I ordered have arrived! I'm happy.

注文したお皿が届いた！ うれしいな。

I've just finished my report. Whew.

ちょうど報告書を書き終えた。フ～。

I haven't made the handouts for the meeting yet. What should I do?

まだ会議の資料を作っていない。どうしよう？

❸「経験」の用法

「～したことがある」とこれまでの経験を表す場合にも、〈have/has ＋動詞の過去分詞〉を使います。「一度も～したことがない」という否定の文は、never（一度も～ない）を使って〈have/has never ＋動詞の過去分詞〉と表します。

「～へ行ったことがある」と訪れた場所について表すときは、go（行く）の過去分詞 gone ではなく、be の過去分詞 been を使って、〈have/has been to ＋場所〉のように表す点に注意しましょう。

また、「完了」の用法と同じく、「経験」を表す現在完了形でも、過去の一時点を表す語句と一緒に使うことはできません。例えば、「彼は子どものときアメリカへ行ったことがある」という場合、He has been to America when he was a child.（×）とするのは誤りです。when he was a child（彼が子どものとき）のような「過去の一時点」を表す語句を用いる場合は、He went to America when he was a child. のように過去形で表しましょう。

このほか、16 years ago（16 年前に）や in 2021（2021 年に）、in my college days（大学時代に）などの語句も、現在完了形とは一緒に使えません。ただし、before（以前に）は広い範囲の過去を表すので、現在完了形と一緒に使うことができます。次ページの例文で確認してくださいね。

彼は子どものとき、アメリカへ行ったことがある。

✕ **He has been to America when he was a child.**

○ **He went to America when he was a child.**

彼は以前、アメリカへ行ったことがある。

○ **He has been to America before.**

「経験」を表す現在完了形は、次のような語句と一緒によく用いられます。

●「経験」の用法でよく使われる語句

【文末に置く語句】

once 1度

twice 2度

a few times 数回

many times 何度も

before 以前に

【have や has の直後に置く語句】

never 一度も～ない

【疑問文で使われる語句】

ever これまでに

例えばこう書く！

Ryo has lived in Paris, London and New York. Lucky him!

リョウはパリやロンドン、ニューヨークに住んだことがある。いいなぁ！

Marie has been to Disneyland many times, but I've never been there.

マリエは何度もディズニーランドに行ったことがあるけど、私は一度もない。

文法 10 「〜される」を表す［受け身］

「〜される」「〜された」という受け身の意味を表したいときは、〈be ＋動詞の過去分詞〉の組み合わせを使います（過去分詞については、p. 655 を参照）。例えば、This sweater is made in France.（このセーターはフランスで作られている［＝フランス製だ］）といった具合です（made は make の過去分詞）。否定文は、be 動詞の後ろに not を入れます。過去のことを表すなら、be 動詞を過去形にします。

「このセーターはフランス製だ」のような場合は、「誰がセーターを作るのか」は重要ではないので、それについては述べられていません。受け身の文で「誰がしたのか」を明確にする場合は、〈by ＋人・物〉を付け加えます。The cake was made by Aki.（このケーキはアキによって作られた）という具合です。

受け身には、さまざまなパターンがあります。完了形の受け身の文は、〈have[has/had] ＋ been ＋動詞の過去分詞〉で表します（例：My bike has just been repaired. ＝自転車は修理されたばかりだ）。進行形の受け身の文なら、〈be ＋ being ＋動詞の過去分詞〉です（例：The boy is being scolded. ＝男の子が叱られているところだ）。助動詞を含む受け身の文は、〈助動詞＋ be ＋動詞の過去分詞〉という形になります。例えば、This novel can be read in many languages.（この小説はさまざまな言語で読むことができる）といった具合です。

例えばこう書く！

These cookies are made from okara. They're nice!

このクッキーはおからでできている。おいしい！

I was invited to a tea party! I'm a little nervous.

お茶会に招待された！　少し緊張するなぁ。

文法 11

助動詞の使い方

助動詞は、動詞にちょっとしたニュアンスを加える言葉です。**助動詞は必ず動詞の前に置き、助動詞に続く動詞は原形**にします。

助動詞のない文とある文を比較して、意味の違いを見てみましょう。

 **I ski.**（私はスキーをする）

I can ski.（私はスキーができる）

I do my homework.（私は宿題をする）

I should do my homework.（宿題をしたほうがいいだろう）

He has a cold.（彼は風邪をひいている）

He may have a cold.（彼は風邪をひいているのかもしれない）

●覚えておきたい助動詞

will	～でしょう、～だろう、～するぞ［未来や推量、意志］
can	～できる、～でありうる、(否定文で)～なはずがない［能力や可能性］
may / might	～かもしれない、～してもよい［可能性や許可］
should	～したほうがいいだろう、たぶん～だ、当然～のはずだ［弱い義務や提案、推量］
must	～しなくてはならない、絶対に～なはずだ［必要性や推量］

右ページの例文で、これらの助動詞の具体的な使い方を見てみましょう。

例えばこう書く！

Tetsu can speak English fluently.
テツは英語を流ちょうに話すことができる。

Yuki should be on the airplane now.
ユキは今ごろ飛行機の中にいるはずだ。

She may〈might〉be angry with me.
彼女は私に腹を立てているかもしれないな。

I must leave home at 6:00 tomorrow morning. I should go to bed early tonight.
明日は朝 6 時に家を出ないといけない。今夜は早く寝たほうがいいだろう。

助動詞は 2 つ連続して使わない

助動詞は、will can（×）のように 2 つ連続して使うことはできません。2 つ以上の助動詞のニュアンスを出したいときは、次のように表します。

「(将来) ～できるようになるだろう」

✕ **will can ～**

○ **will be able to ～**

例 **I'll be able to move into my new house next month.**
（来月には新居に引っ越せるだろう）

「～しなくてはならないかもしれない」

✕ **may must ～**

○ **may have to ～**

例 **He may have to work this Saturday.**
（彼は今週土曜日に仕事をしなくてはならないかもしれない）

過去についての推量や確信を表す場合

助動詞を使って過去のことについて推量や確信を表す場合は、〈助動詞 have ＋動詞の過去分詞〉の形を使います（過去分詞については、p. 655 を参照）。下の表のうち、could have は could've、should have は should've、must have は must've と短縮することもよくあります。

●過去のことについて推量などを表す助動詞

could have	〜だったかもしれない［推量］ （〜しようと思えば）〜できただろう［可能］
can't have	〜だったはずがない［否定の推量］
should have	〜したはずだ［当然、確信］ 〜しておけばよかった［後悔］
may have / might have	〜だったかもしれない［推量］
must have	〜だったに違いない［確信］

※could have と may have / might have はいずれも「〜だったかも［〜したかも］しれない」を表しますが、多少、ニュアンスが異なります。could は「実際には起こらなかったことについて、そうなる可能性があった」場合に使います。may や might は「実際に起きたかどうかにかかわらず、そうなっていたかもしれないと推測する」場合に使います。

例えばこう書く！

The coat I bought last week is now 30% off. I should have waited for a week.

先週買ったコートが、今は３割引きになってる。１週間待てばよかった。

Shinji was kind of quiet today. He might have been tired.

シンジは今日、なんだか静かだった。疲れていたのかもしれないな。

文法12

不定詞の使い方

不定詞とは、to と動詞の原形を組み合わせた形のことで、さまざまな用法があります。ここでは、日記で使いやすい不定詞の用法を見てみましょう。

❶動作の目的を表す

例えば、I went to the library.（図書館へ行った）という文があるとします。これだけでも文として成り立ちますが、本を借りに行ったのか返しに行ったのか、あるいは勉強をしに行ったのかなど、その目的を表せばより具体的になります。これらの目的は、〈to ＋動詞の原形〉を使って次のように表します。

例 **I went to the library to borrow some books.**
（本を借りに図書館へ行った）

I went to the library to return the books.
（本を返却しに図書館へ行った）

I went to the library to study English.
（英語の勉強をしに図書館へ行った）

例えばこう書く！

I went to the hair salon to get a perm.
パーマをかけに美容院へ行った。

I went to a department store to buy a present for my mother.
母へのプレゼントを買いにデパートへ行った。

❷名詞に説明を加える

I have some books.（本が何冊かある）という文を見てみましょう。たいていの人は、「読むための本」を想像するのではないでしょうか。でも、作家であれば「書かなくてはならない本」を指しているかもしれませんし、人によっては「捨てる本」や「人にあげる本」を指すかもしれません。

このような場合、名詞に〈to ＋動詞の原形〉を続けることで、名詞に説明を加えて内容を明確にすることができます。

例 **I have some books to write.**（書かなくてはならない本が何冊かある）

I have some books to throw away.（捨てる本が何冊かある）

I have some books to give Yuki.（ユキにあげる本が何冊かある）

例えばこう書く！

I have a lot of things to do. (Sigh)

やるべきことがたくさんある。はぁー。

I have friends to rely on. I'm grateful.

私には頼れる友人たちがいる。ありがたいことだな。

❸感情の原因を表す

I was happy.（うれしかった）やI was sad.（悲しかった）などの感情を表す文に〈to ＋動詞の原形〉を続けると、「～してうれしかった」「～して悲しかった」のように、その感情の原因を表すことができます。

例 **I was happy to hear from Mike.**（マイクから連絡をもらってうれしかった）

I was sad to lose my favorite pen.
（お気に入りのペンをなくして悲しかった）

これらの不定詞は、自分の行動についての感情を表すときに用います。人の行動について自分がどう感じたかを表すときは、I'm happy (that) he passed the exam.（彼が試験に合格してうれしい）のように、〈(that +) 文〉を続けます。

例えばこう書く！

I was excited to watch Samurai Japan's game.
侍ジャパンの試合を見て興奮した。

I was delighted to meet a lot of great people.
たくさんの素晴らしい人に出会えて、光栄だった。

❹「〜するのが（やさしい・難しい）」といった意味を表す

形容詞の後に不定詞を置くと、「〜するのに」「〜するという点で」という意味を表すことができます。例えば、easy は「楽な、簡単な、やさしい」という意味ですが、これに〈to +動詞の原形〉を続けると、「どんな点で」楽なのかを明確にできるのです。

例 **Professor Ishii's class is easy.**（イシイ教授の授業は楽だ）

Professor Ishii's class is easy to understand.
（イシイ教授の授業は理解するのが楽だ［＝理解しやすい］）

● 「〜するのに（…だ）」という意味の不定詞と一緒によく使う形容詞

easy 簡単な	**safe** 安全な	**necessary** 必要である
important 大切な	**dangerous** 危険な	**pleasant** 気持ちのよい
difficult 難しい	**comfortable** 心地いい	**fun** 楽しい ※ fun は名詞ですが、不定詞と一緒に用いることが多いので覚えておきましょう。
hard 難しい、大変な	**convenient** 便利な	
tough 難しい、大変な	**impossible** 不可能な	

また、〈It's ＋形容詞〉に〈to ＋動詞の原形〉を続けると、「〜することは…だ」という意味を表します。この場合、to 以降が意味上の主語です。

例 It's important to practice **every day.**（毎日練習することが大切だ）

It's **not so** hard to play **the guitar.**
（ギターを弾くことはそんなに難しくない）

例えばこう書く！

It's pleasant to hear **the sound of birds singing.**
鳥の鳴き声を聞くのは気持ちよい［＝耳に心地よい］。

Haruka is friendly and easy to get along with.
ハルカは気さくで、付き合うのが楽だ［＝付き合いやすい］。

It's important to fix **the furniture to the wall and ceiling.**
家具を壁や天井に固定することは大切だ。

❺「(人に)～するように(言った)」といった意味を表す

「(人に)～するように言った〈言われた〉」や「(人に)～するように頼んだ〈頼まれた〉」などと言うときにも、〈to＋動詞の原形〉を使います。次に紹介する構文は日記でよく使うので、ぜひ覚えておきましょう。

●「(人に)～するように(言った・言われた)」の構文

A told me (not) to ～　Aが私に～するように(しないように)言った
＝Aに～するように(しないように)言われた

I was told (not) to ～　私は～するように(しないように)言われた

A asked me (not) to ～　Aが私に～するように(しないように)頼んだ
＝Aに～するように(しないように)頼まれた

I was asked (not) to ～　私は～するように(しないように)頼まれた

※「～しないように」は、not to ～の形で表します。

例えばこう書く！

My boss told me to go to Indonesia next week.
上司に、来週インドネシアに行くようにと言われた。

I was asked to translate the document by this Friday.
今週の金曜日までに資料を翻訳するように頼まれた。

He told me not to call him anymore. Why?
彼に、もう電話しないでと言われた。どうして？

文法13 関係代名詞の使い方

関係代名詞とは、一言で言うと「名詞を詳しく説明するときの接着剤」で、**who、which、that** などを指します。

名詞は、形容詞を付けることで説明を加えることができます。book（本）なら、thick book（分厚い本）、expensive book（値段の高い本）といった具合です。しかし、「ケンが薦めてくれた本」や「石原真弓によって書かれた本」のように、形容詞だけでは表せない説明もありますね。そういうときに使えるのが、関係代名詞です。

a book which〈that〉 Ken recommended
（ケンが薦めてくれた本）

a book which〈that〉 was written by Mayumi Ishihara
（石原真弓によって書かれた本）

上の例のように、関係代名詞を使った部分は〈名詞＋関係代名詞＋説明〉の形で表します。ここでの名詞はbook（本）です。**名詞が「物」のとき、関係代名詞はwhichかthatを使います**（ただし、日常的にはthatを用いることが多いです）。**名詞が「人」の場合は、whoかthatを使います。**

「本」は物ですから、bookの後に関係代名詞which（またはthat）を続けます。この後に、「ケンが薦めてくれた（Ken recommended）」を続ければOK。全体で、a book which〈that〉 Ken recommended（ケンが薦めてくれた本）となります。

「石原真弓によって書かれた本」も、bookの後に関係代名詞which（またはthat）を続けるところまでは同じです。「石原真弓によって書かれた」は、受け身（be＋動詞の過去分詞／p. 681参照）で表します。「～によって」はby ～で表すので、was written by Mayumi Ishiharaとなりますね。これを、which（またはthat）の後にそのまま続けます。全体で、a book which〈that〉 was written by Mayumi Ishiharaとなります。受け身が難しければ、視点を変えて、a book which〈that〉 Mayumi Ishihara wrote（石原真弓が書いた本）とするのも手です。

関係代名詞の後に続くもの

関係代名詞の後ろには、〈主語＋動詞〉が続くときと、〈動詞〉が続くときがあります。まず、例を見てみましょう。

■関係代名詞に〈主語＋動詞〉が続く例

the friend who I met in Montreal　（私がモントリオールで出会った友達）
the teacher who I respect　（私が尊敬する先生）
the mug which my sister gave me　（姉が私にくれたマグカップ）
the smartphone which I bought yesterday　（私が昨日買ったスマートフォン）

■関係代名詞に〈動詞〉が続く例

the friend who lives in Montreal　（モントリオールに住んでいる友達）
the teacher who taught me English　（英語を教えてくれた先生）
the mug which was made in Britain　（イギリスで作られたマグカップ）
the smartphone which takes great pictures　（いい写真が撮れるスマートフォン）

このように、「人が～する（した）…（名詞）」と言いたいときは、〈名詞＋関係代名詞〉の後に〈主語＋動詞〉を続けます。

「～する（した）…（名詞）」や「～される（された）…（名詞）」と言いたいときは、〈名詞＋関係代名詞〉の後に〈動詞〉を続けます。

関係代名詞を省略できる場合

関係代名詞に〈主語＋動詞〉が続く場合は、関係代名詞を省略することができます。くだけた英語では、関係代名詞を省略するのが一般的です。

「ケンが薦めてくれた本」

a book which〈that〉 Ken recommended
= a book Ken recommended

「石原真弓が書いた本」

a book which〈that〉 Mayumi Ishihara wrote
= a book Mayumi Ishihara wrote

関係代名詞を用いた文

では、関係代名詞を用いた語句を文の中に組み込んでいきましょう。例えば、「ケンが薦めてくれた本はとてもよかった」と言いたいなら、The book (which/that) Ken recommended was very good. とします。**The book Ken recommended** が、「ケンが薦めてくれたその本」という１つのまとまりになっているんですね。

「石原真弓によって書かれた本を読んだ」なら、I read a book which〈that〉was written by Mayumi Ishihara. となります。ここでも、**a book which〈that〉was written by Mayumi Ishihara** が、１つのまとまりになっています。

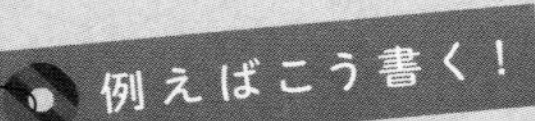

The hairdryer (which/that) I bought last year already broke.

去年買ったヘアドライヤーが、もう壊れた。

I've found the watch (which/that) I lost. I'm very happy.

なくした時計を見つけた。すごくうれしい。

A newcomer who graduated from XYZ University came to my section.

XYZ 大卒の新人がうちの課に入ってきた。

文法 14 時制の一致

時制の一致とは？

1つの文の中に、2つ以上の動詞が出てくる場合があります。例えば、I thought (that) she was older.（私は彼女のほうが年上だと思っていた）という文には、thought と was という2つの動詞・be 動詞が含まれています。このような場合、**文の主となる動詞が過去形なら、that 以下の動詞（助動詞）も過去形や過去完了形にする**というルールがあります。つまり、この例文では、thought は think の過去形なので、that 以下の動詞も is ではなく was という過去形になっているわけです。このルールを**時制の一致**と呼びます。

もう少し具体的に見ていきましょう。「リクは疲れていると言っていた」という文を書く場合、Riku said that ～（リクは～と言っていた）に he is tired（疲れている）を続ければよいと考えてしまいそうです。しかし、この場合は文の主となる動詞が過去形（said）なので、これに合わせて that 以下の動詞も過去形にする必要があります。正しい英文は、**Riku said (that) he was tired.** となるわけです。

もう一つ例を挙げてみます。「彼はエジプトに行ったことがあると言っていた」という文を英語で書くとしましょう。He told me that ～（彼は～と言っていた）に he has been to Egypt（彼はエジプトに行ったことがある）を続ければよいでしょうか？　この場合は、that 以下の動詞 has been（現在完了形）を had been（過去完了形）にして、**He told me (that) he had been to Egypt.** のように表します。

まとめると、文の主となる動詞が過去形の場合、that 以下の文が現在形で表す内容なら動詞を過去形に、過去形や現在完了で表す内容なら動詞を過去完了形（had＋動詞の過去分詞）にするというわけです。

ただし、文の主となる動詞が heard（～だと聞いた）や said（～だと言っていた）などの場合、くだけた英語では時制の一致を無視するネイティブ・スピーカーも多くいます。ですから、慣れないうちは、それほど厳密にとらえなくても構いません。

「アレックスが春に日本に来ると聞いた」

△ **I heard (that) Alex is coming to Japan this spring.**

○ **I heard (that) Alex was coming to Japan this spring.**

「マリはやってみると言っていた」

△ **Mari said (that) she will try it.**

○ **Mari said (that) she would try it.** ※ would は will の過去形。

「彼は手術したと言っていた」

△ **He said (that) he had an operation.**

○ **He said (that) he had had an operation.** ※ had は過去分詞も had。

ただし、主となる動詞が現在形の場合、that 以下の動詞は時制の一致を受けません。

例 **I think (that) she is older.**（私は彼女のほうが年上だと思う）

I know (that) he loved her.（私は彼が彼女を愛していたと知っている）

時制の一致の例外

ことわざ、自然現象などの不変の真理、現在でも変わらない事実や習慣、歴史上の事実は、時制の一致を受けません（例：He said the earth goes around the sun. = 彼は地球が太陽の周りを回っていると言った）。

例えばこう書く！

Kaoru told me (that) she was pregnant.

カオルが妊娠していると教えてくれた。

Eriko said (that) she could come to my birthday party.

エリコは、私の誕生日パーティーに来られると言っていた。

3章

英語日記でよく使う構文

日常的な英語表現でよく使う 74 の構文を収録。
日記に書く英文が、よりバリエーション豊かになります。

強制・必要・義務

構文1 ～しなければならない。 I have to ～.

こんなふうに使います

I have to ～(動詞の原形)は、「～しなければならない」という意味の構文です。特に、周囲からの指示や希望を受けて、あるいは状況的に判断して「～しないといけない」「～するより仕方がない」という「外からの強制」を表します。「面倒だけれど」「あまり気が進まないけれど」「そういう決まりだから」といったニュアンスを含みます。

例えば、「早く宿題をやりなさい」と親に注意されて、I have to do my homework.(宿題をやらないといけない)と書く場合や、医者に「このままだと肥満症になりますよ」と注意を受けて、I have to go on a diet.(ダイエットをしないといけない)と書く場合などにぴったりの表現です。また、規則でそうしなければならないときにも have to ～を使います。I have to go back to my dorm by 11:00.(11 時までに寮へ戻らないといけない)という具合です。

否定文は I don't have to ～(～しなくてもよい)、過去形は I had to ～(～しなければならなかった)、I didn't have to ～(～しなくてもよかった、～する必要がなかった)で表します。

こんなふうに書きます

1 I have to **get up early tomorrow.**
明日は早く起きないといけない。

2 I have to **make a haircut appointment.**
美容院の予約を入れないといけない。
※haircutは「ヘアカット」のこと。状況に応じて、perm（パーマ）やhair coloring（ヘアカラー）、hair dye（白髪染め）などと入れ替える。

3 I have to **finish my graduation thesis by the 10th.**
10 日までに卒業論文を書き終えなければならない。

4 I had to **work overtime again today.**
今日も残業しなければならなかった。

5 I had to **make a detour.**
迂回（うかい）しなければならなかった。
※detourは[ディートゥア]は「迂回路」という意味。

6 I don't have to **make lunch for Hana tomorrow.**
明日はハナに弁当を作らなくてよい。

7 I didn't have to **go to school today.**
今日は学校に行かなくてよかった。

ポイント

- have to ～は「外からの強制」を表す。
- 否定文は I don't have to ～で、「～しなくてもよい」という意味。
- 過去形は I had to ～、I didn't have to ～で表す。

必要・義務

構文 2 ～しなければならない。 I must ～.

こんなふうに使います

I must ～(動詞の原形)は、話し手が主体的に考えて「(絶対に)～しなければならない」と感じるときに使う構文です。「義務」や「強い必要性」のニュアンスがあるため、We must solve our environmental problems.(私たちは環境問題を解決しなければならない)のように、スピーチや論文などでよく使われます。ですから、「買い物に行かなきゃ」「ジョニーにえさをやらなきゃ」などと表すときにmustを使うと、大げさな印象になります。

否定文はI mustn't ～で表し、この場合は「～してはいけない」という禁止の意味に変わります（mustn't は［マスンㇳ］のように発音)。「～しなくてもよい」という意味ではないので注意してください。「～しなくてもよい」と表現したい場合は、構文１の have to を使って I don't have to ～(動詞の原形)としましょう。

must には、過去形がありません。そのため、「～しなければならなかった」と表したいときは、I had to ～(動詞の原形)で代用します。

こんなふうに書きます

1. I must find a job.
仕事を探さなければならない。

2. I must think about my future seriously.
将来のことを真面目に考えなければならない。

3. I must cut down on my living expenses.
生活費を切り詰めないといけない。

4. I mustn't spend so much time playing games.
ゲームで遊んでばかりいてはいけない。

必要・義務

構文3 ～しなくちゃ。 I need to ～.

こんなふうに使います

I need to ～(動詞の原形)は、「～しなくちゃ、～する必要がある」という意味の構文です。have to のような「強制」の意味はなく、日常的な「必要性」や「義務」を表しますが、must ほど強くはありません。

否定文は I don't need to ～で、「～しなくてもよい、～する必要はない」という意味です。過去のことは I needed to ～（～しなければならなかった）、I didn't need to ～（～しなくてもよかった、～する必要はなかった）で表します。

こんなふうに書きます

1 **I need to cut my bangs.**
前髪を切らなくちゃ。

2 **I need to explain it to her tomorrow.**
明日、彼女に説明しなくちゃ。

3 **I need to pick up my clothes from the cleaners.**
クリーニング店に服を取りに行かなきゃ。

4 **I needed to cancel my dentist appointment.**
歯医者の予約を取り消さなければならなかった。

5 **I didn't need to work overtime today.**
今日は残業しなくてもよかった。

必要・義務

～しなくちゃ。 I've got to ～.

こんなふうに使います

I've got to ～(動詞の原形)も「～しなくちゃ」という意味の構文です。I've は I have の短縮形。I've got to ～は、構文３の I need to ～よりもさらにカジュアルな響きがあります。感情的で差し迫ったニュアンスになることが多いため、「毎朝６時半のバスに乗らなければならない」のような習慣的な事柄を表すには適していません。

この表現は会話でよく使われるほか、日記や親しい間柄とのメールなど、くだけた書き言葉でも使われます。さらにくだけて、I've gotta ～(動詞の原形)と表すこともあります。gotta は [ガダ] のように発音します。

否定文や過去を表す文では、have to で代用します。否定文は I don't have to ～(～しなくてもよい)、過去のことは I had to ～ (～しなければならなかった)、I didn't have to ～(～しなくてもよかった、～する必要がなかった) で表しましょう。

こんなふうに書きます

1 **I've got to return the books.**
本を返却しなくちゃ。

2 **I've got to iron my shirt.**
シャツにアイロンをかけなくちゃ。
※iron[アイアン]は「～にアイロンをかける」という意味。

3 **I've got to wash his PE clothes.**
彼の体操着を洗濯しなくちゃ。

4 **I've got to call my grandchildren tomorrow.**
明日、孫たちに電話しなきゃ。

5 **I've got to send something to my mom for Mother's Day.**
母の日に何か送らなくちゃ。

6 **I've got to do my packing.**
荷造りしなくちゃ。

7 **Oh, I've got to apply for the TOEIC!**
あっ、TOEICに申し込まなくちゃ！

ポイント

- I've got to ～は「～しなくちゃ」というカジュアルな表現。
- I've got to ～には、感情的で差し迫ったニュアンスがある。
- くだけて I've gotta ～(動詞の原形) と表すこともある。

必要・義務

構文5 〜したほうがいいだろうな。 I should 〜.

こんなふうに使います

shouldを「〜すべきだ」という訳で覚えている人も多いと思いますが、実際はそれほど強いニュアンスではありません。**I should 〜（動詞の原形）**のように主語をIにすると、「〜したほうがいいだろうな、〜すべきかな」といった**自分の判断に基づく弱い義務**を表します。**Maybe I should 〜**（〜したほうがいいかな、〜しようかな、〜したほうがいいかも）という形もよく使われます。

You should 〜 や He should 〜のように主語をほかの人にすると、「あなたは（彼は）〜したほうがいいと思うけどなぁ」といった**穏やかな提案**を表します。ただし、相手との関係や状況、言い方によっては、「〜すべきだ！」という忠告や非難を表すこともあります。

否定文は**I shouldn't 〜**（〜しないほうがよい）で表します。

こんなふうに書きます

1 **I should eat more vegetables.**
もっと野菜をとったほうがいいだろうな。

2 **I should see a doctor tomorrow.**
明日、医者に診てもらうほうがいいだろうな。

3 **I should leave a little early.**
少し早く出発するほうがいいだろうな。

4 **Maybe I should send her a thank-you letter.**
彼女にお礼状を書いたほうがいいかな。

5 **Maybe he should try a different approach.**
彼は別の方法を試したほうがいいと思うけどなぁ。

6 **I shouldn't hold a grudge against him.**
彼のことを恨むのはよくない。
※hold a grudge against ～は「～に恨みを持つ」という意味。

7 **I shouldn't worry too much.**
気にし過ぎないほうがいいだろうな。

8 **We shouldn't see each other anymore.**
僕たちはもう会わないほうがいいだろう。

ポイント

■ I should ～は、自分の判断に基づく弱い義務を表す。
■ 主語をほかの人にすると、一般的に穏やかな提案を表す。
■ Maybe I should ～という形もよく使われる。

必要・義務

～したほうがよさそうだ。 I'd better ～.

こんなふうに使います

I'd better は、I had better を短縮した形です。くだけた会話では had（= 'd）を省略し、I better とすることもあります。

had better を「～したほうがよい」という意味で覚えている人も非常に多いと思いますが、こうしたソフトなニュアンスになるのは、主語が I または We の場合のみです。I'd〈We'd〉better ～（動詞の原形）で「～したほうがよさそうだ、～しなくちゃ」といった意味になります。

ところが、You'd〈He'd〉better ～ のようにほかの人を主語にすると、「絶対に～すべきだ、～しなさい」といった強い助言や命令になります。場合によっては、「～するほうが身のためだぞ、～しないと後でどうなっても知らないぞ」という脅迫めいた響きになることもあるので、had better は自分以外には使わないほうがよいでしょう。人に対して had better が使われるのは、先生が生徒に、親が子に、上司が部下になど、上下関係がはっきりしているときだけです。むやみに用いると、ひんしゅくを買うので気を付けましょう。

否定文は I'd better not ～で、意味は「～しないほうがよい」です（I または We 以外が主語のときは「～するなよ、～すると後でどうなっても知らないぞ」というニュアンス）。

こんなふうに書きます

1 **I'd better think twice.**
よく考えたほうがよさそうだ。
※think twiceは「よく考える」という意味。

2 **I'd better stay home this weekend.**
今週末は家にいるほうがいいだろう。

3 **I'd better stay away from him.**
彼に関わらないほうがいいだろう。

4 **I'd better start working on the project now.**
そろそろ企画に取りかかったほうがよさそうだ。

5 **I'd better report it to the police.**
警察に届けておいたほうがよさそうだ。
※reportは「～を（警察などに）届け出る」という意味。

6 **I'd better not sell the stock now.**
今はその株を売らないほうがいいだろう。

7 **I'd better not tell him about it.**
そのことは彼に言わないほうがいいだろう。

ポイント

- I'd〈We'd〉 better ～は、「～したほうがよさそうだ」という意味。
- ほかの人を主語にすると強い命令口調になるので注意。
- 否定文は I'd better not ～で表す。

未来・予定や計画

構文7 〜する(予定だ)。 I'm going to 〜.

こんなふうに使います

be going to 〜を用いたI'm going to 〜(動詞の原形)は、前々から決まっている予定を表します。「すでに日時や場所などが決まっている場合」と、「詳細は決まっていないものの、そうする予定がある場合」のいずれにも使えます。会話ではくだけてgoing toの部分をgonna[ガナ]と短縮し、I'm gonna 〜と言うこともあります。

状況から判断して「(この様子だと)〜するだろう、〜になるだろう」と推測する場合にも、be going to 〜を使います。例えば、応援しているスポーツチームがとんとん拍子に勝ち進み、このままいけば優勝するだろうという状況で、They're going to win the championship.(彼らは優勝するだろう)のように使います。

また、be going to 〜はあらかじめ決まっている事柄について用いることから、「〜するぞ」と心に決めた強い意志を述べるときにも使われます。

否定文はI'm not going to 〜で、「〜するつもりはない」という意味。そうする意志がないことを明確に表す表現です。過去形はI was going to 〜で、「〜するつもりだった(けれど実際はしなかった、できなかった)」という意味です。

こんなふうに書きます

1 We're going to **have a BBQ this Sunday.**
日曜日にバーベキューをする。

2 My daughter is going to **have a baby soon.**
娘にもうすぐ赤ちゃんが生まれる。

3 My sister's family is going to **come see us this summer.**
今年の夏、妹の家族が遊びに来る。

4 I'm going to **stop wasting money!**
お金のむだ遣いをやめるぞ！

5 I'm not going to **change jobs.**
転職するつもりはない。

6 I was going to **clean my room this afternoon, but I didn't.**
午後に部屋を片付けるつもりだったけど、しなかった。

7 I was going to **just browse, but I bought a hat.**
ただ見るだけのつもりだったけど、帽子を買っちゃった。
※browse［ブラウズ］は「見て回る」という意味。

ポイント

- I'm going to ～は、前々から決まっている予定を表す。
- 状況から判断して「（この様子だと）～するだろう」という場合や、「～するぞ」と心に決めた強い意志を表す場合にも使える。
- 否定文はI'm not going to ～、過去形はI was going to ～で表す。

未来・予定や計画

～する(予定だ)。 I'm ～ing.

こんなふうに使います

「あれ？〈be 動詞＋動詞の -ing 形〉って、現在進行形じゃないの？」と思った人がいるかもしれません。その通り、形は現在進行形と同じです。でも、これに「未来の時」を表す語句を続けると、そうすることが確実に決まっている近未来の予定を表せるのです。ニュアンスは I'm going to ～とほとんど変わりませんが、それを実行する確実性は I'm ～ing のほうがやや高いといえます。また、I'm going to ～は日時などが決まっていない事柄にも使えますが、I'm ～ing はいつ、誰と、どこでそれをするのかといった詳細が決まっていることが前提です。そのため、「いつ」すなわち「未来の時」を表す言葉を続けるのが基本です。

否定文は I'm not ～ing、過去のことは I was going to ～で代用します。

こんなふうに書きます

1 I'm having dinner with Reo tomorrow night.
明日の夜はレオとディナー。

2 I'm helping my sister move tomorrow.
明日は妹の引っ越しのお手伝い。

3 Yoko and I are going to the movies this Saturday.
土曜日はヨウコと映画を見に行く。

4 I'm not staying up late tonight.
今夜は夜ふかししない。

未来・予定や計画

構文9 ～しようかと考えている。 I'm thinking about〈of〉～ing.

こんなふうに使います

決定してはいないものの、そうしようかと考えている事柄は、I'm thinking about ～（動詞の-ing 形）で表します。about の代わりに of を使って、I'm thinking of ～（動詞の-ing 形）としても OK です。どちらかというと、about は綿密に考えている段階のことに、of は実行する気持ちが強いことに用います。I'm thinking about ～は「～しようかと考えている」、I'm thinking of ～は「～しようと思う」というニュアンスで覚えておくとよいでしょう。状況によっては「～することを検討中」や「～しようか迷っている」という意味にもなります。

否定文の場合は I'm not thinking about〈of〉～ing、過去のことは I was thinking about〈of〉～ing で表します。

こんなふうに書きます

1 I'm thinking about learning **Spanish.**
スペイン語を習おうかと考えている。

2 I'm thinking of getting **a pet.**
何かペットを飼おうと思う。

3 I'm not thinking about getting **a divorce.**
離婚することは考えていない。

4 I was thinking about renting **an apartment, but I decided to buy a house.**
マンションを借りようか検討していたけど、家を買うことにした。

未来・予定や計画

～する計画を立てている。 I'm making plans to ～.

こんなふうに使います

実行を目指して計画段階にある事柄は、I'm making plans to ～(動詞の原形)で表します。構文９の I'm thinking about〈of〉～ing (～しようかと考えている) よりも、計画が具体化している場合に使います。そのため、「～する計画を立てている」のほかに、「～するつもりだ」というニュアンスで使うこともできます。

似た表現で「～を計画している」と表す場合は、I'm planning ～(名詞)とします。I'm planning a going-away party for her. (彼女の送別会を計画している) という具合です。I'm planning to ～(動詞の原形) で「～することを計画している」という使い方もできます。

こんなふうに書きます

1 **I'm making plans to go to Canada this winter.**
この冬、カナダへ行く計画を立てている。

2 **I'm making plans to buy a condo next year.**
来年、マンションを買うつもりだ。
※「分譲マンション」はcondo(condominiumの略)、「賃貸マンション」はapartmentと使い分けることが多い。

3 **We're making plans to remodel our kitchen this spring.**
今年の春にキッチンをリフォームする計画を立てている。

4 **I'm making plans to have my teeth straightened.**
歯列矯正をするつもりだ。

5 **She's making plans to open a café.**
彼女はカフェをオープンする計画を立てている。

条件付きの未来

(もし)～だったら、…しよう。 If ～, I'll ...

こんなふうに使います

実現する可能性がある事柄について「(もし) ～だったら…しよう」と書きたいときは、If ～, I'll ... を使いましょう。「～」には「もし～なら」という条件が文の形で入ります。「～」に入る文は、未来のことでも現在形で表します。

後半の I'll ... には、実際にそうなったときにとる行動を動詞の原形で表します。状況によって、I'll ... を I should ...(…したほうがいいかな)、I may〈might〉...(…するかも) などに変えることもできます。

こんなふうに書きます

1 **If the price goes down, I'll buy it.**
値段が下がったら、それを買おうっと。

2 **If she goes to karaoke, I'll go, too.**
彼女がカラオケに行くなら、私も行こうかな。

3 **If I don't hear from him by tomorrow night, I'll call him.**
明日の夜になっても彼から連絡がなければ、電話してみようっと。

4 **If the typhoon is coming, I should cancel my trip.**
台風が接近するようなら、旅行を取りやめたほうがよさそうだ。

5 **If he says sorry from the bottom of his heart, I may forgive him.**
彼が心の底から謝ったら、許してあげるかも。

構文 12 未来

もうすぐ〜だ。
〜 is coming up soon.

こんなふうに使います

近付きつつある記念日やイベントなどについて、「もうすぐ〜だ」というときは、〜(名詞) is coming up soon で表します。「〜」には、誕生日や結婚式、試験などを表す名詞が入ります。この come up は「(出来事や時期が) 近付く」という意味で、通常、進行形 (be 動詞＋coming up) で表します。soon は省略することもあります。

具体的にいつのことなのかを表したい場合は、文末を、soon の代わりに this weekend (今週末)、in three days (3 日後に) などの語句にしましょう。

こんなふうに書きます

1 **Christmas is coming up soon.**
もうすぐクリスマスだ。

2 **The election is coming up soon.**
もうすぐ選挙だ。

3 **The mid-terms are coming up.**
中間試験が近付いている。

4 **My 60th birthday is coming up in five days.**
5 日後に還暦を迎える。

5 **My son's graduation ceremony is coming up next week.**
来週は息子の卒業式だ。

未来

構文 13 もうすぐ～だ。
～ is just around the corner.

こんなふうに使います

構文 12 の ～ is coming up soon（もうすぐ～だ）と同じく、～(名詞) is just around the corner も、まもなく控えている記念日やイベントについて使います。

around the corner は「(すぐそこの) 角の辺りに」が直訳で、「～がすぐそこまで来ている」というニュアンスです。just の代わりに right を入れることもあり、いずれも記念日やイベントなどが間近に迫っていることを強調しています。この構文は、in three days（3 日後）や next month（来月）などの具体的な「時」を表す言葉と一緒に用いることはできません。

ちなみに、イベントなどに限らず、Success is just around the corner.（成功は目前だ）や Happiness is just around the corner.（幸せはすぐそこにある）といった使い方もできます。あわせて覚えておくとよいでしょう。

こんなふうに書きます

1 **The TOEIC test** is just around the corner.
もうすぐ TOEIC（の試験日）だ。

2 **My son's wedding** is right around the corner.
もうすぐ息子の結婚式だ。

3 **The Olympics** are just around the corner.
もうすぐオリンピックだ。
※The Olympics（＝Olympic Games）は通例、複数形で用いられ、be動詞もareとなる。

4 **My daughter's violin recital** is right around the corner.
もうすぐ娘のバイオリン・リサイタルだ。

未来

…まで、あと〜日。
〜 more day(s) before …

こんなふうに使います

予定やイベント、記念日などについて「…まで、あと〜日」と書きたいときは、〜（数）more day(s) before …（名詞）を使います。これは、「…まで、あと〜日ある」という意味の There is/are 〜 more day(s) before … の There is/are が省略された形です。「…」にはイベントや出来事を表す語句を、「〜」にはそれまでの日数を入れます。イベントは名詞で入れてもいいですし、右ページの例文⑦の I can see him のように〈主語＋動詞〉の形で入れることもできます。また、楽しみなことだけでなく、緊張するようなことについても使えます。

〜 more days（あと〜日、もう〜日）を、日本語の語順につられて more 〜 days（×）などとしないように注意しましょう。

「あと１日」の場合は、one more day のように day を単数形にします。「あと２週間」や「あと１カ月」などという場合は、day(s) を week(s) や month(s) に変えて、two more weeks や one more month のように表しましょう。

こんなふうに書きます

1 **Four more days before my graduation.**
卒業まで、あと4日。

2 **Ten more days before our tenth wedding anniversary.**
結婚10周年まで、あと10日。

3 **Two more days before the complete medical checkup.**
人間ドックまで、あと2日。
※checkupは「検査、健康診断」という意味。

4 **Three more days before the entrance exam.**
入学試験まで、あと3日。

5 **Two more weeks before the interview.**
面接まで、あと2週間。

6 **One more week before the test result announcement.**
試験の結果発表まで、あと1週間。

7 **Five more days before I can see him!**
彼に会える日まで、あと5日！

ポイント

- ～ more day(s) before ... の「～」には数、「...」にはイベントを表す語句を入れる。
- days（日）を weeks（週）、months（月）にしても OK。
- 日本語につられて、more ～ days（×）としないように注意。

過去の習慣

構文15 昔はよく～したなぁ。 I used to ～.

こんなふうに使います

過去を振り返って「昔はよく～したなぁ」と書くときはI used to ～(動詞の原形)、「昔は～だったなぁ」と書くときはI used to be ～(形容詞または名詞)で表します。この構文は、今はそうではないことを暗示しているので、後にbut I don't do it anymore(でも今はもうしていない)や、but now I'm not(でも今は違う)といった内容の文を続ける必要はありません。

「昔は～しなかったなぁ」という否定は、I didn't use to ～のように表現します。never(絶対に～ない)を用いて、I never used to ～(昔は絶対～しなかったなぁ)と強調することもできます。

ちなみに、used toは[ユーストゥ]と発音します。下線部は「ズ」ではなく「ス」に近い音なので、会話では注意してください。

こんなふうに書きます

1 I used to **stay up all night.**
昔はよく徹夜したなぁ。

2 I used to **play the guitar.**
昔はよくギターを弾いたなぁ。

3 I used to **be popular.**
昔はモテたんだけどなぁ。

4 I didn't use to **cook.**
昔は料理をしなかったなぁ。

希望・願望

構文 16

～が欲しいな。
I want ～.

こんなふうに使います

欲しい物は、I want ～(名詞)を使って表します。「～」には、a dog（犬〈を1匹〉）やan oven（オーブン〈を1台〉）、some nice coffee cups（ステキなコーヒーカップ〈をいくつか〉）のように、名詞を入れましょう。

ほかの人を主語にすると、「…は～を欲しがっている、…は～が欲しいと言っている」という意味になります。

「～がすごく欲しい」「～が欲しくてたまらない」と強調する場合は、wantの前にreally（すごく、とても）を入れてI really want ～のように表すことができます。「～は欲しくない」という否定は、I don't want ～で表します。

こんなふうに書きます

1. **I want a new smartphone.**
   新しいスマホが欲しいな。

2. **I want some time alone.**
   1人になれる時間が欲しいな。

3. **I really want a day off.**
   ホント、休みが欲しい。
   ※day offは「(仕事のない)休日」という意味。

4. **I don't want a boyfriend for a while.**
   しばらく彼氏は欲しくない。

5. **My son wants a unicycle for his birthday.**
   息子は誕生日に一輪車が欲しいと言っている。

希望・願望

構文17 ～したいな。／～してみたいな。 I want to ～.

こんなふうに使います

「～したいな、～してみたいな」という希望や願望は、I want to ～(動詞の原形)で表します。「すごく～」と強調するには、want to の前に really（すごく、とても）を入れましょう。くだけた会話や文章では want to を wanna[ワナ] とすることもあります。「～したくないな」「～するのはイヤだな」と書きたい場合は、I don't want to ～で表しましょう。

こんなふうに書きます

1 I want to **lose weight.**
やせたいな。

2 I want to **be a good speaker.**
話し上手になりたいな。

3 I want to **get a driver's license.**
自動車の免許を取りたいな。

4 I want to **visit the Maldives someday.**
いつかモルジブに行ってみたいな。

5 I don't want to **work with her.**
彼女と仕事をするの、イヤだな。

6 I didn't want to **break up with him.**
彼と別れたくなかった。
※break up with ～は「～(恋人など)と別れる」という意味。

構文 18

希望・願望

～できるようになりたい。 I want to be able to ～.

こんなふうに使います

「～（今うまくできないこと）が将来できるようになりたい」と書きたいときは、I want to be able to ～(動詞の原形)で表します。

be able to は can と同じく「～できる」という意味です。want to の後に can を続けて want to can ～（×）とすることはできないので、want to be able to ～と表します。

以前できなかったことができるようになった場合は、Now I'm able to ～(動詞の原形)や Now I can ～(動詞の原形)で表します。「(今では)～ができるようになった」という意味です。

こんなふうに書きます

1 I want to be able to **speak English well.**
英語がうまく話せるようになりたい。

2 I want to be able to **put on a kimono on my own.**
自分で着物が着られるようになりたい。

3 I want to be able to **watch movies without English subtitles.**
英語字幕なしで映画を見られるようになりたいな。

4 Now my grandma is able to **use the Internet.**
おばあちゃんがインターネットを使えるようになった。

5 Now I can **finally have time for myself.**
ようやく自分の時間が取れるようになった。

構文 19 希望・願望

〜に…してほしい。 I want 〜 to ...

こんなふうに使います

構文 17 の I want to 〜（〜したいな）は自分自身の望みについて述べる表現ですが、「〜に…してほしい」といったほかの人に対する望みや願望は、I want 〜（人）to ...（動詞の原形）で表します。〜にはそうしてもらいたい人を、…にはしてもらいたい行動を入れます。この構文は人だけでなく、I want the summer to end soon.（早く夏が終わってほしいな）のように、「物」や「物事」についても使えます。

「〜に…してほしくない」という否定は、I don't want 〜 to ... で表しましょう。

こんなふうに書きます

1 I want my parents to stay healthy.
両親にはずっと健康でいてもらいたい。

2 I want my wife to talk to me in a gentle manner.
妻には、私に優しく話してほしい。

3 I want my husband to help with the housework sometimes.
たまには夫に家のことを手伝ってもらいたい。

4 I don't want him to call me so often.
彼には、こんなにしょっちゅう私に電話しないでほしいな。

5 I didn't want it to happen.
そうなってほしくなかった。

希望・願望

構文20 ～できるといいな。 I hope to ～.

こんなふうに使います

構文17のI want to ～（～したいな）と同じく、**I hope to ～（動詞の原形）**も願望を表します。「～できるといいな」という意味で、実現する可能性のある事柄について期待を込めて願望を表すときに使います。不可能なことや、実現の可能性がかなり低い望みについては、構文22のI wish ～（～だったらいいのに）を参照してください。

こんなふうに書きます

1. I hope to **get an interpreter job.**
通訳の仕事に就けるといいな。

2. I hope to **see her again.**
彼女にまた会えるといいな。

3. I hope to **move to Australia someday.**
いつか、オーストラリアに移住できるといいな。

4. I hope to **meet someone nice this year.**
今年はすてきな人に出会えるといいな。

5. I hope to **have a Labrador.**
ラブラドールを飼えるといいな。

6. I hope to **win a lot of money in the lottery.**
宝くじで大金を当てたいな。

希望・願望

構文21 ～だといいな。 I hope ～.

こんなふうに使います

構文20のI hope to ～（～できるといいな）は、自分がそうできたらいいなと思うことを書くときに使いますが、**I hope ～(文)**は**「ほかの人や事柄がそうなるといいな」**と願う気持ちを表せます。**I hope I can ～(動詞の原形)**という形を使えば、I hope to ～と同じように、「(自分が) ～できるといいな」という自分自身の願望について表すこともできます。

hopeの後にはthatが省略されています。日記やくだけた会話などでは、主語のIを省略し、Hope ... で文を始めることもあります。また、I hope to ～と同様、この構文も、**実現する可能性のある望み**について期待を込めて使います。

未来のことについて書く場合、I hope ～の「～」に入る文は未来を表す形にします。ただし、くだけて現在形で表すこともあります。

「明日は暖かくなるといいな」
- **I hope** it'll be warm tomorrow.
- **I hope** it's warm tomorrow.

こんなふうに書きます

1 **I hope he's happy.**
彼が幸せだといいな。

2 **I hope she's having a good time.**
彼女が（今ごろ）楽しくやっているといいな。

3 **I hope she will like〈likes〉 the present.**
彼女がプレゼントを気に入ってくれるといいな。

4 **I hope it won't〈doesn't〉 rain tonight.**
今夜、雨が降らなければいいけど。
※won'tはwill notの短縮形。

5 **Hope he can get the ticket.**
彼がチケットを取れるといいけど。

6 **I hope she will come back〈comes back〉 safe and sound.**
彼女が無事に戻ってきますように。
※safe and soundは「無事に」という意味。

7 **I hope I can finish the report by the deadline.**
締め切りまでにレポートを終えられるといいな。

ポイント

- I hope ～（文）は「～だといいな」という意味。
- 「ほかの人や事柄がそうなるといいな」という願望を表せる。
- 実現の可能性がある望みについて期待を込めた表現。

希望・願望

～だったらいいのに。 I wish ～.

こんなふうに使います

構文 20 の I hope to ～(～できるといいな)や構文 21 の I hope ～(～だといいな)が「実現の可能性があることに対する期待を込めた表現」であるのに対し、I wish ～(過去形の文)は、実現の可能性がない、または限りなく低い望みについて、半ばあきらめの気持ちを表す構文です。「(実際はそうではないけれど)～できたらいいのに」という現実に反する願望や、「(絶対に無理だとわかっているけれど)～だったらいいのに」「(まずそうはならないだろうけれど)そうなったらいいなぁ」というはかない望みなどを表します。wish の後には、that が省略されています。

現在や未来のことでも、I wish ～の「～」には過去形の文が入る点に注意しましょう。例えば、「(実際は行けないけれど) そのコンサートに行けたらいいのに」という場合は、I can go to the concert (コンサートに行ける) を過去形にして、I wish I could go to the concert. とします。実際は結婚している人が「独身だったらなぁ」と願う場合は、I wish I was single. や I wish I wasn't married. のように表現します。

実は、文法的には I wish I were single. や I wish I weren't married. のように、主語にかかわらず be 動詞は were にするのが正しいのですが、現在では、主語が I、he、she、it の場合、was を使うのが一般的です。

また、過去を振り返って、「(実際はそうではなかったけれど、あの時)～だったらよかったのになぁ」という場合は、I wish ～(過去完了形の文)と表します。過去完了形は、〈had ＋動詞の過去分詞〉で表します。

こんなふうに書きます

1 I wish I had **a big brother.**
お兄ちゃんがいたらよかったな。

2 I wish I made **more money.**
もっと稼ぎがあったらいいのに。

3 I wish he lived **near me.**
彼が私の近くに住んでいたらなぁ。

4 I wish I was〈were〉 **ten years younger.**
私があと10歳若かったらなぁ。

5 I wish I didn't have **to work on New Year's Eve.**
大みそかの日に仕事を休めたらいいのに。

6 I wish I could go **back to my 20s.**
20代の頃に戻れたらなぁ。

7 I wish I could win **300 million yen in the lottery.**
宝くじで3億円当たったらいいのに。

8 I wish I had studied **much harder in my school days.**
学生時代にもっとしっかり勉強していればなぁ。

ポイント

- I wish 〜(過去形の文)は、実現の可能性がない、または限りなく低い望みについて、半ばあきらめの気持ちを表す。
- I wish 〜の「〜」には、現在や未来のことであっても過去形の文が入る。

希望・願望

構文 23

～したい気分だ。 I feel like ～ing.

こんなふうに使います

「～したい気分だ」という気持ちを書くときは、I feel like ～(動詞の-ing 形)で表します。構文 17 の、希望や願望を表す I want to ～（～したいな）と同じような感覚で使える表現です。

「～したい気分だった」と過去の気持ちについて書く場合は、feel を過去形の felt にして、I felt like ～ing としましょう。

否定文は、I don't feel like ～ing（～する気分ではない）や I didn't feel like ～ing（～する気分ではなかった）のように表します。

こんなふうに書きます

1 I feel like having **some fun.**
パーッとやりたい気分だ。

2 I feel like changing **my hairstyle.**
髪型を変えたい気分だな。

3 I don't feel like seeing **anyone.**
誰とも会う気分じゃない。

4 I felt like drinking**.**
酒を飲みたい気分だった。

5 I didn't feel like doing **anything today.**
今日は何もする気にならなかった。

構文
24 〜(すること)が楽しみだ。 I'm looking forward to 〜.

楽しみ・期待

こんなふうに使います

楽しみにしている事柄は、I'm looking forward to 〜(名詞または動詞の -ing 形)で表します。「〜が楽しみだ」と書きたいなら「〜」に名詞を、「〜するのが楽しみだ」なら「〜」に動詞の -ing 形を入れます。

to の後に動詞の原形を続ける表現が多いせいか、I'm looking forward to の後にも動詞の原形を続けてしまうミスが多いようです。しかし、この構文の to は「to 不定詞」ではなく、「前置詞の to」です。そのため、to の後ろには「〜すること」という意味を表す動詞の -ing 形(動名詞) が入ります。

「イタリアに行くのが楽しみだ」

○ I'm looking forward to going to Italy.

✕ I'm looking forward to go to Italy.

待ちきれない気持ちを強調する場合は、I'm really looking forward to 〜 としましょう。I'm very much looking forward to 〜 でも OK です。

こんなふうに書きます

1 **I'm looking forward to my payday.**
給料日が楽しみ。

2 **I'm really looking forward to my daughter's homecoming.**
娘の帰省がとても楽しみだ。

3 **I'm looking forward to going out with her this Sunday.**
日曜日に彼女とデートするのが楽しみ。

楽しみ・期待

～が待ち遠しいな。
I can't wait ～. / I can hardly wait ～.

こんなふうに使います

楽しみにしていることは、I can't wait ～を使って表すこともできます。直訳すると「～を待つことができない」ですが、これで「～が待ち遠しい、～が楽しみだ、早く～したい」といった意味になります。

「物事やイベントが待ち遠しい」という場合は、I can't wait の後ろに for ～（名詞）を続けます。「～するのが待ち遠しい」という場合は、I can't wait の後に to ～（動詞の原形）を続けます。また、I can't wait for A to ～（動詞の原形）とすれば、「A が～するのが待ち遠しい」という気持ちを表すことができます。

- I can't wait for ～(名詞) 「～が待ち遠しい」
- I can't wait to ～(動詞の原形) 「～するのが待ち遠しい」
- I can't wait for A to ～(動詞の原形) 「A が～するのが待ち遠しい」

この構文は、hardly(ほとんど～ない) を使って次のように表現することもできます。can hardly は「とても～できない」というニュアンスです。

- I can hardly wait for ～(名詞) 「～がとても待ち切れない」
- I can hardly wait to ～(動詞の原形) 「～するのがとても待ち切れない」

hardly は否定の意味を持つ言葉なので、can't ではなく can を用います。I can't hardly ～（×）としないように注意してください。

こんなふうに書きます

1 I can't wait for **my bonus.**
ボーナスが待ち遠しいな。

2 I can't wait for **the New Year's holidays.**
年末年始の休暇が楽しみだ。

3 I can't wait to **drive my new car.**
新車に乗るのが待ち遠しい。

4 I can't wait to **receive my order.**
注文した商品が届くのが待ち遠しいな。

5 I can't wait for **spring** to **come.**
春が来るのが待ち遠しい。

6 I can't wait for **my grandchildren** to **come see me.**
孫たちが遊びに来るのが待ち遠しい。

7 I can hardly wait for **the music festival.**
音楽フェスがとても待ち切れない。

8 I can hardly wait to **go out in the outfit I bought the other day.**
この前買った服で、早くお出かけしたいな。

ポイント

- I can't wait for ～(名詞) で「～が待ち遠しい」。
- I can't wait to ～(動詞の原形) で「～するのが待ち遠しい」。
- I can hardly wait for/to ～で表すこともできる。

楽しみ・期待

構文 26 ～がすごく楽しみ。 I'm excited ～.

こんなふうに使います

うれしくてワクワクする気持ちや興奮、ときめきなどは、I'm excited ～で表します。直訳は「ワクワクしている、興奮している」ですが、「～が待ちきれない（くらい興奮している）」や「～がすごく楽しみ（でワクワクしている）」というニュアンスがあると覚えておくと、日記で使いやすくなります。

この構文は、次のような形で用います。

- I'm excited to ～(動詞の原形) 「～するのがすごく楽しみ」
- I'm excited about ～(名詞) 「～がすごく楽しみ」
- I'm excited (that) ～(文) 「～ということがすごく楽しみ」

excited の前に so や really、very などを入れると、「すごく楽しみ、すごくワクワクしている」という気持ちをさらに強調することができます。

また、excited の代わりに thrilled（ワクワクして）を用いることもできます。この場合も、I'm thrilled to ～(動詞の原形)／I'm thrilled about ～(名詞)／I'm thrilled (that) ～(文)の形で表します。

こんなふうに書きます

1 I'm excited to **visit Mont Saint-Michel.**
モンサンミッシェルを訪れるのが、すごく楽しみ。

2 I'm excited to **meet Emma tomorrow!**
明日エマに会うのが待ちきれない！

3 I'm excited about **her homemade cooking.**
彼女の手料理がすごく楽しみ。

4 I'm **so** excited about **tomorrow's game.**
明日の試合がすごく楽しみ。

5 I'm **so** excited about **the announcement of the Summer Jumbo winning numbers.**
サマージャンボ宝くじの当選発表がメチャクチャ楽しみ。

6 I'm excited **my house will be completed this summer.**
今年の夏に家が完成するのが、すごく楽しみ。

7 I'm **so** excited **I'm going to be a grandma this April.**
4月におばあちゃんになる（＝孫が生まれる）のがすごく楽しみ。

8 I'm **very** excited **Taylor Swift is coming to Japan.**
テイラー・スウィフトの来日が、ものすごく楽しみ。

ポイント

■ I'm excited ～は「すごく楽しみでワクワクしている」というニュアンス。
■ excited の後には〈to ＋動詞の原形〉、〈about ＋名詞〉、〈文〉が続く。

安心・喜び

構文 27 〜でよかった。／〜でうれしかった。 I was glad 〜 .

こんなふうに使います

状況や結果などについて「（その時）よかった、うれしかった（と感じた）」と書くときは、I was glad 〜で表します。I was glad 〜は、「安心した、ホッとした」というニュアンスを含む表現です。この構文は、次のような形で用います。

- I was glad to 〜（動詞の原形）「〜してうれしかった」
- I was glad (that) 〜（文）「〜でよかった・〜ということがうれしかった」

「（今）よかった、うれしかった（と感じている）」場合は、I'm glad 〜と現在形で表します。「本当によかった、とてもうれしかった」と強調したい場合は、glad の前に so や very、really などを入れましょう。

こんなふうに書きます

1 **I was glad to talk with him.**
彼と話ができてうれしかった。

2 **I was glad it didn't rain.**
雨が降らなくてよかった。

3 **I was so glad my wife got promoted.**
妻が昇進して、とてもうれしかった。

4 **I'm glad he liked my cooking.**
彼が私の手料理を喜んでくれてよかった。

安心

構文 28 ～にホッとした。 I was relieved ～.

こんなふうに使います

「ホッとしたこと」や「安心したこと」について書くときは、I was relieved ～ で表します。構文 27 の I was glad ～（～でよかった）も「ホッとした、安心した」というニュアンスを含みますが、I was relieved ～は、その気持ちをより明確に表現します。この構文は、次のような形で用います。

- I was relieved at ～（名詞）「～にホッとした」
- I was relieved to ～（動詞の原形）「～してホッとした」
- I was relieved (that) ～（文）「～ということにホッとした」

「（今）ホッとしている、安心している」場合は、I'm relieved ～と現在形で表します。「本当にホッとした」と強調する場合は、relieved の前に so や very、really を入れましょう。

こんなふうに書きます

1 **I was relieved at the success of his operation.**
彼の手術の成功にホッとした。

2 **I was relieved to hear he had arrived safe and sound.**
彼が無事に着いたと聞いてホッとした。
※safe and soundは「無事に」という意味。

3 **I was relieved to learn I managed to pass the test.**
何とか試験に合格できたとわかってホッとした。
※manage to ～は「どうにか～する」という意味。

4 **I'm really relieved my daughter decided to get married.**
娘が結婚を決めて本当にホッとしている。

喜び・満足

構文29 ～してうれしい。／～に満足している。I'm happy〈satisfied〉～.

こんなふうに使います

現状や結果などについて「(今) 満足している、うれしい」と書くときは、I'm happy ～または I'm satisfied ～を使います。この構文は、次のような形で用います。

- I'm happy〈satisfied〉with ～(名詞) 「～に満足している」
- I'm happy〈satisfied〉to ～(動詞の原形) 「～してうれしい・～して満足している」
- I'm happy〈satisfied〉(that) ～(文) 「～ということに満足している」

「かなり満足している、とてもうれしい」と強調したい場合は、happy や satisfied の前に so や very、really などを入れましょう。

I'm not happy〈satisfied〉～と否定文にすると、「～には満足していない、～には納得がいかない」という不満を表します。

こんなふうに書きます

1 **I'm happy〈satisfied〉with my score.**
自分のスコアに満足している。

2 **I'm really happy〈satisfied〉with my new place.**
新居にはとても満足している。

3 **I'm not happy〈satisfied〉to work for a low wage.**
低賃金で働くことに不満だ。

4 **I'm very happy〈satisfied〉my sons grew up to be fine young men.**
息子たちが立派な青年に成長して、とてもうれしい。

喜び

～のおかげでいい一日になった。
～ made my day.

こんなふうに使います

～ made my day を直訳すると「～が私の日を作ってくれた」ですが、これで「～のおかげでいい一日になった」という意味になります。祝日やクリスマスなどのイベントと同じように、カレンダーに「私の日」と記したくなるような特別な日を作ってくれた、つまり、そのくらいすてきな一日になってうれしい、というニュアンスです。プレゼントをもらったり、いい知らせを耳にしたりして、思わず笑顔になったときなどに使うとぴったりです。

～ made my day の「～」に「人」を入れると「～のおかげでいい一日になった」、「～」に「物・物事」を入れると「～がすてきな一日にしてくれた、～がとてもうれしかった」というニュアンスになります。

こんなふうに書きます

1 **He made my day.**
彼のおかげでいい一日になった。

2 **Her smile made my day.**
彼女の笑顔がすてきな一日にしてくれた。

3 **My son's kind words made my day.**
息子の優しい言葉のおかげでいい一日になった。

4 **The letter from Hana made my day.**
ハナからの手紙がとてもうれしかった。

5 **Getting a compliment made my day.**
褒められて、とてもうれしかった。
※complimentは「褒め言葉」という意味。

驚き・感嘆

構文31 すごく～だ！／なんて～だろう！ How ～！

こんなふうに使います

「すごく～だ！」「なんて～なんだろう！」という驚きや感動などの強い気持ちは、How ～！で表すことができます。「～」には、形容詞が入ります。誰のことなのか、何のことなのかを具体的に表すために、〈How ＋形容詞〉の後に〈主語＋ be 動詞〉を続けることもあります（例文❹と❺）。

また、下の例文❻のように、〈How ＋副詞〉の後に〈主語＋動詞〉を続けることもできます。

こんなふうに書きます

1 **How lucky!**
超ラッキー！

2 **How weird!**
ヘンなの～！（奇妙だなぁ！）

3 **How selfish!**
なんて自分勝手な！

4 **How delicious the curry was!**
カレーは本当においしかったな！

5 **How smart she is!**
彼女はなんて賢いんだろう！

6 **How fast he spoke!**
彼は本当に早口だったなぁ！

驚き・感嘆

すごい〜だ！／なんて〜だろう！ What 〜！

こんなふうに使います

「すごい（すごく）〜だ！」「なんて〜なんだろう！」という驚きや感動などの強い気持ちは、What 〜！で表すこともできます。

構文 31 の How 〜！の場合、「〜」には形容詞（または副詞）が入りますが、What 〜！の場合は常に名詞または〈形容詞＋名詞〉が入ります。数えられる名詞の場合、単数なら〈What a/an 〜!〉、複数なら〈What 〜s!〉としましょう。また、誰のことなのか、何のことなのかを具体的に表すために、〈主語＋動詞〉を続けることもあります（例文5）。

こんなふうに書きます

1 **What a surprise!**
すごくビックリ！

2 **What a coincidence!**
すごい偶然！

3 **What a shame!**
とっても残念！

4 **What cute puppies!**
なんてかわいい子犬たち！

5 **What a beautiful house she lives in!**
彼女はすごくすてきな家に住んでいるんだなぁ！

驚き

～に驚いた。 I was surprised ～.

こんなふうに使います

驚いたことは、I was surprised ～で表します。この構文は、次のような形で用います。

- I was surprised at〈by〉～(名詞)「～に驚いた」
- I was surprised to ～(動詞の原形)「～して驚いた」
- I was surprised (that) ～(文)「～ということに驚いた」

「(今) 驚いている」場合は、I'm surprised ～と現在形で表します。「とても驚いた、すごく驚いた」と強調する場合は、surprised の前に so や really、very などを入れましょう。

こんなふうに書きます

1 **I was surprised at〈by〉the rent of the apartment.**
そのマンションの家賃に驚いた。

2 **I was surprised at〈by〉his rudeness.**
彼の無礼さに驚いた。

3 **I was surprised to get a call from my ex-girlfriend.**
元カノから電話があってびっくりした。

4 **I was really surprised to hear about her career.**
彼女の職歴を聞いて、とても驚いた。

5 **I'm surprised she has five children.**
彼女に５人、子どもがいることにびっくり。

失望

～にがっかりした。
I was disappointed ～.

こんなふうに使います

がっかりしたことや残念に思ったことは、I was disappointed ～で表します。この構文は、次のような形で用います。

- I was disappointed with〈at〉～(名詞)　「～にがっかりした」
- I was disappointed in ～(人)　「～（人）に失望した」
- I was disappointed to ～(動詞の原形)　「～してがっかりした」
- I was disappointed (that) ～(文)　「～ということにがっかりした」

「(今) がっかりしている」場合は、I'm disappointed ～と現在形で表します。「とてもがっかりした、すごくがっかりした」と強調する場合は、disappointed の前に so や really、very などを入れましょう。

こんなふうに書きます

1 I was disappointed with〈at〉 **the ending of the drama.**
そのドラマの結末にがっかりした。

2 I was **really** disappointed in **the new mayor.**
新市長には本当に失望した。

3 I was disappointed to **find out the restaurant was closed 〈had been closed〉.**
そのレストランが閉店したと聞いて残念だった。

4 I'm disappointed **no one said anything about my new hairstyle.**
髪型を変えたのに誰も何も言ってくれなくて、がっかり。

いら立ち

構文35 ～にむっとした。／～にイライラした。 I was upset ～.

こんなふうに使います

I was upset ～は気を悪くしたときに使う構文で、何かに対して悔しかったり、がっかりしたりして「むっとした、イライラした、取り乱した、動揺した」といったニュアンスです。この構文は、次のような形で用います。

- I was upset about ～（名詞）「～にむっとした」
- I was upset to ～（動詞の原形）「～してむっとした」
- I was upset (that) ～（文）「～ということにむっとした」

「（今）むっとしている」場合は、I'm upset ～と現在形で表します。「すごく～」と強調する場合は、upset の前に so や really、very などを入れましょう。

こんなふうに書きます

1 **I was upset about his attitude.**
彼の態度にむっときた。

2 **My children were upset to transfer to another school.**
転校することになって、子どもたちは動揺していた。

3 **I was really upset nobody believed me.**
誰も私を信じてくれなくて、本当に腹立たしかった。

4 **I'm always upset about the way my boss makes decisions.**
上司の物事の決め方にいつもイライラしている。

後悔

～したことを後悔している。 I feel bad about ～ing.

こんなふうに使います

自分の行動に対する後悔は、I feel bad about ～(動詞の -ing 形)で表します。直訳は「～したことを悪いと感じている」で、「～したことを後悔している・申し訳なく思っている」という意味です。逆に、「～しなかったことを後悔している・申し訳なく思っている」と書きたいなら、動詞の -ing 形の前に not を置いて、I feel bad about not ～ing とします。

過去の気持ちを振り返り、「～したことを（あの時）後悔した」と書く場合は、feel の過去形 felt を使って、I felt bad about ～ing と表します。

「すごく～」と強調する場合は、feel の前に really を入れましょう。後悔している行動をすでに述べた後なら、I feel bad about it.（そのことを後悔している）と書き添えるだけでも OK です。

こんなふうに書きます

1 **I feel bad about rebelling against my parents.**
親に反抗したことを申し訳なく思っている。
※rebelは「反抗する」という意味。

2 **I really feel bad about taking it out on my wife.**
妻に八つ当たりしてしまったことを、とても後悔している。
※take it out on ～で「～に八つ当たりする」の意味。

3 **I really feel bad about not inviting her.**
彼女を招待しなかったことを、心から申し訳ないと思っている。

4 **I felt bad about lying to him.**
彼にうそをついたことを後悔した。

後悔

～しておけばよかった。 I should've ～.

こんなふうに使います

しなかったことへの後悔の気持ちは、I should've ～(動詞の過去分詞)で表すことができます。「～しておけばよかった」という意味で、should've は should have の短縮形です。

反対に、してしまったことへの後悔の気持ちは I shouldn't have ～(動詞の過去分詞)で表します。「～するんじゃなかった」という意味で、shouldn't は should not の短縮形です。

こんなふうに書きます

1 **I should've made a reservation.**
（乗り物やホテルなどの）予約をしておけばよかった。
※美容院や歯科医などの予約は、an appointment。

2 **I should've waited one more day.**
もう１日待てばよかったな。

3 **I should've seen a doctor earlier.**
もっと早く医者に診てもらえばよかった。

4 **I shouldn't have bought it.**
それを買わなきゃよかった。

5 **I shouldn't have told him my secret.**
彼に秘密を言うんじゃなかった。

6 **I shouldn't have drunk that much in front of her.**
彼女の前であんなに飲むんじゃなかったな。

感謝

構文38 〜に…のことで感謝している。 I thank 〜 for ...

こんなふうに使います

「ありがとう」という訳でおなじみの Thank you. ですが、thank はもともと「〜に感謝している」という意味です（過去形は thanked）。thank の後ろに〈人＋for ＋名詞〉を続けると「〜（人）に…のことで感謝している」、thank の後ろに〈人＋for ＋動詞の -ing 形〉を続けると「〜（人）に…してもらって感謝している」という意味を表すことができます。

「心から感謝している」と強調する場合は、thank の前に really を入れましょう。

こんなふうに書きます

1 **I thank him for his kindness.**
彼の親切に感謝している。

2 **I thank her for her thoughtfulness.**
彼女の思いやりに感謝している。

3 **I really thank them for their advice.**
彼らの助言には心から感謝している。

4 **I thank them for giving me this opportunity.**
このような機会を与えてもらって、彼らに感謝している。

5 **I thank him for helping me with the project.**
彼にプロジェクトを手伝ってもらって感謝している。

6 **I thanked her for caring about me.**
私を気にかけてくれたことを、彼女に感謝した。

感謝

～のことで感謝している。 I'm grateful ～.

こんなふうに使います

感謝の気持ちは、構文 38 の I thank ～ for ...（～に…のことで感謝している）のほかに I'm grateful ～で表すこともできます。特に、相手の親切な行為などに対する感謝で、恩に着るイメージです。感謝の気持ちを強調したい場合は、grateful の前に so や really を入れましょう。この構文は、次のような形で用います。

- I'm grateful to ～（人）for ...（名詞）「…のことで～に感謝している」
  ※ to ～（人）を省略することもあります。
- I'm grateful to ～（人）for ...（動詞の -ing 形）「…してくれて～に感謝している」
- I'm grateful (that) ～（文）「～であることに感謝している」「～で私は幸せ者だ」

こんなふうに書きます

1. **I'm grateful to them for all their support.**
   彼らの支援に感謝している。

2. **I'm grateful to her for lending me money.**
   お金を貸してくれて、彼女に感謝している。

3. **I'm so grateful to my wife for taking care of me while I was sick.**
   体調を崩したとき、妻に世話してもらい心から感謝している。

4. **I'm really grateful my boss let me take a month off.**
   1カ月の休暇を取らせてくれて、上司には心から感謝している。

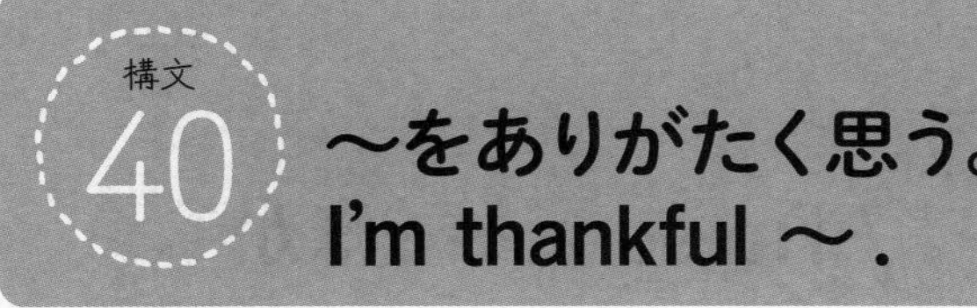

構文 40 ～をありがたく思う。 I'm thankful ～.

感謝

こんなふうに使います

構文39のI'm grateful ～が人の親切な行為に対する感謝を表すのに対し、I'm thankful ～は幸運や恩恵などを「ありがたく思う」ときに使います。感謝の気持ちを強調したい場合は、thankful の前に so や really を入れましょう。この構文は、次のような形で用います。

※ grateful と thankful のどちらを使っても、意味に差がない場合もあります。

- I'm thankful for ～(名詞) 「～をありがたく思う」
- I'm thankful to ～(人) 「～に感謝している」 ※toの代わりにforを用いることもあります。
- I'm thankful to ～(動詞の原形) 「～することをありがたく思う」
- I'm thankful (that) ～(文) 「～であることをありがたく思う」

こんなふうに書きます

1 **I'm thankful for my good health.**
健康でいられることをありがたく思う。

2 **I'm so thankful for a good harvest.**
豊作で本当にありがたい。

3 **I'm really thankful to my parents for their love.**
両親の愛情に、心から感謝している。

4 **I'm thankful to be friends with her.**
彼女と友達でいられることを、ありがたく思う。

5 **I'm thankful my family can live in peace.**
家族が平穏に暮らせることに感謝している。

考え・感想

構文41 ～だと思う。 I think ～. / I'm sure ～. ほか

こんなふうに使います

以下の構文は、すべて「～だと思う」というときに使います。確信の度合いや、根拠のあるなしによって使い分けましょう。どの構文も、「～」には思っている内容を文の形で入れます。「～」の前には、that が省略されています。

- I think ～　「～だと思う」の最も一般的な語。
- I'm sure ～ / I bet ～　「きっと～だろう」と自信のある「～だと思う」。
- I believe ～　ある程度の確信がある「～だと思う」。
- I assume ～　確証はないものの、事実と推測して「（当然）～だと思う」。
- I suppose ～　確信はないものの、そうだろうと仮定して「（たぶん）～だろうと思う、なんとなく～だと思う」。
- I guess ～　与えられた情報から推測したり、言い当てたりするときの「～だろう（と思う）」。くだけて、I suppose ～の代わりに用いることもある。
- I feel ～　漠然と「～だと思う・感じる、～な気がする」。
- I have a feeling ～　「～な気がする、～な感じがする」という予感。

こんなふうに書きます

1 **I don't think I'm cut out for this job.**
私はこの仕事に向いていないと思う。
※be cut out for ～は「(生まれつき)～に向いている」という意味。通常、否定文で用いる。

2 **I'm sure he will make a good father.**
彼はきっといい父親になるだろう。

3 **I believe she's telling the truth.**
彼女は本当のことを言っていると思う。

4 **I assume he is under great stress.**
たぶん、彼はかなりストレスがたまっているのだろう。

5 **I suppose she didn't want to trouble me.**
彼女は私に迷惑をかけたくなかったのだと思う。

6 **I guess she's not so interested in sports.**
彼女はスポーツにあまり興味がないのだろう。

7 **I feel he's avoiding me.**
彼は私のことを避けているような気がする。

8 **I have a feeling something nice will happen.**
何かいいことが起こりそうな気がする。

ポイント

- 「～だと思う」を表す表現はいろいろあり、確信の度合いによって使い分ける。
- 最も一般的な言い方は I think ～。
- どの構文も、「～」には思っていることを文の形で入れる。

構文 42

考え・感想

～かなぁ。 I wonder ～.

こんなふうに使います

自分自身に「～かなぁ」「～だろうか」と問いかけるような軽い疑問や考えは、I wonder ～で表します。知りたいと思うことを間接的に述べるときに便利です。

「明日は晴れるかなぁ」や「彼らは疲れていたのかなぁ」というように、yes/noで答えられる疑問を表すときは、I wonder if ～(文) とします。

疑問に思っている内容が理由や時、場所などの場合はI wonder why ～(どうして～かなぁ)、I wonder when ～(いつ～かなぁ)、I wonder where ～(どこで～かなぁ)のように表します。いずれも、〈I wonder ＋疑問詞＋文〉の形にします。

同じように、「誰に～かなぁ」はI wonder who ～で、「何を～かなぁ」はI wonder what ～で表します。右ページの❻や❽のように、疑問に思う部分 (who や what) が主語になることもあります。

まとめると、以下のような形になります。

- I wonder if ～(文) 「～かなぁ」
- I wonder why ～(文) 「どうして～かなぁ」
- I wonder when ～(文) 「いつ～かなぁ」
- I wonder where ～(文) 「どこで～かなぁ」
- I wonder who ～(文) 「誰に (誰と、誰を) ～かなぁ」
- I wonder who ～(動詞) 「誰が～かなぁ」
- I wonder what ～(文) 「何を～かなぁ」
- I wonder what ～(動詞) 「何が～かなぁ」
- I wonder how ～(文) 「どのように～かなぁ」
- I wonder＋how で始まる疑問詞＋～(文) 「どのくらい～かなぁ」

こんなふうに書きます

1 I wonder if it'll be sunny tomorrow.
明日は晴れるかなぁ。

2 I wonder why she always acts like that.
彼女はどうしていつもあんな態度なんだろう。

3 I wonder when I'll get a raise.
いつになったら昇給するんだろう。

4 I wonder where he was last night.
彼はゆうべ、どこにいたんだろう。

5 I wonder who he's talking to.
彼は誰と話しているのかなぁ。

6 I wonder who told her that.
誰が彼女にそれを言ったんだろう。

7 I wonder what she will do after graduation.
彼女、卒業後は何をするのかなぁ。

8 I wonder what went wrong.
何が間違っていたんだろう。

9 I wonder how she is doing.
彼女は元気にしているかなぁ。

10 I wonder how old he is.
彼はいくつだろう。

考え・感想

構文43 ～するのがよさそう。 I might as well ～.

こんなふうに使います

状況的に「～するのがよさそう」と判断したときは、I might as well ～(動詞の原形)を使います。それがよい選択と思われるので「～することにしよう」と受け入れたり、ほかにいい案がないため「～するしかない」と受け入れざるを得なかったり、といった消極的なニュアンスです。「せっかくだから」「どうせなら」という状況でも使います。might の代わりに may を使うこともあります。

こんなふうに書きます

1. I might as well **go by train.**
（気乗りしないが）電車で行くのがよさそうだ。

2. I might as well **ask for his opinion.**
彼の意見を聞くだけ聞いてみてもいいか。

3. I might as well **save my breath.**
（言ってもムダだから）黙っていたほうがいいか。
※save one's breathは「黙っている、余計なことは言わない」という意味。

4. I might as well **go to the movies with him.**
（暇だし）彼と映画を見に行くのも悪くないのかも。

5. I might as well **upgrade my hotel room.**
（割引がきくし）せっかくだからホテルの部屋をアップグレードしようかな。

考え・感想

それは～だと感じた。 I found it ～.

こんなふうに使います

「それは～だと感じた」、「それは～だった」と感想を書くときは、I found it ～(形容詞または名詞)で表します。経験して感じたことや、わかったことに使います。このfound は find（～だと感じる・わかる）の過去形です。

it の代わりにほかの代名詞（him、her など）や具体的な名詞を入れたり、I found (that) ～(文)の形で書いたりすることもできます。

I found it ～の後に to ...（動詞の原形）を続けると、「…することは～だと感じた」という意味になります。

こんなふうに書きます

1 **I found it interesting.**
それは興味深いと感じた。

2 **I found it very easy to use.**
とても使いやすいと思った。

3 **I found the class a lot of fun.**
その授業はとても楽しかった。

4 **I found him friendly.**
彼は気さくな人だと思った。

5 **I found commuting to work by bike wasn't so bad.**
自転車通勤はそれほど悪くないと思った。

6 **I found it impossible to live with him.**
彼と暮らしていくのは無理だと感じた。

考え・感想

A は思ったほど～ではなかった。 A wasn't as ～ as I thought.

こんなふうに使います

想像や期待、予測と比べて「思ったほど～ではなかった」と感想を書くときは、A wasn't as ～(形容詞) as I thought と表します。wasn't は was not の短縮形です。not as ～ as ... は「…ほど～でない」という意味で、ここでは「...」に I thought (私が思っていた)を入れて、「思ったほど～ではなかった」と表しています。

I thought は I expected(期待していた)と入れ替えて、A wasn't as ～ as I expected とすることもできます。

こんなふうに書きます

1 **The movie wasn't as good as I thought.**
その映画は思ったほどよくなかった。

2 **Okinawa wasn't as hot as I thought.**
沖縄は思ったほど暑くなかった。

3 **The roller coaster wasn't as scary as I thought.**
そのジェットコースターは思ったほど怖くなかった。

4 **The restaurant wasn't as expensive as I thought.**
そのレストランは思ったほど高くなかった。

5 **The party wasn't as formal as I thought.**
そのパーティーは思ったほど堅苦しくなかった。

考え・感想

A は思ったより〜だった。 A was ~ than I thought.

こんなふうに使います

想像や期待、予測と比べて「思ったより〜だった」と感想を書くときは、A was 〜（形容詞の比較級）than I thought と表します。〈形容詞の比較級 + than ...〉は「…より（もっと）〜だ」という意味で、ここでは「...」に I thought（私が思っていた）を入れて、「思ったより〜だった」と表しています。

I thought は I expected（期待していた）と入れ替えて、A was 〜 than I expected と表すこともできます。

また、A was much 〜 than I thought とすると、「思ったよりはるかに〜だった」と強調することができます。A was very 〜 than I thought（×）とは言えないので、注意してください。

こんなふうに書きます

1 **The interview was easier than I thought.**
面接は思ったより簡単だった。

2 **The exhibition was more crowded than I thought.**
展覧会は思ったより混んでいた。

3 **Their prices were lower than I thought.**
その店の価格は思ったより安かった。

4 **His new book was less interesting than I thought.**
彼の新刊は思ったより面白くなかった。

5 **The scenery was much better than I thought.**
その景色は思ったよりはるかによかった。

断定・推量

構文47 ～は…に違いない。 ～ must be ... / ～ must ...

こんなふうに使います

現在または未来のことについて、確固たる証拠はないもののおそらく間違いないだろうという確信のある事柄は、～ must be ...(名詞、形容詞、動詞の-ing 形)または ～ must ...(動詞の原形)で表すことができます。

このmust は「きっと…なはずだ、…に違いない」という意味です。「...」に動詞の原形が入るパターンでは、通常、know(～を知っている)や love(～を愛している、～を気に入っている)などの状態を表す動詞が入ります。

なお、「～は…ではないはずだ、～は…であるはずがない」は、～ can't be ... / ～ can't ... で表すのが一般的です。must の否定形 mustn't は「～してはいけない」という禁止の意味で使われることが多いです。

こんなふうに書きます

1 **She must be an artist.**
彼女はきっと芸術家なのだろう。

2 **He must be stressed.**
彼はストレスがたまっているに違いない。

3 **He must know what happened.**
何があったのか彼なら知っているはずだ。

4 **She must still love him.**
彼女は今でもきっと彼のことを愛しているのだろう。

5 **It can't be true.**
それは本当であるはずがない（＝そんなはずはない）。

断定・推量

～は…だったに違いない。 ～ must've been ... / ～ must've ...

こんなふうに使います

過去のことについて、確固たる証拠はないもののおそらく間違いないだろうという確信のある事柄は、～ must've been ...（名詞、形容詞）または ～ must've ...（動詞の過去分詞）で表します。「～はきっと…だったのだろう、～は…だったに違いない」という意味です。must've は must have の短縮形で、［マスタヴ］のように発音します。

なお、「～は…ではなかったはずだ、～は…であったはずがない」は、～ can't have been ... / ～ can't have ... で表すのが一般的です。

こんなふうに書きます

1 **He must've been a chef before.**
彼は以前、料理人だったに違いない。

2 **Her parents must've been very strict.**
彼女の両親はとても厳しかったに違いない。

3 **He must've graduated from a prestigious university.**
彼は名門大学の出に違いない。
※prestigiousは「権威のある」という意味。

4 **They must've broken up.**
彼らはきっと別れたのだろう。

5 **It can't have been a real diamond for that price.**
その値段では、本物のダイヤモンドだったとは考えられない。

推量

～は(もしかしたら)…かもしれない。
～ might be ... / ～ might ...

こんなふうに使います

現在または未来のことについて、自信がないながらもその可能性があると推量するときには、～ might be ...(名詞、形容詞、動詞の -ing 形)または～ might ...(動詞の原形)で表します。

この might は「(もしかしたら)…かもしれない」という意味です。might は may(…かもしれない)の過去形ですが、過去の意味を表すわけではなく、might と may のどちらを使っても意味の差はあまりありません。

「…ではないかもしれない」という否定の文は、～ might not ... か ～ may not ... で表します。

こんなふうに書きます

1 **It might snow tomorrow.**
明日は雪が降るかもしれない。

2 **My daughter might be hiding something.**
娘は隠し事をしているかもしれない。

3 **There might be a better way.**
もっとよい方法があるかもしれない。

4 **He might not like me.**
彼は私のことが好きじゃないのかもしれない。

5 **I might not be able to get a seat if I don't hurry.**
急がないと席が取れないかもしれない。

推量

構文50 〜は(もしかしたら)…だったのかもしれない。〜 might have ...

こんなふうに使います

過去のことについて、その可能性があったかもしれないと推量するときには、〜 might have ...(動詞の過去分詞)で表します。「〜は（もしかしたら）…だったのかもしれない、〜は（もしかしたら）…したのかもしれない」という意味です。構文49の〜 might ... と同様、might の代わりに may を用いることもできます。

「〜は(もしかしたら)…ではなかったのかもしれない」という否定の文は、〜 might not have ... や 〜 may not have ... で表します。

こんなふうに書きます

1 **I might have hurt her feelings.**
彼女を傷つけてしまったかもしれない。

2 **He might have known everything.**
彼はすべて知っていたのかもしれない。

3 **She might have been at the concert, too.**
彼女もそのコンサートに行っていたのかもしれない。

4 **He might have changed his number.**
彼は電話番号を変えたのかもしれない。

5 **Something might have happened to her.**
彼女に何か起きたのかもしれない。

6 **I might not have understood correctly.**
私が正しく理解していなかったのかもしれない。

印象

構文 51 まるで〜のようだった。It was like 〜.

こんなふうに使います

見たものや聞いたこと、出来事などについて、「まるで〜のようだった」と何かに例えながら印象や感想を書くときは、It was like 〜(名詞または動詞の -ing 形)が便利です。この like は「〜のような」という意味です。「〜」に名詞を入れると「まるで〜のようだった」、「〜」に動詞の -ing 形を入れると「まるで〜しているかのようだった」となります。like の前に just を置いて It was just like 〜とすると、「まさに〜のようだった」と強調することができます。

こんなふうに書きます

1 **It was like a dream.**
まるで夢のようだった。

2 **It was just like a movie.**
まさに映画のようだった。

3 **It was like the scenery on a postcard.**
絵はがきにある景色のようだった。

4 **It was like listening to foreign music.**
まるで外国の音楽を聞いているかのようだった。

5 **It was like being in New York.**
まるでニューヨークにいるかのようだった。

6 **It was like relaxing in my own living room.**
まるで自分の家の居間でくつろいでいるかのようだった。

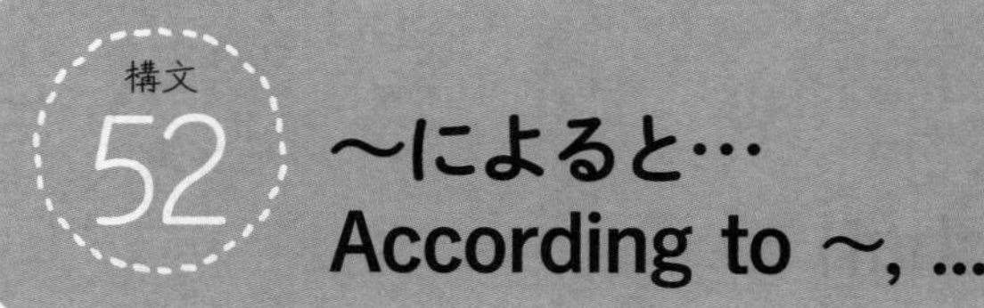

～によると…
According to ～, ...

こんなふうに使います

According to ～, ... は、聞いた内容を情報源を明確にして表すときに使う構文です。通常、文頭に置きます。「～」には、天気予報、新聞、文献、テレビ、ラジオ、調査結果、人など、情報源となるものが入ります。「～によると…らしい、～が…と言っていた」というニュアンスです。

こんなふうに書きます

1 According to **the weather forecast, it'll be burning hot tomorrow.**
天気予報によると、明日はうだるような暑さらしい。

2 According to **TV, grapefruit is good for burning body fat.**
グレープフルーツは脂肪燃焼に効くと、テレビで言っていた。

3 According to **the salesperson, it's the best-selling item at their shop.**
その店ではそれが一番売れていると、店の人が言っていた。

4 According to **statistics, the average person spends over two hours a day on social media.**
統計によると、平均的な人は1日2時間以上をSNSに費やしているらしい。

5 According to **a magazine, the best way to improve your memory is to get enough sleep.**
ある雑誌によると、記憶力をよくする一番の方法は十分な睡眠らしい。

構文 53 伝聞

～らしい。 I heard (that) ～.

こんなふうに使います

耳にしたことを述べるときは、I heard (that) ～(文) を用います。情報源は書かなくて OK ですが、「友だちから聞いた」「ラジオで耳にした」のように、from my friend や on the radio を添えることもできます。heard は hear(～を耳にする、～を聞く)の過去形で、「～」には、聞いた内容を文の形で入れます。that は省略しても OK です。

文法的には、that 以下の文は、I heard ～という過去形の文に時制を一致させます (時制の一致については、p. 693 を参照)。つまり、it will be ～や she has ～といった文が後に続く場合は、it would be ～や she had ～と過去形にするわけです。ただ、実際には時制の一致を無視するネイティブ・スピーカーも多いようです。また、I heard ～は I hear ～と現在形で表すこともあり、この場合、時制の一致は受けません。

こんなふうに書きます

1 **I heard their sweets were〈are〉 really good.**
その店のスイーツはすごくおいしいらしい。

2 **I heard his son entered〈had entered〉 A University.**
彼の息子さんが A 大学に入学したそうだ。

3 **I heard there would〈will〉 be a convenience store across the street.**
道路の向かい側にコンビニができるらしい。

4 **I heard there will〈would〉 be more cedar pollen in the air this spring than ever before.**
この春のスギ花粉の量は、過去最高になるようだ。

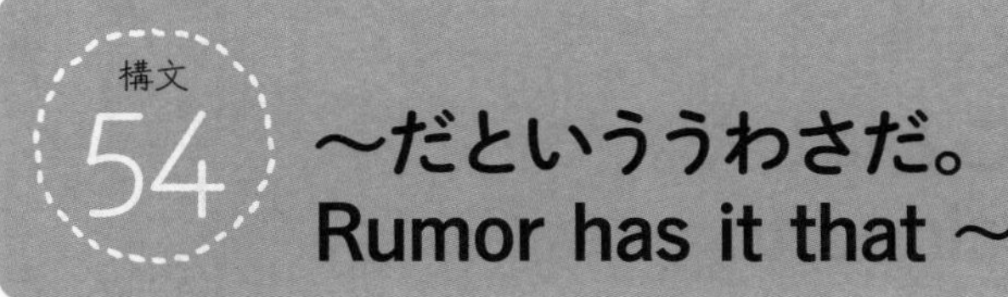

～だというううわさだ。 Rumor has it that ～.

こんなふうに使います

Rumor has it that ～(文)は、構文 53 の I heard (that) ～（～らしい）と同じく、耳にしたことについて書くときに使います。「～だというううわさだ、～だとうわさで聞いた、うわさでは～らしい」というニュアンスです。There's a rumor that ～や The rumor is that ～と表すこともあります。

こんなふうに書きます

1. Rumor has it that **his wife is having an affair.**
彼の妻は浮気をしているというううわさだ。

2. Rumor has it that **Yamada-san is moving to Hokkaido.**
うわさでは、ヤマダさんは北海道へ引っ越すらしい。

3. Rumor has it that **her new movie is a must-see.**
彼女の新作映画は必見らしい。

4. Rumor has it that **the company is going to downsize.**
会社が人員削減をすると、うわさで聞いた。

5. Rumor has it that **Ms. Sato is in the hospital.**
サトウ先生が入院しているというううわさだ。

6. Rumor has it that **Ikumi is getting married in September.**
イクミが 9 月に結婚する予定だと、うわさで聞いた。

決意

～することにした。 I've decided to ～.

こんなふうに使います

「～することにした」という決断は、I've decided to ～(動詞の原形)で表します。I decided to ～と過去形で表しても構いません。

「～しないことにした」と否定文にする場合は、not の位置に注意が必要です。I've decided not to ～(動詞の原形)のように、not を to の前に置きます。

いずれの場合も、on second thought（いろいろ考えて、考え直した結果)や in the end(結局、最終的には、なんだかんだ言ってやっぱり)などのフレーズを加えてもよいでしょう。

こんなふうに書きます

1 **I've decided to tell her how I feel.**
彼女に思いを伝えることにした。

2 **I've decided to take over my father's business.**
父の商売を継ぐことにした。

3 **I've decided to drive to Osaka.**
大阪へは車で行くことにした。

4 **On second thought, I've decided to accept the transfer to Tokyo.**
いろいろ考えて、東京への赴任を受け入れることにした。

5 **In the end, I've decided not to quit my job.**
結局、仕事を辞めないことにした。

決意

何があっても～するぞ。 No matter what, I will ～.

こんなふうに使います

「何があっても～するぞ」という強い意志は、No matter what, I will ～(動詞の原形)で表します。No matter what は No matter what happens(何が起きても、どんなことがあっても)を短くした形です。

「何があっても～しないぞ」という否定は、No matter what, I will not ～(動詞の原形)で表します。No matter what, I will never ～(動詞の原形)のように not を never にすると、「何があっても絶対に～しないぞ」という強い意志をさらに強調できます。

こんなふうに書きます

1 No matter what, I will **support him!**
何があっても彼を支える！

2 No matter what, I will **love her forever.**
何があっても彼女を一生愛し続ける。

3 No matter what, I will **become a lawyer.**
何があっても弁護士になるぞ。

4 No matter what, I will **lose 10kg!**
何がなんでも 10 キロやせるぞ！

5 No matter what, I will never **lose to him!**
何があってもあいつには絶対に負けないぞ！

目的

構文57 ～するために、～しに (in order) to ～

こんなふうに使います

「すしを食べに築地へ行った」の「すしを食べに」のような、「～しに、～するために」という目的は、to ～(動詞の原形)またはin order to ～(動詞の原形)で表します。in order to ～のほうが「～するために」という意味が強調され、また、少しかしこまった響きがあります。

こんなふうに書きます

1. **I went to Kanazawa to eat fresh seafood.**
新鮮な海の幸を食べに金沢へ行った。

2. **I went to Denver to see Peggy.**
ペギーに会いにデンバーへ行った。

3. **I went to the library to return the books.**
本を返却しに図書館へ行った。

4. **My boyfriend called me to say he loves me.**
好きだよと言うために、彼氏が電話をくれた。

5. **I stopped at the gas station to check my tire pressure.**
タイヤの空気圧をチェックするために、ガソリンスタンドに寄った。

6. **I'm saving money in order to buy a car.**
車を買うために、お金を節約中。

原因・理由

構文58 〜で、〜のせいで、〜のため because of 〜 / due to 〜

こんなふうに使います

「雨で試合が延期になった」の「雨で」のような、「〜で、〜のせいで、〜のため」といった原因や理由は、because of 〜（名詞）または due to 〜（名詞）で表します。

どちらも同じ意味ですが、because of 〜はより口語的なニュアンスで、どんな状況でも使うことができます。一方、due to 〜は、交通機関の遅延理由や会議に出席できなかった理由など、よりかしこまった状況を表すときに使います。

こんなふうに書きます

1 **The game was postponed because of the rain.**
雨で試合が延期になった。

2 **I was late because of him.**
彼のせいで遅刻しちゃった。

3 **We lost the match because of me.**
私のせいで試合に負けちゃった。

4 **The train stopped for about 30 minutes due to the earthquake.**
地震のため、電車が 30 分ほど運転を見合わせた。

5 **I couldn't attend the seminar due to other commitments.**
ほかに約束があったため、セミナーに出席できなかった。
※commitmentは「（破れない）約束」という意味。

原因・理由

構文 59

～なので because ～ / as ～ / since ～

こんなふうに使います

「疲れていたので、1日中家にいた」のように「～なので」と理由を表すときは、because ～(文)、as ～(文)、since ～(文)で表します。

because ～は、理由を強調した表現です。文の後半に置くのが一般的で、結果を表す文の直後に because ～を続けます(右の例文❶～❸参照)。because ～の前にコンマは不要です。ちなみに、会話では、理由を尋ねる疑問文に対する答えは Because で始めるのが一般的です（例：Why are you mad at him?［どうして彼のこと怒ってるの？］→ Because he forgot my birthday.［だって私の誕生日を忘れてたんだもん］)。

as ～と since ～も同じく理由を表すときの表現で、because より弱い意味です。会話では、相手がすでに知っている、または想像がつく理由を述べるときによく使います。これらは文頭に置くのが一般的です（右の例文❹～❼参照)。As ～, や Since ～, のように、理由を表した後にコンマを置いてから結果を続けます。

as ～には「～なため」といった、ややフォーマルな響きがあります。since はどのような状況でも使える表現で、特にアメリカ英語でよく使われます。

こんなふうに書きます

1 **I stayed home all day because it was very hot.**
暑かったので、一日中家にいた。

2 **I broke up with him because he cheated on me.**
彼が浮気をしたので別れた。
※cheat on ～は「～を裏切って浮気をする」という意味。

3 **I did all the household chores today because it was my wife's birthday.**
妻の誕生日だったので、今日は家事を全部僕がやった。
※do the household choresは「家事をする」という意味。choreは［チョア］のように発音。

4 **As the plane was delayed, I missed my connection flight.**
飛行機が遅延したため、乗り継ぎの飛行機に乗れなかった。

5 **As the meeting was canceled, we got some free time.**
会合が中止になったため、自由時間ができた。

6 **Since I was full, I gave my dessert to Julia.**
おなかがいっぱいだったので、デザートをジュリアにあげた。

7 **Since it was getting late, we decided to call it a day.**
遅くなってきたので、切り上げることにした。
※call it a dayは「（仕事などを）終わりにする、打ち切る」という意味。

ポイント

- 理由は because ～（文）、as ～（文）、since ～（文）で表す。
- because ～は、結果を表す文の直後に続けるのが一般的。
- as ～、since ～は文頭に置くことが多い。

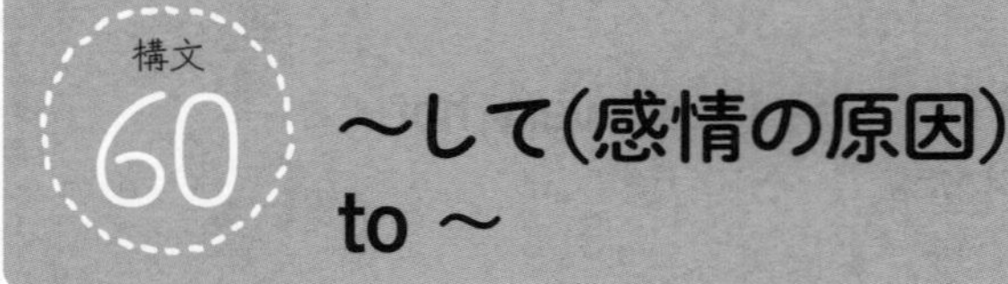

～して（感情の原因）to ～

こんなふうに使います

「お会いできてうれしかったです」のように、「～して（うれしかった、驚いた、がっかりしたなど）」という感情の原因は、to ～（動詞の原形）で表します。

こんなふうに書きます

1 **I was happy to meet her.**
彼女に会えてうれしかった。

2 **I was sad to lose my favorite key ring.**
お気に入りのキーホルダーをなくして悲しかった。

3 **I was surprised to hear his mother went to New York by herself.**
彼のお母さんが１人でニューヨークへ行ったと聞いて驚いた。

4 **I was disappointed to find out the book is out of print.**
その本が絶版になっていると知ってがっかりした。

5 **I was so excited to see a movie being filmed.**
映画の撮影現場を見て、すごく興奮した。
※being filmedは「撮影されている」という意味。

6 **I was upset to learn I didn't get the job.**
自分がその仕事に採用されなかったと知って動揺した。

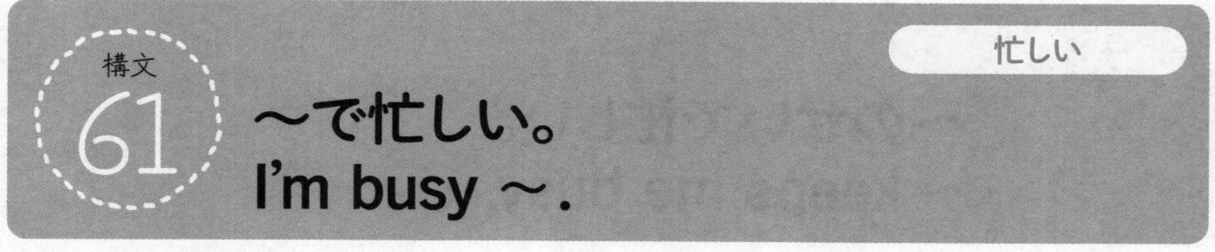

～で忙しい。 I'm busy ～.

こんなふうに使います

忙しい理由について書くときは、I'm busy ～を使って、次のように表します。

- I'm busy with ～(名詞) 「～で忙しい」
- I'm busy ～(動詞の -ing 形) 「～するのに忙しい、忙しく～している」

１日を振り返って、「今日は～で(～するのに)忙しかった」と日記に書くなら、I was busy with ～または I was busy ～ing と過去形で表します。「ここのところ～で(～するのに)忙しい」のように、忙しさが続いていることを強調する場合は、現在完了形で I've been busy with ～または I've been busy ～ing と表しましょう。

こんなふうに書きます

1 I'm busy with the housework every day.
毎日、家事で忙しい。

2 I'm very busy with my club activities.
部活動ですごく忙しい。

3 I was busy with the report all day today.
今日は一日中、報告書（を書くこと）で忙しかった。

4 I've been busy running errands.
ここのところ、雑用で忙しい。
※run errandsは「用事をする」という意味。

5 We've been really busy preparing for our wedding.
ここのところ、結婚式の準備ですごく忙しい。

忙しい

構文 62

～のせいで忙しい。
～ keeps me busy.

こんなふうに使います

～（名詞）keeps me busy は、忙しい理由を主語にした構文です。I が主語の文が続いて日記が単調になったときは、こうした構文を使ってみるのもいいでしょう。

～には、「人」と「物」のどちらも入れることができます。人の場合は「～のせいで忙しい、～の世話で忙しい」、物の場合は「～で忙しい」というニュアンスです。～に入る名詞が複数形の場合は、～ keep me busy としましょう。

一時的に忙しいなら、～ is〈are〉keeping me busy と現在進行形で表します。「～で忙しかった」と過去のことについて書くなら、～ kept me busy と keep を過去形（kept）にします。

こんなふうに書きます

1 **My job keeps me busy.**
仕事で忙しい。

2 **Household chores keep me busy every day.**
毎日、家事で忙しい。
※household chores[チョアズ]は「家事」という意味。

3 **My grandchildren keep me busy.**
孫たちの世話で忙しい。

4 **Giving the students their grades is keeping me very busy.**
（教員が）生徒に成績をつけるのにとても忙しい。

5 **PTA meetings kept me busy last year.**
去年は PTA の会合で忙しかった。

不可能

あまりに…だったので～できなかった。 A was too ... to ～.

こんなふうに使います

「Aがあまりに…だったので～できなかった」と書くときは、A was too ...（形容詞） to ～（動詞の原形）を使います。直訳すると「Aは～するには…過ぎた」ですが、これで「～できなかった」という否定の意味を表します。

また、to ～の前に〈for ＋人〉を入れると、「（人）にとってAはあまりに…だったので、～できなかった」という意味を表せます（例文5参照）。

こんなふうに書きます

1 **I was too tired to cook tonight.**
今夜はあまりに疲れていて、料理できなかった。

2 **We were too busy to see each other last year.**
去年は、お互い忙し過ぎて会えなかった。

3 **I was too sleepy to drive.**
あまりに眠くて車を運転できなかった。

4 **The steak was too hard to eat.**
そのステーキは、あまりに硬くて食べられなかった。

5 **The jeans were too tight for me to wear.**
そのジーンズは、私にはあまりにきつくてはけなかった。

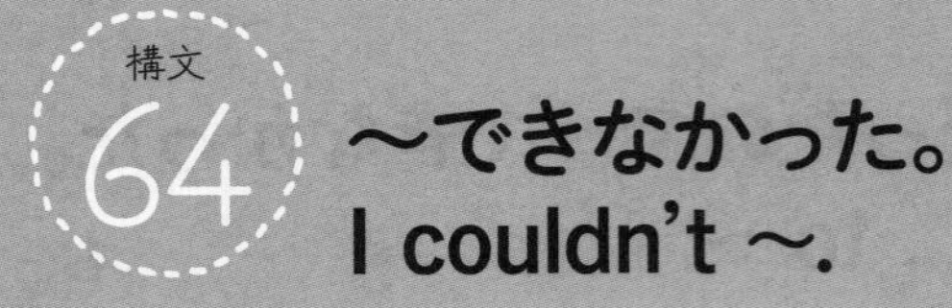

不可能

構文64 〜できなかった。I couldn't 〜.

こんなふうに使います

「〜できなかった」は、I couldn't 〜（動詞の原形）で表します。couldn't は could not の短縮形で、could は can（〜できる）の過去形です。

「予定していたり、そうしたいと思っていたけれどできなかった」ことは、I was going to 〜, but I couldn't.（〜するつもりだったけれど、できなかった）、あるいは、I wanted to 〜, but I couldn't.（〜したかったけれど、できなかった）で表しましょう。いずれも、couldn't の後には do it が省略されています。

こんなふうに書きます

1. **I couldn't get the ticket.**
   チケットが取れなかった。

2. **I couldn't sing very well.**
   あまりうまく歌えなかった。

3. **I couldn't explain it well.**
   うまく説明できなかった。

4. **We couldn't enter the art museum because it was closed.**
   閉まっていたので、美術館の中に入ることができなかった。

5. **I was going to answer all the questions, but I couldn't.**
   すべての問題を解くつもりだったけど、できなかった。

6. **I wanted to see the polar bears, but I couldn't.**
   ホッキョクグマが見たかったけど、見られなかった。

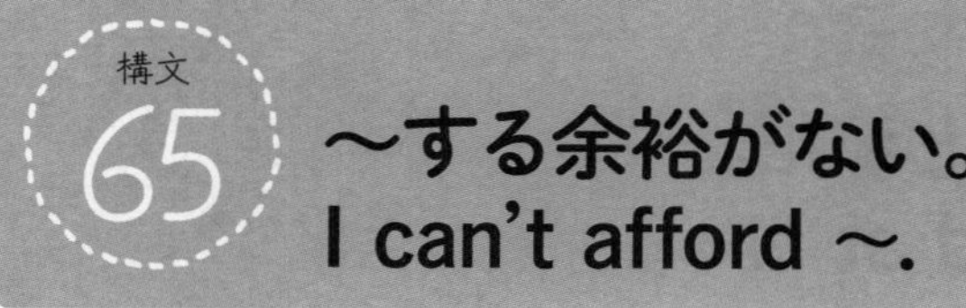

不可能

～する余裕がない。 I can't afford ～.

こんなふうに使います

「（時間的、金銭的に）～する余裕がない」と書きたいときは、I can't afford ～で表します。～には名詞または〈to＋動詞の原形〉が入ります。「～」に入るのが名詞の場合でも、日本語に訳すときは動詞を補った形で考えると自然です。例えば、I can't afford a new car. は直訳すると「新車の余裕がない」ですが、「新車を買う余裕がない」のように「～を買う」を補った訳にするとわかりやすくなります。

また、状況によっては「～は許されない」や「～するわけにはいかない」というニュアンスにもなります（例文❹❺）。toの前にnotを入れてI can't afford not to ～（動詞の原形）とすると、「～しないわけにはいかない」という意味になります。

こんなふうに書きます

1 **I can't afford a new car.**
新車を買う余裕なんてない。

2 **I can't afford to eat out.**
外食する余裕がない。

3 **I can't afford time to travel.**
旅行に行く時間がない。

4 **I can't afford to fail on this project.**
この企画で失敗は許されない。

5 **I couldn't afford not to accept the conditions.**
その条件をのまないわけにはいかなかった。
※acceptは「～を受け入れる」という意味。

得意

～は…が上手だ。
～ is good at ...

こんなふうに使います

人の趣味や特技などについて「～は…が上手だ、～は…が得意だ」と書くときは、～(人) is good at ...(名詞または動詞の -ing 形)で表します。

「…がとても上手だ・かなり得意だ」と強調するときは、～ is really good at ... や～ is great at ... としましょう。

反対に「～は…が上手ではない」なら、～ isn't so good at ... で表すことができます。so は、very としても構いません。また、～ is poor at ... とすると、「～は…が下手だ」という直接的な表現になります。

自分のことを言うときには、～ is〈isn't〉の部分を I'm〈I'm not〉に替えます。

こんなふうに書きます

1. **Rio is good at cooking.**
リオは料理が上手だなぁ。

2. **Masako is really good at drawing.**
マサコは絵を描くのがとてもうまい。

3. **Tetsu is good at all sports.**
テツはスポーツ万能だ。

4. **He is great at making friends.**
彼は友達をつくるのがとても上手だ（＝誰とでもすぐ友達になれる）。

5. **I'm not so good at organizing.**
私は整理整頓があまり得意じゃない。

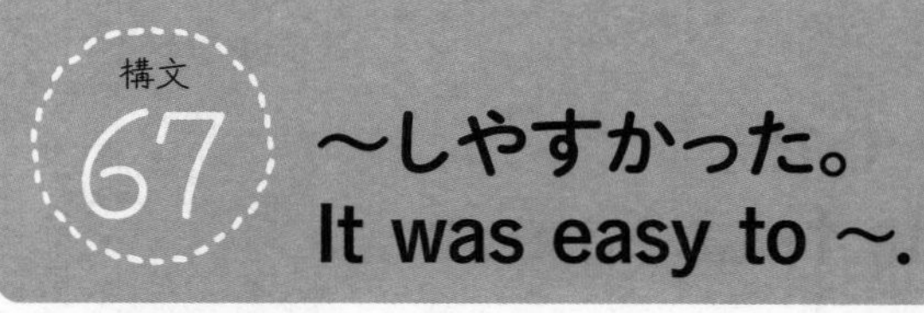

容易

構文 67 ～しやすかった。 It was easy to ～.

こんなふうに使います

「～しやすかった、～するのは容易だった」と書くときは、It was easy to ～(動詞の原形)と表します。反対に「～しづらかった、～するのは大変だった」と書きたいなら、It was hard to ～(動詞の原形)とします。

日記を書いているときにそう感じているなら、It's easy〈hard〉 to ～のように現在形で表します。It の部分は、具体的な名詞や人にしても OK です。

こんなふうに書きます

1 It was easy to **use.**
使いやすかった。

2 It was easy to **understand.**
わかりやすかった。

3 It was easy to **remember.**
覚えやすかった。

4 Michelle's English is easy to **understand.**
ミッシェルの英語はわかりやすい。

5 Kaoru is easy to **talk to.**
カオルは話しかけやすい人だ。

6 The restaurant was hard to **find.**
そのレストランは見つけにくかった。

時間の経過

構文68 …ぶりに〜した。 I ~ for the first time in ...

こんなふうに使います

久しぶりにした行動について書くときは、I ～ for the first time in ... と表します。「～」には動詞の過去形を、「...」にはどのくらい久しぶりなのかを表す期間を入れます。

for the first time は「初めて」という意味です。この構文からもわかるように、英語では「～ぶりに」を、for the first time in ...(…の期間で初めて)と表現します。「2年ぶりに」なら for the first time in two years(2年間で初めて)という具合です。「久しぶりに」と書く場合は、「長い間で初めて」と考えて、for the first time in ages とします。ages は「長い間」という意味で、an age や a long time としても OK です。また、for the first time in a while という言い方もあります。

これからする事柄について「…ぶりに～する」と書く場合は、I'm going to ～(動詞の原形) for the first time in ... / I'm ～ing for the first time in ... で表しましょう。

関連表現として、the first ～（名詞）in ... も覚えておきましょう。「…ぶりの～」という意味で、the first trip in two years（2年ぶりの旅行）のように使います。

こんなふうに書きます

1 **I did my laundry** for the first time in **three days.**
3日ぶりに洗濯した。

2 **I had okonomiyaki** for the first time in **two months.**
2カ月ぶりにお好み焼きを食べた。

3 My husband and I **ate out** for the first time in **a month.**
夫と1カ月ぶりに外食した。

4 **I took my children to Disneyland** for the first time in **five years.**
子どもたちを5年ぶりにディズニーランドへ連れていった。

5 **I listened to Shania Twain's songs** for the first time in ages.
久しぶりにシャナイア・トゥエインの歌を聞いた。

6 My co-workers and I **went bowling** for the first time in **a few years.**
同僚たちと数年ぶりにボウリングをしに行った。

7 I'm meeting **my old friends this weekend** for the first time in **ten years.**
今週末、10年ぶりに昔の友人たちに会う。

ポイント

- 「…(期間)ぶりに」は for the first time in ... で表す。
- 「...」には two years(2年)、five months(5カ月)などが入る。
- 「久しぶりに」は、for the first time in ages で表す。

時間の経過

構文69 …して以来、～(期間)になる。It's been ～ since ...

こんなふうに使います

過去を振り返り、「(ある時から)～の期間がたつなぁ」と懐かしく思ったり、時の早さに驚いたりしたことを日記に書くときは、It's been ～ since ... で表します。It's been ～ はIt has been の短縮形で、「～」にどのくらい時間がたったのかを表す語句を入れると、「～の期間になる、～の時がたつ」という意味を表せます。期間の前にonly を入れると、「まだ～（しかたっていない）」となり、期間の浅さを表せます（右ページの例文❹参照）。

since ... は「…(して)以来」という意味です。... には普通、過去形の文を入れますが、my graduation（卒業）のように名詞が入ることもあります（右ページの例文❻参照）。

「…して以来、明日で～(期間)になる」と書く場合は、It'll be ～ tomorrow since ... としましょう。

こんなふうに書きます

1 **It's been 30 years since we got married.**
結婚して 30 年になる。

2 **It's been a year since I quit drinking.**
禁酒して 1 年になる。

3 **It's been almost 15 years since we moved here.**
ここに引っ越してきて 15 年近くになる。

4 **It's been only one month since I started working for this company.**
この会社で働き始めて、まだ 1 カ月だ。

5 **It's been ten years since I started writing in my diary in English.**
英語で日記を書き始めて 10 年になる。
※write in a diaryは「日記を書く」の意味。

6 **It's already been 40 years since my graduation.**
卒業してもう 40 年になる。

7 **It'll be five years tomorrow since I started my own business.**
起業して、明日で 5 年になる。

ポイント

- It's been ～の「～」には、どのくらい時間がたったかを表す語句を入れる。
- since の後には、過去形の文または名詞を続ける。
- 「…して以来、明日で～(期間)になる」は、It'll be ～ tomorrow since …で表す。

時間の経過

構文70 ここ～(期間)…していないなぁ。 It's been ～ since I last ...

こんなふうに使います

構文69のIt's been ～ since ...(…して以来、～［期間］になる)は、出来事や行動を起こした日を起点としてその経過を振り返る構文です。一方、It's been ～ since I last ... は最後にその行動をした時点から今までを振り返り、「しばらく…していないなぁ」と書くときの表現です。「...」には行動を動詞の過去形で入れ、「～」には、その行動をしていない期間を入れましょう。since I last ... は「最後に…してから」が直訳で、構文全体で「最後に…してから～の期間がたつ」、つまり「ここ～(期間)…していないなぁ」というニュアンスになります。

「私が最後に…してから、明日で～(期間)になる」と書くなら、It'll be ～ tomorrow since I last ... とします。

こんなふうに書きます

1 **It's been a few years since I last went to the movies.**
ここ2～3年、映画を見に行っていないなぁ。

2 **It's been three weeks since I last aired my futon.**
ここ3週間、布団を干していないなぁ。

3 **It's been several years since my wife and I last went on a trip.**
ここ数年、妻と旅行に出かけていないなぁ。
※個人により感覚の違いはあるものの、several yearsは4～6年くらいを指す。

4 **It'll be six months tomorrow since we last contacted each other.**
私たちが最後に連絡を取り合ってから、明日で半年になる。

構文 71

忘れたこと

～し忘れた。／～のことを忘れてた。 I forgot to ～. / I forgot about ～.

こんなふうに使います

「やろうと思っていたのにし忘れた」ことは、I forgot to ～(動詞の原形)で表します。forgot to ～は「～し忘れた、～するのを忘れた」という意味です。I forgot ～ing とすると、「(実際はそれをしたのに) ～した事実を忘れていた」という別の意味になるので注意しましょう。例えば、I forgot to buy a present for her. なら「彼女へのプレゼントを買い忘れた」ですが、I forgot buying a present for her. なら「彼女へのプレゼントを買ったことを忘れていた」という意味になります。

I forgot about ～(名詞または動詞の -ing 形)なら、「(うっかりして)～のことを忘れていた」という意味になります。I totally forgot about ～や I completely forgot about ～とすると、「～のことをすっかり忘れていた」となり、そのことが完全に頭から抜けていた、と強調できます。

こんなふうに書きます

1 **I forgot to say thank you to Hitomi.**
ヒトミにお礼を言い忘れた。

2 **I forgot to take my suit to the cleaners.**
スーツをクリーニング店に出し忘れた。

3 **I forgot to return the pen to Keita again.**
またケイタにペンを返すのを忘れちゃった。

4 **I forgot about the three-day weekend!**
3連休だってこと忘れてた！

5 **I totally forgot about my dentist appointment.**
歯医者を予約していたことを、すっかり忘れてた。

結果

～せずにはいられなかった。 I couldn't help ～ing.

こんなふうに使います

「手伝う」や「助ける」という意味でおなじみの help ですが、I couldn't help ～(動詞の -ing 形)の形で用いると、「～せずにはいられなかった、つい～してしまった、思わず～してしまった」という意味になります。

少しくだけた表現として、I couldn't help but ～(動詞の原形)もあります。意味は I couldn't help ～ing と同じです。

こんなふうに書きます

1 I couldn't help **worrying about her.**
彼女のことを心配せずにはいられなかった。

2 I couldn't help **telling him about it.**
思わずそのことを彼に話してしまった。

3 I couldn't help **complaining.**
つい愚痴を言ってしまった。

4 I couldn't help **feeling sorry for her.**
彼女に同情せずにはいられなかった。

5 I couldn't help but **cry when I remembered my late father.**
亡き父を思い出して、思わず泣いてしまった。
※この late は「亡くなった」という意味。

構文 73

結果

結局～してしまった。 I ended up ～ing.

こんなふうに使います

意思や予定に反して「結局～してしまった」と書く場合は、I ended up ～(動詞の -ing 形) で表しましょう。この構文は、「そうするつもりはなかったのに、誘惑に負けて～してしまった」「そうするつもりはなかったのに、気が付いたら～していた」「そうしたくはなかったのに、～するはめになった」といったニュアンスを含んでいます。

「結局～できなかった、結局～できずじまいだった」は、I ended up not ～ing で表します。not の位置に注意しましょう。

こんなふうに書きます

1 **I ended up eating too much.**
結局、食べ過ぎてしまった。

2 **I ended up speaking Japanese at the international party.**
国際交流パーティーでは、結局、日本語を話してしまった。

3 **I was going to just take a nap, but I ended up sleeping until morning.**
ちょっと仮眠するつもりが、朝まで寝てしまった。

4 **I ended up buying more than I needed.**
結局、必要以上に買ってしまった。

5 **I ended up not eating soki-soba in Okinawa.**
結局、沖縄でソーキそばを食べずじまいだった。

慣れ

ようやく～に慣れた。 I've finally gotten used to ～.

こんなふうに使います

不慣れなことに「ようやく慣れた」ときや、今までうまくできなかったことが「慣れてできるようになってきた」ときなどには、I've finally gotten used to ～(名詞または動詞の -ing 形)と書くことができます。I've は I have の短縮形です。「～」に名詞を入れると「ようやく～に慣れた」、動詞の -ing 形を入れると「ようやく～することに慣れた」という意味になります。I finally got used to ～と過去形を使って表しても OK です。

「～に慣れつつある、～に慣れてきた」と書きたいなら、I'm getting used to ～とします。「まだ～に慣れない」という否定の文は、I haven't gotten used to ～ yet としましょう。

こんなふうに書きます

1 I've finally gotten used to **my new job.**
新しい仕事にようやく慣れた。

2 I've finally gotten used to **living alone.**
1 人暮らしにようやく慣れた。

3 I've finally gotten used to **commuting by train.**
電車通勤にもようやく慣れた。

4 I'm getting used to **speaking English.**
英語を話すことに慣れてきた。

5 I haven't gotten used to **the new model** yet.
まだ新機種に慣れない。

Memo

1章 英語日記フレーズ集 さくいん

あ

い

か

き

せ

そ

た

ち

つ

て

石原真弓 Mayumi Ishihara

英語学習スタイリスト。高校卒業後アメリカに留学。コミュニティカレッジ卒業後、通訳に従事。帰国後は英会話を教える傍ら、執筆やメディア出演、講演などで幅広く活躍。30年以上書き続けている英語日記や英語手帳の経験をもとに、身のまわりのことを英語で発信する学習法を提案している。主な著書に、『新・英語で日記を書いてみる』『今すぐ言える！ 英会話フレーズブック』（Gakken）、『気持ちを表す英単語辞典』『まいにち英会話』（ナツメ社）、『小学生のための聞ける！話せる！英語辞典』（旺文社）、『タッチペンで音がきける！はじめての英検5級』『タッチペンで音がきける！はじめての英検4級』（講談社）など。中国語や韓国語などに翻訳された著書も多数。

STAFF

編集	いしもとあやこ
編集協力	大塚智美、挙市玲子、鈴木香織、高木直子 A to Z English（デイビッド・セイン、小松アテナ） 今居美月、佐藤玲子、髙橋龍之助、西岡小央里
英文校正	A to Z English (Shelley Hastings, Trish Takeda)
表現作成協力	鈴木美里、土屋 檀、東 雄介、森村繁晴［ポルタ］
デザイン	山口秀昭［Studio Flavor］
イラスト	大高郁子
写真（石原真弓）	井上佐由紀［井上佐由紀写真事務所］
ヘアメイク（石原真弓）	徳田郁子
スタイリング（石原真弓）	真島京子